YOUNG ADULT LITERATURE
EXPLORATION, EVALUATION, AND APPRECIATION

Katherine Bucher
Old Dominion University

M. Lee Manning
Old Dominion University

PEARSON

Merrill
Prentice Hall

Upper Saddle River, New Jersey
Columbus, Ohio

Library of Congress Cataloging-in-Publication Data

Bucher, Katherine Toth
  Young adult literature: exploration, evaluation, and appreciation / Katherine Bucher,
M. Lee Manning.
      p. cm.
  Includes bibliographical references and index.
  ISBN 0-13-111841-2
    1. Young adult literature—History and criticism. 2. Young adults—Books and reading.
  3. Young adult literature—Study and teaching (Secondary) I. Manning, M. Lee. II. Title.

PN1009.A1B79 2006
809.8'9283—dc22   2005041581

Vice President and Executive Publisher: Jeffery W. Johnston
Senior Editor: Linda Ashe Montgomery
Senior Development Editor: Hope Madden
Senior Production Editor: Mary M. Irvin
Senior Editorial Assistant: Laura Weaver
Production Coordination: Amy Gehl, Carlisle Publishers Services
Design Coordinator: Diane C. Lorenzo
Cover Designer: Jason Moore
Cover Image: Corbis
Production Manager: Pamela D. Bennett
Director of Marketing: Ann Castel Davis
Marketing Manager: Darcy Betts Prybella
Marketing Coordinator: Brian Mounts

This book was set in Galliard by Carlisle Communications, Ltd. It was printed and bound by Courier
Stoughton, Inc. The cover was printed by Courier Stoughton, Inc.

Pearson Education Ltd.   Pearson Education Australia Pty. Limited
Pearson Education Singapore Pte. Ltd.   Pearson Education North Asia Ltd.
Pearson Education Canada, Ltd.   Pearson Educación de Mexico, S. A. de C. V.
Pearson Education—Japan   Pearson Education Malaysia Pte. Ltd.

10 9 8 7 6 5 4 3 2 1
ISBN: 0-13-111841-2

PREFACE

For quite a while, we have wanted to write a book that would open the door for readers to explore young adult literature. To do so, we would have to establish a foundation of knowledge about young adult literature while providing pathways leading to the literature itself.

A young adult literature text must allow you to find a balance between actual literature and the instructional text. For you to be able to guide young adult readers, you will need to read age and developmentally appropriate literature, finding your own favorites and learning firsthand how enjoyable and meaningful these books can be.

You'll need more than just your own experiences with the literature. To use this literature effectively with young adults, you'll need to

- know what literature is available and be familiar with a wide range of genres

- appreciate, understand, and evaluate the literature

- develop ways to connect readers with the literature

This balance is important to us because young adult literature is a significant aspect of middle and secondary school curricula as well as an invaluable source of enjoyment.

With the current emphasis on literature-based instruction, literature across the curriculum, reading to learn across the curriculum, and the use of literature to integrate curricular areas, the use of young adult literature will become increasingly important for all middle and high school educators. Slim enough to guarantee that you have the opportunity to read the books themselves and comprehensive enough to ensure that you understand adolescents, their literature, and how to connect the two, *Young Adult Literature: Exploration, Evaluation, and Appreciation* will help you provide a rich educational experience for adolescents while nourishing their love of reading.

DRIVING PRINCIPLES

For a young adult literature text to be truly valuable, it must accomplish a few things.

- It must provide readers with the knowledge of quality, age-appropriate books.

- It needs to offer information on literary exploration, emphasizing the evaluation, teaching, and appreciation of young adult literature.

- It should be sufficiently concise, allowing readers the time to read the literature itself.

- It must use technology as a means of learning more about young adult literature and about making it an integral part of the middle and secondary curriculum.

- Finally, it must recognize and value schools' increasing diversity.

RECOGNITION OF AND COMMITMENT TO DIVERSITY

Diversity must be respected and recognized in the middle and secondary school curriculum, and a young adult literature text needs to reflect our nation's and schools' growing diversity. Rather than segregating multicultural literature in a single genre chapter, we interweave diversity and multiculturalism throughout the text. The following threads will help you address and celebrate diversity in your classroom:

- exploring diversity—cultural, gender, ability, and sexual orientation

- identifying multicultural literature

- selecting and evaluating multicultural literature

- uncovering multicultural literature for and about specific cultural groups

- investigating award-winning books with multicultural representations

- integrating multicultural literature throughout the curriculum

- discovering appropriate literature that crosses curricular boundaries

EXPLORING, EVALUATING, AND APPRECIATING YOUNG ADULT LITERATURE

Special features blend with chapter content to support the book's three underlying and unifying themes:

Exploration: Get to Know the Students You Teach and the Literature That Interests Them

- Chapter 2 discusses adolescence and how it affects your students.

- Chapter 3 examines fantasy, science fiction, and horror, all popular genres with adolescents, and explains how to use a reader's interest in these areas to literacy's advantage.

- Chapter 10 explores the popular and burgeoning areas of graphic novels, comic books, and other nontraditional literature, providing an excellent way to motivate young readers.

- Diversity and multicultural literature are major threads that run throughout the book.

- *Suggested Readings* in each chapter list journal articles and books that will benefit your teaching. Visit the Companion Website to find related recommendations.

Evaluation: Learn What Makes a Young Adult Title Great

- Chapter 2, Evaluating and Selecting Young Adult Literature, sets the stage for a text intended to help you select the finest examples of young adult literature.

- *Considerations for Selecting Young Adult Literature* features in every genre chapter provide clarity on how to determine the value of specific titles.

- *Young Adult Books* features in each chapter help you choose the best titles for your students. Each feature is expanded on the text's Companion Website.

Appreciation: Help Young Adults Learn from and Love Young Adult Literature

- Chapter 11, Teaching, Using, and Appreciating Young Adult Literature, helps you see how best to use young adult literature in your classroom, including ways of integrating curricular areas.

- Chapter 12, Protecting Intellectual Freedom, as well as discussions in various genre chapters, will help you learn how to address censorship.

- *Expanding Your Knowledge with the Internet* features enrich your teaching with technology.

- *Connecting Adolescents and Their Literature* features include activities for teaching, exploring, and helping young adults appreciate young adult literature.

- *From Page to Screen* features in each genre chapter explore the best film adaptations of young adult literature, providing opportunities to engage readers and compare films to books.

- *Suggestions for Collaborative Efforts* features provide pre-service and in-service teachers and library media specialists ideas for collaboration on topics being addressed in the text.

TEXT SUPPLEMENTS

Companion Website

Available at **www.prenhall.com/bucher**, this robust online support system offers many rich and meaningful ways to deepen and expand the information presented to you in the text. Included on this site is an extensive Author and Title Index.

- *Expanding Your Knowledge with the Internet* modules further develop the text features, helping you integrate technology in your exploration of young adult literature.

- *Suggested Readings* features from the text are expanded in this online environment.

- *Young Adult Books* features are expanded in this online environment.

- *Self-Assessments* help users gauge their understanding of text concepts.

- *Web Links* provide useful connections to all standards and many other invaluable online sources.

- *Chapter Objectives* provide a useful advance organizer for each chapter's online companion.

- *Syllabus Manager*™ is a tool for the professor, providing an easy, step-by-step process to create and revise syllabi, with direct links into the Companion Website and other online content without having to learn HTML.

Electronic Instructor's Manual:

This useful tool for instructors provides rich instructional support, including:

- A test bank of multiple choice and essay tests

- PowerPoints specifically designed for each chapter

- Chapter-by-chapter materials, including chapter objectives, suggested readings, discussion questions, and in-class activities

To access these items online, go to **www.prenhall.com** and click on the Instructor Support button and then go to the Download Supplements section. Here you will be able to log in or complete a one-time registration for a user name and password. If you have any questions regarding this process or the materials available online, please contact your local Prentice Hall sales representative.

ACKNOWLEDGMENTS

Authors always have a number of people to whom they are grateful—people who motivated them, inspired them, challenged them, and provided actual assistance with the writing and preparation of the book. Therefore, we thankfully acknowledge the assistance of Linda Montgomery, Ben Stephen, and Hope Madden at Merrill Education for their encouragement and patience. We are particularly grateful to the following individuals who served as reviewers for this book and offered numerous constructive suggestions: M. Linda Broughton, Kennesaw State University; Pauline W. U. Chinn, University of Hawaii-Manoa; Jacquelyn M. Culpepper, Mercer University; Debbie East, Indiana University; Cyndi Giorgis, UNLV; Jackie Glasgow, Ohio University; Joan F. Kaywell, University of South Florida; Rodney D. Keller, Brigham Young University, Idaho; Patricia P. Kelly,

Virginia Tech; Leanna Manna, Villa Maria College; Barbara Stein Martin, University of North Texas; Marcy Merrill, California State University, Sacramento; Harold Nelson, Minot State University; Holly G. Willett, Rowan University; and Terrell Young, Washington State University.

KTB
MLM
Old Dominion University

EDUCATOR LEARNING CENTER: AN INVALUABLE ONLINE RESOURCE

Merrill Education and the Association for Supervision and Curriculum Development (ASCD) invite you to take advantage of a new online resource, one that provides access to the top research and proven strategies associated with ASCD and Merrill—the Educator Learning Center. At **www.educatorlearningcenter.com**, you will find resources that will enhance your students' understanding of course topics and of current educational issues, in addition to being invaluable for further research.

HOW THE EDUCATOR LEARNING CENTER WILL HELP YOUR STUDENTS BECOME BETTER TEACHERS

With the combined resources of Merrill Education and ASCD, you and your students will find a wealth of tools and materials to better prepare them for the classroom.

Research

- More than 600 articles from the ASCD journal *Educational Leadership* discuss everyday issues faced by practicing teachers.
- A direct link on the site to Research Navigator™ gives students access to many of the leading education journals, as well as extensive content detailing the research process.
- Excerpts from Merrill Education texts give your students insights on important topics of instructional methods, diverse populations, assessment, classroom management, technology, and refining classroom practice.

Classroom Practice

- Hundreds of lesson plans and teaching strategies are categorized by content area and age range.
- Case studies and classroom video footage provide virtual field experience for student reflection.
- Computer simulations and other electronic tools keep your students abreast of today's classrooms and current technologies.

LOOK INTO THE VALUE OF EDUCATOR LEARNING CENTER YOURSELF

A four-month subscription to Educator Learning Center is $25 but is **FREE** when packaged with any Merrill Education text. In order for your students to have access to this site, you must use this special value-pack ISBN number **WHEN** placing your textbook order with the bookstore: 0-13-195966-2. Your students will then receive a copy of the text packaged with a free ASCD pincode. To preview the value of this website to you and your students, please go to **www.educatorlearningcenter.com** and click on "Demo."

BRIEF CONTENTS

CONTENTS

PART THREE   Connecting Adolescents and Their Literature   305

Note: Every effort has been made to provide accurate and current Internet information in this book. However, the Internet and information posted on it are constantly changing, so it is inevitable that some of the Internet addresses listed in this textbook will change.

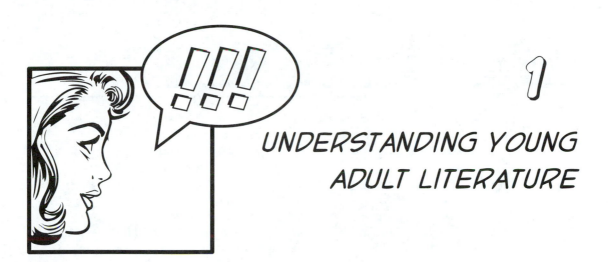

UNDERSTANDING YOUNG ADULT LITERATURE

CHAPTER OVERVIEW   "Like an awkward kid who's finally shed the braces and baby fat, young adult literature is coming into its own" (Crocker, 2003). Attracting the attention of middle and high school readers as well as their teachers and library media specialists, well-written young adult literature provides adolescents with considerable reading enjoyment; assists in the development of their sense of self; allows them to explore life experiences and realities; and helps them understand the many joys, trials, successes, and problems of life. With excellent authors writing high-quality literature especially for adolescents, young adult literature has earned a respected place between children's and adult literature. Young adult literature can be used throughout the school curriculum, either with an integrating theme across subjects, as part of an interdisciplinary unit, or in specific content areas to expand the information found in textbooks.

| FOCUSING POINTS | In this chapter, you will read about: |

> 1. Characteristics of adolescents.
> 2. Definitions of young adult literature and how it reflects adolescents' ages and development, contemporary interests, and their world.
> 3. The history of young adult literature, its qualities, and its place as transitional literature between children's and adult literature.
> 4. Genres of young adult literature and selected authors.
> 5. Young adult literature and the school curriculum and how this literature can be integrated throughout the curriculum.

DESCRIBING ADOLESCENTS

Today's young adults differ significantly from the individuals found in the 12- to 20-year-old age group 30 or 40 years ago. Contemporary adolescents develop faster.

- Physically, they mature earlier;

- Cognitively, they know more (although their cognitive experiences might not be the types that are valued in school); and

- Socially, many have a preoccupation with friends and peers (Manning & Bucher, 2005).

They also face issues—such as eating disorders, including crash diets; alcohol, drugs, and tobacco; AIDS and STDs (sexually transmitted diseases); peer pressure; and physical and psychological safety concerns—that previous generations might not have confronted as young adults. Knowing adolescents' developmental characteristics will assist teachers and library media specialists in selecting appropriate literature as well as planning learning experiences around young adult literature. Table 1–1 lists some adolescent developmental characteristics in more detail. It is important to remember that these developmental characteristics are complex and interrelated. For example, physical development affects self-esteem, socialization tendencies, and abilities to handle social tasks.

Although developmental characteristics can be listed with considerable certainty, educators must remember the importance of individuality and diversity. The wide range of physical developmental characteristics can readily be seen. For example, some 14-year-olds look like 18-year-olds while others resemble 10-year-olds. Other characteristics are more subtle. Psychosocially, some adolescents place priority on friendships and socialize at every opportunity; others might continue to be somewhat shy and may

TABLE 1–1	*Developmental Characteristics During Adolescence*

Physical
- Physical changes (e.g., growth spurt and skeletal and structural changes) are rapid and visually apparent
- Considerable diversity in physical developmental rates occur due to genetics, environmental factors, and health issues
- Distinct gender differences are evident in size, strength, and age of growth spurt (e.g., girls around age 12 and boys around age 14)
- Health risks increase due to behavioral issues such as eating disorders, sexual experimentation, and drug use

Psychosocial
- Friendships form and social interactions increase, which have the potential for boosting self-esteem and reducing anxiety
- Distinct gender differences occur in socialization patterns (e.g., females tend to have smaller numbers of close friends and males tend to have larger "social networks")
- Allegiance and affiliation shifts from parents and teachers to friends and peers
- Social tasks and situations are handled without adult supervision and advice
- Self-esteem changes due to adolescents' home and school lives
- Preoccupations with the self lead to critical self-examination and, subsequently, to the formation of self-perceptions
- Argumentative and aggressive behaviors become evident and often disturb parents and teachers

Cognitive
- Higher levels of cognitive functioning (e.g., reasoning and higher-level thought processes) develop
- Moral and ethical choices are now possible and often guide behavior
- Developmental diversity leads to varying abilities to think and reason
- Cognitive ability is often affected by overall socialization
- Perspectives about past, present, and future develop that allow enhanced perspectives of time
- Language and overall verbalization skills increase, allowing improved communication in both school and home situations

Source: Manning, M. L., & Bucher, K. T. (2005). *Teaching in the middle school.* Upper Saddle River, NJ: Merrill/Prentice Hall.

avoid social opportunities. Cognitive development is even less evident, with some younger adolescents performing formal and higher level thinking, while others continue to think in concrete terms. Every adolescent is maturing, but each is taking a different road and going at a different speed on his or her journey from childhood to adulthood (Manning & Bucher, 2005). Thus, it is important to know adolescents on an individual basis and to use this knowledge to select appropriate young adult literature.

In addition to the internal changes happening to adolescents, the environment or "communities" in which a young adult lives also molds the individual. These communities, including the family and its socioeconomic group, the neighborhood (including the school), the ethnic/racial/religious community, and young adolescent peers, impact the development of adolescents. Often these communities exert conflicting influences. Expectations from an ethnic community may be different from those of peers or the neighborhood, while family expectations may conflict with the neighborhood or peer norms.

All of these developmental and community factors have an affect on young adults and an impact on their reading. However, the outcomes are as diverse as young adults themselves. Some adolescents may read to escape the confines of their homes and communities while others may choose not to read because of peer pressure or the lack of importance placed on reading by their families. Although some young adults prefer literature that realistically addresses the problems of growing up, depicts their culture, or delves into the conflicting emotions they are experiencing, others prefer literature that will allow them to forget day-to-day life and vicariously experience adventures, travel to a fantasy world, or just have a good laugh.

DEFINING YOUNG ADULT LITERATURE

The term *young adult literature* can be difficult to define. Is it the literature that young adults select, on their own, to read? If so, some mainstream adult novels by Danielle Steele or John Grisham might be classified as young adult literature. Or, is young adult literature any book that is written specifically for a young adult audience? In that case, consider that highly recognized young adult authors such as Bruce Brooks and Robert Cormier actually became young adult authors because of their publishers. Their books, which were written as adult novels, were sent to the juvenile editors because their subjects "captured the tone and mood of a teenage character" (Aronson, 2001, p. 35). Publishers sometimes go into the final sales conference not knowing whether to market a book as a young adult or adult title (Maughan, 2000).

In fact, there really is no consensus among publishers, librarians, teachers, reviewers, and booksellers about exactly what young adult literature is (Aronson, 2002). There is not even agreement about who is a young adult. When Joan F. Kaywell (2001) surveyed members of the Conference on English Education Commission on the Study and Teaching of Young Adult Literature, she found the following definitions of young adults:

"an age group roughly between 11 and 16"

"kids between 10–21, grades 4–college"

"adolescents who are 12 to 18 in grades 6–12"

"between the ages of 12 and 22" (Kaywell, 2001, p. 325)

Even professional associations and award committees do not agree on an age span. A 2-year overlap exists between the ages noted for children's literature's Newbery Award (up to age 14) and young adult literature's Michael L. Printz Award (ages 12–18). While the members of the National Council of Teachers of English Conference on English Education Commission on the Study and Teaching of Young Adult Literature could not reach a consensus on an age range (Kaywell, 2001), most committee members did put the range somewhere between age 11 and 18 with a grade range between 6th and 12th grades.

Adding to the difficulty of defining young adult literature is a lack of agreement on the exact term that should be used to refer to it. Poe, Samuels, and Carter (1995) noted that finding research on young adult literature can be difficult because it may be indexed as children's literature, juvenile literature, or sometimes as adult literature. Barnes and Noble, a major bookseller, has changed its signage so that the term *Young Adult* has been replaced by the terms *Teen Fiction* and *Teen Series* (Maughan, 2000).

A Brief History of Young Adult Literature

Perhaps a definition of young adult literature lies in its history. Poe, Samuels, and Carter (1995) contend that, in the 1960s, young adult literature separated from both children's literature and adult literature with the publication of S. E. Hinton's *The Outsiders* (1967) and Paul Zindel's *The Pigman* (1968). Other critics add Robert Lipsyte's *The Contender* (1967) (Cart, 2001) as well as Ann Head's *Mr. and Mrs. Bo Jo Jones* (1967) (Campbell, 2003) to this list of groundbreaking books. These early young adult books were mainly novels that addressed the problems of growing up (Aronson, 2001) with "hard-edged realism" (Cart, 2001, p. 96) and "issues of relevance to the real lives of teen readers" (p. 96). *Go Ask Alice* (Sparks, 1971), published with "anonymous" listed as the author, became a best seller, showing publishers the value of young adult literature in paperback format (Campbell, 2003). Then, in 1974, Robert Cormier's *The Chocolate War* (1974) shook young adult literature, opening the door for "honest, fresh, stylistically daring, startling, terrifying, and wonderful fiction" (Campbell, 2003, p. 183). The following year, Judy Blume pushed the boundaries of sexual content for adolescents in her novel *Forever* (1975). In libraries, the new young adult literature was promoted to high school or college students, while students in sixth and seventh grades were still being directed to the children's collection (Campbell, 2003).

Between the 1970s and the 1990s, "the media that surrounded adolescence expanded and changed both its form and its substance" (Aronson, 2001, p. 34). Talk shows, cable television, and the Internet began to address teenagers' problems and concerns. The decline in young adult readership in the 1980s resulted in changes by publishers. There was a growth of series books such as *Fear Street* and *Sweet Valley High* (Campbell, 2003; Cart, 2001), and an increased interest by young adult readers in fantasy and science fiction, multicultural novels, and poetry (Aronson, 2002). By the late 1980s, publishers "youthen[ed]" (Cart, 2001, p. 95) their main characters in an attempt to target middle school students.

Young adult literature continued to evolve throughout the 1990s. Theme-based short story collections became popular, as did novels in verse such as those by authors Mel Glenn and Karen Hesse. Visual elements worked their way into young adult literature and changed the way books looked (Cart, 2001). "Graphic novels—the comic book come of age . . . [showed] how words and pictures are working together in fresh, original, and exciting ways" (p. 97). These new graphic formats asked readers to examine both the words and pictures when "reading" a story (Dresang, 1999). While the *Harry Potter* phenomenon rekindled an interest in fantasy and science fiction books, there were changes in the traditional linear plot style of realistic fiction. Books began to reflect the interactivity and connectivity of the digital world with shifting perspectives, diverse voices, and even multiple genres within a single book, such as Avi's *Nothing But the Truth* (1991) and Virginia Walter and Katrina Roeckelein's *Making Up Megaboy* (1998) (Dresang, 1999). In *Seedfolks* (1997), Paul Fleischman simultaneously used several storylines and, in *Holes* (1998), Louis Sachar created a multilayered story. When the first Michael L. Printz Award for Excellence in Young Adult literature was given in 1999, it changed "the way young adult literature is regarded and published" (Michael Cart quoted in Crocker, 2003, p. 77). Now, young adult literature had its own national award equal in status to the Newbery Medal, which is given for excellence in writing in children's literature. No longer were young adult books forced to compete for recognition with books for younger readers. Aronson (2001) noted that "the constraint, the box into which we used to try to fit YA books," had vanished (p. 10).

By 2000, both young adult literature and its readers had changed significantly from its founding in the 1970s. Campbell (2003) maintains that, today, most young adult readers are in sixth to ninth grade; and Cart (2001) notes that "one of the fastest-growing segments of publishing is the book market designated for readers 10–14 years old" (p. 95). Publishers have taken advantage of the fact that the teen population has a yearly disposable income in excess of $100 billion (Kiesling, 2002). According to Michael Wood of the marketing firm Teenage Research Unlimited, for the next two decades, teenagers will be the majority of the adult population (the marketing battle for generation Y, 2004).

Publishers are capitalizing on this new, large, more sophisticated audience. As Campbell (2004) points out, more books are speaking "directly to teens themselves, not teachers or librarians" (p. 63). To take advantage of the changes in literature, librarians and teachers need to continually update their collections and booklists. Suggestions for Collaborative Efforts 1–1 provides some information on the importance of keeping things like summer reading lists current.

Young Adult Literature Today

As young adult literature has matured, authors have begun to "tackle more serious subjects and to introduce more complex characters and considerations of ambiguity" (Cart, 2001, p. 96). The boundaries of young adult literature have expanded as authors explore topics of cruelty and crime, personal abuse, and racial violence (Dresang, 1999), accompanied by a change in the perspectives represented in literature. The previously

1-1 SUGGESTIONS FOR COLLABORATIVE EFFORTS

If your school provides summer reading lists for students, it is important to form a team of school library media specialists, teachers, and public librarians to assist in their development. They can take nonbinding recommendations from adolescents as well. The team should know what the goal for summer reading is (i.e., create lifelong readers) and should develop a reading list that actually promotes that goal. The team needs to remember that adolescents, like adults, do not all like the same type of book. Therefore, plenty of choices need to be on the list. Williams (2003) indicated that one-third of Connecticut school summer reading programs in 2003 gave "students complete freedom to choose their own reading" (p. 369). However, most "offered suggested lists" (p. 369) but made it clear that "it was not necessary to read from the list" (p. 369). Check the Companion Website for this book to find additional resources on summer reading.

The following links will appear on the Companion Website:

Summer Reading Resources

http://ct.webjunction.org/do/DisplayContent?id=6087

Summer Reading Collaborative

http://www.summerlibraryprogram.org/about.html

unheard voices of gays, lesbians, the homeless, and people with disabling conditions now join the voices of adolescents who are speaking out in books through their journals, diaries, and letters. Young adult literature is "as varied as the multimedia mix of teenagers' lives, as complex as their stormy emotional landscapes, as profound as their soul-shaping searches for identity, as vital as their nation-forming future" (Aronson, 2001, p. 11). In Expanding Your Knowledge with the Internet 1–1, you will find the URLs for a few general young adult literature web sites.

EXPANDING YOUR KNOWLEDGE WITH THE INTERNET 1-1

A variety of Internet sites have information on young adult literature such as the High School Teachers' Site at Random House http://www.randomhouse.com/highschool/ and *The ALAN Review* (Assembly on Literature for Adolescents of NCTE) at http://www.alan-ya.org/. Links to these and many additional sites are found on this book's Companion Website at http://www.prenhall.com/bucher.

What, then, is contemporary young adult literature? Aronson (2002) calls it a blend of enduring adolescence and constant change.

> An agglomeration of instabilities . . . [i]t requires us simultaneously, to define three inherently unstable terms: what are young adults, what is literature, and what is the literature that has some special link to those readers. (Aronson, 2001, pp. 31–32)

For our purposes, young adult literature will be defined as literature in prose or verse that has excellence of form or expression. *Merriam-Webster's Encyclopedia of Literature* (1995) provides a unique adolescent point of view (Herz & Gallo, 1996) and reflects the concerns, interests, and challenges of contemporary young adults (Brown & Stephens, 1995). In sum, it provides a roadmap for readers 12 to 20 years of age (Bean & Moni, 2003).

Criticism, Praise, and the Future

There are some who believe young adult literature only attracts the poorer readers who do not have the reading and analytical skills to enjoy the classics of literature (e.g., the plays of William Shakespeare, *The Odyssey,* or the works of Charles Dickens) that are part of the traditional literary canon. Christenbury (1997) related comments she had heard about young adult literature such as "It's just for younger kids;" "It's for weaker readers;" "We are a high school, and the parents would complain if we gave their children this watered-down stuff;" and "Our students would be bored by these books" (p. 11). Aronson (1997) maintained that some adolescents, often those praised as the best readers, purposely avoid young adult books and gravitate to adult science fiction and fantasy in an effort to avoid the conciseness of much young adult literature.

Other critics downplay the role of young adult literature, especially in the high school curriculum. Jago (2000) rationalized that, because young adults do not need guidance to understand a young adult novel, young adult literature should be used for independent, pleasure reading, not studied in the curriculum. He found that the characters were frequently one dimensional, and that the books lacked the rich language and complex themes found in the classics (Jago, 2000). Other critics advocated the use of young adult literature primarily for developmental English classes, in middle schools, or for unmotivated students who would find the traditional literary canon of the high school English curriculum too challenging (Knickerbocker & Rycik, 2002).

Perhaps because of the criticism surrounding it, or because of other factors such as the widening gap between young adult literature and the media-saturated world of modern adolescents, as "recently as the mid-'90s, teen-oriented literature seemed *thisclose* to extinction" (Crocker, 2003, p. 76). Thankfully, this changed in 1999 (Maughan, 2000) as authors found ways to "present information—both visually and stylistically—to a generation reared on MTV, the Internet, and video games" (Crocker, 2003, p. 78). As Michael Cart, former president of the Young Adult Library Services Association, stated, "Young adult literature may have had a near-death experience, but it's very very alive now . . . it's sort of like how the cosmos must have looked after the Big Bang, just expanding exponentially" (Crocker, 2003, p. 76).

Some literary critics (Hipple, 2000; Moore, 1997) note the excellence in some contemporary young adult literature. As Patty Campbell, young adult critic for *Horn Book Magazine,* noted, there are "risk-taking, exciting books being published" (Crocker, 2003, p. 76) with the current young adult literature being some of "the finest literature you can find today . . . it is finely crafted literature that's readable and accessible . . . [with stories that are] taut and intense and utterly focused" (pp. 76–77).

While young adult literature helps younger adolescents find themselves in books and begin to think critically about literature, older adolescents use young adult literature to help them explore social issues and examine their role in society (Knickerbocker & Rycik, 2002). When adolescents perceive books, especially those in the traditional literary canon, as less relevant, they become disconnected and lose interest in reading. In contrast, many young adult novels "possess themes that merit and reward examination and commentary" (Hipple, 2000, p. 2) and appeal to adolescents. According to Knickerbocker and Rycik (2002):

> Experiences that provide opportunities for adolescents to read young adult literature, make connections between literary works, orally interpret literature and respond to literature will help create more satisfying literary experiences for adolescents, contributing to the likelihood that they will become lifelong readers. (p. 208)

Qualities of Young Adult Literature

Although some children's and adult's books appeal to young adults, literature written primarily for young adults should reflect several criteria.

- It should reflect young adults' age and development by addressing their reading abilities, thinking levels, and interest levels.

- It should deal with contemporary issues, problems, and experiences with characters to whom adolescents can relate. This includes topics such as dealing with parents and other adults in authority; facing illness and death; dealing with peer pressure, specifically relating to drugs, alcohol, and sexual experimentation; and facing the realities of addiction and pregnancy.

- It should consider contemporary world perspectives including cultural, social, and gender diversity; environmental issues; global politics; and international interdependence.

Characteristics. Young adult literature reflects the changes that adolescents are experiencing. Making their first excursions into adult territory, adolescents are learning to take responsibility for their own actions. Thus, young adult literature reflects their experiences with conflicts, focuses on themes that interest young people, includes young protagonists and mostly young characters, and has language common to young adults (Vogels, 1996). Rather than being watered down in content of style, it is often sophisticated, artistic, and compelling (Christenbury, 1997).

Although young adult fiction no longer shies away from plots that center on topics once considered only for adults, authors of young adult literature use less graphic details while still conveying the reality of the situation (Vogels, 1996). However, the literature is not boring in subject matter or in its appeal to young people. Rather, it contains exciting and intriguing plots and characters (Christenbury, 1997). Also, young adult fiction usually has a concise plot with a time span of 2 months or less, as well as a focus on the present and future in the life of one central character (Vogels, 1996).

Purposes. Young adult literature serves a number of purposes. It:

- teaches adolescents about diverse peoples and the world beyond their community,
- provides pleasure reading,
- demonstrates the range of human emotions and allows adolescents to experience them as a result of reading quality literature,
- reveals the realities of life,
- provides vicarious experiences,
- focuses on "essentials" that make order out of chaos,
- depicts the functions of institutions of society,
- allows readers to escape into the realms of fantasy,
- introduces readers to excellent writers and writing, and
- increases literacy and the ability to analyze literature.

Of course, young adult literature cannot provide these benefits unless adolescents actually read the books. In Connecting Adolescents and Their Literature 1–1, Patrick Jones (2003) provides a different idea on purchasing young adult literature.

CONNECTING | *ADOLESCENTS AND THEIR LITERATURE 1–1*

One key to getting adolescents to read is providing access to the types of materials that they want to read. Patrick Jones (2003) suggests an interesting approach to purchasing literature for school libraries or classroom collections. In addition to selecting books from the best booklists, look at the books that are lost, long overdue, or missing (stolen) from the local school and public library. If the library's circulation system provides the necessary information, also look at the books with the most circulation and the items that have the highest turnover rate or the greatest amount of circulations per copy. Then, use these lists to order additional books. Keep in mind that, as Jones notes, "an old book is new to teens if they've never read it before" (Jones, 2003, p. 49). If you have not read these books, read them so that you can talk to adolescents about the books they are reading.

Young Adult Literature as Transitional Literature

Young adult literature should be appreciated and enjoyed "in and of itself" and young adults should have access to books written especially for them. Young adult literature should not be considered merely a stepping stone to "better" literature or a "holding ground" until readers are ready for adult literature. It is imperative that teachers and library media specialists provide young adults with excellent, well-written books that deal with important adolescent issues and that reflect their interests and concerns. Throughout this book, especially in Chapter 2, you will read about ways to identify this outstanding young adult literature.

However, there is no question that reading excellent young adult literature can help adolescents make the transition from children's books to adult books. By serving as a bridge, young adult novels provide the perfect vehicles to help adolescents cross from literature for children into the traditional literary canon that is studied in high school and college. Generally shorter than adult novels, sometimes less complex in structure, but often well-written and tightly constructed, young adult novels can lead students to a better understanding of the novel form and the elements of fiction. By studying these novels, young adults can understand the craft of fiction so that they are better able to read and comprehend the message and the literary conventions of the classics.

According to Gillet and Temple (2000), students move through stages of reading development. Independent reading begins in the Building Fluency State (usually second or third grade) and continues into Reading for Pleasure/Reading to Learn, and finally into Mature Reading, which includes critical reading and analysis. When teachers understand both the developmental and reading appreciation levels of their students, they are best able to help adolescents find appropriate materials that will simultaneously challenge and entertain them (Bushman & Haas, 2001). In Connecting Adolescents and Their Literature 1–2, Knickerbocker and Rycik (2002) suggest four broad categories of literature experiences that all young adults should have as they move toward becoming mature readers.

In addition to using young adult novels to teach literary conventions, educators can pair young adult novels with the more sophisticated books in the literary canon. Through pairing, teachers can introduce adolescents to a theme, situation, or setting the students find appealing and manageable. After a positive reading experience in which the adolescents become familiar with the concepts presented in the young adult novel, the teacher can introduce the students to the more complex format and ideas of the adult book. Teachers can use the pairing system to match books or authors (Samuels, 1992). A variation of this is to select one adult novel as the core book and then to identify a number of young adult novels that relate to it. The teacher can divide the class into groups with each group reading a different young adult novel. Following discussions within the individual groups, the teacher can host a whole class discussion on the various young adult novels before moving to a study of the core book.

Joan F. Kaywell (1993–2000) has edited a series of books that provide detailed instructional guides for linking young adult literature with the classics. A few of the combinations include linking Arthur Miller's *Death of a Salesman* with Cynthia Voight's *The Runner* (1985); Ibsen's *A Doll House* with Sue Ellen Bridgers' *Permanent*

| CONNECTING | ADOLESCENTS AND THEIR LITERATURE 1-2 |

Knickerbocker and Rycik (2002) believe that "it is inappropriate to make sharp divisions in the instructional practices for middle and high school students" (p. 200). Instead, they suggest four types of literary experiences that all adolescents should have:

- Reading young adult literature.
- Developing bridges between young adult literature and more complex texts and revisiting texts to apply "new understandings or methods of analysis" (p. 201).
- Interpreting literature by listening to dramatic oral readings by skilled individuals such as teachers and library media specialists.
- Responding to literature in ways including discussion groups, journals, and group conversations.

Connections (1987); or *The Tragedy of Julius Caesar* with several novels including Lois Duncan's *Killing Mr. Griffin* (1978), Will Hobbs' *Downriver* (1991), and Bruce Brooks' *No Kidding* (1989).

Genres and Authors

Young adult literature consists of a number of different genres or categories that serve unique purposes and satisfy individual reading choices. Many books overlap genres, making the distinction between types difficult to see.

However, for our purposes, we will use the following categories: fantasy, science fiction, horror fiction, contemporary realistic fiction, adventure, mystery, humor, historical fiction, biography, nonfiction/information, poetry, drama, short stories, comic books, graphic novels, and magazines.

Whether selecting science fiction or poetry, teachers and library media science specialists must be familiar with the literature, reasons for teaching or encouraging young adults to read the literary types, the characteristics of the genre, and the ways to evaluate it. With this knowledge, educators have the basic tools to select quality young adult literature to place in libraries and classrooms and to recommend to adolescents. The following sections provide only a brief overview of the genres and mention just a few titles that are different from the ones you will find in the individual chapters of this book.

Science Fiction, Fantasy, and Horror. There is no doubt that science fiction, fantasy, and horror, the categories discussed in Chapter 3, appeal to many young adults. The Young Adult Library Services Association (YALSA), a division of the American Library

Association, sponsored the first Teens' Top Ten list during Teen Read Week in October 2003. Over 1,700 12- to 18-year-olds voted online for their favorite books. Six of the top ten books were science fiction/fantasy books, including *The Thief Lord* (Funke, 2001); *Tithe, A Modern Faerie Tale* (Black, 2002); and *Abhorsen* (Nix, 2003) ("Fantasy books top the list for teens," 2004). While fantasy books took a majority of the places in the 2003 Teens' Top Ten, horror books were the topic of the 2004 Teen Read Week sponsored by the American Library Association with the slogan "It's Alive @ Your Library®." Teens eagerly read horror stories by R. L. Stine, Christopher Pike, and Stephen King as well as science fiction and fantasy books by Anne McCaffrey, Ursula K. LeGuin, Orson Scott Card, Eoin Colfer, and J. K. Rowling.

In fantasies, readers can go to magical places while, in science fiction, they can explore the possibilities of science and technology both on earth and on other worlds. Horror books allow readers to confront the terrors that populate their worst nightmares. As with all young adult literature, quality among these three genres varies from excellent to mediocre at best. Careful selection is necessary before adding a book to a school library or the curriculum. For example, while some horror books may glorify or sensationalize violence, others are just good, scary stories.

Contemporary Realistic Fiction. The topic of Chapter 4, contemporary realistic fiction, sometimes called the problem novel, appeals to many adolescents and uses plots, themes, settings, and characters to reflect the world as we know it and the problems and challenges that many young people face daily. By reading about characters in situations similar to their own, some adolescents can see that their personal problems are difficult yet not unique. For other adolescents, realistic fiction provides a vicarious experience through which they learn to overcome their fears and accept responsibilities, and to deal with problems related to adoption, divorce, disabilities, disease, sexual relationships, changes within their families, relationships, sexual orientation, alienation, alcohol and drug abuse, and suicide.

Several issues surround realistic fiction. First, teachers and library media specialists should carefully determine whether the violence in a book has meaning and significance or whether the violence is used solely as sensationalism. Also, a few authors in the past tended to portray females and cultural groups stereotypically. Finally, some realistic fiction runs the risk of a censorship challenge. As Chapter 12 suggests, the threat of censorship should not be a reason to avoid teaching a book or encouraging young adults to read the book; however, a planned and deliberate process should be in place for dealing with censorship concerns.

Adventure, Mystery, and Humor. In looking for excitement, many adolescents are attracted to books about adventure and survival or mystery and suspense. Adolescents enjoy the usually fast-paced plots found in adventure stories and the challenges to find out "who-done-it" in mystery novels. Some young adults read humorous novels to have a good laugh and to escape the problems of everyday life. Chapter 5 provides information on these genres.

Historical Fiction. By helping adolescents experience the past, explore misfortunes and triumphs, and examine the background of current events, historical fiction can be both interesting and informative. Young adults can read and learn new perspectives of cultural diversity; perceive challenges associated with disabling conditions; examine societal ills such as poverty, drug addiction, crime, and racism; and explore almost any historical period. As discussed in Chapter 6, historical fiction includes fictional stories based in actual events as well as stories set in the past with little or no reference to recorded history or actual people. Recurring topics include wars and clashes of people, the quest for freedom and equality, and the overcoming of disabling conditions.

Biography. Through biographies, young adults read more than descriptions of individuals' lives. They also explore the frustrations, obstacles, and achievements of people from the past and the present. From the lives of the historically famous to contemporary leaders and names in the news, as well as those who have persevered through challenging circumstances, biographies can add new perspectives to young adults' learning and reading pleasure. Chapter 7 discusses this genre of young adult literature.

Nonfiction/Information. While many adolescents read fiction, others enjoy well-written informational books. A poll of adolescents ages 12 to 18 found that 26% prefer reading nonfiction books ("Reading remains popular among youth, according to poll," 2001). Authors and publishers try to meet young adults' needs and expectations by providing books on timely topics that are written on appropriate reading and interest levels. In fact, some nonfiction authors write with reluctant readers in mind and provide lots of photographs and other illustrations. Chapter 8 discusses nonfiction in more detail.

Poetry, Drama, and Short Stories. Poetry, drama, and short stories are important categories for many young adults, especially for readers who prefer shorter pieces over longer books. Rather than relying on the classics, many adolescents look for works that deal with their contemporary concerns and daily interests and that speak directly to them with words they can understand and situations they can relate to. Identifying works that appeal to young adult readers and that young adults *want* to read, teachers and library media specialists can look for anthologies as well as works written by members of diverse cultural groups. Information on these categories is located in Chapter 9.

Comic Books, Graphic Novels, and Magazines. Growing up in a visual and digital society, contemporary adolescents are comfortable with the visual styles found in comic books, graphic novels, and magazines. These formats differ dramatically from the genres that educators have traditionally encouraged adolescents to read. However, these formats contain the same visual impact and clipped, pared-down writing style that adolescents have grown accustomed to. Their appeal was reflected in the American Library Association 2002 Teen Read Week theme of "Getting Graphic @ Your Library.™" For many young adults, these three genres represent a welcome move away from what they consider traditional "school" reading. Thus, educators need to be able to select quality interesting items that teens will appreciate as well as items that will contribute to the formal and informal education of adolescents. Chapter 10 discusses these categories in more detail.

Authors of Books For Young Adults. There are a number of excellent writers of young adult literature. During spring 1998, McElmeel and Buswell (1998) published the results of a survey of teachers, librarians, and adolescents to determine the most important authors of books for young adults. Although they based their survey on one conducted by Donald Gallo in 1988, McElmeel and Buswell (1998) changed the survey and sampled a wider population. Survey forms with a list of 150 authors compiled by the researchers appeared in the *Iowa Reading Journal* and *The Book Report,* a national journal for secondary school library media specialists. Table 1–2 shows the individuals identified in this survey as the most important authors for young adults.

Then, in June of 2001, the magazine *Voice of Youth Advocates* published its list of books receiving its highest ratings for quality and popularity from 1996 to 2000 and compared them to the American Library Association's Best Books for Young Adults list (Jones, 2001). The authors who appeared on both lists are shown on Table 1–3.

New, exciting, and skillful authors continue to enter the field of young adult literature each year. Educators often strive to help adolescents make connections with outstanding authors. Expanding Your Knowledge with the Internet 1–2 features URLs of some Internet sites where you can find information about authors of young adult literature. Suggestions for Collaborative Efforts 1–2 contains ideas for planning an author visit to your school or community.

TABLE 1-2	**The Most Important Authors of Books For Young Adults**

Identified by 80% of the respondents

R. L. Stine

Identified by 60–79% of the respondents

Beverly Cleary	Anne Frank	Robert Frost
Jack London	C. S. Lewis	

Identified by 50–59% of the respondents

Scott O'Dell	Shel Silverstein	E. B. White
Langston Hughes	Laura Ingalls Wilder	

Identified by 40–49% of the respondents

Louisa May Alcott	Avi	Lewis Carroll
Ray Bradbury	Betsy Byars	Lois Lowry
S. E. Hinton	Washington Irving	Richard Peck
Madeleine L'Engle	Gary Paulsen	
Christopher Pike	Judy Blume	

(continued)

TABLE 1-2	Continued

Identified by 10–39% of the respondents

C. S. Adler	Lloyd Alexander	William Bell
Bruce Brooks	Eve Bunting	Matt Christopher
Patricia Clapp	Bill Cleaver	Ellen Conford
Arthur Connan	Caroline Cooney	James Fenimore Cooper
Robert Cormier	Paula Danziger	Daniel DeFoe
Lois Duncan	Paul Fleischman	Esther Forbes
Paula Fox	Jean Fritz	Jean Craighead George
Nikki Giovanni	Bette Greene	Winston Groom
Jesse Harris	Will Hobbs	Dean Hughs
Irene Hunt	Shirley Jackson	M. E. Kerr
Rudyard Kipling	Jim Kjelgaard	Norma Klein
Katherine Lasky	Marie Lee	Robert Lipsyte
Jack London	Norma Fox Mazer	Ann McCaffrey
Robin McKinley	Walter Dean Myers	Joan Lowrey Nixon
Katherine Patterson	Robert Newton Peck	Susan Beth Pfeffer
Ken Rappaport	Marjorie K. Rawlings	Lois Ruby
Cynthia Rylant	Saki	Josepha Sherman
William Sleator	Gary Soto	Elizabeth Speare
Jerry Spinelli	Nancy Springer	Barbara Steiner
Richie Tankersley	Theodore Taylor	Julian Thompson
Cynthia Voight	Bill Wallace	Luke Wallin
Rob White	Maia Wojciechowski	Jane Yolen
Paul Zindel		

Source: Adapted from McElmeel, S., & Buswell, L. (1998). Readers' choices: The most important authors of books for young adults. *The Book Report, 16*(4), 23–24.

TABLE 1-3	Outstanding Authors From 1996 to 2000

The following authors appeared on both the VOYA Perfect Ten List 1996–2000 and the American Library Association's Best Books for Young Adults list for the same years.

Caroline Cooney	Anita Lobel	Gary Paulsen
Robert Cormier	Albert Marrin	Philip Pullman
Sarah Dessen	Carol Matas	J. K. Rowling
Jackie French Koller	Walter Dean Myers	Cynthia Voight

Source: Developed from Jones, P. (2001). The perfect tens: The top forty books reviewed in Voice of Youth Advocates 1996–2000. *Voice of Youth Advocates, 24*(2), 94–99.

EXPANDING	**YOUR KNOWLEDGE WITH THE INTERNET 1–2**

 There are a variety of Internet sites where you can find information about authors of young adult literature such as Judy Blume at http://www.judyblume.com or Chris Crutcher at http://www.aboutcrutcher.com/. Links to these and many additional sites are found on this book's Companion Website at http://www.prenhall.com/bucher.

 1–2   ## SUGGESTIONS FOR COLLABORATIVE EFFORTS

Meeting an author can generate enthusiasm for reading not only that author's books but also books that are similar.

Schools and public libraries can combine resources to sponsor an author visit to the local community. If several schools and libraries participate, the costs become more affordable for individual schools. Another way to control costs is to combine the visit with an author's presentation at a nearby state convention or to see if a local bookstore will help with financial support. Sometimes humanities councils have grants that can be used to support authors.

Preplanning is very important. As part of your plan, determine where the author will make her/his presentation(s) (i.e., in several schools, in one large auditorium, etc.); if the presentations will be open to all students in the community as well as parents or if invitations will be issued; who will receive invitations (i.e., members of school book clubs, students in particular English classes, students who work in the school or public library,

etc.); and whether there will be any charge for attending the presentation(s).

Asking young adults to nominate a favorite author can be one way to involve them in the process. However, it may be better to start with a suggested list from which adolescents can make their recommendations. Once the author has been determined, teachers and librarians should promote the author's books either through library book discussion groups or in classroom discussions. Be sure that students have read at least some of the books written by the author.

Contact a local bookstore or paperback distributor as soon as you know the name of the author and be sure that copies of the author's books are available for sale before, during, and after the visit. Decide whether you will have a special autograph session with the author during the visit (some authors prefer to send autographed bookplates) and if you will need to limit the number of books that any one individual can have autographed at one time.

Young Adult Literature and the School Curriculum

The importance of having quality young adult literature available in schools is reflected in the International Reading Association's Adolescent Literacy Commission's position statement, which notes that "adolescents deserve access to a wide variety of reading material that they can and want to read" (Moore, Bean, Birdyshaw, & Rycik, 1999, p. 4).

One way to encourage young adults to read is to use "both high-powered young adult literature [that is] linked to content-area concepts and interpretive activities and discussions that engage students" (Bean, 2002, p. 37). Thus, there is an increasing trend to incorporate young adult books and other forms of literature across the middle and high school curriculum. In fact, Chapter 11 focuses entirely on this topic.

All educators agree that reading is an important skill. However, when voluntary reading declines, the problems of struggling readers are only aggravated (Worthy, Patterson, Salas, Prater, & Turner, 2002). By allowing adolescents to read good young adult literature, educators are able to encourage the independent reading, which will, in turn, help adolescents develop the skills necessary to succeed. "If educators are serious about developing students' lifelong love of reading, they need to incorporate in the curriculum literature that is captivating and issue-based" (Bean, 2002, p. 37).

Richardson and Miller (2001) cite four reasons for using literature in the curriculum. Although they targeted the social studies curriculum, their reasons are valid in other subjects as well. They found that literature can:

- help students become emotionally involved with events and people,

- aid students in understanding reality,

- provide stories with satisfactory endings, and

- provide a common, shared experience for the teacher and all students.

You have already read about the use of young adult literature as a transition to the classics and the pairing of young adult and adult literature. In addition, newer trends such as using literature across the curriculum and creating a literature plan have provided more productive ways to use young adult literature not just in the English classroom but also in science, social studies, art, and physical education. By working collaboratively, teachers and library media specialists can implement a literature program that reflects the abilities and interests of young adults, that encourages adolescents to read for enjoyment, and that develops an awareness of authors and literary works. This literature program should also teach adolescents to interpret literature and develop literary awareness. When the entire school environment reflects literature and a respect for reading, young adults learn the importance the school places on literature and reading.

However, as Chapter 11 explains, the effort to use young adult literature across the curriculum does not have to be an "all or nothing" approach. Teachers may elect to implement literature-based approaches of varying degrees at various times during the year. What is essential is that teachers and library media specialists recognize the need to use a variety of materials ranging from books, magazines, and graphic novels to short stories and poetry and provide time for adolescents to read. By varying their approaches to literature in the content areas, teachers can assure that fiction is read from an aesthetic stance and nonfiction from an efferent stance to ensure learning for all adolescents (Galda & Liang, 2003).

Rather than working in isolation, many educators now make collaborative decisions on curricular themes and use young adult literature that crosses subject areas and helps students see new and different perspectives about issues and subject content. In addition, Bean (2002) suggests that educators provide a variety of ways for adolescents to interpret literature through the use of book clubs, journals, graphic organizers, readers' theater, or even a "dinner party" (p. 36) at which students who are playing a character from a novel are interviewed by a moderator. Contemporary adolescents will also welcome the opportunity to produce multigenre papers that, like some recent young adult novels, depart from the traditional linear report format and employ a variety of styles (i.e., graphic novel, essay, poetry, drama, or magazine article) as well as a number of voices and perspectives to provide "multilayered, nonlinear stories and information" (Glasgow, 2002, p. 49).

CONCLUDING THOUGHTS

Since its beginnings in the 1960s, young adult literature has come a long way in its quest for respectability and acceptance. More and more teachers and library media specialists have recognized the need for and value of quality literature that speaks directly to the interests, needs, and desires of adolescents. Also, professionals working with young adults are increasingly seeing the reasons and techniques for implementing young adult literature throughout middle and high school curricula. However, young adult literature is not static. It is changing along with the students who read it and the society in which it is written. Boundaries are pushed as new forms of graphics and multigenre or nonlinear plots become part of the accepted body of work that is young adult literature. For teachers and library media specialists, the challenge remains to identify the most appropriate strategies to provide young adult readers with quality and well-written literature that they can appreciate and enjoy. Visit this book's Companion Website at http://www.prenhall.com/bucher for additional information about young adult literature including review questions, self-assessments, sites, and readings.

Young Adult Books

This section includes young adult titles recommended or mentioned in this chapter. Check the Companion Website at prenhall.com/bucher to find additional suggestions of current young adult literature.

Avi. (1991) *Nothing but the truth*. New York: Orchard.

Black, H. (2002). *Tithe, a modern faerie tale*. New York: Simon & Schuster.

Blume, J. (1975). *Forever*. Scarsdale, NY: Bradbury.

Bridgers, S. E. (1987). *Permanent connections*. New York: Harper & Row.

Brooks, B. (1989). *No kidding*. New York: Harper & Row.

Cormier, R. (1974). *The chocolate war*. New York: Pantheon.

Duncan, L. (1978). *Killing Mr. Griffin*. Boston: Little, Brown.

Fleischman, P. (1997). *Seedfolks*. New York: HarperCollins.

Funke, (2001). *The thief lord*. New York: Scholastic.

Head, A. (1967). *Mr. & Mrs. Bo Jo Jones*. New York: Putnam.

Hinton, S. E. (1967). *The outsiders*. New York: Viking.

Hobbs, W. (1991). *Downriver*. New York: Bantam.

Lipsyte, R. (1967). *The contender*. New York: Harper & Row.

Nix, G. (2003). *Abhorsen*. New York: HarperCollins.

Sachar, L. (1998). *Holes*. New York: Farrar, Straus and Giroux.

Sparks, B. (1971). *Go ask Alice*. Upper Saddle River, NJ: Prentice Hall.

Voight, C. (1985). *The Runner*. New York: Ballantine.

Walter, V., & Roeckelein, K. (1998). *Making up megaboy*. New York: DK Publishing.

Zindel, P. (1968). *The pigman*. New York: Harper & Row.

Suggested Readings

Blasingame, J. (2004). James Blasingame's interview with Robert Lipsyte. *Journal of Adolescent & Adult Literacy, 47*(5), 428–429.

Gauthier, G. (2002). Whose community? Where is the "YA" in YA literature? *English Journal, 91*(6), 70–76.

Hinchman, K. A., Alvermann, D. E., Boyd, F. B., Brozo, W. G., & Vacca, R. T. (2003/2004).

Supporting older students' in- and out-of-school literacies. *Journal of Adolescent & Adult Literacy, 47*(4), 307–310.

Weber, M. (2003). Winning young adult authors. *Oregon Library Association Quarterly (OLA Q), 9*(3), 2–7.

References

(Note: All young adult literature referenced in this chapter are included in the Young Adult Books list and are not repeated in this list.)

Aronson, M. (1997). The challenge and glory of young adult literature. *Booklist, 93*(16), 1418–1419.

Aronson, M. (2001). *Exploring the myth: The truth about teenagers and reading*. Lanham, MD: Scarecrow Press.

Aronson, M. (2002). Coming of age. *Publishers Weekly, 249*(6), 82–86.

Bean, T. W. (2002). Making reading relevant for adolescents. *Educational Leadership, 60*(3), 34–37.

Bean, T. W., & Moni, K. (2003). Developing students' critical literacy: Exploring identity construction in young adult fiction. *Journal of Adolescent & Adult Literacy, 46*(8), 638–648.

Brown, J., & Stephens, E. (1995). *Teaching young adult literature*. Belmont, CA: Wadsworth.

Bushman, J., & Haas, K. P. (2001). *Using young adult literature in the English classroom*. Upper Saddle River, NJ: Merrill/Prentice Hall.

Campbell, P. (2003). *The outsiders*, Fat Freddy, and me. *The Horn Book, 79*(2), 177–183.

Campbell, P. (2004). The sand in the oyster: YA biblio-bullish trends. *The Horn Book, 80*(1), 61–65.

Cart, M. (2001). The evolution of young adult literature. *Voices from the Middle, 9*(2), 95–97.

Christenbury, L. (1997). From the editor. *English Journal, 86*(3), 11–12.

Crocker, K. C. (2003, November/December). Teen books: The new generation. *Pages,* 11 (11/12) 76–78.

Dresang, E. (1999). *Radical change: Books for youth in a digital age.* New York: H. W. Wilson.

Fantasy books top the list for teens: Young adults choose their favorite books as part of YALSA Teen Read Week. (2004). *School Library Journal, 50*(1), 23.

Galda, L., & Liang, L. A. (2003). Literature as experience or looking for facts: Stance in the classroom. *Reading Research Quarterly, 38*(2), 268–277.

Gillet, J. W., & Temple, C. (2000). *Understanding reading problems.* New York: Longman.

Glasgow, J. N. (2002). Radical change in young adult literature informs the multigenre paper. *English Journal, 92*(2), 41–51.

Herz, S. K., & Gallo, D. R. (1996). *From Hinton to Hamlet: Building bridges between young adult literature and the classics.* Westport, CT: Greenwood Press.

Hipple, T. (2000). With themes for all: The universality of the young adult novel. In V. R. Monseau & G. M. Salvner (Eds.), *Reading their world: The young adult novel in the classroom* (pp. 1–14). Portsmouth, NH: Heinemann.

Jago, C. (2000). *With rigor for all: Teaching classics to contemporary students.* Portland, ME: Calendar Islands.

Jones, P. (2001). The perfect tens: The top forty books reviewed in Voice of Youth Advocates 1996–2000. *Voice of Youth Advocates, 24*(2), 94–99.

Jones, P. (2003). To the teen core: A librarian advocates building collections that serve YA readers. *School Library Journal, 49*(3), 48–49.

Kaywell, J. F. (Ed.). (1993–2000). *Adolescent literature as a complement to the classics.* Norwood, MA: Christopher Gordon.

Kaywell, J. F. (2001). Preparing teachers to teach young adult literature. *English Education, 33*(4), 323–327.

Kiesling, A. (2002). Tuning in to the teen soul. *Publishers Weekly, 249*(10), 30–32.

Knickerbocker, J. L., & Rycik, J. (2002). Growing into literature: Adolescents' literary interpretation and appreciation. *Journal of Adolescent & Adult Literacy, 46*(3), 196–208.

Manning, M. L., & Bucher, K. T. (2005). *Teaching in the middle school.* Upper Saddle River, NJ: Merrill Prentice Hall.

The marketing battle for Generation Y. (2004. February). *Life Insurance International,* 15. Retrieved February 11, 2005 from http://proquest.umi.com

Maughan, S. (2000). Teenage growing pains. *Publishers Weekly, 247*(3), 28–32.

McElmeel, S., & Buswell, L. (1998). Readers' choices: The most important authors of books for young adults. *The Book Report, 16*(4), 23–24.

Merriam-Webster's encyclopedia of literature. (1995). Springfield, MA: Merriam-Webster.

Moore, D. W., Bean, T. W., Birdyshaw, D., & Rycik, J. A. (1999). *Adolescent literacy: A position statement.* Newark, DE: International Reading Association.

Moore, J. N. (1997). *Interpreting young adult literature: Literary theory in the secondary classroom.* Portsmouth, NH: Heinemann.

Poe, E., Samuels, B. G., & Carter, B. (1995). Past perspectives and future directions: An interim analysis of twenty-five years of research on young adult literature. *The ALAN Review, 22*(2), 46–50.

Reading remains popular among youth, according to poll (National Education Association survey). (2001, June). *Reading today.* Retrieved January 5, 2004, from http:www.findarticles.com/cf_dls/m0HQZ/6_18/76332780/print.jhtm1.

Richardson, M. V., & Miller, M. B. (2001). Motivating students to read: Using authors and literature from their home state. *Reading Improvement, 38*(3), 119–124.

Samuels, B. G. (1992). The young adult novel as transitional literature. In V. R. Monseau and G. M. Salvner (Eds.), *Reading their world: The young adult novel in the classroom* (pp. 28–47). Portsmouth, NH: Boynton/Cook.

Vogels, M. (1996). Young adult literature/Adult literature: What's the difference? Paper presented at National Council of Teachers of English, November 23, 1996, Chicago, IL.

Williams, L. (2003). Summer belongs in the hands of the students: Celebrating choice in school reading lists. *Voice of Youth Advocates, 26*(5), 368–371.

Worthy, J., Patterson, E., Salas, P., Prater, S., & Turner, M. (2002). More than just reading: The human factor in reading resistant readers. *Reading Research and Instruction, 41*, 177–202.

2

EVALUATING AND SELECTING YOUNG ADULT LITERATURE

In order to identify and recommend young adult literature to adolescents and to incorporate young adult literature into lesson and unit plans, educators must be able to evaluate and select the best and most appropriate literature. While the literature's popularity is one consideration, quality or literary merit is also important. By consulting recognized selection aids, checking the winners of book awards and prizes, and actually examining books for literary elements such as plot, character, theme, setting, style, and point of view, teachers and library media specialists can identify good young adult literature.

Educators must also consider the religious, ethnic, social, racial, physical, sexual, and other diversities found in contemporary society and examine the way all groups are represented in young adult literature. Although there has been a concerted effort in the last decade to depict all groups with respect and understanding in young adult books, the challenge remains to identify appropriate literature, examine it for literary merit, evaluate it accurately and fairly, and take the steps necessary to acquaint young adults with it. When selecting and recommending literature for adolescents, educators must also recognize gender differences and reading preferences and take them into consideration. Good books, even in the genres of science fiction or fantasy, should contain:

> interesting, realistic characters who play out important themes against an accurately depicted and realistically detailed backdrop. . . . If we demand good literature, we will get . . . the lasting pleasure that comes when we finish reading a memorable piece of writing. (Jordan, 1996c, pp. 20–21)

FOCUSING POINTS   **In this chapter, you will read about:**

1. The purpose for selecting young adult literature.
2. The use of selected awards, book lists, review journals, and bibliographies in the book selection process.
3. The elements of literature that library media specialists and teachers can consider when evaluating and selecting young adult literature.
4. Our increasingly multicultural nation and the need to select young adult literature that reflects our schools' diversity.
5. The need to consider gender differences and preferences when selecting young adult literature for both females and males.

THE PURPOSE OF SELECTING YOUNG ADULT LITERATURE

Thousands of new young adult books are published each year. When these are added to the books already in print, teachers and library media specialists often face a difficult task in selecting appropriate, quality literature that meets the developmental, intellectual, and social needs of adolescents as well as the school's curricular standards. Perhaps the ideal way to accomplish this is for educators to read young adult literature and make their own judgments about its quality and appropriateness. Unfortunately, given the large number of young adult books published each year, it is not possible for any educator to read more than a sample of the new young adult literature that reaches the market. For example, 900 newly published books were nominated for the annual Best Books for Young Adults list for 2004 (Best Books for Young Adults honors 84 books, 2004). Given that these were just a portion of the total number of books published, teachers and library media specialists have developed other strategies for selecting quality literature.

RELYING ON OTHERS WHEN SELECTING YOUNG ADULT LITERATURE

Many teachers and all library media specialists have learned to rely on the recommendations of others when selecting materials. However, it is important not to rely on just anyone for these recommendations. Publishers include glowing blurbs in the catalogs and advertisements that they publish, but these publicity reviews are not recognized review sources. As one school library media specialist said, "I never met a book that its publisher didn't love."

Thankfully, a number of resources or selection aids such as book awards, book lists, book length bibliographies, and review journals exist that teachers and library media specialists can use to help them select appropriate young adult literature. In addition, Expanding Your Knowledge with the Internet 2–1 provides links where you will find detailed information about many of these resources. In later chapters, you will read about additional selection aids that target specific genres of young adult literature.

Book Awards

While any group can give an award, it is important to identify awards that are given by recognized groups and associations with established committees that read and evaluate a wide range of books. Not only must the review committee members consider the impact of the book on the reader, but they must also consider the quality of the book and its appeal to teenagers (Gentle, 2001). Some younger adolescents enjoy reading books that have won the Newbery Medal, which is presented annually by the American Library Association (ALA) for excellence in literature for children; the Boston Globe-Horn that Award, which is given by the *Boston Globe* newspaper and the *Horn Book Magazine;* or the Carnegie Medal, which is presented by the British Library Association. Other young adults, however, are ready for books that are intended specifically for an older adolescent audience.

General Awards. A number of specialized awards are discussed later in this book, such as those given to books in specific genres or to specific categories of authors. A number of general awards are also given to young adult literature. While these awards honor specific authors, they also promote quality young adult literature in general by heightening "public awareness of excellent literature and increas[ing] the readership of good

---

EXPANDING | **YOUR KNOWLEDGE WITH THE INTERNET 2–1**

 Information on book awards such as the Michael L. Printz Award www.ala.org/yalsa/printz and the Coretta Scott King Award www.ala.org/ala/srrt/corettascottking/corettascott.htm, as well as Best Books lists and review journals can be found on the Internet. Links to many of these resources can be found on this book's Companion Website at www.prenhall.com/bucher.

books" (Gentle, 2001, p. 27). For example, the **Margaret A. Edwards Award** is given to an author for her or his lifetime contribution to writing for young adults. Winners have included Anne McCaffrey, Paul Zindel, and Nancy Garden.

Established in 1999 by the Young Adult Library Services Association (YALSA) of the ALA and *Booklist* magazine, the **Michael L. Printz Award** recognizes, honors, and promotes excellence in young adult literature for ages 12 to 18. The award is not limited to any specific genre. Each year, a committee selects one award winner and up to four "honor" books. For example, in 2004, the winner was Angela Johnson's *The First Part Last* (2003), while the honor books were Jennifer Donnelly's *A Northern Light* (2003), Helen Frost's *Keesha's House* (2003), K. L. Going's *Fat Kid Rules the World* (2003), and Carolyn Mackler's *The Earth, My Butt and Other Big Round Things* (2003).

Given yearly since 1998 by the Adult Books for Young Adults Task Force of YALSA, the **Alex Award** identifies up to 10 adult books, such as Mark Haddon's *The Curious Incident of the Dog in the Night-time* (2003) or Audrey Niffenegger's *The Time Traveler's Wife* (2003), that will appeal to young adult readers. The award is named after Margaret Alexander Edwards, a public librarian who believed that adult books can help adolescents "broaden their experiences and . . . enrich their understanding of themselves and their world" (YALSA announces 2002 Alex Awards, 2002, p. 58).

A number of other awards also have a category for young adult literature. For example, the **National Book Award** has a category of Young People's Literature. Newspapers also often give awards that have categories for young adult fiction such as the **Los Angeles Times Book Prize** and the **Chicago Tribune Young Adult Fiction Prize.** Several state library associations have young adult literature awards including the **Garden State Teen Book Award** (New Jersey), the **Utah Beehive Award for Young Adult Fiction,** and the **Virginia Young Reader's Award.** Suggestions for Collaborative Efforts 2–1 encourages participation in the state or award process.

Awards with Multicultural Perspectives. Several awards have multicultural perspectives. Given by the National Council for the Social Studies, the **Carter J. Woodson Award** recognizes books, like James Tackach's *Early Black Reformers* (2003) or Harvey

SUGGESTIONS FOR COLLABORATIVE EFFORTS

Adolescents may not be able to select the Academy Award winners, but they can vote for the best books in their state or in the nation. For example, the national Teens' Top Ten Books is sponsored by the Young Adult Library Services Association, a division of the American Library Association (www.ala.org/ala/yalsa/teenreading/teenstopten/ TTTnominations.htm).

Check your state library association(s) or your state reading association for information on existing state awards. If there is not an existing award for adolescent literature in your state, lobby for one, or start your own local or regional award.

Fireside's *The "Mississippi Burning" Civil Rights Murder Conspiracy Trial: A Headline Court Case* (2002), which authentically depict ethnicity in the United States and examine race relations sensitively and accurately. **The Sydney Taylor Book Award** for outstanding Jewish content in children's books is given by the Association of Jewish Libraries and has a category for older readers. Given since 1953 by the Women's International League for Peace and Freedom and the Jane Addams Peace Association, the **Jane Addams Children's Book Award** honors children's books that promote peace, social justice, and world community, and has a category for older children through age 14.

Although not specifically given for young adult literature, a few awards honor multicultural literature and may include young adult literature among the award or honor winners. These include the **Coretta Scott King Award** for African American authors and illustrators of outstanding literature for children and young adults. Winners and honor books have included Mildred Taylor's *The Land* (2001) and Jacqueline Woodson's *Miracle's Boys* (2000). The **Pura Belpré Award** is given for books that portray the Latino cultural experience for children and youth, and has honored books like Julia Alvarez's *Before We Were Free* (2002) and Victor Martinez's *Parrot in the Oven: Mi Vida* (1996). Providing an international viewpoint, the **Mildred L. Batchelder Award** is given to a book originally published in a foreign language and translated into English. It has honored books like Uri Orlev's *Run, Boy, Run* (2003) and Tatjana Wassiljewa's *Hostage to War: a True Story* (1997). Other multicultural awards are mentioned later in this chapter.

Best Books Lists

In addition to awards, a number of organizations and associations develop lists of outstanding books for young adults. While the New York Public Library issues an annual **Books for the Teen Age,** the Young Adult Library Services Association (YALSA), a division of ALA) produces a number of these lists including: **Best Books for Young Adults, Top 10 Best Books for Young Adults, Outstanding Books for the College Bound, Popular Paperbacks for Young Adults, Quick Picks for Reluctant Young Adult Readers, Selected Audiobooks for Young Adults,** and **Selected DVDs & Videos for Young Adults.** Some of the lists are general in nature, while others are more specific. For example, each year the YALSA popular paperbacks committee identifies several themes (not necessarily in specific genres) and selects materials related to those themes. The 2004 themes were heroes, music and musicians, mystery and suspense, and science fiction.

Some lists are based on suggestions by young readers themselves. The **Young Adults' Choices** is a yearly list created by adolescents in grades 7 to 12 at participating schools throughout the United States. Students make their selections from books nominated by publishers; in order to be nominated, each book must have received at least two positive reviews from recognized review sources. The Literature for Young Adults Committee of the International Reading Association supervises the voting. A companion **Teacher's Choices** list includes a category for grades 6 to 8. The American Library Association also sponsors an annual **Teens Top Ten** where adolescents vote online for their favorite books.

Each year, the Children's Literature and Reading Special Interest Group of the International Reading Association identifies the **Notable Books for a Global Society, K–12.** The books, including past notables such as Walter Dean Myers' *The Beast* (2003), Beverly Naidoo's *Out of Bounds: Seven Stories of Conflict and Hope* (2001), and Pegi Deitz Shea's *Tangled Threads: A Hmong Girl's Story* (2003), are culturally authentic and enhance understanding of world cultures while showing the common bonds that exist (2000 Notable Books for a Global Society, 2001).

Review Journals

A number of reputable journals exist that include reviews of young adult literature, such as:

- *Booklist* (published by ALA)
- *Bulletin of the Center for Children's Books*
- *Horn Book Magazine*
- *Kirkus*
- *Library Media Connection* (combination of *Library Talk* and *Book Report*)
- *School Library Journal*
- *Voice of Youth Advocates (VOYA)*

These journals devote a significant number of pages in each issue to reviews or, in the case of *Booklist* and *Kirkus,* contain only reviews. In addition to the regular reviews in each issue, a number, such as *School Library Journal, Booklist,* and *Voice of Youth Advocates (VOYA),* publish yearly best books lists. While most of the journals evaluate young adult literature for quality and literary merit, VOYA includes both a quality and a popularity rating with each review.

Other journals may also include reviews or bibliographies of suggested young adult literature in addition to articles. These include *The ALAN Review* [affiliated with the National Council of Teachers of English (NCTE)], *Journal of Adolescent & Adult Literacy, Journal of Youth Services in Libraries* (affiliated with ALA), *Language Arts* (affiliated with NCTE), *English Journal* (affiliated with NCTE), *Multicultural Review, Voices from the Middle* (affiliated with NCTE), and *Children's Literature in Education.* Taking a thematic approach, *Book Links* publishes curriculum-related bibliographies and essays on linking books with topics of interest to children and young adults. You can find links to all of these on this book's Companion Website at www.prenhall.com/bucher.

Book-Length Bibliographies

In addition to the awards and review journals, a number of books contain bibliographies of recommended books for young adults. Table 2–1 contains a list of some recent titles. A number of books also examine the literary elements of young adult fiction. These include the series *Adolescent Literature as a Complement to the Classics* (Kaywell, 1993–), and the multivolume *Beacham's Guide to Literature for Young Adults* (Beetz &

TABLE 2-1	Recent Bibliographies of Young Adult Literature

Title	Author	Date
Best Books for Young Adults	Carter, Estes, & Waddle	2000
Best Books for Young Teen Readers, grades 7 to 10	Gillespie	2000
Books for You	Beers & Lesesne	2001
British Literature for Young People	Eccleshare	2001
A Core Collection for Young Adults	Jones, Taylor, & Edwards	2003
Helping Teens Cope	Jones	2003
High/Low Handbook	LiBretto & Barr	2002
Radical Reads	Bodart	2002

Niemeyer, 1989–), the latest volumes of which were issued in 2000. In the *Twayne Young Adult Author Series* edited by Patricia Campbell, each volume in the series focuses on a specific young adult author and includes information about the author's works.

Evaluating Review Sources

While Internet sites such as Amazon.com and Barnesandnoble.com are not review sources, they do include reviews from reputable selection journals as part of their descriptions of many of the books found on their sites. By knowing the legitimate, quality selection aids, you can identify appropriate reviews on the web sites of these and other Internet superstores. However, beware of reviews from sources that you do not know or from "readers." Some sources are nothing more than publishers' or distributors' catalogs. In addition, in 2004, Internet users discovered that a number of so-called "reviews from readers" at Internet bookstores were actually written by the book's author or by his or her friends using a variety of fictitious names in order to promote specific books. The best approach is to use only reviews from reputable sources that you know and trust.

RELYING ON YOUR OWN JUDGMENT TO EVALUATE YOUNG ADULT LITERATURE

While, in many cases, you can rely on selection aids to identify appropriate young adult literature, there are cases where you must rely on your own judgment. For example, there may have been conflicting reviews about a book; or you may not be able to locate reviews from recognized sources. In other instances, there may only be a publisher's advertisement that catches a school library media specialist's attention, a mention of a new book in an article, or a display at a conference or bookstore. Certainly, all teachers will want to read and review the young adult books that they assign in their classes or put on their reading lists. When a personal review is needed, you must have a set of guidelines to use when evaluating literature.

Elements of Literature

Throughout this book, you will read about criteria for evaluating each of the genres of literature. Behind all of these specific criteria are the literary elements such as character, plot, theme, setting, style, point of view, and tone. Although these elements are found in all good literature, they can vary according to the genre or type of literature as well as the age of the intended audience. While we can provide guidelines that you can use when examining these elements in books, it is important that you remain flexible when using them to select appropriate materials for a specific group of adolescents. Connecting Young Adults and Their Literature 2–1 presents one educator's view of the study of literary elements by adolescents themselves. Expanding Your Knowledge with the Internet 2–2 provides links that discuss some of these elements in more detail than we can present in this chapter.

Plot. The plot is the "plan or the main story of a literary work . . . also known as the narrative structure" (*Merriam-Webster's Encyclopedia of Literature*, 1995, p. 890). Acting

---

CONNECTING | **YOUNG ADULTS AND THEIR LITERATURE 2–1**

While agreeing that it is important for adolescents to understand and evaluate the elements of literature, Arthea J. S. Reed (1994) suggested that educators should not lecture young adults about the literary elements of young adult novels. Rather, she believed that educators must allow young adults to discover, experience, and respond to the elements of a literary work by examining the work as a whole rather than dissecting the elements. When students are asked to dwell on the elements, they may lose sight of the work as a whole. This does not mean that readers cannot be encouraged to understand how these literary elements work. However, the elements should not be emphasized to a point where adolescents no longer enjoy reading.

EXPANDING | **YOUR KNOWLEDGE WITH THE INTERNET 2–2**

 A number of Internet sites provide information on the elements of literature such as the Elements of Fiction Chart at www.allamericareads. org/lessonplan/strategies/during/elemfict.htm or a Lesson Plan on the Elements of Fiction at www.yale.edu/ynhti/curriculum/units/1983/3/ 83.03.07.x.html. Links to these and additional sites with information on the elements of literature are found on this book's Companion Website at www.prenhall.com/bucher.

as a thread to hold the book together, the plot shows the characters in action and makes the reader want to continue reading (Lukens, 2003).

In young adult literature, the plot's importance cannot be overemphasized. For many reluctant readers, it is the action and movement of the plot rather than the detailed descriptions of the setting or the characters that draw them into the story. Young adults seem to prefer books with interesting plots to which they can relate. In books with well-written plots, events seem logical and natural, not contrived or artificial, and reflect the interests of adolescents. Successful authors such as Walter Dean Myers and Karen Hesse know when to allow readers to predict actions and when to surprise them.

Conflict is at the core of the plot and usually takes one or more of the following forms:

- Person against person

- Person against society (culture)

- Person against nature (environment)

- Person against self

Some critics add another form of conflict as person against fate (spirit or deity).

A number of plot features exist that writers of young adult literature can employ. A plot may be linear/chronological or it may contain flashbacks that move the action between the past and the present. At times, an author may use two or more parallel plots, such as those in Robert Cormier's *I Am the Cheese* (1978), or an episodic plot that consists of a series of loosely connected stories or scenes (*Merriam-Webster's Encyclopedia of Literature*, 1995). Considerations for Evaluating Young Adult Literature: *Plot* provides several guidelines for evaluating plot.

Characters. In literature, character refers to the individuals (human and nonhuman persons, animated objects, or personified animals) about whom the book is written.

CONSIDERATIONS | *For Evaluating Young Adult Literature* | **PLOT**

- Is the plot enjoyable and interesting?

- Is the plot logical or contrived? Natural or artificial?

- Is the plot credible and believable?

- Is there the right amount of predictability for the intended audience and the genre of the book?

- Are the themes/topics of the book represented appropriately by the actions within the plot?

- Is the plot carefully constructed?

- Does the plot lead to a well-defined, logical, and identifiable climax?

| CONSIDERATIONS | For Evaluating Young Adult Literature | CHARACTER |

⊚ Are the characters' emotions, actions, thoughts, and words believable, credible, and consistent?

⊚ Are the characters realistic rather than contrived?

⊚ Do the characters complement each other?

⊚ Do the characters contribute to the action and believability of the plot?

⊚ Do the characters avoid being stereotypes?

⊚ What will the readers learn from the characters?

⊚ Will adolescents relate to or understand the characters?

⊚ In series books, will the characters make adolescents want to continue with the series?

While the plot or action drives some books, in others, effective characterization maintains the reader's interest. When adolescents identify closely with the characters, they become involved with the experiences in the book. Authors reveal information about individual characters in a number of ways: what the character says, thinks, and does; what others say or think about the character or how they relate to the character; and how the book's narrator describes the character.

A number of terms are used to describe the characters within a book. The *protagonist* or principal character (*Merriam-Webster's Encyclopedia of Literature,* 1995) is usually confronted with the *antagonist* or the "principal opponent or foil of the main character" (*Merriam-Webster's Encyclopedia of Literature,* 1995, p. 56). While *round or dynamic characters* are "complex and undergo development throughout the story" (*Merriam-Webster's Encyclopedia of Literature,* 1995, p. 420), *flat or static characters,* although essential, are "two-dimensional . . . uncomplicated, and do not change" (p. 420). Stereotypes or stock characters are usually flat and static. The static or dynamic nature of characters helps the reader understand the ideas behind the action in the plot (Lukens, 2003). Considerations for Evaluating Young Adult Literature: *Character* details several guidelines for examining this literary element.

Setting. Basically, the setting is the time and place in which the action takes place (*Merriam-Webster's Encyclopedia of Literature,* 1995). However, the setting can be much more than a physical description with "the makeup and behavior of fictional characters often depend[ing] on their environment quite as much as on their personal characteristics" (*Merriam-Webster's Encyclopedia of Literature,* 1995, p. 1015). Sounds, smells, kinds of buildings, quality of light, and climate may combine to create the mood and atmosphere for the characters and the conflict (Lukens, 2003). Anne Devereaux Jordan (1996c) suggested that setting can assume the role of a character, especially in situations where nature or the environment helps or hinders characters. By alluding to past literary and philosophical traditions, the use of setting as character adds depth to a story. For example, when

CONSIDERATIONS	For Evaluating Young Adult Literature	SETTING
⦿ Even if imaginary, is the setting appropriate and consistent? ⦿ Does the setting complement the other literary elements? ⦿ Does the setting contribute to an understanding of the time and place?		⦿ Is the setting authentic and credible? ⦿ Does the author use the setting effectively?

nature is brought to life within a story, readers may be reminded of past mythological tales and of the pastoral and Romantic traditions (Jordan, 1996c).

While some works such as historical fiction may depend heavily on a specific realistic setting, other books may have a setting that expands rather than limits the universality of the story (Lukens, 2003). Perhaps the setting is totally imaginary or it may be loosely defined to provide additional interpretations to the book. A setting may create a mood, create conflict, provide historical background, or add to the symbolism in the plot. Considerations for Evaluating Young Adult Literature: *Setting* provides several suggestions for examining this literary element.

Theme. A theme is sometimes described as the "dominant idea of a book" (*Merriam-Webster's Encyclopedia of Literature,* 1995), or the underlying or unstated ideas that provide organization. "If the plot tells us what happens in a story, the theme tells us why it happens" (Russell, 2001). You may forget the exact events in a novel, but the theme will often remain with you because it goes beyond the action of the plot to reach a level of deeper meaning. This does not mean that all themes are serious; however, they should be substantial, not trivial.

Although some authors openly state an explicit theme, in most cases, the theme is implicit or implied and is revealed through the characters, the conflict, and the setting of the book. Sometimes, a book has several themes, with one often being more important than the others. Common themes in young adult books usually present the author's perspective on concepts such as growing into adulthood or "coming-of-age;" accepting responsibility; confronting problems in life such as death and dying, illness, or poverty; and learning to deal with parents, other adults, and friends. Considerations for Evaluating Young Adult Literature: *Theme* provides several guidelines for examining this literary element.

Point of View. The author's perspective in telling the story is called the point of view, with the three main points of view being first person, third person singular, and third person omniscient (*Merriam-Webster's Encyclopedia of Literature,* 1995). For readers, the

CONSIDERATIONS	For Evaluating Young Adult Literature	THEME

- ◉ What is the theme?
- ◉ Is the theme appropriate/worthwhile for adolescents?
- ◉ Will adolescents be able to understand the theme?
- ◉ What will adolescents learn from the theme?
- ◉ Is the theme too "preachy" or blatant or is it natural and objective?

- ◉ Does the theme complement the other literary elements?
- ◉ Does the theme provide cohesion to the work?
- ◉ How is the theme revealed to the reader?

point of view determines what the readers know, how involved they are in the story, and how the story develops.

In the first person point of view, "the story is told by 'I,' one of the characters involved in the story" (*Merriam-Webster's Encyclopedia of Literature,* 1995, p. 894) and the reader sees everything through the eyes of that character, who may or may not be the protagonist. Sometimes authors present the first person point of view through a diary or journal written by the character. When an author writes in the third person singular, he/she "writes from the point of view of a single character, describing or noticing only what that character has the opportunity to see and hear and know, but not in the voice of that character" (p. 894). Sometimes this is referred to as looking over the shoulder of one of the characters. Finally, using the third person omniscient point of view, an author is all-knowing about the details of the plot as well as the conscious or unconscious feelings of all of the characters (Lukens, 2003). Sometimes, authors use multiple points of view, perhaps by having different chapters told by different characters, switching between two major characters for alternating chapters, or interspersing short first person reflections in an otherwise third person omniscient narrative. Considerations for Evaluating Young Adult Literature: *Point of View* provides several guidelines for evaluating this literary element.

Style of Writing. In writing, the word *style* refers to the author's "distinctive manner of expression" (*Merriam-Webster's Encyclopedia of Literature,* 1995, p. 1077) or how the writer chooses and arranges words (Lukens, 2003). Using the most appropriate words and phrases, the author adds details and meanings to plots, shows characters' thoughts and reasons for actions, and provides more intricate descriptions of settings. Whether in exposition, dialogue, vocabulary, imagery, figurative language, or sentence structure, the author's style conveys information, feelings, and perspectives. By putting them together, the author creates the book's mood or overall atmosphere.

The author's style also sets the tone of the book or the author's attitude toward both the book and the intended readers. According to Lukens (2003), the author's choice of

| **CONSIDERATIONS** | *For Evaluating Young Adult Literature* | **POINT OF VIEW** |

- ◎ Is the point of view appropriate for the plot and characters?
- ◎ Is the point of view appropriate for the developmental level of the intended reader?
- ◎ Is the point of view consistent and does it add to the understanding and appreciation of the story?
- ◎ Does the point of view complement the other literary elements?

- ◎ Is the point of view clear to the reader, and is the reader able to determine how objective or subjective it is?
- ◎ Does the point of view contribute to the reader's understanding of the book?
- ◎ Is the point of view credible and maintained throughout the book?

| **CONSIDERATIONS** | *For Evaluating Young Adult Literature* | **STYLE AND TONE** |

- ◎ What literary devices comprise the author's style?
- ◎ Is the author's style appropriate for the plot and the theme?
- ◎ Is the author's style appropriate for adolescents?
- ◎ What mood does the style create?
- ◎ Does the author's style complement the other literary elements?
- ◎ Does the style contribute to the understanding of the book?

- ◎ Does the author maintain the same style throughout the book? If not, why, and is the change effective?
- ◎ Does the tone of the book help young adults to understand the author's perspectives and biases?
- ◎ Will the tone appeal to adolescents?
- ◎ Is the tone consistent throughout the book?

words is a means of showing attitude toward the subject. Condescending, moralizing, didactic, sensational, cynical, or sentimental tones are usually not appropriate (Russell, 2001). In contrast, serious, humorous, passionate, sensitive, zealous, poignant, and warm tones are common in young adult literature. Considerations for Evaluating Young Adult Literature: *Style* and *Tone* provides several guidelines for evaluating these elements.

 This book's Companion Website includes a sample evaluation of a young adult book based on all of the elements of literature.

SELECTING MULTICULTURAL LITERATURE FOR YOUNG ADULTS

The U.S. population is becoming more diverse, so educators are attempting to reflect this diversity in both the literature that is available to adolescents and in the school's curriculum. The importance of this is indicated, in part, by information from the U.S. Census reports which show that in 1900, 85% of immigrants came from Europe. In contrast, in 1990, only 22% came from Europe (U.S. Bureau of the Census, 2003). By the 2000 census, 2.4% of the population claimed a multiracial heritage (Yakota & Frost, 2003). As the anticipated growth in selected minority groups (Table 2–2) continues, there will be an increase in the school-age population from these groups. Also, with the continued practice of inclusion, there will be even more diversity within classrooms.

Responding to Diversity: Values of Multicultural Literature

What is a common pleasure for mainstream students—connecting with a character who has a similar name and a familiar experience—truly delights children who don't typically see themselves reflected in the books they use. (Carger, 2003, p. 34)

James Baldwin [cited in Boyd (2002)] maintained that literature is "vital to how people perceive reality and the world in which they live" (Boyd, 2002, p. 59). Described as a "vehicle for socialization and change" (Harris, 1997, p. 51), multicultural literature allows readers to connect to people from other cultures in a way that the Western male writers in the traditional literary canon are unable to do (Chew, 1997).

Through multicultural literature, young adults can:

- Learn about their own and others' cultural backgrounds

- Realize the many similarities that all people share and experience

- Begin to understand the injustices of the past

- Develop self-esteem and cultural identity

- Understand the problems faced by refugees and immigrant groups

- Develop a respect for a variety of cultural and individual characteristics

- "[B]uild a positive self-image by . . . [observing] characters like themselves and their families who are able to work out problems and succeed in various ways" (McGlinn, 2002, p. 50).

In addition, "good stories from other cultures and languages help connect . . . [readers] to people around the world" (Lo, 2001, p. 87). By using universal themes such as justice, friendship, survival, or conflict resolution, authors of multicultural literature are able to make connections across cultures (Gonzalez, Huerta-Macias, & Tinajero, 1998). Authors are also able to "raise the consciousness and awareness of differences between and among people across contexts, countries, and cultures" (Boyd, 2002, p. 89). For example, in a study by Athanases (1998), a diverse group of 10th-grade students eliminated stereotypes as they read multicultural literature and learned about diversity in race, religion, ethnicity, gender, and sexual orientation.

TABLE 2-2	*Major Cultural Groups in the United States*	

Cultural Group	2002	Projected 2010
Hispanic American	38.761 million	47.756 million
African American	36.746 million	40.454 million
Asian American & Pacific Islanders	12.043 million	14.241 million
Native American	2.752 million	NA

Source: U.S. Bureau of the Census. (2003). *Statistical abstracts of the United States: 2003* (123rd ed.) Washington, DC: Government Printing Office.

As all adolescents begin to shape their identity, minority students begin to develop their ethnic identity (Gonzalez, Huerta-Macias, & Tinajero, 1998). In addition to learning about other cultures, multicultural literature helps adolescents "of diverse backgrounds shape cultural identity" (De León, 2002, p. 51) and their personal identity (Klein, 1992). Multicultural literature "frees the many voices in the reader" (Aronson, 2001, p. 17) and encourages the reader to "explore all of her selves: the master and the slave, the male and the female, the black and the white" (p. 17).

Although Morales (2001) was writing about "Chicano/a" (p. 16) students, her thoughts hold true for other adolescents as well. Adolescents must learn about their cultural identity and "how it fits into their complex identity" (p. 20). When teachers promote a "shared experience" (p. 18) through multicultural literature while also "fostering an exuberance for one's own identity" (p. 18), the result will be a multicultural classroom that will empower all students.

A Brief History of Multicultural Literature

For many decades, children's and young adult literature focused primarily on middle class Anglo American populations, and, of course, dealt with situations, problems, and challenges representative of this cultural group. Other groups, if represented at all, were usually shown as minor characters or in menial and subservient positions. For example, American Indians were often stereotyped as savages and African Americans were portrayed only as servants. These representations had the potential to distort the views of readers toward an entire culture of people. Table 2–3 outlines some of the historical events in the development of multicultural literature.

Recent years have brought about improvements in this representation, as authors and publishers have attempted to produce books that show more balanced perspectives of cultural differences. However, in a study of the publishing industry, Hill (1998) identified three "gatekeepers" who influence the amount of multicultural literature that is published and made available. First, she found that many publishers focus on the profitability of a book and do not seek out minority authors and illustrators. Also, review journals, knowing that they do not have the space in their issues to review all books, focus on literature that they believe will have a wide appeal to schools and libraries. Finally, she cited bookstore buyers and librarians who rely on the publishers

TABLE 2-3	Historical Events in the History of Multicultural Literature

Date	Event
1885	Mark Twain's *Huckleberry Finn* depicted attitudes of that time toward culturally diverse individuals.
1900–1930s	Books included stereotypical perspectives.
1940s–1950s	Books included other cultures only on a superficial level.
1960s–1970s	African American authors such as Virginia Hamilton, Alice Childress, Rosa Guy, and Walter Dean Myers began to be published.
1965	*The Saturday Review* published Nancy Larrick's article entitled "The All-White World of Children's Books."
1968/1969	The ALA established the Mildred L. Batchelder Award for translated books and the Coretta Scott King Award for African American authors.
1970s	Books for children and young adults began to reflect a multicultural viewpoint as authors such as Nicholasa Mohr (Puerto Rican experience), Jamake Highwater (American Indian experience), and Laurence Yep (Asian American experience) were published.
1976	Mildred D. Taylor wrote *Roll of Thunder, Hear My Cry*, which challenged stereotypes of Black life in the South.
1980s	Retrenchment occurred as some established minority writers had difficulty getting their books published and many award-winning books went out of print. Small, independent presses such as Arte Publico began to publish multicultural literature.
Late 1980s–1990s	Rebirth of multicultural publishing among the major publishers.
Late 1990s–2000s	Establishment of multicultural book awards such as the Pura Belpré Award.

Source: Developed in part from Miller-Lachman, L. (1992). *Our family, our friends, our world: An annotated guide to significant multicultural books for children and teenagers.* New Providence, NJ: R. R. Bowker, pp. 5–10.

and the review journals to identify the books that they will carry on their shelves or purchase for their collections (Hill, 1998).

The Cooperative Children's Book Center of the School of Education at the University of Wisconsin–Madison has kept records on the multicultural books published for children and teens. Although there is not a specific breakdown for just adolescent literature, Table 2–4 illustrates their statistics.

As Table 2–4 illustrates, although improvements are still needed, considerable progress has been made as the number of books focusing on multicultural individuals, themes, and issues is growing in quantity and quality. According to Dresang (1999), "the subjugated, unheard voices that are emerging in contemporary literature are not related to ethnicity alone, but speak out on previously unrecognized aspects of gender,

TABLE 2–4	Statistics in Multicultural Publishing For Children and Young Adults

Year	Total Number of Books	African Americans		Asian Americans	American Indian	Latinos
		By	About	By & About	By & About	By & About
1985	2,500	18	NA	NA	NA	NA
1990	5,000	51	NA	NA	NA	NA
1995	4,500	100	167	91	83	70
1998	5,000	92	183	50	54	66
2001	5,000–5,500	99	201	96	60	76
2002	5,000	69	166	91	64	94

NA = Not available.

Source: Developed from Cooperative Children's Book Center. (n.d.). *Children's books by and about people of color published in the United States.* Retrieved May 18, 2004, from www.soemadison.wisc.edu/ccbc/pcstats.htm.

sexual orientation, occupation, socio-economic level, and ability/disability" (p. 26). Discussing literature for Hispanic Americans, Isabel Schon (2004) pointed out that, "from the joys and disappointments of Mexican migrant workers and Cuban exiles in the United States, to Gary Soto's . . . depictions of Mexican American family dynamics, to well-known legends and serious political accounts" (p. 44), today's literature addresses the "dreams, feelings, and celebrations" (p. 44) of different cultures.

Evaluating Multicultural Literature

According to De León (2002), "a multicultural approach to literature . . . is essential because it can foster a self worth and motivation in students of diverse cultural backgrounds that was not present before" (p. 49). This will require a change in secondary English curricula and the ways in which literature is taught (Burroughs, 1999). Chew (1997) supports the study of multicultural literature with the traditional canon by pointing out that an understanding of classical literature can actually assist in the reading of multicultural works. However, the sole responsibility should not reside with the English department (Morales, 2001). Suggestions for Collaborative Efforts 2–2 suggests a book selection team developed from educators throughout the school.

While teachers and library media specialists should evaluate and select all young adult books with care, it may be even more important to select appropriate multicultural literature. As Rochman (1993) noted, a good book can help to "break down [barriers] . . . [and] can make a difference in dispelling prejudice and building community . . . with good stories that make us imagine the lives of others" (p. 19). "Fact and details should emerge naturally in description, action, and dialogue and not detract or derail the storyline or

SUGGESTIONS FOR COLLABORATIVE EFFORTS

Build a book selection team in your school. Too often school librarians and teachers forget that "if . . . collections are to be relevant to the folks we serve, we must strive to respect, and collect, materials that serve tastes not our own" (Benedetti, 2003, p. 29).

- Involve others in the selection process
- Overcome your personal biases
- Identify books that are related to the curriculum
- Determine what young adults are reading in classes and for pleasure
- Read magazines like *Teen People* to see what books are being advertised directly to adolescents
- Check *Entertainment Weekly* to identify the new films based on novels (Benedetti, 2003)

exposition. . . . Themes dealt with in the books should be of significance both to the cultural group portrayed and to the reader" (Jordan, 1996a, p. 23).

Currently, peoples from all cultures are shown from more objective perspectives, more multicultural populations are being written about, and more multicultural authors are being published. However, too many inaccuracies, extreme dialectical differences, and stereotypical perspectives and illustrations still populate current young adult literature. As a result, teachers and library media specialists need to select and use multicultural literature that is free from bias, distortion, stereotypes, racism, and sexism. As Miller-Lachman (1992) pointed out, stereotyping may occur in characterizations (stock physical, social, and behavioral qualities are depicted), the plot (characters play set roles or are unable to solve their own problems), theme (problems are faced by all members of a cultural group, and are specific to only those individuals), setting (all members of a group live in one type of house; i.e., all American Indians live in teepees), language (all members of a group have the same dialect), and illustration (all members of a group look alike).

In spite of the fact that "Ten quick ways to analyze children's books for racism and sexism" (1974) is 30 years old, its suggestions have been a reliable and respected evaluation tool. We have combined this information with ideas from Miller-Lachman (1992) and other sources to provide, in Considerations for Evaluating Young Adult Literature: *Multicultural Books,* a set of questions you can ask when examining multicultural literature. Throughout this book, you will find examples of multicultural literature that, in addition to demonstrating the qualities of outstanding books in their genres, exhibit the characteristics of quality multicultural literature. In addition, Expanding Your Knowledge with the Internet 2–3 provides links where you will find additional information on multicultural young adult literature.

EXPANDING	YOUR KNOWLEDGE WITH THE INTERNET 2-3

 The Internet contains a variety of sites such as the Center for Research on Education, Diversity, and Excellence (www.crede.ucsc.edu/), where you can find information about multicultural diversity, and sites such as How to Choose the Best Multicultural Books—From Scholasticteacher, (scholastic.com/products/instructor/multicultural.htm) where you can find information on multicultural literature. Links to these and many additional sites are found on this book's Companion Website at www.prenhall.com/bucher.

CONSIDERATIONS	*For Evaluating Young Adult Literature*	MULTICULTURAL BOOKS

Ask the following questions when evaluating multicultural books for young adults:

Literary Qualities

◎ Does the book meet the qualifications for good literature?

◎ Does the book exhibit the qualities expected in its genre?

Accuracy and Currency of Facts and Interpretation

◎ Are thoughts and emotions portrayed authentically?

◎ In historical fiction, is the content realistic for the time period?

◎ Does the content intensify the reader's sensitivity to the feelings of others?

◎ Does the author present a balanced view of the issues in the book, especially nonfiction?

Stereotypes in Lifestyles

◎ Are culturally diverse characters and their settings contrasted unfavorably with an unstated norm of Anglo American middle class suburbia?

◎ Does the story go beyond oversimplifications of reality and offer genuine insights into another lifestyle or culture?

Plot

◎ Do European Americans in the story have all the power and make the decisions?

◎ Do people from diverse backgrounds function in essentially subservient roles?

◎ Does a character from a diverse background have to exhibit superior qualities (excel in sports, get A's) to succeed?

◎ How are "problems" presented, conceived, and resolved in the story?

◎ Are people from diverse backgrounds considered to be "the problem"?

◎ Do solutions ultimately depend on the benevolence of a European American?

◎ Are the achievements of girls and women based on their own initiative and intelligence, or is their success due to their good looks or to their relationships with boys?

(continued)

CONSIDERATIONS | For Evaluating Young Adult Literature | **MULTICULTURAL BOOKS**

- Are sex roles incidental or paramount to characterization and plot?

- Could the same story be told if the sex roles were reversed?

Theme

- Would the book limit or promote an adolescent's self-image and self-esteem?

- Would the book limit or promote an adolescent's aspirations?

- Can a reader from any culture become so involved with the book that he or she can identify with the characters and vicariously experience their feelings?

Language

- Is terminology current or appropriate for the time period?

- Does the language refrain from including pejorative terms unless germane to the story?

- Do any dialects reflect the varieties found in contemporary life?

- Does the dialect reflect negatively on an entire culture?

Author's Perspective

- What qualifications does the author (or illustrator) have to write about a multicultural topic?

- Is the author (or illustrator) able to think as a member of another cultural group and to intellectually and emotionally become a member of that group?

- If the author (or illustrator) is not a member of the culturally diverse group being written about, is there anything in the author's (or illustrator's) background that would specifically recommend her or him for this book?

- If a book has to do with the feelings and insights of women, does a male author (or illustrator) present these appropriately?

Illustrations

- Are there stereotypes, oversimplifications, and generalizations in the illustrations?

- Do pictures demean or ridicule characters?

- Is there tokenism or European Americans with tinted or colored faces?

- Is sufficient individuality and diversity depicted within cultural groups?

Sources: Questions developed, in part, from the following:

Jordan, A. D. (1996a). Books of other cultures. *Teaching and Learning Literature, 5*(4), 23–25.

Jordan, A. D. (1996c). Welcome to my world: Books of other cultures. *Teaching and Learning Literature, 5*(4), 15–22.

Miller-Lachman, L. (1992). *Our family, our friends, our world: An annotated guide to significant multicultural books for children and teenagers.* New Providence, NJ: R. R. Bowker.

Ten quick ways to analyze children's books for racism and sexism. (November 3, 1974). *Interracial Books for Children, 5*(3), 6–7.

Selecting Materials for a Diverse Society

In addition to evaluating multicultural literature, teachers and library media specialists must be aware of and use reputable selection tools to assist in identifying quality multicultural literature for young adults. Thankfully, several awards and a number of bibliographies exist (Table 2–5) that educators can turn to.

Gillespie, Powell, Clements, and Swearingen (1994) conducted a study of the Newbery Medal books between 1922 and 1994 to determine the ethnicity of their characters. The results showed 90% of the books had white, Anglo Saxon characters as opposed to 26% with African American characters, 5% with Native Americans, 10% with Asian/Pacific Islanders, and 10% with Hispanic characters. Perhaps because of that, a number of awards for multicultural literature were started. Several of them, such as the Coretta Scott King Award, Pura Belpré Award, and Mildred L. Batchelder Award, were mentioned earlier in this chapter. In addition, the **Américas Award** from the Consortium of Latin American Studies is given to works that portray Latin America, the Caribbean, or Latinos in the United States and includes some titles suitable for adolescents. The **Asian Pacific American Award for Literature,** which is co-sponsored by the Asian Pacific American Librarians Association and the Chinese American Librarians Association, includes young adult literature. Finally, the **Tomás Rivera Mexican American Children's Book Award,** presented by Southwest Texas State University, has included some books that would appeal to younger adolescents. Internet information on these awards is included with the other awards in Expanding Your Knowledge with the Internet 2–1 on this book's Companion Website (www.prenhall.com/bucher).

TABLE 2-5	Bibliographies of Multicultural Literature

Title	Author	Date
The *Best of Latino Heritage, 1996–2000*	Schon	2003
Coretta Scott King Award Books	Stephens	2000
Hearing All the Voices	Darby & Pryne	2002
Latina and Latino Voices in Literature	Day	2003
Lesbian and Gay Voices: An Annotated Bibliography and Guide to Literature for Children and Young Adults	Day	2000
Many Peoples, One Land	Holbig & Perkins	2001
Multicultural Voices in Contemporary Literature	Day	1999
Native Americans Today	Hirschfelder & Beamer	2000
Recommended Books in Spanish for Children and Young Adults, 1996–1999	Schon	2000
Voices from the Margins	Ward	2002

GENDER PERSPECTIVES IN YOUNG ADULT LITERATURE

There are two primary gender issues surrounding young adult literature, both of which will be important to understand when selecting literature for adolescents. One involves the representation of gender in books for adolescents. The other is the differences in reading habits of male and female young adults.

Gender and Reading Preferences

Worldwide literacy scores indicate that boys do not perform as well as girls. For example, in England, girls score higher than boys in English when tested at ages 7, 11, 14, and 16 (Haupt, 2003) while, in Australia, a 1996 survey found that literacy scores for boys declined over a 10 year period (Bantick, 1996). Von Drasek (2002) reported on the National Center for Educational Statistics National Assessment for Educational Progress of 1992–2000 reading assessments in the United States. Between 1998 and 2000, "the gap between boys' and girls' scores increased" (p. 72). Although the percent of girls at or above the proficient level in 2000 was higher than in 1992, for "boys, the percentage in 2000 was not significantly different than in 1992" (p. 72).

In *Reading Don't Fix No Chevys,* Smith and Wilhelm (2002) identified a number of general research findings about boys, girls, and reading:

- Girls comprehend fiction better than boys.

- Boys seem to prefer nonfiction, magazines, and newspapers.

- Boys tend to prefer short texts or texts with short sections.

- Girls enjoy leisure reading more than boys.

- Many boys enjoy reading about sports and hobbies.

- Some boys enjoy fantasy and science fiction.

- Graphic novels and comic books are more popular with boys than girls.

- Boys prefer visual texts.

- Boys really do judge a book by its cover.

However, Wilhelm and Smith (Wilhelm, 2001) went on to caution educators that boys can be "more different than alike" (p. 60) and that depending on statistics alone can cause educators to "lose sight of individual differences" (p. 60). Citing Millard (1997) and Telford (1999), Wilhelm and Smith (Wilhelm, 2001) noted that "teachers tend to use conventional wisdom to reinforce traditional notions of gender and gender preferences, thereby denying boys wider choices and chances to expand their tastes" (p. 60).

Gurian (2001) pointed out that most of the "reading traumatized and reading-deficient high school students" (p. 297) are boys. In a national survey conducted during the 2001 Teen Read Week, adolescents responded to the question: "If you don't read much or don't like reading, why?" Boys reported the following as obstacles to reading: boring/not fun (39.3%), no time/too busy (29.8), like other activities better (11.1%), and can't get into the stories (7.7%). Other responses constituted less than 5% (Jones & Fiorelli, 2003).

In a survey of Arizona high school students that was repeated in 1982, 1990, and 1997, Hale and Crowe (2001) found that, while contemporary boys' favorite books are about adventure, sports, science fiction, and mystery, contemporary girls rank mystery and romance/love stories as their favorites. The lowest-rated categories of books for both boys and girls were historical, western, and biography/autobiography. Although humor books were favorites in 1982, they dropped significantly in popularity by 1997. It should be noted there was no category for realistic fiction on the survey and that the top pleasure reading titles in 1997 were from the genres of fantasy/science fiction/horror, mystery, contemporary realistic fiction, and historical fiction.

While these findings cannot be applied across the board to all adolescents, it is necessary to keep them in mind when selecting young adult literature. Reading takes practice. A coach would never say to a basketball player, "You know how to shoot a basket so you don't need to practice anymore." Instead, both the coach and the player know that practice improves performance. The same holds true with reading. Von Drasek (2002) notes that "skilled readers read an average of 11 pages a day" (p. 72). However, if teachers and library media specialists are not providing the kinds of materials that boys and/or girls enjoy reading, there is a lower probability that adolescents will spend time practicing their reading skills and thus developing reading proficiency.

To encourage boys to read, Allison Haupt (2003), coordinator of Children's and Young Adults' Services at the North Vancouver District Public Library, declared: "I've decided to be overtly and blatantly sexist in everything from the way I approach storytelling to the books I promote. It's not that I don't think that boys and girls . . . can't read and enjoy the same books. . . . But [I am convinced] . . . that our ability to promote reading can be greatly enhanced by recognizing biological and developmental differences between the guys and the gals" (p. 20). Both boys and girls need to see that reading is important and that it can blend with their academic or professional goals. For boys, if "reading is identified as being 'soft' or feminine, then reading would diminish rather than develop . . . [a boy's] fragile sense of self and growing masculinity" (Haupt, 2003, p. 21). Connecting Adolescents and Their Literature 2–2 has some suggestions for encouraging boys to read.

Traditional Perspectives Toward Gender

"Everything we read . . . constructs us, makes us who we are, by presenting our image of ourselves as girls and women, as boys and men" (Fox, 1993, p. 152). A number of writers (Brown & Gilligan, 1992; Orenstein, 1994; Pipher, 1994; Sadker & Sadker, 1994; Thorne, 1993; Walker & Foote, 1999/2000) have focused on the issue of gender in education and the need for gender equity. In their research, these and other researchers have documented gender inequities in educational experiences, as well as differences in socialization and ways in which educational experiences reflect gender.

Traditionally, in schools, educators have provided educational experiences that are based on gender-specific mind-sets. For example, males, both at the top and the bottom of the class, attract a great deal of the teacher's attention (Sadker & Sadker, 1994) while textbooks and other curricular materials cater to males and their learning styles (Textbook sexism, 1994). Clark (1994) found that educators often use teaching strategies that reflect primarily male learning styles, while Levine and Orenstein (1994)

CONNECTING | *ADOLESCENTS AND THEIR LITERATURE 2-2*

A number of strategies exist that teachers and library media specialists can use to encourage adolescent boys to read.

- Identify role models and "catch" them reading. The American Library Association has a series of Read posters that reinforce this, but local personalities, male mentors, coaches, and community leaders can work just as well.
- Find things boys like to read and make them available.
- Include comics and graphic novels in the library and classroom.
- Make sure that both boys' and girls' reading interests are included on reading lists.
- Introduce an "all boys book club" (Haupt, 2003).
- Make magazines and newspapers available.
- Identify books that feature Brozo's 10 positive male archetypes that are relevant to male development: King, Patriarch, Warrior, Magician, Pilgrim, Wildman, Healer, Trickster, Prophet, and Lover (Brozo, 2002).
- Visit author Jon Scieszka's website for ideas: www.guysread.com.
- Display books where boys will notice them.

---

found that educators often perpetuate gender-specific attitudes and beliefs about appropriate motivation and learning behaviors of males and females.

Beginning in the 1960s and gaining momentum from the women's movement of the 1970s, feminist criticism began as some women resisted the exclusion of women and the female consciousness in the accepted literary canon that was taught in schools. By identifying with women writers and their works and by focusing attention on the repression, trivialization, and misinterpretation of female texts, these critics called for studies of the images of women in literary works and, consequently, a feminist revision of the literary canon itself. Female critics pointed out that women bring different experience to a piece of literature than men do. They also believed that male critics not only suppressed female works but also tried to convince women that their interests reflected immature tastes. To reinterpret the literary world and change readers' consciousness, feminist criticism focused on rediscovering female authors and on establishing an alternative historical criticism that would relate literary events to both female and male social concerns (Vandergrift, 1993).

Contemporary Gender Issues

Thankfully, there have been changes over the years in the ways genders are represented in adolescent literature. Fouts (1999) reported a move away from traditional role perspectives for female characters in Spanish children's literature; and Houdyshell and Kirkland (1998) found strong, independent heroines with a sense of self in the most recent Newbery Medal books. In 2002, the Feminist Task Force of the American Library Association's Social Responsibilities Round Table instituted the **Amelia Bloomer List of Recommended Feminist Books for Youth** to recognize risk-taking and life-changing books about women.

In addition to traditional male and female roles, young adult literature has also begun to include gay and lesbian perspectives. Building on John Donavan's *I'll Get There: It Better Be Worth the Trip* (1969) and Nancy Garden's *Annie on My Mind* (1982), young adult realistic novels often address gay and lesbian themes while nonfiction books "provide role models of successful and creative gays and lesbians (Aronson, 2001, p. 60). "Instead of merely telling stories whose punch line is that a character is different and that is okay, we are now getting books in which a character is ambiguous, sorting out a mixed identity, and that is okay too" (p. 88). Today, books that include gay-related themes have received awards such as a National Books Award for Virginia Euwer Wolff's *True Believer* (2001) and a Printz Honor Award for Garrett Weyr's *My Heartbeat* (2002). In 2003, Nancy Garden won a Margaret A. Edwards Award for lifetime contributions to young adult literature.

Selecting Literature for Diverse Gender Perspectives

Teachers and library media specialists need to be aware of gender perspectives when selecting and using young adult literature. This is important because the ways in which genders are depicted in books has an impact on attitudes and the perception of gender-appropriate behavior (Singh, 1998). Both genders deserve fair and equitable treatment. Thus, educators must identify literature that reflects respect for both females and males, shows both genders in non-stereotypical ways, and represents both female and male perspectives. When gender stereotypes are present in young adult literature, both girls and boys are deprived of a range of strong alternative role models.

Everything adolescents read, from advertisements and magazines to sports stories and romance novels, helps develop perceptions and mind-sets (Fox, 1993). Too often, young adult literature portrays individuals in stereotypical ways—girls who are overly concerned with their clothes, hair, makeup, and figure, or are victims in need of a male's help; men who are unable to express emotions or evidence fear. Just as educators should avoid generalizing about a particular culture, they should also avoid selecting literature that perpetuates stereotypes, false perceptions, and half-truths about both males and females.

As with multicultural literature, some critics make the argument that a book with a main character of one gender cannot be written by a writer of another gender. While having "lived" a particular gender perspective might be an advantage, requiring writers to write only about experiences they have encountered limits their imagination and creativity. Would these same critics suggest that an author must have personally been an alcoholic, drug user, or abused child to write about these realistic problems? In an interview with female young adult author M. E. Kerr, B. Allison Gray (1991) asked Kerr why she often wrote from a teenage male's perspective. Kerr responded that many males do not like to read stories about females. Thus, in an effort to encourage boys to read, she decided to write from a male perspective.

Contemporary young adult literature reflects the "complex identities of today's teens" (Pavo, 2003, p. 23) and "readers of all ages are proving that they are ready to move into more complex territory" (p. 25). As authors and publishers continue to diversify the representation of gender in the books that they write and publish, educators must select appropriate titles that support the social, physical, and intellectual needs of adolescents. Considerations for Evaluating Young Adult Literature: *Gender Representations* includes some guidelines for examining all gender representations in contemporary young adult literature. In Expanding Your Knowledge with the Internet 2–4, you will find additional information on gender in education and in young adult literature.

CONSIDERATIONS | *For Evaluating Young Adult Literature:* | **GENDER REPRESENTATIONS**

When examining young adult literature for gender and sexuality, ask the following:

◉ Are the characters developed as individuals, no matter what their gender or sexuality?

◉ Do the descriptions, words, and actions of the characters expand gender roles or reflect traditional stereotypes?

◉ Are occupations, aspirations, and achievements gender neutral?

◉ Do both males and females evidence emotional as well as logical characteristics?

◉ Do both males and females ask questions, confront others, interrupt, and initiate conversations?

◉ Are females "trapped in passive and whiny roles" (Singh, 1998)?

◉ Are females competitive with a desire to meet high expectations?

◉ Do the illustrations depict gender stereotypes?

◉ Does the book include any reversals of traditional gender roles (Rose, 2000)?

◉ Are various family structures shown?

◉ How do males and females gain status (sports, competitions, nurturing, or goodness)?

◉ How does the author want readers to view members of the genders?

◉ What effect does the author's gender have on the book?

◉ Is the book truthful and does it respect its readers (Aronson, 2001)?

◉ Does the book help readers overcome their personal discomfort with sexual roles (Pavo, 2003)?

Additional sources used to develop this list include:

Mitchell, D. (1996). Approaching race and gender issues in the context of the language arts classroom. *English Journal, 85*(8), 77–81.

Roberts, P., Cecil, N. L., & Alexander, S. (1993). *Gender positive!: A teachers' and librarians' guide to nonstereotyped children's literature, K–8.* Jefferson, NC: McFarland.

Rudman, M. (1995). *Children's literature: An issues approach.* White Plains, NY: Longman.

> **EXPANDING**   **YOUR KNOWLEDGE WITH THE INTERNET 2-4**
>
> The Internet contains a number of resources that focus on gender representation and literature. Among these is the Amelia Bloomer List of Recommended Feminist Books for Youth libr.org/FTF/bloomer.html and the Chicago Public Library: Books for Guys www.chipublib.org/007bibliographies/booksforguys.html. Links to these and many additional sites are found on this book's Companion Website at www.prenhall.com/bucher.

CONCLUDING THOUGHTS

In spite of the number of awards, best books lists, and book-length bibliographies, evaluating and selecting young adult books will never be an easy task for teachers and library media specialists. With more books published, the realities of school budgets, and an increasing demand to select books and other forms of literature that can be integrated or at least used across the middle and secondary curricula, educators feel the pressure to select the best and most appropriate young adult literature that will, hopefully, also appeal to young adult readers. Added to the selection dilemma will be the increased diversity within school-age populations that will call for more multicultural literature in the school. Then, too, educators will likely see more accurate and realistic reflections of gender in young adult literature with increased powerful female protagonists, more books written by exceptional female writers, an increasing number of female critics, and a more balanced view of all gender perspectives.

 In response, educators will need to make the commitment to read and thoughtfully consider young adult literature and to seek out reviews in journals and resources that review young adult literature. If they are successful, the lives of all young adults and their respective needs and perspectives will be represented accurately and fairly in the literature in their school. Visit this book's Companion Website at www.prenhall.com/bucher for additional information about selecting young adult literature including review questions, self-assessments, Internet sites, and readings.

Young Adult Books

This section includes young adult titles recommended or mentioned in this chapter. Check the Companion Website at www.prenhall.com/bucher to find additional suggestions of current young adult literature.

Alvarez, J. (2002). *Before we were free*. New York: Knopf.

Cormier, R. (1978). *I am the cheese*. New York: Dell.

Donnelly, J. (2003). *A northern light*. San Diego: Harcourt.

Donovan, J. (1969). *I'll get there: It better be worth the trip*. New York: Harper & Row.

Fireside, H. (2002). *The "Mississippi burning" civil rights murder conspiracy trial: A headline court case*. Berkely Heights, NJ: Enslow.

Frost, H. (2003). *Keesha's house*. New York: Farrar, Straus and Giroux.

Garden, N. (1982). *Annie on my mind*. New York: Farrar, Strauss and Giroux.

Going, K. L. (2003). *Fat kid rules the world*. New York: Putnam.

Haddon, M. (2003). *The curious incident of the dog in the night-time*. New York: Doubleday.

Johnson, A. (2003). *The first part last*. New York: Simon & Schuster.

Mackler, C. (2003). *The earth, my butt and other big round things*. Cambridge, MA: Candlewick.

Martinez, V. (1996). *Parrot in the oven: Mi vida*. New York: HarperCollins.

Myers, W. D. (2003). *The beast*. New York: Scholastic.

Naidoo, B. (2001). *Out of bounds: Seven stories of conflict and hope*. London: Puffin.

Niffenegger, A. (2003). *The time traveler's wife*. San Francisco, CA: MacAdam/Cage.

Orlev, U. (2003). *Run, boy, run*. Boston: Houghton Mifflin.

Shea, P. D. (2003). *Tangled threads: A Hmong girl's story*. New York: Clarion Books.

Tackach, J. (2003). *Early black reformers*. San Diego: Greenhaven.

Taylor, M. (1976). *Roll of thunder, Hear my cry*. New York: Dial.

Taylor, M. (2001). *The land*. New York: Fogelman.

Wassiljewa (Vasil'eva), T. (1997). *Hostage to war: A true story*. New York: Scholastic.

Weyr, G. (2002). *My heartbeat*. New York: Speak.

Wolff, V. E. (2001). *True believer*. New York: Atheneum.

Woodson, J. (2000). *Miracle's boys*. New York: Putnam.

Suggested Readings

Angel, A. (2003). Voices of cultural assimilation in current young adult novels. *The ALAN Review, 30*(2), 52–55.

Colby, S. A., & Lyon, A. F. (2004). Heightening awareness about the importance of using multicultural literature. *Multicultural Education, 11*(3), 24–28.

Daniels, H. (2004). Building a classroom library. *Voices from the Middle, 11*(4), 44–45.

Glenn, W. J. (2003). Consider the source: Feminism and point of view in Karen Hesse's *Stowaway* and *Witness*. *The ALAN Review, 30*(2), 30–34.

Jago, C. (2004). The heart and soul of literature. *Voices from the Middle, 11*(3), 60–61.

References

(Note: All young adult literature referenced in this chapter are included in the Young Adult Books list and are not repeated in this list.)

2000 notable books for a global society: A K–12 list. (2001). *The Reading Teacher, 54*(5), 464–470.

Aronson, M. (2001). *Exploding the myths: The truth about teenagers and reading.* Lanham, MD: Scarecrow.

Athanases, S. Z. (1998). Diverse learners, diverse texts: Exploring identity and difference through literary encounters. *Journal of Literacy Research, 30,* 273–296.

Bantick, C. (1996). Literacy survey. *Youth Studies, 15*(4), 5–6.

Beers, G. K., & Lesesne, T. S. (2001). *Books for you: An annotated booklist for senior high.* Urbana, IL: National Council of Teachers of English.

Beetz, K. H., & Niemeyer, S. (1989–). *Beacham's guide to literature for young adults.* Washington, DC: Beacham Pub.

Benedetti, A. (2003). Falling off my pedestal: A slippery defense of popular taste. *Alki: The Washington Library Association Journal, 19*(3), 28–29.

Best Books for Young Adults honors 84 books. (2004). Accessed January 28, 2004, from www.ala.org/ala/pr2004/prjan2004/2004best booksforya.htm.

Bodart, J. R. (2002). *Radical reads: 101 YA novels on the edge.* Lanham, MD: Scarecrow.

Boyd, F. B. (2002). Conditions, concessions and the many tender mercies of learning through multicultural literature. *Reading Research and Instruction, 42*(1), 58–92.

Brown, L. M., & Gilligan, C. (1992). *Meeting at the crossroads: Women's psychology and girls' development.* Cambridge, MA: Harvard.

Brozo, W. (2002). *To be a boy, to be a reader: Engaging teen and preteen boys in active literacy.* Newark, DE: International Reading Association.

Burroughs, R. (1999). From the margins to the center: Integrating multicultural literature into the secondary English curriculum. *Journal of Curriculum and Supervision, 14*(2), 136–155.

Carger, C. L. (2003). A pool of reflections: The Américas Award. *Book Links, 12*(3), 34–39.

Carter, B., Estes, S., & Waddle, L. L. (2000). *Best Books for Young Adults.* Chicago: American Library Association.

Chew, K. (1997). What does e pluribus unum mean?: Reading the classics and multicultural literature together. *The Classical Journal, 93*(1), 55–78.

Clark, C. S. (1994). Education and gender: The issues. *Congressional Quarterly Researcher, 4*(21), 483–487, 490–491.

Cooperative Children's Book Center. (n.d.). *Children's books by and about people of color published in the United States.* Retrieved May 18, 2004, from www.soemadison.wisc.edu/ ccbc/pcstats.htm.

Darby, M. A., & Pryne, M. (2002). *Hearing all the voices: Multicultural books for adolescents.* Lanham, MD: Scarecrow.

Day, F. A. (1999). *Multicultural voices in contemporary literature.* Portsmouth, NH: Heinemann.

Day, F. A. (2000). *Lesbian and gay voices: An annotated bibliography and guide to literature for children and young adults.* Westport, CT: Greenwood.

Day, F. A. (2003). *Latina and Latino voices in literature: Lives and works.* Westport, CT: Greenwood.

De León, L. (2002). Multicultural literature: Reading to develop self-worth. *Multicultural Education, 10*(2), 49–51.

Dresang, E. T. (1999). *Radical change: Books for youth in a digital age.* New York: H. W. Wilson.

Eccleshare, J. (2001). *British literature for young people: A bibliography 1990–2000.* Great Britain: British Council.

Fouts, E. (1999). Gender and generation in contemporary Spanish children's literature.

Journal of Youth Services in Libraries, 12(2), 31–36.

Fox, M. (1993). *Radical reflections: Passionate opinions on teaching, learning, and living.* San Diego: Harcourt Brace.

Gentle, M. (2001). The Printz Award for young adult literature. *Book Report, 20*(1), 27.

Gillespie, C. S., Powell, J. L., Clements, N. E., & Swearingen, R. A. (1994). A look at the Newbery Medal books from a multicultural perspective. *The Reading Teacher, 48*(1), 40–50.

Gillespie, J. T. (2000). *Best Books for Young Teen Readers, grades 7 to 10.* New Providence, NJ: Bowker.

Gonzalez, M. L., Huerta-Macias, A., & Tinajero, J. V. (Eds.). (1998). *Educating Latino students: A guide to successful practice.* Lancaster, PA: Technomic Publishing.

Gray, B. A. (1991). Her, her, her: An interview with M. E. Kerr. *Voices of Youth Advocates, 13*(6), 337–342.

Gurian, M. (2001). *Boys and girls learn differently: A guide for teachers and parents.* San Francisco: Jossey-Bass.

Hale, L. A., & Crowe, C. (2001). "I hate reading if I don't have to": Results from a longitudinal study of high school students' reading interests. *The ALAN Review, 28*(3), 49–57.

Harris, V. (Ed.) (1997). *Using multiethnic literature in the K–8 classroom.* Norwood, MA: Christopher-Gordon.

Haupt, A. (2003). Where the boys are . . . . *Teacher Librarian, 30*(2), 18–24.

Helbig, A. K., & Perkins, A. R. (2001). *Many peoples, one land: A guide to new multicultural literature for children and young adults.* Westport, NH: Greenwood.

Hill, T. (1998). Multicultural children's books: An American fairy tale. *Publishing Research Quarterly, 14*(1), 36–45.

Hirschfelder, A., & Beamer, Y. (2000). *Native Americans today: Resources and activities for education, grades 4–8.* Englewood, CO: Libraries Unlimited.

Houdyshell, M. L., & Kirkland, J. (1998). Heroines in Newbery Medal award winners: Seventy-five years of change. *Journal of Youth Services in Libraries, 11*(3), 252–262.

Jones, J. B. (2003). *Helping teens cope: A guide to teen issues using YA fiction and other resources.* Worthington, OH: Linworth.

Jones, P., & Fiorelli, D. C. (2003). Overcoming the obstacle course: Teenage boys and reading. *Teacher Librarian, 30*(3), 9–13.

Jones, P., Taylor, P., & Edwards, K. (2003). *A core collection for young adults.* New York: Neal-Schuman.

Jordan, A. D. (1996a). Books of other cultures. *Teaching and Learning Literature, 5*(4), 23–25.

Jordan, A. D. (1996c). Welcome to my world: Books of other cultures. *Teaching and Learning Literature, 5*(4), 15–22.

Kaywell, J. F. (1993–). *Adolescent literature as a complement to the classics.* Norwood, MA: Christopher-Gordon.

Klein, D. (1992). Coming of age in novels by Rudolfo Anaya and Sandra Cisneros. *English Journal, 81*(5), 21–26.

Levine, E. Z., & Orenstein, F. M. (1994). *Sugar and spice and puppy dog tails: Gender equity among middle school children.* ERIC NO: ED389457.

LiBretto, E. V., & Barr, C. (2002). *High/low handbook: Best books and websites for reluctant teen readers.* Englewood, CO: Libraries Unlimited.

Lo, D. E. (2001). Borrowed voices: Using literature to teach global perspectives to middle school students. *The Clearing House, 75*(2), 84–87.

Lukens, R. (2003). *Critical handbook of children's literature*. Boston: Allyn & Bacon.

McGlinn, J. (2002). Seeing themselves in what they read. *Book Links, 11*(3), 50–54.

Merriam-Webster's encyclopedia of literature. (1995). Springfield, MA: Merriam-Webster.

Millard, E. (1997). *Differently literate*. London: Falmer.

Miller-Lachman, L. (1992). *Our family, our friends, our world: An annotated guide to significant multicultural books for children and teenagers*. New Providence, NJ: R. R. Bowker.

Mitchell, D. (1996). Approaching race and gender issues in the context of the language arts classroom. *English Journal, 85*(8), 77–81.

Morales, C. A. (2001). "Our own voice": The necessity of Chicano literature in mainstream curriculum. *Multicultural Education, 9*(2), 16–20.

Orenstein, P. (1994). *Schoolgirls: Young women, self-esteem, and confidence*. New York: Doubleday and American Association of University Women.

Pavo, K. (2003). Out of the closet. *Publisher's Weekly, 250*(24), 23–25.

Pipher, M. (1994). *Reviving Ophelia: Saving the lives of adolescent girls*. New York: Grosset/Putnam.

Reed, A. J. S. (1994). *Reaching adolescents: The young adult book and the school*. Columbus, OH: Merrill.

Roberts, P., Cecil, N. L., & Alexander, S. (1993). *Gender positive!: A teachers' and librarians' guide to nonstereotyped children's literature, K–8*. Jefferson, NC: McFarland.

Rochman, H. (1993). *Against borders: Promoting books for a multicultural world*. Chicago: American Library Association.

Rose, R. (2000). Collection development and the search for positive female characters in children's literature. *Current Studies in Librarianship, 24*(1–2), 107–115.

Rudman, M. (1995). *Children's literature: An issues approach*. White Plains, NY: Longman.

Russell, D. L. (2001). *Literature for children: A short introduction*. New York: Longman.

Sadker, M., & Sadker, D. (1994). *Failing at fairness: How America's schools cheat girls*. New York: Scribner.

Schon, I. (2000). *Recommended books in Spanish for children and young adults, 1996–1999*. Lanham, MD: Scarecrow.

Schon, I. (2003). *The best of Latino heritage 1996–2000: A guide to the best juvenile books about Latino people and cultures*. Lanham, MD: Scarecrow.

Schon, I. (2004). Latinos, Hispanics, and Latin Americans. *Book Links, 13*(3), 44–48.

Singh, M. (1998). *Gender issues in children's literature: ERIC digest*. (ERIC Document Reproduction Service No. ED424591.)

Smith, M. W., & Wilhelm, J. D. (2002). *"Reading don't fix no Chevys": Literacy in the lives of young men*. Portsmouth, NH: Boynton/Cook.

Stephens, C. G. (2000). *Coretta Scott King Award books: Using great literature with children and young adults*. Englewood, CO: Libraries Unlimited.

Telford, L. (1999). A study of boys' reading. *Early Childhood Development and Care, 149,* 87–124.

Ten quick ways to analyze children's books for racism and sexism. (November 3, 1974). *Interracial Books for Children, 5*(3), 6–7.

Textbook sexism. (1994). *Congressional Quarterly Researcher, 4*(21), 496.

Thorne, B. (1993). *Gender play: Girls and boys in school.* New Brunswick, NJ: Rutgers.

U.S. Bureau of the Census. (2003). *Statistical abstracts of the United States: 2003* (123rd ed.). Washington, DC: Government Printing Office.

Vandergrift, J. E. (1993). A feminist research agenda in youth literature. *Wilson Library Bulletin, 68*(2), 22–27.

Von Drasek, L. (2002, October). Boy, oh, boy—books! *Teaching K–8, 33*(2), 72–75.

Walker, C., & Foote, M. M. (1999/2000). Emergent inquiry: Using children's literature to ask hard questions about gender bias. *Childhood Education, 76*(2), 88–91.

Ward, M. (2002). *Voices from the margins: An annotated bibliography of fiction on disabilities and differences for young people.* Westport, CT: Greenwood.

Wilhelm, J. (2001). It's a guy thing. *Voices from the Middle, 9*(2), 60–63.

Yakota, J., & Frost, S. (2003). Multiracial characters in children's literature. *Book Links, 12*(3), 51–57.

YALSA announces 2002 Alex Awards. (2002). *Journal of Youth Services in Libraries, 15*(3), 58.

EXPLORING SCIENCE FICTION, FANTASY, AND HORROR

One look at the phenomenal success of the Harry Potter and *Lord of the Rings* series of fantasy books and movies; the continued popularity of the horror novels of Stephen King, R. L. Stine, and Dean Koontz; or the record-breaking box office ticket sales for the science fiction movie *The Matrix* will reveal that people in general, and young adults in particular, are interested in speculative fiction or works of fantasy, science fiction, and horror. Why, you might wonder, are the fantastic genres so popular with young adults? Perhaps because they provide an escape from the difficulties of life and allow readers to enjoy vicarious experiences, or because young adults enjoy investigating worlds where the impossible becomes possible or where technology makes dreams come true. Regardless of the reasons, young adults do enjoy viewing and reading speculative fiction. Because of this, perceptive teachers, library media specialists, and others who work with young adults need to be aware of the wealth of books that are available and the need to share this literature with adolescents.

SPECULATIVE FICTION: SCIENCE FICTION, FANTASY, AND HORROR

While young adults enjoy reading about the past in historical fiction and about the present in contemporary realistic fiction, they also enjoy escaping to the strange worlds of speculative fiction. Science fiction, fantasy, and horror books allow readers to enter imaginative worlds that are full of endless possibilities. Readers can vicariously face the future, explore the possibilities of science and technology, wrestle with the fantastic in a make-believe world, or confront the horrors that populate their worst nightmares.

It can sometimes be difficult to distinguish between science fiction, fantasy, and horror. Some critics place all speculative fiction in the genre of fantasy, and consider science fiction and horror to be subgenres. Others use the term *fantastic* (Clute & Grant, 1999) or *speculative fiction* (Card, 1990) as an umbrella to cover all three categories, and then discuss each of the three independently. In this book, we will take the latter approach and rely on the term *speculative fiction* to refer to all nonrealistic fiction including fantasy, science fiction, and horror.

Orson Scott Card (1990), a writer of both science fiction and fantasy, and the only author to win both the Nebula Award and the Hugo Award 2 years in a row for the best science fiction novel (*Ender's Game,* 1985; *Speaker for the Dead,* 1986), provides the following way to differentiate between science fiction and fantasy: "If the story is set in a universe that follows the same rules as ours, it's science fiction. If it's set in a universe that doesn't follow our rules, it's fantasy" (Card, 1990, p. 22). He goes on to say that, while plot devices such as time travel can be found in both fantasy and science fiction, if the story contains metal, plastic, and/or heavy machinery, it is science fiction; and the reader can assume, until told otherwise, that the known laws of science apply. If the story contains talismans or magic, it is fantasy; the reader must then rely on the author to describe the natural laws that exist in this fantasy world (Card, 1990). Horror, the final type of speculative fiction, looks at topics that young adults like to read about but would not want to experience, such as vampires, monsters, werewolves, and the supernatural.

Although we will try, it is difficult to put books into categories. Thus, you must realize that some books will cross the lines. For example, some horror books can also fit into the categories of fantasy or science fiction. Some time travel or time warp books are considered science fiction while others are considered fantasy. Some ghost stories are more adventure (Chapter 5) than horror. In the end, we tried to make logical decisions based on certain guidelines which you will find throughout the chapter. Also, although short stories are discussed in Chapter 9, we have included a few collections of speculative fiction in the bibliographies for this chapter. In addition, some books that are classified as nonfiction are directly tied to speculative fiction, such as *Star Wars Episode One: A Visual Dictionary* (Reynolds, 1999) or *Star Wars™ Galactic Phrase Book and Travel Guide* (Burtt, 2001), which provide detailed information about the characters and creatures from this popular science fiction series. Rather than worry about categorizing these works, we encourage you to read them, enjoy them, and recommend them to young adults.

Popularity of Speculative Fiction

In a survey of high school students, Diaz-Rubin (1996) found that horror and fantasy were two of the top 10 areas of interest out of a list of 49 categories. Interest in speculative fiction has been spurred by the continued success of series books and movies such as the Harry Potter and *Lord of the Rings* fantasy books and movies, the release of the new *Star Wars* film trilogy and the *X-Men* films with accompanying books, among others. In 2001, J. K. Rowling's *Harry Potter and the Goblet of Fire* (2000) topped the list of the 100 fastest sellers in Great Britain. In 2003, when *Harry Potter and the Order of the Phoenix* (Rowling, 2003) was published, there were more than 1.3 million advance orders on Amazon.com and more than 13 million copies printed worldwide. Philip Pullman's *The Amber Spyglass* (2000) won the British Whitbread Children's Book of the Year and went on to win the overall Whitbread Award, something never before accomplished by a children's or young adult book.

Science Fiction

By transporting readers to a world where science makes dreams—and sometimes nightmares—come true, science fiction stories appeal to many middle and high school students. Paperbacks, comics, and magazines combine with movies, television shows, and computer games to provide young adults with an opportunity to escape from the difficulties and tedium of everyday life and enter a world that is based on current science as well as trends and technology (Ochoa & Osier, 1993). Clute and Grant (1999) define science fiction as "a text whose story is explicitly or implicitly extrapolated from scientific or historical premises" (p. 844). While science fiction was originally written for adults (although young adults read it as well), writers such as Ursula LeGuin began to write science fiction aimed specifically at the young adult reader (Owen, 1987). Currently, adolescents read a mixture of young adult as well as mainstream adult science fiction.

Many literature critics dismiss science fiction as a literary genre and consider it unworthy of the time of any serious reader. This may be, in part, because much original science fiction is still published in paperback rather than hardback format. Other critics point out that the stories are plot-driven or setting-driven (rather than character-driven), almost to the exclusion of believable and likable characters (Hughes, 1992). In addition, good science fiction demands a high level of scientific accuracy, as errors and inconsistencies found in many science fiction books ruin the credibility of the story (Ochoa & Osier, 1993). Still other readers may see the scientific information as detracting from the story. Then too, many science fiction books have lurid, pin-up style covers or contain steamy sex scenes. Finally, fearing censorship challenges, some teachers and librarians may be reluctant to use novels that present alternative worlds, challenge the supremacy of life on Earth, or present alternatives to contemporary religious beliefs.

However, there are those individuals who maintain that science fiction can be a means of opening student minds and imaginations. Anne Devereaux Jordan (1995) stated that "science fiction for both adults and young people has developed into a sophisticated literary form worth reading and worthy of study" (p. 17). According to author David Brin, science fiction is the "jazz" or most American of all literary genres (Moltz, 2003). Because good science fiction is alive, vibrant, and exciting, its use may yield unexpected dividends (Hughes, 1992). As science fiction challenges readers to think about the past, present, and future, imagination comes into play. As readers begin to consider the future of the world presented in the novel they are reading, they also begin to consider the world in which they live. Well-written science fiction both warns and teaches readers to build the future they want, based upon logic and knowledge, and does so in a pleasing and entertaining manner (Jordan, 1995). Science fiction writing is full of magic moments, "when the writer discovers more in her work than she believed she had put into it. They happen at the subconscious level, perhaps more readily in science fiction and fantasy because the setting and situations therein are removed from the mundane to the more mythical, containing elements that echo the folk tales and legends of the past" (Hughes, 1992, p. 4).

A Brief Look at Science Fiction's Predecessors. When did science fiction begin? Some would argue that the first science fiction book was Mary Shelley's *Frankenstein* in 1818—a book that warned about tampering with science and the unknown. Surely the genre was helped along by books such as *From the Earth to the Moon* (Verne, 1865) and *The Time Machine* (Wells, 1895). Traditionally using either a paperback or magazine format, science fiction publishing began in earnest in the 1950s with authors such as Robert Heinlein and Ray Bradbury (Louvisi, 1997) as well as Isaac Asimov, Frank Herbert, and Robert C. Clarke. In these "pulp" formats (so called because of the cheap pulp paper on which they were printed), the stories were often more concerned with action and scientific gadgets than with the plausibility and logic of the plot (Jordan, 1995). Frequently, the writing was poor, plots were heavily dependent upon coincidence, and the themes were limited to "good versus evil" (p. 19). Fortunately, since the 1950s, science fiction has grown into a respected and popular field of literature (Jordan, 1995).

Types of Science Fiction. It is always difficult to categorize literature, especially with the diversity found in science fiction. Too often, readers lump all science fiction into a category known as "space opera," which takes the old "good guys versus bad guys" scenario of western movies and places it in the realm of outer space. This may have been true with early works such as Edgar Rice Burroughs' *A Princess of Mars* (1912), in which the protagonist John Carter, after being teleported to Mars, battles his way across a planet filled with villains and ultimately wins the hand of Princess Deiah Tjoris. In contrast, contemporary science fiction is much more complex.

In creating the following list of types of science fiction, we have combined the work of Card (1990) and Jordan (1995). As you read through this list, remember that any attempt to categorize literature is fraught with problems since elements from more than one category may be found in a single book. For a listing of recommended science fiction books of all types for young adults, see the annotated bibliography at the end of this chapter.

Earth's Future. The first category of science fiction books includes books that focus on the future of Earth and its inhabitants. There are books that deal with the threat of nuclear or biological war, holocaust brought about by pollution or toxic wastes, the decline of humans and the development of robots or super-intelligent machines or beings, and alien invasions. While, in films, the alien is often portrayed as a threatening entity, in books aliens may arrive either to help or to threaten humankind. Representative young adult novels in this category include *The White Fox Chronicles* (Paulsen, 2000), *Ender's Shadow* (Card, 1999), *Parable of the Talents* (Butler, 1998), *The Kindling* (Armstrong & Butcher, 2002), *Feed* (Anderson, 2002), and *Memory Boy'* (Weaver, 2001).

Contradiction of known laws. A second type of science fiction books focuses on Earth with a contradiction of known laws of nature such as time travel. Time travel was firmly established as a convention in science when H. G. Wells used it in his story *The Time Machine* (1895). Caroline Cooney (2001), Roger Allen (2002), and others build on this idea in contemporary YA novels. By creating an alternative Earth society that is not bound by our laws of nature, Lois Lowry has explored closed utopian communities in books such as *The Giver* (1993), *Gathering Blue* (2002), and *The Messenger* (2004). In a future world, Margaret Haddix in *Turnabout* (2000) allowed people to un-age and go back to their childhoods.

Other worlds. The next group of science fiction books are those set on other (sometimes alien) worlds. The difficulty a writer faces in constructing an alien world is that it cannot be too alien. The characters must share some of the basic fears, needs, and drives humans have—otherwise, the reader cannot identify with or understand them. Anne McCaffrey, the first science fiction author to win the Margaret A. Edwards Award for lifetime achievement in young adult literature, created a classic series of this type of science fiction with her books set on the planet of Pern. One of the early entries in this series, *Dragonsinger* (McCaffrey, 1977), tells of the struggles of a girl, Menolly, who is growing up and trying to find her place within her world. The search for self and a place in the adult world is a task all young people confront as they grow up, and one with which they can identify even if the story is set on a foreign planet. A good introduction to Pern is McCaffrey's *A Gift of Dragons* (2002). Other writers who have created successful worlds include C. J. Cherryh, Ian Banks, Frank Herbert, Nancy Kress, and Kathy Tyers.

Alternative history. Finally, there are the science fiction books that focus on an alternate history of the world or of a prehistoric Earth. Sometimes using time travel, this type of science fiction may present an alternate reality which is often the result of a rewriting of history. Both Henry Turtledove, with a number of alternative history series [e.g., *Best Alternative History Stories of the 20th Century* (Turtledove & Greenberg, 2001)], and Orson Scott Card, with his Alvin Maker books set in North America without the American Revolution, have created series of books based on the premise of contrahistory.

Reasons For Using and Teaching Science Fiction. Science fiction puts an emphasis on imagination and an escape from the demands and practicalities of the real world that appeals to many readers. However, science fiction is more that just "the good versus the bad." Current science fiction reflects many topics such as future worlds, super-intelligent mechanical and human beings, time travel and altered historical events, robots, DNA experiments, nuclear holocaust and survival, toxic wastes, and germ warfare. Thus, science fiction encourages a reader to investigate social concerns and ecological problems (Harris, 1996). In addition, science fiction books attract some adolescents who reject other kinds of books or who are interested in scientific concepts. Adolescents can read these books and evaluate the extent to which science is accurately reflected (Harris, 1996). In fact, a strength of science fiction is its diversity and appeal to adolescents of various reading abilities and on a wide range of grade levels (Bucher & Manning, 2001). Suggestions for Collaborative Efforts 3–1 illustrates how a science fiction novel can be a springboard to scientific inquiry.

Characteristics of Good Science Fiction. With the interest in science fiction, a wide range of books are published each year. While some are excellent, others fall far short of meeting even the basic requirements for any work of fiction. Considerations for Selecting Young Adult Literature: *Science Fiction* presents a list of items to consider in evaluating science fiction.

Suggestions For Selecting and Using Science Fiction. It can be very difficult for teachers and librarians to select, use, and recommend good science fiction, especially

SUGGESTIONS FOR COLLABORATIVE EFFORTS

Link literature and science. As students read a science fiction book, encourage them to use a Possible, Plausible, or Futuristic chart to identify the elements in the book that are currently possible and scientifically accurate, those that are plausible and an extension of current science, and those that are truly futuristic. When in doubt, students can consult a science teacher or use the library media center for research. They can also visit the Internet sites such as www.qrc.nasa.gov/WWW/PAO/warp.htm, the NASA site that discusses space travel.

X **CONSIDERATIONS** | *For Selecting Young Adult Literature* | **SCIENCE FICTION**

When evaluating science fiction books, look for the following:

1. Strong themes that are basic to human existence and that do not rely on time or place.
2. Nonstereotypical characters who believe in the science and who rise to overcome challenges.
3. Well-developed and plausible plots.
4. Believable details.
5. Accurate and well-researched science and/or technology.
6. Rules for imaginary or invented science.
7. Details that support the science.
8. Pleasing writing style that does not talk down to the reader.
9. Escapist qualities with an interesting story.
10. Consistency in the plot, characters, and setting.
11. A reliance on science; not on coincidence.

if they, individually, do not enjoy reading novels in the genre. Fortunately, there are many resources that educators can use to aid in the selection of quality science fiction titles. In Expanding Your Knowledge with the Internet 3–1 you will find information on many of these resources.

X   ***Awards and best books lists.*** First, there are awards and annual best books lists that feature science fiction. Two of the most prestigious awards are the Nebula Award, which is given by the Science Fiction Writers of America, and the Hugo Award, which is presented by the World Science Fiction Convention. Although the Hugo Awards are given in more categories, the Nebula Awards have been called the academy awards of science fiction (Card, 1990). Annual lists of both the Hugo nominees and the Nebula winners can usually be found in the June issue of *Science Fiction Chronicle: The Science Fiction and Fantasy Newsmagazine*. This magazine issue also usually contains information on the Arthur C. Clarke Award for science fiction published in Great Britain, as well as brief listings of a variety of other award winners and nominees such as the Prix Aurora Award for Canadian science fiction and fantasy. Another excellent source of information on science fiction is *Locus: The Newspaper of the Science Fiction Field* (magazine) and *Locus online,* which features the comprehensive Locus index to science fiction awards. Super-Con-Duck-Tivity, a group of parents, teachers, and librarians based in Illinois, presents Golden Duck Awards for Excellence in Children's

EXPANDING | *YOUR KNOWLEDGE WITH THE INTERNET 3–1*

On the Internet you can find information about science fiction awards such as the Hugo Awards (www.wsfs.org/hugos.html) or ideas for teachers such as Reading for the Future (readingforfuture.com). Links to these and many additional sites are found on this book's Companion Website at www.prenhall.com/bucher.

Science Fiction Literature including the Hal Clement Award for Young Adult science fiction and the Eleanor Cameron Award for Middle Grades.

Another excellent source to help teachers identify outstanding science fiction books is the annual best books list published in the April issue of *Voice of Youth Advocates (VOYA)* magazine. Featuring fantasy and horror as well as science fiction, this annotated bibliography consists of excerpts from the reviews of highly rated titles that were published in *VOYA* in the previous year (June to April). One outstanding feature of this list is that, in addition to identifying the suggested grade level for each title (middle school through senior high), the reviewers rate each title for both popularity (1P to 5P) and the quality (1Q to 5Q) of the writing. Included on the list are adult-marketed titles that the reviewers recommend for young adults.

Print review resources. In 1999, *Science, Books and Films,* a publication of the American Association for the Advancement of Science, began to include science fiction reviews. With background in the pure and applied sciences, its reviewers are qualified to evaluate the scientific as well as the literary qualities of the novels (Gath, 1999). Subscribers can view a database of reviews online as well as in the traditional hard copy periodical format.

Other professional resources are available to aid in book selection. One helpful source is *What Fantastic Fiction Do I Read Next?* edited by Neil Barron (1999b). Featuring over 4,800 fantasy, science fiction, and horror titles, this well-indexed volume includes best books of the 1990s. Suzanne Elizabeth Reid's *Presenting Young Adult Science Fiction* (1998) provides the historical background of science fiction as well as individual chapters on authors such as Orson Scott Card and Octavia Butler with biographical information and bibliographies of their works. Finally, *Strictly Science Fiction* (Herald & Kunzel, 2002) uses a symbol to designate titles that are suited for adolescents.

Online resources. Naturally, the Internet has become the home to a number of excellent sites with information on science fiction. Many of the Web-based magazines or "Webzines" can be located through *SF Zines WebRing.* Additional information about science fiction and a categorized list of links to sites throughout the world can be found at *Science Fiction Resources.* Finally, the University of Michigan maintains a page for all who wish to study fantasy and science fiction. This would be especially useful in high schools that offer specialized classes on speculative fiction.

Reviews and information on the major science fiction awards can also be found on the Internet. Author Orson Scott Card and *Omni* magazine fiction reviewer Ellen Datlow both have large databases of reviews at their web sites. In addition to information on science fiction award winners, *The Internet Speculative Fiction DataBase* indicates sources of reviews and contains information on both published and forthcoming books.

For information on science fiction authors, a good starting point is the *SFF Net* site. With more than 1,200 members, the web site of the Science Fiction and Fantasy Writers of America provides news, reviews, and information on writing speculative fiction. Promoting their publications, major science fiction publishers such as Del Rey Books, Tor, HarperCollins, Voyager, and Penguin Putnam/Ace also provide information at their web sites. Links to these resources can be found in Expanding Your Knowledge 3–1 on this book's Companion Website at (www.prenhall.com/bucher).

Evaluating science fiction. In addition to using the checklist for good science fiction, if you want to evaluate individual science fiction titles, you should apply many of the same standards used to evaluate any work of fiction. While the plot, setting, and characters might be simpler in science fiction than in other genres, simplicity does not imply poor quality. Contrived plotting, stereotypical characterization, and ineptly portrayed settings are weaknesses in any work of fiction (Harris, 1996). As Jordan (1995) maintains, good science fiction must be believable. Readers will be skeptical and fail to believe the setting or events if the science fiction does not present a logical world or if the story shows poorly researched and flawed science. A discussion of this important part of science fiction writing can be found in an installment of the National Public Radio Program *Talk of the Nation: Science Friday* on the Web.

Teaching with science fiction. When selecting a science fiction book to use in a classroom, teachers must consider their purpose for using the work and the context in which it will be used. Certainly, a novel that is taught for its literary concepts may be judged differently than one that is taught for other concepts such as ecological or social awareness. Teachers must also determine whether the book meets the materials-selection standards of the local governing bodies for the school. Many of the early works of science fiction might appear sexist by today's standards, but the introduction of strong female characters has led to the inclusion of sexual situations that might cause difficulties in many classrooms (Harris, 1996). To help teachers and librarians promote science fiction, writers Greg Bear and David Brin have developed Reading for the Future, a Web project that includes answers to questions posted by teachers. While Brin's Webs of Wonder web site looked for ways to integrate science fiction into the curricula, Julie Czerneda's site provides information on linking science fiction and the science curriculum (Moltz, 2003).

The Internet also has a number of other resources that teachers can use to teach specific science fiction books. Connecting Adolescents and Their Literature 3–1 lists a number of web sites that have ideas for teaching Lois Lowry's award-winning book, *The Giver.*

Fantasy

One of the most recent genres to be accepted in young adult literature, fantasy has its roots in fairy tales, myths, and legends. For children and younger adolescents, fantasy stories often consist of "modern" fairy tales, stories of magical or talking animals or toys, or travels to imaginary lands. In books targeted at adolescents, the emphasis is often on high fantasy where the story is set in whole, or in part, in a created or secondary world and where the focus is on the epic and heroic.

One thing you cannot deny is the popularity of fantasy in our modern culture. For confirmation, just look at the sales of fantasy video/computer games, the success of the Harry Potter books, or the box-office draw of *The Lord of the Rings* film trilogy. Why are fantasy items so popular? While some educators write off fantasy as escapist and insufficiently serious for young people to read (Charmas, 1992), others suggest that fantasy replaces the boredom of everyday life with the strange and unusual and provides an escape from the problems of modern society (Sanders, 1996). With its appeal

---

CONNECTING | *ADOLESCENTS AND THEIR LITERATURE: TEACHING The Giver 3–1*

 The Internet has a number of excellent resources available to help you teach young adult novels, including works of speculative fiction. You can start with reviews from reputable review sources (that we studied in Chapter 2) which can be found on sites such as Amazon.com or Barnesandnoble.com.

In addition, if you are planning to teach a novel, you might consult web sites where you will find sample lessons and ideas that you can incorporate into your own lessons. Other sites may have background information on the author. For example, on this book's Companion Website, you can find links to some resources that you would be able to use if you were developing a unit on Lois Lowry's award-winning young adult novel *The Giver.* After viewing these resources, select another novel of speculative fiction and locate links that you think will be helpful in teaching that novel.

---

to the senses, fantasy may provide adolescents with a feeling of overcoming the odds and being triumphant at a time when their own lives are often a series of "battles" that they lose or never even get to fight (Bucher & Manning, 2000).

Like other writers of speculative fiction, writers of fantasy often receive less respect than other fiction writers and their works (Service, 1992) and experience problems that other fiction writers might not experience. While some critics consider writing fantasy to be a literary copout (there are no rules except those the author creates, so the author can make up anything he or she wants), Service (1992) disagrees and suggests that writing fantasy involves considerable mental effort. Fantasy writer Terry Brooks claims that it is "harder to write good fantasy than any other form of fiction" *(The Writers' Complete Fantasy Reference,* 1998, p. 1). Even when a writer invents a completely new world, consistency is important. In addition, all fantasy must speak to the reader, reflect the human condition, and "resonate in some identifiable way with truths we have discovered about ourselves" *(The Writers' Complete Fantasy Reference,* 1998, p. 1).

If you think back to your own school days, you can probably recall reading and enjoying favorites such as C. S. Lewis' Narnia books, Susan Cooper's books in the Dark Is Rising Series, Lloyd Alexand Prydain series, Diane Duane's Young Wizards series, Diana Wynne Jones' Chrestomanci series, or even Brian Jacques' Redwall books, Robin McKinley's Damar books, and J. R. R. Tolkein's Middle-Earth books. The fantasy genre has been enriched in recent years by authors such as J. K. Rowling, Philip Pullman, and Gerald Morris. In addition, writers such as Donna Jo Napoli, Patricia McKillip, Katherine Kurtz, Mercedes Lackey, L. E. Modesitt, Patricia Wrede, Jane Yolen, Philip Pullman, Tamora Pierce, Sherwood Smith, and Tanith Lee have created strong characters and series. Many of these fantasy favorites bridge the gap between adolescent and adult fantasy.

A Brief Look at Fantasy's Predecessors. Certainly, fantasy has its roots in the myths, epic tales, and legends that existed in the oral tradition before the spread of literacy. However, fantasy became its own genre when, in the mid-1800s, Hans Christian Anderson began writing literary fairy tales and Lewis Carroll wrote *Alice's Adventures in Wonderland* (1865). By the early 1900s, fantasy reached the United States with the publication of *The Wonderful Wizard of Oz* (1909). Then, in the middle of the 20th century, C. S. Lewis's Narnia books and Tolkein's works created a renewed interest in fantasy, which was strengthened by the success of Terry Brooks' (e.g., 1997) Shannara series, J. K. Rowling's Harry Potter books (e.g., 1998, 2000, 2003), Philip Pullman's (e.g., 1996, 2000) His Dark Materials trilogy, and the popularity of other series such as Brian Jacques' Redwall books (e.g., 2001, 2002), a number of series by Tamora Pierce (e.g., 1999), and books based on computer games such as *Mage Knight*. Still, according to Cushman (1999), only 55 young adult fantasy books were published in 1998. Because many of these fantasy books were written for younger adolescents, older adolescents have turned to reading adult fantasy novels.

Types of Fantasy Books. According to Clute and Grant (1999), fantasy is a "self-coherent narrative" (p. 338) that, if set in our world, "tells a story which is impossible in the world as we perceive it" (p. 338) or, if set in another world, is possible only in terms strictly relating to that other world. Young adult fantasy has been influenced by an array of diverse factors including traditional folk literature. It builds on the categories of children's fantasies including animal and toy fantasy, the imaginary worlds of high fantasy (including religious allegories and heroic quests), time fantasy (including time travel and timeslips), exaggerated characters and preposterous situations, ghosts and the supernatural, and magic. Even comics and graphic novels, which we will discuss in Chapter 10, often feature fantasy themes.

High fantasies, which are popular with older readers, are defined as fantasies that are set in other worlds and that "deal with matters affecting the destiny of those worlds" (Clute & Grant, 1999, p. 466). Often the hero or heroine in these books is engaged in a quest to save the fantasy kingdom from an all-powerful evil force or a dark menace that is threatening to take over. Consisting of a series of emotional and sometimes tragic adventures, high fantasies center on the conflict between good and evil and the ultimate triumph of the forces of right and justice.

Reasons For Using and Teaching Fantasy. Why is fantasy literature often forgotten in many secondary schools? Do educators "teach" out the fantasy in students by focusing on the critical things students need to know and by ignoring the need of many students to escape? In an effort to prepare students to respond with the "right answer" on standardized tests, do educators fail to encourage students to dream? Are teachers and librarians afraid of censorship when they exclude fantasy titles? Do educators allow their own preferences for realistic and historical fiction to overshadow this genre?

While adults often ignore fantasy literature, some young adults, especially boys, are devouring it. Research into reading habits (Fronius, 1993; Leonhardt, 1996; Moffitt & Wartella, 1992; Thomason, 1983; Traw, 1993;) has shown that adolescent boys and girls have different reading preferences. Many girls are "suspicious of anything called fantasy" (Harris, 1996). Thankfully, with the success of the Harry Potter books and the growth of strong female characters in fantasy literature by authors such as Philip Pullman, Garth Nix, Tamora Pierce, Tanith Lee, Patricia Wrede, and Robin McKinley, fantasy is now reaching a wider audience of readers. Expanding Your Knowledge with the Internet 3–2 guides you to the web sites of a number of authors of speculative fiction for young adolescents. Our own observations show that students who read fantasy books are not always those who follow directions. They are often divergent thinkers who use fantasy books as a focal point for thinking, creating, and imagining.

Fantasy books provide a way for young adults to look at codes of behavior and the human psyche. As Rockman (2001) notes, allegory and metaphor are two excellent techniques that authors use to explore the concepts of good and evil. In fantasy, readers can consider concepts that are often too scary to consider in real life. Through fantasies, readers can contemplate dark forces of evil. Often, adolescents find that courage, friendship, their own resourcefulness, and the help of trusted elders help the characters in the books overcome these evil forces (Rockman, 2001). Suggestions for Collaborative Efforts 3–2 shows how to involve a number of people in a discussion of fantasy.

Characteristics of Good Fantasy. Whether written for adults or young adults, there are two things that readers demand from fantasy: it cannot contain nonsense or treachery (Snyder, 1986). According to successful fantasy writer Terry Brooks, fantasy must be grounded "in both truth and life experience if it is to work" (*The Writer's Complete Fantasy Reference,* 1998, p. 1). The impossible must seem to be possible, characters must behave in reasonable and expected ways, magic must work consistently, rules must be followed, and the fantasy world must bear a relationship to our own. Also, the fantasy should not be unfairly taken away at the book's end under the pretext that everything that happened was just a dream. Once the reader is committed to the fantasy world, the author should never trick or deceive the reader. Considerations for Selecting Young Adult Literature: *Fantasy* lists some characteristics to look for in evaluating fantasy.

Of all fantasy's characteristics, originality may be most important. Jon Scieszka (e.g., 1993) may not be a great writer, but the books in his Time Warp series are so original and so imaginative that they have gained a wide following among younger adolescents. The characters of good fantasy—Alice and her friends from Wonderland, Harry Potter and his classmates at Hogwarts, Bilbo Baggins and the other inhabitants of Middle-Earth, Lyra

EXPANDING | **YOUR KNOWLEDGE WITH THE INTERNET 3–2**

 A number of authors of speculative fiction such as David Almond (www.davidalmond.com/) and Tamora Pierce (www.tamora-pierce.com/) have web sites. Visit this book's Companion Website to link directly to these and many other authors of speculative fiction at www.prenhall.com/bucher.

SUGGESTIONS FOR COLLABORATIVE EFFORTS

Plan a movie discussion and comparison of a specific fantasy book such as one of the Harry Potter books or another fantasy that has been adapted to film. After selecting an appropriate work, plan your discussion carefully with either adult or student discussion leaders. Read reviews of both the book and the movie to learn what the critics have said. Then, develop a list of questions to help students compare the two.

Sample questions might be:

- Were there any parts of the book that were not included in the movie?

- Why do you think they were omitted? Did this help or hurt the story?

- Were the characters in the movie true to what you expected after reading the book?

- Why do you think the changes were made? If you could change any one thing about the book or movie, what would it be?

- Do you agree or disagree with the critics' comments?

- If you were writing a review of either the book or the movie, what would you say?

While you can hold the discussion in your classroom or in the school library media center, you can also work with a local public library in this project. For more information on conducting a book/movie discussion, consult the article in *VOYA* by Benée J. Vaillancourt and Julie Gillispie (2001).

CONSIDERATIONS | *For Selecting* *Young Adult Literature* | **FANTASY**

When evaluating science fiction books, ask the following:

- Is there consistency—with rules or "laws of nature" for the fantasy world?

- Are the plot and setting believable— through vivid descriptions?

- Is the story original and/or imaginative?

- Are there restraints or limits to the fantastic or magical?

- Does realism root the fantasy in reality and human nature?

- Are there worthwhile themes such as struggles of good vs. evil, heroism, or order vs. anarchy?

Belacqua and the armored bears, or Taran the assistant pigkeeper to the wizard Dalben—remain indelibly marked in our minds, and become the standard against which we measure all other characters. We believe in them and in the values that they represent for, although they are make-believe people residing in fantasy worlds, they are rooted in human nature and are imbued with a strong sense of reality and a deep seriousness (Russell, 2001).

A good fantasy writer should provide vivid descriptions of things so that readers can actually visualize the scenes. In doing so, the fantasy world begins to exist, if only in the mind of the individual reader. In contrast to the sparseness in folk tales, in a fantasy, "description lends weight and substance to ideas" (*The Writer's Complete Fantasy Reference*, 1998, p. 2) so that a reader can see, taste, smell, hear, and feel the new world. A good fantasy must "establish a whole new set of natural laws, explain them right up front, and then faithfully abide by them throughout" (Card, 1990, p. 23). These rules prevent the story from slipping into sheer absurdity because there are consistent limits on even magical powers. For example, Princess Cimorene in Patricia Wrede's (e.g., 1990) dragon stories learns that soapy water is very powerful against even the strongest wizard.

Suggestions For Selecting and Using Fantasy. You can use many of the same resources (such as *VOYA, Locus,* and *Speculative Fiction Book Awards*) that you use to select science fiction to help you select fantasy. In addition, there are a number of specialized resources such as the following:

- *What Fantastic Fiction Do I Read Next?* (Barron, 1999b)

- *Reference Guide to Science Fiction, Fantasy, and Horror* (Burgess & Bartle, 2002)

- *Alternative Worlds in Fantasy Fiction* (Hunt & Lenz, 2001)

- *Encyclopedia of Fantasy* (Clute & Grant, 1999)

- *Presenting Young Adult Fantasy Fiction* (McRae, 1998)

- *Fluent in Fantasy: A Guide to Reading Interests* (Herald, 1999)

- *Fantasy and Horror: A Critical and Historical Guide to Literature, Illustration, Film, TV, Radio, and the Internet* (Barron, 1999a)

- *Barlowe's Guide to Fantasy* (Barlowe, 1996)

Do not forget to check the lists of winners of general young adult book awards and prizes to locate outstanding fantasy books. As we mentioned before, Philip Pullman's *The Amber Spyglass* (2000) won the Whitbread Award. *Skellig* (1999), the first young adult book written by David Almond, won both the British Carnegie Medal and the Whitbread Award and was an honor book for the Michael L. Printz Award.

When evaluating fantasy on your own, look for the qualities of good fantasy books found in the list of characteristics earlier in this chapter and be sure to evaluate how the elements of fiction (listed in Chapter 2) are treated in the book as well. Ask yourself, does the story reflect the good characteristics of fantasy? Are the plot and the characters believable and original? What has the author done to make the story believable? What message does the story convey? In addition to a well-constructed plot, are there higher-level meanings in the story? How do the setting (e.g., visual aspects, smells, and sounds) and the characterization (e.g., language, actions, and attitudes) contribute to the believability of the story? Connecting Adolescents and Their Literature 3–2 illustrates one way to keep track of the large number of characters that are found in many fantasies.

CONNECTING	ADOLESCENTS AND THEIR LITERATURE 3-2

Fantasy books often have a complex cast of characters. Use a graphic organizer such as the computer program *Inspiration* to keep track of the characters in the book and their relationships. Here is an example of the beginning of a web for the characters in the first Harry Potter novel.

Mr. Dursley — Dudley Dursley — Mrs. Norris (Cat) — Argus Filch (Janitor) — Mrs. Dursley — Dursley Family — Others at Hogwarts — Hagrid — Ron Weasley — Fellow students — Harry Potter — Ghosts — Nearly Headless Nick — Hermione Granger — Draco Malfoy — Instructors — Peeves — Dumbledore — McGonagall — Flitwick

Horror

Horror is the only form of literature that is named "solely after the effect it is intended to produce" (Clute & Grant, 1999, p. 337). According to Card (1990), horror books include "believable events that are so gruesome or revolting that the audience reacts with fear or disgust" (p. 19). While some science fiction and fantasy books may have a "horror 'feel'" (Clute & Grant, 1999, p. 478), true horror fiction creates a feeling of something "obscenely, transgressively impure" (p. 478). Along with this comes the belief that there is a "threat to one's body and/or culture and/or world" as well as "a sense that there is something inherently monstrous and wrong. . . in the invasive presence" (p. 478). Although Dracula, Frankenstein, and the Headless Horseman continue to be popular with adolescents (Lodge, 1996), modern horror stories frequently include elements of romance, mystery, and even comedy. Vampires and werewolves can have human dimensions; serial killers can acquire immortality and possess supernatural powers. Good still triumphs over evil, but the hero or heroine often pays with his or her life.

Perhaps the best known writers of horror fiction are R. L. Stine (e.g., 1999, 2001, 2002) and Stephen King (e.g., 1999). In his current Goosebumps 2000 for children and younger teens and the Fear Street Series for older adolescents, R. L. Stine creates both easy reading tales and spine-chilling dramas that have attracted a wide audience of readers and made Stine the best-selling author in the United States (Jones, 1998). His works "give kids a positive reading experience to which they can respond since the horror is fun, yet also familiar" (p. 211). In addition, in his works, it is the teenagers themselves who, through their own talents and ingenuity, overcome the evil forces. Writing for teenagers and adults, Stephen King also masterfully blends the mundane with the fiendish and fantastic. Many of King's characters are basically decent, normal folk who reside in small towns and lead uneventful lives until some powerful, inexplicable, and usually evil force (such as the vampire in *Salem's Lot*) invades their peaceful existence. Others (such as the main character in *Carrie* or *Firestarter*) have special talents or psychic abilities.

A Brief Look at Horror's Predecessors. Some of the early horror fiction that is still read today was written in the 19th century. Edgar Allan Poe's works, including stories such as *Mask of the Red Death* (1842), a tale of terror, and *Berenice* (1835), a vampire story, were followed by Sheridan Le Fanu's *Carmilla* (1871–72) and Bram Stoker's *Dracula* (1897). There were also Mary Shelley's *Frankenstein* (1818) and a penny dreadful about Varney the Vampire. In the 20th century, the pulp magazine *Weird Tales,* which was published from 1923 until 1954, presented authors such as H. P. Lovecraft, Frank Belknap Long, and Robert Bloch.

In the later part of the 20th century, several horror writers became popular with young adults. R. L. Stine produced a number of series of books, from the Goosebumps for the upper elementary grades to the Fear Street Books for older adolescents. His popularity was indicated in a 1997 survey of 3,200 English educators (McElmell & Buswell, 1998) in which 80% included R. L. Stine on a list of the 100 most important authors of books for young adults, compared with only 17–45% who included award-winning author Virginia Hamilton. Also popular with young adults are the horror novels written by Stephen King (e.g., 1999) and Dean Koontz (e.g., 1998, 1999). In addition, fueled by the popularity of the former television series about Buffy, the Vampire Slayer, teens have turned to the vampire novels of Amelia Atwater-Rhodes (e.g., 2001) and Annette C. Klause (e.g., 1997), as well as those by adult author Anne Rice. Recently, there has been increased interest in novels that deal with the paranormal. While not as scary as mainstream horror books or psycho-slasher novels, these books include demons, witches, and ancient gods and goddesses (Herald, 2002).

Types of Horror Books. It is difficult to categorize horror books. There are "dark fantasies" or "gothic fantasies," which incorporate a feeling of horror but are set in a fantasy world (Clute & Grant, 1999). In contrast, books of supernatural horror, which may include vampires, ghosts, werewolves, and the occult, are set in the normal world and are often called "weird fiction" (p. 478). Included in this type are *Blood and Chocolate* (Klause, 1997) and *The Transition of H. P. Lovecraft* (Lovecraft, 1996). Books of "pure horror" (p. 478) are shaped entirely by the sense of horror that they produce. In them, both the protagonist and the reader recognize that a threat exists from a monstrous, invasive presence (Clute & Grant, 1999). Representative of this type are books such as *Fear Nothing* (Koontz, 1998), *The Girl Who Loved Tom Gordon* (King, 1999), *Haunting Hour: Chills in the Dead of Night* (Stine, 2001), *Nightmare Hour: Time for Terror* (Stine, 1999), *Coraline* (Gaiman, 2002), or one of the Point Horror Trilogy: *The Fog* (Cooney, 1989), *The Snow* (Cooney, 1990), or *The Fire* (Cooney, 1990). Finally, books of the paranormal or unexplained phenomena include series such as the Circle of Three (e.g., Bird, 2001), Daughters of the Moon series (e.g., Ewing, 2000), and the YA Witches' Chillers series (e.g., Ravenwolf, 2000). From Page to Screen lists a number of films based on speculative fiction including some horror movies.

FROM PAGE TO SCREEN

Science Fiction, Fantasy, and Horror
Imaginative tales of fantasy are often turned to film, but their dense and complicated stories are sometimes difficult to fit in a feature-length running time. Compare these films with their novel counterparts and consider how well these stories make the leap to the big screen.

The Lord of the Rings Trilogy
2001–2003, PG-13
★ ★ ★ ★

Peter Jackson's breathtakingly realized vision of J. R. R. Tolkien's classic epics of Hobbits, elves, kings, and evil is surprisingly faithful to the original text. Andrew Lesnie's cinematography, superb performances by Sir Ian McKellen and Sean Astin, and Jackson's brilliant visual style combined with his apparent love of Tolkien's work create a masterful celebration of the beloved novels.

Harry Potter and the Prisoner of Azkaban
2003, PG
★ ★ ★

The third and most impressive adaptation of J. K. Rowling's phenomenally successful novels of witchcraft and wizardry, Prisoner of Azkaban boasts a cinematic quality lacking in the previous Potter films. Director Alfonso Cuaron creates a magical atmosphere in the film that mirrors the tenor of Rowling's text. The stellar supporting cast, impressive visual effects, and more exciting storyline buoy the lead actors' struggle with their performances.

(continued)

FROM PAGE TO SCREEN

Tuck Everlasting
2003, PG

★ ★ ★

Natalie Babbitt's beloved story of an ageless family and the girl who stumbles upon them takes a surprising turn in director Jay Russell's hands. By re-envisioning Winnie as an adolescent, the film adaptation turns the story of a girl who latches on to new parent figures into a story of budding romance. While much of the balance of the story line remains the same, some of the innocence of Babbitt's work is lost. Beautiful camera work and supporting turns from Sissy Spacek, William Hurt, and Ben Kingsley make this an engaging film to watch.

Frankenstein
1931, Unrated

★ ★ ★ ★

Director James Whale's classic interpretation of the Mary Shelley novel no longer packs the scares that thrilled audiences of old, but his principled direction and fantastic eye for gothic staging, alongside Boris Karloff's heartbreakingly humane performance as the monster, create a wonderful film to watch in tandem with a reading of the novel.

Nosferatu
Unrated, 1922

★ ★ ★ ★

F. W. Murnau was unable to get the rights from Bram Stoker's widow to bring the novel Dracula *to the screen, so he improvised, changing just enough to avoid prosecution. Murnau's groundbreaking directorial style, including location shooting and uniquely fluid camera work, give the film an eerie quality far ahead of its time, but it is Max Schreck's astonishing performance as Count Orlock that makes this silent picture a true classic.*

Reasons For Using and Teaching Horror Books. Given that mysteries, thrillers, and horror capture the adult best seller lists, it should not be surprising that horror books also capture the attention of adolescents (Dunleavey, 1995) who want to experience, albeit vicariously, frightening situations. They enjoy reading about the vampires, the walking dead, the invasions, and the assaults because they realize that everything is just make-believe. Perhaps this is an extension of the thrill that children get when they sit in the dark and tell ghost stories. In horror fiction, young adults can read about situations with everyday events (such as school, proms, malls, sports, and parties) in which they, not adults, are in control. By confronting imaginary fears, they are confronting their own anxieties in a safe place while they are learning to accept the responsibilities associated with becoming adults.

Many educators, however, are reluctant to use horror novels in the classroom. This may be, in part, because horror stories, like science fiction, have a history based in pulp magazines. Horror fiction is often seen as sensational rather than serious, and with a focus on popularity rather than quality. Then, too, there may be a reluctance to use horror fiction because of anticipated complaints from parents or others in the community. However, not all horror fiction can be written off so easily. Certainly, works by Edgar Allen Poe have entered the canon of respected literature. Also, the appeal of this type of literature among young adults provides an avenue to reach even reluctant readers. The key is to balance quality and popularity and to find books that both entertain and enrich us.

Characteristics of Horror Books. Horror literature shares several similar characteristics with well-written science fiction and fantasy as identified in Considerations for Selecting Young Adult Literature: *Horror.* Horror, however, has at least one special characteristic—the horror should not be just for sensationalism. It should encourage the reader to explore the reasons behind the actions rather than merely portray a terrifying or gory situation. For example, Dean Koontz's *By the Light of the Moon* "casts a mirror on social responsibility in a world that has become both increasingly dangerous and overly self-absorbed" (Halem, 2003, p. 57).

Suggestions For Selecting and Using Horror. You need to select horror fiction the same way that you select other literature—by looking for books that are well-written and age-appropriate. Look to see if females are singled out as victims or stereotyped as being helpless and in particular need of assistance because of their gender. The events of violence or horror in the novel should teach a lesson or have a meaning and should not be used just for sensationalism. If well-written at a pace that young adults will enjoy, the book should have a believable plot with a setting and characters that contribute to and complement the plot. It should be the characters and the plot, not the events of horror or the paranormal, that hold the reader's attention.

Thankfully, some resources are available that you can consult to help you select horror fiction. The Horror Writers Association gives the Bram Stoker Award each year with a special category that includes books for young people along with awards for adult novels, first novels, story collections, and long fiction. In addition to the information mentioned earlier in this chapter, consult Anthony L. Fonseca and June Michele Pulliam's

CONSIDERATIONS	For Selecting Young Adult Literature	HORROR
When examining young adult horror literature, ask the following: ◉ Does the literature have the characteristics of well-written science fiction and fantasy? ◉ Does it have strong themes, well-developed plots, nonstereotypic characters, and pleasing writing styles?		◉ Does it provide a sense of escapism or sheer enjoyment? ◉ Does it encourage the reader to explore the reasons behind the actions rather than merely portray a terrifying or gory situation?

Hooked on Horror: A Guide to Reading Interests in Horror Fiction (2003) for an in-depth look specifically at horror fiction. Although written primarily about the works of R. L. Stine, *What's So Scary About R. L. Stine?* (Jones, 1998) includes some general information on the horror genre. The classic reference work on vampire literature is J. G. Melton's *The Vampire Book* (1999), which is supplemented by Barron's *Horror Literature: A Reader's Guide* (1990), Ramsland's *The Vampire Companion* (1993), Guiley's and Macabre's *The Complete Vampire Companion* (1994), and Altner's and Ofcansky's *Vampire Readings* (1998). A periodical that covers horror is *Rue Morgue, Horror in Culture & Entertainment* (www.Rue-Morgue.com). Connecting Adolescents and Their Literature 3–3 provides an idea for promoting speculative fiction.

▸ Considering Gender and Speculative Fiction

For many years, speculative fiction was seen as primarily read by boys; female authors were considered "fantasy" writers and male authors were considered "science fiction" writers (Charmas, 1992). Research into reading habits (Fronius, 1993; Leonhardt, 1996; Moffitt & Wartella, 1992; Thomason, 1983; Traw, 1993) has shown that adolescent boys and girls have different reading preferences. In essence, while adolescent girls read more romance and historical romance books, adolescent boys read more fantasy and science fiction. To confirm the research into reading preferences, all you need to do is visit a modern book superstore such as Barnes and Noble or Borders. You'll typically find women browsing through the large sections of romance books, men in the science fiction/fantasy section, and both genders in the mystery and adventure books. However, as more female authors write quality science fiction and the number of strong female characters in these works begins to grow, this gender-related preference is beginning to change.

It is important for teachers and library media specialists to keep these reading preferences in mind when recommending books to adolescents. Unfortunately, in our college young adult literature classes, we often find that secondary teachers and school library media specialists frankly admit that they do not like fantasy, horror, or science fiction and prefer to read realistic and historical fiction. As a result, they are less likely to use speculative fiction in their classrooms, or suggest it to their students.

CONNECTING | **ADOLESCENTS AND THEIR LITERATURE 3–3**

To promote the reading of speculative fiction, put displays of science fiction, fantasy, and horror books in the classroom, near the computers in the school library media center, or on the school's web site. Bookmark approved web sites for speculative fiction and provide the information as links off the school, class, or library homepage.

While educators need to take special care to identify, select, and use appropriate speculative fiction with all adolescents, they need to use science fiction books, in particular, to attract male adolescents to reading.

CONCLUDING THOUGHTS

Speculative fiction is a genre that will continue to attract young adult readers. Fueled by the popularity of the Harry Potter series and a variety of other books and movies, the number of quality science fiction, fantasy, and horror books should continue to grow. Although many educators and library media specialists may not personally enjoy reading works of speculative fiction, they need to appreciate the fact that young adults are reading their favorites with enthusiasm. The main point is that many young people enjoy science fiction, fantasy, and horror and should be allowed (and, in fact, encouraged) to read quality books of their choice. This chapter has provided you with some of the basics to identify, select, and use quality speculative fiction. Be sure to visit this book's Companion Website at www.prenhall.com/bucher for additional information about speculative fiction including review questions, self-assessments, Internet sites, and young adult literature and readings.

Young Adult Books

 This section includes young adult titles recommended or mentioned in this chapter. Check the Companion Website at www.prenhall.com/bucher to find additional suggestions of current young adult literature.

Science Fiction

Adams, D. (1979). *Hitchhiker's guide to the galaxy.* New York: Harmony Books. Join Arthur Dent, his friend Ford Prefect, and a cast of strange fellow travelers for a comical trip through the galaxy aided by the unusual advice from the *Hitchhiker's Guide.*

Allen, R. M. (2002). *The depths of time.* New York: Bantam. Journey to A.D. 5211 and a galaxy where timeshaft wormholes permit time travel through outer space. However, these warmholes can also allow intruders to enter.

Anderson, M. T. (2002). *Feed.* Cambridge, MA: Candlewick. Imagine a world where a communications system that can influence your life is installed in your head at birth.

Armstrong, J., & Butcher, N. (2002). *The kindling.* New York: HarperCollins. In this first volume of the Fire-Us Trilogy, a small group of children form their own community after a virus kills most of the inhabitants of Earth. Their story continues in *The Keepers of the Flame* (2002).

Banks, I. M. (1997). *Excession.* New York: Bantam. When something from another dimension appears in the galaxy, every civilization rushes to control it.

Barnes, J. (1997). *Washington's dirigible: Timeline wars #2.* New York: HarperPrism. It's a battle through multiple timelines when Mark Strang faces the Closers.

Bear, G. (1999). *Darwin's radio.* New York: Ballantine. What is the strange disease that causes women to miscarry and then become pregnant again?

Bennett, C., & Gottesman, J. (2001). *Anne Frank and me.* New York: Putnam. When Nicole Burns goes back in time to the camps of World War II, will she be able to help her family survive the horrors?

Blacker, T. (2002). *The angel factory.* New York: Simon & Schuster. If Thomas Wisdom's parents are not food researchers or CIA spies, what are they?

Burtt, B. (2001). *Star Wars™ galactic phrase book and travel guide: Beeps, bleats, and other common intergalactic verbiage.* New York: Ballantine. This phrasebook accompanies the popular series.

Butler, O. (1998). *Parable of the talents.* New York: Seven Stories Press. Lauren and her daughter try to survive in a post-apocalyptic world.

Card, O. S. (1985). *Ender's game.* New York: Tor. When aliens attack Earth, young Ender Wiggin and his battle skills may be the only hope for survival.

Card, O. S. (1986). *Speaker for the dead.* New York: Tor. In this award-winning sequel to *Ender's Game,* Ender confronts a new group of aliens on the planet Lusitania.

Card, O. S. (1993). *Seventh son.* New York: Tor. Alvin Maker begins this series of alternative histories in 19th-century America.

Card, O. S. (1999). *Ender's shadow.* New York: Tor. Building on the story in *Ender's game* (1985), this is the story of Bean, a classmate of "Ender" during the war with the insectile race of aliens called the Buggers. Sequels include *Shadow of the Hegemon* (2002) and *Shadow Puppets* (2002).

Cherryh, C. J. (2001). *Defender.* New York: DAW. Can the starship Phoenix successfully reach the damaged station in outer space before disaster strikes?

Cooney, C. B. (2001). *For all time.* New York: Delacorte. Annie, a time-traveler, goes back to the 1899 Lightner Expedition.

Dann, J., & Doxois, G. (Eds.). (1999). *Armageddons.* New York: Ace. This is an anthology of 12 end-of-the-world stories.

Farmer, N. (1994) *The ear, the eye, and the arm.* New York: Orchard. The year is 2194 and the children of the military ruler of Zimbabwe begin an adventure to earn a scouting badge. They end up being captured by gangsters, working in a plastic mine, and are tracked by mutant detectives.

Farmer, N. (2002). *The house of the scorpion.* New York: Atheneum. El Patrón rules the fiefdom of Opium on the border of the United States and Mexico. Matt is his clone whose only chance to survive is to flee.

Flint, E. (2000). *1632.* Riverdale, NY: Baen. What will happen when members of the United Mine Workers from West Virginia wind up in central Europe in 1632?

Gerrold, David. (2000). *Jumping off the planet.* New York: Tor. This is the first in a trilogy that includes *Bouncing off the Moon* (2001) and *Leaping to the Stars* (2002).

Gurney, J. (1992). *Dinotopia: A land apart from time.* New York: HarperCollins. Dinosaurs and humans live together in this utopia.

Haddix, M. P. (2000). *Turnabout.* New York: Simon & Schuster. The year is 2085. Melly and Anny Beth are going to un-age, going back from their 16 years to the time of their birth. Another futuristic book by this author is *Among the Hidden* (1998).

Haldeman, J. (1997). *Forever peace*. New York: Bantam. A soldier in a remote-controlled war tries to bring peace to the world.

Heneghan, J. (2000). *The grave*. New York: Farrar, Straus and Giroux. After falling into a gravesite in 1974, Tom winds up in Ireland in 1847 during the famine.

Herbert, F. (1965). *Dune*. Philadelphia: Chilton. On the desert planet Arrakis, when Duke Paul Atreides is exiled after the overthrow of his father's government, the results are felt throughout the interstellar empire.

Kress, N. (2003). *Crossfire*. New York: Tor. Selecting between two alien races will determine the future of mankind.

Lee, G. (1999). *Double full moon night*. New York: Bantam Spectra. Who is responsible for the mysterious sphere in which the Mars colonists are trapped? Is the sphere a paradise or a prison?

Lowry, L. (1993). *The giver*. Boston: Houghton Mifflin. When Jonas is chosen as the Receiver of Memories, he learns the truth about his utopian world.

Lowry, L. (2000). *Gathering blue*. Boston: Houghton Mifflin. Kira has exceptional weaving skills that save her from death. But will the Council of Guardians really protect her?

Lowry, L. (2004). The *messenger*. Boston: Houghton Mifflin. This story returns to the worlds of her earlier books *The Giver* (1993) and *Gathering Blue* (2000).

Marsden, J. (1995). *Tomorrow when the war began*. New York: Houghton Mifflin. Imagine going on a camping trip in the Australian bush and returning to find that your country has been invaded and your family taken prisoner. Would you surrender, hide, or seek revenge? This is the first in a series of books about Ellie and her friends.

McCaffrey, A. (1977). *Dragonsinger*. New York: Atheneum. Menolly begins her studies to become a Harper of Pern and learns about firelizards and dragons.

McCaffrey, A. (2002). *A gift of dragons*. New York: Del Rey. These four short stories are a good introduction to the land of Pern.

Nylund, E. (2001). *Halo: The fall of reach*. New York: Del Rey. In 2552, when a group of aliens known as the Covenant threaten to eliminate humans, the humans' defense depends on their genetically and mechanically enhanced soldiers.

O'Brien, R. (1974). *Z for Zachariah*. New York: Simon & Schuster. After a nuclear holocaust, 16-year-old Ann Burden believes she is the only survivor. But she finds that may not be true.

Paulsen, G. (2000). *The white fox chronicles*. New York: Delacorte. When dissidents overthrow the U.S. government in 2057, 14-year-old Cody Pierce is thrown into a prison camp.

Reynolds, D. W. (1999). *Star Wars Episode One: A visual dictionary*. New York: DK Publishing. This is a "nonfiction" style dictionary of this fictional series.

Roberts, J. M. (2002). *Hannibal's children*. New York: Ace. What would have happened if Hannibal had defeated the Romans in 202 B.C. and won the Second Punic War?

Scarborouch, E. A. (Ed.). (1999). *Past lives, present tense*. New York: Ace. In a series of short stories, past and present figures meet with a variety of results.

Shusterman, N. (2002). *Shattered sky*. New York: Tor. The Star Shards fight to save planet Earth from aliens in the third volume of the *Star Shards* trilogy.

Sleator, W. (2002). *Parasite pig*. New York: Dutton. This is the sequel to the popular *Interstellar Pig* (1985).

Turtledove, H., & Greenberg, M. H. (Eds.). (2001). *Best alternative history stories of the 20th century.* New York: Del Rey. Byzantium falls seven centuries early, Mozart becomes a cyberpunk, and Shakespeare is shipwrecked in North America in this anthology of stories.

Tyers, K. (1999). *Firebird.* Minneapolis: Bethany House. Lady Firebird Angelo of the planet Netaia joins a Federate Sentinel to fight the development of genocidal bombs.

Vande Velde, V. (2002). *Heir apparent.* San Diego: Harcourt. In a future world, a girl is trapped in a virtual reality game.

Vizzini, N. (2004). *Be more chill.* New York: Hyperion. Jeremy Heere, a high school nerd, swallows a pill that will put a supercomputer in his brain.

Weaver, W. (2001). *Memory boy.* New York: HarperCollins. As the ash from volcanoes covers the world and chaos reigns, Miles Newell has a plan to get his family out of Minneapolis to a safe haven.

Fantasy

Adams, R. (1972). *Watership down.* New York: Macmillan. As developers destroy their community, a warren of Berkshire rabbits begins the search for a new home.

Almond, D. (1999). *Skellig.* New York: Delacorte. Why is Skellig, the man-owl-angel, crumpled in the abandoned garage behind Michael's new house? Another book by Almond is *Kit's Wilderness* (2000).

Anthony, P. (1997). *Faun & games.* New York: Tor. This, along with *Roc and a Hard Place* (1995), is a title in the popular Xanth series.

Babbitt, N. (1975). *Tuck everlasting.* New York: Farrar, Straus and Giroux. The Tuck family drinks from the fountain of youth and comes to question the wisdom of eternal life.

Barron, T. A. (1996). *The lost years of Merlin.* New York: Philomel. This is the first in a five-book epic about the life of Merlin.

Bradley, M. Z. (1999). *Traitor's sun, A novel of darkover.* New York: DAW Books. Try this or any other book in the Darkover series and read about the attempts of the Terran Federation to overthrow the rulers of Darkover.

Brooks, T. (1986). *Magic kingdom for sale—sold!* New York: Ballentine. What would it be like to buy an entire magic kingdom?

Brooks, T. (1997). *First king of Shannara.* New York: Ballantine. Breman tries to unite the Four Lands in this book in popular Shannara Cycle. *Morgawr* (2002) is a recent title in the Voyage of the Jerle Shannara series.

Carus, M. (Ed.). (2002). *Fire and wings: Dragon tales from east and west.* Chicago: Cricket Books. These stories from China, Korea, Japan, and Europe provide an overview of the best of modern dragon tales.

Colfer, E. (2001). *Artemis fowl.* New York: Hyperion Books. In this first in the series, a 12-year-old master thief tries to steal the gold of the fairies by outsmarting Captain Holly Short of the LEPrecon (Lower Elements Police Reconnaisance) Unit. The second book in the series is *Artemis Fowl: The Arctic Incident* (2002).

Datlow, E., & Windling, T. (Eds.). (2002). *The green man: Tales from the mythic forest.* New York: Viking. Eighteen contemporary authors have contributed a story or poem about the magic in a forest. Also included is a bibliographic essay that lists additional titles.

De Lint, C. (2002). *Waifs and strays.* New York: Viking. This collection of urban fantasy stories blends contemporary everyday life with the fantastic.

Duane, D. (1983). *So you want to be a wizard.* New York: Delacorte. This is the first in the Young Wizards series that features a teenage wizard and her friends. A more recent title in the series is *A Wizard Alone* (2002).

Ferris, J. (2002). *Once upon a marigold.* San Diego: Harcourt. Christian, the adopted son of a troll, falls in love with the princess Marigold. But Marigold's evil mother has other plans.

Funke, C. (2002). *Thief lord.* New York: Scholastic. Prosper and Bo try to escape their aunt by going to Venice where they are taken in by the Thief Lord. But a mysterious request for the Thief Lord and his gang to steal a wooden wing begins a chase that ends with a magical merry-go-round.

Goodkind, T. (1995). *Stone of tears.* New York: Tor. When the veil to the Underworld is torn, Richard the Seeker must stop the evil that enters the world.

Hambly, B. (1998). *Icefalcon's quest.* New York: Ballantine. In this sequel to the Darwath Trilogy, Icefalcon must rescue Tir before the kingdom is destroyed.

Hobb, R. (1996). *Assassin's apprentice.* New York: Bantam. Fitz may be treated as an outcast, but King Shrewd plans to use his magical skill and have him trained as an assassin. This is the first book of the Farseer Trilogy for mature readers.

Hoeye, Michael. (1999). *Time stops for no mouse: A Hermux Tantamoq adventure.* New York: Putnam's. A daredevil aviatrix and a broken watch begin an adventure for the gentle watchmaker Hermux Tantamoq. The second book in the series is *Sands of Time* (2001).

Huntington, G. (2002). *Sorcerers of the nightwing.* New York: ReganBooks. In the first title in the Ravenscliff series, orphan Devon March discovers that he is a great sorcerer.

Jacques, B. (2001). *Taggerung.* New York: Philomel. Deyna, a young otter, is captured by the ferret leader of a vermin clan who wants to use Deyna in his evil plans. This is part of the Redwall series.

Jacques, B. (2002). *Triss.* New York: Philomel. Join Triss, a squirrelmaid, and her friends as they elude the evil ferret king and discover Brockhall, the ancient home of the badgers.

Jordan, R. (2002). *From the two rivers.* New York: Starscape. This is part one in the Eye of the World, the beginning of the wheel of time fantasy series. It is followed by part two, *To the Blight.*

Kurtz, K. (2000). *King Kelson's bride: A novel of the Deryni.* New York: Ace. In the conclusion to the King Kelson series, Kelson is pressured to find a wife and keep his ward Prince Liam safe.

Lackey, M. (2001). *Take a thief.* New York: DAW. After a mysterious fire, Skif sets out with vengeance on his mind in this prequel to the Valdemar tales.

Lee, T. (2000). *Wolf tower.* New York: Dutton. Escaping from the house where she is a maid, Claidi journeys through the Waste with a stranger only to find a worse fate in Wolf Tower.

LeGuin, U. (1968). *A wizard of earthsea.* Berkeley, CA: Parnassus Press. LeGuin begins her tales of wizards, mages, and dragons that continue in *The Tombs of Atuan* (1971), *The Farthest Shore* (1972), *Tehanu* (1990), and *Tales from Earthsea* (2001).

Levine, G. C. (1997). *Ella enchanted.* New York: HarperCollins. The gift of obedience turns into a curse.

Levine, G. C. (2001). *The two princesses of bamarre.* New York: HarperCollins. Addie has always been the timid princess. Now, however, only she can save her sister from the Gray Death.

McKillip, P. (1999). *Riddle master, the complete trilogy.* New York: Ace. This reissue of the Riddle-Master trilogy contains *The Riddle-Master of Hed, Heir of Sea and Fire,* and *Harpist in the Wind,* an epic tale.

McKinley, R. (1978). *Beauty: A retelling of the story of Beauty and the Beast.* New York: Harper & Row McKinley tells her own version of this traditional tale.

McKinley, R. (1982). *The blue sword.* New York: Greenwillow. Corlath, the King of the Hillfolk of Damar, kidnaps Harry Crewe and trains her to fight the evil forces threatening his country.

Modesitt, L. E. (1997). *The Chaos balance.* New York: Tor. Can Nylan the Smith use the forces of Chaos to help the world survive? Try others in Modesitt's Saga of Recluse series or the Spellsong Cycle.

Morris, G. (2000). *The savage damsel and the dwarf.* Boston, MA: Houghton Mifflin. Will Lady Lynet find a champion to save her castle from the Knight of the Red Lands?

Napoli, D. J. (1998). *Sirena.* New York: Scholastic. A young siren rescues Philoctetes, a Greek soldier. But can she release him to face his destiny?

Nix, G. (1996). *Sabriel.* New York: HarperCollins. Can Sabriel save the Old Kingdom from destruction by the undead and rescue her necromancer father who is trapped in Death? The saga continues in *Lirael* (2001) and *Abhorsen* (2003).

Nix, G. (2003). *The keys to the kingdom: Mister monday.* New York: Scholastic. This is the first in a new fantasy series.

Paolini, C. (2003). *Eragon.* New York: Knopf. In this first book in the Inheritance Trilogy, a 15-year-old boy finds a mysterious stone that will change his life.

Pierce, T. (1999). *Protector of the small.* New York: Random House. Ten-year-old Keladry of Mindalen begins her quest to become a knight in this first book in the Protector of the Small series. Other series by Pierce include the Trickster's books (e.g., *Trickster's Choice,* 2003), Circle of Magic (e.g., *Sandry's Story,* 1997), The Circle Opens (e.g., *Cold Fire,* 2002), The Immortals (e.g., *Realm of the Gods,* 1996), and Song of the Lioness.

Pullman, P. (1996). *The golden compass.* New York: Knopf. In this first of the His Dark Materials trilogy, Lyra Belacqua begins her quest to learn about the mysterious Dust and to rescue the missing children in the far north. The second book in the trilogy is *The Subtle Knife.*

Pullman, P. (1998). *Clockwork, or all wound up.* New York: Arthur A. Levine. Can Karl, the apprentice clockmaker, find a way to make a new figure for the Glockenheim town clock or must he make a bargain with the devil?

Pullman, P. (2000). *The amber spyglass.* New York: Knopf. Will sets out to rescue Lyra in the conclusion to the trilogy.

Rowling, J. K. (1998). *Harry Potter and the sorcerer's stone.* New York: Scholastic. Harry Potter is rescued from the home of his Muggle aunt and uncle Dursley to begin school at Hogwarts School of Witchcraft and Wizardry.

Rowling, J. K. (2000). *Harry Potter and the goblet of fire.* New York: Scholastic. In his fourth year at Hogwarts Academy, Harry Potter is mysteriously entered in an unusual contest.

Rowling, J. K. (2003). *Harry Potter and the order of the phoenix.* New York: Scholastic. In this fifth book in the series, Harry Potter learns to face new challenges as he studies for his Ordinary Wizarding Levels and begins the transition into adulthood.

Scieszka, J. (1993). *The time warp trip, your mother was a neanderthal.* New York: Viking. When Sam, Joe, and Fred look at the pictures of cavemen in a book, the time travel mist appears and the three boys are transported back to prehistoric times.

Smith, S. (1997). *Crown duel.* New York: Harcourt. Will Meliara be able to keep her promise to her father and protect her country?

Springer, N. (1998). *I am Mordred: A tale of Camelot.* New York: Philomel. Mordred tells his side of the legend of King Arthur.

Taylor, C. (2001). *On wings of a dragon.* Markham, Ont: Fitzhenry & Whitside. Who is Kor'el, a young girl with amnesia, and why is Queen Mariah summoning all the village maidens?

Thomsen, B. M. (Ed.). (2002). *American fantasy tradition.* New York: Tor. From folk tales and tall tales to fantastic historical stories and glimpses of enchantment in everyday life, this collection covers the realm of fantasy in America.

Wrede, P. C. (1990). *Dealing with dragons.* New York: Harcourt Brace. Not content with being a bored princess, Cimorene runs away to live with a dragon. This is the first book in the series.

Yolen, J. (1982). *Dragon's blood.* New York: Delacorte. In the first of the Pit Dragons series, Jakkin steals a dragon hatchling and trains it to become a fighter.

Horror

Atwater-Rhodes, A. (2001). *Shattered mirror.* New York: Delacorte. Sarah is a high school vampire-hunter. Other vampire books by this author include *Demon in My View* (2002), *Midnight Predator* (2002), and *In the Forests of the Night* (1999).

Bird, I. (2001). *So note it be.* New York: Avon. In this first book in the Circle of Three series, Morgan uses a spell in a book and then must locate others who have checked out the book in an attempt to undo the damage she caused.

Butler, C. (2000). *Timon's tide.* New York: McElderry. Who is hiding in the woods near Daniel's home?

Cooney, C. (1989). *The fog.* New York: Scholastic. In this first book of the Losing Christina series or the Point Horror Trilogy, the Shevvingtons almost destroy Christina's friend Anya. Other books in the series are *The Snow* (1990) and *The Fire* (1990).

Ewing, L. (2000). *Goddess of the Night.* New York: Hyperion. Meet Vanessa, a typical teenager except for her special talents, in this first book in the Daughters of the Moon series.

Gaiman, M. (2002). *Coraline.* New York: Harper. Coraline is living the good life until she wants to return home.

Kiln, G. (1996). *Horror show.* New York: Tor. Strange things happen during the making of a low-budget 1950s creature film.

King, S. (1999). *The girl who loved Tom Gordon.* New York: Scribner. What is the beast that is following Trisha McFarland through the Maine woods?

Klause, A. C. (1997). *Blood and chocolate.* New York: Delacorte. Vivian and her werewolves are blamed for unexplained deaths of humans. Another vampire tale by Klause is *Silver Kiss* (1990).

Koontz, D. (1998). *Fear nothing.* New York: Bantam. Can Chris Snow come out of the darkness and save his world? A sequel is *Seize the Night.*

Koontz, D. (1999). *False memory.* New York: Bantam. Can Martie protect herself from herself?

Lovecraft, H. P. (1996). *The transition of H. P. Lovecraft: The road to madness*. New York: Ballantine. Here are 29 weird tales by a master of the genre.

Martin, E. B. (Ed.). (2000). *Campfire collection: Spine-tingling tales to tell in the dark*. San Francisco: Chronicle. You might not want to read these 17 tales late at night.

Matheson, R. (Ed.). (2002). *Nightmare at 20,000 feet*. New York: Tor. This is a collection of classic horror tales.

Naylor, P. R. (2000). *Jade green: A ghost story*. New York: Atheneum. Why did Jade die? Judith must find the answer before disaster strikes her family.

Pearce, P. (2002). *Familiar and haunting: Collected stories*. New York: Greenwillow. If you enjoy psychological hauntings and extraordinary events, try this collection of stories.

Ravenwolf, S. (2000). *Witches' night out*. St. Paul, MN: Llewellyn. This is the first book in the YA Witches' Chillers series.

Shan, D. (2001). *Cirque du Freak: A living nightmare*. Boston: Little Brown. After he steals a rare spider, Darren Shan must pledge his life to a vampire. This is the first in the series. Other tales in the series are *Cirque du Freak: Tunnels of Blood* (2002) and *Cirque du Freak: Vampire Mountain* (2002).

Shusterman, N. (2003). *Full tilt*. New York: Simon & Schuster. Visit a bizarre carnival with truly frightening rides.

Stine, R. L. (1999). *Nightmare hour: Time for terror*. New York: HarperCollins. These 10 tales of fear and horror are for younger teens.

Stine, R. L. (2001). *Haunting hour: Chills in the dead of night*. New York: HarperCollins. A collection of 10 horror stories. Another collection by Stine is *Beware: R. L. Stine Picks His Favorite Scary Stories* (2002).

Stine, R. L. (2002). *The stepsister*. New York: Simon Pulse. Emily learns a terrifying secret from Jessie's past. This book is from the Fear Street series.

van Belkon, E. (Ed.). (2000). *Be afraid! Tales of horror*. Toronto: Tundra Books. What start out as realistic stories become tales of terror.

Vande Velde, V. (1995). *Companions of the night*. San Diego: Harcourt. Is Ethan a vampire or is he innocent? Will Kerry find out in time?

Windsor, P. (1996). *The blooding*. New York: Scholastic. Imagine becoming the nanny for a family in which the father is a werewolf.

Suggested Readings

Barbieri, R. (2002). Wizardry at work: The fiction of J. R. R. Tolkien and J. K. Rowling. *Independent School, 61*(4), 99–102.

Barron, T. A. (2001). Truth and dragons. *School Library Journal, 47*(6), 52–54.

Creel, K., & Stern, A. F. (2002). Fantasy for people who don't like fantasy: A booklist. *Voice of Youth Advocates, 25*(1), 17–19.

Decker, C. (2002). Science fiction and fantasy roundup. *The Book Report, 20*(5), 21–24.

Denton, P. H. (2002). What could be wrong with Harry Potter? *Journal of Youth Services in Libraries, 15*(3), 28–32.

Estes, S. (2003). Science fiction in science class: Is there a place for it? *Book Links, 13*(2), 34–36.

Klause, A. C. (1998). Why vampires? A young adult author speaks out. *Voice of Youth Advocates, 21*(1), 28–30.

Pierce, E. (2001). Science fiction and fantasy. *Voices from the Middle, 9*(2), 74–77.

Saltman, J., Denton, P. H., & Opar, T. (2002). Understanding Harry: The Potter frenzy and furor. *Journal of Youth Services in Libraries, 15*(3), 24–29.

Wilson, M. (2000). The point of horror: The relationship between teenage popular horror fiction and the oral repertoire. *Children's Literature in Education, 31*(1), 1–9.

References

(Note: All young adult literature referenced in this chapter are included in the Young Adult Books list and are not repeated in this list.)

Altner, P., & Ofcansky, T. (1998). *Vampire readings.* Lanham, MD: Scarecrow.

Barlowe, W. D. (1996). *Barlowe's guide to fantasy.* New York: HarperPrism.

Barron, N. (1990). *Horror literature: A reader's guide.* New York: Garland.

Barron, N. (Ed.). (1999a). *Fantasy and horror: A critical and historical guide to literature, illustration, film, TV, radio, and the internet.* Lanham, MD: Scarecrow.

Barron, N. (1999b). *What fantastic fiction do I read next? A reader's guide to recent fantasy, horror, and science fiction.* Farmington Hills, MI: Gale.

Bucher, K. T., & Manning, M. L. (2000). A boy's alternative to bodice-rippers. *English Journal, 89*(4), 135–137.

Bucher, K. T., & Manning, M. L. (2001). Taming the alien genre: Bringing science fiction into the classroom. *The ALAN Review, 28*(2), 41–45.

Burgess, M., & Bartle, L. R. (Eds.). (2002). *Reference guide to science fiction, fantasy, and horror.* Englewood, CO: Libraries Unlimited.

Burroughs, E. R., (1912). *A princess of Mars.* Garden City, NY: Nelson Doubleday.

Card, O. S. (1990). *How to write science fiction and fantasy.* Cincinnati, OH: Writer's Digest Books.

Carroll, L. (1865). *Alice's adventures in wonder land.* London: MacMillan.

Charmas, S. M. (1992). A case for fantasy. *The ALAN Review, 19*(3), 20–22.

Clute, J., & Grant, J. (Eds.). (1999). *Encyclopedia of fantasy.* New York: St. Martin's Griffin.

Cushman, C. (February, 1999). 1998 book summary. *Locus: The Newspaper of the Science Fiction Field, 42,* 43–46.

Diaz-Rubin, C. (1996). Reading interests of high school. *Reading Improvement, 33* (Fall 96), 169–175. Retrieved December 30, 2002, from WilsonWeb: http://vnweb.hwwilsonweb.com.

Dunleavey, M. P. (1995). Children's writers plumb the depths of fear. *Publishers Weekly, 242*(13), 28–29.

Fonseca, A., & Pulliam, J. M. (2003). *Hooked on horror: A guide to reading interests in horror fiction.* Englewood, CO: Libraries Unlimited.

Fronius, S. K. (1993). *Reading interests of young adults in Media County, Ohio.* ERIC Document Reproduction Service No. ED367337.

Gath, T. (1999). Exploring new worlds; Finding science in science fiction. *Science, Books and Films, 35*(3). Retrieved July 26, 2000, from http://ehrweb.aaas.org/~sbf/313.htm.

Guiley, R., & Macabre, J. B. (1994). *The complete vampire companion.* New York: Macmillan.

Halem, D. (2003). "Night light; Dean Koontz finds brightness in life's dark mysteries." *Pages, 11*(1/2), 56–59.

Harris, J. (1996). "State of fantasy." *Discussion List* [Online] 28 May 1996. Available at, http://www.igloo-press.com/disc.fantasy.html [accessed 1999, February 9].

Herald, D. T. (1999). *Fluent in fantasy: A guide to reading interests.* Englewood, CO: Libraries Unlimited.

Herald, D. T. (2002). Dead but not gone. *Booklist, 98*(22), 1950.

Herald, D. T., & Kunzel, B. (2002). *Strictly science fiction.* Englewood, CO: Libraries Unlimited.

Hughes, M. (1992). Science fiction as myth and metaphor. *The ALAN Review, 19*(3), 2–5.

Hunt, P., & Lenz, M. (2001). *Alternative worlds in fantasy fiction.* New York: Continuum.

Jones, P. (1998). *What's so scary about R. L. Stine?* Lanham, MD: Scarecrow.

Jordan, A. D. (1995). Future reading: Science fiction. *Teaching and Learning Literature, 4*(5), 17–23.

Le Fanu, S. (1871–72). Carmilla. *The Dark Blue.* Vols. 2–3: Chapters 1–3 (December 1871); 4–6 (January 1872); 7–10 (February); 11–16 (March).

Leonhardt, M. (1996). *Keeping kids reading: How to raise avid readers in the video age.* New York: Crown.

Lodge, S. (1996). Life after Goosebumps. *Publishers Weekly, 243*(3), 24–27.

Louvisi, G. (1997). *Collecting science fiction and fantasy.* Brooklyn, NY: Allicance Publishing.

McElmell, S., & Buswell, L. (1998). Readers' choices: The most important authors of books for young adults. *Book Report, 16*(4), 23–24.

McRae, C. D. (1998). *Presenting young adult fantasy fiction.* Farmington Hills, MI: Twayne.

Melton, J. G. (1999). *The vampire book: The encyclopedia of the undead.* Detroit: Visible Ink Press.

Moffitt, M. A. S., & Wartella, E. (1992). Youth and reading: A survey of leisure reading pursuits of female and male adolescents. *Reading Research and Instruction, 31*(2), 1–17. Available www.cyfc.umn.edu/Documents/C/B/CB1025.html [accessed 1999, February 9].

Moltz, S. (2003). Forging futures with teens and science fiction: A conversation with Greg Bear and David Brin. *Voice of Youth Advocates, 26*(1), 15–18.

Ochoa, G., & Osier, J. (1993). *The writer's guide to creating a science fiction universe.* Cincinnati, OH: Writer's Digest Books.

Owen, L. (October 30, 1987). Children's science fiction and fantasy grows up. *Publishers Weekly, 232,* 32–37.

Poe, E. A. (March, 1835). Berenice. *Southern literary messenger.*

Poe, E. A. (1842). Mask of the Red Death. *Graham's magazine, 20*(5), 257–259.

Ramsland, K. M. (1993). *The vampire companion: The official guide to Anne Rice's* The Vampire Chronicles. New York: Ballantine.

Reid, S. E. (1998). *Presenting young adult science fiction.* Farmington Hills, MI: Twayne.

Rockman, C. (2001). Up for discussion—Give them wings'. *School Library Journal, 47*(12), 42–43.

Russell, D. L. (2001). *Literature for children: A short introduction* (4th ed.). New York: Longman.

Sanders, L. M. (1996). "Girls who do things": The protagonists of Robin McKinley's fiction. *The ALAN Review, 24*(1), 38–42.

Service, P. F. (1992). On writing scifi and fantasy for kids. *The Alan Review, 19*(3), 16–19.

Shelley, M. W. (1818). *Frankenstein, or, the modern Prometheus.* London: Lackington, Hughes, Harding, Mayor & Jones.

Snyder, Z. (1986). Afterword. *Tom's midnight garden* (by Philippa Pearce). New York. Dell.

Stoker, B. (1897). *Dracula.* Garden City, NY: Nelson Doubleday.

Thomason, N. (1983). *Survey reveals truths about young adult readers.* ERIC Document Reproduction Service No. ED237959.

Traw, R. (1993). *Nothing in the middle: What middle schoolers are reading.* ERIC Document Reproduction Service No. ED384864.

Vaillancourt, R. J., & Gillispie, J. (2001). Read any good movie lately? *Voice of Youth Advocates, 24*(4), 250–253.

Verne, J. (1865). *From the Earth to the Moon.* New York: Bantam.

Wells, H. G. (1895). *The time machine: An invention.* London: Heinemann. *The writer's complete fantasy reference.* (1998). Cincinnati, OH: Writer's Digest Books.

EXPLORING CONTEMPORARY REALISTIC FICTION

CHAPTER OVERVIEW

Newborn baby found abandoned in local park! Drunk driver *indicted in death of 16-year-old! Teenage dad charged with physical abuse of infant son! Teenagers riot in Benton Harbor, Michigan! Priest accused of sexually abusing a teenager! Violence continues in Iraq and Liberia! Affirmative action under attack!* These news headlines from a single Thursday in southeastern Virginia are typical of some of the more serious events, problems, and challenges that impact many young people. Had this Thursday fallen within the school year, there might also have been reports of violence or weapons in a school.

As young adults develop and mature, they must cope with a number of issues outside of those that make the news. They must learn to overcome their fears and accept responsibilities, and to deal with problems related to adoption, divorce, disabilities, disease, sexual relationships, changes within their families, relationships, sexual orientation, alienation, alcohol and drug abuse, and suicide. Contemporary realistic fiction, sometimes called the problem novel, uses plots, themes, settings, and characters to reflect the world as we know it and the problems and challenges that many young people face daily. These books often address topics in an open and frank manner. While other books, such as adventure, mystery, and humorous novels, are sometimes considered realistic fiction, we have chosen to discuss these novels in a separate chapter and will focus here on the contemporary problem novel.

1. The background and brief history of contemporary realistic fiction;
2. Common themes and characteristics of realistic fiction;
3. Reasons for using and teaching contemporary realistic fiction;
4. Suggestions for using realistic fiction in a classroom or library;
5. Issues facing realistic fiction such as violence, stereotyping, and censorship; and
6. Representative examples of realistic fiction in the various categories of realism.

CONTEMPORARY REALISTIC FICTION

Some critics believe that putting the word *realistic* with the word *fiction* presents a problem. As Jordan (1995) states:

> We may judge fiction that is labeled "realistic" by how much the various elements that compose it seem to reflect the world as we know it, how closely they mimic reality, but such literature does not nor can it capture reality as we experience it; the term itself is an oxymoron. If a realistic novel were to mirror life truly, it would consist of a plethora of random characters, actions, and events from which no overall meaning would emerge. In a novel, an author takes great pains to choose and arrange events, characters, and actions in a way that, ultimately, they have meaning. Hence, we classify such literature as fiction—made-up, arranged, and graced with meaning. (Jordan, 1995, p. 16)

While Jordan (1995) makes some excellent points, realistic fiction does exist as a category of literature, even though it might not capture the essence of actual events and might not mirror peoples' lives and society exactly as the participants perceive them. What realistic fiction does attempt to do is make meaning out of a number of related events in ways that present readers with new ideas, add new depths to their lives, and allow young adults to see themselves in new ways. By creating a fictional story that is true-to-life, realistic fiction helps young adults explore socially significant themes and events, empathize with others, and examine complex human interactions (Tyson, 1999). Today, a goal of contemporary realistic fiction may be to make adolescents think about the "challenges of life in the multichanneled, disjunctive, digital world" (Aronson, 2001, p. 82). Either because of this realism (or in some cases, sensationalism) or because young adults can often relate to the events in the story and the characters' feelings and concerns, realistic fiction is a popular genre. In 2004, Judy Blume was the first author of young adult literature to receive the Medal for Distinguished Contribution to American

Letters from the National Book Foundation based on her books which provide "help in navigating the travails of growing up and . . . characters with whom [young adults] can identify" (McDuffie, 2004).

A Brief Look at Contemporary Realistic Fiction's Predecessors

Experts differ on the exact beginnings of contemporary realistic fiction. Jordan (1995) proposed that realistic fiction began with moral tales including the didactic and popular English realistic moral tale *The Renowned History of Little Goody Two Shoes,* which was attributed to Oliver Goldsmith and published by John Newbery in 1765. However, most other histories of literature suggest that realistic fiction for children appeared in the latter half of the 19th century with the publication of books such as Mary Mapes Dodge's *Hans Brinker,* or *The Silver Skates* (1865), Louisa May Alcott's *Little Women* (1868), and Mark Twain's *The Adventures of Tom Sawyer* (1876) and *Adventures of Huckleberry Finn* (1884).

By the 1960s and 1970s, when young adult literature was recognized as a separate category from children's literature, realistic young adult novels began to confront contemporary problems. Books included Robert Cormier's *The Chocolate War* (1974), S. E. Hinton's *The Outsiders* (1967), and the anonymously written *Go Ask Alice* (Anonymous, 1971). Often the main character spoke to the reader, saying "I am a teenager just like you and this is my problem." The idea was that if teenagers saw the fictitious person with a problem and the ability to solve it, they would then realize that they, too, could find solutions to their own problems. While these realistic books were often labeled "problem novels," Aronson (2001) called them first-person "self-help and coping" (p. 55) novels. This is not to say that these books were inferior. Indeed, Judy Blume, Robert Cormier, Paul Zindel, and other writers demonstrated that these problem novels could be quality literature. In many instances, the "happily-ever-after" ending and the "phony realism" (Aronson 2001, p. 81) were replaced by uncomfortable and sometimes disturbing endings that encouraged readers to look beneath the surface to tell "truths people don't want to see" (p. 82) and to provoke thought and contemplation rather than provide neat compact answers (Aronson, 2001).

The 1980s brought a temporary turn away from this stark realism, as paperback romance series for young adults including a number of "Sweet Valley" titles grew in popularity. However, in spite of predictions that the Internet and MTV would eliminate young adult fiction publishing in the 1990s, the amount of realistic young adult literature not only grew but also included more multicultural viewpoints. Jacqueline Woodson, Kyoko Mori, Walter Dean Myers, Victor Martinez (1996), Virginia Euwer Wolff, and other writers added their voices among a number of young adult novels.

Today, young adult books address a wide range of themes including religion, sexuality and sexual orientation, ethnicity, and a concern for the future. According to Dresang (1999), books are breaking barriers that formerly "blocked off certain topics, certain kinds of characters, [and] certain styles of language" (p. 13). Authors are also using multiple perspectives and allowing previously subjugated voices to speak in their novels. The result of these changes is books that address previously forbidden subjects, examine overlooked settings and communities, and portray characters in new and more complex ways. Even violence in realistic fiction has changed to become "more central, bold and graphic" (Dresang, 1999, p. 189). In addition to the traditional young adult first-person narrative with a typical linear, sequential plot, books such as Paul Fleischman's *Seedfolks* (1997), Cynthia Voigt's *Bad Girls* (1996), and Virginia Walter and Katrina Roeckelein's *Making Up Megaboy* (1998) use multiple viewpoints. Other writers are changing the format of realistic fiction. For example, Walter Dean Myers' *Monster* (1999) is written as a screenplay; Mel Glenn's *Split Image* (2000) and Virginia Euwer Wolff's *Make Lemonade* (1993) and *True Believer* (2001) are novels in verse; and Paul Fleischman's *Seek* (2001) is written as a radio script. In *Nothing But the Truth* (1991), Avi tells the story, not as a straightforward narrative, but through a series of memos, hand-written messages, diary entries, news releases, and dialogues. Louis Sachar blends three stories in a nonlinear fashion in *Holes* (1998). Realistic graphic novels (based on the traditional comic book format and discussed in Chapter 10) are also common. Connecting Adolescents and Their Literature 4-1 suggests an inexpensive way to add realistic fiction to classroom and library collections.

Themes of Contemporary Realistic Fiction

What makes a young adult book feel real? Jordan (1995), Dresang (1999), Aronson (2001), and others identify characteristics found in most realistic fiction. These books:

- take their settings, characters, and plot from the real world and change the randomness of the world into meaningful patterns;

- mirror the real world and the moral and ethical dilemmas that young people face;

- are believable;

- exhibit the literary qualities (plot, setting, character, point of view, theme, and style) of good fiction;

- comment on the human condition; and

- are direct and often intense or extreme.

CONNECTING | **ADOLESCENTS AND THEIR LITERATURE 4-1**

Don't be afraid of paperbacks. Because of the flimsy nature of paperbacks, some educators and librarians are reluctant to spend money on paperback novels. However, many excellent realistic fiction novels are published in paperback format and can extend a classroom or library collection. Look for bargains at garage sales, thrift stores, and half-price or used book stores. Use your knowledge of review sources and the information from the paperback's cover to select good literature. Often quotes from reviews and lists of awards are included on the back of the book or inside the front cover. Knowing those awards and review journals will help you add quality literature to your collection at a very reasonable price.

Aronson (2001) maintains that, as with a great painter, a writer of realistic fiction must go beneath the surface to explore discontinuities, examine the subconscious, and investigate unsettling truths. The results must not be sugar-coated stories of perfect lives, but frank examinations of the choices that young adults must make. Thus, the themes of realistic fiction are varied and range from gaining the acceptance of others, developing friendships, growing up, and understanding the role of the family to finding a place in society, coping with alienation, finding a sexual identity, and searching for a sense of self. By using multiple voices to tell the same story, some young adult writers have attempted to show the complexities of adolescents' lives. They have also attempted to show that there are "hidden connections between things and that we can never fully know the consequences of our acts" (Aronson, 2001, p. 82). In quality young adult realistic fiction, nothing is diluted and no condescension is permitted. Perhaps this stance is epitomized by the author Robert Cormier who was both "unflinching and full of compassion, often brutal and always uncompromising in his depiction of the individual struggling in the face of power, corruption, victimization, betrayal and conspiracy" (Robert Cormier Remembered, 2001). Expanding Your Knowledge with the Internet 4-1 identifies web sites you can visit to learn more about Robert Cormier as well as a few other authors of contemporary realistic fiction.

Rather than focusing on the subject (sports), the setting (western), or the feeling (romance) of a book, we have chosen to examine young adult contemporary realistic fiction by the theme a novel portrays. Some of the most common themes are discussed in the following text, along with a few recommended "problem" novels for each theme. As with all lists, we caution you that it is not exhaustive, that the categories are not mutually exclusive, and that books can cross categories.

In deciding on the young adult novels to include, we faced the problem of identifying what is contemporary realism and what is historical realism. For example, Walter Dean Myers' *Fallen Angels* is often included on lists of realistic fiction, as many of the teachers and librarians who select realistic fiction see the Vietnam War as a very contemporary event. However, 1968 is a historical time for young adolescents who were born years after the end of the war. In the same manner, while Ann Head's (1967) *Mr. and Mrs. Bo Jo Jones* may address the issue of accepting responsibility for a teenage pregnancy, many modern young adults would find the story dated and unrealistic. Thus, with the exception of a few classic novels, our discussion will focus on more recent novels.

EXPANDING | *YOUR KNOWLEDGE WITH THE INTERNET 4-1*

Laurie Halse Anderson (www.writerlady.com/) and Walter Dean Myers (aalbc.com/authors/walter1.htm) are two of the many authors of realistic fiction who have Internet sites. Visit this book's Companion Website at www.prenhall.com/bucher to link directly to these and many other sites with information on authors of young adult contemporary realistic fiction.

Overcoming Fears and Accepting Responsibilities. In quality young adult literature, major or minor characters are often challenged by others (or by themselves) to meet responsibilities. For example, Tony must confront his weight and his friend's drug abuse in *Fat Kid Rules the World* (Going, 2003); Nick uses basketball to help him cope with his parent's divorce in *Night Hoops* (Deuker, 2000); Benjie fights drugs in the classic *A Hero Ain't Nothin' But a Sandwich* (Childress, 1973); Claudia must accept responsibility for her actions in *The Search* (Holland, 1991); and a young man must determine his own future in *Stetson* (Rottman, 2002). Other books that include this theme are *Because of Winn-Dixie* (DiCamillo, 2000), *Spellbound* (McDonald, 2001), and *My Evil Twin* (McKean, 1997). Connecting Adolescents and Their Literature 4-2 examines one way to create a character description web based on the main character in a contemporary realistic novel.

CONNECTING   *ADOLESCENTS AND THEIR LITERATURE 4–2*

Use a graphic organizer to create a character description web based on the main character in a contemporary realistic novel. The following web is based on Steve Harmon, the main character in Walter Dean Myers' *Monster* (1999).

Protects himself

Outgoing

Confused

Prisoner

My own description

Wants to be accepted

Personality

A good student

Cares about his family

"Bright, talented, compassionate"

Steve Harmon

Physical characteristics

Description by others

A killer

Thin

"Monster"

Important things in his life

Feelings/ thought about himself

"Brown skinned"

16 years old

Innocent

Scared

Film workshop

His brother

"A good person"

Understanding Families, Divorce, and Adoption. Relationships with parents and other family members are important to young adults. Differences of opinion over dress, curfews, and length and color of hair, as well as more serious concerns such as excessive alcohol consumption (either among the parents or the young person), physical or sexual abuse, or neglect, can exact a considerable toll on both adults and young people. While the two-parent family with a couple of children still exists today, many different family makeups and even some dysfunctional or disintegrating families also occur. One-parent homes, as well as homes with stepparents, foster children, and other family arrangements, are common today and are therefore reflected in books that young adults read.

Several authors of young adult novels deal with the problems found in contemporary families. Tracy Mack explores divorce in *Drawing Lessons* (2000), while Ian Lawrence observes a disintegrating family in *The Lightkeeper's Daughter* (2002). Trial separation is a theme in Carolyn Mackler's *Love and Other Four-Letter Words* (2000), and Gary Paulsen explores a single-parent family in *The Glass Café* (2003). Orphans and family tensions are central to the story in Patricia Reilly Giff's *Pictures of Hollis Woods* (2002), and adoption plays an important part in Ingrid Tomey's *The Queen of Dreamland* (1996). The Applewhites are a nontraditional family of writers and artists who take in a juvenile delinquent in Stephanie Tolan's *Surviving the Applewhites* (2002).

A number of young adult realistic fiction novels examine father-son or father-daughter relationships. Although each differs in more than one way, the circumstances are usually the same—differences exist between the parent and the young adult and both have to gain an understanding of himself/herself and the other. For example, Jean Ferris tells the story of Brian and his father in *All That Glitters* (1996). In Walter Dean Myers' classic *Somewhere in the Darkness* (1992), Jimmy Little is surprised when his father returns from jail. *Seek* (Fleischman, 2001) tells the story of Rob Radkovits, who is looking for his father's voice in his life. In a book of family relationships (particularly father-daughter relationships), Kate must cope with being a preacher's daughter as she tries to get into MIT in Laurie Halse Anderson's *Catalyst* (2002).

Families also play a part in a number of other books. Mel Glenn's *Split Image* (2000) is a multi-voice story told in poems that focus on a young Asian American girl who is caught between her parents' expectations and the freedom of America. In *Miracle's Boys* (2000), Jacqueline Woodson writes about three brothers and the pressures of the inner city that keep trying to pull them apart. Ellen Wittlinger's *Hard Love* (1999) uses a modified magazine format to explore a young boy growing up and coping with his parents' divorce. Other stories about a wide range of families include *Tangerine* (Bloor, 1997), *Like Sisters on the Homefront* (Williams-Garcia, 1995), the Alice series by Phyllis Reynolds Naylor, and the works of Todd Strasser and Walter Dean Myers.

Family relationships also spill over into other categories of realistic novels as they touch on alcoholism, the death of a family member, spouse abuse, a gay parent, parents embarrassing young people, and a host of other topics. Any problem that some family has experienced or is experiencing has probably been addressed in young adult realistic fiction. For example, Michael Cadnum's *Taking It* (1995) discusses shoplifting and sexual relationships; Marion Dane Bauer's *A Question of Trust* (1994) explores the issue of trust between parents and children; and Thelma Wyss's classic *Here at the Scenic-Vu Motel* (1988) tells about the Bear Flats, Idaho, school board's decision to stop bussing seven children to town to the high school and, instead, to have them live at the Scenic-Vu Motel during the week.

Finding Friends: Relationships, Alienation, and a Sense of Belonging. Peers and friends are also important to young adults and can play an influential role in many young peoples' choice of dress, mannerisms, and behaviors. Naturally, young adult fiction can portray that relationship. In *Who the Man* (Lynch, 2002), Earl has little control over his own life and resorts to fighting. In contrast, Nick learns that he can control his life and relationships the way he controls a basketball game in *Night Hoops* (Deuker, 2000), and Ben finds he has to challenge his best friend to a wrestling match in *Wrestling Sturbridge* (Wallace, 1996). In Nikki Grimes' *Bronx Masquerade* (2001), as high school students read the poems that they have written, they reveal their secret fears and their real selves to their classmates. Peer pressure is a focus in *The Battle of Jericho* (Draper, 2003), while changing friendships play an important part in *The New Rules of High School* (Nelson, 2003). Other books that present glimpses of adolescent relationships are *The Girls* (Koss, 2000), *Rain Catchers* (Thesman, 1991), *Snail Mail No More* (Danziger & Martin, 2000), *Three Clams and an Oyster* (Powell, 2002), and *How I Changed My Life* (Strasser, 1995).

In an attempt to belong, some teens are searching for their cultural identity while others are only trying to fit in with the majority culture. That is what Tara Mehtas is trying to do in *A Group of One* (Gilmore, 2001) until her grandmother arrives from India. Also from India, Dimple, in *Born Confused* (Desai Hidier, 2002), is an ABCD, American Born Confused Desi, who is too American for her immigrant Indian parents and too Indian for her American friends. Young Ju in An Na's *Step from Heaven* (2001) must balance her Korean heritage with her new life in America and her cruel father's demands. Contemporary American Indians and their search for cultural identity are found in a number of books including *The Window* (Dorris, 1997), *The Heart of a Chief* (Bruchac, 1998), and *Who Will Tell My Brother?* (Carvell, 2002). Other books that include a search for cultural identity are *Breakaway* (Yee, 1997), *Beacon Hill Boys* (Mochizuki, 2002), and *Cuba 15* (Osa, 2003). Connecting Adolescents and Their Literature 4-3 looks at one technique to use when examining the cultural conflict found in some contemporary realistic fiction.

Developing and Maturing. After being bombarded with messages from parents, family, peers, television, the Internet, school, and the community, young adults must search for ways to make sense of this cacophony of voices. While attempting to discover their own identity, they ask: Who am I? What kind of person will I grow up to be? What will I be like? Developing a personal, sexual, and individual identity represents a significant (although often unconscious) task for young adults. The fact that many young adults are turning to realistic fiction for answers can be seen in the phenomenal success of Ann Brashares' *The Sisterhood of the Traveling Pants* (2001), the first young adult debut novel to sell over 100,000 copies.

Contemporary realistic fiction provides an excellent way for teachers and library media specialists to help young adults understand their own cultural identity as well as the cultural background of others. Sometimes a character in a novel will feel torn between the expectations of a culture and his or her own wants and desires. Use the information from the book to complete a graphic organizer that provides a visual representation of these feelings and the conflicts.

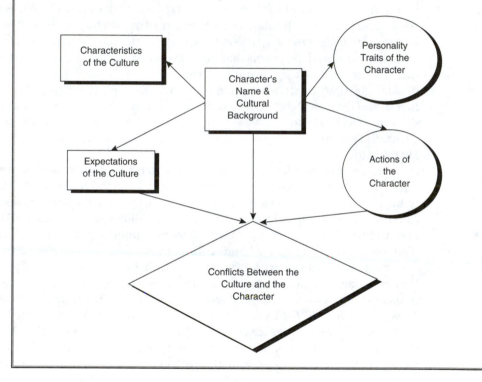

Adolescent protagonists face the challenges and struggles of growing up in many books, from H. F. Simms seeking a sexual identity in *Finding H. F.* (Watts, 2001); overweight outsider Elvin failing at his assigned sport slot in *Slot Machine* (Lynch, 1995); Raspberry equating money with security in *Money Hungry* (Flake, 2001); wise-guy Matt emerging from his bad-boy shell in *Big Mouth and Ugly Girl* (Oates, 2002); and Myrtle trying to determine just exactly who and what she is in *Myrtle of Willendorf* (O'Connell, 2000). While many novels, such as Virginia Euwer Wolff's story of life in the inner city in *Make Lemonade* (1993) and *True Believer* (2001), Victor Martinez's tale of a Mexican American teenager in the California projects in *Parrot in the Oven* (1996), or Rob Thomas'

novel of a gifted but troubled high school senior in *Rats Saw God* (1996), are very serious, more humorous narratives also exist, such as Louise Rennison's funny British tale of Georgia Nicholson that begins in *Angus, Thongs, and Full-Frontal Snogging* (2000) or the diaries of Jonah Black that begin in *Black Book Diary of a Teenage Stud: Girls, Girls, Girls* (2001). In a series of poems, Sonya Sones tells of the maturing of 15-year-old Sophie in *What My Mother Doesn't Know* (2001). Other tales that address these topics include *Alice, I Think* (Juby, 2003), *Bloomability* (Creech, 1998), *Cry Baby* (Karas, 1996), *Goodbye, Amanda the Good* (Shreve, 2000), and *Homeless Bird* (Whelan, 2000).

Coping with Violence, Crime, Alcohol, and Drug Abuse. Unfortunately, violence, crime, alcohol and drug use, and various other forms of abuse are an integral part of our society and, at least in the lives of many people, take precedence over civility. Too many young adults see or experience gang-related violence and death, and feel the resulting fear, anger, and grief. No longer restricted to inner cities, violence even reaches students in rural and suburban schools in places such as Littleton, Colorado, or Red Lake, Minnesota. While shielding or protecting young people from violence and abuse is ideal, it is also impossible. However, through literature, we can present novels that help young adults explore these issues. Sometimes the realistic novels offer hope, while at other times they provide a forum in which readers can explore options and alternatives.

Never one to shy away from violence, Robert Cormier, well-known for his classic novel *The Chocolate War* (1974), often examines the topic from a new perspective. His *We All Fall Down* (1991) looks at violence in a small town and includes trashing a house, attacking a 14-year-old girl, and seeking revenge. Cormier's *The Rag and Bone Shop* (2001) explores the murder of a child and the attitude of authorities to do whatever is necessary to solve the crime, even if it means forcing a 12-year-old boy to confess.

Other authors also examine the issue of violence in our society. S. E. Hinton's classic *The Outsiders* (1967) tells of three brothers who grow up in a world of violent street gangs. While Steve Harmon, in Walter Dean Myers' *Monster* (1999), writes the story of his trial for murder in the form of a screenplay, Ryan Walker in Phyllis Reynolds Naylor's *Walker's Crossing* (1999) must confront his own feelings when his older brother joins a militia group and violence erupts. Looking at violence in a school, Todd Strasser examines a school shooting in *Give a Boy a Gun* (2000).

Violence exists in families as well as in society in general. In *Silent to the Bone* (Konigsburg, 2000), Branwell Zamborska is accused by the family's English au pair of dropping and shaking his baby sister until she stops breathing. A physically abusive father plays a major role in Gloria Velasquez's *Rina's Family Secret* (1998). Vince's violent "family" in Gordon Korman's *Son of the Mob* (2002) is a bit unconventional—his father is really a powerful Mafia boss.

Pressures from peers, television and billboard advertising, and society norms mean that most young adults are familiar with the problems associated with alcohol and drug abuse. However, the desire to experiment with the unknown too often results in disaster for young people as well as their friends and loved ones. By presenting the problems associated with substance abuse, young adult novels include characters who must deal with getting hooked and working toward recovery, experience the despair and desperation associated with substance abuse, face the problems with alcoholic or drug-dependent parents, and confront the violence that often results from substance abuse.

Although published over 30 years ago, Alice Childress' *A Hero Ain't Nothin' But a Sandwich* (1973) continues to be popular. The story realistically addresses addiction problems by following Benjie's experience with drugs and his slip into desperation and despair as his family and friends try to save him. Drinking and alcoholism take center stage in Jan Cheripko's *Imitate the Tiger* (1996), as Chris Serbo plays football and drinks too much. Chris has been sent to a detox clinic and, through his flashbacks, readers learn about his life of despair and self-delusion.

Living with Physical and Mental Disabilities. A primary value of literature is that it provides readers with experiences which, although not always ideal, help them understand their own lives and the world around them. Contemporary realistic fiction may not always present "the best" people or places but, in effective and well-written young adult realistic fiction, the stories are presented in nonsensationalized, realistic terms.

In realistic fiction novels, a number of characters must deal with disabling conditions. For example, in the classic *Deenie* (Blume, 1973), Deenie wears a back brace. Likewise, Mandy is blinded in an automobile accident in *The Window* (Ingold, 1996); and Joey Pigza faces the devastating effects of learning disabilities such as attention deficit disorder in a series of books by Jack Gantos. Young adults face the challenges of cerebral palsy in Ronald Koertge's *Stoner and Spaz* (2002) and in Terry Trueman's *Stuck in Neutral* (2001). In a classic work for mature readers, a crippling automobile accident forces star athlete Willie Weaver to leave his family and friends to rebuild his shattered life in Chris Crutcher's *The Crazy Horse Electric Game* (1987). Some characters must deal, not with their own disabling conditions, but with disabilities in their families. In Norma Fox Mazer's *When She Was Good* (1997), Em is finally liberated from years of torment by her mentally ill older sister.

In contrast to Em, some young adults must face their own mental illness including serious problems of depression. Carrie, in the classic *The Language of Goldfish* (Oneal, 1980), experiences emotional and mental illness; while Dani in *The Game* (Toten, 2001) must deal with a number of problems including physical abuse, a dysfunctional family, and a psychological struggle for her own survival. In Terry Trueman's *Inside Out* (2003), readers see the torment in Zach's life as a schizophrenic when he is taken hostage during a failed robbery attempt. After being directed to see a court-appointed psychologist following her friend Aimee's suicide, Zoe learns to cope with her own depression, guilt, loneliness, and anger in Mary Beth Miller's *Aimee* (2002).

Coping with Death, Disease, Accidents, and Suicide. On a daily basis, many young adults see and hear about death and debilitating diseases. This takes a toll on their emotions, especially when the event is an accident or an unexpected suicide.

Both Jesse and Roxanne cope with death and loss in Martha Moore's *Under the Mermaid Angel* (1995). While Jesse grieves the death of her brother, Roxanne must deal with giving up her child at birth. Bobby, in the classic *My Brother Stealing Second* (Naughton, 1989), is also grief-stricken about his brother: Although his brother Billy was a star athlete, he killed both himself and a couple celebrating their wedding anniversary while driving drunk. In Deborah Froese's *Out of the Fire* (2002), Dayle is seriously burned in an accident and must go through therapy and treatment for her burns. Other books in which teenagers must face the death of a family member or friend include *Facing the Music* (Willey, 1996) and *Dinah Forever* (Mills, 1995).

Too often, murder and suicide find their way into the lives of young adults. In Colby Rodowsky's *Remembering Mog* (1996), the Fitzhugh family remembers Mog's violent death and tries to move toward healing. Todd, a 16-year-old African American teenager living in Denver in *Soulfire* (Hewitt, 1996), experiences grief over the death of his cousin, Tommy. Will in *Freewill* (Lynch, 2001) must deal with the suicides in his town and wonder what part, if any, he is playing.

While an accident or violence can cause a very sudden death, characters who have, or know someone who has, a life-threatening disease must struggle to cope with their feelings. Samantha and Juliana, better known as Sam and Jules, are close friends in Davida Wills Hurwin's *A Time for Dancing* (1995). Their story becomes one of death and dying when Jules learns she has cancer. In Liza Hall's *Perk!* (1997), bulimia becomes a life-threatening disease. Other books that examine this topic are *Hope Was Here* (Bauer, 2000), the various books by Lurlene McDaniel, and the classics *A Summer to Die* (Lowry, 1977) and *Tiger Eyes* (Blume, 1981).

During the later 1980s and 1990s, as the AIDS epidemic spread, there was an increase in the quantity and quality of young adult books that addressed the topic by looking at the loneliness of the disease, the change of relationships (and sometimes outright rejection) with parents and friends, attempts to make others aware of AIDS, the transmission of the disease (whether from a blood transfusion or sexual contact), and HIV-positive babies. For example, Joel keeps the memory of his uncle Michael alive in his thoughts after Michael dies of AIDS in Patricia Quinlan's *Tiger Flowers* (1994). In M. E. Kerr's classic *Night Kites* (1986), 17-year-old Jim's relationship with his family and friends changes when his older brother announces he has AIDS. A similar thing happens to Liam in *The Eagle Kite* (Fox, 1995). In *Diving for the Moon* (Bantle, 1995), Bird struggles through her mixed emotions when she discovers that her best friend Josh is HIV positive. Also, in *Earthshine* (Nelson, 1994), living with her father means that Slim will also be living with her father's long-time companion, Larry, who has AIDS.

Developing Sexual Relationships and Surviving Pregnancy, Incest, Rape, Abortion, and Sexually Transmitted Diseases. As teenagers grow up, they constantly deal with problems related to their sexuality. Not only must they cope with their own feelings, but they must also confront peer pressures and their families' expectations. In addition, they must factor in the things that they see on television and in movies. Stories of sexual relationships and pregnancy began to be published in the late 1960s and early 1970s when some of the taboos about these areas broke down. Now, books on these and other topics dealing with sexuality are accepted in most circles, although some are still challenged, especially for younger adolescents. Many of the books contained in other categories of this list show young adults facing the difficulties of dating and establishing relationships.

Some teens have to cope with unwanted pregnancies. Two uncompromising looks at the realities of life for some teenage girls are found in Rita Williams-Garcia's *Like Sisters on the Homefront* (1995) and Connie Rose Porter's *Imani All Mine* (1999). Margaret E. Bechard's *Hanging on to Max* (2002) and Angela Johnson's *The First Part Last* (2003) look at teenage fathers who try to raise their children. In *Second Choices* (Brinkerhoff, 2000), Nikki's conversion to Christianity helps her deal with her choice to give her baby up for adoption.

In the past, rape and sexual abuse often went unreported and unaddressed in young adult realistic fiction. Although the victims' emotional scars may have lasted a lifetime, especially in the case of sexual abuse by a family member, the violence remained hidden. Therefore, books on these topics received sharp criticism from censors and other groups who wanted to limit what young people read. Those restrictions have been lifted as more novels address these topics. In Hadley Irwin's classic *Abby, My Love* (1985), Chip loves Abby and questions her reluctance to be close, both psychologically and physically, with him. Then, Abby reveals that she has been sexually abused by her father. In *Out of Control* (1993), Norma Fox Mazer presents the story of Valerie Michon, who is assaulted by three respected teenage boys; and in *Speak* (Anderson, 1999), Melinda deals with the aftermath of date rape. While safe in the United States, 14-year-old Mardi tries to hide the fact that she was raped by soldiers in Haiti as she was leaving the country in Jaira Placide's *Fresh Girl* (2002).

Understanding Sexual Orientation. In the past, few young adult authors wrote about sexual orientation, in part because of the nature of the topic and, perhaps, the fears of censorship. However, an increasing number of writers now provide frank looks at differing sexual orientations and their surrounding challenges. One of the first books to address this topic was Nancy Garden's classic *Annie on My Mind* (1982), in which two high school girls accept their feelings for one another as their relationship develops and they fall in love. In *Deliver Us from Evie* (1994), M. E. Kerr explores the reactions of Evie Burrman's family and the small town in which she lives when Evie reveals her sexual orientation and her affair with Patsy Duff, the daughter of a banker who holds the loan on the Burrman farm. Dirk McDonald confronts his sexual identity in Francesca Lia Block's *Baby Be-Bop* (1995), and Heavenly Faith Simms learns who she really is in Julia Watts' *Finding H. F.* (2001).

Some young adults are challenged to understand the sexual orientation of friends and other family members. Mel in *From the Notebooks of Melanin Sun* (Woodson, 1995) keeps detailed notebooks telling of his anger, confusion, and denial in this story of mothers, sons, and lesbians. In *Brad's Universe* (Woodbury, 1998), Brad's father sexually harasses boys; and in *True Believer* (Wolff, 2001), LaVaughn finds out why the boy she likes is not interested in having a girlfriend.

Understanding the Difficulties Associated with Growing Old. When you are not even 20 years old, it is difficult to think about what it is like to be a senior citizen. However, many young adults do form very strong ties to older people only to realize that, just as there are problems with growing up, there are problems with growing old. In

River Boy (2000), Tim Bowler writes about the death of a grandfather. In *Stone Water* (1996), Barbara Snow Gilbert tells about a serious choice that a teenager's grandfather asks him to make. Teenagers share unique relationships with elderly neighbors in both Paul Zindel's classic *The Pigman* (1968) and in Kazumi Yumoto's *The Friends* (1996). Alzheimer's and its effects on a family plays an important part in Barbara Park's *Graduation of Jake Moon* (2000).

Living in a Global Society: Prejudice, Politics, Conflicts, and War. Not only does realistic fiction reflect on issues and problems that young adults find in their everyday lives in America, but it also asks young adults to look at issues in a global society. These multicultural themes, while often containing some of the previously addressed issues such as developing and maturing or family relationships, focus on other cultures or on global issues. Books such as Suzanne Fisher Staples's *Shabanu* (1989), Naomi Shihab Nye's *Habibi* (1997), Gloria Whelan's *Homeless Bird* (2000), Nancy Farmer's *A Girl Named Disaster* (1996), and Anton Ferreira's *Zulu Dog* (2002) present pictures of teenagers in other cultures.

Prejudice can be found almost anywhere. Kate, who is half-white, finds it in Hawaii in *Dance for the Land* (McLaren, 1999), and Zack, who has a Jewish father and a black mother, finds it with his grandfather in Mississippi in *Zack* (Bell, 1999).

Although the Cold War is over, teenagers today hear and read about conflicts, strife, and terrorism both at home and abroad. Several young adult novels look at the problems faced by teenagers throughout the world as they try to cope with conflict. In Deborah Ellis's *Parvana's Journey* (2002), a young girl tries to survive in Taliban-threatened Afghanistan, while in Jan Simeon and John Nieuwenhuizen's *What About Anna?* (2002), Anna tries to learn the truth about her brother's death from a landmine in Bosnia. Because Slade's father is a muckraking journalist, she and her brother must flee Nigeria in Beverley Naidoo's *The Other Side of Truth* (2001).

Understanding Religion and Its Role in Society. While many young adults are beginning their own search for spirituality and trying to determine the place that religion will or will not have in their lives, others are trying to understand the religious choices that others have made and how those choices will affect relationships. The inspirational Clearwater Crossing series of books by Laura Peyton Roberts features a diverse group of teenagers who face a series of crises that force them to increasingly rely on each other and on their faith. Lurlene McDaniel addresses the importance of religious beliefs in several of her books, including *Angel of Hope* (2000) and *Angels Watching Over Me* (1996). In Sonia Levitin's *The Singing Mountain* (1998), Mitch Green, a California teen, visits Israel and decides to join an Orthodox yeshiva there. Other books in which religion plays a strong role are *Blind Fury* (Shands, 2001), *The Book of Fred* (Bardi, 2001), and *Conflict in California* (Stuckey, 2001).

Some young adults must deal with religious fanaticism. For example, Dorry, in *Leaving Fishers* (Haddix, 1997), finds that the group of students who befriend her are really members of a religious cult. In *The Last Safe Place on Earth* (Peck, 1995), Todd's little sister is brainwashed by his fundamentalist babysitter.

Many works of contemporary realistic fiction have been made into movies. Some of these are listed in From Page to Screen.

FROM PAGE TO SCREEN

Contemporary Realistic Fiction

Share these screen adaptations of young adult literature worthy of an adolescent audience. Each film is rated appropriately for adolescents, and each film is worthy of thoughtful viewing. Consider comparing the film adaptations with the original texts and discuss the ways the original was altered for the screen. Why were the changes made? Was the running time the main consideration, or were filmmakers hoping to attract a specific audience? How do the changes affect the overall quality of the piece?

Holes
★★★★

2003, PG

Louis Sachar adapted his own Newbery Award-winning novel for the screen in this delightful, funny, clever film that follows Stanley Yelnats, victim of the Yelnats bad luck, to Camp Green Lake to uncover a generations-old mystery that starts with Kissin' Kate Barlow and ends with camp inmates digging holes.

The Mighty
1998, PG-13
★★★1/2

This adaptation of Rodman Philbrick's novel Freak the Mighty *tracks the unlikely friendship between Max, the underachieving son of a convict, and Kevin, a physically handicapped genius. Solid performances by Sharon Stone, James Gandolfini, and Elden Henson as Max provide touching clarity to Philbrick's story.*

Tex
1982, PG
★★★1/2

Tex is a well crafted, beautifully acted adaptation of S. E. Hinton's authentic and layered tale of the realities and dangers of adolescence as seen by two abandoned brothers living outside Tulsa. Her revered novel is treated with genuine respect.

Man Without a Face
1993, PG-13
★★★

Mel Gibson's directorial debut highlights the intelligent dialogue and subtle themes of Isabelle Holland's novel, and boasts a beautifully bold and nuanced performance by Nick Stahl as the fatherless boy who learns the value of trust from an ostracized, disfigured mentor.

The Outsiders
1983, PG
★★1/2

Director Francis Ford Coppola gives a fascinating, stylized look to S. E. Hinton's novel of the culture clash between the haves and the have-nots in 1960s Oklahoma, *although his vision threatens to suffocate the story itself. Screenwriter Kathleen Rowell's simplified version of Hinton's story has to fight with Coppola's overpowering look, but some talented young actors help the film meet Hinton's emotional purpose.*

Reasons for Using and Teaching Contemporary Realistic Fiction

Why use contemporary realistic fiction in a classroom or add it to a library collection? Perhaps because the genre developed as a didactic moral tale, many critics attempt to link realistic fiction with morality by examining a realistic novel in light of the messages that it delivers (Aronson, 2001). Thus, they focus on whether the novel "teaches" a lesson or provides a positive role model that young adults can emulate. However, Aronson (2001) maintains that "realism is not concerned with morality; it is about verisimilitude" (p. 80). While morality shapes beliefs or behaviors and does provide role models, realism reflects life and focuses on the conflicts that young adults face. Young adults do not want "predigested morals and fake realities" (p. 83). What they do want are works that will force them to confront their own beliefs, to identify their own messages in the story, and to grow in their own way (Aronson, 2001). Thus, some contemporary realistic fiction novels are uncomfortable to read while others raise more questions than they solve.

It is important for young adults to be exposed to books that reach and move them because, as Aronson notes (2001), "it can affect them as at no other age" (p. 81). Rather than looking for books that are contrived or didactic, young adults seem to be looking for novels that speak to them and about them in an honest and realistic way. These books will range on a continuum from lighthearted, even romantic, stories to more dark and disturbing examinations of the frustrations, events, and challenges of the real world in which contemporary adolescents live. Realistic characters are not always comfortable to know. As author Paul Zindel (2002) said about the protagonists he created, they are ornery, troubled, and "have an irksome itch. They always demanded a realistic story that was more than a comfortable grocery list" (p. 30).

There are many values of contemporary realistic fiction. Young adults can:

■ Identify with characters who have similar interests and who must deal with similar problems.

■ Realize that, while their problems and challenges are difficult, they are shared by other adolescents.

■ Extend their horizons and broaden their interests.

■ Better cope with grief, fear, and anger as they read about other young adults or characters who have dealt with adversity.

Aronson (2001) believes that good realistic fiction has the potential "to touch readers deeply so that, in the struggle with it, they begin to see and to shape themselves" (p. 119). Suggestions for Collaborative Efforts 4-1 suggests the use of contemporary realistic fiction as a basis for middle school advisory sessions.

Characteristics of Good Realistic Fiction

Mirroring life as some people experience it, realistic fiction deals with many complex problems and situations from understanding sexual orientation to dealing with family problems. At its core, a good realistic fiction novel is about people, their problems, and their challenges. The characters in the novel should be believable and their language and actions should be appropriate for the setting of the story and reflective of the culture and social class in which they live. An author writing about a gang in an urban setting has a responsibility to use appropriate words, slang, phrases, and dialects. However, while realism prevails, people are still considered with sensitivity; a good author is always aware of the fine line between stereotyping and realistic, objective writing. Although readers learn a lesson or a value such as being accountable for one's actions, or accepting the cultural, physical, or sexual differences of other people, good realistic fiction novels do not dictate specific moral and ethical beliefs. Rather, they challenge readers to learn the importance of moral and ethical behavior by drawing their own conclusions after they consider the events and facts from their personal perspectives using their own moral and ethical judgments. Some realistic fiction is expected to include violence; in fact, the genre would be failing in its mission if some novels did not mirror the violence that many young people experience. However, violence should be used appropriately and to make a point—never just for sensationalism. To Aronson (2001), a good book "recognize[s] the depth of darkness within teenagers

SUGGESTIONS FOR COLLABORATIVE EFFORTS

Middle schools often provide time within the curriculum for advisory sessions. A realistic novel (which can also be used in the English/language arts/reading classes) can provide a basis for discussion of contemporary problems and can allow young adults to explore their feelings freely. Teachers, school library media specialists, and counselors can work together to identify age-appropriate books and to develop group discussion guides. Discussion leaders need to beware of moralizing, oversimplifying situations, or suggesting that reading a book will solve all problems. However, the books can provide an excellent springboard for discussion and an examination of contemporary problems. While teachers can select the initial books, young adults should be encouraged to suggest books that they would like to discuss as well.

and yet also assume[s] that readers have the intelligence and the imagination to deal with ambiguity" (p. 120).

Due to the popularity of contemporary realistic fiction among young adults, many excellent books are published each year. Unfortunately, many others claim to be problem novels but lack the qualities that define good young adult literature. Considerations for Selecting Young Adult Literature: *Contemporary Realistic Fiction* lists some of the characteristics of good realistic fiction.

When selecting realistic fiction to use with reluctant young adult readers, you should also look for fast-paced books that begin with a hook to get the reader's interest and that have a limited number of characters, flashbacks, or subplots. These books should focus on high-interest topics and real-life situations that will keep the reader's interest. In the writing, look for familiar words and short sentences and paragraphs. A book for reluctant readers will ideally have visual appeal with an attractive cover, an easy-to-read typeface, and fewer than 200 pages in a paperback format (Jones, 1994).

Suggestions for Selecting and Teaching Realistic Fiction

Young adults are a diverse group, so selecting literature for them is never easy. Teachers and librarians need to balance the interests of individual adolescents with the reviews

---

CONSIDERATIONS	For Selecting Young Adult Literature	CONTEMPORARY REALISTIC FICTION

When evaluating a contemporary realistic fiction novel, ask:

1. Are there engaging and true-to-life, well-rounded characters who are both wise and foolish while they are growing and changing?
2. Is there an accurate reflection of the human condition and contemporary life without stereotyping?
3. Is there a sensitivity to all people regardless of sex or sexual orientation, race, religion, age, socioeconomic level, social group, or culture?
4. Does the plot appeal to young adults; address the challenges, hopes, and fears as well as the problems faced by contemporary adolescents; and offer hope for the future?

5. Does the plot ask young adults to consider or reconsider their own values and beliefs, inspire without providing "handy resolutions" (Aronson, 2001, p. 119), and not talk down to readers or tell them what to think?
6. Is the setting believable?
7. Is there an appropriate treatment of violence that never glamorizes violence, records it more graphically than necessary, or includes it gratuitously?
8. Does the language accurately reflect the characters as well as their educational status, social class, culture, and the place in which they live?

written by adults who work with young people. The ideal is to identify contemporary realistic fiction novels that interest young adults and that also receive laudatory reviews and critics' accolades and then to determine ways to use that literature in classrooms.

Awards and Best Books Lists. Fortunately, contemporary realistic novels are often found on many of the best books lists that are discussed in Chapter 2 such as the *School Library Journal,* the Young Adult Library Services Association best books lists, or the ALA Quick Picks for Reluctant Young Adult Readers. Others go on to win honors or awards such as the Michael L. Printz Award. Several of the multicultural book awards, such as the Pura Belpré Award, Jane Addams Book Award, or the Americas Award, may include contemporary realistic fiction in their list of winners. In addition, many of the books of recommended young adult literature such as the National Council of Teachers of English series, including *Books for You* (Beers & Lesesne, 2001), list a variety of contemporary realistic fiction novels.

Print Review Resources. A number of more specific print selection aids also include realistic fiction. Print resources include:

- *Helping Teens Cope: A Guide to Teen Issues Using YA Fiction and Other Resources* (Jones, 2003),

- *Radical Reads: 101 YA Novels on the Edge* (Bodart, 2002),

- *Hearing All the Voices: Multicultural Books for Adolescents* (Darby & Pryne, 2002), and

- *Rocked by Romance: A Guide to Young Adult Romance Genre Fiction* (Carpan, 2004).

Greenwood Press has issued the Using Literature to Help Troubled Teenagers series of books that include titles such as:

- *Using Literature to Help Troubled Teenagers Cope with End-of-Life Issues* (Allen, 2002),

- *Using Literature to Help Troubled Teenagers Cope with Health Issues* (Bowman, 2000), and

- *Using Literature to Help Troubled Teenagers Cope with Societal Issues* (Carroll, 1999).

Each book in the series includes a number of essays that review important issues and books, as well as provide suggestions for using the books in a classroom or library.

Online Resources. Other selection aids can be found on the Internet. A special issue of *The ALAN Review* was devoted to the problem novel and multicultural literature as well as books about eating disorders, health issues, inclusion, and capital punishment. The Gay, Lesbian, Bisexual, and Transgendered Round Table of the American Library Association makes available an excellent bibliography of fiction for gay teens. Expanding Your Knowledge with the Internet 4-2 provides links to these resources on the Web along with links to lesson plan ideas for teaching contemporary realistic fiction novels.

EXPANDING   *YOUR KNOWLEDGE WITH THE INTERNET 4–2*

Internet resources provide additional information about selecting and using contemporary realistic fiction. *The ALAN Review*–Spring 1998—issue on Realistic Fiction (scholaar.lib.vt.edu/ejournals/ALAN/spring98) and the Bibliography for Teens from the Gay, Lesbian, Bisexual, and Transgendered Round Table of the American Library Association (www.ala.org/Content/NavigationMenu/Our_Association/Round_Tables/GLBTRT/Publicat) both have selecting information, while *The Chocolate War* (www.randomhouse.com/teachers/catalog/display.pperl?isbn=0394828054&view=rg) has information for teaching the novel. Visit this book's Companion Website to link directly to these and many other sites.

Rasinski and Padak (1990) noted that:

> . . . there are few stimuli with greater potential to move people to action than literature. Because it tells the stories of human events and the human condition and not simply the facts, literature does more than change minds; it changes people's hearts. (p. 580)

In light of the impact that literature can have, contemporary realistic fiction is often used for **bibliotherapy,** which, in its broadest sense, is defined as the "use of books to help people solve problems" (Aiex, 1993, p. 1). When bibliotherapy is used with individual students:

1. The reader identifies with a character in the book **(Identification).**

2. The character is faced with and is able to resolve a difficult situation or problem **(Catharsis).**

3. A reader reflects on the events in the story, relates them to his/her life, and internalizes them to develop personal coping strategies or problem-solving skills **(Insight)** (Afolayan, 1992; Halsted, 1994).

However, bibliotherapy is more than just locating a book that discusses a problem or issue, giving the book to an adolescent, and letting him or her read it to find the answers to personal or societal problems. When bibliotherapy is used to help a specific young person cope with a personal problem, it is most effective if it is used as a group or individual therapeutic treatment with clearly defined roles for student(s), teacher(s), and counselor(s) (Wolpow & Askov, 2001). Furthermore, Linda Goettina (1999), a psychoanalyst working with both adults and young people, cautions that it is important for the individuals to have the "freedom and opportunity" (p. 13) to select the book that they find helpful to meet their emotional needs rather than have an adult select the book. Sometimes books are able to "provide escape when denial is the only means of coping," to provide an "opportunity for expression of the unthinkable and undoable desires," or "to test the boundaries between what one is and what one hopes to be" (p. 14).

While some educational professionals regard bibliotherapy as a tool to be used only by skilled counselors working with individuals or with groups of students who share a similar problem, others see it as one way to help a wide range of students learn problem-solving skills. Although Forgan (2002) used bibliotherapy with students who had behavioral or learning disabilities to help them learn problem-solving strategies, he stressed that all students can benefit when they explore strategies in books as ways to solve typical personal and social problems. It can also be used to provide role models for students such as a gifted girl who feels pressures to conform academically to a lower group standard or an African American boy who is ridiculed by his peers because he applies himself academically rather than in athletics (Ford, Tyson, Howard, & Harris, 2000). Whether used for small-group or whole-class problem solving, developmental bibliotherapy (Doll & Doll, 1997) allows young adults to focus on their developmental needs. It is important for teachers and library media specialists to select the realistic fiction novel(s) carefully and to introduce the novel(s) so that adolescents can begin to make connections between their own experiences and those of the characters in the novel(s). Connecting Adolescents and Their Literature 4-4 outlines a process that can be used with young adults. Then, Suggestions for Collaborative Efforts 4-2 links realistic fiction to the social studies classroom.

Issues Facing Realistic Fiction

In discussing the topics and issues that are really important to young adults, contemporary realistic fiction brings a sense of freedom and often includes subjects that were heretofore taboo. Beginning with the 1970s' publication of books such as *Deenie* (Blume, 1973), which mentions masturbation, this emergence of new topics did not go unnoticed by censors who sought to remove realism from the shelves. While Chapter 12 looks at censorship more comprehensively, in this section we look briefly at three selected issues facing realistic fiction: violence and profanity, stereotyping, and the frequent challenges to intellectual freedom.

Issue: The Extent of Violence. How much violence and profanity can be used in a young adult novel? How much makes the intended point and how much do authors include just for sensationalism? In Robert Cormier's classic *We All Fall Down* (1991), the violence occurs in a small town and includes trashing a house, attacking a 14-year-old girl, and seeking revenge. Did Cormier need the violence to make his point? While some censors and critics might suggest otherwise, Cormier was doing more than simply showing acts of violence. Rather than sensationalizing, he was showing the nature of violence; showing how violence affects people, both physically and psychologically; and making the point that suitable alternatives to violence need to be considered. Still, questions exist. As you read contemporary realistic fiction, you need to consider the following: How much violence or profanity can readers and censors tolerate? How much is needed to make a point? What is the effect of violence in realistic fiction on

CONNECTING | *ADOLESCENTS AND THEIR LITERATURE 4–4*

To use bibliotherapy as a developmental strategy for problem solving, educators can use or modify the following approach depending on the level of the students involved and their experience in discussing literature.

Prereading:
1. Teacher(s) and library media specialist determine the structure of the reading. Will everyone in the class read the same book or will small groups read different books?
2. Teacher(s) and library media specialist carefully select the novel(s).
3. Teacher(s) and/or library media specialist introduce or booktalk the novel(s) and relate them to current or developmental issues while remaining sensitive to individuals within the group.

During Reading:
1. Depending on the group, teacher(s) and/or library media specialist may provide students with questions to guide their reading.
2. Depending on the group, students may read all or portions of the novel(s) before any discussion.
3. Students are encouraged to record their thoughts in their journals as they read and to write questions that they may have for the discussion.

Follow-Up Discussion:
1. Conduct a discussion by using a variety of questions, moving from simple recall of facts and comprehension to more complex analytical and evaluative questions.
2. Encourage students to ask the questions that they wrote as they read the novel(s).
3. Ask students to move beyond the novel(s), explain the problem-solving strategies they found in the book, and explain how these strategies could or could not be applied in real-life situations.

Forgan (2002) suggests using an I Solve strategy as part of the discussion with younger readers by having students identify the problem, the solutions to the problem (both those found in the book and other alternatives), and the obstacles to the solutions. Then, after examining all solutions, select one. For simple problems it may be possible to test the solution and evaluate the outcome.

4-2   SUGGESTIONS FOR COLLABORATIVE EFFORTS

English teachers, library media specialists, and social studies teachers can work together to use contemporary realistic fiction. Many issues that are found in realistic books—such as homeless individuals, substance abuse, diversity in the community and nation, and individual and community responsibilities—are also studied in social studies classes. Library media specialists can booktalk various titles, social studies teachers can use the books for discussion, and English teachers can use the books as required or supplemental reading or for book reports.

young adults, even those who see violence daily in their communities? Does reading profanity legitimize or encourage its use? These questions and the overall issue of violence and profanity in realistic fiction will not be settled anytime soon, and may never be settled to the satisfaction of readers, censors, and people who believe that young adults should have considerable freedom in their reading.

Issue: *Gender, Sex Role, and Cultural Stereotyping.* Writers of realistic fiction have to use considerable caution to avoid stereotyping by gender, sex role, social group, and/or culture. Such a task may be difficult, especially when the protagonist fits into a particular category. Consider Walter Dean Myers' *Slam!* (1996) which, first, tells the story in 17-year-old Greg "Slam" Harris' engaging African American voice, and second, tells of Slam's obsession with basketball. While some might say that this book stereotypes African American boys as basketball players, it is a genuine story about a young man who is trying to cope with the illness of his grandmother, the prejudice at school, and the possible loss of his best friend to drugs. The question must always be: how far can an author take the characters before they are victims of stereotyping? A fine line exists between portraying what a character might have done in a particular situation and stereotyping that character according to some preconceived notion of what a member of a particular group might have done. Like the question of violence or profanity, the issue of stereotyping must be considered in realistic fiction.

Issue: *Likelihood of Censorship.* What do Shakespeare, Harper Lee, Robert Cormier, and Judy Blume have in common? They all have been the target of censorship, with someone or some group trying to tell adolescents that they cannot read a particular book or have it in a school library or English curriculum. As A. C. LeMieux (1998) stated:

> . . . the banning of controversial young adult problem novels serves to reinforce a most immoral precept: turn your eyes away from any problem too disturbing, too culturally unacceptable for comfort, or potentially subversive in the issues and questions raised. [The result will be] a generation with a shrinking or atrophied ability to discern, to evaluate, perhaps even to question. (p. 5)

Judging from the number of articles written about censorship (e.g., Agee, 1999; Curry, 2001; Donelson, 1997; Weiss, 2002), intellectual freedom continues to be an issue. Increased violence, gang activity and the accompanying street language, and references to sexual issues, especially sexual orientations in realistic fiction novels, will likely motivate censors to continue and perhaps escalate their attacks. Realistic novels are often challenged because of their bleakness and lack of positive role models. What many adults seem to want is a book that will act as a guidebook for life or a manual for living. In contrast, what adolescents seem to want is a book that will help them explore who they are and who they want to be; a book that speaks to them on several levels, that asks them to evaluate their feelings, and that helps them as they mature. In Chapter 12, we will provide some ideas to help educators, library media specialists, and other professionals, especially those involved with realistic fiction, be prepared to counter the censors' attacks.

CONCLUDING THOUGHTS

Contemporary realistic fiction or the problem novel provides young adult readers with an excellent look at other people's lives—their problems and challenges as well as their families and relationships. Although realistic fiction, while not designated using those specific labels, has been around for decades in one form or another, the literature of today is much more graphic in terms of violence, sex, and language. Unfortunately, for many young people, explicit violence and sex are everyday occurrences. The literature only mirrors the world they see. Even though censors will continue to attack many of its themes and topics, the future of realistic fiction or the problem novel looks bright: There are excellent realistic fiction writers, topics abound, and many young adults enjoy the books. Visit this book's Companion Website at www.prenhall.com/bucher for additional information about realistic fiction including review questions, self-assessments, Internet sites, and young adult literature and readings.

Young Adult Books

This section includes young adult titles recommended or mentioned in this chapter. Check the Companion Website at www.prenhall.com/bucher to find additional suggestions of current young adult literature.

Anderson, L. H. (1999). *Speak*. New York: Farrar, Straus and Giroux. After she is raped at a party, Melinda does not tell anyone what happened. In fact, she does not speak at all.

Anderson, L. H. (2002). *Catalyst*. New York: Viking. Relating her life to chemistry, Kate finds that a catalyst is about to bring major changes.

Anonymous. (1971). *Go ask Alice*. Upper Saddle River, NJ: Prentice Hall. A 15-year-old drug user struggles to escape the pull of the drug world.

Avi. (1991). *Nothing but the truth*. New York: Orchard. In this story told through multiple voices, Phillip Malloy is suspended for humming along with the national anthem.

Bantle, L. F. (1995). *Diving for the moon*. New York: Macmillan. Bird finds that her best friend Josh, a hemophiliac, is HIV positive.

Bardi, A. (2001). *The book of Fred*. New York: Washington Square Press. Can teenaged Mary Fred Anderson adjust to the world when she leaves her fundamentalist community and is placed in foster care? Or will she change the people that she meets?

Bauer, J. (2000). *Hope was here*. New York: Putnam. Sixteen-year-old Hope and her aunt work as the waitress and cook in the Welcome Stairways diner when the owner finds he is dying of leukemia.

Bauer, M. D. (1994). *A question of trust*. New York: Scholastic. Brad and his younger brother devise a plan to get their mother to return home.

Bechard, M. E. (2002). *Hanging on to Max*. Brookfield, CT: Roaring Brook Press. Sam wants to keep his infant son even though Brittany wants to give the baby up for adoption.

Bell, W. (1999). *Zack*. New York: Simon & Schuster. Searching for his mother's roots, Zack, the son of a Jewish father and a black mother, drives to Mississippi to meet his grandfather.

Black, J. (2001). *Black book diary of a teenage stud: Girls, girls, girls*. New York: Avon. In this fictional diary, Jonah is a vulnerable, humorous, likable teenage boy, but girls are a real problem for him.

Block, F. L. (1989). *Weetzie bat*. New York: Harper & Row. You will either love or hate this story of a young girl and her very unusual friends in Los Angeles.

Block, F. L. (1995). *Baby be-bop*. New York: HarperCollins. Dirk has to come to terms with his own sexual identity.

Bloor, E. (1997). *Tangerine*. San Diego, CA: Harcourt Brace. Paul lives in the shadow of his brother Eric, a football hero. But, what is the hidden secret about his life that Paul is trying to remember?

Blume, J. (1973). *Deenie*. Scarsdale, NY: Bradbury. Deenie's modeling career may be over when she discovers that she has scoliosis.

Blume, J. (1981). *Tiger eyes*. Scarsdale, NY: Bradbury. After the murder of her father, Davey and her family try to begin a new life in Los Alamos, New Mexico. Another classic is *Forever* (1975).

Bowler, T. (2000). *River boy*. New York: Margaret K. McElderry Books. Can grandfather finish his final painting before he dies?

Brashares, A. (2001). *The sisterhood of the traveling pants*. New York: Delacorte. Were they just ordinary jeans from the thrift store or was there something about them that helped everyone who wore them?

Brinkerhoff, S. (2000). *Second choices*. Minneapolis, MN: Bethany House. In this conclusion to the Nikki Sheridan Series, Nikki relies on her faith to help her live with the difficult choices that she has made in her life.

Brooks, B. (1984). *The moves make the man*. New York: Harper & Row. Basketball provides a bridge between a black boy and a troubled white boy.

Brooks, B. (1999). *Vanishing*. New York: HarperCollins. Alice goes on a hunger strike to keep from leaving the hospital. Are there cases where death is really better than life?

Bruchac, J. (1998). *The heart of a chief*. New York: Dial. The story of Chris, a Penacook Indian, looks at some major issues in contemporary American Indian culture: gambling, alcoholism, and the racist use of American Indian names in sports.

Burgess, M. (2004). *Doing it.* New York: Henry Holt. Three boys confront the joys and fears of maturing and are sometimes confused about their changing relationships.

Cadnum, M. (1995). *Taking it.* New York: Viking. Anna shoplifts as a way to vent her anger, but things seem to be getting out of control.

Carvell, M. (2002). *Who will tell my brother?* New York: Hyperion. Evan protests the use of Indian names for mascots in his high school.

Cheripko, J. (1996). *Imitate the tiger.* Honesdale, PA: Boyds Mills Press. From a detox clinic Chris Serbo reflects on his life of despair and self-delusion.

Childress, A. (1973). *A hero ain't nothin' but a sandwich.* New York: Coward-McCann. A 13-year-old Harlem boy is becoming a confirmed heroin addict. His story is told by his family and friends.

Cole, B. (1987). *The goats.* New York: Farrar, Straus and Giroux. As a joke at summer camp, misfits Howie and Laura are naked and stranded on a nearby island.

Cooney, C. (1996). *The voice on the radio.* New York: Delacorte. This is the third book in the *Face on the Milk Carton* trilogy.

Cormier, R. (1974). *The chocolate war.* New York: Knopf. Jerry Renault does not realize consequences of refusing to sell chocolate for his private school.

Cormier, R. (1991). *We all fall down.* New York: Delacorte. Why did four boys victimize Karen Jerome and her family and who is the Avenger?

Cormier, R. (2001). *The rag and bone shop.* New York: Delacorte. Since Alicia was Jason's friend, he could not have killed her, could he? Another novel by this author is *Tenderness* (1997).

Creech, S. (1998). *Bloomability.* New York: HarperCollins. Dinnie has a chance to spend a year in Switzerland.

Crutcher, C. (1987). *The Crazy Horse electric game.* New York: Greenwillow. After being disabled by an accident, a high school athlete regains his mental and physical health.

Crutcher, C. (1995). *Ironman.* New York: Greenwillow. After he blows up in class, Bo Brewster has to attend an anger management group to stay in school. However, school is not the only place that Bo has problems.

Crutcher, C. (2001). *Whale talk.* New York: HarperCollins. T. J. champions the underdog Chris and forms a swimming team in this dark novel of hatred, anger, and revenge. Earlier works by Crutcher include *Running Loose, Chinese Handcuffs, Staying Fat for Sarah Byrnes,* and *Stotan!*

Danziger, P., & Martin, A. (2000). *Snail mail no more.* New York: Scholastic. Elizabeth and Tara try to use e-mail to maintain their friendship.

Desai Hidier, T. (2002). *Born confused.* New York: Scholastic. Dimple's parents are from India and Dimple seems caught between their traditional beliefs and the culture of her American friends.

Deuker, C. (2000). *Night hoops.* Boston: Houghton Mifflin. Through basketball, Nick learns that life is full of choices and, like basketball, you can make adjustments to succeed.

DiCamillo, K. (2000). *Because of Winn-Dixie.* Cambridge, MA: Candlewick. When India Opal Buloni found a dog in the grocery store, she named him Winn-Dixie after the store. Her life then began to change.

Dorris, M. (1997). *The window.* New York: Hyperion. When her mother goes into alcohol rehabilitation, Rayona begins to find out about her heritage.

Draper, S. (1994). *Tears of a tiger.* New York: Atheneum. Andy's world has come crashing down around him. Is the only person he has left really his 5-year-old brother?

Draper, S. (2003). *The battle of Jericho.* New York: Atheneum. Jericho wants to join the Warriors of Distinction, an elite club. But he begins to feel uncomfortable with the initiation process.

Dressen, S. (1999). *Keeping the moon.* New York: Viking. Being a waitress might be the best thing for 15-year-old Colie, but living with her eccentric aunt is sometimes a challenge.

Ellis, D. (2002). *Parvana's journey.* Toronto: Groundwood Books. As the Taliban takes over Afghanistan, Parvana disguises herself as a boy and tries to find her mother. Another novel about Parvana is *The Breadwinner* (2001).

Farmer, N. (1996). *A girl named Disaster.* New York: Orchard Books. Fleeing Mozambique and an unwanted marriage, Nhamo struggles to reach Zimbabwe.

Ferreira, A. (2002). *Zulu dog.* New York: Farrar, Straus and Giroux. In postapartheid South Africa, a young Zulu boy seeks to become the friend of a white girl.

Ferris, J. (1996). *All that glitters.* New York: Farrar, Straus and Giroux. Brian is faced with leaving Chicago and spending 6 weeks in the Florida Keys with his father, Leo, after his mother remarries.

Flake, S. G. (2001). *Money hungry.* New York: Hyperion. Money is important to 13-year-old Raspberry, but her schemes to raise some do not always work out as she planned. Another book by Flake is *The Skin I'm In* (1998).

Fleischman, P. (1997). *Seedfolks.* New York: HarperCollins. Each person tells his or her story as they rehabilitate an abandoned downtown lot and turn it into a garden.

Fleischman, P. (2001). *Seek.* New York: Simon & Schuster. When Rob Radkovitz is assigned to write his autobiography, he looks back at the voices in his life, especially that of his long-absent father.

Fox, P. (1995). *The eagle kite.* New York: Orchard Books. Liam's father has AIDS and Liam has a secret that he does not want to share with his family.

Fredericks, M. (2003). *The true meaning of cleavage.* New York: Atheneum. Can two girls' friendship survive when one of them becomes obsessed with an older boy?

Froese, D. (2002). *Out of the fire.* Toronto: Sumach Press. When Pete tries to light a bonfire with gasoline both he and Dayle are burned. As she recovers, Dayle thinks about revenge.

Gantos, J. (1998). *Joey Pigza swallowed the key.* New York: Farrar, Straus and Giroux. A follow-up novel is *Joey Pigza Loses Control*. Joey tries so hard to be good. But when his meds do not work, Joey has problems following directions and paying attention in class. In fact, Joey can get into real trouble if he is not careful.

Garden, N. (1982). *Annie on my mind.* New York: Farrar, Straus and Giroux. Liza met Annie at the Metropolitan Museum of Art. Now they must try to hide their love from people who would not understand. Garden has also written *Good Moon Rising* (1996), *Holly's Secret* (2000), and *The Year They Burned the Books* (1999).

Giff, P. R. (2002). *Pictures of Hollis Woods.* New York: Wendy Lamb Books. Although Hollis Woods is an orphan, she may have found a home with an elderly artist who needs her. But what happened at the last foster home she was in?

Gilbert, B. S. (1996). *Stone water.* Arden, NC: Front Street. When his grandfather is placed in the skilled personal care wing of the nursing home, Grant has a difficult choice to make.

Gilmore, R. (2001). *A group of one*. New York: Henry Holt. When Tara Mehtas' grandmother arrives from India, Tara must begin to deal with her own feelings about her cultural heritage.

Glenn, M. (2000). *Split image*. New York: HarperCollins. Laura Li tries desperately to determine who she is. For some of her fellow students, she's too smart, too pretty, and too perfect. But for Laura, nothing can illuminate the gray of her days.

Going, K. L. (2003). *Fat kid rules the world*. New York: Putnam's. After Curt saves overweight Troy Billings from committing suicide when he jumps off a New York City subway platform, Troy begins to confront the problems in his life.

Grimes, N. (2001). *Bronx masquerade*. New York: Dial. A group of high school students express their fears, concerns, joys, and values as they read the poems that they have written.

Guy, R. (1973). *The friends*. New York: Holt, Rinehart and Winston. This book shows it's easier to blame your mother's death or your father's behavior than your own actions when you lose your best friend.

Haddix, M. P. (1996). *Don't you dare read this, Mrs. Dunphrey*. New York: Simon & Schuster. Tish's journal becomes an outlet after her abusive father returns home.

Haddix, M. P. (1997). *Leaving fishers*. New York: Simon & Schuster. Going to a new high school, Dorry is lonely until she is befriended by the members of a religious cult.

Hall, L. F. (1997). *Perk! The story of a teenager with bulimia*. Carlsbad, CA: Gurze. It takes a near disaster before anyone recognizes the serious problem that is taking over Perk's life.

Hautman, P. (2003). *Sweetblood*. New York: Simon & Schuster. Linking her disease to vampires, Lucy Szabo, a diabetic teen, frequents an Internet chat room for so-called vampires and becomes involved with the mysterious Draco.

Hewitt, L. (1996). *Soulfire*. New York: Dutton. What will happen when Ezekiel tries to end the problem of gang violence in his Denver neighborhood?

Hinton, S. E. (1967). *The outsiders*. New York: Viking. Ponyboy feels the world is made up of two kinds of people, those with money (the socs) and those like him who live on the outside (the greasers). He has always been willing to fight the socs until the night his friend Johnny kills a soc.

Hobbs, V. (2000). *Charlie's run*. New York: Farrar, Straus and Giroux. When Charlie learns that his parents are separating, he runs away. But it takes more than $43.75 and his Boy Scout skills to survive on the road.

Holland, I. (1991). *The search*. New York: Ballantine. Although Claudia gave her baby up for adoption, she tries to find out what happened to him.

Hurwin, D. W. (1995). *A time for dancing*. Boston: Little Brown. Life changes when 17-year-old Juliana finds that she has cancer.

Ingold, J. (1996). *The window*. San Diego: Harcourt Brace. Blind since the automobile accident that killed her mother, Mary is sent to live with relatives in Texas.

Irwin, H. (1985). *Abby my love*. New York: Atheneum. Chip cannot understand why Abby will not let him get close to her. Then he learns the horrible truth.

Johnson, A. (2003). *The first part last*. New York: Simon & Schuster. Sixteen-year-old Bobby is trying to raise his infant daughter, but sometimes the pressure gets too much to bear.

Johnson, K. J. (2003). *Target*. Brookfield, CT: Roaring Brook Press. Grady is hiding the secret that he was raped by two men.

Juby, S. (2003). *Alice, I think*. New York: Harper Tempest. Home schooled since first grade, Alice is now attending a public high school. But, with her unusual background can she fit into the mainstream teen culture in a small town?

Kantor, M. (2004). *Confessions of a not it girl*. New York: Hyperion. Jan doesn't have what it takes to be an IT girl, but maybe that's okay after all.

Karas, P. (1996). *Cry baby*. New York: Avon. With three successful older sisters, a pregnant 47-year-old mother, a friend with an eating disorder, and a crush on her best friend's boyfriend, Sam has just a few problems in her life.

Kerr, M. E. (1986). *Night kites*. New York: Harper & Row. Life can sure get complicated when your best friend's girl makes a play for you and you find out that your brother is dying of AIDS.

Kerr, M. E. (1994). *Deliver us from Evie*. New York: HarperCollins. Things become difficult in rural Missouri for 16-year-old Parr Burrman and his family when his lesbian older sister begins a relationship with the daughter of the town's banker.

Koertge, R. (2002). *Stoner and Spaz*. Cambridge, MA: Candlewick Press. It takes drugged-out Colleen to show Ben that his cerebral palsy does not have to keep him from living.

Konigsburg, E. L. (2000). *Silent to the bone*. New York: Atheneum. Branwell Zamborska is accused by the English au pair of dropping and shaking his baby sister. Now his sister is in a coma and Branwell has lost the ability to talk.

Korman, G. (2002). *Son of the mob*. New York: Hyperion. In this humorous tale, Vince, the son of a Mafia boss, falls in love with Kendra, the daughter of the FBI agent who is investigating his "family."

Koss, A. G. (2000). *The girls*. New York: Dial. Although she was once part of the group, Maya now finds herself on the outside.

Lawrence, I. (2002). *The lightkeeper's daughter*. New York: Random House. Only the McCrae family lives on Lizzie Island, but it can be a refuge from the events that threaten to tear the family apart. However, it also may be a prison that forces them to live together in captivity.

Levitin, S. (1998). *The singing mountain*. New York: Simon & Schuster. On a trip to Israel, a California teen decides to stay and join an Orthodox yeshiva, but his family is sure he has been brainwashed.

Lowry, L. (1977). *A summer to die*. Boston: Houghton Mifflin. Molly, who was always pretty and popular, is now dying.

Lynch, C. (1995). *Slot machine*. New York: HarperCollins. Will overweight 13-year-old Elvin Bishop ever be able to find the sport that is right for him?

Lynch, C. (2001). *Freewill*. New York: HarperCollins. Is there really a relationship between Will, the woodcarvings, and the suicides that begin to happen in town? Lynch has also written the Blue Eyed Son series that includes *Blood Relations* (1996), *Dog Eat Dog* (1996), and *Mick* (1996).

Lynch, C. (2002). *Who the man*. New York: HarperCollins. Just who is Earl Pryor? Is he the giant freak that his classmates see, a beloved son as his parents claim, or someone else?

Mack, T. (2000). *Drawing lessons*. New York: Scholastic. What is the relationship between Rory's father and the female art model?

Mackler, C. (2000). *Love and other four-letter words*. New York: Delacorte. When her parents agree to a trial separation, Samantha "Sammie" Davis learns about several four-letter words including *hate, gain,* and *grow.*

Martinez, V. (1996). *Parrot in the oven: Mi vida.* New York: HarperCollins. We see life in the projects of a California city through the eyes of a Mexican American teenager.

Mazer, N. F. (1993). *Out of control.* New York: Morrow. Valerie Micho is assaulted by three respected teenage boys.

Mazer, N. F. (1997). *When she was good.* New York: Scholastic. Em's life is complicated by her abusive, emotionally disturbed sister.

McDaniel, L. (1996). *Angels watching over me.* New York: Bantam. While Leah is in the hospital, she meets Rebekah, an Amish girl with strong religious beliefs.

McDaniel, L. (2000). *Angel of hope.* New York: Random House. When Heather (the central character in *Angel of Mercy*) (1999) becomes ill with hepatitis, her sister Amber decides to return to Africa in Heather's place.

McDonald, J. (2001). *Spellbound.* New York: Farrar, Straus and Giroux. When 16-year-old Raven becomes a single mother, she drops out of school and her dreams of college evaporate. Another excellent title by this author is *Swallowing Stones.*

McKean, T. (1997). *My evil twin.* New York: Avon. When Jellimiah tries to get his first name taken out of his school record before it is sent to a new school, he winds up with two identities instead of one.

McLaren, C. (1999). *Dance for the land.* New York: Atheneum. When her father moves the family to his home in Hawaii, Kate is ostracized because she is half-white and longs to return to California.

Miller, M. B. (2002). *Aimee.* New York: Dutton. After being acquitted of helping her best friend Aimee commit suicide, Zoe begins a journal to help her understand her life and her unhappiness.

Mills, C. (1995). *Dinah forever.* New York: Farrar, Straus and Giroux. Dinah Seabrook has a lot on her mind: her elderly friend Mrs. Briscoe, school, and Nick Tribble.

Mochizuki, K. (2002). *Beacon hill boys.* New York: Scholastic. As a Japanese American, Dan searches for his cultural identity.

Moore, M. (1995). *Under the mermaid angel.* New York: Delacorte. Jesse grieves the death of her brother while Roxanne feels the loss of the child she gave up at birth.

Mori, K. (1993). *Shizuko's daughter.* New York: Henry Holt. Shizuko commits suicide and her husband marries his mistress. Now Shizuko's daughter Yuki must try to make sense of her life.

Myers, W. D. (1992). *Somewhere in the darkness.* New York: Scholastic. Jimmy Little's life in New York with Mama Jean changes dramatically when Crab, his father, returns from jail and takes Jimmy away to Chicago and Arkansas.

Myers, W. D. (1996). *Slam!* New York: Scholastic. Greg Harris faces more challenges from his Harlem neighborhood than he ever did on the basketball court. Other books by this popular author include *Hoops* and *Somewhere in the Darkness.*

Myers, W. D. (1999). *Monster.* New York: HarperCollins. Sixteen-year-old Steve Harmon is being called a monster, as he's on trial for murder.

Na, A. (2001). *Step from heaven.* Asheville, NC: Front Street. Korean immigrant Young Ju must adjust to her new life in America and the unraveling of her family as changes begin to drive her father toward violence.

Naidoo, B. (2001). *The other side of truth.* New York: HarperCollins. Because their father is a muckraking journalist, two Nigerian children must flee to England. But even there, they still face problems.

Naughton, J. (1989). *My brother stealing second.* New York: Harper & Row. Bobby's brother might have been a star athlete, but when he was drunk, he killed himself and a couple celebrating their wedding anniversary.

Naylor, P. R. (1997). *Outrageously Alice*. New York: Atheneum. In this entry in the popular series of Alice books, Alice is suffering an identity crisis. Other recent books in the popular series include *Alice on the Outside* (1999), *The Grooming of Alice* (2000), *Alice Alone* (2001), and *Simply Alice* (2002).

Naylor, P. R. (1999). *Walker's crossing*. New York: Atheneum. When his older brother Gil joins a local militia group, Ryan Walker must balance his love for his brother against his distaste of violence and bigotry.

Nelson, B. (2003). *The new rules of high school*. New York: Viking. One day Max has it all— good grades, editor of the school newspaper, and debate team captain with a beautiful girlfriend. The next day, his whole life starts to change dramatically.

Nelson, T. (1994). *Earthshine*. New York: Orchard. Slim watches her father die of AIDS.

Nye, N. S. (1997). *Habibi*. New York: Simon & Schuster. When her Palestinian-American family moves from St. Louis to Jerusalem, Liyana finds herself in the middle of the conflict between Arabs and Israelis.

Oates, J. C. (2002). *Big mouth and ugly girl*. New York: HarperCollins. Everyone believes Matt really threatened to blow up the school and Ursula lost the basketball game on purpose. Can two misunderstood high school juniors help each other learn who they really are?

O'Connell, R. (2000). *Myrtle of Willendorf*. Asheville, NC: Front Street. Myrtle, soon to be a college sophomore, looks back at her years in high school and tries to find out who she really is underneath the layers of fat.

Olson, G. (1998). *Joyride*. Honesdale, PA: Boyds Mills. To repay the damage from his joyride, affluent Jeff works with Hispanic laborers on a strawberry farm.

Oneal, Z. (1980). *The language of goldfish*. New York: Viking. Something is happening to 13-year-old Carrie as she experiences dizzy spells and her mind begins to wander. But no one seems to realize how serious the problem is.

Osa, N. (2003). *Cuba 15*. New York: Delacorte. Violet Paz is preparing for her quincera-ero, a celebration of womanhood, but she is having problems relating her Cuban heritage with her life in suburban Chicago.

Park, B. (2000). *Graduation of Jake Moon*. New York: Atheneum. Granddad has Alzheimer's disease and is becoming increasingly irresponsible.

Paulsen, G. (2003). *The glass café*. New York: Wendy Lamb Books. The trouble began when 12-year-old Tony drew pictures of the dancers at the Kitty Kat Club where his mother works.

Peck, R. (1995). *The last safe place on earth*. New York: Delacorte. Walden Woods looks like the perfect suburban community to raise a family, safe from the violence of the city. But Todd and his family soon find out that things are not what they seem.

Placide, J. (2002). *Fresh girl*. New York: Wendy Lamb Books. Mardi's uncle is a political activist in Haiti, and Mardi blames him for all of her problems, even after she escapes to the United States.

Porter, C. R. (1999). *Imani all mine*. Boston: Houghton Mifflin. Fifteen-year-old Tasha loves her daughter Imani, even though Imani was conceived as the result of a rape.

Powell, R. (2002). *Three clams and an oyster*. New York: Farrar, Straus and Giroux. When Cade, the "Oyster," misses the first four-man flag football game, Rick, Dwight, and Flint have a weekend to find a replacement or be dropped from the league.

Quinlan, P. (1994). *Tiger flowers*. New York: Dial. When his uncle Michael dies of AIDS, Joel uses his thoughts and dreams to keep Michael's memory alive.

Rennison, L. (2000). *Angus, thongs, and full-frontal snogging*. New York: HarperCollins. Fourteen-year-old Georgia Nicholson shares her crazy life in this humorous diary. Follow-ups include *On the Bright Side, I'm Now the Girlfriend of a Sex God* (2001), *Knocked Out by my Nunga-Nungas* (2002), and *Dancing in my Nuddy-Pants* (2003).

Reynolds, M. (1997). *The starlite drive-in*. New York: Morrow. Is there more to life than what Callie can see at the drive-in?

Roberts, L. P. (1999). *Get a life: Clearwater crossing #1*. New York: Random House. Eight teenagers are working to raise money for Kurt, a student who has cancer. But a tragedy changes their plans.

Rodowsky, C. (1996). *Remembering Mog*. New York: Farrar, Straus and Giroux. Annie struggles to deal with the murder of her sister.

Rottman, S. L. (2002). *Stetson*. New York: Viking. If being abandoned by his mother and living with his alcoholic father isn't enough of a challenge, 17-year-old Stetson suddenly finds he has a 14-year-old sister and she is moving in with him.

Sachar, L. (1998). *Holes*. New York: Farrar, Straus and Giroux. Stanley Yelnats is sent to a correctional camp in the Texas desert where he finds a friend, a treasure, and himself.

Shands, L. I. (2001). *Blind fury*. Grand Rapids, MI: Fleming H. Revell. Fifteen-year-old Wakara Sheridan watches as her mother's death changes everyone in the family in a different way.

Shreve, S. (2000). *Goodbye, Amanda the good*. New York: Knopf. Purple hair, dark clothes, and a new boyfriend are all signs that Amanda is changing.

Simeon, J., & Nieuwenhuizen, J. (2002). *What about Anna?* New York: Walker. Anna is living in Belgium when she learns that her brother may not have been killed by a landmine in Bosnia.

Sones, S. (2001). *What my mother doesn't know*. New York: Simon & Schuster. In a series of poems, Sophie must decide between her own feelings and those of her friends.

Soto, G. (1997). *Buried onions*. San Diego, CA: Harcourt Brace. Eddie, a Mexican American and a college drop-out, tries to pull his life back together, but he's living in the wrong neighborhood to do that. Soto also wrote *Taking Sides* (1991).

Staples, S. F. (1989). *Shabanu: Daughter of the wind*. New York: Knopf. Only 11 years old, Shabanu, a Pakistani girl, wonders if she will be able to obey her father and marry an older man.

Strasser, T. (1995). *How I changed my life*. New York: Simon & Schuster. There is a modern prom queen/football hunk/wallflower triangle when overweight Bo decides to change her image.

Strasser, T. (1996). *Girl gives birth to own prom date*. New York: Simon & Schuster. When the boy she likes does not invite her to the senior prom, Nicole decides to mold her neighbor into the ideal date.

Strasser, T. (2000). *Give a boy a gun*. New York: Simon & Schuster. Strasser provides a multi-viewpoint look at a shooting at a high school dance.

Stuckey, K. (2001). *Conflict in California*. Grand Rapids, MI: Baker Books. The members of the Thunderfoot Ballet Company, the support crew for a racing team, are attending the drag races where they use their Christian faith to help others.

Thesman, J. (1991). *Rain catchers*. Boston: Houghton Mifflin. Each of the women in Grayling's family has her own story to tell, but Grayling must learn about her past before she can tell her own tale.

Thomas, R. (1996). *Rats saw God*. New York: Simon & Schuster. Steve was an outstanding student. Now he's on drugs. What happened?

Tolan, S. S. (2002). *Surviving the Applewhites*. New York: HarperCollins. Add Jake, the juvenile delinquent, to the unconventional Applewhite family's Creative Academy and you get a crazy, humorous story.

Tomey, I. (1996). *The queen of dreamland*. New York: Atheneum. Julie's life is changed forever when she discovers her birth mother Loretta, the palm reader, is the direct opposite to her adopted mother.

Toten, T. (2001). *The game*. Calgary: Red Deer Press. Will Dani ever be able to confront the truth about her own family and the reasons that she is now in a New York clinic for detox?

Trueman, T. (2001). *Stuck in neutral*. New York: HarperCollins. Would Shawn's father really try to kill him just because Shawn has cerebral palsy?

Trueman, T. (2003). *Inside out*. New York: HarperCollins. Can Zach's schizophrenia help him survive in a hostage crisis?

Vail, R. (1998). *If only you knew*. New York: Scholastic. This is the first in a series of books about a group of seventh-grade girls. Other books are *Please, Please, Please* (1998) and *Not That I Care* (1998).

Velasquez, G. (1998). *Rina's family secret*. Houston, TX: Arte Publico. Rina cannot understand how her mother can continue to

put up with the beatings from her alcoholic husband. Check out other books in the Roosevelt High School series.

Voigt, C. (1986). *Izzy, willy-nilly*. New York: Atheneum. Popular Izzy finds that her life changes dramatically after losing her leg in an accident.

Voigt, C. (1994). *When she hollers*. New York: Scholastic. Trish has to do something to stop her abusive father.

Voigt, C. (1996). *Bad girls*. New York: Scholastic. Margalo and Mikey help each other in and out of trouble. A follow-up is *Bad, Badder, Baddest* (1997).

Wallace, R. (1996). *Wrestling Sturbridge*. New York: Knopf. Wrestling provides a focus for Ben's life, but it seems that things are always stacked against him.

Walter, V., & Roeckelein, K. (1998). *Making up megaboy*. New York: DK Publishing. Robbie Jones shot the old man in the liquor store, but he will not tell anyone why he did it.

Watts, J. (2001). *Finding H. F.* Los Angeles, CA: Alyson. Heavenly Faith Simms left her home in Kentucky to find her mother and wound up finding herself.

Whelan, G. (2000). *Homeless bird*. New York: HarperCollins. Koly is 13 years old, a widow, and alone in modern India.

White, R. (1992). *Weeping willow*. New York: Farrar, Straus and Giroux. Tiny finally tells her mother about her sexually abusive stepfather.

Willey, M. (1996). *Facing the music*. New York: Delacorte. After her mother's death, Lisa turns to music to help her understand her feelings.

Williams-Garcia, R. (1995). *Like sisters on the homefront*. New York: Lodestar. When

14-year-old Gayle gets pregnant for the second time, she is sent to live with her relatives in the country.

Wittlinger, E. (1999). *Hard love.* New York: Simon & Schuster. In this 'zine format novel, John/Gio struggles to find out who he really is in the aftermath of his parents' divorce.

Wolff, V. E. (1993). *Make lemonade.* New York: Holt. In a novel in free verse, Verna LaVaughn tries to help a teenage mother with two small children without letting go of her own dreams.

Wolff, V. E. (2001). *True believer.* New York: Atheneum. In another novel in poetic form, LaVaughn finds her life is changing as her friends join a Christian group, her mother starts dating, and she falls in love. But she learns that things are not always what they seem on the surface.

Woodbury, M. (1998). *Brad's universe.* Victoria, BC, Canada: Orca. Did Brad's father really spend a year in a mental hospital, or was there some other reason that he had to leave the family?

Woodson, J. (1995). *From the notebooks of Melanin Sun.* New York: Blue Sky Press. What do you do when you find out that your mother is in love with another woman?

Woodson, J. (2000). *Miracle's boys.* New York: Putnam. After Mamma dies, all Lafayette has left are his brothers. But, while Ty'ree works to support the family, Charlie seems changed by those years in Rahway Correctional. Will anything bring the brothers back together again? Three other books by Woodson are *I Hadn't Meant to Tell You This* (1994), *Hush* (2002), and *Locomotion* (2003).

Wyss, T. H. (1988). *Here at the Scenic-Vu Motel.* New York: Harper & Row. Living too far from town to commute to school, Jake and six other teenagers spend each week at the Scenic-Vu Motel.

Yee, P. (1997). *Breakaway.* Toronto: Groundwood Books. Family traditions and adolescent dreams clash and present problems for Kwok Wong.

Yumoto, K. (1996). *The friends.* New York: Farrar, Straus and Giroux. The friendship between three boys and their elderly neighbor changes all of them.

Zindel, P. (1968). *The Pigman.* New York: Harper & Row. Sophomores John and Lorraine meet Mr. Pignati, the Pigman, but then something destroys the happiness that they found. A follow-up is *The Pigman's Legacy* (1981).

Suggested Readings

Boyd, F. B. (2003). Experiencing things not seen: Educative events centered on a study of *Shabanu. Journal of Adolescent & Adult Literacy, 46*(6), 460–474.

Carrol, P. S. (2003). An interview with author, teacher, mom, coach (Whew!) S. L. Rottman. *The ALAN Review, 30* (3), 15–17.

Gillis, C. (2002). Multiple voices, multiple genres: Fiction for young adults. *English Journal, 93* (2), 52–59.

Liang, L. A. (2002). On the shelves of the local library: High-interest, easy reading trade books for struggling middle and high school readers. *Preventing School Failure, 46* (4), 183–188.

Prater, M. A. (2003). Learning disabilities in children's and adolescent literature: How are characters portrayed? *Learning Disability Quarterly, 26* (1), 47–62.

Tigner-Rasanen, M. (2001). Meeting a censorship challenge: *Scorpions and the Chocolate War. English Journal, 90* (3), 126–129.

Wasserman, E. (2003). The epistolary in young adult literature. *The ALAN Review, 30* (3), 48–51.

References

(Note: All young adult literature referenced in this chapter are included in the Young Adult Books list and are not repeated in this list.)

Afolayan, J. A. (1992). Documentary perspective of bibliotherapy in education. *Reading Horizons, 33,* 137–148.

Agee, J. M. (1999). "There it was, that one sex scene": English teachers on censorship. *English Journal, 89* (2), 61–69.

Aiex, N. K. (1993). *Bibliotherapy.* (Report NO. EDO-CS-93-05). Bloomington: Indiana University, Office of Educational Research and Improvement. (ERIC Document Reproduction Service No. ED357333)

Alcott, L. M. (1868). *Little women, or, Meg, Jo, Beth, and Amy.* Boston: Roberts Bros.

Allen, J. (Ed.). (2002). *Using literature to help troubled teenagers cope with end-of-life issues.* Westport, CT: Greenwood Press.

Aronson, M. (2001). *Exploring the myths; The truth about teenagers and reading.* Lanham, MD: Scarecrow.

Beers, G. K., & Lesesne, T. S. (Eds.). (2001). *Books for you: An annotated booklist for senior high.* Urbana, IL: National Council of Teachers of English.

Bodart, J. R. (2002). *Radical reads: 101 YA novels on the edge.* Lanham, MD: Scarecrow Press.

Bowman, C. A. (Ed.). (2000). *Using literature to help troubled teenagers cope with health issues.* Westport, CT: Greenwood Press.

Carpan, C. A. (2004). *Rocked by romance: A guide to young adult romance genre fiction.* Westport, CT: Libraries Unlimited.

Carroll, P. (Ed.). (1999). *Using literature to help troubled teenagers cope with societal issues.* Westport, CT: Greenwood Press.

Curry, A. (2001). Where is Judy Blume? Controversial fiction for older children and young adults. *Journal of Youth Services in Libraries, 14*(3), 28–37.

Darby, M. A., & Pryne, M. (2002). *Hearing all the voices: Multicultural books for adolescents.* Lanham, MD: Scarecrow Press.

Dodge, M. (1865). *Hans Brinker,* or *The silver skates: A story of life in Holland.* New York: Scribner's.

Doll, B., & Doll, C. (1997). *Bibliotherapy with young people: Librarians and mental health professionals working together.* Englewood, CO: Libraries Unlimited.

Donelson, K. (1997). "Filth" and "Pure filth" in our schools—Censorship of classroom books in the last ten years. *English Journal, 86*(2), 21–25.

Dresang, E. T. (1999). *Radical change: Books for youth in a digital age.* New York: H. W. Wilson.

Ford, D. Y., Tyson, C. A., Howard, T. C., & Harris, J. J. (2000). Multicultural literature and gifted Black students: Promoting self-understanding, awareness, and pride. *Roper Review, 22*(4), 235–240.

Forgan, J. W. (2002). Using bibliotherapy to teach problem solving. *Intervention in School and Clinic, 38*(2), 75–82.

Goettina, L. (1999, Spring). When books help. *Riverbank Review,* Spring, 12–14.

Halsted, J. W. (1994). *Some of my best friends are books: Guiding gifted readers from pre-school to high school.* Dayton, OH: Ohio Psychology Press.

Head, A. (1967). *Mr. and Mrs. Bo Jo Jones.* New York: Putnam.

Jones, J. B. (2003). *Helping teens cope: A guide to teen issues using YA fiction and other resources.* Worthington, OH: Linworth Publishing.

Jones, P. (1994). THIN books, BIG problems: Realism and the reluctant teen reader. *The ALAN Review, 20*(2), 18–28.

Jordan, A. D. (1995). True-to-life: Realistic fiction. *Teaching and Learning Literature, 5*(1), 16–22.

LeMieux, A. C. (1998). The problem novel in a conservative age. *The ALAN Review, 25*(3), 4–6.

McDuffie, C. (2004). 2004 Medal for Distinguished Contribution to American Letters. Retrieved 11/19/2004 from www.nationalbook.org/dcal_2004_pr.html.

Myers, W. D. (1988). *Fallen angels.* New York. Scholastic.

Rasinski, T. V., & Padak, N. D. (1990). Multicultural learning through children's literature. *Language Arts, 67*(6), 576–580.

Robert Cormier Remembered—1/1/2001. *Publishers Weekly.* Retrieved 12/30/2002 from http://publishersweekly.reviewsnews.com/index/asp?layout:articlePrint&articleID=CA16892.

Twain, M. (1884). *Adventures of Huckleberry Finn (Tom Sawyer's comrade).* New York: Charles L. Webster.

Twain, M. (1876). *The adventures of Tom Sawyer.* Hartford, CT: American Publishing.

Tyson, C. A. (1999). "Shut my mouth wide open": Realistic fiction and social action. *Theory into Practice, 38*(3), 155–159.

Weiss, M. U. (2002). Rumbles! Bangs! Crashes! The roar of censorship. *The ALAN Review, 29*(3), 54–57.

Wolpow, R., & Askov, E. N. (2001). Widened frameworks and practice: From bibliotherapy to the literacy of testimony and witness. *Journal of Adolescent & Adult Literacy, 44*(7), 606–609.

Zindel, P. (2002). The 2002 Margaret A. Edwards Award Acceptance Speech. *Journal of Youth Services in Libraries, 15*(4), 30–34.

5

EXPLORING ADVENTURE, MYSTERY, AND HUMOR

Americans seem to be fascinated with mystery, adventure, and humor. According to the *Library Journal,* mystery books make up the highest percent of book expenditures by libraries for adult genre fiction (Hoffert, 1998). True-life adventure stories such as Sebastian Junger's *The Perfect Storm* (1998) and Jon Krakauer's *Into Thin Air* (1998) and *Into the Wild* (1996), as well as the humorous books by Bill Bryson, regularly top the best seller lists. While some adolescents read contemporary realistic fiction or speculative fiction, others follow the adult trend and turn to adventure and survival, mystery and suspense, or humorous novels to provide an escape from the problems of everyday life. While these books may explore values and social morality, they also examine the disruption and restoration of order in a person's life in an exciting or funny way. Young adults enjoy the usually fast-paced plots found in adventure stories, the challenges to find out "who-done-it" in mystery novels, and the laughs in humorous books. Some might suggest that these books provide a sense of escapism whereby adolescents can leave the day-to-day routine they often perceive as troubling or boring and vicariously feel the thrill and excitement of the unknown. Regardless of the reasons, educators and library media specialists can take advantage of this popularity.

1. Predecessors of adventure, mystery, and humor novels.
2. Types of adventure, mystery, and humor novels.
3. Reasons for using and teaching adventure, mystery, and humor novels.
4. Characteristics of adventure, mystery, and humor literature.
5. Suggestions for selecting and using adventure, mystery, and humor literature.
6. Recommended titles and authors of adventure, mystery, and humor for young adults.

THE GENRES: ADVENTURE, MYSTERY, AND HUMOR

Through vicariously experiencing adventure, using their sleuthing abilities to solve murders and other mysteries, outwitting a criminal in a suspense novel, and enjoying a laugh that results from a funny situation, young adults have demonstrated a liking for novels of adventure, mystery, and humor. In addition to applauding the fact that so many young people enjoy reading these books, teachers and library media specialists should also be glad that these books can be used to support the curriculum and to encourage reluctant readers. This chapter looks at various aspects of these types of books and offers suggestions for books that are appropriate for young adults.

Adventure

From *The Odyssey* and *Gilgamesh* to *Beowulf* and the Hindu epic of the Mahabharata, the ancient stories of wars and the challenges to survive, which began in the oral tradition, have progressed to today's adventure books. Whether looking to escape their everyday problems or sense of everyday boredom, becoming caught in the fast-moving plots, or simply enjoying a good story, many young adults enjoy reading about other peoples' adventurous events. Faced with fighting to survive and the possibility of death, the main characters, either the protagonist alone or a group of people, struggle against the people and/or elements that place them in dangerous situations. Writers such as Caroline Cooney, Mary Casanova, Will Hobbs, and Gary Paulsen—just to name a few—provide stories that attract the interest of many young adults.

A Brief Look at Adventure's Predecessors. With their roots in oral tradition stories and the quests of the knights in medieval tales, written adventure stories became popular in the 18th century with the publication of Daniel Defoe's *Robinson Crusoe* (1719), which featured the theme of survival on a desert island. In the 19th century, books such as James Fenimore Cooper's *Leather-Stocking Tales* (1850–1851), Robert Louis Stevenson's *Treasure Island* (1883), and Mark Twain's *The Adventures of Tom Sawyer* (1876) and *Adventures of Huckleberry Finn* (1884) continued the adventure genre (Rigby, 1999). By the end of the 19th century, adventure books or "boy's stories" (p. 12) dominated children's literature, with American stories set at home and British stories set in foreign countries or waters (Russell, 2001). In the 20th century, survival stories in which the hero or heroine adapted to, rather than conquered, the environment became popular with children's books such as Scott O'Dell's *Island of the Blue Dolphins* (1960) and Jean Craighead George's *My Side of the Mountain* (1959) and *Julie of the Wolves* (1972).

Types of Adventure Books. According to Rigby (1999), adventure stories have a basic theme of exile, physical challenge, and survival/return of the hero or the group. While he divides the adventure into two main categories, the human and the superhuman, our discussion will be only of realistic human adventures. (Superhuman adventures that appear in fantasy novels are discussed in Chapter 3, and those in graphic/comic book novels are discussed in Chapter 10.)

Russell (2001) points out that modern adventure and survival stories have taken on a new meaning. With "technology and impersonal bureaucracy threatening the individual's identity and . . . even the nature of society and civilization" (p. 215), adventure stories today are set not only in a wilderness but also in an urban environment. However, no matter what the setting, the protagonist(s) must locate food and shelter and provide "protection from threatening forces" (p. 215). In contemporary stories, rescue is no longer an overarching concern. Instead, the focus is on the individual achieving a "sense of identity and self-actualization" (p. 216).

As you have seen with other genres, it is difficult to divide young adult literature into discrete categories. Thus, the types of adventure and survival books overlap with some of the other genres that we discuss in this book. For example, we have chosen to discuss many excellent nonfiction adventure stories in Chapter 8, and many realistic stories are included in Chapter 4.

Person against nature adventures. Among the most popular types of adventure novels are those in which an individual or group is pitted against nature. These are often tales of survival in the wilderness; a good example is the series of novels by Gary Paulsen about Brian and his life in the woods of northern Canada, beginning with *Hatchet* (1988), as well as the stories by Mary Casanova (1995, 1997, 2002). In *Wild Man Island* (Hobbs, 2002), Andy washes ashore on a wild and remote Alaskan island with bears, wolves, and a mysterious bearded man; and in *Lucy the Giant* (Smith, 2002), 15-year-old Lucy runs away from her alcoholic father to work on a commercial fishing boat in Alaska where she must survive not only the seas but someone who wants to tell the truth about her age and identity. However, not all adventures are set in current times. In Karen Hesse's *Stowaway* (2000), a young boy keeps a diary of his adventures with Captain James Cook on board *The Endeavor* during its round-the-world trip from 1768–1771.

Person against person and nature adventures. Adventure stories become even more complex when a person-to-person conflict is added to the challenges supplied by nature. In *Downriver* (Hobbs, 1991) and *River Thunder* (Hobbs, 1997), Jessie and her friends must survive the Colorado River rapids and each other. Likewise, in the Everest series by Gordon Korman (2003), a group of teenagers must learn to work together to conquer the world's tallest mountain. Other wilderness adventure stories include Robb White's *Deathwatch* (1972), Jean Craighead George's *Julie's Wolf Pack* (1997), Harry Mazer's *The Island Keeper* (1981), Roland Smith's *Jaguar* (1997), and Curtis Parkinson's *Storm-Blast* (2003).

Disasters. Disasters often feature prominently in adventure stories as nature unleashes floods, famine, epidemics, blizzards, and wildfires, while accidents or conflicts produce plane crashes, shipwrecks, or massacres. For example, Nory tries to save her family when the blight attacks Ireland's potato crop in *Nory Ryan's Song* (Giff, 2000), and 14-year-old Emily fights to survive after the sinking of a ferry off Sumatra in *Overboard* (Fama, 2002). In *Walks Alone* (Burke, 1998), a young Apache girl and her family try to survive capture and imprisonment by the "White Eye" soldiers in 1880, and in Alexandria, Egypt, in 45 B.C., Damon has just begun a quest to find his father when his ship sinks and he is attacked by sharks in *The Wadjet Eye* (Rubalcaba, 2000). Caroline Cooney has written a number of novels with adventure/survival themes including *Flight Number 116 Is Down* (1992), in which a 747 crashes behind a rural estate and a group of teenagers must find the skills to help the survivors; and *Flash Fire* (1995), in which a group of teens have to outrun a wildfire that has suddenly spread to the canyon where they live.

Urban adventures. Not all stories of adventure and survival are set in the wilderness. In fact, some adventure and survival novels are set in the suburbs or in the city and may include a different type of conflict and survival. With a focus on the conflict of person against other person(s) or person against society, these novels are sometimes considered problem novels and may contain gangs and violence. Several of those novels were previously mentioned in Chapter 4 with the contemporary realistic fiction titles. In Francine Prose's *After* (2003), Tom and Becca try to survive the aftermath of a school shooting and find something just as deadly as the shooting itself. Four classic urban survival stories are Virginia Hamilton's *The Planet of Junior Brown* (1971), in which a group of homeless boys survive against the odds; Felice Holman's *Slake's Limbo* (1974), in which Aremis Slake tries to escape his problems by going underground in the New York subway; Walter Dean Myers' *Scorpions* (1988), in which Jamal must decide whether to join his brother's gang; and Ineke Holtwijk's *Asphalt Angels* (1999), in which Alex joins a group of street children in Rio de Janeiro.

Terrorists, assassins, and kidnappers. Other person-against-person conflicts are found in adventure and survival stories of terrorists, assassins, kidnappers, and threats of revenge. Toswiah and her family must enter the witness protection program in Jacqueline Woodson's *Hush* (2002), and Laura becomes involved with terrorists when a package carried by her brother explodes in Carolyn Cooney's *The Terrorist* (1997). Sometimes teens assume the role of eco-terrorist, such as Mullett Fingers in *Hoot* (Hiaasen, 2002). Finally, in *The Kidnappers* (Roberts, 1998), Joey loves to tell tall tales so, when he witnesses a kidnapping, no one believes him.

Reasons for using and teaching adventure books. Extreme sports may not appeal to you, but many young people relish the prospect of snowboarding Mt. Everest, kayaking 13 of the world's greatest rivers, climbing all 15 of California's 14,000-plus foot peaks in less than four-and-a-half days, or sailing solo in the 29,000 mile "Around Alone" yacht race around the world. Many adolescents, especially reluctant readers who do not usually pick up a book unless it is part of a school assignment, willingly read books about adventure and survival.

One way to encourage reluctant readers, especially boys, may be to recommend some of the excellent adventure and survival books that are currently available. At one time, this was barely possible. When Gary Paulsen, a leading author of adventure and survival fiction, was beginning to write for children and young adults, he asked why there were not more books written for boys. After being told that people do not write for boys because boys do not read, Paulsen noted the paradox in this reply. Thus, drawing on his own experiences in the wilderness and his passion about writing, Paulsen began to write adventure novels that, while they are read by both boys and girls, have a special attraction for many male reluctant readers. Connecting Adolescents and Their Literature 5-1 suggests another way to encourage reluctant readers by using adventure and survival books.

Characteristics of Adventure Novels. Characterized by exciting, fast-moving plots, adventure and survival novels are set in realistic places, although they may be remote or exotic. For the most part, the characters are believable and the protagonist is usually a strong individual, although those attributes may not be apparent until he/she is placed in a survival situation. However, the focus is always on the interaction between the protagonist and the forces pitted against him or her. Considerations for Selecting Young Adult Literature: *Adventure* outlines the characteristics of good adventure novels.

CONNECTING | *ADOLESCENTS AND THEIR LITERATURE 5–1*

To build good readers, you have to encourage young adults to read on a daily basis. One way to do that is to capitalize on the interests of teenagers and to use a variety of literary formats including magazines. Two periodicals that regularly contain articles on adventures and survival are

National Geographic Adventure

(www.nationalgeographic.com/adventure)

Outside

(www.outsideonline.com)

You can use articles from these magazines or their web sites to create an interest in a topic. Then provide suggestions of both fiction and nonfiction adventure and survival books that will expand the topic while appealing to a wide range of readers.

| **CONSIDERATIONS** | *For Selecting Young Adult Literature* | **ADVENTURE** |

When examining young adult adventure literature, ask yourself the following questions:

◉ Is there an exciting, clearly defined plot that develops naturally and logically from the actions and decisions of the characters—one that grabs readers' attention at the beginning of the book?

◉ Are the basic conflicts believable and credible (i.e., conflicts may result from people, nature, or events, but readers must believe that the conflict could have happened)?

◉ Can young adults understand and relate to the protagonist?

◉ Are the characters convincingly real, multidimensional (i.e., having good and bad traits like most people), and lifelike (personalities and mannerisms that readers can believe)?

◉ Is there a detailed setting, whether in snow-filled mountains or the streets of an inner city, that contributes to and reflects adventure?

Suggestions For Selecting and Using Adventure Novels. Historically, adventure stories were viewed as primarily appealing to boys, while girls read family stories. However, thanks to the growth of female protagonists in adventure and survival stories, this view has changed. Today, young adults, including many reluctant readers, enjoy reading adventure stories, many of which are written on a middle school/junior high school level. However, few readers, male or female, will struggle through an adventure book (or any other type of book) if they find it dull and not believable. By carefully selecting contemporary adventure books with fast-paced plots and interesting characters, you should be able to encourage reluctant young adult readers. Although no specific awards exist for this type of literature, many adventure and survival novels do win major book awards or honors and are included on some of the best books lists that are published each year, especially the lists for reluctant young adult readers. *More Rip-Roaring Reads for Reluctant Teen Readers* (Ammon & Sherman, 1999) includes adventure novels as well as mystery and humor stories. Some excellent booklists of adventure and survival stories are also available on the Internet (see Expanding Your Knowledge with the Internet 5-1). Connecting Adolescents and Their Literature 5-2 suggests another way you can help adolescents discover good adventure novels.

Mystery

People who read mysteries hate mysteries. What they like are solutions. A mystery novel is the only kind of book a reader can pick up knowing that, after some two hundred pages of turmoil, order will be restored at the end. Questions will be answered, problems will be solved, and the disruptive force in the world of the book will be routed out to allow that world to return to its own norm. (Paul, 1999, p. 121)

| EXPANDING | YOUR KNOWLEDGE WITH THE INTERNET 5-1 |

 You can find information on adventure stories and selected authors on the Internet, including booklists from

The Logan Utah Public Library
www.logan.lib.ut.us/booklist/ya/advnturb.htm (for boys)
www.logan.lib.ut.us/booklist/ya/advnturg.htm (for girls)
www.logan.lib.ut.us/booklist/ya/survive.htm

and links to adventure novelists such as Will Hobbs www.willhobbsauthor.com/
Visit this book's Companion Website at www.prenhall.com/bucher to link directly to these and many other sites.

A good mystery encourages reasoning and problem solving as well as questioning and examining evidence, fact, and motives. Like a problem novel, a good mystery also explores values and social morality. Behind the plot of each mystery is "good versus evil, order versus chaos, illusion versus reality, and the necessity of thought as a tool for survival" (DeAndrea, 1994, p. ix).

Mystery books for young adults reflect a wide array of topics such as murders, missing or disappearing people, missing items, lies and deceit, games ending in questionable deaths, perplexing or sinister letters and phone calls, and a host of other suspicious occurrences. While some mysteries just tell an interesting story, others make an effort to improve people's lives (such as promoting Civil Rights). In a mystery, the "real message . . . is that even in the worst of circumstances, a [person] . . . can make things right using courage, tenacity, and brainpower" (DeAndrea, 1994, p. ix). Although some mysteries are written as novels, others are short stories; some are written in narrative form, while others—such as Mel Glenn's *Who Killed Mr. Chippendale?* (1996)—are written in free verse. Taken as a whole, mysteries comprise 28.1% of all popular fiction sales in North America (Charles, Morrison, & Clark, 2002).

A Brief Look at Mystery's Predecessors. The mystery first became popular among adults in the early 19th century, thanks to Wilkie Collins (e.g., *The Woman in White* and *The Moonstone*) and Edgar Allan Poe (e.g., *The Murders in the Rue Morgue* and *The Purloined Letter*). The trend continued in the late 19th and early 20th century courtesy of Sir Arthur Conan Doyle and his adventures of Sherlock Holmes (e.g., *A Study in Scarlet* and *The Hound of the Baskervilles*). In addition, mystery has long been a favorite of young readers. The 1920s and 1930s saw mystery series growth with juvenile detectives including the Hardy Boys, Nancy Drew, Judy Bolton, the Dana girls, and Cherry Ames (Herbert, 1999). These books were very popular, although they rarely involved the crime of murder and included no ghosts that could not be rationally explained at the end of the story (Nixon, 1994).

CONNECTING | *ADOLESCENTS AND THEIR LITERATURE 5–2*

Do not forget something as simple as a bookmark to lead adolescents to good literature. Reproducible mystery bookmarks appear each year in the December issue of *Voice of Youth Advocates* journal. Or, you can make your own. Just visit a few of the web sites mentioned in this chapter or use the list of books that we provide and develop your own. Keep the list short with 10 or fewer titles on a wide variety of reading levels. Be sure that your school library has the titles that you include. In addition, contact your local public library and let them know about the title on your list.

On our sample bookmark, we have included some fantasy and historical adventure stories as well as contemporary ones to appeal to a wide variety of readers.

Adventure and Survival Past, Present, and Future

For adventure in the past:

Adaline Falling Star by Mary Pope Osborne. 2000.
Kit Carson's "half-breed" daughter runs away from her cruel relatives to find her father somewhere in the Rocky Mountains.

Stones in Water by Donna Jo Napoli. 1997.
Captured by German soldiers, Roberto escapes into the Ukrainian winter.

Wish Me Luck by James Heneghan. 1997.
When Jamie's ship is torpedoed by a German U-boat, he and his friends are thrown into the frigid waters of the north Atlantic.

For present-day adventure:

Shipwreck by Gordon Korman. 2003.
In this first in the Island series, things go wrong when a big storm throws six troubled kids together in order to survive in the middle of the Pacific Ocean. Follow-up with the other books in the series: *Survival* and *Escape.*

Too Cool by Duff Drenna. 1998
Escaping from reform school, Elbert Earl Evans heads away from the law and into a Colorado blizzard.

For a monstrous adventure:

Raptor by Paul Zindel. 1998.
Zack and his friend Uta follow a dinosaur hatchling into the den and come face-to-face with the deadly Utahraptor dinosaur.

These parameters changed when young adult literature broke away from children's literature in the 1960s. Authors became free to include more situations and problems in longer novels that provided more opportunities for character and plot development. Lois Duncan included murder in *Killing Mr. Griffin* (1978), Norma Fox Mazer had a kidnapping by a parent in *Taking Terry Mueller* (1983), Joan Lowery Nixon wrote of a suspicious suicide in *Secret Silent Screams* (1988), and Robert Peck introduced the psychic Blossom Culp in *The Ghost Belonged to Me* (1975) (Nixon, 1994). In addition, Rosa Guy and Virginia Hamilton brought a multicultural voice to the mystery field.

Currently, a wide variety of mysteries, both stand-alone and series books, are written by a number of outstanding authors for teens of all interests and all reading levels. In addition, many older adolescents are reading adult mystery and suspense novels by John Grisham, Sharyn McCrumb, Mary Higgins Clark, and others, while more serious mystery fans read P. D. James, Ruth Rendell, Ian Rankin, Ed McBain, and Tony Hillerman. A spinoff of the genre consists of the many CD-ROM interactive mysteries and role-playing games now available.

Types of Mystery Books. According to young adult mystery author Lesley Grant-Adamson, "labels are for jam; a novel is too subtle a blend for simple tagging" (Moody, 1990, p. 77). Nevertheless, many attempts have been made to categorize mysteries, with people talking about classic British mysteries or locked room and coded mysteries. Novelist Carol Gorman broke the genre into two categories by maintaining that, in a mystery, you do not know who committed the crime or what the answer is to the mystery until the end of the story; while, in a suspense novel, there is a race against time because the protagonist knows who committed the crime but must prove it before the criminal is able to silence her or him (Crowley, 1998). Another simple way to categorize mysteries is to divide the genre into two types, the cozy (which has an optimistic outlook) and noir (which is dark and despairing with a bleak view of life) (DeAndrea, 1994). Others look at the theme of the novel and identify culinary, legal, and animal mysteries. However, the categories that we have chosen to use are those that are found in the yearly mystery review in the December issue of *Voice of Youth Advocates (VOYA)* and shown in Table 5-1.

In our discussion of mysteries, we made several decisions. Like *VOYA*, because of young adults' great interest in adult mysteries, we have chosen to include a few of them in the following discussion. Also, given the popularity of mystery series, we decided to mention a number of them in our discussion. In doing so, we have usually identified the first book in the series. Later in this chapter, we will discuss a number of sources that you can use to identify all of the books in a particular mystery series.

P. I. mysteries. Teenagers enjoy reading private investigator (P. I.) novels, even though most are written for adult audiences. However, teenagers may enjoy them because they respond to the "lone seeker of truth. . . who, although disillusioned and even cynical, is never afraid to plunge into the seamy underside of society in the search for truth" (Charles & Morrison, 2000, p. 318). Although this subgenre began primarily with male protagonists in the classic mystery stories of Sir Arthur Conan Doyle, Dashiell Hammett, and Raymond Chandler or the contemporary stories by Robert Parker, female

TABLE 5-1	Types of Mysteries

Private Investigator (P. I.)
Amateur Sleuths
Police Procedural
Historical Mysteries
Suspense and Thriller
     (including Gothic mysteries, which are now known as romantic suspense)
Mystery Blends
     (Mystery blended with fantasy or science fiction)

private investigators are now very popular. Sara Paretsky's V. I. Warshawski is based in Chicago, Sue Grafton's Kinsey Millhone works in California, and Linda Barnes' Carlotta Carlyle calls Boston home.

Amateur sleuths. While many older teens read the adult mysteries about amateur sleuths such as those written by Earlene Fowler and Sujata Massey, a number of amateur sleuth mysteries are written specifically for young adults. For younger adolescents, Wendelin Van Draanen's series of books focuses on seventh-grade sleuth Sammy Keyes, while Gloria Skurzynski and Alane Ferguson's series of mysteries are set in national parks. Another popular series is Mark Delaney's Misfits, Inc.

Books for older teens many include murder, even though the actual killing does not occur in the book. In Willo Davis Roberts' award-winning *Twisted Summer* (1996), Cici's summer at the beach becomes a search to solve last year's murder, while, in Tim Wynne-Jones's *The Boy in the Burning House* (2001), Jim Hawkins tries to solve the mystery of what happened to his father by looking into the past. While not really a series, Daniel Parker's *The Wessex Papers* (2002) is a mystery trilogy set in a ritzy boarding school. Joan Lowery Nixon is a perennial favorite among teens for her books such as *The Name of the Game Was Murder* (1993) and *The Trap* (2002), as is Caroline B. Cooney, the author of books such as *Burning Up* (1999). Other books with amateur sleuths include *Facing the Dark* (Harrison, 2000), *Close to a Killer* (Qualey, 1999), and *The Night the Penningtons Vanished* (Heusler, 2002).

Police procedurals. While police play a role in many mysteries featuring amateur sleuths, mysteries in the police procedural subgenre take the reader directly into the professional world of law enforcement, both the criminal investigations and the routine work. Big-city cops are the main focus in the adult novels of Deborah Crombie and Ridley Pearson. Perennial favorites among adolescents are Tony Hillerman's Lt. Joe Leaphorn and Sgt. Jim Chee novels, which are set on the Navajo Reservation; and stories of Ute tribal policeman Charlie Moon in the series by James D. Doss. We have already mentioned Robert Cormier's *The Rag and Bone Shop* (2001) in our discussion of realistic fiction; however, it is also a first-class young adult mystery story with the police as main characters.

Historical mysteries. Historical mysteries are very popular, as a number of authors create adult series that appeal to adolescents. While these books are good mysteries, they are also able, like good historical fiction, to make another time and place come alive in the reader's mind. Beginning in *The Beekeeper's Apprentice* (1994), Laurie King writes about teenager Mary Russell and her future husband Sherlock Holmes. In *The Cater Street Hangman* (1979), Anne Perry begins the story of Victorian British policeman Thomas Pitt and his upper-class wife Charlotte. In other series, Diane Day takes readers to early San Francisco, Barbara Hambly writes of antebellum New Orleans, Lynda S. Robinson sets her mysteries in ancient Egypt, and Ellis Peters makes her hero a medieval monk.

Several excellent historical mysteries are available for adolescents. In Virginia Hamilton's *The House of Dies Drear* (1968), a young African American boy learns about his heritage while solving a mystery at a former station on the Underground Railroad. Philip Pullman sets his mysteries, beginning with *Ruby in the Smoke* (1985), in 1870s England. Dorothy and Thomas Hoobler take readers back to 18th century Japan in *The Ghost in the Tokaido Inn* (1999). Middle school reluctant readers may also enjoy the Roman Mysteries series by Caroline Lawrence.

Suspense novels. Many suspense novels have as their protagonist an innocent individual in a familiar everyday setting who is drawn into a threatening situation. It may be that the protagonist has to deal with "the results of the villain's conspiracies and plots," or that the innocent person is "drawn into committing a crime" (Reid, 1999, p. 438). Some suspense novels have romantic themes and were formerly called gothic novels. Adult suspense authors who are favorites of young adults include Mary Higgins Clark and Thomas Perry.

Several authors of young adult literature write in the mystery subgenre of suspense. An early suspense novel for young adults was Richard Peck's *Are You in the House Alone?* (1976), one of the first novels to address the terror of date rape. More recently, in Nancy Werlin's *The Killer's Cousin* (1998), David, acquitted of murder in the accidental death of his girlfriend, finds that his cousin Lily may really be a killer. In Elaine Marie Alphin's *Counterfeit Son* (2002), the abused son of a serial killer assumes the identity of one of his father's victims. Many teens who enjoy a story of intrigue and action-packed adventure will enjoy reading the suspenseful spy series of Anthony Horowitz. His books, featuring 14-year-old Alex Rider as the protagonist, include *Stormbreaker* (2001) and *Skeleton Key* (2003). Another suspense series is Jordan Cray's danger.com, which features crimes related to the Internet. In Carol Plum-Ucci's *The Body of Christopher Creed* (2000), when the class outcast disappears, some of his class are suspected of playing a role in his disappearance. Several other young adult novels of suspense include Nancy Werlin's *Locked Inside* (2000), Robert Cormier's *Tenderness: A Novel* (1997), Shelley Sykes's *For Mike* (1998), and Gail Giles' *Shattering Glass* (2002).

Mystery blends. Finally, there are the mystery blends, many of which combine elements from speculative fiction with a mystery. Adult fantasy writer Katherine Kurtz's *St. Patrick's Gargoyle* (2001) follows Paddy, a gargoyle who witnesses an act of vandalism at the church. Michael Crichton's *Timeline* (1999) involves a time-travel mystery, and Jim Butcher's *Grave Peril* (2001) (part of the Dresden File series) has professional wizard Harry Dresden solving mysteries in Chicago. Writing for adolescents, Vivian Vande Velde blends history, mystery, and the supernatural in her medieval mystery *Never Trust a Dead Man* (1999), and Joyce McDonald takes a 17-year-old boy back 200 years to meet the ghost of a murderer in *Shades of Simon Gray* (2001). Jenny Carroll (who also writes under the name Meg Cabot) writes one of the books in the popular 1-800-WHERE-R-YOU mystery series about Jessica and her psychic visions. Other mystery blends include Lois Duncan's *Gallows Hill* (1997), Elizabeth Chandler's *Dark Secrets: Legacy of Lies* (2002), and Kathryn Reiss's *PaperQuake* (1998).

Reasons For Using and Teaching Mystery Books. According to young adult novelist Laurence Yep:

> a good mystery challenges the mind. It presents a set of clues, some of which appear so contradictory they seem as tangled as the mythological Gordian knot. The detective wields reason like a knife slicing though the knot to the truth. . . . The stroke must be exact and sure because a mystery must reveal some truth about society and what we hope are the workings of our universe. The knife that cuts is also the knife that shapes us as creatures of reason, as social beings, as readers and writers. (Yep, 2003, p. 1521)

Although the mystery author creates an exciting or dangerous plot, he or she cleverly plants clues to help the reader solve the mystery along with the protagonist. With the many interesting stand-alone books and series currently available on a wide range of reading levels, there is a mystery to appeal to the reading tastes of almost every young adult.

Series mysteries continue to be popular with readers who enjoy the ongoing characters and the familiar settings. Not only do readers want to solve the mystery, but they also want to know more about the characters and watch them grow and change, something that did not happen in the early formula mystery series about Nancy Drew or the Hardy Boys. In contemporary series, readers can connect with the characters and enjoy reading the solid and orderly format in a very disorderly time. As editor Kate Miciak states: "If a mystery is about disrupting order, then reinstating it, a series mystery is about how the characters who shape the plot not only bring order to their world, but also about how they change and grow because of what has just happened" (Dahlin, 2002). Connecting Adolescents and Their Literature 5-3 suggests one way to use mysteries across the curriculum.

Characteristics of Good Mystery Literature. Plot and characters are very important in both mysteries written for young adults and the adult mysteries that adolescents read. In true young adult mysteries, the protagonist is usually an adolescent who assumes the role of the amateur sleuth, sometimes following in the footsteps of a parent or adult friend who is a P. I. or police officer. The characters should be engaging, interesting, and multidimensional; and most of them, with the exception of the protagonist, could be the murderer or perpetrator of the crime.

The plot usually begins with action, intrigue, or suspense to hook the reader. Then, through a series of clues, the protagonist eventually solves the mystery, sometimes placing himself or herself in jeopardy by facing real or perceived danger. All information

CONNECTING   *ADOLESCENTS AND THEIR LITERATURE 5–3*

Every teacher has days when the lesson ends early or the class activities are completed in record time. For a change of pace, have a collection of short mysteries close at hand. Teens will enjoy listening to and solving the puzzles without realizing that they are developing their problem-solving skills.

- Check with your library media specialist to identify some collections such as Vicki Cameron's *Clue Mysteries: 15 Whodunits to Solve in Minutes* (2003).

- Join the Two Minute Mystery "Solve-It" club, which is sponsored by the Quebec English Schools Network on the Web, at: www.qesnrecit.qc.ca/cc/2mmsolve/index.html.

- Use short mysteries as a springboard to writing in the English classroom.

in the plot (clues) could be important in solving the case, yet in some cases, the author presents misleading information (a red herring) to challenge the reader and the detective. With foreshadowing often used to heighten the suspense, there usually will be several motives for the crime, lots of plot twists, and plenty of alibis that must be investigated. The solution to the crime must come from known information, not a surprise villain introduced in the last chapter of the book; however, the clues must be cleverly planted so that the mystery is not solved too easily or too soon. In a suspense novel, the setting often becomes very important with violent storms, a deserted island, an abandoned mine, or a spooky old house playing an important role. Considerations for Selecting Young Adult Literature: *Mystery* summarizes some of the characteristics of a good mystery. Then, Suggestions for Collaborative Efforts 5-1 shows an example of teachers who used good mysteries to develop an interdisciplinary unit.

Suggestions For Selecting and Using Mystery Novels. In addition to reading mysteries and evaluating them by looking for the characteristics of good mysteries, a number of guides can help you select quality mysteries for young adults.

    Awards and best books lists. The Edgar Awards (short for the Edgar Allan Poe Awards), given by the Mystery Writers of America, Inc., have had categories for both children's and young adult mysteries since 1989. Before that only a single children's mystery category existed. The Agatha Award, given by Malice Domestic for traditional or cozy mysteries, has a combined children's/young adult category. Other awards for adult mysteries include the Anthony and the Macavity. A number of excellent magazines also review mystery books, including *Sherlock, Mystery Scene, Drood Review of Mystery,* and *Mystery Readers Journal.* We have already mentioned that the December issue of *VOYA* has, since 1997, featured adult mysteries that are recommended for young adults.

CONSIDERATIONS	For Selecting Young Adult Literature	MYSTERY

When examining young adult mystery books, ask the following questions:

- ◎ Does the author provide clues and endings that seem realistic rather than contrived and phony?

- ◎ Are there well-developed and believable characters?

- ◎ Does the setting create a mood or present information about a time or a place (e.g., a period in history, a type of art or music, or a particular location) without becoming didactic?

- ◎ Are there clear descriptions of the locale, the events, the characters, and other descriptive material that might lead to or suggest clues?

- ◎ Is there a "twist in the plot" to challenge readers to think and consider new clues?

- ◎ At the end, after the conflict is convincingly resolved, is the mystery solved although there can be some uncertainty about the future of some characters?

- ◎ Does the book provide enjoyment for the reader—a chance to enjoy reading, to be challenged to think and consider all clues, and to want to read additional mysteries or books by the same author?

SUGGESTIONS FOR COLLABORATIVE EFFORTS

Amy Shimberg and Heidi Meehan Grant (1998) developed a mystery thematic unit combining English and science to build on their students' interest in criminology, forensics, and law.

- ■ Begin with a mystery genre study in the English classroom.

- ■ Ask local attorneys to visit and answer questions about legal procedures.

- ■ Ask police to visit the science class to demonstrate fingerprinting and other basic forensic sciences.

- ■ Host a simulated murder investigation with a "murder" in the school's hallway, clues planted by the teachers, and science labs to allow for ink, poison, fabric, fingerprint, and handwriting analysis.

Print review resources. Several excellent reference sources exist about mysteries, which, although they cover primarily adult mysteries, provide information on the genre. Examples include the following:

- ■ *Detecting Women* (Heising, 2000) and *Detecting Men* (Heising, 1998)

- ■ *The Mammoth Encyclopedia of Modern Crime Fiction* (Ashley, 2002)

- *The Encyclopedia of Murder and Mystery* (Murphy, 1999)

- *Killer Books* (Swanson & Dean, 1998)

- *Silk Stalkings* (Nichols & Thompson, 2000)

- *Crime & Mystery:* The *100 best books* (Keating, 1987)

- *100 Favorite Mysteries of the Century* (Huang, 2000)

- *St. James Guide to Crime & Mystery Writers* (Pederson, 1996)

The listing of adult mysteries for young adults that appears in the December issue of *VOYA* often includes a listing of additional mystery reference sources.

Online resources. A number of Internet sources have information about writing mysteries and incorporating mystery writing into the English curriculum. The Two Minute Mystery Writing Club provides detailed information on the writing process as well as specific guidelines for creating the essential ingredients of a good mystery. Project activities and teaching ideas can also be adapted for working with a wide range of adolescents; for example, Joan Lowery Nixon provides an entire mystery writing workshop on the Web. Expanding Your Knowledge with the Internet 5-2 provides links to some of the previously mentioned sources as well as to Internet sites with additional information about mysteries.

Muse (1999) notes that young adult mysteries often include themes of social responsibility and social realism. By centering the moral debate around the conflict between good and evil, mysteries encourage readers to question values and even to combine entertainment with lessons on history and culture. Thus, mystery units can go beyond the English classroom and involve a number of other subjects. Suggestions for Collaborative Efforts 5-2 identifies some Internet WebQuests that incorporate mysteries throughout the

EXPANDING | **YOUR KNOWLEDGE WITH THE INTERNET 5-2**

On the Internet you can find information on mysteries including awards and prizes, periodicals, booklists, teaching guides, and selected writers at sites such as the following:

Mystery Writers of America, Inc., an organization for mystery writers and other professionals in the mystery field, has a database of the Edgar Award winners and nominees.

Mystery Writers of America, Inc.
www.mysterywriters.org/

Drood Review of Mystery
www.droodreview.com

Lois Duncan
loisduncan.arquettes.com/

Links to these and many additional sites are found on this book's Companion Website at www.prenhall.com/bucher.

curriculum. Then, Connecting Adolescents and Their Literature 5-4 identifies some additional ways to share mysteries with adolescents.

Finally, From Page to Screen identifies some mystery and adventure novels that have been released as movies.

SUGGESTIONS FOR COLLABORATIVE EFFORTS

Teachers can work together and with the library media specialist and/or technology facilitator to have students complete WebQuests, a number of which center around mysteries. Here are a few examples. Links to these and many additional sites are found on this book's Companion Website at www.prenhall.com/bucher.

A forensic mystery WebQuest in which students use logical thought processes and scientific inquiry skills to determine whether or not the science accurately explains the crime.

projects.edtech.sandi.net/kearny/forensic/

Was It Murder? The Death of King Tutankhamun—A social studies and science WebQuest

www.pekin.net/pekin108/wash/webquest/

CONNECTING ADOLESCENTS AND THEIR LITERATURE 5-4

Look for ways to capitalize on the interest of young adults in mysteries.

- Host a mystery night program in the school or public library and allow adolescents to help solve an imaginary case. Visit the following web site for more information on a successful program: www.ala.org/Content/NavigationMenu/YALSA/For_Members_Only/YAttitudes/Archives

- *The Mystery Readers' Advisory: The Librarian's Clues to Murder and Mayhem* (Charles, Morrison, & Clark, 2002) has a number of suggestions for marketing mysteries that both teachers and librarians can use:
  - Annotated booklists, bookmarks, and bibliographies
  - Displays that focus on topics (culinary mysteries, crime around the world, teens as sleuths), types (historical mysteries), or authors
  - Mystery book discussion groups
  - Booktalks of mysteries
  - Linking mystery films and books
  - Celebrations of events in the history of mysteries

FROM PAGE TO SCREEN

Adventure, Mystery, and Humor

Good cinematography can add a visual thrill to stories of adventure and mystery, but simplified and shortened stories sometimes compromise the details that make the original texts riveting. Compare the following films with their origins to see how well these filmmakers realized their cinematic potential.

Hounds of the Baskervilles
Unrated, 1959
★ ★ ★

Infamous British blood and gore film studio Hammer produced an uncharacteristically atmospheric and subdued adaptation of Sir Arthur Conan Doyle's classic mystery. Although Peter Cushing's Sherlock Holmes is singularly logical, director Terence Fisher's film re-imagines Doyle's world of logic as a realm of evil. His version is spooky and effective, if often far afield from the original novel. This adaptation makes for an interesting comparison to the original text when considering artistic interpretation.

Jaws
1975, PG
★ ★ ★ ★

Peter Benchley's novel is a favorite among adolescents. Charged with the task of coscripting his own work for the screen, Benchley succeeded where most screen adaptations fail: he wrote a movie that is superior to the novel. Aided in large part by young director Steven Spielberg, who coaxed excellent performances from Robert Shaw, Roy Scheider, and Richard Dreyfuss—all of whom benefited from a very temperamental mechanical shark—the result is a classic adventure tale that still packs a thrill.

Something Wicked This Way Comes
1983, PG
★ ★ ★

Ray Bradbury adapted his own novel for the screen, focusing as much on the mystery behind Dark's Pandemonium Carnival as on the fantasy that made the novel famous. The spooky, atmospherically staged film boasts a beautiful rhythm and language, as well as a stellar performance by Jason Robards.

A Cry in the Wild
1990, PG
★ ★ ½

This adaptation of Gary Paulsen's Hatchet *moves erratically through plot points and sometimes loses focus, but contains powerful moments and fine supporting performances. Catherine Cyran's screenplay often veers from the original novel, providing an opportunity to discuss the possible reasons filmmakers have for altering novels for the screen.*

Humor

According to author James Howe (1995), "humor is nature's way of saying, 'Lighten up' " (p. 5). Many young adults want a good laugh or maybe a polite chuckle. By reading about others' antics, sayings, mishaps, and puns, adolescents may see themselves in the humorous situations or they may just want to escape from the ordeals they perceive themselves experiencing in their everyday lives. Either way, young adult readers enjoy the humorous works of such authors as Joan Bauer, Richard Peck, Todd Strasser, Terry Pratchett, and Gordon Korman.

Joan Bauer, a writer of humorous fiction, regards humor as a survival tool. Believing that humor in life illustrates that an individual has moved from looking at life as a series of problems to gaining a greater sense of clarity and control over one's life, Bauer sees humor as a series of mirrors. When young adults look into these mirrors, they learn to distinguish between the laughter that shames and ridicules and the laughter that brings redemption and good-hearted feelings (Bauer, 1996).

A Brief Look at Humor's Predecessors. "Humor is seeing the Emperor without his clothes" (Howe, 1995, p. 7). Humorous stories may have begun with the droll, simpleton, or noodlehead tales and the tall tales found in the oral folk tradition, which often poked fun at human foolishness and the stupidity of some people. Miguel de Cervantes incorporated these characteristics into his classic 16th century novel of Don Quixote. Adding foolishness to their own children's stories written in the late 1800s and early 1900s, Lucretia P. Hale (e.g. 1880) told stories of the Peterkin family, and P. L. Travers (e.g., 1934) recounted the adventures of Mary Poppins.

By the middle of the 20th century Beverly Cleary (e.g., 1955) was writing about Ramona and her family, Sid Fleischman (e.g., 1965) told stories about McBroom, Judy Blume (e.g., 1972) provided funny stories of Fudge and his family, and James Howe (e.g., 1979) invented a vampire rabbit named Bunnicula. For adolescents, Douglas Adams added humor to space travel in *The Hitchhiker's Guide to the Galaxy* (1979), Sue Townsend penned *The Secret Diary of Adrian Mole, Aged 13 3/4* (1984), Paula Danziger wrote *The Cat Ate My Gymsuit* (1988), and Jill Pinkwater introduced Brenda Tuna and her friend India Ink Tiedlebaum in *Buffalo Brenda* (1989). Now, a number of writers continue this tradition by writing humorous tales for adolescent readers.

Types of Humor in Books. Humor can be found in any type of novel (historical fiction, science fiction, realistic fiction, or mystery) as well as in short stories, poetry, and graphic novels. There have been many attempts to categorize humor, but as Max Eastman noted in 1936 in the introduction to *Enjoyment of Laughter* "nothing kills the laugh quicker than to explain a joke" (Howe, 1995, p. 4). Thus, rather than try to categorize humorous books, we have decided, in Table 5-2, to list some of the types of humor that are found in young adult literature.

In addition to some of the novels that we have already mentioned in Chapter 4, a number of young adult novels combine humor and realistic fiction. In *Confess-O-Rama* (Koertge, 1996), when Tony calls the self-help hotline, he does not realize who he is telling all his secrets. In *Behaving Bradley* (Nodelman, 1998), Brad tries to gather student opinion for the school's new code of conduct.

TABLE 5-2	Types of Humor That Are Found in Young Adult Literature

Strange and/or funny characters
Impossible, absurd, and/or ridiculous situations
Suspense, surprise, and/or unexpected actions and endings
Wordplay: jokes, puns, malapropisms
Exaggeration, fabrications, irony, and incongruity
Slapstick comedy
Satire
Hyperbole
Innuendoes and double-entendres
Tricks and twists
Sarcasm

Diary and journal formats are popular with adolescents. In *Truth or Dairy* (Clark, 2000), Courtney Von Dragen Smith shares her feelings as she tries to survive her senior year and breaking up with her boyfriend. In *Absolutely Normal Chaos* (Creech, 1995), Mary Lou documents the ups and downs of a typical 13-year-old girl interspersed with her thoughts about her summer reading assignments.

Several authors have written a number of humorous novels for young adults. Gordon Korman is a perennial favorite with novels such as *No More Dead Dogs* (2000), *The Chicken Doesn't Skate* (1996), and *Losing Joe's Place* (1993). In *Squashed* (1992), Joan Bauer writes of overweight Ellie Morgan who has a fascination with growing giant pumpkins, while in *Rules of the Road* (1998) she sends shoe-selling sophomore Jenna Boller on a road trip with elderly Mrs. Gladstone.

Humor crosses genres. Fantasy author Patricia Wrede has written several humorous books including *Dealing with Dragons* (1990) and, with Caroline Stevermer, *Sorcery and Cecelia, or the Enchanted Chocolate Pot* (2003). Todd Strasser also combines speculative fiction and humor in books such as *Help! I'm Trapped in an Alien's Body* (1998) and *How I Spent My Last Night on Earth* (1998). In *A Fate Totally Worse Than Death* (1995), Paul Fleischman provides a parody of a horror novel, while novel and cartoon combine in Gary Larson's story of an earthworm in *There's a Hair in My Dirt! A Worm's Story* (1998). For younger adolescents, Lemony Snicket has produced a Series of Unfortunate Events, 13 melodramas filled with the misery and misadventures that befall the three Baudelaire children. Finally, Terry Pratchett has created the bizarre land of Discworld with his fantasy spoofs and madcap adventures that begin in *The Colour of Magic* (1983) and continue into *Men at Arms* (1993) and *Thief of Time* (2001).

Historical novels also incorporate humor. In Karen Cushman's *Catherine, Called Birdy* (1994), readers meet a medieval girl with a determination not to get married. In Richard

Peck's *A Long Way from Chicago* (1998), a brother and sister visit their grandmother in rural Illinois during the Great Depression and find that Grandma is constantly involved in outlandish schemes.

Reasons For Using and Teaching Humor. Humor for adolescents is "not just a weapon. It helps them deflect some of life's more perplexing problems" (Davis, 1999, p. 15) that they experience everyday in their own lives and vicariously through the media. By helping them work through and with their own emotions, humor can be both a barrier and a tool for overcoming that barrier. An author must find a balance between the serious and the humorous to make the humor effective. Laughter can be a positive force when, even in the midst of pain, it can bring hope for the future and help characters overcome fears and adversity. It can also allow readers to look at social problems and cultural differences because it lowers barriers to discussion while providing a look a problems and issues in a new light. As Paul Lewis (1995) states:

> The suggestion that we should work the study of humor into English curricula starting in middle school is based . . . on a sense that humor can be a powerful force in the expression of any value or idea . . . we should take [students] inside jokes to expose the subtle way humor can convey information, images, and assertions. (p. 10)

A number of researchers (Gentile & McMillan, 1978; Jalonga, 1985; Klesius, Laframboise, & Gaier, 1998; Kuchner, 1991; McGhee, 1979; Monson & Sebesta, 1991) have studied the humor preferences of various developmental groups. While children enjoy books with incongruous events, riddles, and linguistic wordplay, younger adolescents usually enjoy more complex, aggressive, or "sick" humor as well as slapstick comedy. When puberty begins, humor often becomes more aggressive and sexual with lewd jokes and with authority figures bearing the brunt of the humor. The interest in riddles is replaced with an appreciation of humor in real-life stories. Finally, adolescents develop an understanding of more complex intellectual humor including parody.

Characteristics of Humor. Humor comes from unusual, ludicrous, or incongruous events, characters, and/or settings and appeals to adolescents across a wide range of ages, developmental levels, and reading abilities. Humor can range from perfectly normal people who wind up in funny, but realistic, situations to zany, whimsical, nonsensical characters. While some humorous books are straight narratives, others, like books in contemporary realistic fiction, break from the traditional narrative pattern and include clippings, drawings, memos, newspaper ads, and other artifacts that add to the story. No matter the format of the book, the adolescent protagonist should be placed in realistic situations where he or she can do things that readers can relate to. In addition to being well-written stories, humorous novels should make the reader laugh; since different things make different people laugh, humorous tales need to reflect the wide-ranging interests of adolescents. Considerations for Selecting Young Adult Literature: *Humor* points out some attractive features of quality humor.

| CONSIDERATIONS | For Selecting Young Adult Literature: | HUMOR |

When evaluating humor, ask the following questions:

◉ Is the humor well-written? Are wording, sentences, and paragraphs well-constructed?

◉ Is the plot interesting and does it capture and hold the readers' attention?

◉ Are the chapters easy to read and of a length that will appeal to young adult readers?

◉ Are the characters developed to a point where readers can see both strengths and weaknesses?

◉ Is the humor developmentally appropriate (i.e., do various ages of readers understand and appreciate the humor)?

Suggestions For Selecting and Using Humor. According to Teri Lesesne (2000), while there is an abundance of humorous books for children, humor is "in terribly short supply for middle and high school readers" (p. 60). Unfortunately, there are not any awards given specifically for humorous stories. However, a number of web sites do include lists of recommended titles. Expanding Your Knowledge with the Internet 5-3 contains some pertinent information on humor.

The March 1999 issue of *English Journal,* the publication of the National Council of Teachers of English (NCTE) for secondary educators, and the September 1995 issue of *Voices from the Middle,* the publication of the NCTE for educators in the middle grades,

| EXPANDING | YOUR KNOWLEDGE WITH THE INTERNET 5-3 |

A number of Internet sites are available where you can find information about humor, including booklists and author information, such as:

The American Library Association's list of recommended humor books

www.ala.org/Content/NavigationMenu/YALSA/Booklists_and_Book_Awards/Popular_
Paperbacks_for_Young_Adults/2001_Popular_Paperbacks_for_Young_Adults.htm#humor

Information on author Gordon Korman

www.gordonkorman.com/

Links to these and many additional sites are found on this book's Companion Website at www.prenhall.com/bucher.

focused on using humor in the English classroom. Barbara S. Morris (1999) discussed the use of character studies from comedy television shows, Colleen A. Ruggieri (1999) explained how she uses humor to capture her students' attention as well as to teach a lesson, and Tom Tatum (1999) wrote about the use of puns as part of his vocabulary reviews with college-bound students. For a clever bulletin board idea, Andrew Dunn (1999) described how he uses paper cutouts of tee shirts and prints literature-related slogans on them such as "Ahab Was a Whale of a Guy" or "King Arthur Used a Knight Light" (p. 65). While teaching in a middle school, Michele McInnes (1995) explained how she uses humor with her advisees, and Dan Rothermel (1995) wrote about how he takes everyday events, twists and turns them, and comes up with the unexpected in his writing workshop. We encourage you to read these and other articles to discover ways to use humor and humorous literature in your classroom.

CONCLUDING THOUGHTS

Obviously, adventure and survival, mystery and suspense, and humorous novels are a very important part of young adult literature. While we have tried to include many of them in this chapter, we encourage you to consult the many selection guides mentioned in the chapter to locate additional titles. Because these books provide vicarious experiences, a sense of enjoyment, and an opportunity to get away from the trials of everyday life, they should remain popular with adolescents. Realizing this popularity, educators and library media specialists should seek to incorporate quality and age-appropriate books into both classroom and media center book collections and to integrate these books into the middle and secondary school curriculum. This book's Companion Website at www.prenhall.com/bucher features additional information about adventure and survival, mystery and suspense, and humorous novels, including review questions, self-assessments, Internet sites, and young adult literature and readings.

Young Adult Books

This section includes young adult titles recommended or mentioned in this chapter. Check the Companion Website at www.prenhall.com/bucher to find additional suggestions of current young adult literature.

Adventure and Survival—Fiction

Anderson, L. H. (2000). *Fever 1793*. New York: Simon & Schuster. Can Mattie and her mother survive now that the yellow fever epidemic has begun in Philadelphia?

Burke, B. (1998). *Walks alone*. San Diego: Harcourt Brace. A young Apache girl struggles to survive after an attack on her village.

Casanova, M. (1995). *Moose tracks*. New York: Hyperion. Twelve-year-old Seth lives an exciting life in northern Minnesota.

Casanova, M. (1997). *Wolf shadows*. New York: Hyperion. Seth becomes involved in the conflict over the wolves in northern Minnesota.

Casanova, M. (2002). *When eagles fall*. New York: Hyperion. After she paddles to a remote island to band some eaglets, Alex is stranded by a storm.

Cooney, C. (1992). *Flight number 116 is down*. New York: Scholastic. A group of teenagers become involved in the rescue effort to help the survivors of a 747 crash.

Cooney, C. (1995). *Flash fire*. New York: Scholastic. When an out-of-control wildfire threatens their homes, Danna and her friends have to find a way to escape.

Cooney, C. (1997). *The terrorist*. New York: Scholastic. Everything changes when a package carried by Laura's brother explodes.

Fama, E. (2002). *Overboard*. Chicago: Cricket Books. When the ferry Emily is on sinks off the coast of Sumatra, she fights to save herself and a young Indonesian boy.

George, J. C. (1997). *Julie's wolf pack*. New York: HarperCollins. This continues the story begun in *Julie of the Wolves* (1972). Julie begins a third adventure with the wolf pack that saved her life.

Giff, P. R. (2000). *Nory Ryan's song*. New York: Delacorte. Can Nory and her family survive the 1845 Irish potato famine?

Hamilton, V. (1971). *The planet of Junior Brown*. New York: Macmillan. Street-wise Buddy Clark leads a group of homeless boys and befriends Junior Brown as Junior begins to slip into madness.

Hesse, K. (2000) *Stowaway*. New York: Margaret K. McElderry Books. Join Captain James Cook as he sets out on an around the world trip in 1768.

Hiaasen, C. (2002). *Hoot*. New York: Knopf. By putting alligators in the portable toilets and releasing cottonmouth snakes to terrorize the guard dogs, Mullett Fingers and his friends sabotage the site for the proposed Pancake House to save the burrowing owls.

Hobbs, W. (1991). *Downriver*. New York: Atheneum. Jessie and her friends ditch their guide from "Hoods in the Woods" camp and decide to run the rapids of the Grand Canyon on their own.

Hobbs, W. (1996). *Far north*. New York: Morrow. When their floatplane is destroyed, Gabe and Raymond must fight to survive the winter in the Canadian Northwest Territories.

Hobbs, W. (1997). *River thunder*. New York: Delacorte. This is the sequel to *Downriver*. Jessie and her crew from the book *Downriver* return for another adventure on the Colorado River. Can they forget their differences and work together as a team?

Hobbs, W. (1998). *The maze*. New York: Morrow Junior Books. After escaping from a juvenile detention facility, Rick joins a biologist who is introducing condors in Canyonlands National Park.

Hobbs, W. (2002). *Wild man island*. New York: HarperCollins. When Andy tries to visit the site of his father's death, his sea kayak is blown to a remote Alaskan island. Other adventure books by Hobbs that are set in Alaska include *Jason's Gold* (1999) and *Down the Yukon* (2001).

Holman, F. (1974). *Slake's limbo*. New York: Scribner. As his life seems to crumble all around him, Aremis Slake flees into the New York City subway tunnels where he intends to spend the rest of his life.

Holtwijk, I. (1999). *Asphalt angels*. Asheville, NC: Front Street. The Asphalt Angels, a gang of street kids, provide protection and support but there is a price to pay for security.

Korman, G. (2003). *The contest*. London: Scholastic. Four adolescent boys want to be the youngest expedition to climb Everest, but their troubles begin before they leave Base Camp. Other books in the series are *The Climb* (2003) and *The Summit* (2003).

Mazer, H. (1981). *The island keeper*. New York: Delacorte. Cleo tries to escape personal problems by fleeing to a desolate Canadian island where her major problem becomes survival.

Myers, W. D. (1988). *Scorpions*. New York: Harper & Row. With his older brother Randy in jail, Jamal must decide whether to join the gang known as the Scorpions.

Parkinson, C. (2003). *Storm-blast*. New York: Random House. Regan does not get along with his sister Carol and cousin Matt. But when the three are swept out to sea, they will only survive if they learn to cooperate with each other.

Paulsen, G. (1988). *Hatchet*. New York: Viking Penguin. After a plane crash in northern Canada, Brian learns to survive in the wilderness with only a hatchet. Sequels include *The River* (1991), *Brian's Winter* (1996), and *Brian's Return* (1999).

Prose, F. (2003). *After*. New York: HarperCollins. The school shooting was bad enough. Now Tom and his friends find that friends who refuse to conform to the new school rules are disappearing.

Roberts, W. D. (1998). *The kidnappers*. New York: Atheneum. Joey sees the men kidnapping Willie Groves. But will anyone believe his story before it's too late?

Rubalcaba, J. (2000). *The wadjet eye*. New York: Clarion. Damon leaves Alexandria, Egypt, in 45 B.C. to find his father in the Roman army in Spain.

Smith, R. (1997). *Jaguar*. New York: Hyperion. Jacob finds adventure on the Amazon River when he accompanies his father to a jaguar preserve.

Smith, S. L. (2002). *Lucy the giant*. New York: Delacorte. Leaving her alcoholic father, 15-year-old Lucy takes a job on a commercial fishing boat in Alaska.

Sweeney, J. (1996). *Free fall*. New York: Delacorte. When they decide to explore a cave, four teens are caught underground.

White, R. (1972). *Deathwatch*. Garden City, NY: Doubleday. A college boy accepts a job as a guide on a desert hunting trip and soon finds that he is the hunted, not the hunter.

Woodson, J. (2002). *Hush*. New York: Penguin. When her father testifies against two of his fellow police officers, Toswiah's family must enter the witness protection program.

Mystery and Suspense—Fiction

Alphin, E. M. (2002). *Counterfeit son*. San Diego: Harcourt. After the police shoot Hank Miller, a serial killer, his son assumes the identity of one of his father's victims.

Barnes, L. (1987). *Trouble of fools*. New York: St. Martin's. When P.I. Carlotta Carlyle takes a missing person case, she does not expect to find ties to the IRA. A more recent novel in this series is *The Big Dig* (2002).

Butcher, J. (2001). *Grave peril*. New York: Roc. Magician Harry Dresden and his friend Michael, a knight, take on the vengeful ghosts loose in modern-day Chicago as they try to find who is behind the violence.

Cameron, V. (2003). *Clue mysteries: 15 whodunits to solve in minutes*. Philadelphia: Running Press. These 15 short mysteries take only minutes to solve.

Carroll, J. (2002). *Safe house*. New York: Pocket Pulse. Should Jess try to keep a low profile or use her psychic powers to find a missing girl?

Chandler, E. (2002). *Dark secrets: Legacy of lies*. New York: Pocket Books. In this first of the Dark Secrets series, Megan visits her grandmother and finds that her nightmares are coming true. The second book in the series is *Dark Secrets: Don't Tell* (2002).

Chandler, R. (1939). *The big sleep*. New York: Knopf. This is the first of the Philip Marlowe, private investigator stories.

Clark, M. H. (2001). *On the street where you live*. New York: Simon & Schuster. Someone is trying to re-create three old murders and have Emily as one of the victims.

Cooney, C. B. (1999). *Burning up*. New York: Delacorte. Macey's school project leads her to investigate a 1959 arson case and uncover prejudice in her Connecticut town.

Cormier, R. (1997). *Tenderness: A novel*. New York: Delacorte. Eric Poole is a serial killer and Lori is the 15-year-old runaway who is drawn to him.

Cormier, R. (2001). *The rag and bone shop*. New York: Delacorte. Since Alicia was his friend, Jason could not have killed her, could he?

Cray, J. (1997a). *Firestorm*. New York: Aladdin. Randy discovers a fanatical group in an Internet chat room.

Cray, J. (1997b). *Gemini 7*. New York: Aladdin. After meeting a girl on the Internet, Jonah's life begins to fall apart.

Crichton, M. (1999). *Timeline*. New York: Knopf. Historians travel back in time to 1357 to rescue a colleague who is stuck in the past.

Crombie, D. (1993). *A share in death*. New York: Scribner's. Scotland Yard Superintendent Duncan Kincaid's holiday ends when he discovers a dead body in the hotel's swimming pool. A more recent novel in this series is *And Justice There Is None* (2002).

Day, D. (1995). *The strange files of Fremont Jones*. New York: Doubleday. After escaping an arranged marriage, Fremont Jones opens a typewriting business in San Francisco in 1905 and soon becomes involved in murder. A more recent novel in this series is *Beacon Street Mourning* (2000).

Delaney, M. (1998). *The vanishing chip*. Atlanta: Peachtree. Four high school students try to find out who stole a valuable computer chip in this first book in the series. Another title is *Hit and Run* (2002).

Doss, J. D. (1994). *The shaman sings*. New York: St. Martin's. Ute tribal police sergeant Charlie Moon, his colleague Scott Parris, and Shaman Daisy Perika join forces to solve the murder of a graduate student. A more recent novel in this series is *White Shell Woman* (2002).

Duncan, L. (1978). *Killing Mr. Griffin*. Boston: Little, Brown. Playing a trick on a high school English teacher leads to his death.

Duncan, L. (1997). *Gallows hill*. New York: Delacorte. When Sarah runs the fortune-telling booth at the Halloween carnival, her fortunes and nightmares come true! Other suspense books by this author include: *The Third Eye* (1985), *Twisted Window* (1987), and *Stranger with my Face* (1981).

Fowler, E. (1994). *Fools' puzzle*. New York: Berkley. After a murder at the Folk Art Museum that she manages, Benni Harper starts looking for the killer. A more recent novel in this series is *Sunshine and Shadow* (2003).

Giles, G. (2002). *Shattering glass*. Brookfield, CT: Roaring Brook Press. Rob and his friends transformed Simon Glass from a nerd to a popular guy. Then, they killed him.

Glenn, M. (1996). *Who killed Mr. Chippendale?* New York: Lodestar. As the school day begins, a high school teacher is shot to death. Fellow teachers, students, and others describe their reactions in free verse poems.

Grafton, S. (1982). *"A" is for alibi*. New York: Holt, Rinehart and Winston. Kinsey Millhone is hired to clear Nikki Fife of the charge of murder. A more recent novel in this series is *"Q" Is for Quarry* (2002).

Guy, R. (1979). *The disappearance*. New York: Delacorte. When the 7-year-old daughter of a Brooklyn family disappears, everyone suspects the young boy from Harlem who has been living with them.

Hambly, B. (1997). *A free man of color*. New York: Bantam. Benjamin January, a Paris-trained Creole surgeon, is framed for murder. A more recent novel in this series is *Die Upon a Kiss* (2001).

Hamilton, V. (1968). *The house of Dies Drear*. New York: Macmillan. A young boy examines his African American heritage as he investigates the strange happenings at a former station on the underground railroad. Hamilton revisits this setting in *Mystery of Drear House* (1987).

Hammett, D. (1930). *The Maltese falcon*. New York: Knopf. When a beautiful redhead asks P. I. Sam Spade for help, there is trouble ahead.

Harrison, M. (2000). *Facing the dark*. New York: Holiday House. Did Simon's father kill Charley's dad? The two teens decide to find out the truth.

Heusler, M. (2002). *The night the Penningtons vanished*. Prides Crossing, MA: Larcom Press. Two love birds vanish and Isabella is determined to recover them even if it means hunting a murderer.

Hillerman, T. (1970). *The blessing way*. New York: Harper & Row. While investigating a ritual murder, Lt. Joe Leaphorn is soon trailing a Wolf-Witch.

Hillerman, T. (1986). *Skinwalkers*. New York: Harper & Row. This is the first novel in which Sgt. Jim Chee and Lt. Joe Leaphorn of the Navajo Tribal Police combine their resources.

Hoobler, D., & Hoobler, T. (1999). *The ghost in the Tokaido inn*. New York: Philomel Books. After risking his life to defend a girl who is accused of stealing a jewel from a samurai warrior, Seikei tries to find the real criminal.

Horowitz, A. (2001). *Stormbreaker*. New York: Philomel Books. After his uncle's death, Alex is approached by the British government to follow in his uncle's footsteps as a spy.

Horowitz, A. (2003). *Skeleton key*. New York: Philomel Books. Alex goes to Wimbledon and finds Chinese gangs, illegal nuclear weapons, and a possible Russian psychopath.

King, L. (1994). *The beekeeper's apprentice*. New York: St. Martin's. A young teenager stumbles across Sherlock Holmes on the Sussex downs and goes on to join him in a series of adventures. A more recent novel in this series is *Justice Hall* (2001).

Kurtz, K. (2001). *St Patrick's Gargoyle*. New York: Ace. In Dublin, Ireland, a gargoyle witnesses a crime and decides to bring the perpetrator to justice.

Lawrence, C. (2002). *The thieves of Ostia: A Roman mystery*. Brookfield, CT: Roaring Brook Press. Four children investigate the beheading of a pet dog in A.D. 79.

Massey, S. (1997). *The salaryman's wife*. New York: HarperPaperbacks. A 27-year-old Japanese American living in Japan visits an ancient castle and becomes involved in a murder.

Mazer, N. F. (1983). *Taking Terry Mueller*. New York: Morrow. When Terri is 14, she learns that her mother is still alive and that her father kidnapped her after the divorce.

McDonald, J. (2001). *Shades of Simon Gray*. New York: Delacorte. What has caused the plagues of frogs and crows in a New Jersey town and does it have anything to do with Simon Gray breaking into the school computers?

Nixon, J. L. (1988). *Secret silent screams*. New York: Delacorte. Almost everyone thinks that Marti's friend Barry committed suicide, but Marti is convinced it was murder.

Nixon, J. L. (1993). *The name of the game was murder*. New York: Delacorte. When her great-uncle blackmails a group of celebrities, Samantha doesn't realize that the game will lead to murder. Other books by Nixon include *Shadowmaker* (1994), *Candidate for Murder* (1991), and *The Weekend Was Murder* (1992).

Nixon, J. L. (2002). *The trap*. New York: Delacorte. When valuables begin to go missing, Julie realizes that a murderer may be nearby.

Paretsky, S. (1982). *Indemnity only*. New York: Dial. What starts as a missing person investigation leads to murder and insurance fraud. A more recent novel in this series is *Total Recall* (2001).

Parker, D. (2002). *The Wessex papers: Trust falls*. New York: Avon. Although each book in this trilogy tells its own story, together they tell one long mystery. The other titles are *Fallout* (2002) and *Outsmart* (2002).

Parker, R. (1973). *The Godwulf manuscript*. Boston: Houghton Mifflin. In this first of the tales of Spencer, a tough private eye, a stolen manuscript leads to murder. A more recent novel in this series is *Potshot* (2001).

Pearson, R. (1988). *Undercurrents*. New York: St. Martin's. Detective Lou Boldt and psychologist Daphne Matthews investigate a series of murders of young women in Seattle. A more recent novel in this series is *Art of Deception* (2002).

Peck, R. (1975). *The ghost belonged to me*. New York: Viking. In 1913, Blossom Culp and friends set out to exorcize a ghost.

Peck, R. (1976). *Are you in the house alone?* New York: Viking. Whenever she babysits, sixteen-year-old Alison gets threatening phone calls.

Perry, A. (1979). *The Cater Street hangman*. New York: St. Martin's. Someone is killing women on Cater Street and it is up to Investigator Thomas Pitt to find the secrets hiding behind the walls of the Victorian mansions. A more recent novel in this series is *Seven Dials* (2003).

Perry, T. (2001). *Pursuit*. New York: Random House. What is the meaning behind the massacre of 13 diners in a local restaurant?

Peters, E. (1977). *A morbid taste for bones*. New York: Morrow. When Brother Cadfael accompanied a group of monks to Wales to bring some holy relics back to England, he was not counting on murder.

Plum-Ucci, C. (2000). *The body of Christopher Creed*. New York: Harcourt. Tory finds that things are not always what they appear to be when he begins a search for a boy in his class who has disappeared.

Pullman, P. (1985). *Ruby in the smoke*. New York: Knopf. In 19th-century London, a young girl looks for the man who killed her father and for a valuable ruby. Other books in this series are *Shadow in the North* (1988) and *Tiger in the Well* (1990).

Qualey, M. (1999). *Close to a killer*. New York: Delacorte. Just because all of the stylists in Barrie's mother's hair salon are convicted murderers doesn't mean that they are involved in the string of killings in Dakota City.

Reiss, K. (1998). *PaperQuake*. San Diego: Harcourt Brace. A force from the past tries to help Violet solve a mystery.

Roberts, W. D. (1996). *Twisted summer*. New York: Atheneum. Cici is trying to solve a murder that took place last summer at the beach. Another book by Roberts is *Undercurrents* (2002).

Robinson, L. (1994). *Murder in the Place of Anubis.* New York: Walker. Egyptian Pharaoh Tutankhamun sends Lord Meren to investigate a murder in the sacred Place of Embalming. A more recent novel in the series is *Slayer of Gods* (2001).

Skurzynski, G., & Ferguson, A. (2002). *Escape from fear.* Washington, DC: National Geographic Society. In St. John National Park, a young boy is searching for his birth mother who, he believes, is in danger. Other books in the series include *Over the Edge* (2002) and *Buried Alive* (2003).

Sykes, S. (1998). *For Mike.* New York: Delacorte. In a blend of mystery, suspense, and romance, Jeff begins an investigation into the disappearance of his friend Mike.

Van Draanen, W. (2003). *Sammy Keyes and the art of deception.* New York: Knopf. Sammy is off to investigate the strange things that are happening at an art gallery. Another book about Sammy is *Sammy Keyes and the Search for Snake Eyes* (2002).

Vande Velde, V. (1999). *Never trust a dead man.* San Diego: Harcourt Brace. When Selwyn is sealed in the tomb of the man he is accused of killing, only a witch can save him.

Werlin, N. (1998). *The killer's cousin.* New York: Delacorte. Acquitted of murder, David goes to live with his aunt and uncle and finds that there is something wrong with his young cousin Lily—she may really be a murderer.

Werlin, N. (2000). *Locked inside.* New York: Delacorte. The story begins with the computer game Paliopolis and ends with Marnie locked in a windowless basement.

Wynne-Jones, T. (2001). *The boy in the burning house.* New York: Farrar, Straus and Giroux. Jim does not know what to believe. Did his father commit suicide or did the local pastor kill him?

Humor—Fiction

Adams, D. (1979). *The hitchhiker's guide to the galaxy.* New York: Harmony. Arthur Dent and Ford Perfect take a very funny journey through outer space.

Bauer, J. (1992). *Squashed.* New York: Delacorte. Ellie stakes everything on winning the Rock River Pumpkin Weigh-In contest with her 611-pound pumpkin.

Bauer, J. (1998). *Rules of the road.* New York: Putnam's. Jenna accepts a summer job driving the elderly president of a shoe company from Chicago to Texas. Other books by Bauer include *Thwonk* (1995) and *Sticks* (1996).

Clark, C. (2000). *Truth or dairy.* New York: HarperTempest. Can Courtney really give up boys until she graduates?

Creech, S. (1995). *Absolutely normal chaos.* New York: HarperCollins. It's a summer of reading, romance, and growing up for 13-year-old Mary Lou.

Cushman, K. (1994). *Catherine, called Birdy.* Boston: Houghton Mifflin. Peek into the diary of a 14-year-old girl in the middle ages and read her attempts to keep her father from finding her a rich husband.

Danziger, P. (1988). *The cat ate my gymsuit.* New York: Dell. Marcy hates everything including herself. Then something changes her life.

Fleischman, P. (1995). *A fate totally worse than death.* Cambridge, MA: Candlewick Press. Is the new exchange student really a ghost? And why are some girls aging so rapidly? Will arthritis and liver spots replace acne as a teenage worry?

Fleischman, S. (1998). *Bandit's moon.* New York: Dell. Joaquin, the bandit, is helping Annyrose Smith find her brother, but there is a reward for Joaquin—dead or alive.

Koertge, R. (1996). *Confess-o-rama*. New York: Orchard. Tony calls the self-help hotline and gets more than he bargained for.

Korman, G. (1993). *Losing Joe's place*. New York: Scholastic. Jason and his friends have Jason's older brother's apartment for the summer until they lose their jobs, fight over girls, and deal with a difficult landlord.

Korman, G. (1996). *The chicken doesn't skate*. New York: Scholastic. Henrietta the chicken goes from being Milo's science project to serving as the mascot of the hockey team.

Korman, G. (2000). *No more dead dogs*. New York: Hyperion. Wallace Wallace, a football player, gets to serve his detention by working on the school play. Other titles by Korman include *Something Fishy at McDonald Hall* (1995), *Semester in the Life of a Garbage Bag* (1987), and *The Twinkie Squad* (1992).

Larson, G. (1998). *There's a hair in my dirt: A worm's story*. New York: HarperCollins. When a young worm finds a hair in his supper, father worm tells him how the hair got there.

Nodelman, P. (1998). *Behaving Bradley*. New York: Simon & Schuster. Eleventh-grader Brad Gold learns about school politics and bureaucracy when he tries to get input for the new code of conduct.

Peck, R. (1998). *A long way from Chicago*. New York: Dial. Grandma Dowdel has her own ways of surviving in the Great Depression as she lies, trespasses, and outwits her neighbors in rural Illinois.

Pinkwater, J. (1989). *Buffalo Brenda*. New York: Macmillan. Things begin to happen when Brenda Tuna takes over the high school newspaper and suggests a live bison for the school mascot.

Pratchett, T. (1983). *The colour of magic*. New York: St. Martin's. Twoflower, the tourist, and Rincewind, his wizard guide, set off into the zany Discworld.

Pratchett, T. (1993). *Men at arms: A novel of Discworld*. New York: Harper. While investigating a murder, Captain Vimes runs into affirmative action in fantasy land.

Pratchett, T. (2001). *Thief of time: A novel of Discworld*. New York: HarperCollins. If Jeremy Clockson builds a totally accurate glass clock, will he be able to put the Grim Reaper out of business?

Snicket, L. (1999). *The bad beginning: A series of unfortunate events, book I*. New York: HarperCollins. Following the sudden death of their parents, the three rich Baudelaire children find they must live with the miserable, mean, money-hungry Count Olaf!

Strasser, T. (1998). *Help! I'm trapped in an alien's body*. New York: Scholastic. Jake switches bodies with a funny looking alien and now Jake wants his own body back.

Strasser, T. (1998). *How I spent my last night on earth*. New York: Simon & Schuster. Allegra "Legs" Hanover does not know whether to believe the rumor about an asteroid headed for earth, but, just in case, there are a few things she wants to do. This is one of the books in the Time Zone High series.

Townsend, S. (1984). *The secret diary of Adrian Mole, aged 13 3/4*. New York: Avon. A 13-year-old English boy keeps a diary of his funny, funny life.

Welter, J. (1996). *I want to buy a vowel: A novel of illegal alienation*. Chapel Hill, NC: Algonquin Books. It's going to be a long summer for Eva Galt after a lady sees the image of the Virgin Mary in a stamp-vending machine and Eva finds a skeleton that may be evidence of ritual sacrifice.

Wrede, P. (1990). *Dealing with dragons*. San Diego: Jane Yolen Books. Cimorene is a very unconventional princess who volunteers to become the captive of the female king of the

Dragons. Other funny books in this fantasy series are *Searching for Dragons* (1991), *Calling on Dragons* (1993), and *Talking to Dragons* (1993).

Wrede, P., & Stevermer, C. (2003). *Sorcery and Cecelia, or the enchanted chocolate pot.*

Orlando: Harcourt. Cecilia and Kate keep each other informed of events in London and the country through their letters about their silly families and the mysterious wizards that they meet.

Suggested Readings

Carroll, S. (2003). Adolescent readers *Flip* for David Lubar. *The ALAN Review, 30*(3), 21.

Nilsen, A. P., & Nilsen, D. L. F. (1999). The straw man meets his match: Six arguments for studying humor in English classes. *English Journal, 88*(4), 34–42.

Reid, R. (2003). *Something funny happened at the library: How to create humorous programs for children and young adults.* Chicago: American Library Association.

Truett, C. (2001). Sherlock Holmes on the Internet: Language arts teams up with the computing librarian. *Learning and leading with technology, 29*(2), 36–41.

Zanarini, A. (2001). Who dun it? Mysteries. *Voices from the Middle, 9*(2), 85–87.

References

(Note: All young adult literature referenced in this chapter are included in the Young Adult Books list and are not repeated in this list.)

Ammon, B. D., & Sherman, G. W. (1999). *More rip-roaring reads for reluctant teen readers.* Englewood, CO: Libraries Unlimited.

Ashley, M. (2002). *The mammoth encyclopedia of modern crime fiction.* New York: Carroll & Graf.

Bauer, J. (1996). Humor, seriously. *The Alan Review, 23*(2), 2–3.

Blume, J. (1972). *Tales of a fourth grade nothing.* New York: Dutton.

Charles, J., & Morrison, J. (2000). Clueless? Adult mysteries with young adult appeal 2000. *Voice of Youth Advocate, 23*(5), 318–321.

Charles, J., Morrison, J., & Clark, C. (2002). *The mystery readers' advisory: The librarian's clues to murder and mayhem.* Chicago: American Library Association.

Cleary, B. (1955). *Beezus and Ramona.* New York: Morrow.

Collins, W. (1860). *The woman in white.* London: Sampson Low.

Collins, W. (1868). *The moonstone: A romance.* London: Tinsley Brothers.

Cooper, J. F. (1850–51). *The leather-stocking tales.* New York: G. P. Putnam.

Crowley, C. (1998). Pathways, pointers and pearls: Interview with Carol Gorman. In J. Grape, D. James, & E. Nehr (Eds.), *Deadly women: The woman mystery reader's indispensable companion* (pp. 255–257). New York: Carroll & Graf.

Dahlin, R. (2002). Publishers are getting really series-ous. *Publisher's Weekly 4/22/2002.* Accessed 12/30/02 http://publishersweekly.reviewsnews.com/index.asp?layout=articlePrint&articleID=CA21357.

Davis, J. (1999). Speaking my mind: On humor. *English Journal, 88*(4), 14–15.

DeAndrea, W. L. (Ed.). (1994). *Encyclopedia mysteriosa: A comprehensive guide to the art of detection in print, film, radio, and television.* New York: Prentice Hall.

Defoe, D. (1719). *The farther adventures of Robinson Crusoe being the second and last part of his life, and of the strange surprising accounts of his travels round three parts of the globe.* London: W. Taylor.

Doyle, A. C. (1900). *The hound of the Baskervilles.* Garden City, NY: Doubleday.

Doyle, A. C. (1887). *A study in scarlet.* London: Ward Lock.

Dunn, A. (1999). "Lit-TEE-raries," or "Getting it off your chest." *English Journal, 88*(4), 56.

Fleischman, S. (1965). *McBroom tells the truth.* New York: W. W. Norton.

Gentile, L. M., & McMillan, M. M. (1978). Humor and the reading program. *Journal of Reading, 21,* 343–349.

George, J. C. (1959). *My side of the mountain.* New York: Dutton.

George, J. C. (1972). *Julie of the wolves.* New York: Harper & Row.

Hale, L. P. (1880). *The Peterkin papers.* Boston: James R. Osgood.

Heising, W. L. (1998). *Detecting men: A reader's guide and checklist for mystery series written by men.* Dearborn, MI: Purple Moon Press.

Heising, W. L. (2000). *Detecting women: A reader's guide and checklist for mystery series written by women.* Dearborn, MI: Purple Moon Press.

Herbert, R. (Ed.). (1999). *Oxford companion to crime and mystery writing.* New York: Oxford University Press.

Hoffert, B. (1998). The book report: What public libraries buy and how much they spend. *Library Journal, 123*(3), 106–110.

Howe, J. (1979). *Bunnicula: A rabbit tale of mystery.* New York: Atheneum.

Howe, J. (1995). Mirth & mayhem: Humor and mystery in children's books. *Voices from the Middle, 2*(3), 4–9.

Huang, J. (Ed.). (2000). *100 favorite mysteries of the century: Selected by the Independent Mystery Booksellers Association.* Carmel, IN: Crum Creek Press.

Jalonga, M. R. (1985). Children's literature: There's some sense to its humor. *Childhood Education, 62,* 109–114.

Junger, S. (1998). *The perfect storm: A true story of men against the sea.* New York: HarperPaperbacks.

Keating, H. R. F. (1987). *Crime & mystery: The 100 best books.* New York: Carroll & Graf.

Klesius, J., Laframboise, K. L., & Gaier, M. (1998). Humorous literature: Motivation for reluctant readers. *Reading Research and Instruction, 37*(4), 253–261.

Krakauer, J. (1996). *Into the wild.* New York: Villard Books.

Krakauer, J. (1998). *Into thin air: A personal account of the Mount Everest disaster.* New York: Anchor Books.

Kuchner, J. (1991). *The humor of your children.* (Report No. PS 020 516.) Paper presented at the National Association for the Education of Young Children. (Eric Document Reproduction Service No. 348-139)

Lesesne, T. (2000). A passion for humor: An interview with Joan Bauer. *Teacher Librarian, 27*(3), 60–62.

Lewis, P. (1995). Why humor. *Voices from the Middle, 2*(3), 10–16.

McGhee, P. E. (1979). *Humor: Its origin and development.* San Francisco: Freeman.

McInnes, M. (1995). Backing into the hallway, one step at a time. *Voices from the Middle, 2*(3), 17–19.

Monson, D., & Sebesta, S. (1991). Reading preferences. In J. Flood, J. M. Jensen, D. Lapp, & J. R. Squire (Eds.), *Handbook of research on teaching the English language arts* (pp. 664–673). New York: Macmillan.

Moody, S. (Ed.). (1990). *Hatchards crime companion: The top 100 crime novels selected by the Crime Writer's Association.* London: Hatchards.

Morris, B. S. (1999). Why is George so funny? Television comedy, trickster heroism, and cultural studies. *English Journal, 88*(4), 47–52.

Murphy, B. F. (1999). *The encyclopedia of murder and mystery.* New York: St. Martin's Minotaur.

Muse, D. (1999). Detectives, dubious dudes, spies, and suspense in African-American fiction for children and young adults. *Multicultural Education, 6*(3), 37–41.

Nichols, V., & Thompson, S. (2000). *Silk stalkings: More women write of murder.* Lanham, MD: Scarecrow Press.

Nixon, J. L. (1994). Juvenile mysteries. In W. L. DeAndrea (Ed.), *Encyclopedia mysteriosa: A comprehensive guide to the art of detection in print, film, radio, and television* (pp. 186–187). New York: Prentice Hall.

O'Dell, S. (1960). *Island of the blue dolphins.* Boston: Houghton Mifflin.

Paul, B. (1999). Putting an end to the mystery. In H. Windrath (Ed.), *They wrote the book: Thirteen women mystery writers tell all* (pp. 121–130). Duluth, MN: Spinsters Ink.

Pederson, J. P. (Ed.). (1996). *St. James guide to crime & mystery writers.* Detroit: St. James Press.

Poe, E. A. (1841). *The murders in the Rue Morgue.* Philadelphia. (No publisher is listed)

Poe, E. A. (1844). The purloined letter. *Chamber's Edinburgh Journal, 2*(48), 343–347.

Reid, R. A. (1999). Suspense novel. In R. Herbert (Ed.), *Oxford companion to crime and mystery writing* (pp. 437–438). New York: Oxford University Press.

Rigby, N. (1999). Adventure story. In R. Herbert (Ed.), *The Oxford companion to crime and mystery writing* (pp. 7–8). New York: Oxford University Press.

Rothermel, D. (1995). What's so funny in 303? *Voices from the Middle, 2*(3), 20–25.

Ruggieri, C. A. (1999). Laugh and learn: Using humor to teach tragedy. *English Journal, 88*(4), 53–58.

Russell, D. L. (2001). *Literature for children: A short introduction.* New York: Longman.

Shimberg, A., & Grant, H. M. (1998). Who-dun-it? A mystery thematic unit. *Science Activities, 35*(3), 29–35.

Stevenson, R. L. (1883). *Treasure island.* London: Casell.

Swanson, J., & Dean, J. (1998). *Killer books: A reader's guide to exploring the popular world of mystery and suspense.* New York: Berkley Prime Crime.

Tatum, T. (1999). Cruel and unusual PUNishment (LOW humor is better then NO humor). *English Journal, 88*(4), 62–64.

Travers, P. L. (1934). *Mary Poppins.* New York: Harcourt, Brace.

Twain, M. (1876). *The adventures of Tom Sawyer.* Hartford, CT: American Publishing.

Twain, M. (1884). *Adventures of Huckleberry Finn (Tom Sawyer's comrade).* New York: Charles L. Webster.

Yep, L. (2003). The knife that cuts: Writing mysteries for young readers. *Booklist, 99*(17), 1521.

EXPLORING
HISTORICAL FICTION

In addition to telling a good story, historical fiction provides readers with information about life, customs, and events in the past while it takes readers into the lives of the characters.

> [Historical fiction] makes us feel . . . what otherwise would be dead and lost to us. It transports us into the past. And the very best historical fiction presents to us a TRUTH of the past that is NOT the truth of the history books, but a bigger truth, a more important truth—a truth of the HEART. (Lee, 2000)

Although many young adults know the important dates and events in history and realize that historical events occurred many years ago, it is often difficult for adolescents to comprehend the magnitude of historical changes and also how historical events affected many aspects of people's lives. By going beyond the mere presentation of facts, young adult historical fiction allows adolescents to explore history though the eyes of characters their own age. They can see how the Civil War changed families and the nation; how the Salem witchcraft trials brought fear and threats; and how people have struggled to achieve personal and national freedom.

Thankfully, both adult and young adult readers can enjoy the current resurgence of interest in historical novels. Not only have a number of mainstream adult writers such as Michael Crichton, John Grisham, and Amy Tan begun to write in the genre (Nesbeitt,

2002), but a number of historical fiction books have won major awards and prizes. In 2001, historical novels won the Pulitzer Prize for Fiction in the United States, the Booker Prize in Great Britain, and the Governor General's Literary Award in Canada. Recent historical fiction adult best sellers have included Charles Frazier's *Cold Mountain* (1997), Tracy Chevalier's *Girl with a Pearl Earring* (1999), and Arthur Golden's *Memoirs of a Geisha* (1997). In the children's and young adult world, from 1996 to 2005, seven historical fiction novels won the Newbery Award. The award went to Avi in 2003 for *Crispin, The Cross of Lead* (2002); Linda Sue Park in 2002 for *A Single Shard* (2001); Richard Peck in 2001 for *A Year Down Yonder* (2000); Christopher Paul Curtis in 2000 for *Bud, Not Buddy* (1999); and Karen Hesse in 1998 for *Out of the Dust* (1997). Books such as Laurie Halse Anderson's *FEVER 1793* (2000) have shown up as an ALA Best Book for Young Adults, a New York Public Library Best Books for the Teen Age, and an IRA Teacher's Choice, while Aidan Chambers' *Postcards from No Man's Land* (2002), a book that interweaves contemporary and historical fiction, won both Britain's Carnegie Medal and America's Michael Printz award. In 2002, historical fiction author Karen Hesse became the second young adult author (the first was Virginia Hamilton) to win a prestigious "Genius" fellowship from the John D. and Catherine T. MacArthur Foundation.

FOCUSING POINTS   *In this chapter, you will read about:*

1. *The historical predecessors of historical fiction;*
2. *Types, themes and values of historical fiction;*
3. *Reasons for using and teaching historical fiction;*
4. *Criteria for evaluating and selecting well-written historical fiction;*
5. *Changing perspectives toward historical fiction and the issues surrounding historical fiction today; and*
6. *Recommended titles and authors of historical fiction for young adults.*

HISTORICAL FICTION

What exactly is historical fiction? Most writers and educators agree that it is fiction that is set in the past. The problem seems to revolve around the definition of "the past." Is a contemporary novel that was written 5 years ago now historical fiction? What about a contemporary novel that was written 50 years ago? Does a novel have to be written orig-inally as historical fiction or can a contemporary novel become historical fiction as time marches forward and the contemporary events become history? What role does the age of the author and/or the age of the reader play in this definition?

According to *Merriam Webster's Encyclopedia of Literature* (1995), a historical novel is one that

> has as its setting a period of history and that attempts to convey the spirit, manners, and social conditions of a past age with realistic detail and fidelity to historical fact. (p. 549)

Some others set additional criteria. For example, the periodical *Historical Novels Review* indicates that a historical novel must be set at least 50 years in the past and that the au-thor must base the book on historical research rather than on personal experiences (Nesbeitt, 2002). While these criteria might be appropriate for adult historical fiction, young adult novels are written for readers to whom anything that happened 15 years ago is historical. Thus, in our discussions, we will define historical fiction as a novel that was set in the past when it was originally written and that takes place at least one generation (approximately 15 to 20 years) in the past from the date of its original pub-lication. We will also apply Nesbeitt's (2002) criteria that the historical period is so well represented in the novel that the story could not have been set in any other time or place in history. Suggestions for Collaborative Efforts 6–1 explores one way to use his-torical fiction as a basis for examining history.

SUGGESTIONS FOR COLLABORATIVE EFFORTS

In addition to its literary value, historical fiction, with its links to actual events and people, can be used in social studies classes as well as language arts classes.

- One technique to use historical fiction is to have students do fact checking by identifying elements of the story pertaining to food, clothing, shelter, social norms, government, and education. Then, with the help of the library media specialist and social studies teacher, students can check these elements against the facts of history.

- Pair historical fiction books with nonfiction books that cover the same events or time periods. Then have students compare and contrast the information from both books, checking for accuracy of the information. Thus, the *Diary of Anne Frank,* a biography, can be paired with a historical fiction book such as *The Devil's Arithmetic* (Yolen, 1988) or *Good Night, Maman* (Mazer, 1999).

- Use the American Memory Website of the Library of Congress to check facts; to correlate the fictional events in a historical novel to actual historical photographs, recordings, and other primary source materials; and to provide information that students can use to create their own historical fiction.

However, regardless of the historical period being written about, good writers of historical fiction achieve a sense of authenticity, whereby readers believe that the cultural, social, and political events as well as the feelings, joys, disappointments, and frustrations of the characters actually could have happened. Without using artificiality or sensationalism, good historical novels genuinely relate historical perspectives to the plot, setting, and characters so that, as contemporary adolescents view the past through the eyes of characters who are their own age, they learn not only about the past, but how that past has contributed to the world as it exists today. As author Katherine Paterson says: "When we write about . . . the past, we are really writing about our present . . . shedding light on our own time . . . . History becomes a pair of spectacles to focus our vision on the chaotic present" (Johnson & Giorgis, 2001/2002, p. 400).

A Brief Look at Historical Fiction's Predecessors

Historical fiction began as a genre for adults in the 1800s with the writings of Sir Walter Scott such as The *Waverley* novels (1822) and *Ivanhoe* (1820) and continued with classics such as Leo Tolstoy's *War and Peace* (1869). Along the way, a number of other not-so-notable novels featured a historical setting only as a backdrop for improbable adventures (*Merriam Webster's Encyclopedia of Literature,* 1995).

During the late 19th century, Charlotte Yonge's *The Dove in the Eagle's Nest* (1866) and Howard Pyle's *Otto of the Silver Hand* (1888) were among a number of historical fiction books written for children. After a decline in popularity during the early 20th century, children's historical fiction flourished again after the 1930s with books such as Laura Ingalls Wilder's *Little House* series, Elizabeth Forbes' *Johnny Tremaine* (1943), and Elizabeth George Speare's *Witch of Blackbird Pond* (1958) (Hillman, 2003).

Another decline came in the 1970s when the youth rebellion and the maxim of not trusting anyone over 30 led to a rejection of historical fiction (Russell, 2001). In the 1980s, according to Leo Garfield, historical fiction was "something of an embarrassment . . . tolerated out of a sense of duty and reluctantly supported in a condition of genteel poverty" (Brown, 1998, p. 7). The emphasis in young adult literature was, instead, on contemporary realistic fiction and nonfiction.

However, by the late 1990s, historical fiction was again popular with adolescents as publishers produced both series and stand-alone novels (Brown, 1998). A number of writers of young adult literature turned to the genre including Avi, Christopher Curtis, Karen Cushman, Karen Hesse, Walter Dean Myers, Katherine Paterson, Anne Rinaldi, and Mildred Taylor. Expanding Your Knowledge with the Internet 6–1 provides links to information about a few of these authors.

Types of Historical Fiction

While a number of ways exist to categorize historical fiction, perhaps the most basic is to divide the genre into two broad types. First, some novels are set in the past but not directly tied to specific historical events or to actual historical characters. While the characters and their behaviors are appropriate for the historical setting, they are the creation of the author. In contrast, some novels relate directly to actual historical events with factual supporting characters and, perhaps, a fictitious protagonist. In between

EXPANDING | *YOUR KNOWLEDGE WITH THE INTERNET 6–1*

 The Internet has information on some of the outstanding authors of young adult historical fiction. Here are a few samples. Links to these and many additional sites are found on this book's Companion Website at www.prenhall.com/bucher.

Ann Rinaldi
www.annrinaldi.com/

Karen Cushman
www.eduplace.com/author/cushman/

Walter Dean Myers
www.randomhouse.com/teachers/authors/myer.html

these two extremes are novels with a mixture of historical and fictional events and characters (see Figure 6–1).

For example, Anne Rinaldi's *Mine Eyes Have Seen* (1998) is based on historical events and actual characters. Through the eyes of his adolescent daughter, readers watch abolitionist John Brown plot the attack on the U.S. Arsenal at Harper's Ferry, West Virginia, and a slave revolt. In contrast, using an actual historical event, Laurie Halse Anderson sets her novel *FEVER 1793* (2000) during the yellow fever epidemic in Philadelphia, Pennsylvania, but has a cast of fictional characters. While the book provides an accurate description of the life and times of the busy port city, protagonist Mattie Cook is the author's creation. Finally, although Robert Cormier sets his *Frenchtown Summer* (1999) in a post-World War I community, the novel is mainly about a young boy facing problems and trying to understand his conflicting emotions about his life and family.

FIGURE 6–1 *Continuum of Historical Fiction*

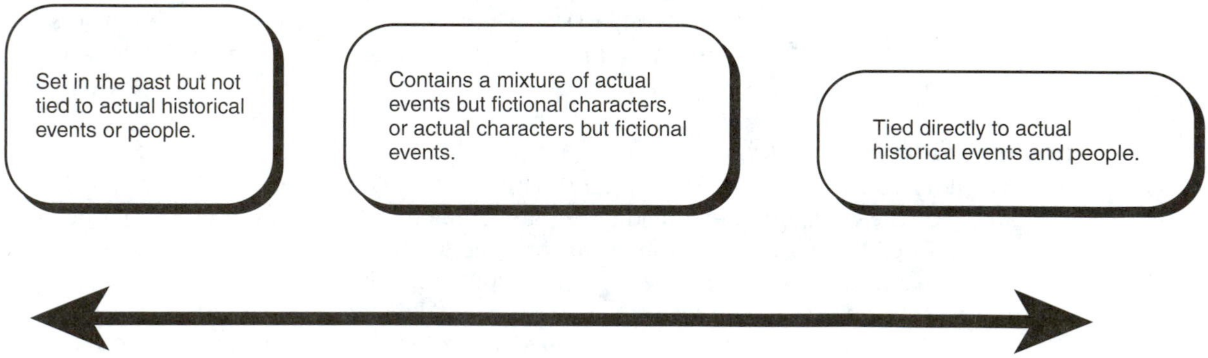

Set in the past but not tied to actual historical events or people.

Contains a mixture of actual events but fictional characters, or actual characters but fictional events.

Tied directly to actual historical events and people.

Themes in Historical Fiction

Another way to categorize historical fiction is to look at some of the recurring themes that appear in the novels. As you might expect, historical novels often focus on the clash of cultures, the human cost of war, the quest for individual and group freedom, the overcoming of disease and disabling conditions, and the struggle to survive the challenges of everyday life.

Clashes of Cultures. People have long fought to protect and to honor their cultures for a number of reasons: they considered their culture superior and thought others should embrace their culture as well; they thought others wanted to destroy their culture; and/or they considered their cultural heritages and traditions worthy of honor and worthy of protection. Understandably, young adult literature reflects these cultural clashes and their effects on peoples' lives.

Authors such as Kirkpatrick Hill in *Minuk: Ashes in the Pathway* (2002), Scott O'Dell in the classic *The King's Fifth* (1966), Caroline Cooney in *The Ransom of Mercy Carter* (2001), Joseph Bruchac in *The Arrow Over the Door* (1998), and Beatrice Harrell in *Longwalker's Journey: A Novel of the Choctaw Trail of Tears* (1999) have written young adult novels about the clash of American Indian and European cultures. In Virginia Euwer Wolff's *Bat 6* (1998), cultural prejudices left over from World War II simmer in a community and come to the surface during a girl's softball game, and in *Beacon Hill Boys* (Mochizuki, 2002), a young boy becomes an activist for Asian American rights in Seattle.

Other books look at cultural clashes in other countries. In *Forgotten Fire* (Bagdasarian, 2000), the tensions between Turks and Armenians erupt in the Armenian massacres of the early 20th century, and in *Neela: Victory Song* (Divakaruni, 2002), a 12-year-old girl becomes involved in India's fight for independence. Cathryn Clinton's *A Stone in My Hand* (2002) is set in a Palestinian community during the intifada of the late 1980s and provides some background on the current fighting in the region.

Wars and Conflicts. Many times clashes over culture and individual or group freedoms lead to war. Figure 6–2 shows a web of young adult historical fiction novels related to the American Civil War, while Figure 6–3 is a book web of novels related to World War II. Other novels about war include Theresa Breslin's *Remembrance* (2002), which shows the effect of World War I on five British teenagers; Walter Dean Myers' *Fallen Angels* (1988), which looks at the Vietnam War; and Brian Burks' *Soldier Boy* (1997), which follows a young boy from Chicago to Custer's Cavalry.

The Quest For Freedom. Throughout history, freedom has meant different things to different people. While some protagonists may be attempting to flee the bonds of actual slavery or imprisonment, other protagonists may be attempting to break free of the social or cultural rules and traditions which limit their freedom. Juan in the classic *I, Juan De Pareja* (de Trevino, 1965) risks everything to paint in spite of the fact that he is a Spanish slave to the artist Velazquez, while Lyddie tries to escape the servitude of being a mill girl in the Lowell, Massachusetts, textiles mills in *Lyddie* (Paterson, 1991).

FIGURE 6-2 Historical Fiction About the American Civil War

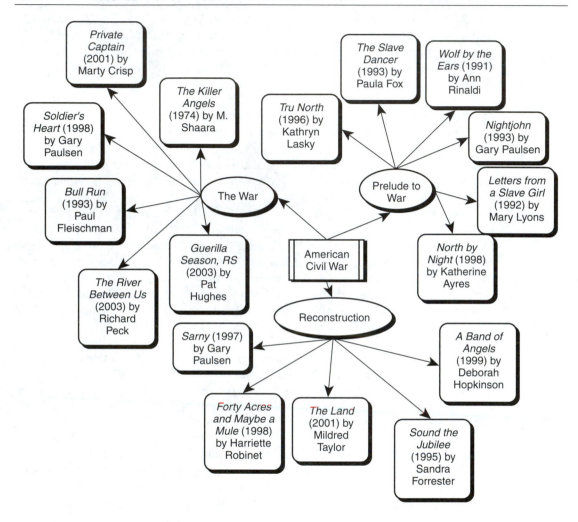

Many times, freedom is associated with attaining civil rights and equal treatment under the law. In Karen Hesse's *Witness* (2001), a young Jewish girl and an African American girl both learn about bigotry when the Ku Klux Klan comes to Vermont. In *The Watsons Go to Birmingham, 1963* (1995), Christopher Paul Curtis contrasts the full loving Watsons' life with the terror of a church bombing in Birmingham, Alabama. Other historical fiction books that look at Civil Rights in the United States include John Armistead's *The Return of Gabriel* (2002), Sue Monk Kidd's *The Secret Life of Bees* (2002), and Chris Crowe's *The Mississippi Trial, 1955* (2002).

FIGURE 6-3 *Historical Fiction About World War II*

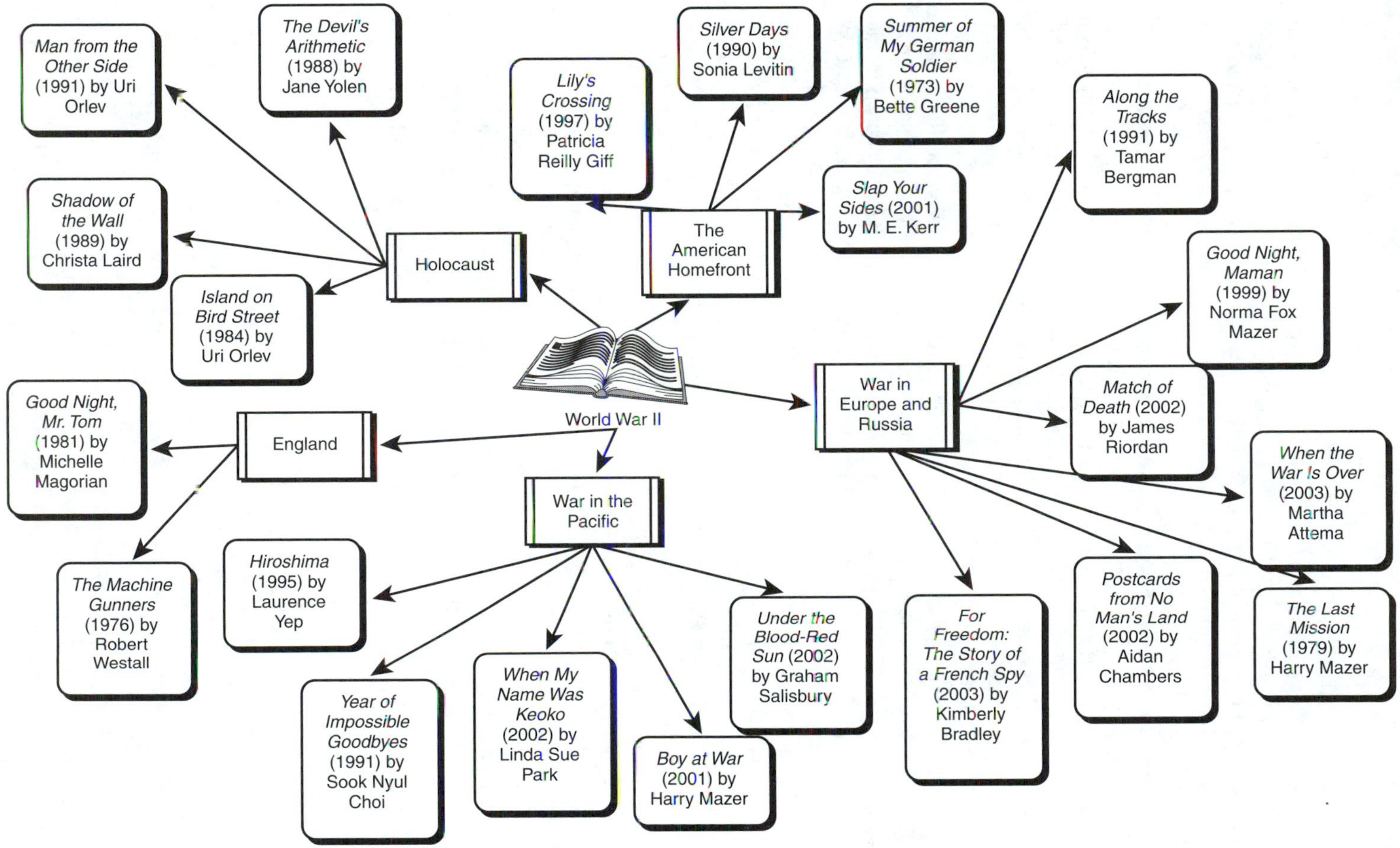

World War II

War in Europe and Russia
- Along the Tracks (1991) by Tamar Bergman
- Good Night, Maman (1999) by Norma Fox Mazer
- When the War Is Over (2003) by Martha Attema
- The Last Mission (1979) by Harry Mazer
- Match of Death (2002) by James Riordan
- Postcards from No Man's Land (2002) by Aidan Chambers
- For Freedom: The Story of a French Spy (2003) by Kimberly Bradley

The American Homefront
- Summer of My German Soldier (1973) by Bette Greene
- Slap Your Sides (2001) by M. E. Kerr
- Silver Days (1990) by Sonia Levitin
- Lily's Crossing (1997) by Patricia Reilly Giff

Holocaust
- The Devil's Arithmetic (1988) by Jane Yolen
- Island on Bird Street (1984) by Uri Orlev
- Man from the Other Side (1991) by Uri Orlev
- Shadow of the Wall (1989) by Christa Laird

England
- Good Night, Mr. Tom (1981) by Michelle Magorian
- The Machine Gunners (1976) by Robert Westall

War in the Pacific
- Under the Blood-Red Sun (2002) by Graham Salisbury
- Boy at War (2001) by Harry Mazer
- When My Name Was Keoko (2002) by Linda Sue Park
- Year of Impossible Goodbyes (1991) by Sook Nyul Choi
- Hiroshima (1995) by Laurence Yep

161

Other authors look at freedom in other parts of the world. In *Before We Were Free* (Alvarez, 2002), Anita and her family are involved in the underground movement that is trying to end dictator General Trujillo's rule in the Dominican Republic. Su Phan tells about her life growing up in North Vietnam in *Sing for Your Father, Su Phan* (Pevsner & Tang, 1997), and Ying flees an arranged marriage in China in *Child Bride* (Russell, 1999).

Overcoming Natural Disasters, Death, Disease, and Disabling Conditions. The overcoming of a variety of tragedies and disabilities is another recurring theme in young adult historical fiction. Billie Jo in Karen Hesse's *Out of the Dust* (1997) not only copes with the Dust Bowl in Oklahoma, but also the violent death of her mother. Nat Field's response to his father's suicide in Susan Cooper's *The King of Shadows* (1999) is to journey back in time to Elizabethan London to perform at the Globe Theater where he meets William Shakespeare.

At many times in history, people have had to fight to survive pestilence and disease. In *FEVER, 1793* (Anderson, 2000), Mattie flees the yellow fever epidemic. In *A Time of Angels* (Hesse, 1995), Hanna strives to help her family survive the Boston influenza epidemic of 1918. A young girl and her family try to survive the Irish potato famine in *Nory Ryan's Song* (Giff, 2000), and a plague almost destroys an English village in *A Parcel of Patterns* (Walsh, 1983).

There are many types of disabling conditions. In *The Dark Light* (Newth, 1998), a young girl in the 19th century is diagnosed with leprosy. The 14-year-old boy in *Charlie Wilcox* (McKay, 2000) tries to disprove everyone's belief that his club foot makes him unfit for work in his Newfoundland community in 1915 by stowing away on what he thinks is a seal hunting ship only to find himself on a troop ship headed for Europe. Sometimes a disabling condition comes after a trauma. In *Motorcycle Ride on the Sea of Tranquility* (Santana, 2002), a young Hispanic girl tries to help her brother deal with his emotional problems when he returns home from the Vietnam War.

Surviving the Challenges of Everyday Life. In the past, the mere attempt to survive from day to day has often been a struggle for a number of people. In *The Birchbark House* (1999), Louise Erdrich tells about the daily life of an Ojibwa family in 1847; in *The Ballad of Lucy Whipple* (1996), Karen Cushman tells about life in the California gold fields; in *Search of the Moon King's Daughter* (2002), Linda Holeman describes life in Dickensian London; and in *The Borning Room* (1991), Paul Fleischman tells the history of a single family through the events that take place in one room in their home. Sometimes survival is a life or death matter as Mary Chase finds out in Kathryn Lasky's *Beyond the Burning Time* (1994) when her mother is accused of being a witch.

Humor can go a long way toward helping people through the challenges of everyday life. Richard Peck is a master with several stories set in the past, including *Fair Weather* (2001), *A Long Way from Chicago* (1998), and *A Year Down Yonder* (2000). In *Harris and Me* (1993), Gary Paulsen tells the very funny tale of a young city boy who is sent to live with his country cousins for the summer.

By using a diary format, authors can take readers inside the daily lives of characters. In *Catherine, Called Birdy* (1994), Karen Cushman goes back to 1290 as a young girl tells about her attempts to keep her father from selecting her husband. Sometimes the diary keepers come from higher stations in life. In the Royal Diaries series, Carolyn Meyer tells the story of *Anastasia: The Last Grand Duchess, Russia, 1914* (2000), while Kathryn Lasky provides the diary of *Marie Antoinette: Princess of Versailles, Austria-France, 1769* (2000). These diaries take readers into the lives of historical characters through fiction rather than through biographies. Connecting Adolescents and Their Literature 6–1 explores using literature to examine social issues.

Chronology of Young Adult Historical Fiction

A final way to categorize historical fiction for young adults is to arrange books chronologically according to the time period presented in the book. Many of the bibliographies listed later in this chapter categorize historical fiction by historical period. In Figure 6-4, we have tried to provide a list of a few selected young adult historical fiction novels that present a worldview of historical events. Of course, the books mentioned earlier in this chapter or in Figures 6–2 and 6–3 could also be added to the chronology.

Reasons for Using and Teaching Historical Fiction

Why should we encourage young adults to read historical fiction? Haven't most professionals at some time heard young people complain of reading about history? Don't many young adults prefer contemporary realism? While there might be some validity

---

CONNECTING   **ADOLESCENTS AND THEIR LITERATURE 6–1**

Developmentally, adolescents begin to explore their feelings about themselves and the world around them when they are in middle school. Toni Sills-Briegel and Deanne Camp (2001) suggest using excerpts from a variety of genres to focus on selected social issues or problems. This idea can be expanded by using entire works of historical fiction rather than just excerpts and by using the technique with older adolescents as well. Here are a few examples:

Facing the constraints of family and society
A Northern Light (Donnelly, 2003)

Rights and freedoms for all people
Saturnalia (Fleischman, 1990)

Growing up in an inner city
Jazmin's Notebook (Grimes, 1998)

Civil Rights for everyone
Kinship (Krisher, 1997)

Challenges for immigrants
An Ocean Apart, a World Away (Namioka, 2002)

Figure 6-4   Chronology of Selected Historical Fiction

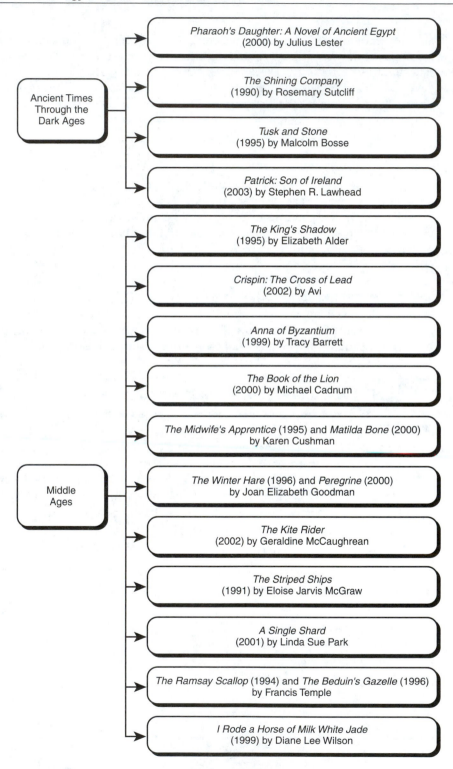

Ancient Times Through the Dark Ages

- *Pharaoh's Daughter: A Novel of Ancient Egypt* (2000) by Julius Lester
- *The Shining Company* (1990) by Rosemary Sutcliff
- *Tusk and Stone* (1995) by Malcolm Bosse
- *Patrick: Son of Ireland* (2003) by Stephen R. Lawhead

Middle Ages

- *The King's Shadow* (1995) by Elizabeth Alder
- *Crispin: The Cross of Lead* (2002) by Avi
- *Anna of Byzantium* (1999) by Tracy Barrett
- *The Book of the Lion* (2000) by Michael Cadnum
- *The Midwife's Apprentice* (1995) and *Matilda Bone* (2000) by Karen Cushman
- *The Winter Hare* (1996) and *Peregrine* (2000) by Joan Elizabeth Goodman
- *The Kite Rider* (2002) by Geraldine McCaughrean
- *The Striped Ships* (1991) by Eloise Jarvis McGraw
- *A Single Shard* (2001) by Linda Sue Park
- *The Ramsay Scallop* (1994) and *The Beduin's Gazelle* (1996) by Francis Temple
- *I Rode a Horse of Milk White Jade* (1999) by Diane Lee Wilson

Figure 6-4   Continued

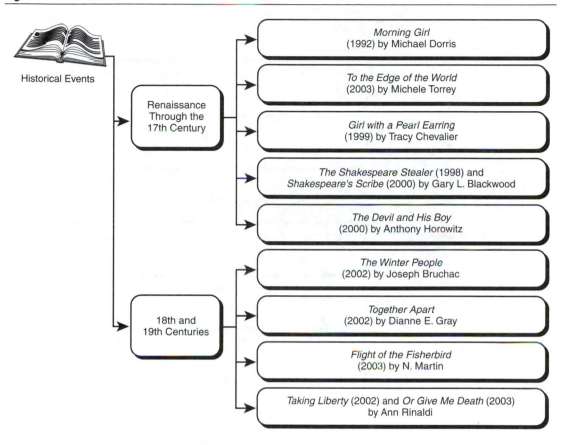

Historical Events

Renaissance
Through the
17th Century

Morning Girl
(1992) by Michael Dorris

To the Edge of the World
(2003) by Michele Torrey

Girl with a Pearl Earring
(1999) by Tracy Chevalier

The Shakespeare Stealer (1998) and
Shakespeare's Scribe (2000) by Gary L. Blackwood

The Devil and His Boy
(2000) by Anthony Horowitz

18th and
19th Centuries

The Winter People
(2002) by Joseph Bruchac

Together Apart
(2002) by Dianne E. Gray

Flight of the Fisherbird
(2003) by N. Martin

Taking Liberty (2002) and Or Give Me Death (2003)
by Ann Rinaldi

to each of these viewpoints, a number of reasons exist to use interesting, well-written historical fiction with adolescents.

Historical fiction helps adolescents make connections between the past and the present, to view problems and situations over a period of time, and to place events in a historical context. As adolescents vicariously experience the past with its conflicts, joys, and challenges, they can see how a single decision may have far-reaching ramifications. Young adults, like most people today, feel a sense of preoccupation with daily events. These preoccupations vary with age and developmental period, and may differ from those of previous times. However, through historical fiction, readers may see that there are some concerns that have remained constant throughout the ages. For example, while adolescents today do not concern themselves with traveling west in a covered wagon, many contemporary young adults do deal with problems that have concerned individuals for centuries: honesty, developing friendships, overcoming loneliness, dealing with crime and criminals, finding a place in society, and dealing with family members.

Figure 6-4 Continued

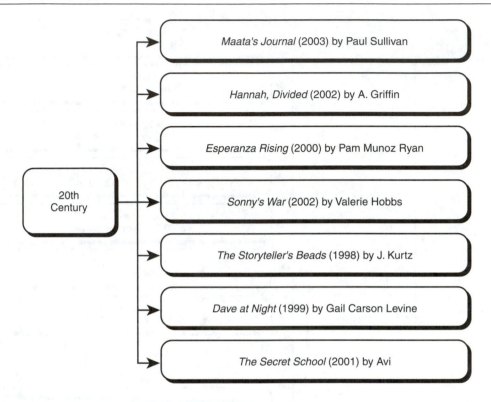

Charlotte in *The True Confessions of Charlotte Doyle* (Avi, 1990) faces a personal struggle. In other examples, Stone confronts discrimination in *Just Like Martin* (Davis, 1992), Ben learns about the challenges associated with family problems in *Borderlands* (Carter, 1990), and Celeste appreciates the power of friendships in *The Starplace* (Grove, 1999). By reading about these characters, their lives, and the difficult decisions that they needed to make, readers are drawn into the decision-making process. By exploring the extremes of human behavior, readers can focus on the cause and effects of events, the results of human behavior, and the consequences of human actions as well as the impact that events can have on personal choices (Nawrot, 1996).

Young adult historical fiction also encourages readers to think beyond historical events. Adolescents can read social studies and history texts to learn "facts"—those events that shaped the nation and the world. However, much is lost when young adults learn historical events yet fail to perceive the human perspectives surrounding the events. Historical fiction helps readers develop a context for the names, dates, and events of history. While textbooks focus on the results of an action, historical fiction allows readers to look at why that action occurred. Although history provides objective analysis, historical fiction offers synthesis. With a textbook, the reader is on the outside, looking in. With historical fiction, the reader becomes involved in the events and the lives of the people in the story (Nawrot, 1996).

For example, many history books provide the events of the Civil War—the reasons, the states, the battles, and numbers killed. While this information is undoubtedly important, young adults also need an understanding of the human perspectives such as the suffering the war brought, its effects on family relationships, and the terror and worry. War tears friends apart in *The Best of Friends* (Rostokowski, 1989) and families apart in *My Brother Sam Is Dead* (Collier & Collier, 1974). Readers can begin to appreciate the feelings that convince an escaped slave to join the Union Army in *Which Way to Freedom* (Hansen, 1986) and can wonder at the hostile attitudes of Americans during the Vietnam War in *The Road Home* (White, 1995).

Young adult historical fiction also helps readers to identify and judge the mistakes of the past. Our nation and its peoples, both collectively and individually, have made errors in the past—attitudes and actions that young adults will want to understand and strive to avoid. Bilof suggests using historical fiction in high schools to provide a "credible insight into the motive forces and values of the era or society under study" (Bilof, 1996, p. 19). Because historical fiction allows readers to see historical and societal events from various perspectives, it is an excellent genre to help adolescents understand their own cultural heritage as well as the heritage of other ethnic groups.

Finally, historical fiction is ideal for use in an integrated curriculum and with literature-based approaches across the disciplines. Young adult historical fiction can address the problem of history being taught from a singular dimension void of human emotion or from an approach that does not show the interrelationships among the disciplines. Readers can benefit when they learn about the "human" aspects of historical and societal events and when they see relationships among subject areas.

Characteristics of Good Historical Fiction

As we have cautioned with other genres of young adult literature, you should select historical fiction for young adults carefully. Perhaps, more than in any other genre, historical fiction calls for interweaving of both fiction and nonfiction because historical fiction should be both good history and good fiction. Without stereotyping, historical fiction must be true to the time period and reflect the values and attitudes of the historical period presented in the novel. The accurate details of daily life in a given time period dictate what a character can and cannot do (Clarke, 1999). For example, a character cannot use a kerosene lamp or take photographs in the 1600s or talk about being strong as steel or escaping a mob in the 1700s. These inventions and expressions simply did not exist at that time. While being well written and entertaining, historical fiction must also be well researched with characters who are true to their time period. In addition, the language must fit the period and the person while still being understandable to a modern reader.

Because some readers may accept everything in the novel as true, an author must constantly ask himself or herself two questions: (a) How historically accurate must this be? (b) What fiction is acceptable and/or necessary? According to author Chris Crowe, it is difficult to blend fact and fiction because "the fictional plot and characters . . . [keep]

bumping up against real history" (Blassingame, 2003, p. 24). Thus, an author must constantly recheck facts in an attempt to be faithful to the actual historical events.

However, historical accuracy is not everything. Caro Clarke (1999) maintains that good historical fiction demonstrates a balance between story and fact and that a good writer must know what history to include and what to omit. "The good historical novel is the wise selection of the right fact for the right effect. It doesn't surfeit . . . [readers] by too much information; it doesn't starve them with too little . . . in the end, it is the story that must rule" (Clarke, 1999).

While authors of historical fiction are writing about the past, they are still influenced by their own political, economic, social, or religious biases. Even historical fiction is a reflection of the time in which it is written as well as the time that it portrays (Brown, 1998). Some authors of historical fiction have a definite agenda to present, a cause to advance, or a perceived wrong to right. In addition, history is constantly being revised as contemporary society reflects on its own past (Lee, 2000). Views on topics such as colonialism and imperialism, the role of women, yesterday's heroes, the contributions of minorities, and the government treatment of individuals and groups have changed through the years. These changes are often reflected in historical fiction and are discussed in more detail later in this chapter. Considerations for Selecting Young Adult Literature: *Historical Fiction* outlines additional criteria that you will want to keep in mind when examining historical fiction.

Suggestions for Selecting and Teaching Historical Fiction

Unless you are a historian, it may be difficult for you to evaluate the historical accuracy in historical fiction. Thankfully, there are a number of awards, prizes, bibliographies, and web sites that can help you select quality historical fiction. Expanding Your Knowledge with the Internet 6–2 provides information on Internet resources.

CONSIDERATIONS | **For Selecting Young Adult Literature:** | **HISTORICAL FICTION**

When evaluating historical fiction, ask the following questions:

◉ Is the plot interesting and enjoyable?

◉ Are the historical events accurate and authentic?

◉ Do the background details reflect the historical period?

◉ Do the events, attitudes, and behaviors reflect the values and spirit of the time?

◉ Are various points of view represented?

◉ Is the dialogue realistic and conversational in tone?

◉ Are the characters and situations believable?

◉ Are the events, actions, and situations historically possible and plausible?

◉ Do the themes provide insights into contemporary problems?

EXPANDING	YOUR KNOWLEDGE WITH THE INTERNET 6-2

 On the Internet, you can find information on many awards and prizes, bibliographies, and teaching resources. Here are just a few of them:

Awards and Prizes

Scott O'Dell Historical Fiction Award www.scottodell.com/sosoaward.html

Bibliographies of Historical Fiction For Young Adults

New Lenox Public Library www.newlenoxlibrary.org/historicalfiction.htm

Library of Congress—American Memory

memory.loc.gov

Links to these and many additional sites are found on this book's Companion Website at www.prenhall.com/bucher.

Awards and Best Books Lists. The oldest award for historical fiction is the Scott O'Dell Award for Historical Fiction, which was established in 1982 by author Scott O'Dell. The annual award is given to a children's or young adult book that is set in the New World and that will help readers understand the history that has helped shape their world and their country. The next year, the Virginia Library Association established the Jefferson Cup, which is awarded for quality writing in either historical fiction, biography, or U.S. history. The Geoffrey Bilson Award is given annually by the Canadian Children's Book Center for a work of historical fiction by a Canadian author. In addition, historical fiction books regularly appear on many of the young adult book lists (e.g., Best Books for Young Adults, Quick Picks for Reluctant Readers, Notable Children's Trade Books in the Social Sciences).

Print Review Sources. There are also a number of excellent bibliographies of outstanding historical fiction, some in print and some that are provided on the Internet by public and school libraries. Lynda Adamson has written a number of guides that include historical fiction, including:

- *American Historical Fiction: An Annotated Guide to Novels for Adults and Young Adults* (1999a),

- *World Historical Fiction: An Annotated Guide to Novels for Adults and Young Adults* (1999b),

- *Literature Connections to American History: Resources to Enhance and Entice, 7–12* (1997), and

- *Literature Connections to World History: Resources to Enhance and Entice, 7–12* (1998).

Other print bibliographies include:

- *America as Story: Historical Fiction for Middle and Secondary Schools* (Coffey & Howard, 1997),

- *An Annotated Bibliography of Historical Fiction for the Social Studies, Grades 5–12* (Silverblank, 1992),

- *Recasting the Past: The Middle Ages in Young Adult Literature* (Barnhouse, 2000), and

- *American in Historical Fiction: A Bibliographic Guide* (Van Meter, 1997).

Other references focus on individual authors such as Jeanne M. McGlinn's *Ann Rinaldi: Historian and Storyteller* (2000) or on topics such as Edward T. Sullivan's *Holocaust in Literature for Youth: A Guide and Resource Book* (1999).

Online Resources. The Internet resources on historical fiction are varied. Although not limited to young adult fiction, the *Copperfield Review* is a quarterly journal for writers and readers of historical fiction, the *Historical Fiction Review* provides reviews of historical fiction, and the Historical Novel Society has excellent information. Another comprehensive site for historical fiction is Soon's Historical Fiction Site. All four sites maintain links to other historical fiction sites.

Several other Internet sites have information on using historical fiction in the curriculum. Although Tarry Lindquist's article was written for teachers of intermediate and middle school children, her "seven reasons I teach with historical fiction" provides an excellent rationale for using historical fiction in any grade. In addition, the Social Studies for Kids web site provides ideas for incorporating historical fiction into social studies lessons. Finally, the SecondaryEnglish.com web site contains reviews of historical fiction along with ways to use the genre in the English classroom.

Nawrot (1996) maintains that, while historical fiction is not the most efficient way to teach history, it is the most effective. By reliving the past and internalizing the feelings, emotions, and events, readers can remember more than the facts found in a textbook. Therefore, teachers can use historical fiction to help students make comparisons of life today and in the past, create timelines, write a sequel, produce a newspaper based on the novel, write letters to characters, or keep a diary. Because some writers of historical fiction even attempt to revise history, challenge existing ideas, or refute previous theories about the way things were, it is always important to select young adult historical fiction carefully. One book that discussed a mystery in history when it was written is *Wolf by the Ears* (Rinaldi, 1991). Connecting Adolescents and Their Literature 6–2 provides a unit to use with this historical novel.

Changing Perspectives in Historical Fiction

As the world has changed, so has our view of history. At one time, young adults read only about majority culture males with little negative said or implied about them. Flaws and weaknesses went undiscussed and societal ills were ignored. Within the past 25 years, perspectives in historical fiction have changed somewhat so that young adult historical fiction increasingly includes characters from all backgrounds; looks at all sides of

CONNECTING	*ADOLESCENTS AND THEIR LITERATURE 6-2*

Instructional Unit for Wolf by the Ears *1819–1822 by Ann Rinaldi*

Summary

Harriet Hemings was born in 1798 at Monticello to Sally Hemings, an educated slave owned by Thomas Jefferson. Now, Harriet's 21st birthday is approaching and she must make a decision. Will she stay at Monticello, will she receive her freedom and leave as a free person of color, or will she receive her freedom and leave Monticello to pass as a white woman? As Harriet watches her brother Beverly, who wants to leave to go to college but cannot do so, she realizes that if she decides to take her freedom, she will have to leave behind the security of her family and everything that she loves. She finally makes her decision, fully understanding its cost.

Through the eyes of Harriet, readers see the conflict that Thomas Jefferson felt about the issue of slavery when he says ". . . As it is, we have the wolf (slavery) by the ears, and we can neither hold him, nor safely let him go. Justice is in one scale, and self-preservation the other."

Introducing the Book

1. Explore the setting of the book. Use the Internet to view Monticello and other southern plantations. What would you expect daily life to be like at Monticello? How would you expect life at Monticello to differ from your life today?
2. Explore the social situation of the early 1800s. What constraints does this put on the book?
3. Explore the recent DNA findings about the parentage of some of Sally Hemings' children.
4. Have you ever wondered what life would be like if your father was someone rich or famous? How would you feel if people in your neighborhood said your dad was a member of an important or wealthy family but your mother refused to tell you if you were really that person's child? How would you feel if that man had other children who lived with him and enjoyed his lifestyle, but you were his servant?

Discussing the Book

1. What changes take place in Harriet from the time Mr. Jefferson gives her the diary until she makes her last entry almost 2 years later? Why did Jefferson give her the diary?
2. What role did each of the following people play in Harriet's life: Sally Hemings, Isobel's Davie, Mammy Ursula, Charles Bankhead, Thad, and Thomas Jefferson?
3. Why does Sally Hemings have such passionate feelings about freedom? Why does Harriet call these feelings a sickness?

(continued)

CONNECTING | *ADOLESCENTS AND THEIR LITERATURE 6-2*

4. What most influences Harriet's final decision? Would you have made the same choice? Why or why not?

5. Why did Harriet and Beverly make different choices?

6. Sally Hemings could have stayed in France as a free woman. Why didn't she? What did she lose/gain?

7. Alienation is a theme in this novel. For example, Beverly and Jefferson are alienated as are Martha and Sally. Who else feels alienation? Why are these feelings so strong?

8. Examine the way that Rinaldi portrays Jefferson. Does she put him on a pedestal or does she try to take him off one? Is she sympathetic or unsympathetic to his feelings and actions?

9. Why does Jefferson tell Beverly the Wythe story?

10. Why is Randolph confused about his feelings for his father-in-law?

11. What are Harriet's feelings toward Thruston? What role do they play in her decision?

12. When Harriet leaves Monticello, she called Jefferson "mister" rather than "master." What does this signify?

Moving Beyond the Book

1. Thomas Jefferson, the third president of the United States and author of the Declaration of Independence, was rumored to be the father of Sally Hemings' children. What have been the findings of recent DNA investigations? Why do you believe that Thomas Jefferson refused to comment on the allegations during his lifetime?

2. Some writers put historical figures on a pedestal and show only the good side of them. Other writers prefer to debunk the hero and focus on the flaws in his or her character. How has Rinaldi treated Thomas Jefferson?

3. As president, what actions, if any, did Jefferson use to curtail slavery or to curb its spread?

4. Contrast life on Monticello to life on other southern plantations. Would you consider Jefferson to be an "enlightened" slave owner?

5. Find a map of the United States as it was in 1819. Use the book and other resources to identify the free states and the slave states. Locate your town on the map if you can. Was it part of the United States in 1819? If so, was it in a free or slave state?

6. Thomas Jefferson was known as an inventor and an amateur scientist. What things did he invent?

CONNECTING | *ADOLESCENTS AND THEIR LITERATURE 6–2*

7. Harriet may be a slave, but she is also a well-educated woman of the early 19th century. Contrast her education to education for women today as well as to education for other women in her time period.

8. While little is known about Harriet after she leaves Monticello, there is information on some of her brothers. Locate that information and explain what it adds to your knowledge about Thomas Jefferson and his relationship with Sally Hemings.

Literature Activities

1. Research is very important in historical fiction. However, in researching the novel, Rinaldi found very little direct information about Harriet. Thus, much of her portrayal of Harriet is indeed fiction. That means, using your imagination and common sense, you could create a very different young woman in the same setting. You could make her a rebel or a coward. Write a summary that gives a character sketch of the Harriet you would write.

2. Rinaldi tells the story from Harriet's point of view. What constraints does this put on her as an author? How does she deal with these constraints? Is she effective?

3. Discuss the ways in which Rinaldi uses figurative language throughout the story, identifying similes, metaphors, oxymorons, and symbols.

4. How does Rinaldi use both dialect and formal speech to advance the story?

5. Select a scene from the story that you would like to dramatize. What does this scene show about Harriet's life and/or her relationship to Thomas Jefferson?

6. Little is known about Harriet after she leaves Monticello. Use your imagination to continue her diary. Remember to anticipate that she will encounter both success and sorrow. Go back and reread Thad's words to Harriet about leaving her friends and family.

individuals to present strengths, weaknesses, and challenges; portrays realism; and examines societal ills. Because every piece of history, whether fiction or nonfiction, reflects the author's interpretations of the events complete with his or her biases (Brown, 1998), these changes have presented some challenges for both the writer and the reader of historical fiction.

From Page to Screen looks at the historical accuracy of some films based on historical fiction novels.

Increased Diversity. Our nation's increased diversity shows the need to have historical fiction that accurately reflects the many cultures, races, and ethnic groups in our nation as well as all genders. As you look at the books discussed in this chapter, you can

FROM PAGE TO SCREEN

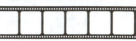

Historical Fiction

Consider the historical authenticity of these films compared to their original text. Does the visual aspect of the film clarify the time period, or does the book feel more historically true?

Sounder
1972, G
★★★★

Adapted from William H. Armstrong's novel, this film is tenderly and truthfully told, boasting powerful performances by Cicely Tyson, Paul Winfield, and Taj Mahal, as well as an unburdened but nuanced screenplay by Lonne Elder. Its simplicity helps the film maintain the attention of younger audiences, while performances and a beautifully crafted script keep older audiences entranced.

Dances with Wolves
1990, PG-13
★★★★

Michael Blake adapted his own young adult novel for the screen in Kevin Costner's directorial debut. Dean Semler's stunning cinematography captured Blake's words and Costner's vision, together garnering a Best Picture Oscar for this tale of 1860s hardship, humanity, and cultural identity.

Old Yeller
1957, G
★★★ ½

The classic Walt Disney movie showcases the harsh yet wholesome tale of Travis, an adolescent trying to fill in for his absent father in the 1860s American frontier. Fred Gipson co-wrote the screenplay adaptation of his novel, and the central themes help the film maintain its relevance today.

Little Big Man
PG-13, 1970 (2002 re-rated)
★★★ ½

This entertaining adaptation of Thomas Berger's novel boasts an engaging Dustin Hoffman as the 120-year-old spinner of yarns, whose tales, though fantastic and unlikely, provide insight into the tragedy that befell the Cherokee nation. A brilliant supporting turn by Chief Dan George and a touchingly comic screenplay come together in a film worth seeing.

Johnny Got His Gun
1971, PG-13 (re-rating; originally rated R)
★★★★

Dalton Trumbo directs the screen adaptation of his own disturbing novel of a World War I soldier mutilated by a landmine. More appropriate for older audiences, Trumbo's honest, human direction keeps the film almost alarmingly personal, and he manages to avoid

(continued)

FROM PAGE TO SCREEN

 a soapbox while still telling a powerful tale. It will be interesting for students to compare Trumbo's cinematic vision with his own novel, and question why certain changes were made. Consider listening to Metallica's song "One" with readers, as well, and discuss how Trumbo's work is re-imagined in the song.

see this diversity reflected in the protagonists and supporting characters in these novels. But merely changing names or identifying the ethnicity of the characters is not enough. As contemporary writers look back on the past, it is important to reflect that past as accurately as possible. In addition, we need to remember that we cannot erase bigotry or racism from our history by writing historical fiction books that portray relations as we wish they would have been. For example, today, shameful and hurtful words to describe certain cultural groups have, for the most part, been removed from the vocabularies of all but the most extreme racists. But these terms were used in the past. As we examine historical fiction, we must determine whether the use of what we now consider racial or ethnic slurs provides accuracy and advances the plot of the novel or whether the words are used gratuitously or for their shock value.

Suggestions for Collaborative Efforts 6–2 looks at some ways educators can work together to select multicultural historical fiction.

6-2 SUGGESTIONS FOR COLLABORATIVE EFFORTS

The library media specialist and members of an interdisciplinary team (or just two or three other teachers if your school does not have interdisciplinary teams) can work together to plan an integrated curriculum unit and to select appropriate books that accurately portray the realities of diversity in historical fiction.

- Take advantage of the perspectives of all the educators on the team. For example, opinions may vary on accurate portrayals of historical events, depictions of people with culturally diverse backgrounds, and the extent the diversity contributes to or diminishes the overall worth of the book.

- Explain:
  - (a) how the diversity (e.g., characters, plot, setting) makes a genuine contribution to the book.
  - (b) how the diversity makes a genuine contribution to the unit.

- Use only books that have merit and that make a legitimate contribution to the unit.

CONNECTING | *ADOLESCENTS AND THEIR LITERATURE 6–3*

In an informal survey of girls in grades 6–12, Samantha Melnick (2002) found that 66% of the respondents indicated that "there had been characters in books that they felt they could use as role models in their lives" (p. 44). Melnick was surprised when an "overwhelming number of girls" (p. 45) mentioned a historical person as being an inspiration to them. She concluded that "fictional characters that display good qualities and traits, such as honesty, bravery, creativity, and kindness, can teach the girls . . . to possess these same qualities in their own lives" (p. 45). Thus, teachers and library media specialists need to:

- Identify historical fiction books that contain positive role models for girls.

- Use these books in displays.

- Incorporate these books into instructional activities.

- Include these books on book lists.

Connecting Adolescents and Their Literature 6–3 suggests a way to use the strong historical characters as role models for students.

Increased Look at All Types and All Sides of Individuals. At one time in our history, authors created many stereotyped, single-dimensional characters. For example, Indians were portrayed as ignorant savages who would be rescued from their pitiful lives by turning over their lands and submitting to the demands of the white settlers. The settlers, in contrast, were depicted as hard-struggling individuals who embodied the best qualities of the American pioneer. Now, however, as writers of historical fiction do more accurate research, multifaceted characters populate historical novels. Not all of the pioneers were upstanding individuals. As Kathryn Lasky has pointed out, some of the pioneers who went west in the wagon train robbed, killed, and raped other settlers; and not all of the women who went west were school marms (Brown, 1998). The problem for writers of historical fiction is whether to produce accurate characters or to maintain the myth of the American pioneer. Thankfully, in deciding to debunk many of the myths of history, authors have incorporated a wider variety of characters from all ethnic, religious, and cultural groups and all genders in their historical novels.

Also, in the past, many people considered disabling conditions to be evil, a jinx, or an imperfection to be ignored and, certainly, not written about. While exceptions exist, contemporary perceptions of disabling conditions today are more accepting and positive; and more characters with disabling conditions are included in historical fiction. As Baskin and Harris (1984) said in the preface of their book, *Notes from a Different Drummer: A Guide to Juvenile Fiction Portraying the Handicapped:*

Like everyone else, people with impairments are still just people—individuals who are good and bad, wise and foolish, congenial and aloof. Their core human needs are the same, and their differences are in degree, not in kind. Undeniably, their pursuit of goals is affected by the fact and severity or complexity of their disabilities. (p. xv)

Increased Realism. With interest in multiculturalism and in representing all peoples fairly in historical fiction, authors have begun to sharpen their sensitivities and to re-examine historical events and viewpoints (Brown, 1998). The concern is that, in doing so, these authors must still retain historical accuracy. A racist view, while not accepted today, might have been the norm in the 1700s. Likewise, what is acceptable behavior today might have been unthinkable in the past. Most young adult novels have adolescents as the protagonist and/or main characters. Usually these characters are able to overcome obstacles and to succeed in spite of their youth and lack of power. However, "by inflating their valor and courage, an author may diminish or even sacrifice their humanity as well as challenge the reader's suspension of disbelief" (Brown, 1998, p. 7). For example, although it is true that, today, authors create many strong positive women and girls as role models, many critics have questioned whether a young, sheltered, upper class girl in the early 1899s, such as Charlotte in *The True Confessions of Charlotte Doyle* (Avi, 1990), would have actually been able to lead a rough crew of sailors and captain a trading ship (Brown, 1998).

There is also the issue of the inclusion of violence in realistic fiction. For example, although some would have us believe that, in the 1700s and 1800s, most slave owners were benevolent individuals, this was not the case in a majority of the situations. Thus, any writers who incorporate these settings in their novels will need to deal with the unsavory, cruel, and repugnant aspects of the situations. In *Nightjohn* (1993), Gary Paulsen realistically includes references to forced sex, castration, and cruel punishments to slaves.

Increased Examination of Societal Ills. Historical fiction increasingly addresses societal ills, situations such as racism, injustice, discrimination, and inhumane treatment of others that once were not considered ills or were simply ignored. In some instances similar situations may even exist today. For example, in the 1800s and early 1900s, the owners of coal mines were not always fair and honest individuals who were looking out for the good of their "employees." Thus, in *Breaker* (1988), Perez shows the deplorable conditions that led to the coal miners' strike of 1902. Increasingly, authors have addressed societal ills in an attempt to improve society; to help young adults understand prejudice, discrimination, and inhumane treatment; and to recognize the need to improve all people's living and social conditions. The problem is that, in looking at these issues, novelists may ignore complexities and nuances and "forego the expansive canvas that historians use in order to create clear characterizations and forward-moving plot lines that arrive, finally, at resolutions often denied to history" (Brown, 1998, p. 8). Thus, Brown (1998) cautions teachers to look for books that blend literary art with historical information. Suggestions for Collaborative Efforts 6–3 contains ideas for combating "isms" in schools.

6-3 SUGGESTIONS FOR COLLABORATIVE EFFORTS

Most teachers believe they have a responsibility to work toward justice in schools and society. Many think social ills need to be addressed whenever possible. While teachers cannot address all societal ills, they can make significant contributions toward eliminating or at least reducing them.

Four or five teachers (working collaboratively with the library media specialist) can discuss societal ills (e.g., racism, sexism, and classism) to determine the effects of these issues on students in their school. Next, they can:

- Select historical fiction that accurately portrays these ills and shows some deliberate action to lessen their effects;
- Include the selected books in lessons and units (being sure to choose books that students will see as relevant to contemporary society); and
- Identify Internet sites that complement or enhance the selected books.

CONCLUDING THOUGHTS

Well-written young adult literature has the potential to add a personal dimension to history. By carefully evaluating and selecting historical fiction, you will be able to provide young adult readers with interesting, enjoyable, and accurate books with background details that reflect the historical period. These books will help adolescents see how historical events affected people and families. They can vicariously experience the character's feelings when wars tore families apart, when prejudice and racial hatred limited opportunities and often resulted in death, and when freedom required sacrifice. In addition, quality historical fiction can help readers learn about people in the past, how they struggled, and how they overcame obstacles and their own fears. Many adolescents will appreciate recent historical fiction and its changing perspectives toward cultures and societal ills. By using carefully selected historical fiction, you can help young adults see that there is more to history than bare facts and dates and that their heritage is a rich tapestry of feelings, emotion, fears, joys, and satisfactions.

Visit this book's Companion Website at www.prenhall.com/bucher for additional information about historical fiction including review questions, self-assessments, Internet sites, and young adult literature and readings.

Young Adult Books

This section includes young adult titles recommended or mentioned in this chapter. Check the Companion Website at www.prenhall.com/bucher to find additional suggestions of current young adult literature.

Alder, E. (1995). *The king's shadow.* New York: Farrar, Straus and Giroux. After his tongue is cut out by bullies, Evyn becomes a slave to Harold Godwinson, the future King of England.

Alvarez, J. (2002). *Before we were free.* New York: Knopf. In the 1960s, Anita and her family become involved in the attempts to overthrow Trujillo's dictatorship in the Dominican Republic.

Anderson, L. H. (2000). *FEVER, 1793.* New York: Simon & Schuster. It seems like any other hot August in Philadelphia until disease begins to spread and Mattie begins to wonder if she can outrun it even if she flees from the city.

Arington, F. (2003). *Prairie whispers.* New York: Putnam. Life on the South Dakota prairie can be harsh. There is a dead baby with a living mother and, in a nearby covered wagon, a living baby with a dying mother. What will happen if Colleen switches the two babies?

Armistead, J. (2002). *The return of Gabriel.* Minneapolis, MN: Milkweed Editions. When the Civil Rights movement and the Klan both come to their Mississippi hometown in 1964, the lives of three young boys are changed forever when their families and friends start taking opposite sides.

Attema, M. (2003). *When the war is over.* Custer, WA: Orca. Sixteen-year-old Janke joins her father and brother in the resistance movement in Holland in World War II.

Avi. (1990). *The True confessions of Charlotte Doyle.* New York: Orchard. As a passenger on a sailing ship in 1832, Charlotte is accused of murder.

Avi. (1999). *Midnight magic.* New York: Scholastic. Mystery and history mix in a tale of Renaissance Italy.

Avi. (2001). *The secret school.* San Diego: Harcourt. When their teacher leaves the one-room school, 14-year-old Ida takes over the classes.

Avi. (2002). *Crispin, The cross of lead.* New York: Hyperion. After a 13-year-old orphan is declared a "wolf's head" (meaning that he is anyone's prey), he flees across' England and

meets a juggler named Bear in this adventure story from the middle ages.

Ayres, K. (1998). *North by night.* New York: Delacorte. Through Lucy's journal, readers learn the rules of hiding slaves and the operation of a station on the underground railroad.

Bagdasarian, A. (2000). *Forgotten fire.* New York: Dorling Kindersley. When the Turkish leaders begin to massacre Armenians, young Vahan must flee for his life.

Baker, J. (2002). *Up Molasses Mountain.* New York: Random House. When West Virginia miners try to unionize in 1953, there is trouble for everyone.

Barrett, T. (1999). *Anna of Byzantium.* New York: Delacorte. Through the eyes of princess Anna Comnena, we see the royal court of 12th-century Constantinople.

Bergman, T. (1991). *Along the tracks.* New York: Houghton Mifflin. After the German invasion of Russia, a young Jewish boy learns to survive by fleeing east.

Blackwood, G. L. (1998). *The Shakespeare stealer.* New York: Dutton. When Widge is sent to copy the script of Will Shakespeare, his first job is to survive in London. The sequel is *Shakespeare's Scribe* (2000).

Bosse, M. (1995). *Tusk and stone.* Arden, NC: Front Street. In seventh-century India, a Brahman's son is kidnapped and forced into the army.

Bradley, K. (2003). *For freedom: The story of a French spy.* New York: Delacorte. Sixteen-year-old Suzanne becomes a spy for the French Resistance.

Breslin, T. (2002). *Remembrance.* New York: Delacorte. By watching five teenagers, we see the reality of war, the slaughter on the battlefield, and the changes that World War I made in the lives of women.

Bruchac, J. (1998). *The arrow over the door.* New York: Dial. A Quaker boy and an Abenaki Indian scout explore their beliefs in this tale of the American Revolution.

Bruchac, J. (2002). *The winter people.* New York: Dial. A young Abenaki boy tries to rescue his mother and sister from Rogers' Rangers in the French and Indian War.

Burks, B. (1997). *Soldier boy.* San Diego: Harcourt. After Johnny "The Kid" McBane throws a boxing match, he ends up in Custer's Cavalry at the Battle of the Little Big Horn.

Cadnum, M. (2000). *The book of the lion.* New York: Viking. Edmund travels to the Holy Land as the squire of a crusader.

Carter, P. (1990). *Borderlands.* New York: Farrar, Straus and Giroux. Ben Curtis learns that there is both cruelty and adventure in the Old West.

Chambers, A. (2002). *Postcards from no man's land.* New York: Dutton. In this novel for mature readers, two stories, one contemporary and one set during World War II, come together as a young British boy goes to the Netherlands to learn about his grandfather.

Chevalier, T. (1999). *Girl with a pearl earring.* New York: Dutton. After becoming a model for Vermeer, the 17th-century Dutch painter, a young maid describes life in his household.

Choi, S. N. (1991). *Year of impossible goodbyes.* Boston: Houghton Mifflin. World War II changes the life of a young Korean girl as first the Japanese and then the Russian troops arrive.

Clinton, C. (2002). *A stone in my hand.* Cambridge, MA: Candlewick. Through the eyes of a young Palestinian girl, we see life in Gaza during the intifada of the 1980s.

Collier, J. L., & Collier, C. (1974). *My brother Sam is dead.* New York: Four Winds Press. Sam runs away to join the army of Benedict Arnold in the American Revolution. But no one anticipates how he dies. Another book about the Colliers that is set in the same time period is *Jump Ship to Freedom* (1981).

Cooney, C. B. (2001). *The ransom of Mercy Carter.* New York: Delacorte. Captured by Mohawks in 1704, Mercy Carter recounts her life and her hopes to return to her home.

Cooper, S. (1999). *The king of shadows.* New York: McElderry Books. After his father's suicide, Nat Field goes back in time to the Elizabethan England of William Shakespeare.

Cormier, R. (1999). *Frenchtown summer.* New York: Delacorte. In the aftermath of World War I, Eugene watches his tenement community and thinks about the unanswered questions in his life.

Crisp, M. (2001). *Private captain: A story of Gettysburg.* New York: Philomel. Searching for his older brother, Ben leaves home with his brother's dog and his cousin Danny and arrives at Gettysburg, where he helps bury the bodies and nurse the wounded.

Crowe, C. (2002). *The Mississippi trial, 1955.* New York: Dial. Hiram meets Emmett Till, an African American boy who is visiting his town and who is soon murdered for speaking to a white woman. Now Hiram begins to look at the people he knows who might have been involved in the killing.

Curtis, C. P. (1995). *The Watsons go to Birmingham, 1964.* New York: Delacorte. Kenny and his family lead a funny life until they travel south to visit a family in Alabama where there is a church bombing.

Curtis, C. P. (1999). *Bud, not Buddy.* New York: Delacorte. After his mother's death, Bud begins his search for his father in the depths of the Great Depression.

Cushman, K. (1994). *Catherine, called Birdy.* New York: Clarion. In 1290, Birdy's diary shows the lengths to which she will go to discourage all suitors.

Cushman, K. (1995). *The midwife's apprentice*. New York: Clarion. Lying in a dung heap to keep warm, Brat is taken in by Jane, the local midwife who begins to teach her a trade.

Cushman, K. (1996). *The ballad of Lucy Whipple*. New York: Clarion. When Lucy Whipple's mother moves the family from New England to the California gold fields, everyone is in for a major change in life. Another title by Cushman is *Rodzina* (2003).

Cushman, K. (2000). *Matilda Bone*. New York: Clarion. Matilda is shocked when she leaves the castle she grew up in to become the apprentice of Red Peg, the Bonesetter of Blood and Bone Alley.

Davis, O. (1992). *Just like Martin*. New York: Simon & Schuster. When Stone's father keeps him from attending the March on Washington in 1963, he decides to find other ways to protest.

de Trevino, E. B. (1965). *I, Juan De Pareja*. New York: Bell Books. Although he is a slave, Juan De Pareja risks his life to follow his dream of being a painter like his master Velazquez.

Divakaruni, C. B. (2002). *Neela: Victory song*. Middleton, WI: Pleasant Company. In this book in the Girls of Many Lands series, a young girl searches for her father and becomes involved in India's fight for independence from Great Britain.

Donnelly, J. (2003). *A northern light*. San Diego: Harcourt. In 1906, waitress Matie Gokey seeks to find a balance between her dreams of becoming a writer and the expectations of her family.

Dorris, M. (1992). *Morning Girl*. New York: Hyperion. Life changes for Morning Girl and her brother when the white men land on their Caribbean island.

Erdrich, L. (1999). *The birchbark house*. New York: Hyperion. In this book for younger teens, we see the life of a young Ojibwa girl in 1847.

Fleischman, P. (1990). *Saturnalia*. New York: Harper & Row. At the end of the Indian War, William, a Narraganset Indian, tries to find his twin brother in a Boston that is tombstone-cracking cold.

Fleischman, P. (1991). *The borning room*. New York: HarperCollins. The Civil War, World War I, women's suffrage, and medical folklore are all reflected in the events that take place in one room.

Fleischman, P. (1993). *Bull run*. New York: HarperCollins. Soldiers and slaves, men and women, adults and children tell the story of the first battle of the Civil War. Another novel by Fleischman is *Dateline: Troy* (1996).

Forrester, S. (1995). *Sound the jubilee*. New York: Lodestar. Maddie's family joins a colony of former slaves on Roanoke Island, North Carolina.

Fox, P. (1973). *The slave dancer*. Scarsdale, NY: Bradbury. A young boy is kidnapped so that he can provide music on a slave ship to keep the "cargo" in good shape.

Giff, P. R. (1997). *Lily's crossing*. New York: Delacorte. When Lily's father is drafted, her family moves to Long Island where she meets a young refugee boy.

Giff, P. R. (2000). *Nory Ryan's song*. New York: Delacorte. Nory and her family try to survive the Irish Potato Famine of 1845.

Goodman, J. E. (1996). *The winter hare*. Boston: Houghton Mifflin. Twelve-year-old Will Belet becomes involved in the intrigues of the nobles and knights in medieval England.

Goodman, J. E. (2000). *Peregrine*. Boston: Houghton Mifflin. After the death of her husband and her child, a young English girl goes on a pilgrimage to the Holy Land.

Gray, D. E. (2002). *Together apart*. Boston: Houghton Mifflin. After the Great Blizzard of 1888, two children cope with life on the Nebraska prairie and their "luck" at being survivors.

Greene, B. (1973). *Summer of my German soldier.* New York: Dial. What exactly is freedom and what is prison? That is the problem that a young Jewish girl in Arkansas must face when German prisoners of war come to her town.

Griffin, A. (2002). *Hannah, divided.* New York: Hyperion. Against all odds, Hannah wins a scholarship and leaves the farm to attend school in Philadelphia during the Great Depression.

Grimes, N. (1998). *Jazmin's notebook.* New York: Dial. The notebook of 14-year-old Jazmin reflects life in Harlem in the 1960s.

Grove, V. (1999). *The starplace.* New York: Putnam. Celeste, an African American girl, enrolls in a school in Oklahoma in 1961.

Hahn, M. D. (2003). *Hear the wind blow.* New York: Clarion. When Haswell Margurder hides a wounded Confederate soldier, the Yankees retaliate. Escaping with his younger sister, Haswell begins a search for his wounded older brother.

Hansen, J. (1986). *Which way to freedom?* New York: Walker. After escaping from slavery, Obi joins a black Union regiment.

Harrell, B. O. (1999). *Longwalker's journey: A novel of the Choctaw Trail of Tears.* New York: Dial. This short novel for younger adolescents recounts the walk of the Choctaw people from Mississippi to Oklahoma.

Hesse, K. (1995). *A time of angels.* New York: Hyperion. During the Boston influenza epidemic in 1918, Hanna becomes responsible for her younger sisters.

Hesse, K. (1997). *Out of the dust.* New York: Scholastic. As if the Dust Bowl did not provide enough challenges, Billie Jo must also cope with the sudden death of her mother.

Hesse, K. (2001). *Witness.* New York: Scholastic. Everyone has his or her own story to tell when the Ku Klux Klan comes to Vermont in the 1920s.

Hill, K. (2002). *Minuk: Ashes in the pathway.* Middleton, WI: Pleasant Co. A young Yup'ik girl in Alaska watches the arrival of Christian missionaries.

Hobbs, V. (2002). *Sonny's war.* New York: Farrar, Straus and Giroux. The Vietnam War and the Civil Rights Movement become personal for Corin.

Holeman, L. (2002). *Search of the Moon King's daughter.* Toronto: Tundra Books. Emmaline goes to London to search for her brother who has been sold as a chimney sweep in Victorian England.

Hopkinson, D. (1999). *A band of angels: A story inspired by the Jubilee Singers.* New York: Atheneum. After Ella enrolls at Fish, the school for freed slaves, she is invited to join the chorus. But will the school be able to survive the financial difficulties that threaten it?

Horowitz, A. (2000). *The devil and his boy.* New York: Philomel. In 1593, a young boy becomes involved with a group of actors who are really thieves and rebels.

Hughes, P. (2003). *Guerrilla season, RS.* New York: Farrar, Straus and Giroux. In the 1860s, when Quantrill's raiders come closer to his Missouri farm, 15-year-old Matt has to make some difficult choices about a brutal war.

Kerr, M. E. (2001). *Slap your sides.* New York: HarperCollins. When Jubal's brother registers as a conscientious objector during World War II, his Quaker family becomes the target of hostility from residents of his small town.

Kidd, S. M. (2002). *The secret life of bees: A novel.* New York: Viking. Running from racial unrest in the 1960s, Lily and Rosaleen, her adult companion, flee to Tiburon, South Carolina, where Lily hopes to learn more about her mother who was killed when Lily was four.

Krisher, T. (1997). *Kinship*. New York: Delacorte. When Pert's father shows up at her home in a small town in Georgia in 1961, she does not realize that he has brought trouble with him.

Kurtz, J. (1998). *The storyteller's beads*. San Diego: Harcourt. When famine and social unrest strike Ethiopia in the 1980s, two young girls attempt to flee to a refugee camp in the Sudan.

Laird, C. (1989). *Shadow of the wall*. New York: Greenwillow. When a young boy joins a resistance group, he misses the deportations from the Warsaw ghetto to the Treblinka concentration camp. The sequel to this is *Beyond the Wall*. Another book by this author on the Holocaust is *But Can the Phoenix Sing* (1993).

Lasky, K. (1994). *Beyond the burning time*. New York: Blue Sky Press. Mary Chase tries to save her mother from being executed as a witch.

Lasky, K. (1996). *True north: A novel of the Underground Railroad*. New York: Scholastic. Lucy decides to help a young slave escape.

Lasky, K. (2000). *Marie Antoinette: Princess of Versailles, Austria-France, 1769*. New York: Scholastic. Marie Antoinette's diary shows her rise to Queen of France and wife of Louis XVI.

Lawhead, S. R. (2003). *Patrick: Son of Ireland*. New York: William Morrow. This novel fills in the gaps in the life of a young boy who is captured as a slave and who eventually returns to Ireland and becomes a legend.

Lester, J. (2000). *Pharaoh's daughter: A novel of ancient Egypt*. San Diego: Silver Whistle. This is a fictionalized story of the birth of Moses.

Levine, G. C. (1999). *Dave at night*. New York: HarperCollins. In 1920s New York, a young orphan splits his life between the routine of the Hebrew Home for Boys and the fascination of the Harlem Renaissance.

Levitin, S. (1990). *Silver days*. New York: Atheneum. Escaping from Nazi-Germany, the Platts find a home in America.

Lyons, M. (1992). *Letters from a slave girl*. New York: Scribner. Before she is able to escape to the North in 1842, Harriet Jacobs hides where she is able to watch her children grow up.

Magorian, M. (1981). *Good night, Mr. Tom*. New York: Harper & Row. When the Germans begin to bomb London, Willie Beech is among the children who are sent to the country for safety.

Martin, N. (2003). *Flight of the fisherbird*. New York: Bloomsbury. When Clementine rescues an illegal Chinese immigrant on the coast of Washington in 1889, she must decide what to do with him.

Mazer, H. (1979). *The last mission*. New York: Delacorte. A young boy lies about his age so that he can enlist in the U.S. Air Force in World War II and fly bombing missions over Europe until his plane is shot down.

Mazer, H. (2001). *Boy at war: Novel of Pearl Harbor*. New York: Simon & Schuster. Growing up as the son of a U.S. naval officer in Honolulu in 1941 is not easy for Adam. Then the Japanese planes come.

Mazer, N. F. (1999). *Good night, Maman*. San Diego: Harcourt Brace. Karin Levi, her mother, and her brother flee the Nazis who have invaded France. But Karin and her brother must leave their mother behind when they flee on an American refugee ship.

McCaughrean, G. (2002). *The kite rider*. New York: HarperCollins. To save his mother from marriage to the man who killed his father, Haoyou becomes a "wind tester."

McGraw, E. J. (1991). *The striped ships*. New York: M. K. McElderry. Juliana, a Saxon girl, works on the Bayeux Tapestry after the Norman invasion of England.

McKay, S. E. (2000). *Charlie Wilcox*. Toronto: Stoddard Kids. When Charlie tries to stow away on a seal hunting ship, he finds himself on a troop ship headed to the war in Europe where his courage will be tested in the trenches during the Battle of the Somme.

McKissack, P. (2000). *Color me dark*. New York: Scholastic. Nellie Lee Love and her family move to Chicago to escape the Ku Klux Klan in Tennessee in 1919.

Meyer, C. (2000). *Anastasia: The last grand duchess, Russia, 1914*. New York: Scholastic. This book in the Royal Diaries series takes readers inside the life of Russian nobility from 1914–1918.

Mochizuki, K. (2002). *Beacon Hill boys*. New York: Scholastic. Tensions are high in Seattle in the 1970s as a high school student decides to stand up for his rights as an Asian American.

Myers, W. D. (1988). *Fallen angels*. New York: Scholastic. A young African American boy tries to escape his neighborhood by enlisting for the Vietnam War.

Myers, W. D. (1994). *The Glory Field*. New York: Scholastic. Two hundred years of history in an African American family are traced through their attachment to the land they call the Glory Field.

Namioka, L. (2002). *An ocean apart, a world away*. New York: Delacorte. Leaving China for life in the United States in the 1920s, Yanyan finds that she has two strikes against her: she is Asian and she is a woman.

Newth, M. (1998). *The dark light*. New York: Farrar, Straus and Giroux. When Tora is diagnosed with leprosy, she learns that she still may be able to help others.

O'Dell, S. (1966). *The king's fifth*. Boston: Houghton Mifflin. The conquistadors' search for gold is not a peaceful one.

Orlev, U. (1984). *Island on Bird Street*. Boston: Houghton Mifflin. When his father disappears, a young boy tries to survive in an abandoned house in the Warsaw Ghetto.

Orlev, U. (1991). *Man from the other side*. Boston: Houghton Mifflin. Marek learns the secret of the sewers that lead into the Warsaw Ghetto.

Park, L. S. (2001). *A single shard*. New York: Clarion. In 12th-century Korea, a young boy must deliver the work of a master potter.

Park, L. S. (2002). *When my name was Keoko*. New York: Clarion. Sun-hee and her brother Tae-yul lose more than their names when the Japanese invade Korea during World War II.

Paterson, K. (1983). *Rebels of the heavenly kingdom*. New York: Crowell. After Wang Lee is kidnapped by bandits, he is rescued by a mysterious girl who introduces him to a secret society that is dedicated to the overthrow of the Manchu government.

Paterson, K. (1991). *Lyddie*. New York: Lodestar. When tragedy strikes her family, Lyddie runs away to work in the textile mills rather than be bound-out as a servant. But Lyddie finds a different kind of servitude in the mills of Lowell, Massachusetts.

Paterson, K., (1996). *Jip: His story*. New York: Lodestar. Where did Jip come from? Who was his mother? And why is a stranger looking for him?

Paulsen, G. (1993). *Harris and me*. San Diego: Harcourt. Get ready for laughs when a young city boy spends the summer with his country cousins.

Paulsen, G. (1993). *Nightjohn*. New York: Delacorte. Sarny wants to learn to read, but that is forbidden for slaves.

Paulsen, G. (1997) *Sarny, A life remembered*. New York: Delacorte. Leaving the plantation at the end of the Civil War, Sarny journeys south to find her children and begin a new life.

Paulsen, G. (1998). *Soldier's heart: Being the story of the enlistment and due service of the boy Charley Goddard in the First Minnesota*

Volunteers. New York: Delacorte. Charley leaves Minnesota full of the glory he will find in the Civil War. He returns full of the horrible images of the war.

Peck, R. (1998). *A long way from Chicago*. New York: Dial. Two children are sent to rural Illinois to spend the summer with their grandmother during the Great Depression.

Peck, R. (2000). *A year down yonder*. New York: Dial. Because of the Depression, Mary Alice has to spend a year in rural Illinois with her grandmother.

Peck, R. (2001). *Fair weather*. New York: Dial. What's more interesting: The 1893 World's Fair or grandfather?

Peck, R. (2003). *The river between us*. New York: Dial. When Howard visits his grandparents, his grandmother tells him of the strange events of 1861 when two young ladies from New Orleans arrived in their Mississippi town.

Perez, N. A. (1988). *Breaker*. Boston: Houghton Mifflin. As a Polish breaker boy in the Pennsylvania coal mines, Pat tries to survive the brutality of the mine owners and the mistrust of the Irish miners.

Pevsner, S., & Tang, F. (1997). *Sing for your father, Su Phan*. New York: Clarion. Growing up in North Vietnam, Su Phan tells about her life after her father is sent to prison.

Rinaldi, A. (1991). *Wolf by the ears*. New York: Scholastic. Harriet Hemings, a young slave on Thomas Jefferson's plantation, must decide whether to accept her freedom or stay at Monticello. Other books by this author include *Ride the Morning: The Story of Tempe Wick* (1991), *The Secret of Sarah Revere* (1995), and *In My Father's House* (1993).

Rinaldi, A. (1998). *Mine eyes have seen*. New York: Scholastic. Annie follows John Brown, her father, to Maryland where he will plan his raid on the U.S. arsenal at Harpers Ferry, West Virginia.

Rinaldi, A. (2002). *Taking liberty*. New York: Simon & Schuster. Oney Judge was a slave at Mount Vernon and the servant of Martha Washington. But will George Washington really free the slaves when he dies or should she try to escape?

Rinaldi, A. (2003). *Or give me death: A novel of Patrick Henry's family*. San Diego: Harcourt. Through the eyes of his daughters, we see the tensions that may tear Patrick Henry's family apart.

Riordan, J. (2002). *Match of death*. Oxford: Oxford University Press. The Kiev Dinamos are scheduled to play a football match against the Germans in 1942. Then a referee tells the team members that if they win the game, they will all die.

Robinet, H. (1998). *Forty acres and maybe a mule*. New York: Atheneum. At the end of the Civil War, Pascal, his brother, and their friends set out to get the 40 acres that have been promised to all of the freed slaves.

Rostkowski, M. I. (1989). *The best of friends*. New York: HarperCollins. When one of two friends becomes a peace activist and the other enlists as a soldier in the Vietnam War, can two boys remain good friends?

Russell, C. Y. (1999). *Child bride*. Honesdale: Boyds Mills. Eleven-year-old Ying tries to flee an arranged marriage in 1940s China.

Ryan, P. M. (2000). *Esperanza rising*. New York: Scholastic. When her father is murdered by bandits, Esperanza and her mother flee from Mexico to a migrant camp in California during the Great Depression.

Salisbury, G. (1994). *Under the blood-red sun*. New York: Delacorte. Living in Hawaii, Tomakazu Nakaji is a Japanese-American boy whose only worries are baseball and school until the Japanese attack on Pearl Harbor turns his world upside down.

Santana, P. (2002). *Motorcycle ride on the sea of tranquility.* Albuquerque: University of New Mexico Press. When Chuy returns from Vietnam in 1969, his sister is frightened by the emotional changes in him.

Shaara, M. (1974). *The killer angels.* New York: Ballantine. The Battle of Gettysburg comes alive in this classic novel.

Soto, G. (1994). *Jesse.* San Diego: Harcourt. Is Jesse destined to spend his life as a farm worker in California or can he find a way out of the fields?

Spinelli, J. (2003). *Milkweed.* New York: Knopf. A gypsy, a thief, and an orphan, Misha is also a boy growing up in Warsaw under the Nazi occupation.

Sullivan, P. (2003). *Maata's journal: A novel.* New York: Atheneum. Through a young Inuit girl's journal, we learn about survival in the Arctic in 1924.

Sutcliff, R. (1990). *The shining company.* New York: Farrar, Straus and Giroux. A young shield bearer tells the story of the Saxon invasion of Britain in the seventh century. Other books by Sutcliff on early British history include *The Shield Ring* (1957), *Dawn Wind* (1961), *Knight's Fee* (1960), *The Silver Branch* (1959), *The Lantern Bearers* (1959), and *The Eagle of the Ninth* (1961).

Taylor, M. (2001). *The land.* New York: Phyllis Fogelman. The son of a white plantation owner and a slave mother, Paul-Edward Logan tells his tale of the reconstruction south. The sequel to this novel is the classic *Roll of Thunder, Hear My Cry* (1976). Other books about the Logan family include *The Road to Memphis* (1990) and *Mississippi Bridge* (1990).

Temple, F. (1994). *The Ramsay scallop.* New York: Orchard Books. Before they are married, Eleanor and Thomas make a pilgrimage to Spain.

Temple, F. (1996). *The Beduin's gazelle.* New York: Orchard Books. Although Atiyah and Halima are betrothed, politics and war are keeping them apart.

Torrey, M. (2003). *To the edge of the world.* New York: Knopf. A young orphan joins Ferdinand Magellan on his first successful circumnavigation of the world in 1519.

Walsh, J. P. (1983). *A parcel of patterns.* New York: Farrar, Straus and Giroux. In 1665, a plague comes to an English village.

Westall, R. (1976). *The machine gunners.* New York: Greenwillow. A group of English children find a German machine gun and decide to hide it from the adults.

White, E. E. (1995). *The road home.* New York: Scholastic. After spending a year with the soldiers in Vietnam, Becky Phillips comes home to a hostile America.

Wilson, D. L. (1999). *I rode a horse of milk white jade.* New York: HarperCollins. Disguised as a boy, Oyuna joins the army of Kublai Khan.

Wolff, V. E. (1998). *Bat 6.* New York: Scholastic. Tradition had the sixth-grade girls playing a softball game at the beginning of the new school year for 50 years. But this year's game was filled with danger.

Yep, L. (1995). *Hiroshima.* New York: Scholastic. Through Sachi, we see the effects of the atomic bomb on Hiroshima, Japan.

Yep, L. (2003). *The traitor.* New York: HarperCollins. Tensions run high between the American and Chinese coal miners in 1885 in the Wyoming Territory in this book in the Golden Mountain Chronicle series. Another historical novel in the series is *Dragon's Gate* (1993).

Yolen, J. (1988). *The devil's arithmetic.* New York: Viking. Hannah is transported back in time to 1942 when the Nazi soldiers come to her family's village in Poland.

Suggested Readings

Agbaw, V. Y. (2003). Revolutionary War and contemporary students: It happened a L-O-N-G time ago! *The ALAN Review, 31*(1), 53–60.

Glodblatt, P. (2002). Creating credible female characters across time and cultures. *MultiCultural Review, 11*(1), 30–32.

McNulty, M. H. (2001). The girl's story: Adolescent novels set in the Middle Ages. *The ALAN Review, 28*(2), 20–24.

Power, C. L. (2003). Challenging the pluralism of our past: Presentism and the selective tradition in historical fiction written for young people. *Research in the Teaching of English, 37*(4), 425–466.

References

(Note: All young adult literature referenced in this chapter are included in the Young Adult Books list and are not repeated in this list.)

Adamson, L. G. (1997). *Literature connections to American history: Resources to enhance and entice, 7–12.* Englewood, CO: Libraries Unlimited.

Adamson, L. G. (1998). *Literature connections to world history: Resources to enhance and entice, 7–12.* Englewood, CO: Libraries Unlimited.

Adamson, L. G. (1999a). *American historical fiction: An annotated guide to novels for adults and young adults.* Phoenix: Oryx Press.

Adamson, L. G. (1999b). *World historical fiction: An annotated guide to novels for adults and young adults.* Phoenix: Oryx Press.

Barnhouse, R. (2000). *Recasting the past: The Middle Ages in young adult literature.* Portsmouth, NH: Boynton/Cook.

Baskin, B. H., & Harris, K. H. (1984). *Notes from a different drummer: A guide to juvenile fiction portraying the handicapped.* New York: Bowker.

Bilof, E. G. (1996). *The Killer Angels:* A case study of historical fiction in the social studies curriculum. *The Social Studies, 87*(1) 19–23.

Blassingame, J. (2003). "A crime that's so unjust!" Chris Crowe tells about the death of Emmett Till. *The ALAN Review, 30*(3), 22–24.

Brown, J. (1998). Historical fiction or fictionalized history? Problems for writers of historical novels for young adults. *The ALAN Review, 26*(1), 7–11.

Clarke, C. (1999). Writing advice from Caro Clarke: 19. Historical fiction: Who rules, researcher or story-teller? Retrieved August 4, 2003, from http://www.caroclarke.com/historicalfiction.html.

Coffey, R. K., & Howard, E. F. (1997). *America as story: Historical fiction for middle and secondary schools.* Chicago: American Library Association.

Forbes, E. (1943). *Johnny Tremain: A novel for old and young.* Boston: Houghton Mifflin.

Frazier, C. (1997). *Cold Mountain.* New York: Atlantic Monthly Press.

Golden, A. (1997). *Memoirs of a geisha.* New York: Knopf.

Hillman, J. (2003). *Discovering children's literature.* Upper Saddle River, NJ: Merrill/Prentice Hall.

Johnson, N. J., & Giorgis, C. (2001/2002). Stepping back, looking forward. *The Reading Teacher, 55*(4), 400–408.

Lee, R. (2000). *History is but a fable agreed upon: The problem of truth in history and fiction.* Paper presented at the Romantic Novelists'

Association. Retrieved August 4, 2003, from http://www.historicalnovelsociety.com/historyis.htm.

McGlinn, J. M. (2000). *Ann Rinaldi: Historian and storyteller.* Lanham, MD: Scarecrow.

Melnick, S. (2002). Fictional characters in books as positive role models for adolescent females. *Gifted Child Today, 25*(2), 44–45.

Merriam-Webster's encyclopedia of literature. (1995). Springfield, MA: Merriam-Webster.

Nawrot, K. (1996). Making connections with historical fiction. *The Clearing House, 69*(6), 343–345.

Nesbeitt, S. (2002, March). *What are the rules for historical fiction?* (Panel Discussion.) Paper presented at the Associated Writing Programs annual conference. Retrieved August 4, 2003, from http://www.historicalnovelsociety.com/historyic.htm.

Pyle, H. (1888). *Otto of the silver hand.* New York: C. Scribner's.

Russell, D. L. (2001). *Literature for children: A short introduction.* New York: Longman.

Scott, W. (1820). *Ivanhoe: A romance.* Edinburgh: A. Constable.

Scott, W. (1822). *The Waverly novels.* New York: George Routledge and sons.

Sills-Briegel, T., & Camp, D. (2001). Using literature to explore social issues. *The Clearing House, 74*(5), 280–284.

Silverblank, F. (1992). *An annotated bibliography of historical fiction for the social studies, grades 5–12.* Dubuque, IA: Kendall/Hunt.

Speare, E. G. (1958). *Witch of Blackbird Pond.* Boston: Houghton Mifflin.

Sullivan, E. T. (1999). *Holocaust in literature for youth: A guide and resource book.* Lanham, MD: Scarecrow.

Tolstoy, L. (1869). *War and peace.* New York: Modern Library.

Van Meter, V. (1997). *American in historical fiction: A bibliographic guide.* Englewood, CO: Libraries Unlimited.

Wilder, L. I. (1932). *Little house in the big woods.* New York: Harper & Bros.

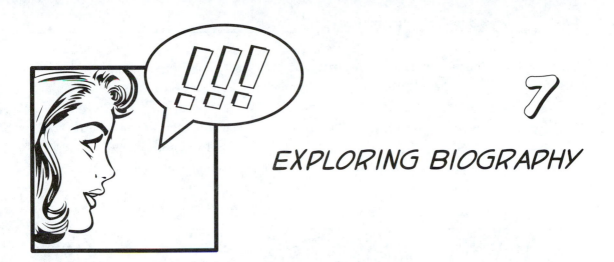

EXPLORING BIOGRAPHY

CHAPTER OVERVIEW

"If democratic citizenship education—the ability to make informed and reasoned decisions for the public good—is the goal . . . , then students must develop an understanding of the lives of those who lived before them, who are different from them, and whose struggles created the kind of world in which they live" (Akmal & Ayre-Svingen, 2002, p. 272). Biographies can provide young adults with these descriptions of individuals' lives, serve as information resources, and offer considerable reading enjoyment by illuminating the frustrations, obstacles, and achievements of a wide spectrum of people from the past and the present. In doing so, biographies can add new perspectives to young adults' learning and reading pleasure.

Many adolescents enjoy reading biographies. According to Moss and Hendershot (2002), 50 to 85% of the juvenile books circulated by libraries are nonfiction, including biographies. David McCullough's books on Truman and on John Adams, Joseph J. Ellis' biography of Thomas Jefferson entitled *American Sphinx*, Alfred Habegger's biography of Emily Dickinson entitled *My Wars Are Laid Away in Books,* and David Levering Lewis' books on W. E. B. DuBois are a few of the serious biographies that have recently appeared on adult best-seller lists and have been read by adolescents. Laura Hillenbrand's best-selling biography *Seabiscuit* was even made into a successful movie. A&E (Arts and Entertainment) television features the television series "Biography" with its Companion Website, magazine, and radio version. For both adults and young adults, biographies continue to be a genre that is read, viewed, and listened to for both enjoyment *and* learning.

In this chapter we will explore the types of biographies that are available for young adult readers, provide guidelines for evaluating and selecting biographies, and identify ways that teachers and librarians can use biographies in schools to help adolescents appreciate biographies.

FOCUSING POINTS　　*In this chapter, you will read about:*

1. The predecessors of contemporary biography;
2. Types of biographies and the contrasts between biography and historical fiction;
3. Various subjects and categories of biographies and the reasons for using and teaching biographies;
4. Characteristics of good biographies;
5. Suggestions for selecting and using biographies; and
6. Recommended titles and authors of biographies for young adults.

BIOGRAPHY

Well-written biographies are more than a series of facts about a biographee (person about whom a biography is written) that are thrown together in more-or-less chronological order. A biographer (the author of the biography) must sort through the truths and fictions, decide what is important and what is inconsequential, identify relevant details, eliminate superfluous trivia, and create a narrative that presents a person's life. Instead of depicting only the best about an individual, contemporary biographies for young adults portray all sides of a person and present a well-rounded, realistic character whom adolescents can relate to or begin to understand. A good biography will encourage curiosity by challenging readers to revisit their own beliefs and prior knowledge about the subject (Carter, 2003). Without ignoring the flaws in the individual, the author must strive to be empathetic (Townsend & Hanson, 2001). While novelists create a legend, biographers portray a life. "Biography's ties to fiction lie in its story narrative; its allegiance to nonfiction, in its history" (Carter, 2003, p. 166). However, it is important to remember that biographies can "easily pass into fiction when rational inference or conjecture pass over into imaginative reconstruction or frank invention" (*Merriam-Webster's Encyclopedia of Literature,* 1995, p. 141). Thus, it is as important to identify and select quality biographies as it is to select quality fiction.

A Brief Look at Biography's Predecessors

According to the *Merriam-Webster's Encyclopedia of Literature* (1995), the earliest biographies were probably funeral oratories that lauded and praised the deceased. In time, these speeches evolved into books that contained biographies of a number of noteworthy rulers and leaders. One early example is Plutarch's moralizing tales of prominent Romans and Greeks. The field of biography was changed in the 18th century and finally recognized as a distinct genre when Samuel Johnson produced his *Lives of the English Poets* and James Boswell wrote *The Life of Johnson* in which he combined psychological insight with exhaustive records of events and conversations. As more biographies were written, Thomas Carlyle voiced the opinion that history was actually the record of great men and that the key to understanding society was through the lives of the individuals who shaped it.

With that in mind, it is surprising that early children's literature did not include more quality biographies. To be sure, there were numerous "wordy, repetitive, and didactic" (Hillman, 2003, p. 229) biographies, but, even during the golden age of children's literature in the 19th and early 20th centuries, there were only "lackluster" (p. 229) biographies. With a few exceptions, including Cornelia Meigs' Newbery Medal-winning *Invincible Louisa* (1933) and James Daugherty's *Daniel Boone* (1939), as well as the autobiography *Diary of a Young Girl* (1952) by Anne Frank, biography was, according to Mary Mehlman Burns (1995), "the stepchild among the genres of children's literature. Not that there were too few but rather that there were too few that qualified as literature, let alone good biography" (p. 60).

Thankfully, there have been changes in the genre with a number of individuals now writing quality biographies for young adults and with more recognition for biographies. Beginning in the 1970s, Milton Meltzer, the recipient of the 2001 Laura Ingalls Wilder Award, has presented a number of excellent biographies including works about Dorothea Lange, George Washington, Mark Twain, Langston Hughes, and Mary McLeod Bethune. Then, in 1988, Russell Freedman's *Lincoln: A Photobiography* (1987) won the Newbery Medal and, in 1997, Diane Stanley won the Orbis Pictus Award for Outstanding Nonfiction for *Leonardo da Vinci* (1996). Expanding Your Knowledge with the Internet 7–1 provides more information on Russell Freedman and Diane Stanley and their biographies.

The focus of book awards began to change as the Orbis Pictus Award (given by the National Council of Teachers of English) was established for nonfiction writing and the Boston Globe-Horn Book Award included a nonfiction category. Then, in 2001, the Association for Library Service to Children created the ALSC/Robert F. Sibert Information Book Award. Although these awards did not specifically target biographies, they did serve to draw attention to well-written nonfiction in general. Several biographies that are suitable for young adults have won these awards.

Types of Biographies

A number of ways are available to categorize biographies. One way is based on the amount of historical evidence in the book. Another is on the amount of a person's life that the biography covers. Still other ways to divide biographies are to consider the author or whether the book is about one or several persons.

EXPANDING   *YOUR KNOWLEDGE WITH THE INTERNET 7–1*

Russell Freedman and Diane Stanley have won a number of awards for their biographies and other informational books. On the Internet, you can find information about them and their books as well as teaching ideas. Links to the following examples and many additional sites are found on this book's Companion Website at www.prenhall.com/bucher.

Russell Freedman
www.eduplace.com/kids/hmr/mtai/freedman.html

Diane Stanley
www.cbcbooks.org/html/dianestanley.html

Pure Biography/Fictionalized Biography/Biographical Fiction. Biographies may be divided into three basic categories—pure or authentic biography, fictionalized biography, and biographical fiction (see Figure 7–1)—based on the emphasis on factual information in the book.

In this biography continuum, the emphasis on the amount of facts changes as you move from left to right. For example, pure or authentic biographies are based only on the known or verifiable facts about a person. Well-documented, researched, and well-written, authentic biographies are gaining in popularity. However, sometimes authentic biographies are very scholarly and are enjoyed most by mature young adults. In contrast, many works about historical figures are fictionalized because little or no primary source documentation exists of their lives. Even when authors can identify primary sources, they might need to add some fictionalized details such as a conversation to make a point about the person, describe the person's thoughts, or show the person's relationship to other historical figures. However, even in fictionalized biography, the invented dialogue is based on actual events and people. It does not matter whether these biographies are contemporary or historical. At the other end of the continuum from pure biography is biographical fiction, which includes accurate historical events and individuals as well as invented characters and events. An easy way to remember the emphasis is to focus on the noun in each phrase—fictionalized **biography** is more factual than biographical **fiction.**

FIGURE 7–1 Types of Biographies

Pure/Authentic Biography   Fictionalized Biography   Biographical Fiction

Informational ← ——————————————————————————— → Historical Fiction

Biography/Autobiography. While a biography is written by the author about the life of another individual, an autobiography is written by the biography's subject. Many autobiographies are fictionalized autobiographies because most people rely on their memories rather than on actual notes of conversations to re-create the story of their life.

Autobiographies may take the form of a personal narrative or a memoir. Some would argue that, when a person writes his or her autobiography but changes details to suit the writer's personal perspective, perhaps by including events as the writer wishes they had happened, the autobiography moves to the right end of the scale to become autobiographical fiction. As you evaluate autobiographies, you will need to keep this in mind.

Partial/Complete Biographies. The various types of biographies can be broken down in other ways, such as partial and complete biographies. In a partial biography, the author focuses on one period in the subject's life. While this may be the period of the subject's greatest accomplishment such as a sports career or the time that an individual spends in public office, it may also be the subject's childhood. In *Jack: The Early Years of John F. Kennedy* (2003), Ilene Cooper looks at the struggles that shaped the life of the future president. Walter Dean Myers' autobiography *Bad Boy: A Memoir* (2001) concentrates on his childhood in Harlem in the 1950s, Jack Gantos' autobiography *A Hole in My life* (2002) focuses on his life before he became a writer, and Esmeralda Santiago's *When I Was Puerto Rican* (1993) tells of growing up in Puerto Rico and New York. In contrast, a complete biography traces the entire life of an individual or the individual's life to the current time such as Freedman's *Eleanor Roosevelt: A Life of Discovery* (1993) or Myers' *At Her Majesty's Request: An African Princess in Victorian England* (1999).

Individual/Collective Biographies. No matter whether authentic or fictionalized, biographies can also be divided into the categories of individual and collective biographies. While individual biographies are written about one individual, collective biographies are collections of biographies about a number of individuals. Although some collective biographies include individuals from many backgrounds such as Kathleen Krull's *Lives of Extraordinary Women: Rulers, Rebels (And What the Neighbors Thought)* (2000), others have an organizing theme such as politicians and world leaders, as in Jill S. Pollack's *Women on the Hill* (1996) or Milton Meltzer's *Ten Kings and the Worlds They Ruled* (2002); scientists, as in Kim K. Zach's *Hidden from History: The Lives of Eight American Women Scientists* (2002); successful business leaders, as in Laura S. Jeffrey's *Great American Businesswomen* (1996); or notable achievers, as in Julie Danneberg's *Women Artists of the West: Five Portraits in Creativity and Courage* (2002). Later, when we look at the criteria for evaluating biographies, we will identify some special things to look for when examining collective biographies. Connecting Adolescents and Their Literature 7–1 provides a suggestion for using collective biographies across the curriculum.

Biography in Contrast to Historical Fiction

In our look at biographies and autobiographies, we will concentrate on pure/authentic and fictionalized biographies. Works of biographical fiction tend to place a greater emphasis on the plot rather than the character and are sometimes categorized as historical

| CONNECTING | ADOLESCENTS AND THEIR LITERATURE 7–1 |

Taylor (2002/2003) describes link-up activities that are ideal to use with younger adolescents and collective biographies. Students should:

- Read the biography of an historical individual.

- Note interesting, intriguing, unique, but factual characteristics of that individual.

- Search newspapers, magazine articles, and biographical databases to identify a contemporary individual who shares a majority of these characteristics.

- Report the results in a paper, electronic presentation, or an art project.

In addition to practicing public-speaking and listening skills, this activity helps students develop critical thinking skills.

fiction. Whether to place a book in the genre of biography or historical fiction depends on the degree to which a historical figure plays a central role in the book and on the amount of accurate information in the book about that individual. Often, in historical fiction, the real individual is included only to advance the central story or to add a sense of authenticity and credibility.

Biographical Subjects

At one time in history, biographies examined the lives and perspectives of only historical people (and mostly Western European or American males) such as explorers; political leaders and social activists; artists, scientists, and sports figures; and people who persevered through difficult or challenging circumstances. Now, however, biographies focus on contemporary people or historical individuals who interest young people. Movie stars, popular artists and musicians, sports figures, characters from sitcoms, and just about anyone who is in the public spotlight has had a biography written of her or him. Some of these subjects will remain important over time. Others are less enduring and demand that teachers and library media specialists who select biographies remain current with the interests of young adults. Connecting Adolescents and Their Literature 7–2 has a suggestion for developing a collection of biographies that are both interesting to young adults and well-written.

Remember, too, that not all biographies are about heroes and people we would want young adults to emulate or revere. For example, James Giblin's award-winning *Life and Death of Adolf Hitler* (2002) asks readers to confront some difficult questions about power and its use or misuse. Carter (2003) suggests that good biographies "present individuals as people readers might *want* to know rather [than] those they *should* know" (p. 170) and helps the reader "understand the historical context that sets the stage for the story" (p. 166). Suggestions for Collaborative Efforts 7–1 provides one way that a number of educators can work together to incorporate collective biographies into the curriculum.

CONNECTING   **ADOLESCENTS AND THEIR LITERATURE 7-2**

Keeping up with the latest sports and entertainment figures can be difficult for educators. To ensure that the biography collection contains information on individuals adolescents will enjoy reading about as well as those they should read about, enlist their help.

- Have a biography advisory board for the library media center that contains representatives from each grade level.

- Use recommendations from teachers and guidance counselors to be sure these students represent a wide range of abilities and interests.

- Have students make a list of the individuals they would like to see in the library collection.

- Have the students themselves, with the assistance of the library media specialist or the staff of the library, determine
  (*a*) if there are any books about the people on the list.
  (*b*) what the reviewers have said about the book.

- Give the group a budget and have them determine the biographies, from their list, that should be added to the collection with the budgeted funds.

Categories of Biographies

Although biographies focus on individuals with achievements in many areas, we have tried to group them into categories and have identified some representative examples in each category. While other groupings can be devised, the following categories show the richness of biographies, both individual and collective, that are currently available for young adults.

Politicians and Leaders. As you might expect, many biographies have been written about American presidents and the founders of the United States. These range from Albert Marrin's portrait of George Washington in *George Washington and the Founding of a Nation* (2001) and Abraham Lincoln in *Commander in Chief: Abraham Lincoln and the Civil War* (1997); to David Adler's *B. Franklin, Printer* (2001); Natalie S. Bober's collective biography of colonial patriots in *Countdown to Independence: A Revolution of Ideas in England and Her American Colonies: 1760–1776* (2001); and Russell Freedman's biographies of a president and his wife in *Eleanor Roosevelt: A Life of Discovery* (1993) and *Franklin Delano Roosevelt* (1990). However, young adult biographies also include other leaders as well. Russell Freedman examines the life of an American Indian leader in *Life and Death of Crazy Horse* (1996). For younger adolescents, Diane Stanley takes a look at a French leader in *Joan of Arc* (1998) and an Islamic leader in *Saladin: Noble Prince of Islam* (2002).

SUGGESTIONS FOR COLLABORATIVE EFFORTS

Using collective biographies, English teachers, social studies teachers, art teachers, and library media specialists can help adolescents explore the lives of important individuals and see the contributions they have made.

- Before beginning the project, the teachers and the library media specialists meet to determine the availability of appropriate collective biographies.

- The social studies teacher introduces the assignment of historical figures and the English teacher begins a study of biography as a genre of literature.

- Students draw names of people that the educators have selected, read about those individuals in the collective biographies, and create a mobile that represents the individuals.

- After the mobiles are hung in the classroom or library, teachers challenge the students to guess the subject of each of them.

Although the individual biographies in the collections are short, they should provide basic information that, if necessary, can be supplemented with additional resources from the school library media center. More detailed information on this project can be found in the article by Akmal and Ayre-Svingen (2002) in the reference section of this chapter.

James I. Robertson, Jr., depicts Civil War General Thomas J. Jackson in *Standing Like a Stone Wall* (2001) and Tracy Barrett explores an 11th-century teenage princess in *Anna of Byzantium* (1999). However, not all biographees are positive subjects. As we mentioned before, James Cross Giblin has written *Life and Death of Adolf Hitler* (2002) and Elaine Landau has presented *Osama bin Laden: A War Against the West* (2002).

Religious Leaders. While there are not a large number of young adult biographies about religious leaders, a few recent books deserve mention, including Russell Freedman's *Confucius: The Golden Rule* (2002), Bruce Feiler's *Abraham: A Journey to the Heart of Three Faiths* (2002), and Stephen Mitchell's controversial *Jesus: What He Really Said and Did* (2002).

Scientists and Inventors. A number of excellent biographies highlight notable scientists and their achievements. M. F. Delano explores the life of Thomas Alva Edison in *Inventing the Future: A Photobiography of Thomas Alva Edison* (2002), Mary Collins examines man's first successful flight in *Airborne: A Photobiography of Wilbur and Orville Wright* (2003), John Severance looks at Albert Einstein in *Einstein: Visionary Scientist* (1999), and Frances A. Karnes describes female inventors in *Girls & Young Women Inventing* (1995). Two collective biographies of women scientists are *Twentieth-Century Women Scientists* (1996) and *Contemporary Women Scientists* (1994), both by Lisa Yount.

Explorers and Adventurers. Some people have lives full of thrills, excitement, and exploits throughout the world. In *Far Beyond the Garden Gate: Alexandra David-Neel's Journey to Lhasa* (2002), Don Brown tells the story of an unconventional woman in 1911; in *Extraordinary Explorers and Adventurers* (2001), Judy Alter appeals to younger adolescents; while in *Sir Walter Ralegh and the Quest for El Dorado* (2000), Marc Aronson provides a carefully researched book for all ages. Biographies of explorers and adventurers include contemporary as well as historical figures. For example, there is David Breashers' recent Alex Award winner *High Exposure: An Enduring Passion for Everest and Unforgiving Places* (1999), and Pam Flowers with Ann Dixon's *Alone Across the Arctic: One Woman's Epic Journey by Dog Team* (2001).

Artists and Writers. Not all interesting people were explorers or adventurers. There are several excellent biographies of artists and authors who led very interesting lives. Looking at photographers, Beverly Gherman wrote *Ansel Adams: America's Photographer* (2002), Elizabeth Partridge penned *Restless Spirit: The Life and Works of Dorothea Lange* (1998), Jan Greenberg and Sandra Jordan chronicled an artist's life in *Runaway Girl: The Artist Louise Bourgeois* (2003), and Russell Freedman compiled *Kids at Work: Lewis Hind and the Crusade Against Child Labor* (1994). Diane Stanley has written a number of picture-book biographies for younger adolescents including *Michelangelo* (2000) and *Leonardo da Vinci* (1996). Jan Greenberg and Sandra Jordan use letters and paintings to help tell an artist's story in *Vincent van Gogh: Portrait of an Artist* (2001), and Barbara O'Connor has written *Leonardo da Vinci: Renaissance Genius* (2003).

A number of biographies are available on a wide range of authors. For example, writers are the subject of several Alex Award-winning autobiographies including Pulitzer Prize-winning correspondent Rick Bragg's memoir *All Over But the Shoutin'* (1997) and poet June Jordan's *Soldier: A Poet's Childhood* (2001). In *Something to Declare* (1998), Hispanic American author Julia Alvarez presents a series of autobiographical essays about her life as a "hyphenated American;" in *Alice Walker: Freedom Writer* (2000), Caroline Lazo tells the story of novelist Alice Walker; in *Shakespeare: His Work and His World* (2001), Michael Rosen combines art and quotes from plays; and in *Sometimes the Magic Works: Lessons from a Writing Life* (2003), Terry Brooks includes advice to aspiring writers in his autobiography. As we mentioned before, a number of other young adult authors have also written autobiographies including Jack Gantos and Walter Dean Myers.

Athletes. Sports are important to many adolescents. Thus, biographies of sports stars, past and present, focus on the achievements of athletes, including their hardships, determination, and trials of endurance. Readers might enjoy biographies of current sports figures in books such as Bill Gutman's *Lance Armstrong: A Biography* (2003) and Glen MacNow's *Sports Great Allen Iverson* (2003); as well as autobiographies like *Dropping in with Andy Mac: The Life of a Pro Skateboarder* (2003) by Andy MacDonald with Theresa Foy DeGeronimo and *A Journey: The Autobiography of Apolo Anton Ohno* (2002) by Apolo Anton Ohno with Nancy Ann Richardson. Biographies of sports greats from the past are popular as well, with some current titles including Jane Leavy's *Sandy Koufax: A Lefty's Legacy* (2002); Jim Haskins' *Champion: The Story of Muhammad Ali* (2002); John

Stravinsky's *Muhammad Ali* (1997); and Thomas Streissguth's *Jesse Owens* (1999). A number of biographies also exist about women athletes, including Russell Freedman's *Babe Didrikson Zaharias: The Making of a Champion* (1999) and Joan Anderson's *Rookie: Tamika Whitmore's First Year in the WNBA* (2000).

Entertainers and Musicians. While there are a number of biographies of popular current and past performers, many are little more than carefully controlled publicity packages. Mixed with these, less-than-quality titles, however, are a few biographies that really examine the lives of performers. These include Rita J. Markel's *Jimi Hendrix* (2001), Elizabeth Partridge's *This Land Was Made for You and Me: The Life & Songs of Woody Guthrie* (2002), Savion Glover, Bruce Weber, and Gregory Hines' *Savion! My Life in Tap* (2000), and Rachel Stiffler Barron's *John Coltrane: Jazz Revolutionary* (2002). Sue Macy reaches back into history in *Bull's Eye: A Photobiography of Annie Oakley* (2001).

Uncommon Individuals. Young adults enjoy reading about individuals who have overcome hardships and struggles in their lives or who have distinguished themselves through their valor, courage, and conviction of beliefs. For example, several biographies have been written by or about Holocaust survivors or rescuers. Anita Lobel recounts her experiences as a Polish Jew in *No Pretty Picture: A Child of War* (1998), Irene Gut Opdyke tells of her experiences in *In My Hands: Memories of a Holocaust Rescuer* (1999), Ruth Jacobsen tells of her family in *Rescued Images: Memories of a Childhood in Hiding* (2001), and Howard Greenfeld examines the struggles of survivors in *After the Holocaust* (2001).

Several biographies tell the stories of individuals who fought for equal rights throughout American history. In *Elizabeth Cady Stanton: The Right Is Ours* (2001), Harriet Sigerman writes of an early feminist. Ruby Bridges remembers the struggle for school integration in *Through My Eyes* (1999); Dennis Brindell Fradin and Judith Bloom Fradin examine the life of an unconventional activist in *Ida B. Wells: Mother of the Civil Rights Movement* (2000); and Marilyn Nelson uses poetry to reveal the life of George Washington Carver in *Carver: A Life in Poems* (2001). Christine M. Hill (2002) explores the life of a civil rights activist in *John Lewis: From Freedom Rider to Congressman.*

Young Adults Growing Up. A number of biographies focus on adolescents' feelings and emotions. Esmeralda Santiago tells of growing up in Puerto Rico and her shock when she moves to New York to live with her grandmother in *When I Was Puerto Rican* (1993), Gary Paulsen recounts his life after running away at the age of 16 in *The Beet Fields: Memories of a Sixteenth Summer* (2000), and Rebecca Walker explores her own identity as the child of a white father and black mother in the Alex Award-winning *Black, White, and Jewish: Autobiography of a Shifting Self* (2002). In *Barefoot Heart* (1999), E. T. Hart remembers her childhood as a Mexican American whose family worked as migrant laborers. Two outstanding biographies examine a child's life in a communist culture. In *Red Scarf Girl: A Memoir of the Cultural Revolution* (1997), Ji-Li Jiang tells about her life in China while, in *Blessed by Thunder: Memoir of a Cuban Girlhood* (1999), Flor Fernandez Barrios recounts her family's struggle for survival in Cuba under Castro and their flight to the United States.

From Page to Screen lists some films that are based on the lives of famous individuals.

FROM PAGE TO SCREEN

Biography

Just as there are many fascinating biographies to share with adolescent readers, there are countless biopics illustrating those same lives these biographies share in their pages. Consider pairing a biography with one of these appropriate biopics, and discuss the commonalities and the differences in the two versions of one life. What could account for some of the differences? Which version seems more authentic? Why?

Anne Frank's Diary
1999, Unrated, Animated
★★★

This provocative animated version of the famous journals of the young Jew hiding from Nazis during World War II explores many of the passages from the actual journal that were cut for publication, providing an image of a more fully realized human than the traditional casting of an upright, well behaved adolescent. There is no cynicism in the characterization, however, and the result remains one of heartbreaking naiveté. Compare the film with The Diary of a Young Girl *and consider the text's omissions, as well as the use of animation to tell the story on screen.*

Amadeus
1984, PG (Note: Director's cut is rated R)
★★★★

While the storylines are not parallel, it is interesting to compare the innocent and ornery nature illustrated in F. N. Monjo's book

Letters to Horseface: Young Mozart's Travels in Italy *with the depiction of Mozart in director Milos Forman's brilliant* Amadeus. *Peter Shaffer adapted his own stage play, emphasizing the maestro's brilliant talent, innocent nature, and the effects of the stress of his genius.*

When We Were Kings
1996, PG, Documentary
★★★

Muhammad Ali, the Greatest
1969, Unrated, Documentary
★★★

Compare these tandem documentaries—first William Klein's 1969 documentary chronicling the iconic boxer's very early career, and Leon Gast's 1996 Academy Award nominee covering the infamous 1974 Zaire bout with George Foreman—with Walter Dean Myers' biography The Greatest: Muhammad Ali. *How do the documentaries mirror Myers' themes? How is the impact on American history, as discussed in the text, highlighted in the films?*

(continued)

FROM PAGE TO SCREEN

Malcolm X
1992, PG-13
★ ★ ★ ★

Follow a reading of Arnold Adoff's Malcolm X *with a screening of the Spike Lee film. Although Lee's version is based on the biography written by* Alex Haley and Malcolm X's own autobiography, Adoff's text is more appropriate for younger adolescent readers. Denzel Washington's powerful performance and Lee's thoughtful storytelling bring the Civil Rights leader's tale vividly to life.

Reasons for Using and Teaching Biographies

At the most basic level, biographies satisfy an adolescent's need to know and a desire to find out more about a person, event, or topic. But there is more than that. According to Hurst (2001), biographies personalize history by focusing on the motivations and driving forces behind personal actions. Through biographies, adolescents can see that, while social constructs can be harmful to some individuals and helpful to others, these constructs can be challenged and changed (Taylor, 1996). By seeing the choices that others have made and how those choices determined the course of an individual's life, adolescents can begin to realize that they too can make choices and that their decisions will influence their future. As Akmal and Ayre-Svingen (2002) note, if adolescents are to realize that history is more than the study of dead people, educators must use the connection between inquiry and biography to help young adults see the relationship between past events and the realities of the present. Connecting Adolescents and Their Literature 7–3 has one suggestion for making individuals from the past come alive.

Characteristics of Good Biographies

According to research cited by Carter (2003), biography reading declines between fourth and tenth grades with the exception of books for the yearly required biography book report. However, sports and entertainment magazines that feature biographies are eagerly read by teenagers. Perhaps, then, these statistics are more a comment on the quality and subjects of many of the biographies written for adolescents than on the interest of young adults in biographies. Just as with all young adult literature, it is important to look for the best biographies. Thus, as in other chapters in this book, we want to explore the characteristics that distinguish excellent biographies from the adequate, mediocre, or unacceptable. Unfortunately, not all biographies that are marketed for adolescents have those characteristics. After examining juvenile biographies in general, Lechner (1997) found inaccuracies occurring as the result of carelessness and oversimplification, inadequate or incomplete data, unreliable primary sources, and social mores and taboos. Based on her own experiences, Carter (2003) suggests dismissing those biographies that feature a

---

CONNECTING | *ADOLESCENTS AND THEIR LITERATURE 7–3*

Engage young adults with biographies by having a Dressing Up for History day. English, social studies, science, mathematics, art, and music teachers as well as the library media specialist can work together or this project can be done by an individual teacher with the help of the library media specialist.

- After reading a biography and exploring other resources about an individual, each student plans a costume that represents the individual and prepares a brief presentation that contains information about the person's accomplishments.

- When the student appears in class dressed as the individual and gives the presentation, classmates attempt to guess who the individual is.

- The student may even prepare a set of questions that others can ask to aid in the identification.

- If this is done with several classes, the best from each class can present for other classes, grade level, or the school.

A variation on this idea is to host a "dinner party" (Buehler, 2003) where everyone attends as a character from history whom they have researched.

---

larger-than-life, near-perfect individual to be honored and emulated; a lack of historical context within which to place the subject; an endless tally of accomplishments that show little relationship to either character or reader; and an organizing structure that revolves around birth and death dates rather than an implied theme concerning the subject's life. (p. 165)

What, then, are the characteristics of excellent biographies? Obviously, good biographies should be authentic and honest and should provide an objective treatment of the subject. But there is much more. First, young adults deserve accurate biographies in which controversial information and personal fallacies are neither omitted nor glossed over. In a good biography, the individual's character is revealed to the reader through the details and events of his or her life and as a complex individual with his or her own share of human strengths as well as weaknesses. Readers can understand and, at least sometimes, relate to the person's feelings of frustration and happiness. A good biography should depict the life of an individual in ways that allow the reader to question, evaluate, and analyze the narrative to identify the pattern or meaning in the person's life.

Next, a good biography should stay away from didacticism. Sermon should not "substitute for story" and fictionalization should not "enhance factual material" (Carter, 2003, p. 168). Included should be the feelings, beliefs, actions, and daily decisions made by the individual (Townsend & Hanson, 2001). However, to keep a biography from becoming a chronology of events or a collection of dates without any unifying theme, there needs to be a definite narrative thread. Grounded in the historical context of the time period in which an individual lived, a biography must tell the story of that person's life in a way that captures and holds the reader's interest (Carter, 2003).

Third, biographies must avoid stereotypes based on things such as gender, culture, religious background, and ethnicity. This does not mean that biographies should distort the truth or contain inaccuracies. For example, one cannot disguise the fact that women received second-class treatment for many decades and this treatment should be accurately portrayed. However, in writing about these times, writers should avoid placing women in stereotypical roles such as being helpless and dependent upon a male. According to Lucy Townsend (Townsend & Hanson, 2001), many earlier biographies of women show them achieving success only through their relationships with others (e.g., wife, mother, daughter). While historical perspectives and events cannot be changed, women need to be shown as individuals with unique strengths as well as weaknesses (Bucher & Manning, 1998). The same can be said about the members of any minority group.

Remember, too, that "biography is as much a product of the times in which it is written as it is of the times and lives it portrays" (Carter, 2003, p. 167). This means that, first, an author must respect the accepted beliefs and traditions of the time period he or she is writing about. Some things (such as segregation or the absence of most women from positions of political power) that are not acceptable today must be included for the sake of historical accuracy. As Steve Weinberg (2003) notes, "the most intellectually honest biographies capture subjects as they lived in their own times, not as an author alive centuries later thinks they ought to have comported themselves" (p. 30). However, while writing a biography, the author is also affected by the social institutions of the time period in which he or she is writing. Thus, a Franklin Roosevelt biography that was written in the 1950s with the idea of the leader as a role model will generally present a less well-rounded portrait than one that was written in the 1990s with a discussion on the motives for his actions and his personal life.

Julia Mickenberg (2002) also pointed out that juvenile literature, especially biography, is used as a vehicle both for activism and to support the status quo. Authors use biographies to deal with race, challenge gender norms, and present stories of lives that provide role models that are outside the prescribed traditional expectations of society. She maintains that by publishing, between 1945 and 1965, a number of biographies of early civil rights leaders, authors were able to lay the groundwork for the involvement of young adults in the Civil Rights movement in the 1960s and 1970s (Mickenberg, 2002).

Finally the treatment of the subject, the theme of the biography, and the style of the writing should be appropriate for adolescent readers. When reviewing biographies, Carter (2003) suggests beginning by thinking about what you know and what you do not know about the person and/or the time period in which the individual lived. Hold this information up against what the author provides. Then think about the author as a "partner in discovery" (p. 172) who will help you learn even more about an individual by showing you the character of the person rather than telling you about it. Considerations for Selecting Young Adult Literature: *Biography* contains additional information for evaluating biographies.

| CONSIDERATIONS | For Selecting Young Adult Literature | BIOGRAPHY |

When evaluating biographies, ask the following questions:

⊚ What are the author's credentials, experience/background, and perspectives that indicate competence to write about this individual?

⊚ Is the biography authentic or fictionalized, and, if fictionalized, is there an explanation of the rationale for creating the fictionalized parts?

⊚ Are the fictionalized parts identified?

⊚ Is the content up-to-date, complete, and objective with language/dialect that reflects the subject of the biography?

⊚ Is the book accurate?

⊚ Does the book avoid misrepresentations of events and facts?

⊚ Is the biography free from bias and not patronizing?

⊚ Does it present all sides of controversial issues?

⊚ Does the book neither debunk the subject nor place him/her on a pedestal?

⊚ Is the biography relevant to young adults?

⊚ Will the style of writing attract young adults?

⊚ Are there a bibliography of sources, endnotes or footnotes, and a list of recommended readings?

⊚ Are there special features such as period art work, photographs, or other illustrations; replicas of documents, letters, and other artifacts; and an index to the biography?

When evaluating collective biographies, ask these additional questions:

⊚ What is the scope of the entire collection?

⊚ What criteria did the author use to select (and exclude) individuals?

⊚ Is the writing consistent across the selections?

⊚ How is the collection organized?

⊚ Is there consistency in the amount of information presented on each individual?

Suggestions for Selecting and Using Biographies

As with all young adult literature, proper selection and evaluation of biographies are absolute essentials. Young adults deserve accurate biographies in which the controversial information and personal fallacies have neither been omitted nor glossed over. Readers should see the biographee as a human being with both strengths and weaknesses and can understand and, at least sometimes, relate to their feelings of frustration and happiness. Remember, too, that not all authors write and not all companies publish accurate and well-written biographies. The result is that educators need to use the characteristics of good biographies when reviewing books for purchase for a school library or for incorporating them into the curriculum.

Awards and Best Books Lists. We have often cited awards as one indication of quality. While there are no specific awards for biographies, the genre is included in a number of best books lists and awards. The Orbis Pictus award, which is given by the National Council of Teachers of English, has honored several biographies, and, in 2002, the ALSC/Robert F. Sibert Information Book Award, which was created in 2001 by the Association for Library Service to Children, was awarded to James Cross Giblin for *Life and Death of Adolf Hitler* (2002) with an honor going to Jack Gantos for *A Hole in My Life* (2002). In addition, the National Science Teachers Association (NSTA) has a biography category in its annual list of Outstanding Science Trade Books for Students K–12 and the Notable Social Studies Trade Books for Young People, which is issued annually by the National Council for the Social Studies (NCSS), has a section on biographies. The Young Adult Library Services Association (YALSA) list of Outstanding Books for the College Bound and Lifelong Learners, features a number of excellent biographies. There are also a variety of Internet resources that educators can use to locate biographies and to cross-check the information in books when evaluating biographies. Expanding Your Knowledge with the Internet 7–2 has the URLs for several of these awards and other resources.

Teaching with Biographies in the Classroom. From reading biographies and autobiographies to creating biographies and autobiographies, teachers and library media specialists can use biographies throughout the curriculum in a number of ways. While expanding adolescents' knowledge about themselves and others, biography study can be an engaging, stimulating, and motivational activity for readers that addresses a number of the NCTE standards for the English Language Arts, including using "a variety of strategies to comprehend, interpret, evaluate, and appreciate texts;" (Taylor, 2002/2003 p. 342) exploring a wide range of print materials in a variety of genres; developing an understanding of themselves and the cultures of the world; communicating with others; and using all the language arts (Taylor, 2002/2003).

EXPANDING	**YOUR KNOWLEDGE WITH THE INTERNET 7-2**

 You can use a number of Internet resources to help identify quality biographies and find biographical information. A few of them are listed below. Links to these and many additional sites are found on this book's Companion Website at www.prenhall.com/bucher.

Orbis Pictus

www.ncte.org/elem/awards/orbispictus

Arts and Entertainment Network's Biography.com

biography.com

While there are a number of excellent activities that teachers and library media specialists can use with the study of biographies, we have room to mention just a few of them. After reading biographies, students can research their own history and write a family genealogy that is more than an ancestor chart. In addition, adolescents can construct their own biographies about the subject of a biography or other interesting people. Based on a biography that they have read, students can write a resume, eulogy, or obituary; appear as a "guest" on an imaginary talk show in the classroom; or write a journal entry about a specific event from the point of view of the biographee. Teachers can also extend the study of the biography by asking adolescents to think critically about the biographies that they have read by having students describe what the subject of the biography might have put in a backpack, make a class or school hero quilt with each square representing a different biography, or develop a class or school biography timeline and have students place their books appropriately. Teachers can also have students create a biopoem or a vanity license plate about the subject of the book. Connecting Adolescents and Their Literature 7–4 has a few examples.

Working with the art teacher, students can make a collage, mobile, sculpture, or model that is based on the book; prepare an ad that could be used to sell the biography; create a new book jacket; design a bulletin board based on the theme of the biography; make a flip book or animated presentation of key events; or illustrate scenes from the person's life.

One interesting way to create a biography is to produce an Interactive BioCriticism of a favorite author. This activity, outlined in Suggestions for Collaborative Efforts 7–2, has students read young adult literature and, then, use databases in the library and Internet resources to create a "biography" of the author. However, instead of copying the information that is available on the Web about the individual, the Interactive BioCriticism provides the links to the appropriate Internet sites. In this project, adolescents learn a number of skills from using search engines to evaluating Internet sites.

Expanding Your Knowledge with the Internet 7–3 provides links to some additional Internet resources to use with biographies across the curriculum of the school.

Using Biographies in Science, Math, and Social Studies. As we have mentioned before, there are a number of benefits of using biographies throughout the curriculum, not just in the English/language arts classroom. Biographies can serve as advanced organizers or as a summarizing activity for the study of a historical time period, can enrich a science unit, or can help build critical thinking skills through the use of concept maps or Venn diagrams. When young adults look at the past through biographies, history is no longer a series of static events but the "intersection of numerous human actors, creative minds, and innovators" (Rudelson, 2003).

Daisey (1996a, 1996b, 1997) noted that the use of biographies in secondary science and mathematics instruction helps promote the construction of knowledge, the development of positive attitudes toward instruction, and positive growth. By presenting information about scientists and mathematicians in a different genre from traditional textbooks, biographies complement secondary instruction, appeal to a wider range of students, and ask both teachers and students to examine the factual, discipline-specific information that is found in the biography (Daisey, 1997).

CONNECTING | ADOLESCENTS AND THEIR LITERATURE 7-4

Encourage adolescents to read biographies by moving beyond the required book report. Two different approaches are bio-poems and vanity license plates.

Here are a few license plates (limited to eight characters) based on biographies:

Shakespeare	IN2WRTNG
Alexandra David-Neel	TIBET-11
Allen Iverson	#1HOOPS

There are a number of different formats for bio-poems. One is to take the letters of the subject's name (last only, first (full or initials) and last) and write a brief description that begins with each of the letters:

L	Leader of the nation
I	Interested in maintaining the union
N	Not supported by all in the country
C	Conflicted over the wisdom of his actions
O	Overcame adversity
L	Left a country that was trying to heal
N	Now revered as a great president

Another form of the bio-poem uses the following format:

Line 1	First name of the subject of the biography
Line 2	Four words that describe the individual
Line 3	"Who is a lover of" (three ideas, objects, things, etc.)
Line 4	"Who believes in" (one idea)
Line 5	"Who learns" (three things)
Line 6	"Who notices" (three things)
Line 7	"Who dreams" (three things)
Line 8	"Who says" (one quote)
Line 9	Last name of the subject of the biography
Line 10	Who is the subject of the biography
	_____ (title) by
	_____ (author).

SUGGESTIONS FOR COLLABORATIVE EFFORTS

On this book's Companion Website at www.prenhall.com/bucher, you will find a sample of the beginning of an Interactive BioCriticism of Philip Pullman that can be taught by an English/Language Arts teacher, library media specialist, and computer resource teacher. Before beginning the unit, the educators can use Web resources to help adolescents learn how to evaluate web sites.

A few of the web sites from the unit include:

To Find a bibliography of Philip Pullman's works visit:

Books by Philip Pullman at:
my.linkbaton.com/bibliography/pullman/philip/

To Find biographical information on Philip Pullman visit:

Random House at:
www.randomhouse.com/features/pullman/philippullman/index.html

To Find information on the awards that Philip Pullman has won visit:

Carnegie Acceptance Speech at:
www.randomhouse.com/features/pullman/philippullman/speech.html

In Suggestions for Collaborative Efforts 7–3, Daisey and José-Kampfner (2002) discuss the use of biographies to develop a positive sense of self in the mathematics classroom. Another way to use biographies in a math class is to create a personal budget, graph, or pie chart illustrating how the subject of a biography would spend his or her money (Taylor, 2002/2003).

Using Biographies in Guidance and Advising. Because biographies can paint compelling portraits of a wide range of individuals, educators have often recommended

EXPANDING | YOUR KNOWLEDGE WITH THE INTERNET 7-3

A number of Internet resources help young adults write and use biographies. A few of them are listed below. Links to these and many additional sites are found on this book's Companion Website at www.prenhall.com/bucher.

Writing with Writers: Biography:

teacher.scholastic.com/writewit/biography/biography_tguide.htm

Student Biographers Lesson Plan for grades 5-8:

222.askeric.org/Virtual/Lessons/Language_Arts/Writing/WCP0034.html

7-3

SUGGESTIONS FOR COLLABORATIVE EFFORTS

In response to a number of studies that have documented the school experiences of Latino teenagers and have highlighted their discouragement and high dropout rate, Peggy Daisey and Cristina José-Kampfner (2002) designed a biographical storytelling project in a middle school.

- Teachers selected biographies that presented Latinas with a number of positive role models.

- In storytelling sessions, the teachers and students told or reenacted the stories for others in their classes.

    We have mentioned some Latino biographies in this chapter. To find additional ones, you can consult the article by Sherry York (2001) that is in the references section of this chapter.

---

biographies to point out role models for adolescents and to use in bibliotherapy. Fortunately, there are excellent biographies of a number of diverse individuals who have struggled against bias or personal circumstances to achieve their goals.

Sue S. Minchew (2002) suggests using sports literature, including biographies, to teach character education. With more states committed to including character education in their standards, the question is not whether to teach character education but how to teach it. Although character education is sometimes taught through mini-lessons on various traits, the trend is now to integrate character education into lessons throughout the curriculum. Minchew (2002) found that sports biographies can help young adults learn about the importance of setting goals, thinking positively, triumphing over adversity while learning from it, overcoming physical fears and demonstrating psychological courage, playing honestly and fairly, developing a sense of humor and an ability to laugh at oneself, learning tolerance and the importance of working with others, developing self-discipline and a strong work ethic, and believing in oneself. While Minchew looked at sports novels, short stories, and poems as well as biographies, it is evident that all of these important character traits are evidenced by the subjects in well-written young adult sports biographies.

CONCLUDING THOUGHTS

Biographies today focus on people from all ethnic, cultural, religious, social, and gender groups and from all nationalities. In doing so, they provide young adults with more than the descriptions of lives of famous individuals. By combining valuable information with an opportunity for reading enjoyment, biographies let young adults share the frustrations, obstacles, and achievements of individuals from all walks of life and in all levels of society. These biographies also add new perspectives to young adults' learning and reading pleasure. By carefully evaluating and selecting biographies and by incorporating these books into the curriculum, teachers and library media specialists can introduce adolescents to quality biographies. Visit this book's Companion Website at www.prenhall.com/bucher for additional information about biographies including review questions, self-assessments, Internet sites, and young adult literature and readings.

Young Adult Books

This section includes young adult titles recommended or mentioned in this chapter. Check the Companion Website at www.prenhall.com/bucher to find additional suggestions of current young adult literature.

Adler, D. A. (2001). *B. Franklin, printer.* New York: Holiday House. Adler takes readers through the multifaceted career of Franklin as a printer, inventor, writer, and patriot.

Aliki. (1999). *William Shakespeare & the Globe.* New York: HarperCollins. This is a carefully researched yet easy to read biography of Shakespeare and a look at the Globe Theater.

Alter, J. (2001). *Extraordinary explorers and adventurers.* New York: Children's Press. With its short biographies, this collection will appeal to reluctant readers. Another book by Alter in this series is *Extraordinary Women of the American West* (1999).

Alvarez, J. (1998). *Something to declare.* Chapel Hill, NC: Algonquin Books. In 24 autobiographic essays, Alvarez shares the story of her youth in the Dominican Republic and America as well as her adult life as a successful author.

Anderson, J. (2000). *Rookie: Tamika Whitmore's first year in the WNBA.* New York: Dutton. Read about the life and basketball career of a player with the New York Liberty in the WNBA.

Aronson, M. (2000). *Sir Walter Ralegh and the Quest for El Dorado.* New York: Clarion. This literary biography provides a fresh look at an important historical figure.

Barrett, T. (1999). *Anna of Byzantium.* New York: Delacorte. In the 11th century, princess Anna Comnena fights for the throne of the Byzantine Empire.

Barrios, F. F. (1999). *Blessed by thunder: Memoir of a Cuban girlhood.* Seattle, WA: Seal Press. From living in Cuba under Castro to moving to America as a 14-year-old, Flor Fernandez Barrios tells the story of her life.

Barron, R. S. (2002). *John Coltrane: Jazz revolutionary.* Greensboro, NC: Morgan Reynolds. Barron looks at the life of an innovative jazz saxophonist.

Bausum, A. (2001). *Our country's presidents.* Washington, DC: National Geographic Society. This collective biography provides portraits and profiles of each of our presidents.

Berenstain, S., & Berenstain, J. (2002). *Down a sunny dirt road: An autobiography.* New York: Random. These famous picture book authors have written a dual autobiography.

Bober, N. S. (2001). *Countdown to independence: A revolution of ideas in England and her American colonies: 1760–1776.* New York:

Atheneum. Bober provides portraits of patriots, both familiar and those less known.

Bragg, R. (1997). *All over but the shoutin'*. New York: Pantheon. Growing up in poverty, Rick Bragg followed his dreams to become a writer and a Pulitzer Prize-winning correspondent.

Breashears, D. (1999). *High exposure: An enduring passion for Everest and unforgiving places*. New York: Simon & Schuster. Mountain climber and filmmaker David Breashers recounts the story of his adventure-filled life.

Bridges, R. (1999). *Through my eyes*. New York: Scholastic. As a 6-year-old, Ruby Bridges walked through a hostile crowd on the first day of school integration in New Orleans. Now she looks back and tells her story. This was the 2000 Orbis Pictus winner.

Brooks, T. (2003). *Sometimes the magic works: Lessons from a writing life*. New York: Del Rey. Fantasy author Terry Brooks reflects on his life and the lessons that he has learned about writing.

Brown, D. (2002). *Far beyond the garden gate: Alexandra David-Neel's journey to Lhasa*. Boston: Houghton Mifflin. Leaving her family behind, a woman journeys to Tibet in 1911 and stays 14 years to study Buddhism.

Burchard, P. (2003). *Frederick Douglass: For the great family of man*. New York: Atheneum. This is a well-rounded look at a leader in the abolitionist movement in America.

Carpenter, A. S. (2003). *Lewis Carroll: Through the looking glass*. Minneapolis: Lerner. This is a realistic look at Charles Lutwidge Dodgson, who wrote as Lewis Carroll.

Chen, D. (2002). *Sounds of the river*. New York: HarperCollins. Da Chen recounts his college years in China. This is a sequel to *Colors of the Mountain* (1999).

Clinton, C. (Ed.). (2003). *Poem of her own: Voices of American women yesterday and today*. New York: Abrams. With a representative poem and a brief biography, Clinton looks at 25 poets from Emily Dickinson to Sylvia Plath.

Collins, M. (2003). *Airborne: A photobiography of Wilbur and Orville Wright*. Washington, DC: National Geographic. The individual personalities of these brothers comes through in this book.

Cooper, I. (2003). *Jack: The early years of John F. Kennedy*. New York: Dutton. This biography for younger adolescents portrays the pressures and struggles that shaped the future president.

Danneberg, J. (2002). *Women artists of the west: Five portraits in creativity and courage*. Golden, CO: Fulcrum Pub. Danneberg looks at five notable women who influenced the art of the western United States.

Dash, J. (2001). *The world at her fingertips: The story of Helen Keller*. New York: Scholastic. Dash provides an honest portrayal of Helen Keller.

Delano, M. F. (2002). *Inventing the future: A photobiography of Thomas Alva Edison*. Washington, DC: National Geographic Society. Photographs bring to life the story of a famous scientist.

Doherty, K. (1999). *William Bradford: Rock of Plymouth*. Brookfield, CT: Twenty-First Century. This is the story of one of the founders of Plymouth Colony in Massachusetts.

Doherty, K. (2002). *Marjory Stoneman Douglas: Guardian of the 'glades*. Brookfield, CT: Twenty-First Century. Douglas was a strong environmentalist who devoted her life to protecting the Everglades.

Donnelly, K. (2003). *Deacon Jones*. New York: Rosen. This biography is part of a series on football hall of famers. Another book in the series is *Fran Tarkenton* (2003) by David Hulm.

Donnelly, M. (2003). *Theodore Roosevelt: Larger than life.* North Haven, CT: Linnett Books. Using primary source materials, Donnelly has created a biography that can be enjoyed by even reluctant readers.

Feiler, B. (2002). *Abraham: A journey to the heart of three faiths.* New York: Morrow. This biography for advanced readers looks at the truth and the fantasy in the life of the patriarch of three religions.

Felix, A. (2002). *Condi: The Condoleezza Rice story.* New York: Newmarket Press. Felix takes readers into the life of the national security advisor to President George W. Bush.

Fleming, C. (2003). *Ben Franklin's almanac: Being a true account of the good gentleman's life.* New York: Atheneum. This nontraditional biography is in scrapbook format, and the information is excellent.

Flowers, P., & Dixon, A. (2001). *Alone across the Arctic: One woman's epic journey by dog team.* Portland, OR: Alaska Northwest Books. Tracing the route of 1923–1924 Norwegian explorers, Flowers takes her dogs from Point Barrow, Alaska, to Repulse Bay, Canada.

Fradin, D. B., & Fradin, J. B. (2000). *Ida B. Wells: Mother of the civil rights movement.* New York: Clarion. Photographs help tell the story of this often forgotten Civil Rights leader.

Freedman, R. (1987). *Lincoln: A photobiography.* New York: Clarion. This 1988 Newbery Medal winner focuses on Lincoln as president and his impact on the country.

Freedman, R. (1990). *Franklin Delano Roosevelt.* New York: Clarion. Although weakened by polio, Roosevelt led the United States through the Depression and World War II.

Freedman, R. (1993). *Eleanor Roosevelt: A life of discovery.* New York: Clarion. Although she began her public life as the wife of an American president, Eleanor remained active as a crusader for human rights, serving as a delegate to the United Nations and as Chairman of the Human Right Commission.

Freedman, R. (1994). *Kids at work: Lewis Hind and the crusade against child labor.* New York: Clarion. Traveling throughout the United States in the early 1900s, Lewis Hind became an investigative photographer who documented the abuses of child labor. This was a 1995 Orbis Pictus honor book.

Freedman, R. (1996). *Life and death of Crazy Horse.* New York: Holiday House. Freedman tells the story of the Oglala leader and his resistance to the takeover of Indian lands.

Freedman, R. (1999). *Babe Didrikson Zaharias: The making of a champion.* New York: Clarion. Constantly testing the boundaries set for women in sports, Babe was named the best female athlete of the first half of the 20th century.

Freedman, R. (2002). *Confucius: The golden rule.* New York: Arthur Levine Books. Freedman explores the life of a religious teacher and the links between his writings and the visions of Thomas Jefferson. Other biographies by Freedman include *Out of Darkness: The Story of Louis Braille* (1997) and *Martha Graham: A Dancer's Life* (1998).

Gantos, J. (2002). *A hole in my life.* New York: Farrar, Strauss and Giroux. Award-winning young adult author Jack Gantos reflects on his youth including his arrest for drug trafficking.

Gherman, B. (2002). *Ansel Adams: America's photographer.* Boston: Little, Brown. With a timeline, bibliography, and notes, the author presents the life of a famous photographer.

Giblin, J. C. (2000). *The amazing life of Benjamin Franklin.* New York: Scholastic. This book for reluctant readers was a 2001 Orbis Pictus Award honor book. Another biography by Giblin is *Charles A. Lindbergh: A Human Hero* (1997).

Giblin, J. C. (2002). *Life and death of Adolf Hitler.* New York: Clarion. This is an award-winning biography.

Glover, S., Weber, B., & Hines, G. (2000). *Savion! My life in tap.* New York: Morrow. This young tap dancer choreographed the Tony Award-winning Broadway show "Bring in da Noise, Bring in da Funk."

Goh, C. H. (2002). *Beyond the dance: A ballerina's life.* Toronto: Tundra. Goh, a prima ballerina with the National Ballet of Canada, looks back at her life.

Gold, A. L. (2000). *A special fate: Chiune Sugihara: Hero of the Holocaust.* New York: Scholastic. This is the story of the Japanese Vice Counsel who issued illegal visas to 6,000 Jews during the Holocaust.

Greenberg, J., & Jordan, S. (2001). *Vincent van Gogh: Portrait of an artist.* New York: Delacorte. Brilliance and intensity filled the life and the paintings of this tortured artist.

Greenberg, J., & Jordan, S. (2003). *Runaway girl: The artist Louise Bourgeois.* New York: Abrams. The authors use Bourgeois' works and words to tell the story of this Franco-American sculptor.

Greenfeld, H. (2001). *After the Holocaust.* New York: Greenwillow. Howard Greenfeld examines the lives of survivors of the Holocaust after their liberation.

Gutman, B. (2003). *Lance Armstrong: A biography.* New York: Simon & Schuster. This biography looks beyond the world of sports to portray the entire life of this Tour de France winner.

Hart, E. T. (1999). *Barefoot heart: Stories of a migrant child.* Tempe, AZ: Bilingual Press. As the youngest of six children, Hart remembers life as part of a family of migrant workers.

Haskins, J. (2002). *Champion: The story of Muhammad Ali.* New York: Walker & Company. Haskins provides a view of the life of a famous sports individual.

Haskins, J., & Benson, K. (2000). *Carter G. Woodson: The man Who put "Black" in American history.* Brookfield, CT: Millbrook. In this easy-reading biography, the authors present the story of the father of African American history.

Hill, C. M. (2002). *John Lewis: From freedom rider to Congressman.* Berkely Heights, NJ: Enslow Publishers. Hill explores the civil rights movement through the eyes of one of the participants.

Hipperson, C. E. (2001). *The belly gunner.* Brookfield, CT: Twenty-First Century Books. This is the account of an American GI in World War II.

Jacobsen, R. (2001). *Rescued images: Memories of a childhood in hiding.* New York: Mikaya Press. Using collages and photographs, Jacobsen tells the story of her family.

Jeffrey, L. S. (1996). *Great American businesswomen.* Springfield, NJ: Enslow. Jeffrey profiles ten 20th-century American women who have achieved success in business. Jeffrey has also written *Betty Shabazz: Sharing the Vision of Malcolm X* (2000).

Jiang, J. (1997). *Red scarf girl: A memoir of the cultural revolution.* New York: HarperTrophy. What can a young girl do when her government wants her to turn her back on her ancestors and inform on her parents?

Jordan, J. (2001). *Soldier: A poet's childhood.* New York: Basic Civitas. Poet and professor of African American Studies June Jordan tells her own story in this coming-of-age autobiography.

Karnes, F. A. (1995). *Girls & young women inventing.* Minneapolis, MN: Free Spirit. Describing how each inventor began and continued the process of inventing, Karnes includes inventions such as laborsaving devices, objects that improve safety, and gadgets that make life more convenient.

Kent, Z. (1999). *Andrew Carnegie: Steel king and friend to libraries*. Springfield, NJ: Enslow. Kent describes the life of an American industrialist and philanthropist.

Kenyon, K. S. (2003). *The Bronte family: Passionate literary geniuses*. Minneapolis, MN: Lerner. Kenyon looks at all the Bronte siblings: Charlotte, Anne, Emily, and Branwell.

King-Smith, D. (2002). *Chewing the cud*. New York: Knopf. Author Dick King-Smith explains how his many jobs prepared him to become an author.

Kraft, B. H. (2003). *Theodore Roosevelt: Champion of the American spirit*. New York: Clarion. Follow FDR from the Rough Riders in the Spanish-American War to his years in the White House.

Krull, K. (2000). *Lives of extraordinary women: Rulers, rebels (And what the neighbors thought)*. San Diego: Harcourt. Krull uses lots of humor to tell the stories of important women throughout history. Another anthology by Krull is *Lives of the Writers: Comedies, Tragedies (and What the Neighbors Thought)* (1994).

Landau, E. (2001). *Heroine of the Titanic: The real unsinkable Molly Brown*. New York: Clarion. The legend and the facts are both presented in this biography.

Landau, E. (2002). *Osama bin Laden: A war against the West*. Brookfield, CT: Twenty-First Century Books. This book presents information about militant Islamic leader Osama bin Laden and the beliefs that fuel his terrorist actions.

Lasky, K. (2000). *Vision of beauty: The story of Sarah Breedlove Walker*. Cambridge, MA: Candlewick. Madame C. J. Walker became the first female African American self-made millionaire.

Lazo, C. (2000). *Alice Walker: Freedom writer*. Minneapolis, MN: Lerner. Using quotations from Walker's writings, Lazo explores the life of an American author.

Lazo, C. E. (2003). *F. Scott Fitzgerald: Voice of the Jazz age*. Minneapolis, MN: Lerner. This easy-to-read biography meshes the private and public lives of a great writer.

Leavy, J. (2002). *Sandy Koufax: A lefty's legacy*. New York: HarperCollins. Although Koufax guards his private life, Leavy has written an excellent biography of one of baseball's greatest pitchers.

Lobel, A. (1998). *No pretty picture: A child of war*. New York: Greenwillow. Anita Lobel takes readers back to her experiences as a Jewish child in Poland in World War II, her capture by the Nazis, and her later life in Sweden after the war. This was a 1999 Orbis Pictus honor book.

MacDonald, A., with DeGeronimo, T. F. (2003). *Dropping in with Andy Mac: The life of a pro skateboarder*. New York: Simon Pulse. This autobiography takes readers into the world of skateboarding.

MacNow, G. (2003). *Sports great Allen Iverson*. Berkeley Heights, NJ: Enslow. Follow this basketball player from the projects to his career as an NBA superstar.

Macy, S. (2001). *Bull's eye: A photobiography of Annie Oakley*. Washington, DC: National Geographic Society. Macy's text along with outstanding photographs and quotes bring this woman of the old west to life.

Markel, R. J. (2001). *Jimi Hendrix*. Minneapolis, MN: Lerner. Markel recounts the life of the famous rock-and-roll guitarist.

Marrin, A. (1997). *Commander in chief: Abraham Lincoln and the Civil War*. New York: Dutton. *School Library Journal* (January 1998) called this the best book on Lincoln since Russell Freedman's Newbery Medal-winning book. Another biography of a Civil War leader is *Unconditional Surrender: U. S. Grant and the Civil War* (1994).

Marrin, A. (2001). *George Washington and the founding of a nation*. New York: Dutton. Using primary resources, Marrin provides an honest portrait of one of the founding fathers. Marrin has also written *Terror of the Spanish main: Sir Henry Morgan and his buccaneers* (1999).

Mason, B. A. (2003). *Elvis Presley: A penguin life*. New York: Viking. Mason looks at all sides of the complex individual who changed the course of American music.

McDonough, Y. Z. (2002). *Peaceful protest: The life of Nelson Mandela*. New York: Walker. In this biography for reluctant readers, McDonough presents the life of a leader in the struggle against apartheid.

Meltzer, M. (1985). *Dorothea Lange: Life through the camera*. New York: Viking Kestrel. Lange's photographs of migrant workers and poverty in rural America became an impetus to social reform. Other biographies by Meltzer include *Langston Hughes* (1997), *Lincoln, in His Own Words* (1993), *Mary McLeod Bethune: Voice of Black Hope* (1987), *Captain James Cook: Three Times Around the World* (2002), and *Starting from Home: A Writer's Beginnings: A Memoir* (1988), his own autobiography.

Meltzer, M. (2002a). *Walt Whitman: A biography*. Brookfield, CT: Twenty-First Century Books. Meltzer explores Whitman's life and the events of the 19th century. Meltzer has also written *Carl Sandburg: A biography* (1999).

Meltzer, M. (2002b). *Ten kings and the worlds they ruled*. New York: Scholastic. Meltzer tells the stories of rulers from Attila and Charlemagne to Kublai Khan, Atahualpa, and Mansa Musa.

Mitchell, S. (2002). *Jesus: What he really said and did*. New York: HarperCollins. Mitchell tries to distinguish fact from legend and to identify the authentic sayings and actions of Jesus.

Myers, W. D. (1999). *At her majesty's request: An African princess in Victorian England*. New York: Scholastic. Saved from becoming a ritual sacrifice, an Egbado princess is taken to London and presented to Queen Victoria as Sara Forbes Bonetta. Myers tells the tragic story of her life and the cultural conflicts she faced. This biography was a 2000 Orbis Pictus honor book.

Myers, W. D. (2001). *Bad boy: A memoir*. New York: HarperCollins. Award-winning author Walter Dean Myers tells of his youth in Harlem in the 1950s.

Nelson, M. (2001). *Carver: A life in poems*. Asheville, NC: Front Street Books. Poems tell the story of Carver's life from slavery to scientist.

O'Connor, B. (2003). *Leonardo da Vinci: Renaissance genius*. Minneapolis, MN: CarolRhoda. O'Connor has written an informative and interesting biography of this famous artist.

Ohno, A. A., with Richardson, N. A. (2002). *A journey: The autobiography of Apolo Anton Ohno*. New York: Simon & Schuster. Olympic speed skater and medalist Ohno recounts the best and the worst of his career on ice.

Opdyke, I. G. (1999). *In my hands: Memories of a Holocaust rescuer*. New York: Knopf. As a young Polish girl, Irene saved Jews during the Holocaust.

Partridge E. (1998). *Restless spirit: The life and works of Dorothea Lange*. New York: Viking. Lange took powerful photographs of migrant workers and Japanese American internees.

Partridge, E. (2002). *This land was made for you and me: The life & songs of Woody Guthrie*. New York: Putnam. Partridge examines the strong political views and personality that made Woody Guthrie an icon in American music.

Paulsen, G. (2000). *The beet fields: Memories of a sixteenth summer*. New York: Delacorte. After running away from home, Paulsen worked in the fields as a migrant laborer and with a carnival.

Pollack, J. S. (1996). *Women on the hill.* New York: Watts. Pollack provides comprehensive profiles of women who have served in the U.S. Congress.

Reef, C. (2000). *Paul Laurence Dunbar: Portrait of a poet.* Berkeley Heights, NJ: Enslow. More than a poet, Dunbar wrote plays, stories, and newspaper articles.

Robertson, J. I., Jr. (2001). *Standing like a stone wall.* New York: Atheneum. Primary resources enhance this biography of a Civil War general.

Rosen, M. (2001). *Shakespeare: His work and his world.* Cambridge, MA: Candlewick. Michael Rosen brings the bard and Elizabethan times to life.

Santiago, E. (1993). *When I was Puerto Rican.* New York: Vintage. A sequel is Santiago's Alex Award-winning *Almost a Woman* (1999). In these classic coming-of-age biographies, Santiago recounts her life in Puerto Rico and in Brooklyn.

Schraff, A. (1999). *Ralph Bunche: Winner of the Nobel Peace Prize.* Springfield, NJ: Enslow. This is the story of a complex man who became a great peacemaker.

Severance, J. B. (1999). *Einstein: Visionary scientist.* New York: Clarion. This is a comprehensive biography of the famous scientist.

Sigerman, H. (2001). *Elizabeth Cady Stanton: The right is ours.* New York: Oxford University Press. Primary sources provide the basis for this biography of a woman and her fight for equal rights.

Sis, P. (2003). *Tree of life: A book depicting the life of Charles Darwin: Naturalist, geologist, and thinker.* New York: Frances Foster Books. Although this is a short biography, Sis has relied on primary documents to look into the private life of a scientist.

Spies, K. B. (1999). *Franklin D. Roosevelt.* Springfield, NJ: Enslow. With a chronology and chapter notes, this is an informative and interesting biography of an American president.

Spinelli, J. (1998). *Knots in my yo-yo string; The autobiography of a kid.* New York: Knopf. Author Jerry Spinelli describes his childhood in rural Pennsylvania.

Stanley, D. (1996). *Leonardo da Vinci.* New York: Morrow. Stanley won the Orbis Pictus for this biography of the great artist.

Stanley, D. (1998). *Joan of Arc.* New York: Morrow. Stanley examines the life of a familiar historical figure against the backdrop of a turbulent time in French history.

Stanley, D. (2000). *Michelangelo.* New York: HarperCollins. Filled with illustrations and art work, this biography will appeal to middle schoolers and reluctant readers.

Stanley, D. (2002). *Saladin: Noble Prince of Islam.* New York: HarperCollins. Stanley uses her art and writing to bring this historical figure to life for younger adolescents.

St. George, J. (2001). *John and Abigail Adams: An American love story.* New York: Holiday House. The letters of John and Abigail form the basis for this biography.

Stille, D. R. (1995). *Extraordinary women scientists.* Chicago: Children's Press. Stille describes the lives and contributions of more than 50 important scientists from many different disciplines.

Stravinsky, J. (1997). *Muhammad Ali.* New York: Random. Photos, text, sidelights, and samples of Ali's poetry combine in this biography.

Streissguth, T. (1999). *Jesse Owens.* Minneapolis, MN: Lerner. Jesse Owens went from being a sharecropper's son to winning four gold medals at the 1936 Olympics in Berlin, Germany.

Torres, J. A. (2003). *Sports great Sammy Sosa.* Berkeley Heights, NJ: Enslow. Growing up in the Dominican Republic, Sosa saw baseball as the path to success.

Walker, R. (2002). *Black, White, and Jewish: Autobiography of a shifting self.* New York: Riverhead Books. Born to a black mother and a white father who were Civil Rights activists, Rebecca Walker finds herself adrift when her parents divorce.

Yount, L. (1994). *Contemporary women scientists.* New York: Facts on File. Yount looks at 10 women who have contributed significantly to the natural sciences.

Yount, L. (1996). *Twentieth-century women scientists.* New York: Facts on File. The author describes the struggles and discrimination that each of these scientists faced.

Zach, K. K. (2002). *Hidden from history: The lives of eight American women scientists.* Greensboro, NC: Avisson. These biographies range from astronomer Annie Jump Cannon to bacteriologist Alice Evans and biologist Nettie Stevens as well as well-known women such as Grace Hooper and Gertrude Elion.

Zoya, with Folian, J., & Cristofari, R. (2002). *Zoya's story: An Afghan woman's struggle for freedom.* New York: Morrow. A young woman from Afghanistan tells of her life under the rule of the Taliban and the Mujahideen.

Suggested Readings

Barbieri, R. (2002). American lives. *Independent School, 62*(1), 97–98. (NOTE: This is not specific to YA biography.)

Brodie, C. S. (2003). Milton Meltzer: History, biography, and social issues. *School Library Media Activities Monthly, 19*(6), 43–46.

Kenyon, K. (2003). Writing a young-adult biography: Bringing the Bronte family to life was a labor of love. *The Writer, 116*(3), 24–25.

Partridge, E. (2002). The creative life. *School Library Journal, 28*(10), 42–43.

References

(Note: All young adult literature referenced in this chapter are included in the Young Adult Books list and are not repeated in this list.)

Akmal, T. T., & Ayre-Svingen, B. (2002). Integrated biographical inquiry: A student-centered approach to learning. *The Social Studies, 93*(6), 272–276.

Bucher, K. T., & Manning, M. L. (1998). Telling our stories, sharing our lives: Collective biographies of women. *The ALAN Review, 26*(1), 12–16.

Buehler, J. S. (2003). Dinner party. *Voices from the Middle, 10*(4), 16–19.

Burns, M. M. (1995). Biography. In A. Silvey (Ed.), *Children's books and their creators.* Boston: Houghton Mifflin.

Carter, B. (2003). Reviewing biography. *The Horn Book, 79*(2), 165–174.

Daisey, P. (1996a). Promoting interest in plant biology with biographies of plant hunters. *The American Biology Teacher, 58*(7), 396–407.

Daisey, P. (1996b). Promoting literacy in secondary content area classrooms with biography projects. *Journal of Adolescent & Adult Literacy, 40*(4), 270–279.

Daisey, P. (1997). Promoting equity in secondary science and mathematics classes with biography projects. *School Science and Mathematics, 97*(8), 413–418.

Daisey, P., & José-Kampfner, C. (2002). The power of story to expand possible selves for Latina middle school students. *Journal of Adolescent & Adult Literacy, 45*(7), 578–587.

Hillman, J. (2003). *Discovering children's literature.* Upper Saddle River, NJ: Merrill/Prentice Hall.

Hurst, C. O. (2001). Personalizing history. *Teaching PreK-8, 32*(1), 106–109.

Lechner, J. V. (1997). Accuracy in biographies for children. *New Advocate, 10*(3), 229–242.

Merriam-Webster's Encyclopedia of Literature. (1995). Springfield, MA: Merriam-Webster.

Mickenberg, J. (2002). Civil rights, history, and the left; Inventing the juvenile black biography. *MELUS, 27*(2), 65–95.

Minchew, S. S. (2002). Teaching character through sports literature. *The Clearing House, 75*(3), 137–141.

Moss, B., & Hendershot, J. (2002). Exploring sixth graders' selection of nonfiction trade books. *The Reading Teacher, 56*(1), 6–17.

Rudelson, C. (2003). *For teachers: Why use biographies?* Retrieved August 25, 2003, from www.whitneystewart.com/ASSK/why_biography.htm.

Taylor, D. (1996). *The healing power of stories: Creating yourself through the stories of your life.* New York: Doubleday.

Taylor, G. (2002/2003). Who's who? Engaging biography study. *The Reading Teacher, 56*(4), 342–344.

Townsend, L. T., & Hanson, C. (2001). The self and the narrative: A conversation on educational biography. *Educational Studies, 32*(1), 38–52.

Weinberg, S. (2003, November/December). American biographies, volume 1. *Bookmarks, 7,* 28–33.

York, S. (2001). What's new in Latino literature? *Book Report, 19*(4), 19–24.

EXPLORING NONFICTION/ INFORMATION BOOKS

Many adults do not think of nonfiction when they talk about young adult literature. For example, Worthy, Moorman, and Turner (1999) noted instances of teachers who will not allow students to read nonfiction in sustained silent reading time in spite of studies showing that some older children and adolescents prefer nonfiction. We do not want you to fall into that trap. Thus, although we have acclaimed the pleasures of reading fiction, we also want to point out that reading well-written informational books is an enjoyable experience for many adolescents. Doiron (1995) found that nonfiction is no longer dry and boring as authors employ "rich writing styles and a variety of forms not just to convey knowledge or list facts but also to infuse their subject with the same sense of wonder and awe that drew them to the topic in the first place" (p. 37). A poll of adolescents ages 12 to 18 found that 35% read mainly to get information and facts and 26% prefer reading nonfiction books ("Reading remains popular among youth, according to poll," 2001). "While still lagging somewhat behind fiction, young adult nonfiction is on the rise . . . [with] teenagers enjoy[ing] biographies and creative nonfiction" (Furi-Perry, 2003). An example of this popularity is Jack Canfield's best-selling inspirational and motivational series of books including *Chicken Soup for the Teenage Soul* (1997) and *Chicken Soup for the Teenage Soul on Tough Stuff* (2001).

Thus, all educators need to be knowledgeable of the many informational books written especially for young adults and with the criteria used to select them. In addition to examining information books and informational series for young adults, library media specialists and teachers have a professional responsibility to make these books an integral part of the curriculum as well as part of young adults' daily reading habits.

FOCUSING POINTS	In this chapter, you will read about:

1. The definition of nonfiction.
2. The types of nonfiction including informational series.
3. The categories of nonfiction.
4. Reasons for using and teaching nonfiction.
5. The characteristics of good nonfiction.
6. Suggestions for selecting and using nonfiction.
7. Suggestions for teaching with nonfiction.
8. Recommendations of quality nonfiction for young adults.

YOUNG ADULT NONFICTION

Do adolescents lose interest in reading as they reach middle school or do they just lose interest in reading what teachers expect them to read? Worthy, Moorman, and Turner (1999) found that the gap between what students want to read and what schools provide them is widening. Adolescents do not find what they want to read in schools and see school reading as an imposition. In addition, some public libraries do not even include nonfiction in the young adult literature collection (Jones, 2001). Aronson (2001) decried the adult mind-set that assumes young adults do not enjoy nonfiction and cited the research of Betty Carter, which pointed out that nonfiction is popular with young adults but not with the school library media specialists who purchase it or teachers who use it in the curriculum.

Why do young adults read nonfiction? To find part of the answer, go back to psychology and child development. As adolescents mature, they evidence a need to know about things and to explore concepts and subjects in more detail. According to Tracey Firestone of the Suffolk (NY) Cooperative Library System, adolescents look to books to find information they do not feel comfortable asking someone else about (Jones, 2001). In addition, rather than focusing on the relationships or character development found in fiction, some boys prefer the action in "visual media—the Internet, nonfiction, newspapers, and magazines—that focus on sports, electronics, and games" (Guzzetti et al., 2002, p. 47). Jones (2001) also reported that the research of Teri S. Lesesne showed that nonfiction is especially important to "at-risk teens . . . [who are] less-than-enthusiastic readers" (p. 44). Lesesne further noted that, although adolescents may read nonfiction on a regular basis, "they do not see themselves as readers because nonfiction is not as valued in the English classroom" (Jones, 2001, p. 44). Lesesne's findings were echoed by Moss and Hendershot (2002), who found that many reluctant middle school readers enjoy reading nonfiction trade books because the books are interesting and useful for learning. Therefore, in this chapter, you will explore young adult nonfiction that "admits its limitations and invites readers into a process of discovery. Like the best literary fiction, it is willing to be ambiguous and to leave space for the reader's own conclusions" (Aronson, 2001). Connecting Adolescents and Their Literature 8–1 suggests one way to build on young adults' enthusiasm for nonfiction.

Definition of Nonfiction

The simplest way to define nonfiction is to say it is literature that is not fiction and that focuses, instead, on facts and information, hence the often used synonym *informational book*. However, the lines between fiction and nonfiction sometimes blur. Adult authors Truman Capote and John Hersey both wrote nonfiction "novels" in which they told the story of actual people and events in the form of a novel without inserting their own comments (*Merriam-Webster's Encyclopedia of Literature*, 1995). Calling a writer of nonfiction a "writer of reality," author Penny Colman reports that some editors see a blurring of the boundaries between fiction and nonfiction to create a new category known as edutainment. While hard-core nonfiction writers do not make up anything, writers of edutainment do. Colman goes on to say that, although she uses a style that she terms *creative nonfiction* or *literary journalism with fictional techniques,* she does not

---

CONNECTING **ADOLESCENTS AND THEIR LITERATURE 8–1**

To encourage adolescents to read nonfiction, educators can build upon an idea discussed by Mary J. Lickteig (2003). While reading nonfiction, students are expected to locate interesting facts, and to share this information with the class. At a given time, the teacher turns to one student and says, "Feed my brain." The student replies by sharing a specific, unusual, and/or interesting fact from the nonfiction book he or she is currently reading. In turn, that student asks another student in the class to "Feed my brain." Lickteig suggests limiting the sharing to three or four students at one time. An extension of this activity would be to gather the shared information into a book of interesting facts or to have the class vote on the "best" facts to place on a bulletin board. This idea can be used in any subject across the curriculum.

TABLE 8–1	A Contrast of Fiction and Nonfiction

Fiction		Nonfiction
Pleasure	**Purpose**	Information
Read from beginning to end	**Structure**	Read in parts or pieces
Specific to the characters	**Language**	Specific to the subject
Created	**Content**	Researched

make anything up including the dialogue, scenes, or characters ("Adventures in non-fiction: Talking with Penny Colman," 2002). The best nonfiction books present, interpret, organize, and document factual materials with an interesting presentation style. Table 8–1 shows the contrast between fiction and nonfiction.

Types of Nonfiction Books

As with other genres of literature, a number of ways exist to divide nonfiction. One way is to divide the literature into series and stand-alone titles.

Individual Works. Like novels, nonfiction books may either be stand-alone works or part of a series. While an individual author may choose to write in a particular discipline or on a particular topic, he or she might write each stand-alone book in a different format with a different style and/or book design. Expanding Your Knowledge with the Internet 8–1 has links to information about a few nonfiction authors.

EXPANDING	YOUR KNOWLEDGE WITH THE INTERNET 8–1

 You can use the Internet to find information about some selected authors of nonfiction for young adults such as the following. Links to these and many additional sites are found on this book's Companion Website at www.prenhall.com/bucher.

Susan Campbell Bartoletti
www.childrenslit.com/f_bartoletti.html

Jim Haskins
www.childrenslit.com/f_haskins.html

Jim Murphy
www/cbcbooks.org/html/jim_murphy.html

Series. In contrast to stand-alone books, nonfiction series consist of a number of books that may or may not be written by the same author. However, they are on the same general topic/subject and are linked by the publisher's book design for the series. Thus, nonfiction series are evaluated not only on the content of the books, but also on the book design for the entire series (Zvirin, 1999). Poor design will detract from a good text while a fancy design does not compensate for poor information. The publisher's challenge is to find a good design that will be appropriate for all of the books in the series. Some nonfiction series are written quickly to a specific formula and do not adhere to the same standards as non-series nonfiction. While they might meet the need to provide information for a specific report, they can be very pedestrian and rapidly become outdated (Lempke, 1999). However, a number of excellent series are available, and there is no doubt that young adults, including reluctant readers, find informational series books appealing, especially those with photographs and other illustrations. Table 8–2 lists a few of the current popular nonfiction series.

One problem for educators is that, because of the number of series and the limited amount of review space in journals, many review journals focus on the series as a whole rather than on individual titles unless a specific book deals with a highly controversial subject (Zvirin, 1999). This can cause problems when the books in a series are very uneven, especially if new books are added to the series over a period of several years. For example, an early review of a series may be very favorable; however, books published after the initial review may be of a lesser quality. Because the journal has only one review of the series, an educator might not be aware of the change in the later books' quality in that particular series. Thus, it is important to review the individual books in nonfiction series with the same care that you would use in evaluating stand-alone nonfiction.

TABLE 8-2	Nonfiction Series

A few popular and well-written current nonfiction series are:

Series Title	Publisher
Crafts of the Ancient World	Rosen
Great Cities Through the Ages	Enchanted Lion Books
Projects for Young Scientists	Franklin Watts
Science Concepts	Twenty-First Century
Sports Greats	Enslow
Teen Health Series	Omnigraphics
Women's Hall of Fame	Second Story Press
Questioning History	Creative Education

Categories of Nonfiction

It is tempting to divide nonfiction into categories based on the content of the school's curriculum. However, Dresang (1999) notes the changing boundaries in young adult nonfiction books with the inclusion of previously ignored or forbidden subjects such as child slavery/labor, contemporary political issues, sexuality, religion, violence, and environmental issues. Therefore, popular young adult nonfiction provides more than curriculum-related information. It is also full of information on growing up, popular culture, and the contemporary world. Seeing the wide range of nonfiction available and knowing that adolescents select nonfiction that goes beyond the subjects taught in school, we have chosen to divide informational books into groups that roughly parallel some categories in the Dewey Decimal System and to highlight a few outstanding books. You will find additional recommended nonfiction titles listed in the bibliography at the end of this chapter. To help you select the categories that your own students will like, Connecting Adolescents and Their Literature 8–2 suggests using surveys to determine reading interests.

General Works. Books of assorted and sometimes apocryphal "facts" are always popular with adolescents. In addition to the usual almanacs, two excellent choices are Jenifer Corr Morse's *Scholastic Book of World Records* (2001) and David Holt and Bill Mooney's *Spiders in the Hairdo: Modern Urban Legends* (1999).

Religion and Mythology. While religion is not a popular topic with all young adults, some adolescents do begin to explore their personal religious beliefs. In Rahel Musleah's *Why on This Night? A Passover Haggadah for Family Celebration* (2000) and Tahar Ben Jelloun's *Islam Explained* (2002), authors explore religions that are in the news. Two excellent historical accounts that provide a background on religion in America are Randall Balmer's *Religion in Twentieth Century America* (2001) and Grant Wacker's *Religion in Nineteenth Century America* (2000). Looking even farther to the past, Margaret Mulvihill looks at the early Christian church in *The Treasury of Saints and Martyrs* (1999), and Sheila Keenan explores mythology in *Gods, Goddesses, and Monsters: An Encyclopedia of World Mythology* (2000).

CONNECTING | **ADOLESCENTS AND THEIR LITERATURE 8–2**

Use surveys to determine the reading preferences of your students. Be sure to include several categories of nonfiction such as "how-to-do-it" books, true sports books, and books of interesting facts. Then, have books in the preferred categories available for students and allow students to read them, especially in sustained silent reading time.

You can find sample inventories on the Internet. Links are found on this book's Companion Website at www.prenhall.com/bucher.

Social Sciences. A number of topics fall into the broad category of the social sciences. Several authors look at the changing face of America in books such as Pearl Fuyo Gaskins' *What Are You? Voices of Mixed-Race Young People* (1999), Milton Meltzer's *There Comes a Time: The Struggle for Civil Rights* (2001b), and Martha E. Kendall's *Failure Is Impossible: The History of American Women's Rights* (2001). Other books in the social sciences include Karen Magnuson Beil's *Fire in Their Eyes: Wildfires and the People Who Fight Them* (1999), Michael L. Cooper's *Indian School: Teaching the White Man's Way* (1999), and Penny Colman's *Corpses, Coffins, and Crypts: A History of Burial* (1997).

Science. Information books can help adolescents explore the interesting world of science. James M. Deem shows the mysteries hidden for centuries in *Bodies from the Bog* (1998). Likewise, Donna Jackson looks at scientists who hunt criminals in *The Wildlife Detectives: How Forensic Scientists Fight Crimes against Nature* (2000). There is tension in Thom Holmes' *Fossil Feud: The Rivalry of the First American Dinosaur Hunters* (1998) and investigation in Diane Swanson's *Nibbling on Einstein's Brain: The Good, the Bad, & the Bogus in Science* (2001). For pleasure and fun, Elizabeth Van Steenwyk takes readers to the ocean in *Let's Go to the Beach: A History of Sun and Fun by the Sea* (2001). Adolescents can see how far weather forecasting has come after reading Jim Murphy's tale of the snowstorm of 1888 in *Blizzard!* (2000). While there are a number of ways to introduce science nonfiction to adolescents, Suggestions for Collaborative Efforts 8–1 provides one example.

Health. With peer pressure and the need to assert their independence, many adolescents consider engaging in risky behaviors or begin to develop health problems. A number of nonfiction books address these issues in a nondidactic manner. Magdalena Alagna has written *Everything You Need to Know about the Dangers of Binge Drinking* (2001); Melanie Ann Apel penned *Cocaine and Your Nose: The Incredibly Disgusting Story* (2000); and Margaret O. Hyde and Elizabeth H. Forsyth presented *Depression: What You Need to Know* (2002). Other health-related nonfiction books include Jeanette Farrell's

SUGGESTIONS FOR COLLABORATIVE EFFORTS

Some adolescents enjoy conducting experiments. Before students develop and implement their own (with sometimes disastrous results), teachers and library media specialists can work together to develop a display of science experiment books. A few to consider are:

■ *Science Is . . . A Source Book of Fascinating Facts, Projects and Activities* (Bosak, 2000)

■ *See for Yourself: More Than 100 Experiments for Science Fairs and Projects* (Cobb, 2001)

■ *Mad Professor: Concoct Extremely Weird Science Projects* (Frauenfelder, 2002).

Invisible Enemies: Stories of Infectious Diseases (1998), Gael Jennings' *Bloody Moments: And Further Highlights from the Astounding in History of Medicine* (2000), and Ellen Schwartz's *I'm a Vegetarian: Amazing Facts and Ideas for Healthy Vegetarians* (2002).

Growing Up as a Teenager. Young adults often turn to nonfiction books to answer the questions that they are reluctant to ask adults. For boys there are Jeremy Daldry's *The Teenage Guy's Survival Guide: The Real Deal on Girls, Growing Up, and Other Guy Stuff* (1999) and Mavis Jukes' *The Guy Book: An Owner's Manual: Safety, Maintenance and Operating Instructions for Teens* (2002). Girls will similarly enjoy Anthea Paul's *Girlosophy: The Love Survival Kit* (2002). Several books provide all teens with a frank look at sexual information including Jane Pavanel's *The Sex Book: An Alphabet of Smarter Love* (2001); Linda Madaras's *What's Happening to My Body* (2000), with editions for both boys and girls; Michael J. Basso's *The Underground Guide to Teenage Sexuality* (1997); and Tania Heller's *Pregnant! What Can I Do? A Guide for Teenagers* (2002). Finally, teenager Aisha Muharrar relates the results of a Teen Labels Survey and frankly discusses the issues in *More Than a Label: Why What You Wear or Who You're with Doesn't Define Who You Are* (2002).

Applied Science and Technology. Many adolescents want to learn how things are made and how they work. Favorite nonfiction books on this subject include Susan Goldman Rubin's *There Goes the Neighborhood: Ten Buildings People Loved to Hate* (2001); John B. Severance's *Skyscrapers: How America Grew Up* (2000); Elizabeth Mann's *Hoover Dam: The Story of Hard Times, Tough People, and the Taming of a Wild River* (2001); Angela Wilkes' *A Farm Through Time: The History of a Farm from Medieval Times to the Present Day* (2001); and David Macaulay's *The New Way Things Work* (1998). For young adults who dream of actually building things, there are books such as David Burgess-Wise's *The Ultimate Race Car* (1999) and Ed Sobey's *How to Build Your Own Prize-Winning Robot* (2002).

The Arts. Art takes many forms and most of them are represented in quality nonfiction for young adults. Michael L. Cooper's *Slave Spirituals and the Jubilee Singers* (2001) looks at music; Kathlyn Gay and Christine Whittington's *Body Marks: Tattooing, Piercing, and Scarification* (2002) explores body art; and Carol Sabbeth's *Monet and the Impressionists for Kids* (2002) examines an artistic movement. In Jim Haskins and Kathleen Benson's *Conjure Times: Black Magicians in America* (2001) and Cherie Turner's *Stunt Performers: Life Before the Camera* (2001), authors look at two different types of entertainers. For budding cartoonists, there is Christopher Hart's *Manga Mania Villains: How to Draw the Dastardly Villains of Japanese Comics* (2003). Finally, in Frank Augustyn and Shelley Tanaka's *Footnotes: Dancing the World's Best-Loved Ballets* (2001) and Olympid Dowd's *A Young Dancer's Apprenticeship: On Tour with the Moscow Ballet* (2002), writers examine the world of ballet.

Sports. Sports books are always popular nonfiction titles. Michael Brooke takes readers behind the scenes in *The Concrete Wave (The History of Skateboarding)* (1999), Steven Krasner presents information on sports with tips on how to be a better player in *Play*

Ball Like the Pros: Tips for Kids from 20 Big League Stars (2002), and Susan D. Bachrach combines sports and history in *The Nazi Olympics: Berlin 1936* (2000). Four historical views of sports are found in *Best Shots: The Greatest NFL Photographs of the Century* (1999), Sandra and Susan Steen's *Take It to the Hoop: 100 Years of Women's Basketball* (2003), Marcos Bretón's *Home Is Everything: The Latino Baseball Story* (2002), and *Baseball's Best Shots: The Greatest Baseball Photography of All Time* (2000). In addition, a number of excellent sports biographies exist such as those in Chapter 7 in this text.

Authors and Writing. Although some authors include information about writing in their autobiographies, others write about the creative process of writing. In *Blood on the Forehead: What I Know about Writing* (1998), M. E. Kerr uses excerpts from her novels to explain the writing process. Leonard W. Marcus's *Author Talk: Conversations with Judy Blume . . .* (2000) presents a series of interviews with fifteen young adult writers who talk about themselves and their craft. Finally, *What Is Poetry: Conversations with the American Avant-Garde* (2003), edited by Daniel Kane, explores poets who usually are not studied in school, and Ron Miller's *The History of Science Fiction* (2001) provides an overview for younger adolescents.

Real Adventures. Nonfiction adventure books can be as exciting as fiction. Sir Earnest Shackleton's ill-fated Antarctic expedition has been chronicled in Jennifer Armstrong's *Shipwreck at the Bottom of the World: The Extraordinary True Story of Shackleton and the Endurance* (1998) and Caroline Alexander's *The Endurance: Shackleton's Legendary Antarctic Expedition* (1998). Suggestions for Collaborative Efforts 8–2 examines the way some high school teachers used this adventure as a basis for an integrated unit. Jon Krakauer takes readers on an Everest expedition in *Into Thin Air* (1997) and Kathy Pelta looks at an ancient mystery in *Rediscovering Easter Island* (2001).

History. In nonfiction books, young adults can find a fresh look at historical events. Tom Feelings uses illustrations to document the Africa to America slave trade in *The Middle Passage: White Ships/Black Cargo* (1995). In Connecting Adolescents and Their Literature 8–3, Julia Johnson Connor (2003) describes how she used this wordless nonfiction book to provide a context for a discussion of African American literature in high school. Milton Meltzer looks at another type of immigration in *Bound for America: The Story of the European Immigrants* (2001a). Susan Campbell Bartoletti examines a great tragedy that led to emigration in *Black Potatoes: The Story of the Great Irish Famine, 1845–1850* (2001).

Many adolescents want to read books about war. G. Clifton Wisler's *When Johnny Went Marching: Young Americans Fight the Civil War* (2001) provides a new view of the American conflict. Karen Zeinert explores another hidden face of war in *Those Extraordinary Women of World War I* (2001), Amy Nathan and Eileen Collins look at another war in *Yankee Doodle Gals: Women Pilots of World War II* (2001), and Allan M. Winkler examines a modern form of conflict in *The Cold War: A History in Documents* (2001). Ted Gottfried records the aftermath of war in *Displaced Persons: The Liberation and Abuse of Holocaust Survivors* (2001).

SUGGESTIONS FOR COLLABORATIVE EFFORTS

Katz, Boran, Braun, Massie, and Kuby (2003) used the nonfiction book *Shipwreck at the Bottom of the World* (Armstrong, 1998) as the basis for an integrated thematic unit for high school students that would allow cooperation among several teachers such as the reading teacher, social studies teacher, library media specialist, and language arts teacher. The strategies that these teachers successfully used were similar to those used with fiction and included the following:

Introductory Activities:

> Linking the book to a video
>
> Making predictions about the story/video
>
> Agree/disagree statements
>
> Quotes from the major character

During Reading Activities:

> Continuation of some of the previous activities
>
> Dramatization of scenes from the book
>
> Vocabulary development activities
>
> Collaboration of facts in the book
>
> Study guide questions on the reading

After Reading Activities:

> Discussion of the book and/or links to fiction on the same topic
>
> Inquiry, research, and electronic slide presentation of a topic from the book

From Page to Screen lists a number of films that can be paired with young adult informational books in different cateopries.

Reasons for Using and Teaching Nonfiction

As we indicated earlier in this chapter, young adult nonfiction is often ignored in schools. However, a number of reasons exist to make nonfiction part of the curriculum and to encourage recreational nonfiction reading.

Reading nonfiction helps adolescents develop information literacy. This is a much needed skill in modern society where students can no longer memorize everything in school that they will need to know as adults. Instead, they must develop the skills to

CONNECTING | *ADOLESCENTS AND THEIR LITERATURE 8–3*

When Julia Johnson Connor (2003) saw the pictures in Tom Feelings' wordless nonfiction book *The Middle Passage: White Ships/Black Cargo* (1995), she decided to use the book in her 11th- and 12th-grade English classes to provide a background for the discussion of slavery in African American literature.

As adolescents examine the book:

- Ask them to consider not only the information that they gained from the pictures but also the feelings that the illustrations evoked.

- Ask students to think about why the author presented a visual representation of the Middle Passage rather than writing about it.

- Question students about their personal reaction to the book.
  Connor found that the use of this nonfiction book with an African American literature unit significantly increased the students' intellectual and emotional understandings of the Middle Passage and created the context for the exploration of other writings about the African American experience in literature.

locate, evaluate, and use information. In other words, they must become information literature. To do this, adolescents need the ability to:

- see the parts within the whole and their relationship,

- solve problems and think analytically,

- work in groups and communicate with others, and

- work independently and assume responsibility (Benson, 2002).

To help adolescents become information literate, educators must use reading and writing strategies and critical thinking skills that focus on nonfiction. For example, in nonfiction, adolescents find tables, charts, graphic organizers, maps, drawings, diagrams, timelines, and other visual representations of information. To survive in contemporary society, adolescents need to develop the skills and abilities to decode the information found in these visuals. Also, Hadaway, Vardell, and Young (2002) argue that, although most educators use fiction in the classroom, high-stakes tests contain more nonfiction than fiction passages for students to read and analyze. Suggestions for Collaborative Efforts 8–3 discusses information literacy, science teachers, and library media specialists.

Several studies have found a link between the reading of nonfiction and the development of literacy skills. Generally, students who read magazines and nonfiction books have higher average reading proficiencies than those who do not (Campbell, Kapinus, & Beatty, 1995). Also, nonfiction that presents concepts and vocabulary in a concrete

FROM PAGE TO SCREEN

Nonfiction and Informational Books

Like biographies, informational books cover topics that are often also the subject of film. Consider pairing a good informational text with one of the following films to deepen students' understanding of the subject matter, and as a means of comparing the authenticity of the tellers' fact gathering.

Titanica
1995, Unrated, Documentary
★ ★ ★

One of several documentaries about the shipwreck of the Titanic, *this poignant, humane look at the infamous tragedy was originally filmed for giant IMAX screens. That cinematic technique makes for a brief film, saturated color and shadow, and beautifully eerie shots. Narration that relies on the power inherent in witness testimony and histories, rather than on the narrator's own response to the tragedy, make this one of the more intriguing films on the topic. It's an interesting version to compare with Canter and Hirschorn's book* Titanic Adventure *and Robert Ballard's* Exploring the Titanic.

Into the Arms of Strangers: The Story of Kindertransport
2000, PG, Documentary
★ ★ ★ ★

This Academy Award winner for best documentary follows the stories of many children who were secretly transported to Britain without their families to escape Nazi persecution. This very moving, expertly crafted film compares poignantly with Hana Volavkova's I Never Saw Another Butterfly, a collection of the writings of children who did not escape the Holocaust.

Spider-Man
2002, PG-13
★ ★ ★ ¹/₂

Compare Sam Raimi's vibrant, exhilarating world of superheroes and villains with Mark Cotta Vaz's Behind the Mask of Spider-Man: The Secrets of the Movie. *Find the secrets Vaz writes about, and find other amazing effects or unanswered questions held in the film.*

Contact
1997, PG
★ ★ ★

This screen adaptation of Carl Sagan's novel is an interesting counterpoint to Ellen Jackson's informational book Looking for Life in the Universe: The Search for Extraterrestrial Intelligence. *Sagan's heroine, played in the film by the incomparable Jodie Foster, is modeled after astrophysicist Jill Tarter, who is the subject of Jackson's nonfiction text.*

8-3　SUGGESTIONS FOR COLLABORATIVE EFFORTS

The National Science Education Standards provide broad, interdisciplinary goals for educators. Noting that both "emergent and sophisticated readers often choose science and nature as their favorite genre of reading material," Terrence E. Young (2003) challenged teachers and school library media specialists to work together to identify quality nonfiction. Although his suggestions pertained only to science, these same principles can be adapted for other subjects in the curriculum.

- Content teachers and library media specialists should collaborate to help young adults understand curriculum concepts.
  They should identify quality nonfiction resources by:

  - Comparing the nonfiction books in a given subject in the school library's collection to a recognized standard.

  - Identifying the most important topics to be developed.

  - Purchasing nonfiction in these areas.

way can help teach literary skills and can provide a bridge to textbooks for non-native as well as native English speakers (Hadaway, Vardell, & Young, 2002).

There are still other benefits of using nonfiction with young adults. Nonfiction:

- helps adolescents learn and understand content-related vocabulary,

- provides current information in a more interesting way than textbooks,

- may be more appealing visually than a textbook (Hadaway, Vardell, & Young, 2002),

- is effective in moving adolescents from the Internet to the library (Jones, 2001),

- generally has a clear focus in less than 200 pages, and

- can provide a pleasurable reading experience.

Characteristics of Good Nonfiction

You should evaluate informational books for young adults as carefully as you evaluate fiction. Just because a nonfiction book presents information does not mean that you should not examine its quality (Broderick, 1995; Jones, 1995) and its appeal to young adults including the writing ability of the author, her or his writing style, and the tone of the book. Fortunately, many nonfiction books have factual and unbiased material, clear photographs, and writing that reflects young adults' reading levels and interests. Unfortunately, not all have these qualities. Thus, teachers and library media specialists must read reviewers' critiques of nonfiction and engage in firsthand evaluation.

What qualities should you look for in evaluating nonfiction? Considerations for Selecting Young Adult Literature: *Nonfiction* outlines a few items that we believe are important to keep in mind when selecting nonfiction books. Obviously, accuracy and objectivity are of prime importance as is an unbiased perspective, (i.e., does the book present accurate representations of people with differing sexual orientations?). Nonfiction should not trivialize a subject. As Sullivan (2000) wonders, how can one book teach you everything you need to know about a topic (as some nonfiction books claim) in 100 pages or less? Important, too, is a style and organization that is appropriate to the content, appealing to young adults' interests, and written on their reading levels. Because some authors write a number of informational books on different topics, it is necessary to look closely at their qualifications or at the amount of research that they have done. Also, examine the organizing features such as the index and glossary. Check the usefulness of the index by trying to locate information in the book and noting whether key topics and concepts are included in the index. Whether the illustrations are in color or black and white, they should be sharp and appropriately positioned on the pages. They should also accurately portray or extend the text, and have correct descriptive captions. Credits for the illustrations should be included. An appealing and compatible book design is important to attract readers. Even the shape of a nonfiction book is important, with short and thick books conveying the impression of serious information while tall and skinny books appeal to reluctant readers.

CONSIDERATIONS	*For Selecting Young Adult Literature*	*NONFICTION*

When evaluating and selecting nonfiction for young adults, ask the following questions:

- Is the content accurate, current, and clear?

- Is there an unbiased presentation and perspective?

- Does the author have a didactic or preachy tone?

- Is there a distinction between fact and conjecture or opinion?

- Is the content well-organized?

- Are the style and tone appropriate for the content and audience?

- What are the qualifications of the author?

- Are there a table of contents, index, glossary, timeline, or other organizers that help make the content accessible?

- Is there a useful index?

- Is the information up-to-date with current research and documentation?

- Is there evidence of research in bibliographies, notes or endnotes, suggestions for further reading, and Internet sites or key words for searching?

- Are the illustrations appropriate, attractive, and accurate with appropriate (and correct) captions?

- Is the book design appealing with:
  Attractive borders
  Crisp, uncluttered pages
  Readable and appropriate typeface
  Features such as symbols and feature boxes

As we have mentioned before, one special consideration when evaluating nonfiction is the number of series books. As Jones (1995) noted, the editors of some journals and magazines that review young adult books believe that evaluating the large number of nonfiction series is an overwhelming task. Thus, elect not to review them. Other journals will review a series one time, based only on the books that are available at that time. Adding to the difficulty of reviewing, just as some series fare better than others, individual books in the series may vary in quality. Unfortunately, publishers often try to get purchasers to buy the entire series by using a quote about one book to generalize the accolades to all books in the series (Jones, 1995). Lempke (1999) cautions against series books where authors insert annoying comments and exclamation points in an attempt to be chatty or perky. In any work of nonfiction, series, or stand-alone book, the ideal is to provide a well-written, attractive, interesting book that makes even complex subjects simple enough for adolescents without trivializing the information.

Like single works of nonfiction, series books must also be evaluated for accuracy and authenticity, content and perspective, style and organization, and author's qualifications. Considerations for Selecting Young Adult Literature: *Nonfiction Series* identifies some special items to look for when evaluating nonfiction series. Although it is tempting to look for well-known authors, it is just as important to determine the qualifications of all of the authors who write books in the series. If the names of well-known authors are listed as editors or consultants for the series, you should determine exactly what their contributions are and whether they have actually written any books in the series. Be sure that the books in the series are more than out-of-print titles that have simply been given new covers and a new series title; in addition, verify that the individual books are not padded with thick sections of incidental information that is repeated from title to title throughout the series (Boardman, 1997).

CONSIDERATIONS	For Selecting Young Adult Literature	NONFICTION SERIES

When evaluating and selecting nonfiction series for young adults, ask the same questions used to evaluate non-series nonfiction. Then, ask the following:

◉ How do the contents of the books compare to the packaging of the series?

◉ Are the books in the series a consistent length?

◉ Is there evidence of consistent research throughout the series?

◉ Do the topics in each book in the series correlate with the curriculum or the interests of young adults?

◉ What are the qualifications of all of the authors who write books in the series?

◉ Is the book design consistent throughout the series?

◉ How much repetition is there in the books in the series?

Suggestions for Selecting and Using Nonfiction

Selecting appropriate nonfiction is just as important as selecting quality fiction. While the impulse may be to choose a book because it addresses a topic that is included in the curriculum or that reflects a current interest of young adults, it is important to evaluate nonfiction by applying the criteria listed previously in this chapter. Adolescents deserve accurate, appealing, well-written nonfiction books and schools need to spend their resources wisely.

Awards and Best Books Lists. As with fiction, the nonfiction books that win book awards and prizes are usually good choices to recommend to adolescents. Although there are no specific awards for young adult nonfiction, a number of awards for nonfiction literature routinely include books that will appeal to young adult readers. These include the Orbis Pictus Award, which is given annually by the National Council of Teachers of English to outstanding nonfiction for children; and the Robert F. Sibert Informational Book Award, which is given annually by the Association for Library Services to Children. The Boston Globe-Horn Book Award also has a category for nonfiction, the Society of School Librarians International gives a nonfiction K–12 award, and the Children's Book Guild has a nonfiction award. In addition, the yearly best books lists prepared by the National Council for the Social Studies (NCSS) and the National Science Teachers Association (NSTA) consist of a large number of nonfiction books.

Nonfiction titles are often found among the winners and honor books in other awards and best books lists. Historical nonfiction books are eligible for consideration for the Jefferson Cup, which is given by the Virginia Library Association. Frequently, the Best Books for Young Adults, Quick Picks for Young Adults, and Popular Paperbacks for Young Adults, all annual lists from the Young Adult Library Services Association, contain some recommended nonfiction titles. However, the best books lists are usually overwhelmingly composed of fiction books.

Print Review Resources. Several journals include information on recommended nonfiction. The journal *Voice of Youth Advocates* presents a nonfiction honor list in its August issue each year. Selected from books that are nominated by publishers, this list consists of books that are recommended for middle school students and, recently, has included some additional comments on the books by adolescents. Published by the American Association for the Advancement of Science (AAAS), the journal *Science, Books & Films* contains reviews of science books including those for adolescents.

Some published bibliographies highlight recommended nonfiction:

- *Nonfiction for Young Adults: From Delight to Wisdom* (Carter & Abrahamson, 1990)

- *Eyeopeners II* (Kobrin, 1995)

- *Earth Works: Recommended Fiction and Nonfiction about the Environment for Adults and Young Adults* (Dwyer, 1996)

- *Building an ESL Collection for Young Adults: A Bibliography of Recommended Fiction and Nonfiction for Schools and Public Libraries* (McCaffrey, 1998)

EXPANDING | *YOUR KNOWLEDGE WITH THE INTERNET 8–2*

The following Internet sites provide a sample of where you can find information about young adult nonfiction. Links to these and many additional sites are found on this book's Companion Website at www.prenhall.com/bucher.

Orbis Pictus Award

www.ncte.org/elem/awards/orbispictus

Outstanding Science Trade Books For Students K–12 (NSTA)

www.nsta.org/ostbc

Online Resources. On the Internet, Search It! Science is a subscription-based database of recommended science trade books that has an option for a free preview. Expanding Your Knowledge with the Internet 8–2 contains additional information on these awards and selection sources.

Teaching with Nonfiction in the Classroom

Educators can use a number of strategies to incorporate young adult nonfiction into the classroom. In many of the content areas, educators can identify nonfiction books to supplement the curriculum. School health professionals and guidance counselors will find nonfiction books very useful in helping adolescents cope with developmental and health problems as well as in career education. In addition, nonfiction can be used as a core book in literature-based instruction with a thematic approach, in interdisciplinary teaching, and for independent reading. Cheryl Thomas (2000), a sixth-grade language arts teacher, cites two professional books that have helped her integrate nonfiction into her classroom: *Nonfiction Matters* (Harvey, 1998) and *Strategies That Work* (Harvey & Goudvis, 2000). In her class Thomas (2000) uses Walter Wick's *A Drop of Water* (1997) as a core book to teach reading, science, and math. Figure 8–1 illustrates her use of this book. In addition, Suggestions for Collaborative Efforts 8–4 provides an idea for incorporating young adult nonfiction into the mathematics classroom.

Here are some additional ideas for using nonfiction in classrooms:

- Have students read two nonfiction books on the same subject and then compare the treatment in both books. Do the authors use the same style? Are the books unbiased? What characteristics make one book better than the other?

- Make nonfiction books the basis for reading activities along with fiction.

- In social studies, have students compare and contrast a fiction and nonfiction book about the same subject.

- Have students use a chart to compare the information from nonfiction books, library reference sources, and Internet resources.

- When assigning readings, make nonfiction one of the choices.

FIGURE 8–1   Nonfiction as a Core Book in the Curriculum

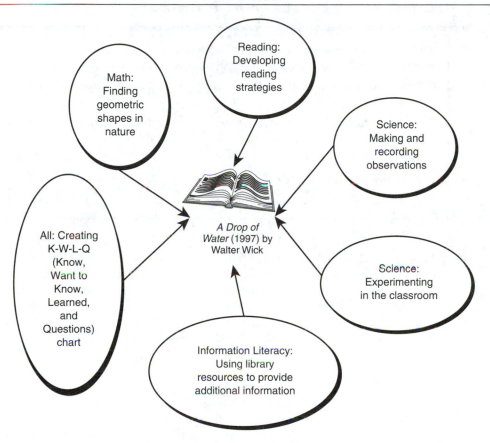

Source: This chart was developed from information in Thomas, C. (2000). From engagement to celebration: A framework for passionate reading. *Voices from the Middle, 8*(2), 16–25.

- Use nonfiction books as the basis for discussion in student advisory sessions.

- Use concept maps to organize the information from nonfiction books.

- Make sure the school library has books that answer the questions that adolescents are afraid to ask adults.

Content Area Reading. A natural use of nonfiction is to supplement or replace the textbook in the various subjects throughout the curriculum. Because nonfiction presents concepts and vocabulary in a concrete way, informational books can also be an excellent tool for teaching literacy development (Hadaway, Vardell, & Young, 2002). However, Benson (2002) maintains that teaching nonfiction in a content area means more than having students read a book. Even though students can decode words by the time they are in middle and high school, they still need help understanding the content that

8-4

SUGGESTIONS FOR COLLABORATIVE EFFORTS

To use nonfiction in the mathematics classroom, work with science and/or social studies teachers to identify books that can also be used in those classes. Then,

- Divide the class into groups and have each group of students read a nonfiction book on a particular subject.
- Have each group take the information from the books that group members have read, and
  - combine it,
  - organize it into a database, and
  - develop graphic representations of the data such as charts, graphs, and tables.

---

they are reading (Donahue, 2003). Reading and information literacy skills require adolescents to go beyond merely accessing information and asks them to evaluate and use it. In other words, young adults must construct their own meaning from a text and must use different strategies for reading different texts. In doing so, they demonstrate comprehension by taking prior knowledge or topic knowledge and building on it to develop text knowledge or an understanding of the global structure of the text, the interrelationship of main concepts, and the organization of the text.

Literacy Skills. To teach these information literacy and content reading skills, teachers must employ a number of different strategies. They cannot assume that young adults know these skills or that the literacy skills that students employ when reading fiction will transfer to nonfiction. As Ogle points out (D'Arcangelo, 2002), students will apply different reading strategies to information text than to fiction. With fiction, they can anticipate the story structure of beginning, middle, and end. With nonfiction, they need help understanding the structure of the information. A number of reading strategies can be used with nonfiction, including predicting, thinking aloud, creating visual representations and graphic organizers, activating prior knowledge, previewing, taking notes, writing to learn, responding to study guides, preparing K-W-L (Know, Want to know, Learned) charts, establishing purposes for reading, developing questions on the reading, participating in directed reading-thinking activities, engaging in peer teaching, creating marginal notes, and participating in discussion webs (Barry, 2002). Text maps, based on the organization features of a book such as the chapter headings, headings, charts and tables, and boldfaced words, can also help readers become fluent in content area reading (Spencer, 2003).

To help students develop content reading skills, educators must model the appropriate strategies and expect students to focus on only one or two new strategies at a time such as making a summary, comparing and contrasting an idea, creating a timeline, or determining cause and effect. When educators help students identify and use appropriate strategies for understanding text structure, students not only become better readers, but they are also able to understand and recall information (Rhoder, 2002).

When helping adolescents develop the appropriate reading and information literacy strategies to use with informational books, content teachers can use young adult nonfiction as a core book, a supplement to the text, a part of interdisciplinary instruction, or for independent reading. Collaborating with the library media specialist, English/language arts teacher, and/or reading specialist, content teachers can identify nonfiction that can be taught in a number of classes throughout the curriculum. Educators can use just nonfiction books or they can use both fiction and nonfiction by relating the books to a central theme. Figure 8–2 shows the use of both fiction and nonfiction books around a single topic or theme, while Figure 8–3 illustrates the use of a fiction book as a springboard to several nonfiction books.

FIGURE 8–2 *Fiction and Nonfiction on a Single Topic or Theme*

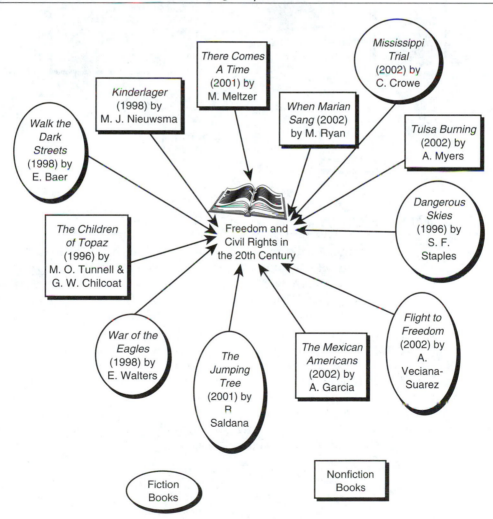

FIGURE 8–3   Fiction as a Springboard to Nonfiction

The Following Web on the Theme of Science, Technology, and Crime in the Modern World Features a Fiction Book as the Core Title Leading to Nonfiction Books

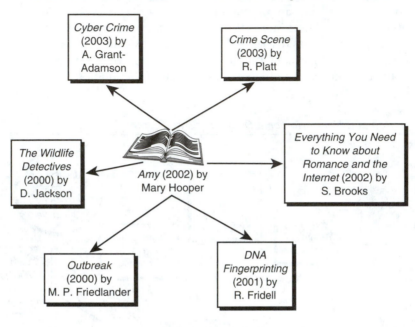

 CONCLUDING THOUGHTS

The wealth of informational books and the number of nonfiction series available today provide young adults with opportunities for both enjoyment and learning. This tremendous selection can be a mixed blessing. While there are many informational books and series from which to choose, educators have a tremendous responsibility to select and suggest well-written and age-level appropriate books for young adults. Although many informational books are attractive and appealing in design and format, teachers and library media specialists need to focus on their accuracy, perspectives, organization, and author's qualifications and purpose in writing the book. Considering today's technological advances, the future will likely bring even more books—larger quantities, enhanced photographs, more current topics, and more writers trying their skills at the market. Visit this book's Companion Website at www.prenhall.com/bucher for additional information about nonfiction including review questions, self-assessments, Internet sites, and young adult literature and readings.

Young Adult Books

 This section includes young adult titles recommended or mentioned in this chapter. Check the Companion Website at www.prenhall.com/bucher to find additional suggestions of current young adult literature.

Alagna, M. (2001). *Everything you need to know about the dangers of binge drinking.* New York: Rosen. Other books in this series include Sheldon Brooks' *Everything You Need to Know about Romance and the Internet* (2001), Cherie Turner's *Everything You Need to Know about the Riot Grrrl Movement* (2001), and Katherine White's *Everything You Need to Know about Relationship Violence* (2001).

Alexander, C. (1998). *The endurance: Shackleton's legendary antarctic expedition.* New York: Knopf. This Alex Award winner is full of adventure.

Alonso, K. (2002). *The Chicago seven political protest trial.* Berkeley Heights, NJ: Enslow. Alonso provides the context for this famous case. Other trial books by Alonso are *Loving v. Virginia: Interracial Marriage* (2000) and *Schenck v. United States; Restrictions on Free Speech* (1999).

Altman, L. J. (1999). *Slavery and abolition in American history.* Berkeley Heights, NJ: Enslow. A well-researched look at slavery in America. Another book by Altman is *The Holocaust, Hitler, and Nazi Germany* (1999).

Apel, M. A. (2000). *Cocaine and your nose: The incredibly disgusting story.* New York: Rosen. After looking at the functions of the nose, Apel examines the effects of cocaine use, and options for treatment for addiction. Another book in this series is Allan B. Cobb's *Speed and Your Brain: The Incredibly Disgusting Story* (2000).

Armstrong, J. (1998). *Shipwreck at the bottom of the world: The extraordinary true story of Shackleton and the Endurance.* New York: Crown. In 1914, Sir Ernest Shackleton's ship was trapped in the Antarctic ice. Another book by this author is *Shattered: Stories of Children and War* (2002).

Arnold, C. (2000). *Easter Island: Giant stone statues tell of a rich and tragic past.* New York: Clarion. Arnold examines the cultural legacies of the people of Easter Island.

Ash, R. (2000). *Great wonders of the world.* New York: DK. This book explores the wonders that humans have constructed.

Augustyn, F., & Tanaka, S. (2001). *Footnotes: Dancing the world's best-loved ballets.* Brookfield, CT: Millbrook Press. The authors introduce seven ballets and the dancers who perform them.

Bachrach, S. D. (2000). *The Nazi Olympics: Berlin, 1936.* Boston: Little Brown. Readers go behind the sports events for the real story.

Balmer, R. (2001). *Religion in twentieth century America.* New York: Oxford University Press. Religion and social issues combine in this history.

Barrett, P. (2001). *National Geographic dinosaurs.* Washington, DC: National Geographic Society. Filled with full-color photographs and drawings, this book is an overview of dinosaurs.

Bartoletti, S. C. (2001). *Black potatoes: The story of the Great Irish Famine, 1845–1850.* Boston: Houghton Mifflin. With period illustrations, Bartoletti presents the story of a great tragedy. Bartoletti has also written *Kids on Strike!* (1999) and *Growing Up in Coal Country* (1997).

Baseball's best shots: The greatest baseball photography of all time. (2000). New York: DK. This was a Quick Pick for Reluctant Young Adults Readers, 2001.

Basso, M. J. (1997). *The underground guide to teenage sexuality.* Minneapolis: Fairview. This is a popular title for young adults.

Batten, M. (2001). *Anthropologist: Scientist of the people.* Boston: Houghton Mifflin. Learn about anthropology by following a scientist into the rain forest.

Beil, K. M. (1999). *Fire in their eyes: Wildfires and the people who fight them.* San Diego: Harcourt. From training to actual experiences on the fire line, Beil presents the story of people who use fire and those who battle it.

Ben Jelloun, T. (2002). *Islam explained.* New York: New Press. After a history of Islam, the author moves to a discussion of Muslim beliefs.

Best shots: The greatest NFL photographs of the century. (1999). New York: DK. A collection of some of the greatest football photographs.

Bial, R. (2002). *Tenement: Immigrant life on the lower east side.* Boston: Houghton Mifflin. Bial looks at the immigrants, their living conditions, and the laws that finally protected them.

Bishop, N. (2000). *Digging for bird-dinosaurs; An expedition to Madagascar.* Boston: Houghton Mifflin. Paleontologist Cathy Foster investigates evidence of bird evolution.

Blumenthal, K. (2002). *Six days in October: The stock market crash of 1929.* New York: Atheneum. More than a look at the crash, this book provides fundamentals of the stock market.

Bodanis, D. (1998). *The secret family: Twenty-four hours inside the mysterious worlds of our minds and bodies.* New York: Simon & Schuster. This Alex Award-winning book looks at the human body through the lives of five members of a single family.

Bosak, S. V. (2000). *Science is . . . a source book of fascinating facts, projects and activities.* New York: Scholastic. Middle schoolers should enjoy the information and projects about weather, matter, energy, and biology.

Bretón, M. (2002). *Home is everything: The Latino baseball story.* El Paso, TX: Cinco Puntos Press. This is a bilingual book on the contributions of Latinos to baseball.

Brooke, M. (1999). *The concrete wave (the history of skateboarding).* Toronto: Warwick. Take a ride through the history of this extreme sport.

Brooks, S. (2002). *Everything you need to know about romance and the Internet: How to stay safe.* New York: Rosen. In addition to information about online relationships, this book emphasizes Internet safety.

Buckley, J. (1999). *Football.* New York: DK. Illustrations tell the history of professional football.

Burgess-Wise, D. (1999). *The ultimate race car.* New York: DK. This was a 2000 Quick Pick for Reluctant Young Adult Readers.

Canfield, J., & Hansen, M. V. (1997). *Chicken soup for the teenage soul.* Deerfield Beach, FL: Health Communications. A collection of inspirational stories about life, love, and learning.

Canfield, J., & Hansen, M. V. (2001). *Chicken soup for the teenage soul on tough stuff.* Deerfield Beach, FL: Health Communications. Another collection of inspirational stories and messages about life.

Cart, M., Aronson, M., & Carus, M. (Eds.). (2002). *911: The book of help.* Chicago: Cricket Books. This collection of essays is designed to help young people cope with the tragedy of September 11.

Cerullo, M. M. (2001). *Sea soup: Zooplankton.* Gardiner, ME: Tilbury House. With microscopic photography, Cerullo brings the invisible microbe to life.

Cobb, V. (2001). *See for yourself: More than 100 experiments for science fairs and projects.* New York: Scholastic. Here are lots of ideas for science fair projects.

Cohen, D. (1999). *The Manhattan project.* Brookfield, CT: Twenty-First Century. Cohen provides a history of the atomic age.

Colman, P. (1997). *Corpses, coffins, and crypts: A history of burial.* New York: Henry Holt. Colman looks at the rituals and customs associated with burials. Other recommended books by Colman are *Rosie the Riveter: Women Working on the Home Front in World War II* (1995) and *Where the Action Was: Women War Correspondents in World War II* (2002).

Cooper, M. L. (1999). *Indian school: Teaching the white man's way.* New York: Clarion. Cooper uses various documents to explore the removal of Indian children to schools where they would learn the white man's culture.

Cooper, M. L. (2000). *Fighting for honor: Japanese Americans and World War II.* New York: Clarion. From the battlefields to the internment camps, Cooper examines the life of Japanese Americans.

Cooper, M. L. (2001). *Slave spirituals and the jubilee singers.* New York: Clarion. Cooper traces the spiritual from its roots to its presentation by the Jubilee Singers. Another book by this author is *Fighting for Honor: Japanese Americans and World War II* (2000).

Crandell, R. (2002). *Headin' for better times: The arts of the Great Depression.* Minneapolis: Lerner. Damon explores the artists of a bleak time in American history.

Daldry, J. (1999). *The teenage guy's survival guide: The real deal on girls, growing up, and other guy stuff.* Boston: Little, Brown. This was on the Quick Picks for Reluctant Young Adult Readers 2000 list.

Deem, J. M. (1998). *Bodies from the bog.* Boston: Houghton Mifflin. The bog of northern Europe has preserved bodies for thousands of years. Now the bodies have a tale to tell about our ancestors.

Dowd, O. (2002). *A young dancer's apprenticeship: On tour with the Moscow Ballet.* Brookfield, CT: Twenty-First Century Books. Follow this teenager as she joins the Moscow City Ballet.

Downs, S. (2000). *Earth's fiery fury.* Brookfield, CT: Twenty-First Century Books. Downs explores volcanoes and geothermal activity.

Farrell, J. (1998). *Invisible enemies: Stories of infectious diseases.* New York: Farrar, Straus and Giroux. From bubonic plague and leprosy to AIDS and smallpox, diseases have brought death throughout the world.

Feelings, T. (1995). *The middle passage: White ships/black cargo.* New York: Dial. This is a stark and moving visual portrayal of the African slave trade.

Ferrie, R. (1999). *The world turned upside down: George Washington and the Battle of Yorktown.* New York: Holiday House. Ferrie uses photos, maps, and charts to bring the battle to life.

Finkelstein, N. H. (1999). *The way things never were: The truth about the "good old days."* New York: Atheneum. This book suggests the good old days of the 1950s and 1960s had their own share of problems.

Frauenfelder, M. (2002). *Mad professor: Concoct extremely weird science projects.* San Francisco: Chronicle. The projects may be strange, but the science is sound.

Freedman, R. (2000). *Give me liberty! The story of the Declaration of Independence.* New York: Holiday House. Freedman looks at the politics behind this document.

Fridell, R. (2001). *DNA fingerprinting: The ultimate identity.* New York: Franklin Watts. Fridell puts a lot of information about the forensic science of DNA fingerprinting in this slim volume.

Friedlander, M. P. (2000). *Outbreak: Disease detectives at work.* Minneapolis: Lerner. Friedlander looks at the way epidemiologists battle infectious diseases.

Garcia, A. M. (2002). *The Mexican Americans.* Westport, CT: Greenwood. In addition to background information, this book explores the effects of immigration on families and cultures.

Gaskins, P. F. (1999). *What are you? Voices of mixed-race young people*. New York: Holt. Eight mixed-race young people describe their lives and the issues that they face.

Gay, K., & Whittington, C. (2002). *Body marks: Tattooing, piercing, and scarification*. Brookfield, CT: Twenty-First Century. This is a history of the art of body decorations and the health risks involved.

Giblin, J. C. (Ed.). (2000): *The century that was: Reflections on the last 100 years*. New York: Atheneum. Eleven authors revisit the 20th century.

Gottfried, T. (2001). *Displaced persons: The liberation and abuse of Holocaust survivors*. Brookfield, CT: Twenty-First Century Books. Unfortunately, anti-Semitism did not end with the fall of the Nazi regime. Another book by Gottfried is *Nazi Germany: The Face of Tyranny* (2000).

Grant-Adamson, A. (2003). *Cyber crime*. Broomall, PA: Mason Crest. This book explores the efforts that law enforcement uses to stay ahead of hackers.

Hart, C. (2003). *Manga mania villains: How to draw the dastardly villains of Japanese comics*. New York: Watson-Guptil. This book shows artists how to move from geometric shapes to characters such as the punk, the monster, and the mad scientist.

Haskins, J. (1999). *The geography of hope: Black exodus from the south after reconstruction*. Brookfield, CT: Twenty-First Century. Going back before the Civil War, Haskins examines the conditions of African Americans and their migration to the West. Haskins has also written *One Love, One Heart: A History of Reggae* (2002).

Haskins, J., & Benson, K. (2001). *Conjure times: Black magicians in America*. New York: Walker. The authors look at African American magicians. Other books by these authors are *Bound for America: The Forced Migration of Africans to the New World* (1999) and *African Beginnings* (1996).

Heller, T. (2002). *Pregnant! What can I do? A guide for teenagers*. Jefferson, NC: McFarland. This is a straightforward nonbiased presentation of all aspects of this issue.

Hicks, B., & Sropf, S. (2002). *Raising the Hunley: The remarkable history and recovery of the lost confederate submarine*. New York: Ballantine. Novelist Clive Cussler led the effort to locate this relic of the Civil War.

Hirschfelder, A., & Wright, B. (2000). *Native Americans*. New York: Dorling Kindersley. Five hundred years of history are presented visually.

Holmes, T. (1998). *Fossil feud: The rivalry of the first American dinosaur hunters*. Parsippany, NJ: Messner. Two 19th-century scientists had a bitter feud about dinosaurs.

Holt, D., & Mooney, B. (1999). *Spiders in the hairdo: Modern urban legends*. Little Rock, AR: August House. This was a 2000 Top 10 Quick Pick for Young Adults.

Hoose, P. (2001). *We were there, too! Young people in U.S. history*. New York: Farrar, Straus and Giroux. This well-researched overview is arranged chronologically.

Hyde, M. O., & Forsyth, E. H. (2002). *Depression: What you need to know*. New York: Franklin Watts. With the rise of teenage depression; this book frankly discusses the causes, symptoms, and treatments of the disease.

Ichord, L. F. (2000). *Toothworms and spider juice: An illustrated history of dentistry*. Brookfield, CT: Millbrook. Fascinating illustrations depict the unusual treatments and techniques of dentistry.

Jackson, D. (2000). *The wildlife detectives: How forensic scientists fight crimes against nature*. Boston: Houghton Mifflin. Environmentalists use science to solve crimes.

Jenkins, S. (1999). *Top of the world: Climbing Mount Everest.* Boston: Houghton Mifflin. Filled with information about the equipment and techniques of mountain climbing, this book takes readers to the slopes of Everest.

Jennings, G. (2000). *Blood moments: And further highlights from the astounding in history of medicine.* Aoronto: Annick Press. Lots of interesting and sometimes gory details from medicine fill this volume.

Johnston, R. D. (2002). *The making of America: The history of the United States from 1492 to the present.* Washington, DC: National Geographic. Paintings, photographs, maps, and documents enhance this history.

Jones, C. F. (1999). *Yukon gold: The story of the Klondike gold rush.* New York: Holiday House. With vintage photos, Jones relates the frenzy of the Canadian gold rush.

Judson, K. (2001). *Medical ethics: Life and death issues.* Berkeley Heights, NJ: Enslow. Judson uses a case study approach to examine ethical behavior.

Jukes, M. (2002). *The guy book: An owner's manual: Safety, maintenance and operating instructions for teens.* New York: Crown. The comparisons between boys and cars helps provide essential information.

Kane, D. (Ed.). (2003). *What is poetry: Conversations with the American Avant-Garde.* New York: Teachers and Writers Collaborative. Rather than presenting poems, Kane focuses on the writers who create them and their approach to writing.

Katz, W. L. (1999). *Black pioneers: An untold story.* New York: Simon & Schuster. This is the story of African Americans on the Great Plains.

Keenan, S. (2000). *Gods, goddesses, and monsters: An encyclopedia of world mythology.* New York: Scholastic. This book contains concise sketches from throughout the world.

Kendall, M. E. (2001). *Failure is impossible: The history of American women's rights.* Minneapolis: Lerner. Kendall traces the movement from its beginning to modern times.

Kerr, M. E. (1998). *Blood on the forehead: What I know about writing.* New York: HarperCollins. Kerr talks about the sources of her ideas and how she turns ideas into stories.

Krakauer, J. (1997). *Into thin air.* New York: Anchor. Krakauer recounts an ill-fated trip to Mount Everest where everything seems to go wrong.

Krasner, S. (2002). *Play ball like the pros: Tips for kids from 20 big league stars.* Atlanta: Peachtree. Along with a little history of sports, there are plenty of tips, anecdotes, and guidance from professional players.

Lanier, S., & Feldman, J. (2000). *Jefferson's children: The story of one American family.* New York: Random. Shannon Lanier looks back at the relationship that started his family.

Lannin, J. (2000). *A history of basketball for girls and women: From bloomers to big leagues.* Minneapolis: Lerner. Meet amateurs as well as members of Olympic and professional teams.

Levine, E. (2000). *Darkness over Denmark: The Danish Resistance and the rescue of the Jews.* New York: Holiday House. This book includes the stories of young people who were rescued from the Holocaust.

Macaulay, D. (1998). *The new way things work.* Boston: Houghton Mifflin. Macaulay illustrates and explains the workings of all kinds of machines. Other works by Macaulay are *Building Bid: A Companion to the PBS Series* (2000) and *Building the Book: Cathedral* (1999).

Madaras, L., with Madaras, A. (2000). *What's happening to my body? Book for boys: Growing up guide for parents and sons.* New York: Newmarket Press. The companion book is *What's Happening to My Body? Book for Girls: Growing Up Guide for Parents and Daughters.*

Maestro, B. (1999). *The story of clocks and calendars: Marking a millennium.* New York: HarperCollins. This book explores the history of time keeping.

Mann, E. (2001). *Hoover Dam: The story of hard times, tough people, and the taming of a wild river.* New York: Mikaya Press. It took an extraordinary feat of engineering to build this dam in the middle of the Great Depression. Another title by Mann is *Machu Picchu* (2000).

Mansir, A. R. (1999). *Stagecoach: The ride of a century.* Watertown, MA: Charlesbridge. From the 1700s to 1910, Mansir recounts the story of the stagecoach.

Marcus, L. S. (Ed.). (2000). *Author talk: Conversations with Judy Blume, Bruce Brooks, Karen Cushman, Russell Freedman, Lee Bennett Hopkins, James Howe, Johanna Hurwitz, E. L. Konisgburg, Lois Lowry, Ann M. Martin, Nicholasa Mohr, Gary Paulsen, Jon Scieszka, Seymour Simon, and Laurence Yep.* New York: Simon & Schuster. Fifteen young adult authors discuss their careers and their writing.

Massof, J. (1999). *Emergency!* New York: Scholastic. This book explores emergency medicine.

Matthews, G. (2000). *American women's history: A student companion.* New York: Oxford University. This is a detailed reference about women in American history.

Maurer, R. (1999). *The wild Colorado: The true adventures of Fred Dellenbaugh, age 17, on the second Powell Expedition into the Grand Canyon.* New York: Random. This is the story of the 1869 expedition of the Colorado River.

Meltzer, M. (2001a). *Bound for America: The story of the European immigrants.* New York: Benchmark Books. Meltzer focuses on the First Great Migration of Europeans from 1829 to 1920. Other books by Meltzer include *In the Days of the Pharaohs: A Look at Ancient Egypt* (2001) and *Piracy & Plunder: A Murderous Business* (2001).

Meltzer, M. (2001b). *There comes a time: The struggle for Civil Rights.* New York: Random. Meltzer presents a concise history of the Civil Rights movement.

Menzel, P., & D'Aluiso, F. (1999). *Man eating bugs: The art and science of eating bugs.* Berkeley, CA: Ten Speed Press. This was a 2000 Top 10 Quick Pick for Young Adults.

Mierau, C. (2000). *Accept no substitutes: The history of American advertising.* Minneapolis: Lerner. From colonial times to the present, advertisers have influenced the consumption patterns of Americans.

Miller, R. (2001). *The history of science fiction.* New York: Franklin Watts. This is an excellent introduction to the genre.

Morse, J. C. (2001). *Scholastic book of world records.* New York: Scholastic. Many adolescents are drawn to books like this that are full of interesting facts.

Muharrar, A. (2002). *More than a label: Why what you wear or who you're with doesn't define who you are.* Minneapolis, MN: Free Spirit. This survey of a thousand teenagers uses personal stories to illustrate the problems of "labeling" people.

Mulvihill, M. (1999). *The treasury of saints and martyrs.* New York: Viking. Mulvihill recounts the lives of 40 saints of the Christian church.

Murphy, J. (2000). *Blizzard!* New York: Scholastic. A single snowstorm paralyzes New York City. Other popular nonfiction books by Jim Murphy include *The Great Fire* (1995) and *An American Plague: The True and Terrifying Story of the Yellow Fever Epidemic of 1793* (2003).

Musleah, R. (2000). *Why on this night? A Passover Haggadah for family celebration.* New York: Simon & Schuster. This book presents the story of the ritual of the Seder.

Myers, A. (2002). *Tulsa burning.* New York: Walker. Myers explores the people and families behind the 1921 race riot.

Nathan, A., & Collins, E. (2001). *Yankee doodle gals: Women pilots of World War II.*

Washington, DC: National Geographic. Meet the Women Airforce Service Pilots (WASPs).

Nelson, P. (2002). *Left for dead: A young man's search for the* USS Indianapolis. New York: Delacorte. An 11-year-old boy finds the true story behind this World War II sinking.

Nieuwsma, M. J. (Ed.). (1998). *Kinderlager: An oral history of young Holocaust survivors*. New York: Holiday. Nieuwsma interviewed survivors of the children's section of Auschwitz in this frank book.

Patent, D. H. (2000). *Shaping the Earth*. Boston: Houghton Mifflin. Photos expand the text in this interesting volume. Another book by Patent is *Animals on the Trail with Lewis and Clark* (2002).

Paul, A. (2002). *Girlosophy: The love survival kit*. St. Leonards, NSW, Australia: Allen & Unwin. The book contains commonsense advice about love and relationships. A companion volume is *Girlosophy: A Soul Survivor Kit* (2001).

Pavanel, J. (2001). *The sex book: An alphabet of smarter love*. Montreal: Lobster Press. Pavanel takes on the myths and provides frank information for teens of all sexual orientations.

Pelta, K. (2001). *Rediscovering Easter Island*. Minneapolis: Lerner. Something about the monoliths of Easter Island have attracted explorers and scholars for ages.

Philbrick, N. (2002). *The revenge of the whale: The true story of the whaleship* Essex. New York: Putnam. Twenty men are adrift in the Pacific after a whale sinks their ship.

Platt, R. (2003). *Crime scene: The ultimate guide to forensic science*. New York: DK. Take a look at the way forensic science aids law enforcement.

Reif, P. (2000). *A dinosaur named Sue: The story of the colossal fossil*. New York: Scholastic. Follow the discovery of Sue, the most complete Tyrannosaurus Rex ever found.

Rubin, S. G. (2001). *There goes the neighborhood: Ten buildings people loved to hate*. New York: Holiday House. Even famous structures like the Eiffel Tower were not always loved when they were first built.

Ryan, M. (2002). *When Marian sang: The true recital of Marian Anderson*. New York: Scholastic. Racism kept this great opera singer from performing in many places in the United States.

Sabbeth, C. (2002). *Monet and the Impressionists for kids*. Chicago, IL: Chicago Review Press. This is an introduction to Monet, Renoir, Degas, Cassatt, Cezanne, Gauguin, and Seurat.

Schwartz, E. (2002). *I'm a vegetarian: Amazing facts and ideas for healthy vegetarians*. Toronto: Tundra Books. This is an excellent overview that looks at both factual issues and social ones.

Severance, J. B. (2000). *Skyscrapers: How America grew up*. New York: Holiday House. Look at the architects and the challenges they faced in building skyscrapers.

Sloan, C. (2002). *SuperCroc and the origin of crocodiles*. Washington, DC: National Geographic Society. Imagine a crocodile the size of a Tyrannosaurus Rex!

Sobey, E. (2002). *How to build your own prize-winning robot*. Berkeley Heights, NJ: Enslow. In addition to information on creating a robot, this book has lists of resources such as clubs and organizations.

Stanchak, J. (2000). *Civil War*. New York: DK. Photographs and prints bring history to life.

Steen, S., & Steen, S. (2003). *Take it to the hoop: 100 years of women's basketball*. Brookfield, CT: Twenty-First Century. This short book provides information on a changing sport.

Steinberg, J. (2002). *The gatekeepers: Inside the admissions process of a premier college*. New York: Viking. The author traces the applications of six prospective students.

Swanson, D. (2001). *Nibbling on Einstein's brain: The good, the bad, & the bogus in science.* Toronto: Annick Press. Go beyond the surface of science to separate the good and the bad research.

Thomas, P. (2000). *Marine mammal preservation.* Brookfield, CT: Twenty-First Century Books. Explore the research and rehabilitation of a number of marine mammals.

Tunnell, M. O., & Chilcoat, G. W. (1996). *The children of Topaz: The story of a Japanese-American internment camp based on a classroom diary.* New York: Holiday. Through the diary of a third-grade teacher, we see the daily life in an internment camp.

Turner, C. (2001). *Stunt performers: Life before the camera.* New York: Rosen. This is a book in the extreme careers series.

Van Steenwyk, E. (2001). *Let's go to the beach: A history of sun and fun by the sea.* New York: Henry Holt. This is a short history of the appeal of the beach.

Vogel, C. G. (2001). *Breast cancer: Questions and answers for young women.* Brookfield, CT: Millbrook Press. This book provides accurate information on everything from diagnosis to coping with loss due to the disease. Another book by Vogel is *Legends of Landforms: Native American Lore and the Geology of the Land* (1999).

Wacker, G. (2000). *Religion in Nineteenth Century America.* New York: Oxford University Press. Wacker looks at the individuals and movements that influenced the developing nation.

Walker, S. M. (2002). *Fossil fish found alive: Discovering the Coelacanth.* Minneapolis: Carolrhoda. Join the hunt for a fish once thought to be extinct for 70 million years.

Weiss, E. (2000). *Odd jobs.* New York: Simon & Schuster. Have you ever considered a job as an armpit sniffer?

Weitzman, D. (1999). *Locomotive: Building an eight-wheeler.* Boston: Houghton Mifflin. Weitzman chronicles the building of a wood-burning steam locomotive.

Wick, W. (1997). *A drop of water.* New York: Scholastic. Wick uses photographs to explore all of the states of water.

Wilcox, C. (2000). *Mummies, bones and body parts.* Minneapolis: Carolrhoda. From ancient Egypt to the present, Wilcox explores the preservation of bodies.

Wilkes, A. (2001). *A farm through time: The history of a farm from medieval times to the present day.* New York: Dorling Kindersley. Farmers change from using hand tools to driving modern machines.

Winkler, A. M. (2001). *The Cold War: A history in documents.* New York: Oxford University Press. Using documents and photographs, Winkler analyzes the Cold War.

Wisler, G. C. (2001). *When Johnny went marching: Young Americans fight the Civil War.* New York: HarperCollins. Wisler shows a less-than-glamorous view of the American Civil War.

Woods, M., & Woods, M. B. (1999). *Ancient medicine: From sorcery to surgery.* Minneapolis: Lerner. The authors discuss the medical practices in Ancient Egypt, India, China, Greece, and Rome.

Wulffson, D. L. (2001). *The kid who invented the trampoline: More surprising stories about inventions.* New York: Dutton. Learn where toilet paper came from and more.

Young, M. B., Fitzgerald, J. J., & Grunfeld, A. T. (Eds.). (2002). *The Vietnam War: A history in documents.* New York: Oxford University Press. The editors use original documents to tell the story of the war.

Zeinert, K. (2001). *Those extraordinary women of World War I.* Brookfield, CT: Millbrook Press. The role of women during World War I is shown in vivid detail. Zeinert has also written *The Valiant Women of the Vietnam War* (2000).

Suggested Readings

Benson, V. (2003). Informing literacy: A new paradigm for assessing nonfiction. *New England Reading Association Journal, 39*(1), 13–20.

Daniels, H. (2002). Expository text in literature circles. *Voices from the Middle, 9*(4), 7–14.

Johannessen, L. R. (2003). Making history come alive with the nonfiction literature of the Vietnam War. *The Social Studies, 94*(4), 171–178.

Mitchoff, K. H. (2003). Bridging the gap between learning to be male and learning to read. *Teacher Librarian, 30*(3), 53–54.

References

(Note: All young adult literature referenced in this chapter are included in the Young Adult Books list and are not repeated in this list.)

Adventures in nonfiction: Talking with Penny Coleman. (2002). *Journal of Children's Literature, 28*(2), 58–61.

Aronson, M. (2001). *Exploding the myths: The truth about teenagers and reading.* Lanham, MD: Scarecrow Press.

Barry, A. L. (2002). Reading strategies teachers say they use. *Journal of Adolescent & Adult Literacy, 46*(2), 132–141.

Benson, V. (2002). Shifting paradigms and pedagogy with nonfiction: A call to arms for survival in the 21st century. *The New England Reading Association Journal, 38*(2), 1–6.

Boardman, E. (1997). Series books: 'Can we buy with confidence?' *The Book Report, 16*(3), 23–24.

Broderick, D. M. (1995). The history the young (and not so young) don't know. *Voice of Youth Advocates, 17,* 330–331.

Campbell, J. R., Kapinus, B., & Beatty, A. S. (1995). *Interviewing children about their literacy experiences.* Washington, DC: U.S. Department of Education.

Carter, B., & Abrahamson, R. F. (1990). *Nonfiction for young adults: From delight to wisdom.* Phoenix, AZ: Oryx.

Connor, J. J. (2003). "The textbooks never said anything about . . . ." Adolescents respond to the *Middle Passage; White Ships/Black Cargo. Journal of Adolescent and Adult Literacy, 47*(3), 240–246.

D'Arcangelo, M. (2002). The challenge of content-area reading. *Educational Leadership, 60*(3), 12–15.

Doiron, R. (1995). An aesthetic view of children's nonfiction. *English Quarterly, 28*(1), 35–41.

Donahue, D. (2003). Reading across the great divide; English and math teachers apprentice one another as readers and disciplinary insiders. *Journal of Adolescent and Adult Literacy, 47*(1), 24–37.

Dresang, E. T. (1999). *Radical change: Books for youth in a digital age.* New York: H. W. Wilson.

Dwyer, J. (1996). *Earth works: Recommended fiction and nonfiction about the environment for adults and young adults.* New York: Neal-Schuman.

Furi-Perry, U. (2003, April–May). "Dude, that book was cool": The reading habits of young adults. *Reading Today.* Retrieved January 5, 2004, from www.findarticles.com/cf_dls/m0HQZ/5_20/100046846/print.jhtml.

Guzzetti, B., Young, J., Gritsavage, M., Fyfe, L., & Hardenbrook, M. (2002). *Reading, writing, and talking gender in literacy learning.* Newark, DE: International Reading Association.

Hadaway, N. L., Vardell, S. M., & Young, T. A. (2002). Highlighting nonfiction literature: Literacy development and English language learners. *The New England Reading Association Journal, 38*(2), 16–22.

Harvey, S. (1998). *Nonfiction matters*. York, ME: Stenhouse.

Harvey, S., & Goudvis, A. (2000). *Strategies that work*. York, ME: Stenhouse.

Jones, P. (1995). Homework helpers: The best in YA nonfiction series. *Voice of Youth Advocates, 17*(6), 324–329.

Jones, P. (2001). Nonfiction: The real stuff. *School Library Journal, 47*(4), 44–45.

Katz, C. A., Boran, K., Braun, T. J., Massie, M. J., & Kuby, S. A. (2003). The importance of being with Sir Ernest Shackleton at the bottom of the world. *Journal of Adolescent & Adult Literacy, 47*(1), 38–49.

Kobrin, B. (1995). *Eyeopeners II*. New York: Scholastic.

Lempke, S. D. (1999). What makes a good nonfiction series? *Booklist, 96*(4), 431.

Lickteig, M. J. (2003). Feed my brain: Involving children with informational books. *School Library Media Activities Monthly, 14*(6), 29–30.

McCaffrey, L. H. (1998). *Building an ESL collection for young adults: A bibliography of recommended fiction and nonfiction for schools and public libraries*. Westport, CT: Greenwood.

Merriam-Webster's encyclopedia of literature. (1995). Springfield, MA: Merriam-Webster.

Moss, B., & Hendershot, J. (2002). Exploring sixth graders' selection of nonfiction trade books. *The Reading Teacher, 56*(1), 6–17.

Reading remains popular among youth, according to poll (National Education Association survey). (2001, June). *Reading Today*. Retrieved January 5, 2004, from www.findarticles.com/cf_dls/m0HQZ/6_18/76332780/print.jhtml.

Rhoder, C. (2002). Mindful reading: Strategy training that facilitates transfer. *Journal of Adolescent & Adult Literacy, 45*(6), 498–512.

Spencer, B. H. (2003). Text maps: Helping students navigate information texts. *The Reading Teacher, 56*(8), 752–756.

Sullivan, E. (2000). More is not always better. *School Library Journal, 46*(4), 42–43.

Thomas, C. (2000). From engagement to celebration: A framework for passionate reading. *Voices from the Middle, 8*(2), 16–25.

Worthy, J., Moorman, M., & Turner, M. (1999). What Johnny likes to read is hard to find in school. *Reading Research Quarterly, 34*(1), 12–27.

Young, T. E. (2003). No pain, no gain . . . the science teacher and you working together. *Library Media Connection, 21*(4), 14–21.

Zvirin, S. (1999). Coping with series books. *Booklist, 96*(4), 432.

EXPLORING POETRY, DRAMA, AND SHORT STORIES

Poetry, drama, and short stories are just as important as the other types of literature discussed in this book and deserve a place in any literature program for adolescents. Although many times these genres are overlooked, books in these categories often appear on some of the recommended lists of young adult literature. For example, the short story collection *Firebirds: An Anthology of Original Fantasy and Science Fiction* (November, 2003) was on the Best Books for Young Adults 2004 list of the Young Adult Library Services Association, a division of the American Library Association, and Naomi Shihab Nye's *19 Varieties of Gazelle: Poems of the Middle East* (2002) made the 2003 Top 10 Best Books from the Best Books for Young Adults 2003 list. Paul Zindel's classic drama *The Effect of Gamma Rays on Man-in-the-Moon Marigolds* (1971) won the Pulitzer Prize. As with other forms of literature, to use this literature successfully with adolescents, educators must identify poetry, drama, and short stories that appeal to young adult readers and that young adults *want* to read. While this may include classics in each genre, it also means that educators need to share contemporary poetry, drama, and short stories with young adults and use appropriate titles that are written specifically for adolescents.

FOCUSING POINTS

In this chapter, you will read about:

1. Types of poetry, drama and short stories.
2. Reasons for using poetry, drama, and short stories.
3. Characteristics of well-written poetry, drama, and short stories.
4. Suggestions for selecting and using poetry, drama, and short stories.
5. Selected titles of poetry, drama, and short stories that are written for and will appeal to young adults.

POETRY, DRAMA, AND SHORT STORIES

While most educators readily recognize the need to provide adolescents with quality poetry, drama, and short stories, they often focus on classics. However, rather than reading only literary works that have claimed fame for years, young adults also want works that deal with their contemporary concerns and daily interests such as beginning and maintaining a romance, coping with parental expectations, and struggling to grow into the adult world. They also want books that speak directly to them with words they can understand and situations they can relate to. Thankfully, there is excellent young adult literature in these formats that both meets the need for quality literature and appeals to adolescent readers.

Poetry

While speaking of poetry in general rather than poetry written specifically for young adults, Charters (1997) maintained that contemporary poetry pleases nearly everyone, from the most traditional to the most avant-garde. "Poetry in America is a diverse, highly contested field, crowded with a variety of practices and philosophies, none of which lends itself easily to generalization" (Charters, 1997, p. 38).

In the not-too-distant past, some people thought "poetry was best left in the hands of experts, those deemed knowledgeable enough to decipher and interpret the enigmatic language poets seem to so enjoy" (Steineke, 2002, p. 8). Fortunately, poetry has changed and, today, students can personally connect to many contemporary poems. Thus, educators must provide adolescents with the tools to understand poetry and help them develop the confidence necessary to read, discuss, and enjoy poetry. When taught effectively and with poetry they enjoy, young adults can meet even a challenging poem with enthusiasm and confidence (Steineke, 2002).

Called the language of emotions, poetry's elusive quality defies exact definition. In general, the emphasis is not on how the reader feels about poetry, but on how poetry makes the reader feel. Poetry is "writing that formulates a concentrated imaginative awareness of experience in language chosen and arranged to create a specific emotional response through its meaning, sound, and rhythm" (*Merriam-Webster's Encyclopedia of Literature*, 1995, p. 893). When the poem and the reader connect, poetry has the power to elicit rich sensory images and deep emotional responses. However, these emotional responses are often age-related. Thus, educators must ensure that the topics in poetry relate to the experiences, emotions, concerns, and feelings of the reader (Knowles & Smith, 1997).

Types of Poetry. Part of what makes it difficult to select poetry for adolescents is that poetry affects readers in different ways (Heartwell, 2002). Some people like rhyming poetry while others enjoy free verse. Some people think poetry should reflect the simple things in life while others believe poetry should explore the depths of a person's most complex emotions. The challenge for teachers and library media specialists is to pique the interest and curiosity of all students and help them learn to appreciate a variety of poetic styles.

As shown in Table 9–1, poetry for young adults comes in various forms. While some readers might like narrative poems, others might prefer lyrical poetry. Looking at studies of poetry preferences of young adults, Abrahamson (2002) found that, while adolescents enjoy narrative poetry, they also like humorous poems, including limericks, with older teens enjoying more subtle humor. Rhythm and rhyme are not as important to older teens as to younger teens, who also find that figurative language interferes with their ability to understand poems. Also, younger adolescents "prefer modern poetry

TABLE 9–1	Selected Types of Poetry

Type	Definition
ACROSTIC	A short verse in which the first, middle, or last letters of each line form words.
BALLAD	An eight-stanza poem, containing four lines, each with eight syllables and with the second and fourth lines rhyming.
CINQUAIN	A five-line verse with two syllables in the first and last lines, and four, six, and eight syllables in the middle lines, respectively.
DIAMANTE	A diamond-shaped poem with seven lines.
FREE VERSE	Poetry that establishes its own pattern without predetermined rules.
HAIKU	A poem in three lines with five, seven, and five syllables, respectively.
LIMERICK	A five-line humorous poem whereby first, second, and fifth lines rhyme and the third and fourth lines rhyme.
LYRIC	A poem that tells about a poet's personal experience or response to a time or moment.
NARRATIVE	A poem that tells a story using a sequence of events.
SONNET	A poetic form that has 14 lines, each with 10 syllables.

over traditional or classic pieces" (Abrahamson, 2002, p. 22). Haiku came in at the bottom of the list in preferred types of poems (Abrahamson, 2002). Thus, to decide what they like and enjoy, adolescents need to have the opportunity to explore various forms of poetry and to develop the skills to understand poetry. To help them, educators must expose young adults to a wide variety of poems and teach them how to find individual poems and collections that appeal to their interests.

Reasons For Using and Teaching Poetry. A number of reasons exist to use poetry with young adults. Poetry "has the power not only to delight but also has the potential to instruct" (Kazemek, 2003, p. 46) especially by providing "non-didactic moral education" (p. 44). In addition,

> Poetry, like painting, reflects a special way of looking at the world. The poet, as the painter, looks at the world with an artist's vision, selecting images as vehicles for thoughts and feelings. The process is the same; only the mode of expression is different. The artist uses paint to convey a personal vision of the world: the poet uses words (Marshall & Newman, 1997, p. 7).

Unfortunately, an emphasis on poetic conventions may keep adolescents from enjoying the "words and music" (p. 23) of poetry (Thomas, 2000). For example, when Andrea Davis (1997) surveyed her eighth-grade students, their comments about poetry ranged from "I love it" to "It's boring, pointless, and mushy" (p. 17). However, she found that, at the end of a carefully planned poetry anthology unit, these same students made the following comments:

> Before we did the anthology I hated poetry, I am glad my opinion changed. You're probably going to think I'm lying, but I thought the anthologies were the best thing we've done all year . . . I even think I learned how to enjoy poetry a little better. (Davis, 1997, p. 20)

Lowery (2003) also found that poetry, with its short, concise thoughts, is an excellent way to help students at risk of failure learn to read. Poetry can help everyone (even preservice teachers) reflect on themselves and move "beyond those self-reflections to understanding the greater worldview" (p. 51).

Characteristics of Poetry For Young Adults. One essential key to identifying the best poetry to use with young adults is to remember their developmental period. While children are not developmentally "ready" for young adult poetry, adolescents do not usually enjoy children's poetry. While there are always some exceptions such as the poems of Shel Silverstein and Jack Prelutsky, in general, young adult poetry should be evaluated on the criteria listed in Considerations for Selecting Young Adult Literature: *Poetry*.

Unfortunately, young adults might not like a poem that possesses all these characteristics because, like adults, adolescents have their own individual tastes, likes, and dislikes. Thomas (2001) goes so far as to contend that many contemporary poets who are writing for young adults disempower adolescent readers by writing in traditional ways and encourages adults to look for poems that push the boundaries of poetry by providing highly complex explorations of the feelings, emotions, and experiences of young

CONSIDERATIONS | *For Selecting Young Adult Literature* | **POETRY**

When selecting poetry for young adults, ask the following questions:

◎ Does the poem have meaning for the young adult—can the young adult relate to the topic, the setting, the theme, or the emotion being conveyed?

◎ Does the poem elicit rich sensory images or deep emotional responses, which young adults appreciate or understand?

◎ Does the poem allow adolescents to experience the power of words and to explore how words can elicit certain emotional responses?

◎ Does the poem have vivid imagery and vibrant language?

◎ Will the poem provide pleasure (i.e., can young adults relate to the poetry in some way either as an event or emotion they have experienced or would like to experience)?

adults. Thus, you must be sure to expose adolescents to a number of different poems in an attempt to interest as many readers as possible.

When identifying poetry to use in a classroom or add to a library collection, educators must remember that females and males differ as readers, writers, and critics and bring unique perspectives to poetry including their expectations for appropriate male and female behavior. To determine the gender messages including the biases and stereotypes in adolescent poetry and the possible impact of poetry on gender identity, Johnson, McClanahan, and Mertz (1999) examined poetry anthologies for young adults. They identified five anthologies (Table 9–2) that "show both females and males

TABLE 9-2 | *Five Gender-Balanced Poetry Collections*

Duffy, C. A. (Ed.). (1993). *I wouldn't thank you for a valentine: Poems for young feminists.* New York: Henry Holt.

Glenn, M. (1982). *Class dismissed! High school poems by Mel Glenn.* New York: Clarion.

Hirschfelder, A. B., & Singer, B. R. (Eds.). (1992). *Rising voices: Writings of young Native Americans.* New York: Scribner.

Lyne, S. (Ed.) (1983). *Ten-second rainshowers: Poems by young people.* Scarsdale, NY: Bradbury.

Medearis, A. S. (1995). *Skin deep and other teenage reflections: Poems by Angela Shelf Medearis.* New York: Macmillan.

Source: Abstracted from Johnson, A. B., McClanahan, L. G., & Mertz, M. P. (1999). Gender representation in poetry for young adults. *The ALAN Review, 26*(3), 39–44.

as complex human beings rather than flat and one dimensional subjects" (p. 39) and that could be used "in valuable ways to initiate classroom dialogue in an attempt to break various gender stereotypes before the stereotypes become permanent in the minds of adolescents" (p. 39).

Poetry Books For Young Adults. Books of poetry usually take one of three formats: edited anthologies consisting of the poems of a number of poets, collections of poems of one poet, or a single poem or group of poems that are meant to be read from beginning to end. One example of this latter category is Mel Glenn's *Split Image* (2000), which is the story of a young Asian American girl and the conflicts she faces at home and at school. In contrast, the poems within an anthology are often meant to be shared individually although the collection as a whole may present a single theme. As poet Nikki Grimes (2000) says, a single poem can be "memorized or sung, or . . . carried in the back pocket of the mind" (p. 33). While you will want to share a number of classic poems with young adults, there are also a number of contemporary poems and collections of poetry which will provide poems that adolescents will want to carry with them.

Anthologies of poetry. There are a number of excellent collections of young adult poetry, some by adult poets and others by adolescents themselves. Patrice Vecchione has edited several anthologies that should appeal to adolescents including *The Body Eclectic: An Anthology of Poems* (2002) and *Truth and Lies* (2000). Another anthology compiler is Paul Janeczko, who often combines information about poets with their poetry. His *Seeing the Blue Between: Advice and Inspiration for Young Poets* (2002) is a compilation of letters and poems from 32 poets that provides advice to adolescent writers. Other excellent poetry anthologies by Janeczko include the classic *Poetspeak: In Their Work, about Their Work* (1983), *The Music of What Happens: Poems That Tell Stories* (1985), *The Place My Words Are Looking For: What Poets Say about and Through Their Work* (1990), and *Looking for Your Name: A Collection of Contemporary Poems* (1993). Some of his more recent anthologies include *Stone Bench in an Empty Park* (2000) and *Blushing: Expressions of Love in Poems and Letters* (2004).

Adolescents often enjoy poems written by teenage authors. For example, the San Francisco Arts Commission's WritersCorps provides a workshop for young authors. Their yearly volume includes excellent poetry that is sometimes combined with prose or even photography. Some of their more recent volumes include *Believe Me, I Know: Poetry and Photography by WritersCorps Youth* (Bush, 2002) and *Jump: Poetry and Prose by WritersCorps Youth* (Bush, 2001). Another collection by teen writers is *Movin': Teen Poets Take Voice* (2000), edited by Dave Johnson. This anthology consists of poems by participants in New York Public Library poetry workshops or by teens who submitted their work via the Internet. Esther Pearl Watson and Mark Todd checked teen magazines and combed Internet sites to develop the anthology *The Pain Tree and Other Teenage Angst-Ridden Poetry* (2000). Finally, *You Hear Me? Poems and Writings by Teenage Boys* (2000), collected by Betsy Franco, contains the frank and sometimes raw emotions of adolescent boys.

While boys and girls often appreciate the same type of poetry, there are times when their interests turn in other directions. In *I Wouldn't Thank You for a Valentine: Poems for Young Feminists* (1993), Carol Ann Duffy has collected poems that explore women's issues;

likewise, in *I Feel a Little Jumpy Around You: Paired Poems by Men & Women* (1996), Naomi Shihab Nye and Paul B. Janeczko present pairs of poems.

Many young adult poetry anthologies incorporate multicultural poetry. Some of the classic collections are *I Am the Darker Brother,* which was compiled by Arnold Adoff in 1968 and expanded and updated in 1997, and *The Whispering Wind: Poetry by Young American Indians* (1972), edited by Terry Allen. *Pierced By a Ray of Sun: Poems about the Times We Feel Alone* (1995), featuring poems selected by Ruth Gordon, is an international collection that focuses on individual alienation and loneliness. Another favorite that focuses on young adult concerns (e.g., school and the future) is Lori M. Carlson's *Cool Salsa: Bilingual Poems on Growing Up Latino in the United States* (1994), in which she includes poets such as Sandra Cisneros and Gary Soto. Other collections about the Latino experience are *Wáchale! Poetry and Prose about Growing Up Latino in America* (2001), edited by Ilan Stavans, and *The Tree Is Older Than You Are: A Bilingual Gathering of Poems and Stories from Mexico with Paintings by Mexican Artists* (1995) by Naomi Shihab Nye. In *Shimmy Shimmy Shimmy Like My Sister Kate: Looking at the Harlem Renaissance Through Poems* (1996), Nikki Giovanni has collected poems that reflect the African American cultural experience in the early 20th century.

There is no doubt that young adults enjoy a wide range of poetry. In *Light-Gathering Poems* (2000), Liz Rosenberg has produced a collection of classic and contemporary poems from throughout the world, including translations of poems from poets such as Issa, Rilke, and Rumi. David Kherdian goes back to the 1960s and the Beat poets in San Francisco in his *Beat Voices: An Anthology of Beat Poetry* (1995). Other collections to consider are June Cotner's collection *Teen Sunshine Reflections: Words for the Heart and Soul* (2002), Naomi Shihab Nye's *What Have You Lost?* (1999), Michael Stipe's *The Haiku Year* (1998), and Zoe Anglesey's *Listen Up! Spoken Word Poetry* (1999).

Collections of a single poet. While Shel Silverstein, Jack Prelutsky, and even Dr. Seuss remain favorites with some adolescents, there are a number of poets who write especially for young adults. In addition to his novels in various genres, Paul Fleischman has written several books of poetry that are meant to be read aloud including his *I Am Phoenix: Poems for Two Voices* (1989), *Joyful Noise: Poems for Two Voices* (1988), and *Big Talk: Poems for Four Voices* (2000). From the pen of Naomi Shihab Nye comes *19 Varieties of Gazelle: Poems of the Middle East* (2002), a collection of her poems about the Middle East and Arab Americans, especially their feelings since September 11, 2001. Selecting works from her adult poems and adding new ones, Pat Mora has produced a collection of free verse poems in *My Own True Name* (2000), while in *Remember the Bridge: Poems of a People* (2002), Carole Boston Weatherford combines poetry and history to chronicle African American history and culture. A perennial favorite is poet Arnold Adoff. In addition to compiling collections' of the works of other poets, he has written a number of volumes of original work including *Slow Dance: Heart Break Blues* (1995), *The Basket Counts* (2000), and *Sports Pages* (1986). Expanding Your Knowledge with the Internet 9–1 provides Internet sites on individual poets as well as young adult poetry in general.

A story in poems. A number of authors have written poetic young adult novels by using a series of poems to tell a complete story. In *You Remind Me of You: A Poetry Memoir* (2002), Eireann Corrigan, a high school student, reflects on her fight against an

EXPANDING   *YOUR KNOWLEDGE WITH THE INTERNET 9–1*

You can use a number of Internet sites to expand your knowledge of poetry. Links to the samples listed below and many additional sites are found on this book's Companion Website at www.prenhall.com/bucher.

Academy of American Poets

www.poets.org/

Favorite Poem Project

www.favoritepoem.org/

Poetry a Day For American High Schools

www.loc.gov/poetry/180/

eating disorder. Although each poem can stand alone, the series of poems present a picture of the conflicting emotions and pressures that teens feel. Another new writer who looks at teenage problems through poetry is Sonya Sones. Her *Stop Pretending* (1999) tells the story of a teenager who is trying to cope with her sister's mental breakdown.

A number of other authors have written stories in poems. In both the Newbery Medal-winning *Out of the Dust* (1997) and *Witness* (2001), Karen Hesse uses free verse to tell very complex tales. *True Believer* (2001) and *Make Lemonade* (1993), Virginia Euwer Wolff's stories of LaVaughn and her struggle to escape from the housing projects, are also written as free verse poems. Popular author Mel Glenn offers several stories in poetry, including his mysteries *Who Killed Mr. Chippendale? A Mystery in Poems* (1996) and *Foreign Exchange: A Mystery in Poems* (1999), as well as *Split Image: A Story in Poems* (2000). Other novels in verse include Robert Cormier's *Frenchtown Summer* (1999), Cynthia Rylant's *Soda Jerk* (1990), and Jacqueline Woodson's *Locomotion* (2003).

Suggestions For Selecting and Using Poetry. According to Georgia Heard (Smith & Zarnowski, 1999), "poetry is about recognizing and paying attention to our inner lives—our memories, hopes, doubts, questions, fears, [and] joys" (p. 66). Why, then, is poetry often a neglected genre? Unfortunately, many preservice teachers and library media specialists tell us that they do not like poetry because they had to analyze it to death in high school or memorize it in elementary school. Rather than focusing on the pleasure that can come from reading a well-crafted poem, these educators remember only the pain that they felt when they were forced to dissect a poem. In an interview, Sonya Sones quoted a poem by poet laureate Billy Collins about people who want to "tie the poem to a chair with rope and torture a confession out of it" (Lesesne, 2002, p. 52). Fortunately, there are as many ways to use poetry as there are individual teachers and library media specialists. The key is to determine "what works" for an individual teacher and what young adults seem to enjoy. While some adolescents like to create anthologies, others enjoy writing poetry, performing poetry, or just discussing poems.

A number of excellent resources are available that educators can use to encourage young adults to read, write, and perform poetry. We have already mentioned several of the works of Paul B. Janeczko that incorporate poems with ideas for writing poetry. Another of his books is *How to Write Poetry* (1999). In addition, Kathi Appelt has written two books for budding poets: *Poems from Homeroom: A Writer's Place to Start* (2002) and *Just People & Paper/Pen/Poem: A Young Writer's Way to Begin* (1997). For teachers, excellent resources include:

- *Teaching Poetry in High School* (Somers, 1999)

- *Today You Are My Favorite Poet: Writing Poems with Teenagers* (Hewitt, 1998)

- *Young Adult Poetry: A Survey and Theme Guide* (Schwedt & DeLong, 2002)

Suggestions for Collaborative Efforts 9–1 explains how teachers and library media specialists can select poetry to complement a specific subject area.

The following are a few selected strategies to help you use poetry in instruction. We encourage you to consult the original source for more detailed information.

- Share poems with young adults, but remember that the way you share them can be important. Abrahamson (2002) reported a study which found that adolescents who listened to poems that were read aloud "favored short poems with rhythm and rhyme. Students who read the poems and listened to them at the same time tended to give all poems the lowest ratings" (p. 21). In addition, poems that were serious, or without rhyme or obvious rhythm, scored highest when students read them silently (Abrahamson, 2002).

- Teach adolescents to read poetry out loud by reading slowly in a normal tone of voice and pausing at the punctuation, rather than at the end of the line. For more practical suggestions, visit *How to Read a Poem Out Loud* at www.loc.gov/poetry/180/p180-howtoread.html.

SUGGESTIONS FOR COLLABORATIVE EFFORTS

Teachers across the curriculum can work with school library media specialists to identify poetry that can be used in specific curricular areas or even in several subjects. While the poems need not be long or difficult, they can set the mood for a unit or a lesson or just provide some humor. Teachers can read the poems aloud to the class or, following copyright guidelines, provide copies of a single poem from an anthology for everyone in the class. For example, social studies teachers might want to explore the poems in *Hour of Freedom: American History in Poetry* (2003), collected by Milton Meltzer, while mathematics teachers can look at *Math Talk: Mathematical Ideas in Poems for Two Voices* (1991) by Theoni Pappas.

- Link poems to a classic novel. Susan Jolley (2002) integrated poetry into the study of *To Kill a Mockingbird* by encouraging students to read poems that enhanced the theme of understanding others. Helping students examine the structure of the assigned poems, she asked them to create couplets or quatrains in their journals (Jolley, 2002).

- Engage in authentic poetry discussions. Students find two poems they like and make four photocopies of each. Then, working in groups of four, the students:

  1. Discuss one of the poems.
  2. Take turns reading the poem in various interpretive ways.
  3. Share general impressions.
  4. Work individually and take notes on impressions of the poem.
  5. Share ideas, making sure each reader has an opportunity to explain her or his personal views.
  6. Spend 10 to 15 minutes to reach a group consensus about the poem.
  7. Repeat the process with a different group member's poem (Steineke, 2002).

- Save words from a poem. Allen (2002) taught poetry by having students read a poem and then look for words they wanted to save for their own use. Using a writing workshop approach, students collected words on word walls or living charts. Some categories included (a) words/images that make me smile or laugh; (b) smells, sights, and sounds that bring tears to my eyes; (c) words/phrases that paint a picture; (d) words that make noise; (e) forbidden words; and (f) action words. By collecting words that capture their eyes and ears, adolescents can explore these words and make them part of their speaking and writing vocabularies.

- Create poems. While some students may enjoy writing poems that follow traditional forms such as haiku, sonnets, or cinquains, others might enjoy creating collage poems, found poems, group poems, character poems, riddle poems, raps, poems for two or more voices, or repeat poster poems. Some of these ideas are explained in detail in an article by Bleeker and Bleeker (1996).

- Create an Internet writer's workshop. Hommel (2003) encourages teachers to create an Internet writer's workshop where students can share their poetry and discuss the poems that other teens have written.

- Host a poetry jam. Connecting Adolescents and Their Literature 9–1 provides information on holding a poetry jam or poetry slam.

Drama

Jean Brown and Elaine Stephens (1995) called drama "probably the most neglected field for young adults" (p. 309). Now, a decade later, drama still has not received its rightful place in young adult literature. This is unfortunate, because carefully selected drama can provide adolescents with varied language situations, thought-provoking scenarios and dialogue, and considerable enjoyment.

ADOLESCENTS AND THEIR LITERATURE 9–1

Educators can build on the popularity of performance poetry by holding a poetry café or hosting a poetry jam/slam. In *Wham! It's a Poetry Jam: Discovering Performance Poetry* (2002), Sara Holbrook provides teenagers with ideas for poetry competitions, advice on presenting poetry, and suggestions for jamming. For a more formal poetry reading without the competition of a jam/slam, try a poetry care. Cheryl Thomas (2000) reported that her students held one for parents, faculty, staff, and friends and found that the experience was "their finest day of the year" (p. 25). Other poetry slam resources are:

- *Slam* (von Ziegesar, 2000)
- *Slam Poetry Manual* (Bladwin, 2003)
- There is also information on the Internet at www.ala.org/ala/yalsa/teenreading/trw/trw2003/wayscelebrate.htm

Types of Dramatic Presentations. Educators can use a number of different styles of drama in the classroom including oral interpretation (usually a one-person performance of a poem or brief prose passage), story theater (a pantomime accompanied by a narrator who reads or tells the story while others act out the plot); Readers' Theater (the reading of a script as opposed to acting it out); creative dramatics (the dramatization of a story with an improvised dialogue); and role-playing (the actors invent both the dialogue and the action as they proceed) (Russell, 1997). In addition, a number of short plays and monologues are written especially for young adults. When any of these dramatic forms are presented by enthusiastic teachers and library media specialists and are based on adolescent interests and developmental levels, middle and high school students usually enjoy dramatic activities.

Reasons for Using and Teaching Drama. Young adults are often eager to confront contemporary problems and relevant world issues. Thus, authors and playwrights who are willing to write for adolescent audiences have an excellent opportunity to help young adults consider themes of diversity in race, religion, gender, and class in a way that profoundly affects them (Bontempo, 1995). Harding et al. (1996) found that watching live theater can help young adults confront contemporary problems such as substance abuse by promoting reflection and stimulating discussion (1996). Drama can transform people by making them think and sometimes by making them feel uncomfortable. However, educators often have to work to help adolescents take these feelings of discomfort that a play may cause and to transfer them to their own lives and the decisions they will personally have to make (Gonzalez, 2002). Therefore, when Abramovitz (2000) wanted to foster an appreciation and acceptance of diversity with her high school classes, she used a number of drama techniques such as Stanislavsian sensitivity exercises, role-playing, and interpretation sessions to help adolescents explore their feelings about ethnic conflicts.

In addition to helping adolescents explore issues and the dilemmas of the human experience, educators can use drama to help secondary students develop their creativity. Another essential purpose of drama should be to help adolescents develop the pleasure and skills in reading and interpreting drama, to acquaint students with dramatic traditions so they can evaluate dramatic performances, and to increase the students' insights into themselves and others.

Characteristics of Drama for Young Adults. When selecting drama to use with young adults, educators have to remember that the key words are *young adults*. Drama that middle and secondary students enjoy and appreciate is usually different than drama for young children and older adults. While the playwright might not have had young adults specifically in mind, his or her drama still must appeal to young adults. Considerations for Selecting Young Adult Literature: *Drama* lists questions when selecting drama for young adults.

Drama for Young Adults. Dramas for adolescents can take several forms. In addition to actual plays and monologues, there are also novels that are written or adapted as dramas or screenplays and poems that are meant to be performed.

There are several excellent anthologies of plays for young adults. In *Center Stage* (1990), Don Gallo compiled short plays by young adult authors such as Walter Dean Myers and Susan Beth Pfeffer. Wendy Lamb collected winning plays from the Young Playwrights Festival, which is sponsored by the Foundation of the Dramatist Guild, in several anthologies including *Ten Out of Ten: Winning Plays from YPF 1* (1992) and *Ground Zero Club* (1987), while Norma Bowles and Mark E. Rosenthal edited *Cootie*

CONSIDERATIONS	For Selecting Young Adult Literature	DRAMA

Ask the following questions when selecting drama for young adults:

- Can young adults relate to the topics or themes (e.g., relationships, struggling for or dealing with increased freedom from significant adults)?

- Will young adults be able to understand the language and communication, both verbal and nonverbal, and are these similar to their own?

- Will the drama provide real pleasure for young adults? Unlike the first item in this list, this item suggests that young adults can actually experience pleasure from either watching or participating in the drama.

- Is the drama cognitively appropriate in content and action so that the drama is neither so low-level that young adults consider it "elementary" nor too advanced for young adults' thinking capacity?

Shots: Theatrical Inoculations Against Bigotry for Kids, Parents and Teachers (2001), a collection of plays created by Fringe Benefits, a Los Angeles-based theatrical company. Other anthologies of dramas include *International Plays for Young Audiences: Contemporary Works from Leading Playwrights* (Ellis, 2000), *Great Scenes for Young Actors* (Slaight & Sharrar, 1991), and *Short Plays for Young Actors* (Slaight & Sharrar, 1996).

Several authors have issued collections of their own plays for young adults. *Most Valuable Player and Four Other All-Star Plays for Middle and High School Audiences* (1999) by internationally known playwright Mary Hall Surface contains scripts that focus on contemporary social issues. In *Nerdlandia* (1999), Gary Soto explores relationships in the Los Angeles Barrio, and in *Perspectives: Relevant Scenes for Teens* (1997), Mary Krell-Oishi provides short scenes that explore the range of teen emotions.

In other chapters of this book, we have discussed realistic and historical fiction. Some of these books are written in the form of a play including Paul Fleischman's *Seek* (2001) and *Mind's Eye* (1999), and Walter Dean Myers' *Monster* (1999). A popular young adult novel by Avi has been adapted into a play by Ronn Smith as *Nothing But the Truth: A Play* (1997).

Adolescents can also create drama through poetry. Some short poems with strong emotional themes are actually mini-dramas, often written in dialogue form, which are suitable for dramatization. While these poems may be found in a number of different anthologies, Paul Fleischman has created three volumes of poetry, *I Am Phoenix: Poems for Two Voices* (1989), *Joyful Noise; Poems for Two Voices* (1988), and *Big Talk: Poems for Four Voices* (2000), which are designed to be performed. Gasparro and Falletta (1994) suggested that teachers of English as a second language (ESL) could especially benefit from a multisensory approach because the dramatization of poetry is a powerful tool in stimulating learning.

Many drama have been released as films. From Page to Screen lists a few of them.

Suggestions For Selecting and Using Drama. We have already mentioned a number of excellent anthologies and collections of plays as well as some complete plays. In addition, the Internet provides many resources that can help teachers and library media specialists select and use drama in schools. Expanding Your Knowledge with the Internet 9–2 features a list of some of these sources.

Earlier in this chapter we mentioned several reasons to use drama with young adults. Barbara T. Bontempo (1995) encourages teachers and young adults to explore prejudice through drama and role-playing. Other suggestions for using drama with young adults include the following:

- Integrate drama into subjects throughout the curriculum. Suggestions for Collaborative Efforts 9–2 recommends the use of Readers' Theater to achieve this.

- After a dramatic performance, build on the play by asking students to:
  1. Write a short review of the play.
  2. Discuss or write about the relationship of the theme of the play to contemporary life.

FROM PAGE TO SCREEN

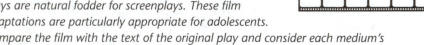

Poetry, Drama, and Short Stories

Plays are natural fodder for screenplays. These film adaptations are particularly appropriate for adolescents. Compare the film with the text of the original play and consider each medium's strengths and weaknesses in terms of the individual tale.

Driving Miss Daisy
1989, PG
★★★★

Alfred Uhry adapted his own Pulitzer Prize-winning stage play for the screen in this charming comedy/drama about aging, race relations, and friendship. Jessica Tandy, Morgan Freeman, and Dan Aykroyd are superb, each finding a natural grace and humanity in the characters that Uhry so beautifully crafted. Bruce Beresford's unobtrusive direction allows his actors to carry the film, which won several Academy Awards, including best picture.

Inherit the Wind
1960, PG
★★★★

Spencer Tracy's magnetic performance in this courtroom drama of creationism vs. evolution, highlighted beautifully by Ernest Laszlo's black and white photography, mirror the power of the Jerome Lawerence, Robert E. Lee play. This adaptation was beautifully crafted to bring drama to the courtroom, creating a riveting centerpiece to the film.

A Man for All Seasons
1966, Unrated
★★★★

Robert Bolt adapted his own stage play of a man forced to choose between standing up for his principles and risking the wrath of a villainous king, or submitting to the will of the king and risking his own corruption. His screenplay is vivid and precise, and in the capable hands of director Fred Zinnemann, the script, cinematography, and performance from Paul Scofield combine in an engaging, powerful film.

Romeo + Juliet
PG-13, 1996
★★★

Director Baz Luhrman's dizzying, hip re-imagining of Shakespeare's classic tale of star-crossed lovers is a surprisingly worthwhile adaptation. Retaining the original dialogue, Luhrman's updating surrounds the couple with modern media, gadgetry, and music, in a visually stunning film. The purpose behind the dissonance between ancient text and modern environment is never clear, which weakens the final product, but it creates an interesting opportunity for discussion.

EXPANDING | *YOUR KNOWLEDGE WITH THE INTERNET 9-2*

 A number of Internet sites have information about drama for young adults. On this book's Companion Website at www.prenhall.com/bucher you will find links to the following examples and many additional sites.

National Standards for Theatre Education

www.byu.edu/tma/arts-ed/

Drama Teacher's Resource Room

www3.sk.sympatico.ca/erachi/

Philadelphia Young Playwrights

www.pypf.org

3. Write an alternative ending to the play.

4. Debate an issue that is presented in the play.

■ Take a scene from a young adult novel and turn it into a dramatic presentation through Readers' Theater, role-playing, or script writing.

■ Encourage young adults to develop their creative talents by performing short plays. Connecting Adolescents and Their Literature 9–2 suggests one way to accomplish this.

■ Use monologues and dialogues in speech classes to develop oral presentation skills.

■ Encourage students to participate in a national, state, or local young playwrights festival or organize a festival in your own school division.

■ Work with other teachers to develop a drama workshop in your school to provide a place for adolescents who want to perform plays and those who want to write them.

 SUGGESTIONS FOR COLLABORATIVE EFFORTS

Teachers and library media specialists can identify short dramas that can be used throughout the curriculum to make subjects and concepts more meaningful and to encourage adolescents to develop their oral and physical communication skills. One excellent starting point is *Readers Theatre for American History* (2001) by Anthony D. Fredericks. Working together, English and social studies teachers could use some of the scripts in this collection to help young adults explore historical events.

- Build on successful workshops such as the Bonderman (Newman, 2003), which was developed to support new playwrights.

- Build on the living newspaper format and use research, play design, scriptwriting, presentation, and puppets to present plays that articulate significant social studies issues (Chilcoat, 1996).

Short Stories

> A short story is, in some ways, like a photograph—a captured moment of time that is crystalline, though sometimes mysterious; arresting, though perhaps delicate. But while a photo may or may not suggest consequences, a short story always does. In the story's moment of time something important, something irrevocable has occurred. The change may be subtle or obvious, but it is definite and definitive. (Singer, 2000, p. 12)

Since the publication of Don Gallo's groundbreaking short story collection *Sixteen: Short Stories by Outstanding Writers for Young Adults* (1984), there has been a relative explosion in the number of quality short stories and short story collections written for young adults. Adolescents have welcomed this, shown their appreciation for short stories, and turned to reading short stories instead of or in addition to young adult novels. Because of their length, many short stories can be read in one sitting, often while waiting for class or for a friend. Through short stories, some young adults have been introduced to popular authors and have gone on to read complete novels by these writers. Expanding Your Knowledge with the Internet 9-3 offers Internet sites that provide helpful information on short stories for young adults.

Types of Short Stories. Emerging as a distinct literary form in the 19th century, the short story's popularity was spurred by the tales of Edgar Allan Poe, especially his *Tales*

CONNECTING | **ADOLESCENTS AND THEIR LITERATURE 9-2**

Athletes are not the only ones who can perform in school activities. Many young adults welcome the opportunity to demonstrate their dramatic abilities. In this chapter, we have already suggested holding a poetry slam. This can be expanded to include the presentation of monologues and short dramatic scenes as well. A number of resources listed in the Young Adult Books section at the end of this chapter can serve as resources, including:

- *Acting Natural: Monologs, Dialogs, and Playlets for Teens* (Kehret, 1991)

- *Forensics Series, Vol. 1 Duo Practice and Competition* (Lhota & Milstein, 2003a)

- *Forensics Series Duo Practice and Competition . . . Vol. 2* (Lhota & Milstein, 2003b)

EXPANDING   *YOUR KNOWLEDGE WITH THE INTERNET 9-3*

 A few of the many Internet sites that provide information about short stories for young adults are listed below. Links to these and many additional sites are found on this book's Companion Website at www.prenhall.com/bucher.

Popular Paperbacks For Young Adults—Short Takes

www.ala.org/ala.valsa/booklistsawards/popularpaperback/2000popularpaperbacks.htm

The Elements of the Short Story From the Yale-New Haven Teachers Institute

www.cis.yale.edu/ynhti/curriculum/units/1983/3/83.03.09.x.html

of the Grotesque and Arabesque. In general, short stories are found in the same genres as novels: fantasy, science fiction, horror, historical and contemporary realism, adventure, mystery, and humor. A short story differs from a novel in that the short story focuses on a single episode or scene with a limited number of characters. In a way, a short story is similar to the episodic plot found in chapter books for beginning readers where each chapter can almost stand on its own. In the short story, however, the entire plot must stand on its own with the author using a concise setting, an economy of narration, and quickly developed characters.

Most frequently, short stories for young adults are collected into anthologies. The collection may be by a single author or by a number of individuals. Sometimes there is a connecting theme while, in other cases, the connecting factor is that the stories are all written for young adults. According to editor Sharyn November,

> A short story collection is the literary equivalent of a Whitman's Sampler. The reader pokes around to see what's interesting—reads some stories the way you'd snap up the truffle or caramel, flips past others the way you'd put back the bad mint cocoanut swirl. (Singer, 2000, p. 13)

Reasons For Using and Teaching Short Stories. With the number of excellent short story collections currently available, a number of reasons exist to include short stories in the curriculum. Many teachers have found that using short stories for required reading helps students with a variety of reading and comprehension abilities. In addition, with their short length and quickly moving plot, short stories can also capture the attention of young adult readers. Finally, while young adults sometimes read short stories written for other age groups, especially short stories written for adults, many authors of short stories for adolescents deal with issues and concerns to which this age group can relate. Rather than just suggesting short stories due to their long literary standing, educators and library media specialists who carefully select young adult short stories make a valuable contribution.

Characteristics Of Short Stories For Young Adults. What attributes or characteristics make a good short story for young adults? What kind of short story do young adults want? What separates the "good" from the mediocre? Like a novel, a short story must have a plot structure that provides the reader with an introduction, development and conclusion, and a character (or characters) who works through a conflict in less than 10,000 (sometimes less than 5,000) words. According to editor Sharyn November, a short story is

> bite-sized. Like good chocolate, it's intense. It's long enough to make you care about the characters—but it resolves in a way that's satisfying, rather than seeming unfinished or overdone. (Singer, 2000, p. 13)

Short stories should have "clarity and directness of vision, with no wasted words, no throwaway sentences . . ." (Pearl, 2002, p. 31). While a novel is completeness, a short story is intensity. Considerations for Selecting Young Adult Literature: *Short Stories* provides several questions you can ask when selecting short stories that young adults might enjoy.

When selecting short stories, educators also need to keep in mind the needs of both proficient and reluctant readers and try to find a balance between a reading level that challenges advanced readers and one that is appropriate for less accomplished readers. Connecting Adolescents and Their Literature 9–3 suggests the use of short story collections to appeal to a wide variety of readers including those who have less than average reading skills or who simply do not enjoy reading.

Short Story Collections For Young Adults. There are several excellent collections of short stories for young adults. As we noted in poetry, some of the collections are by a

---

CONSIDERATIONS	For Selecting Young Adult Literature	SHORT STORIES

When selecting short stories for young adults, ask the following questions:

- Was the short story written specifically *for* young adult readers?

- Will themes interest young adult readers? Will the young adult enjoy and want to continue reading the short story?

- Is the plot believable, interesting, and sufficiently fast-paced to hold readers' attention? Does it seem contrived or artificial in places?

- Is the characterization developed and free of racial, gender, social class, and other stereotypes?

- Is the length appropriate for young adults' attention spans?

- Is the setting appropriate and one with which young adults can relate?

- Will the short story contribute to integrated curricular approaches? Can the short story be related to issues examined in a particular curricular area such as science or history?

CONNECTING	ADOLESCENTS AND THEIR LITERATURE 9–3

"Do we have to read the whole book?" While that question can come from an adolescent who feels pressured to find the time to read an entire novel, it can also come from a student who finds reading a book to be academically challenging. One advantage of short stories is that a complete story can often be read in a single sitting and may be more intellectually accessible for some students. Teachers and library media specialists can work collaboratively to compile a reading list of short stories (and the collection each can be found in) that includes:

- Stories for students who lack reading skills.
- Stories for students who simply do not like to read.
- Stories that vary in theme or subject.

Provide a way for young adults to share what they read—this does not have to be the traditional book report, but some means of response might motivate other readers.

single author while other anthologies feature stories from a number of the best young adult writers. Often the collections are developed around a single theme or contain stories in a specific literary genre.

Don Gallo is credited with creating and popularizing the young adult short story anthology that was more than a collection selected from adult short stories. His *Sixteen* (1984) was a collection of original short stories from popular young adult authors such as Richard Peck, Robert Cormier, and Bette Greene. Subsequent volumes have continued that emphasis with authors such as Ellen Wittlinger, Bruce Brooks, and Chris Lynch. While some collections such as *Visions* (1987) and *Connections* (1989) were eclectic, other anthologies such as *Time Capsule* (1999), *Destination Unexpected* (2003), *On the Fringe* (2001), and *No Easy Answers* (1997) have focused on specific themes such as tough choices for teens, adolescent outsiders, and transforming journeys.

With the popularity of fantasy, horror, and science fiction, it is not surprising that a number of recommended short story collections feature these genres. In *Firebirds: An Anthology of Original Fantasy and Science Fiction* (2003), Sharyn November collected stories from authors such as Megan Whalen Turner, Garth Nix, Nancy Farmer, and Lloyd Alexander. Other similar collections include *On the Edge: Stories at the Brink* (2000), *Trapped! Cages of Mind and Body* (1998), and *Night Terrors: Stories of Shadow and Substance* (1996), which are all edited by Lois Duncan; *Tomorrowland: Ten Stories about the Future* (1999), edited by Michael Cart; *Demons and Shadows: The Ghostly Best Stories of Robert Westall* (1993) by Robert Westall; and *Being Dead* (2001), edited by Vivian Vande Velde.

Some collections are centered around the theme of growing up in a multicultural world. Lori Carlson has collected tales of Asian Americans in *American Eyes: New Asian American Short Stories for Young Adults* (1994), and Paul Yee created 10 ghost stories related to the experiences of early Chinese immigrants in *Dead Man's Gold and Other Stories* (2002). Other anthologies include *Half and Half: Writers on Growing Up Biracial and Bicultural* (1998), edited by Claudine Chiawei O'Hearn, and *America Street: A Multicultural Anthology of Stories* (1993), collected by Anne Mazer. Walter Dean Myers tells of the people who live in Harlem in *145th Street Stories* (2000), Gary Soto writes of life in the barrio in *Petty Crimes* (1998), Graham Salisbury takes readers to Hawaii in *Island Boyz* (2002), and David Rice goes to the Rio Grande Valley in Texas in *Crazy Loco: Stories* (2001).

Girls are the target audience for some collections of short stories. In *No Missing Parts: And Other Stories About Real Princesses* (2003), Anne Carter has collected stories of girls who struggle to overcome adversity and to understand their place in life. Other collections for girls include *Stay True: Short Stories for Strong Girls* (1998), collected by Marilyn Singer, and *Small Avalanches and Other Stories* (2004) by Joyce Carol Oates. Other collections focus on the problems that both boys and girls feel as they mature. Coretta Scott King Award-winning author Angela Johnson has written *Gone from Home* (1998), which contains 12 stories about the pressures and pains of growing up, while James Howe has collected stories about the emotional life of adolescents in *Color of Absence: 12 Stories about Loss and Hope* (2001).

A number of other subjects and themes appear in story collections. There are sports stories ranging from the classic *Athletic Shorts* (1991) by Chris Crutcher to *Sports Stories* (2000), an anthology edited by Alan Durant. Judy Blume collected short stories from authors such as David Klass and Katherine Paterson who have felt the pressures of censorship in *Places I Never Meant to Be* (1999). Finally, in *Shattered: Stories of Children and War* (2002), Jennifer Armstrong collected stories of young people living during times of war.

Suggestions For Selecting and Using Short Stories. Short stories should be selected with the same care and skills that you use to select any quality literature for young adults. In fact, you can apply the criteria for each genre discussed in this book when selecting short stories in that genre. The difference between the novel and the short story is in the focus. You can also apply some of the same ideas for using genre novels to using short stories. With teaching methods that reflect young adults' interests as well as their developmental, reading, and motivational levels, both teachers and library media specialists can enrich the curriculum with well-selected short stories. Short stories can be used to study the elements of fiction writing including plot, characterization, setting, and themes; as the basis for literature discussions; and to practice reading skills by using previewing, during reading, and postreading activities. Some specific lesson plans were referenced in Expanding Your Knowledge with the Internet 9–3, mentioned earlier in this chapter and found on the Companion Website. Suggestions for Collaborative Efforts 9–3 illustrates how a teacher and library media specialist can collaborate to encourage students to read short stories.

To encourage students to read short stories for pleasure, a high school English teacher and a library media specialist worked together on a short story unit.

- Together they selected short story anthologies from the school library collection that had interesting book covers, compelling titles, or topics/themes in which young adults are interested.

- The teacher developed a worksheet that focused on the elements of a short story that the students had been studying and encouraged students to select a story to read on their own.

- The class visited the library, selected stories of their choice, and used the Internet to find information about other books or story collections by the same author.

- Finally, the students completed a brief evaluation of the stories that they selected ("The short of it," 2000).

CONCLUDING THOUGHTS

Carefully selected poetry, drama, and short stories can capture the interest of young adults, especially when educators and library media specialists collaboratively select works that young adults deem relevant. With the amount of quality literature available today, young adults are fortunate that they can enjoy collections and anthologies of poetry, drama, and short stories that include more literature written by women and authors of culturally diverse backgrounds, and literature that caters to their interests in romance, conflicts with parents and other adults, and contemporary issues. However, the challenge still remains for educators to introduce young adults to appropriate poetry, drama, and short stories that will interest them and, whenever possible, to integrate these three types of literature into the various curricular areas in a way that allows adolescents to see new and unique perspectives. When educators and library media specialists achieve these challenges, young adults will be the beneficiaries. Visit this book's Companion Website at www.prenhall.com/bucher for additional information about poetry, drama, and short stories including review questions, self-assessments, Internet sites, and young adult literature and readings.

Young Adult Books

This section includes young adult titles recommended or mentioned in this chapter. Check the Companion Website at www.prenhall.com/bucher to find additional suggestions of current young adult literature.

Poetry

Adoff, A. (1986). *Sports pages*. New York: Lippincott. Here are poems about the feelings and experiences adolescents find in sports.

Adoff, A. (1995). *Slow dance; Heart break blues*. New York: Lothrop Lee & Shephard. Here are poems for contemporary, urban teens.

Adoff, A. (1997). *I am the darker brother: An anthology of modern poems by African Americans*. New York: Aladdin. This is an updated collection of the 1968 edition with 21 new poems.

Adoff, A. (2000). *The basket counts*. New York: Simon & Schuster. Basketball takes center court in this collection.

Allen, T. (Ed.). (1972). *The whispering wind: Poetry by young American Indians*. Garden City, NY: Doubleday. A classic collection of poems by adolescents.

Anglesey, Z. (1999). *Listen up! Spoken word poetry*. New York: One World. A collection of poems that are designed to be used in performance.

Appelt, K. (1997). *Just people & paper/pen/poem: A young writer's way to begin*. Houston, TX: Absey & Co. A book of poems and ideas for young writers.

Appelt, K. (2002). *Poems from homeroom: A writer's place to start*. New York: Holt. Appelt matches the writing process to familiar school places such as study hall and homeroom.

Berman, D. (1999). *Actual air: Poems*. New York: Open City Books. Radical poems from a rock musician turned poet.

Bush, V. C. (Ed.). (2001). *Jump: Poetry and prose by Writerscorps youth*. San Francisco, WritersCorps. Teens work through the problems, joys, and details of their everyday lives in this collection.

Bush, V. C. (Ed.). (2002). *Believe me, I know: Poetry and photography of WritersCorps youth*. San Francisco: WritersCorps. Candid photos

illustrate this collection of poems by young poets.

Carlson, L. M. (1994). *Cool salsa: Bilingual poems on growing up Latino in the United States*. New York: Holt. Carlson's poems are for all adolescents.

Cormier, R. (1999). *Frenchtown summer*. New York: Delacorte. In free verse, Cormier tells of a 12-year-old boy in the summer of 1938.

Corrigan, E. (2002). *You remind me of you: A poetry memoir*. New York: Plush. These are autobiographical poems about a teen's battle with eating disorders.

Cotner, J. (Ed.). (2002). *Teen sunshine reflections: Words for the heart and soul*. New York: HarperCollins. This is an interfaith collection of poems and quotations.

Duffy, C. A. (Ed.). (1993). *I wouldn't thank you for a valentine: Poems for young feminists*. New York: Henry Holt. Women from different cultures share their feelings and their fears.

Fleischman, P. (1988). *Joyful noise; Poems for two voices*. New York: HarperCollins. This is the 1989 Newbery Medal winner.

Fleischman, P. (1989). *I am Phoenix: Poems for two voices*. New York: HarperTrophy. Fleischman's poems celebrate birds.

Fleischman, P. (2000). *Big talk: Poems for four voices*. Cambridge, MA: Candlewick. These color-coded poems cover a range of topics and emotions.

Franco, B. (Ed.). (2000). *You hear me? Poems and writings by teenage boys*. Cambridge, MA: Candlewick. This is a no-holds-barred collection of poems.

Giovani, N. (Ed.). (1996). *Shimmy shimmy shimmy like my sister Kate: Looking at the Harlem Renaissance through poems*. New York: Holt. Giovanni includes poems by many of the writers of the Harlem Renaissance.

Glenn, M. (1996). *Who killed Mr. Chippendale? A mystery in poems*. New York: Lodestar. Poems tell the story when a high school teacher is shot.

Glenn, M. (1999). *Foreign exchange: A mystery in poems*. New York: Morrow. It is easy to blame the visitors when a young girl is killed.

Glenn, M. (2000). *Split image: A story in poems*. New York: Morrow. Is Laura Li really as perfect as she seems?

Gordon, R. (1995). *Pierced by a ray of sun: Poems about the times we feel alone*. New York: HarperCollins. An international anthology of poems.

Hesse, K. (1997). *Out of the dust*. New York: Scholastic. Billie Jo uses poems to tell of her family's life in the Depression.

Hesse, K. (2001). *Witness*. New York: Scholastic. Poems tell the story when the Klan comes to Vermont.

Holbrook, S. (2002). *Wham! It's a poetry jam: Discovering performance poetry*. Honesdale, PA: Boyds Mills. Holbrook turns teens on to the world of performance poetry.

Hughes, L. (1994). *The dream keeper and other poems*. New York: Alfred Knopf. A collection of 66 poems selected by J. Brian Pinkney.

Janeczko, P. (1983). *Poetspeak: In their work, About their work*. New York: Macmillan. A collection of 148 poems by modern writers.

Janeczko, P. (1985). *The music of what happens: Poems that tell stories*. New York: Orchard. A collection of thought-provoking poems.

Janeczko, P. (1990). *The place my words are looking for: What poets say about and through their work*. New York: Macmillan. Thirty-nine American poets share their poems and memories.

Janeczko, P. (Ed.). (1993). *Looking for your name: A collection of contemporary poems*. New York: Orchard. Contemporary poets are featured in this collection.

Janeczko, P. (1994). *Poetry from A to Z: A guide for young writers*. New York: Simon & Schuster.

Janeczko introduces the process of writing poetry.

Janeczko, P. (1999). *How to write poetry*. New York: Scholastic. This is an excellent guide to writing poetry.

Janeczko, P. (Ed.). (2000). *Stone bench in an empty park*. New York: Orchard. Haiku goes to the city in this modern collection in a traditional form.

Janeczko, P. (Ed.). (2002). *Seeing the blue between: Advice and inspiration for young poets*. Cambridge, MA: Candlewick. Thirty-two poets provide poems and letters explaining their craft and giving advice to aspiring writers.

Janeczko, P. (Ed.). (2004). *Blushing: Expressions of love in poems and letters*. New York: Orchard. Janeczko goes beyond the usual romantic poems in this collection.

Johnson, D. (2000). *Movin': Teen poets take voice*. New York: Orchard. This anthology contains poets who participated in a New York Public Library workshop.

Kherdian, D. (1995). *Beat voices: An anthology of beat poetry*. New York: Holt. Both East and West Coast poets are represented in this collection.

Livingston, M. C. (1994). *Animal, vegetable, mineral*. New York: HarperCollins. Included are poems from Arnold Adoff, Carmen Bernos de Gasztold, Barbara Juster Esbensen, Karla Kuskin, David McCord, and Valerie Worth. Other anthologies by Livingston are *Flights of Fancy* (1994) and *Remembering and Other Poems* (1989).

Meltzer, M. (Ed.). (2003). *Hour of freedom: American history in poetry*. Honesdale, PA: Boyds Mills. The major events in U.S. history are reflected in the 59 poems in this volume.

Mora, P. (2000). *My own true name*. Houston, TX: Pinata Books. Although many of the poems reflect Mora's experience as a Latina in the Southwest, this collection will appeal to a wide range of adolescents.

Nye, N. S. (Ed.). (1995). *The tree is older than you are: A bilingual gathering of poems and stories from Mexico with paintings by Mexican artists.* New York: Simon & Schuster. Paintings by contemporary artists enrich this collection of translated poems.

Nye, N. S. (Ed.). (1999). *What have you lost?* New York: Greenwillow. From a lost memory to a lost friendship, these poems look at a range of experiences.

Nye, N. S. (2002). *19 varieties of gazelle: Poems of the Middle East.* New York: Greenwillow. Nye explores the emotions of Arab Americans.

Nye, N. S., & Janeczko, P. B. (1996). *I feel a little jumpy around you: Paired poems by men & women.* New York: Simon Pulse. These poems share the views of both men and women on the same subject.

Pappas, T. (1991). *Math talk: Mathematical ideas in poems for two voices.* San Carlos, CA: Wide World Pub Tetra. From circles and fractions to Fibonacci numbers and tessellations, here are poems to share.

Rosenberg, L. (Ed.). (2000). *Light-gathering poems.* New York: Holt. Biographical sketches accompany the poems in this collection of contemporary and classic poetry.

Rylant, C. (1990). *Soda jerk.* New York: Orchard. Twenty-eight poems tell the story of life in a small Virginia town through the eyes of a boy who works as a soda jerk.

Sones, S. (1999). *Stop pretending: What happened when my big sister went crazy.* New York: HarperCollins. How do you cope when your sister has a mental breakdown? Another book by Sones is *What My Mother Doesn't Know* (2001).

Soto, G. (1994). *Neighborhood odes.* San Diego: Harcourt. Soto's poems describe life in a Hispanic neighborhood.

Stavans, I. (Ed.). (2001). *Wáchale! Poetry and prose about growing up Latino in America.* Chicago: Cricket Books. From a Christmas poem to the verses of José Martí, this book explores the Latino culture.

Stipe, M. (1998). *The Haiku year.* New York: Soft Skull. A collection of haiku poems.

Vecchione, P. (Ed.). (2000). *Truth and lies.* New York: Holt. This collection includes biographic notes and suggested readings along with a variety of poems.

Vecchione, P. (Ed.). (2002). *The body eclectic: An anthology of poems.* New York: Holt. Ruth Schwartz, Reginal Gibbons, and Li-Young Lee are some of the poets in this anthology that celebrates the body. Another collection by Vecchione is *Whisper and Shout* (2002).

von Ziegesar, C. (Ed.). (2000). *Slam.* New York: Penguin Putnam. Ideas and poems pack this book of contemporary poetry.

Watson, E. P., & Todd, M. (Eds.). (2000). *The pain tree and other teenage angst-ridden poetry.* Boston, MA: Houghton Mifflin. In 25 poems, young adults consider the problems of growing up.

Weatherford, C. B. (2002). *Remember the bridge: Poems of a people.* New York: Philomel. Poems complement a photo-essay on African American history.

Wolff, V. E. (1993). *Make lemonade.* New York: Holt. LaVaughn sees the stress of being a teenage single parent when she babysits for Jolly.

Wolff, V. E. (2001). *True believer.* New York: Atheneum. LaVaughn has a crush on Jody, but Jody's feelings are for someone else.

Wong, J. S. (1994). *Good luck gold and other poems.* New York: Margaret K. McElderry. This collection has strong roots in cultural identities and reflects Wong's Asian heritage.

Woodson, J. (2003). *Locomotion.* New York: Putnam. Lonnie discovers poetry as he reflects on the tragedies in his life.

Worth, V. (1994). *All the small poems and fourteen more.* New York: Farrar, Straus and Giroux. Worth celebrates the richness of the ordinary world.

Drama

Bowles, N., & Rosenthal, M. E. (Eds.). (2001). *Cootie shots: Theatrical inoculations against bigotry for kids, parents and teachers.* New York: Theatre Communications Group. Each play, poem, or song in this collection focuses on tolerance and overcoming bigotry.

Ellis, R. (Ed.). (2000). *International plays for young audiences: Contemporary works from leading playwrights.* Colorado Springs, CO: Meriwether. These timely, sometimes edgy, dramas feature young characters. Another collection is *New International Plays for Young Audiences* (2002).

Fleischman, P. (1988). *Joyful noise; Poems for two voices.* New York: HarperCollins. Here are more poems that can be dramatized.

Fleischman, P. (1989). *I am Phoenix: Poems for two voices.* New York: HarperTrophy. Fleischman's poems are meant to be performed.

Fleischman, P. (1999). *Mind's eye.* New York: Holt. Courtney, 16 and a paraplegic, and Elva, 88 and losing her sight, are roommates in a nursing home.

Fleischman, P. (2000). *Big talk: Poems for four voices.* Cambridge, MA: Candlewick. Four people can perform these poems.

Fleischman, P. (2001). *Seek.* Chicago: Cricket Book. Radio sound bits and snippets of conversations create this interesting dramatic novel that includes instructions for performance.

Gallo, D. (Ed.). (1990). *Center stage.* New York: HarperCollins. A collection of 10 one-act plays.

Henderson, H. H., & Zapel, T. (Ed.). (1998). *The flip side: 64 point-of-view monologs for teens.*

Colorado Springs, CO: Meriwether. This collection of monologues is presented in pair to highlight different opinions. A follow-up is *The Flip Side II: 60 More Point-of-View Monologs for Teens* (2001).

Kehret, P. (1991). *Acting natural: Monologs, dialogs, and playlets for teens.* Colorado Springs, CO: Meriwether. These short scripts require no special props or costumes.

Krell-Oishi, M. (1997). *Perspectives: Relevant scenes for teens.* Colorado Springs, CO: Meriwether. From dating and teen pregnancy to family relationships and the problems of growing up, these short scenes explore adolescent life. Krell-Oishi has also written *Scenes That Happen* (1991).

Lamb, W. (Ed.). (1987). *Ground zero club.* New York: Laurel Leaf. These six plays were written by dramatists under the age of 19 for the Young Playwrights Festival.

Lamb, W. (Ed.). (1992). *Ten out of ten: Winning plays from YPF 1.* New York: Delacorte. More plays from the Young Playwrights Festival.

Lhota, B., & Milstein, J. B. (2003a). *Forensics series, vol. 1 duo practice and competition: Thirty-five 8–10 minute original comedic plays* (young actors series). Hanover, NH: Smith & Kraus. This is a collection of short scripts for two actors.

Lhota, B., & Milstein, J. B. (2003b). *Forensics series duo practice and competition: Thirty-five 8–10 minute original dramatic scenes, vol. 2.* Hanover, NH: Smith & Kraus. This is a collection of short scripts for two actors.

Mecca, J. T. (1997). *Real-life drama for real, live students: A collection of monologues, duet acting scenes, & a full-length play.* Nashville, TN: Incentive. A collection of dramas in a variety of formats.

Myers, W. D. (1999). *Monster.* New York: HarperCollins. In this novel written as a screenplay, 16-year-old Steve Harmon is on trial for murder.

Slaight, C., & Sharrar, J. (Eds.). (1991). *Great scenes for young actors.* Newbury, VT: Smith & Kraus. These scenes from contemporary plays focus on the perspectives of young adults. Slaight has also edited *Multicultural Scenes for Young Actors* (1995).

Slaight, C., & Sharrar, J. (Eds.). (1996). *Short plays for young actors.* Newbury, VT: Smith & Kraus. There are both classic and modern plays in this anthology.

Smith, R., & Avi. (1997). *Nothing but the truth: A play.* New York: Avon. When Philip is punished for humming the "Star Spangled Banner," everything gets blown out of proportion.

Soto, G. (1999). *Nerdlandia.* New York: PaperStar. Martin, a nerd, likes Ceci, a chola girl. But, while he is busy trying to become cool, Ceci is turning into a nerdish beauty.

Surface, M. H. (1999). *Most valuable player and four other all-star plays for middle and high school audiences.* Lyme, NH: Smith & Kraus. Surface explores a number of social themes in these plays.

Zindel, P. (1971). *The effect of gamma rays on man-in-the-moon marigolds.* New York: Harper & Row. A widow and her daughters lead very interesting lives.

Short Stories

Appelt, K. (2000). *Kissing Tennessee and other stories from the stardust dance.* San Diego: Harcourt. These are the stories of the students at the Dogwood Junior High School dance.

Armstrong, J. (2002). *Shattered: Stories of children and war.* New York: Knopf. These short stories look at the effects of war on young people.

Blume, J. (Ed.). (1999). *Places I never meant to be.* New York: Simon & Schuster. These stories are accompanied by the author's observations on censorship.

Carlson, L. (Ed.). (1994). *American eyes: New Asian American short stories for young adults.* New York: Holt. These stories explore what it means to be an Asian American.

Cart, M. (1999). *Tomorrowland: Ten Stories about the future.* New York: Scholastic. Stories about a new millennium in a number of different time periods.

Cart, M. (2003). *Necessary noise: Stories about our families as they really are.* New York: Harper Tempest. Cart features stories of the future by authors such as Katherine Paterson and Lois Lowry. Another collection by Cart is *Love & Sex* (2003).

Carter, A. (2003). *No missing parts: And other stories about real princesses.* Calgary: Red Deer College Press. The "princesses" in these stories confront contemporary issues.

Coville, B. (1999). *Odder than ever.* San Diego: Harcourt. Coville has written a selection of outlandish science fiction stories.

Crutcher, C. (1991). *Athletic shorts.* New York: Greenwillow. Popular writer Chris Crutcher debunks the myth of the bonehead jock.

Duncan, L. (Ed.). (1996). *Night terrors: Stories of shadow and substance.* New York: Simon & Schuster. Annette Curtis Klause, Theodore Taylor, and Harry Mazer are some of the authors of these spooky tales.

Duncan, L. (Ed.). (1998). *Trapped!: Cages of mind and body.* New York: Simon & Schuster. Teenagers are emotionally, physically, or mentally trapped in these stories.

Duncan, L. (Ed.). (2000). *On the edge: Stories at the brink.* New York: Simon & Schuster. Suspense is high in this collection.

Durant, A. (Ed.). (2000). *Sport stories.* New York: Kingfisher. These 21 stories cover a range of sports from soccer and basketball to swimming and football.

Gallo, D. (Ed.). (1984). *Sixteen: Short stories by outstanding writers for young adults.* New York:

Delacorte. The first in a series of original short story collections for adolescents.

Gallo, D. (Ed.). (1987). *Visions: Nineteen short stories about outstanding writers for young adults*. New York: Delacorte. A collection from outstanding authors.

Gallo, D. (Ed.). (1989). *Connections: Short stories by outstanding writers for young adults*. New York: Delacorte. Stories by 17 authors including Gordon Korman, M. E. Kerr, and Sue Ellen Bridgers.

Gallo, D. (Ed.). (1997). *No easy answers: Short stories about teenagers making tough choices*. New York: Delacorte. The collection looks at the moral dilemmas adolescents face.

Gallo, D. (Ed.). (1999). *Time capsule: Short stories about teenagers throughout the twentieth century*. New York: Delacorte. Gallo looks at the trends, inventions, and values of the past in this collection.

Gallo, D. (Ed.). (2001). *On the fringe*. New York: Dial. These are stories of the geeks, the poor, the loners, the unathletic, and other outsiders.

Gallo, D. (Ed.). (2003). *Destination unexpected*. Cambridge, MA: Candlewick. In these stories, teenagers are transformed while on a variety of journeys. Published in 2004 is *First Crossing: Stories about Teen Immigrant*.

Howe, J. (Ed.). (2001). *Color of absence: 12 stories about loss and hope*. New York: Atheneum. Stories about the different forms of loss in the lives of adolescents.

Johnson, A. (1998). *Gone from home*. New York: DK. These are 12 stories of young people who face challenges when they leave home.

Mazer, A. (Ed.). (1993). *America street: A multicultural anthology of stories*. New York: Persea. Fourteen authors present stories from diverse cultural and racial backgrounds. Another collection by this editor is *A Walk in My World: International Short Stories about Youth* (1998).

Myers, W. D. (2000). *145th street stories*. New York: Delacorte. Myers writes about the people in Harlem.

Nixon, J. L. (2000). *Ghost town: Seven ghostly stories*. New York: Delacorte. These stories were inspired by western ghost towns.

November, S. (Ed.). (2003). *Firebirds: An anthology of original fantasy and science fiction*. New York: Penguin. Here are 16 short stories from well-known authors.

Oates, J. C. (2004). *Small avalanches and other stories*. New York: HarperTempest. Oates has collected some of her previously published stories in this volume.

O'Hearn, C. C. (1998). *Half and half: Writers on growing up biracial and bicultural*. New York: Pantheon. Writers look at what it is like to grow up in a biracial or bicultural family.

Potok, C. (1998). *Zebra and other stories*. New York: Knopf. Six different young people experience a life-changing event.

Rice, D. (2001). *Crazy loco: Stories*. New York: Dial. These are stories of Mexican Americans in the Rio Grande Valley of Texas.

Rylant, C. (2003). *God went to beauty school*. New York: HarperCollins. God looks at the wonders He created as well as the misses.

Salisbury, G. (2002). *Island boyz*. New York: Wendy Lamb. All of these stories are set in Hawaii.

Singer, M. (Ed.). (1998). *Stay true: Short stories for strong girls*. New York: Scholastic. Coming of age stories by several well-known writers.

Singer, M. (Ed.). (2000). *I believe in water: Twelve brushes with religion*. New York: HarperCollins. Twelve authors look at spiritual traditions.

Soto, G. (1998). *Petty crimes*. San Diego: Harcourt. These are the stories of life in the barrio.

Van Pelt, J. (2002). *Strangers and beggars*. Auburn, WA: Fairwood Press. Stories of things gone wrong.

Vande Velde, V. (2001). *Being dead.* San Diego: Harcourt. Ordinary teens wind up in creepy situations. Vande Velde takes one story and retells it five ways in *The Rumpelstiltskin Problem* (2000).

Westall, R. (1993). *Demons and shadows: The ghostly best stories of Robert Westall.* New York: Farrar, Straus and Giroux. Westall has collected some of his best stories of the strange and supernatural.

Wittlinger, E. (1999). *What's in a name.* New York: Simon & Schuster. All of these stories are about teenagers at Scrub Harbor High.

Yee, P. (2002). *Dead man's gold and other stories.* Toronto: Groundwood. Yee combines ghost stories with the experiences of early Chinese immigrants.

Suggested Readings

Angel, A. M. (2004). Striking pensively, beating playfully: The power of poetic novels. *English Journal, 93*(3), 101–104.

Campbell, P. (2000). Best new short story collections for young adults. *Journal of Youth Services in Libraries, 14*(1), 14–15.

Heartwell, P. (2002). Masters as mentors: The role of reading poetry in writing poetry. *Voices from the Middle, 10*(2), 29–32.

Lowery, R. M. (2003). Dreams of possibilities: Linking poetry to our lives. *The ALAN Review, 30*(2), 49–51.

Smith, B. S. (2003). Haiku measures up: Putting those 17 syllables to work. *Voices from the Middle, 10*(4), 20–21.

A symphony of words: Poets talk about their craft. (2003). *Teacher Librarian, 31*(1), 47–49.

References

(Note: All young adult literature referenced in this chapter are included in the Young Adult Books list and are not repeated in this list.)

Abrahamson, R. F. (2002). Poetry preference research: What young adults tell us they enjoy. *Voices from the Middle, 10*(2), 20–22.

Abramovitz, S. (2000). The power of performance in multicultural curricula. *Multicultural Education, 7*(3), 31–33.

Allen, J. (2002). Painting word pictures: The language of poetry. *Voices from the Middle, 10*(2), 52–53.

Bladwin, M. (2003). *Slam poetry manual.* Chicago: ALA.

Bleeker, G., & Bleeker, B. (1996). Responding to young adult fiction through writing poetry: Trying to understand a mole. *The ALAN Review, 23*(3), 38–40.

Bontempo, B. T. (1995). Exploring prejudice in young adult literature through drama and role play. *The ALAN Review, 22*(3), 31–33.

Brown, J. E., & Stephens, E. C. (1995). *Teaching young adult literature: Sharing the connection.* Belmont, CA: Brooks/Cole.

Charters, M. (1997). The different faces of poetry. *Publisher's Weekly, 244*(9), 38–41.

Chilcoat, G. W. (1996). Living newspaper puppet theater: An inquiry process for exploring—historical social issues in high-school social studies. *The Social Studies, 87*(6), 254–261.

Davis, A. (1997). Salamanca Hiddle is alive and well: Developing a palette for poetry. *Voices from the Middle, 4*(1), 16–21.

Fredericks, A. D. (2001). *Readers theatre for American history.* Englewood, CO: Teacher Ideas Press.

Gasparro, M., & Falletta, B. (1994). *Creating drama with poetry: Teaching English as a second language through dramatization and improvisation.* ED 368214.

Gonzalez, J. B. (2002). From page to stage to teenager: Problematizing "transformation" in theatre for and with adolescents. *Stage of the Art, 14*(3), 17–21.

Grimes, N. (2000). The power of poetry. *Book Links, 9*(4), 32–35.

Harding, C. G., Safer, L. A., Kavanagh, J., Bania, R., Carty, H., Lisnov, L., et al. (1996). Using live theatre combines with role playing and discussion to examine what at-risk adolescents think about substance abuse, its consequences, and prevention. *Adolescence, 31*(124), 783–796.

Heartwell, P. (2002). Masters as mentors: The role of reading poetry in writing poetry. *Voices from the Middle, 10*(2), 29–32.

Hewitt, G. (1998). *Today you are my favorite poet: Writing poems with teenagers.* Portsmouth, NH: Heineman.

Hommel, M. (2003). Slamming on the net: A new writers workshop for teens. *Voice of Youth Advocates, 26*(1), 26–27.

Johnson, A. B., McClanahan, L. G., & Mertz, M. P. (1999). Gender representation in poetry for young adults. *The ALAN Review, 26*(3), 39–44.

Jolley, S. (2002). Integrating poetry and *To Kill a Mockingbird. English Journal, 92*(2), 34–40.

Kazemek, F. E. (2003). "And I wrote my happy songs, Every child may joy to hear": The poetry of William Blake in the middle school classroom. *The ALAN Review, 30*(2), 44–47.

Knowles, E., & Smith, M. (1997). *The reading connection.* Englewood, CO: Libraries Unlimited.

Lesesne, T. (2002). Gaining power through poetry: An interview with Sonya Sones. *Teacher Librarian, 29*(3), 51–53.

Lowery, R. M. (2003). Dreams of possibilities: Linking poetry to our lives. *The ALAN Review, 30*(2), 49–51.

Marshall, S., & Newman, D. (1997). A poet's vision. *Voices from the Middle, 4*(1), 7–15.

Merriam-Webster's Encyclopedia of Literature. (1995). Springfield, MA: Merriam-Webster.

Newman, J. D. (2003). The Bonderman and beyond: Developing new works for young audiences. *Stage of the Art, 15*(2), 9–12.

Pearl, N. (2002). The pleasures of short stories. *Alki, 18*(2), 31.

Russell, D. L. (1997). *Literature for children: A short introduction* (3rd ed.). New York: Longman.

Schwedt, R. E., & DeLong, J. (2002). *Young adult poetry: A survey and theme guide.* Westport, CT: Greenwood.

The short of it. (2000). *The School Librarian's Workshop, 21*(2), 12.

Singer, M. (2000). What is a short story? *Journal of Youth Services in Libraries, 14*(1), 12–13.

Smith, K. P., & Zarnowski, M. (1999). Letting poetry in, sending poetry forth. *New Advocate, 12*(2), 209–213.

Somers, A. (1999). *Teaching poetry in high school.* Urbana, IL: NCTE.

Steineke, N. (2002). Talking about poetry: Teaching students how to lead the discussion. *Voices from the Middle, 10*(2), 8–14.

Thomas, C. (2000). From engagement to celebration: A framework for passionate reading. *Voices from the Middle, 8*(2), 16–25.

Thomas, J. (2001). Mel Glenn and Arnold Adoff: The poetics of power in the adolescent voice-lyric. *Style, 35*(3), 486–500.

10

EXPLORING OTHER FORMATS: COMIC BOOKS, GRAPHIC (COMIC-FORMAT) NOVELS, AND MAGAZINES

CHAPTER OVERVIEW

"All those graphic novels are trash, and I don't have trash in my school library."

"Oh, I guess the boys would like the comic books with those almost naked, well-endowed heroines, but not in my classroom."

"These magazines are just not appropriate—where's the literary value in them?"

"There's too much good literature out there for me to use that stuff. What would parents think?"

These are just a few of the comments teachers and library media specialists may offer when talking about comics, graphic novels, and magazines—the most visual "literature" formats for young adults. However, before educators dismiss these formats, we caution them to remember that contemporary adolescents are growing up in a visual and digital society where the use of pictures to present information is often the norm and where teenagers are comfortable with the visual styles found in these formats. If sales are any indication of popularity, the increase in sales of graphic novels from $75 million in 2001 to $120 million in 2003 (Raiteri, 2003b) points out the growing interest in this visual genre.

Comics and graphic novels are beginning to gain acceptance among some adults. *Maus I,* Art Spiegelman's graphic novel, won the Pulitzer Prize and was later combined with *Maus II* to create *The Complete Maus* (1997). *'Nam*, Doug Murray's graphic novel, won the Best Media of the Vietnam War Award, which is given by Bravo Organization, a veterans group. In 2002, the American Library Association (ALA) annual conference featured a preconference workshop on graphic novels. The ALA 2002 Teen Read Week theme was "Getting Graphic @ Your Library."

FOCUSING POINTS   **In this chapter, you will read about:**

1. Formats, availability, and current popularity of comic books and ways teachers can help connect young adults to this genre.
2. Suggestions for effective use of comic books in middle and secondary classrooms.
3. The recent interest and popularity of graphic novels and how teachers can take advantage of young adults' interest in this genre.
4. Suggestions for using graphic novels in middle and secondary classrooms.
5. Topics that young adults like to read about in magazines.
6. Titles and brief descriptions of magazines published specifically for young adults.
7. Internet sites for teachers and library media specialists who want to learn more about comic books, graphic novels, and magazines.

COMIC BOOKS, GRAPHIC NOVELS, AND MAGAZINES

Many young adults enjoy comic books, graphic novels, and magazines, perhaps because these formats differ so dramatically from the genres that educators have traditionally encouraged adolescents to read—books that were, for the most part, all words and no pictures. In contrast to earlier generations, contemporary young adults have grown up with television and its "sound bites" as well as video games. Looking for print media that contains the same visual impact and a clipped, pared-down writing style, adolescents have turned to comics and to slick magazines that are designed to appeal to the teen market. There is no doubt that these visual print media attract the attention and interest of adolescents and contribute to their enthusiasm for visual rather than written literacy. For many young adults, these three genres represent a welcome move away from what they consider traditional "school" reading.

As you explore each of these formats in this chapter, keep in mind this enthusiasm. Because we believe that one way to encourage young adults to read is to allow them to read things that interest them, we also believe that these three formats belong in every school library and that they should, when appropriate, be incorporated into the school's curriculum. However, this also means that, as with any other formats or genres of literature, educators need to know about comic books, graphic novels, and magazines; the materials that are available; and how to select quality, interesting items for young adults—items that teens will appreciate as well as items that will contribute to the formal and informal education of adolescents.

Comics

Contemporary comic books have come a long way since a comic strip about the Yellow Kid appeared in an 1896 issue of *New York World* and a pamphlet featuring the comic characters Mutt and Jeff was offered as a premium for clipping newspaper coupons in 1911. By the late 1930s, readers could buy Action Comics and the *Superman Quarterly Magazine*. The industry continued to grow, and between 1940 and 1953, comic book sales jumped from 17 million to 68 million copies a year (S. Rep. No. 83–62, 1956). However, this growth was not always met with praise. In fact, many parents and educators questioned the deleterious effects that comics might have on children. These fears led to a U.S. Congress investigation of the links between comic books and juvenile delinquency, a call to raise the standards of decency and good taste in comic books, and the establishment of the Comics Code Authority to monitor the content of comics. Another result was the growth of the underground comics publishing industry, which did not adhere to the code.

After many years of declining sales, comic books have begun to regain their former popularity. Today, comics, along with graphic novels (which you will read about later in this chapter), are moving out of the traditional comic book stores and into the mainstream of American book publishing and sales. Comics are no longer cheap, with an average cost in 2004 of $2.85 (www.comicsworthreading.com). In 2002, Marvel Comics, a major publisher, reported a 400% 3-year sales increase in bookstore sales while DC Comics saw a 25% growth in overall sales (McDonald, 2002). Although some educators question whether this genre actually belongs in school library media centers and classrooms, other teachers and library media specialists have decided to explore the existing comic book formats and identify strategies for making effective use of this genre.

Types of Comics. Several ways exist to categorize comic books. However, as with any listing of categories, there are some overlaps and some comics that just do not fit into one of these categories.

Many comics belong in the publishing category known as serials or works, like magazines, that are issued in successive parts. Thus, one way to group comic books is by publishing frequency. There are:

- Continuing or ongoing series that are published on a regular schedule, such as bimonthly or monthly, with no scheduled ending date.

- Mini-series, which usually have six or fewer issues.

- Maxi-series, which usually have more than six issues but with a definite ending point.

Mini-series and maxi-series are also referred to as limited series to distinguish them from ongoing series.

In addition to the comic book series, there are:

- Annual comics, which are a yearly supplement to a series.

- One-shot comics, which are a single, stand-alone publication.

Sometimes comic books are categorized by their format, including:

- *Standard format* of 32, 7" by 10" pages stapled together. Variations on this are the 48-page *Double-issues* and the 80-page *Giants.*

- *Prestige format* of 8" by 10" pages with a higher quality paper and heavier covers.

- *Treasury editions* or specially published comic books that are issued in a prestige or larger format.

- *Magazines* or a comic book series that is printed on magazine-size paper with stapled binding.

- *Trade paperbacks* or book-like volumes that usually collect and reprint a limited series. However, they may also include a number of different comics that are related to a single theme or are written by a single individual.

- *Graphic novels* or GN, which are complete, book-length stories or collections of original, related short stories that are bound with more durable cardstock or with hardcovers (http://ublib.buffalo.edu/libraries/units/lml/comics/pages/reading.html; and http://bookshelf.diamondcomics.com/glossary.html).

While most comics are issued in color, some publishers economize by producing black and white comics, often with a colored cover.

Reasons For Using and Teaching with Comic Books. With fast-paced action, powerful images, and dramatic plots that feature heroic adventures, contemporary comic books address themes that are important to young adults, including issues of acceptance, nonconformity, prejudice, social injustice, coming of age, triumph over adversity, and personal growth. In comic books, adolescents can explore current and historical events, legends and tall tales, mythology, and visual versions of classic novels and dramas. Some comics are even designed to raise social consciousness and interest in issues such as famine relief and environmental preservation, while others have anti-drug or sex education themes. While some young adults may turn to comics to find familiar characters and cultural icons such as Superman, Batman, and Spider-Man, others are simply looking to enjoy a good story.

Many educators have discovered that they can interest reluctant readers by including comic books in libraries and on reading lists. In addition, comic books appeal to many poor readers and visual learners because, in comics, readers are expected to apply different "reading" skills. No longer following a single line of text, the reader must let the pictures direct the reading. Comics can also help adolescents develop their language arts skills and expand their vocabularies while conveying educational messages and serving as a bridge to other types of literature.

Characteristics of Comic Books For Young Adults. Although the Comics Code Authority (CCA) began as a good way for a business group to police itself, today, with a few exceptions, most comic book publishers do not participate in the CCA. Thus, educators need to examine comic books carefully and identify those that are appropriate for various age levels of young adults and that will appeal to teenage readers. Considerations for Selecting Young Adult Literature: *Comics* contains suggestions for evaluating comic books.

Archie Comics is one publisher who is committed in all of their comic books to WFOP, or wholesome, family-oriented products. Their Web site lists a number of situations in which a character in one of their comics will never participate, such as drinking alcoholic beverages, taking drugs, smoking, or knowingly engaging in illegal activities (www.archiecomics.com/arcade/sunday/stumper/forparents.html).

Comic Books For Young Adults. Because of the serial format of many comic books, one good way to explore comics is to look at the various series that are offered by major publishers. Table 10-1 identifies some of the series that are appropriate for young adults. Other comic book series fall into the categories of crime comics, historical fiction, and literature-based (myths, legends, and visual representations of other classic literature). Although some publishers are offering nonfiction comics, these are often one-shots or graphic novels. However, we advise anyone who is interested in adding comic books to a classroom or school library to visit a local comic book store or one of the Internet sites in Expanding Your Knowledge with the Internet 10-1.

CONSIDERATIONS	For Selecting Young Adult Literature	COMICS

In general, ask the following questions when selecting comic books for young adults:

- Does the comic present positive role models and/or positive themes?

- Is the comic tied to popular movies, video games, or television shows?

- Are there good visual qualities with an interesting layout, quality illustrations (color is not necessary although new comic readers may be attracted to color comics), and good reproduction of the artwork?

- Is there good writing with original characters, an intriguing plot, and a style that will keep the reader's interest?

- Does the comic avoid extreme violence, abusive behavior, or gratuitous profanity?

TABLE 10–1	*Popular Comic Book Series*

The following are a selection of popular comic books series for young adults and their publishers.

Super-Heroes

Batman—DC Comics
Generation X—Marvel Comics
Justice Society of America—DC Comics
Legion of Super-Heroes—DC Comics
Spider-Girl—Marvel Comics
Spider-Man—Marvel Comics
Superman—DC Comics
Wolverine—Marvel Comics
X-Men—Marvel Comics
Young Justice—DC Comics

Humor

Any series published by Archie
Geeksville—3 Finger Prints
Groo—Dark Horse
Sabrina the Teenage Witch—Archie
The Simpsons—Bongo Entertainment
Weirdsville—Blindwolf Comics

Fantasy/Science Fiction

Akiko—Sirius
Bone—Cartoon Books
Castle Waiting—Olio
Elfquest—Warp Graphics
Little White Mouse—Blue Line Pro Comics
Star Wars—Dark Horse
Usagi Yojimbo—Dark Horse
Xeno's Arrow—Cup O'Tea Studios

Manga

Princess Prince—CPM Manga
Tenchi Muyo!—Viz

One type of comic book that has been gaining popularity is known as manga, which, translated from Japanese, means whimsical pictures. Although manga is used in Japan to refer to all comics, in the United States, the term refers to Japanese comics in translation. A spin-off of the Japanese anime or animation industry, manga is distinguished by intricate drawings and textures as well as a sophisticated plot. In the authentic format, manga has a right-to-left format instead of the traditional American left-to-right format. Although some publishers reverse the images for U.S. audiences, Tokyopop publishes manga in the original right-to-left format. Stuart Levy, the founder of Tokyopop, has called manga "chicklit for comics" (Reid, 2003, p. S6), as manga is the only type of comic or graphic novel that is more popular with females than with males (Reid, 2003). *Shojo* is a manga category that is aimed at younger girls, while *shonen* appeals to boys with its action stories. Violent or sexually graphic manga are referred to as *hentai*. Connecting Adolescents and Their Literature 10-1 suggests using manga to introduce young adults to other literature.

Suggestions For Selecting and Using Comic Books. Selecting comic books to use in schools can be difficult because, while educational publications are beginning to review graphic novels, few publish reviews of the more ephemeral comic books. To identify comics you might want to use with young adults, you can examine the winners

CONNECTING | *ADOLESCENTS AND THEIR LITERATURE 10–1*

Use comic books as a bridge to other forms of literature. For example:

- Recommend books on how to draw manga and anime.
- Identify books on other forms of Japanese art or the history of comic books in general.
- Link comics to the longer graphic novels.
- Use manga and anime to inspire adolescents to explore Japanese culture and language.

of several comic awards including the Reuben Awards of the National Cartoonists Society, which has a category for comic books; the Eisner Awards; the Harvey Awards; and the Comics Buyer's Guide Fan Awards. On the Internet, Comics Worth Reading publishes reviews of comics, and AnimeNews Network has information on manga along with very detailed reviews of some of the popular series. Diamond Comics, a distributor, has a special "bookshelf" Web site with information for librarians and teachers and a comic book shop locator, while Comic Books for Young Adults has detailed information on selecting and using comic books. Although no longer being updated, Comic Book Conundrum provides information on many of the issues in the comic book world. Finally, serving as a marketplace for comic book collectors, Comics Buyer's Guide provides news about comics, profiles of artists and writers, and information on new releases.

Because of the nature of comics, we suggest that educators preview all issues before making them available for adolescents. One of the best ways to remain current about comics is to work with a local comic book retailer who can keep you informed about the new series and can identify comics that are popular with teens in your area. If that is not possible, visit the Web sites of some of the major comic book publishers to see what they are producing.

Actually purchasing comic books can also be a challenge because many comic book publishers do not offer subscriptions to their ongoing series. However, in addition to comic book stores, there are Internet sites that sell comics, although it is difficult to preview the comic on the Internet before ordering it. In contrast, trade paperbacks and graphic novels are now available in bookstores and on the Internet at places like Amazon.com. Published primarily for comic book dealers and collectors, the standard reference guide to current and out-of-print comic books is the *Official Overstreet's Comic Book Price Guide* (Overstreet, 2004) from Gemstone Publishing. Expanding Your Knowledge with the Internet 10-1 lists the URLs of some of these sources.

Teachers and library media specialists can incorporate comic books into the school in a number of ways. As Alvermann, Moon, and Hagood (1999) pointed out, when teachers use resources from popular culture, they appeal to the multiple literacies of students. Thus, educators can include comic books in instructional units and use some of the same strategies used in teaching a novel such as making predictions, identifying new vocabulary, preparing new illustrations, and comparing the comic to other literature. After visiting an Internet site (e.g., http:///rec.arts.comics.reviews), young adults can review, compare, and contrast comic books. Suggestions for Collaborative Efforts 10-1 has an idea for working with an art teacher to create comics. Finally, comic books can serve as an introduction to reading for some reluctant readers or teens with limited reading abilities.

Graphic Novels

Graphic novels are one of the most popular and fastest-growing types of young adult literature. The genre began in 1978 when cartoonist Will Eisner created *A Contract with God,* a collection of stories about a poor, crowded Jewish Bronx neighborhood, and coined the term *graphic novel* to describe a complex story told in comic book format in

10–1

SUGGESTIONS FOR COLLABORATIVE EFFORTS

Teachers can work with the art resource specialist to help adolescents plan, write, and illustrate a comic book. For example:

- A science or social studies teacher can help students select a topic.
- An English teacher can help students write the dialogue and other verbal passages.
- An art teacher can help them illustrate the comic.

Writing for Comic Books
www.williamsullivanadvertising.com/joeedkin/writing.html contains information on becoming a comic book author.

64 to 179 pages. More than a collection of comic strips in book format (such as a collection of Garfield comics or Charles Schultz's tales of Charlie Brown), graphic novels are, according to Eisner, "the literary form of comics" (Kennedy, 2003, p. 110), which has finally received recognition and acceptance as a "valid, legitimate medium" (p. 110). Obviously a visual medium, graphic novels are engaging, sometimes edgy, and often written for a mature audience. While traditional book publishers have been slow to recognize the success of graphic novels, comic book publishers have embraced the medium and have issued graphic novels by outstanding artists such as Art Spiegelman, Neil Gaiman, Jeff Smith, and Coleen Doran.

A graphic novel is a "dynamic format of image and word that delivers meaning and enjoyment" (Simmons, 2003, p. 12) and differs in subtle ways from both comic books and picture books. Comprised of boxed pictures and text, a graphic novel may have several boxes per page. As in a picture book, the illustrations enrich and extend the text. However, in a graphic novel, readers must not only decode the words and the illustrations but must also identify what is happening between the visual sequences (Simmons, 2003). Diamond Comics, a major U.S. distributor, distinguishes a graphic novel from a comic book by noting that the graphic novel is longer and that most graphic novels tell a complete stand-alone story, unlike comics that are often issued in successive parts. In addition, many graphic novels go beyond the superheroes found in traditional comic books and address the issues and concerns reflected in more traditional types of literature. Thus, graphic novels have sometimes been called meatier comics (Gorman, 2002a), or "your favorite comics all grown up" (Lubbock (Texas) City-County Library). Graphic novels are usually issued in hardcover; the paperback format is called a trade paperback.

Types of Graphic Novels. Despite their popularity, graphic novels are often seen as nothing more than adventure stories. There are, however, a number of different types of graphic novels including superhero tales; realistic stories; science fiction and fantasy novels; future, contemporary, and historical adventure stories; and manga (Japanese) tales, as well as humorous works, political satires, and adaptations of classics. Although fiction remains the most popular part of the genre (Weiner, 2001), the scope of graphic novels has even widened to include more sophisticated subject matter, including nonfiction, biography, and autobiography. No matter whether fiction or nonfiction, the genre is still called the graphic novel.

Even those graphic novels that focus on the traditional superhero cannot be written off as mere fluff. Robert G. Weiner (2001) sees the superhero tale serving as an allegory to modern life while providing an escape for readers. Others believe that the superheroes can be compared to the heroic figures in classical mythology.

Like manga (Japanese) comics, manga graphic novels and anime (Japanese animation) are very popular with teenagers because of the "dynamic, eccentric, and very often sexy illustrations in combination with fast-paced science fiction, adventure, fantasy and martial arts stories" (Reid, 2003, S6), usually with teens as the main characters. In fact, the growth of English-language manga graphic novels has been phenomenal (Reid, 2002), spurred, in part, by the release of related anime on television and in video/DVD format. Even a small manga publisher like ComicsOne, which publishes the manga version of the hit movie *Crouching Tiger Hidden Dragon,* issued nearly 100 titles in 2002 (Reid, 2002). Like manga comics, manga graphic novels, with their diverse subject matter, are more popular with females than males (Reid, 2003).

Reasons For Using and Teaching with Graphic Novels. Too often educators exclude graphic novels solely because of the format or the erroneous impression that all graphic novels are supernatural horror stories, or an expression of the male power fantasy. Instead, graphic novels are a fusion of text and art that builds on the impact of visuals to offer value, variety, and a new medium for literacy. Because graphic novels appeal to young people, educators can use them to offer alternatives to traditional texts and mass media and to introduce young adults to literature that they might otherwise never encounter. In fact, some educators use graphic novels to teach literary terms and techniques such as dialogue, serve as a bridge to other classics, and act as the basis for writing assignments. Although some educators might worry that reading graphic novels will discourage adolescents from reading other genres of literature, others believe that graphic novels may require young adults to use more complex cognitive skills than are required when reading text alone (Schwartz, 2002).

Characteristics of Graphic Novels For Young Adults. Tabitha Simmons (2003) maintains that

> Graphic novel readers have learned to understand print, but can also decode facial and body expressions, the symbolic meanings of certain images and postures, metaphors and similes, and other social and literary nuances teenagers are mastering as they move from childhood to maturity. (Simmons, 2003, p. 12)

It is, therefore, important to look for graphic novels that have visual impact while presenting a blending of text and art because both the art and the text must be "read." Graphic novels are one genre where it is especially important to select books carefully, preview them when possible, and ensure that they are age-appropriate. Considerations for Selecting Young Adult Literature: *Graphic Novels* contains questions to ask during the selecting process. A number of popular graphic novels deal with controversial themes or have content that is more suited for adult readers, even though adolescents may read them. Thus, Gorman (2002a) advises educators to examine the genre, target audience, quality, and artistic merit as well as the reputation and style of the author and illustrator when evaluating graphic novels.

Graphic Novels For Young Adults. Graphic novels reflect many of the genres of traditional literature from fantasy and science fiction to adventure and nonfiction. In some books, including many by the award-winning Neil Gaiman, authors treat themes and depict situations that are most appropriate for mature young adults or for adult audiences. Therefore, we again mention the importance of previewing graphic novels before using them and recommending them to adolescents.

A number of graphic novels can be used in the curriculum. While Larry Gonick's *Cartoon History of the Universe* (1997) contains facts as well as enough trivia to keep readers interested, several authors of graphic novels have looked at specific historical events for their subjects. In *300* (1999), Frank Miller and Lynn Varley combine fact and fantasy to retell the story of the Spartans and the Battle of Thermopylae, while, in the Age of Bronze series, which begins with *A Thousand Ships* (2001), Eric Shanower writes of the Trojan War. Looking at more recent history, Art Spiegelman examines the Holocaust in *The Complete Maus* (1997), which combines his Pulitzer Prize-winning *Maus I* with its sequel, *Maus 2*.

Several graphic novels present interesting biographies. *Streetwise* (Cooke & Morrow, 2000) is a collection of autobiographies of people in the comic book industry. *Dignifying Science* (Ottaviani, 2003) provides a look at famous women in science, and *Two-Fisted Science* (Ottaviani, 2001b) presents stories of scientists like Newton, Einstein, and Galileo.

Graphic novelists have also successfully adapted some classics, including David Wenzel's graphic novel version of Tolkein's *The Hobbit* (2001), a translation of Proust's *Remembrance of Things Past* (Heuet, 2001), Peter Kuper's rendition of Kafka's

---

CONSIDERATIONS | **For Selecting Young Adult Literature** | **GRAPHIC NOVELS**

When selecting graphic novels, ask the following questions:

⊚ Does the novel have visual impact that showcases the artistic ability of the creator?

⊚ Does the graphic novel blend text and art?

⊚ Does the use of color add to the graphic novel or is it unnecessary?

⊚ Does the story have the best qualities of the literature genre (i.e., mystery, nonfiction, biography) it represents?

⊚ Are the story and illustrations appropriate for adolescents?

The Metamorphosis (2003), and P. Craig Russell's adaptation of *The Ring of the Nibelung* (2002). Will Eisner retold an African legend in *Sundiata: A Legend of Africa* (2002) and gave a new perspective to Charles Dickens' *Oliver Twist* in *Fagin the Jew* (2003).

In other areas of the curriculum, science educators can use *Clan Apis* (Hosler, 2000) to study the life of the honeybee, *The Sandwalk Adventures* (Hosler, 2003) to look at Darwin's theory of natural selection, or *Fallout* (Ottaviani, 2001a) to examine the scientific and social aspects of the development of the atomic bomb. For social studies educators, Joe Kubert takes readers to the Balkans in *Fax from Sarajevo: A Story of Survival* (1998) while Joe Sacco reports on his experiences in the Middle East in *Palestine* (2002) and Ted Rall recounts his travels in *To Afghanistan and Back: A Graphic Travelogue* (2002).

Several graphic novels explore social issues, such as Judd Winnick's look at AIDS in *Pedro and Me* (2000) and Katherine Arnoldi's exploration of rape and pregnancy in *Amazing "True" Story of a Teenage Single Mom* (1998). For mature readers, Bryan Talbot's *The Tale of One Bad Rat* (1995) is a powerful story of sexual abuse. Other powerful graphic novels include collections of stories that look back at the September 11, 2001, attacks including *9-11 Artists Respond* (2002) and *9-11 The World's Finest Comic Book Writers and Artists Tell Stories to Remember* (2002).

Within the genre of graphic novels are many fantasy and science fiction books, with some of them based on comics that feature the same characters. For example, the X-Men move into graphic novels with *The Dark Phoenix Saga* (2003) from Chris Claremont and John Byrne's X-Men series or Peter Sanderson's *X-Men: The Ultimate Guide* (2003). In *Legion of Super-Heroes: The Beginning of Tomorrow* (1999), Tom McCraw tells the stories of teenage superheroes in the 31st century, while in the three volumes of the *Daredevil: Visionaries* series (2000–2001) Frank Miller looks at another superhero. Similarly, Brian Bendis and Mark Bagley take a fresh look at another well-known character in *Ultimate Spider-Man: Power and Responsibility* (2002).

Appealing especially to girls are a number of graphic novels that reflect young adults' love of mystery and horror. *Buffy the Vampire Slayer: Origin* (Golden, 1999) and *Leave It to Chance: Shaman's Rain* (Robinson, 2000) are two books in series that feature female protagonists. Older teens will enjoy the mature subjects in Neil Gaiman's classics *The Sandman* (1993), *Death: The High Cost of Living* (1994), and *Black Orchid* (1996).

Like manga comics, manga graphic novels remain popular. *Rumiko Takahashi's Rumic Theater* (1996) and *Rumic Theater: One or Double* (1998) are excellent collections of the works of Rumiko Takahashi, the popular female artist of the Ranma $1/2$ series. Other popular manga novels and series are Kosuke Fujishima's *Oh My Goddess!* (2003), Stan Sakai's stories of *Usagi Yojimbo* (2000), and Akira Toriyama's *Dragonball* (2002) series. There is even a wordless graphic novel called *Gon* (2000) by Masashi Tanaka. Other popular manga series feature characters such as Astro Boy, Fushigi Yugi, Marmalade Boy, and Peach Girl. Table 10-2 provides selected examples of manga series as well as other popular graphic novel series.

Suggestions For Selecting and Using Graphic Novels. Like comic books, graphic novels have just begun to achieve a level of acceptance by the publishing industry. Professional publications are now starting to include reviews of graphic novels. Some

TABLE 10-2	Graphic Novel Series

Series/Character	Author	Publisher
Akiko	Crilley, Mark	Sirius
Astro Boy	Tezuka, Osamu	Dark Horse
AstroCity	Busiek, Kurt	Homage Comics
Black Panther	Lee, Stan and Priest, Christopher	Marvel Comics
Bone	Smith, Jeff	Cartoon Books
Call Me Princess	Taniguchi, Tomoko	CPM
Electric Girl	Brennan, Michael	Mighty Gremlin
Elfquest	Pini, Wendy and Pini, Richard	Wolfrider Books
Fushigi Yugi	Watase, Yu	Viz
Groo	Aragones, Sergio	Dark Horse Comics
Meridian	Kesel, Barbara and McNiven, Steve	CrossGen Comics
Nausciaa of the Valley of Wind	Miyazaki, Hayao	Viz
Peach Girl	Ueda, Miwa	Tokyopop
Ranma $\frac{1}{2}$	Takahashi, Rumiko	Viz Communications
Simpsons	Groening, Matt	HarperPerennial
SpyBoy	David, Peter	Dark Horse Comics
Tenchi Masaki	Okuda, Hitoshi	Viz
Usagi Yojimbo	Sakai, Stan	Fantagraphics and Dark Horse

graphic novels even show up on the annual best books lists as well as in the comic awards mentioned earlier in this chapter. *School Library Journal* has started to include a "Graphic Novel Roundup" section, while *Voice of Youth Advocates (VOYA)* now has a graphic novel column written by Kat Kan in each issue. Several writers including Philip Crawford (2002, 2003b) and Michele Gorman (2002a, 2002b) have developed lists of recommended graphic novels. In addition to Roger Sabin's *Comics, Comix & Graphic Novels: A History of Comic Art* (2001), there are several publications on selecting graphic novels including Joss O'Kelly's *Son of Invisible Art: Graphic Novels for Libraries* (2001) and Stephen Weiner's *101 Best Graphic Novels* (2001). To learn more about graphic novels and keep informed about trends and new offerings, educators need to develop a relationship with a local comic book shop or a book store that carries graphic novels.

When ordering graphic novels for a school library or a classroom collection of materials that students can check out, it may be more practical to order the trade paperback rather than the hard copy version. Gorman (2002a) recommends taping spines and edges of trade paperbacks with clear, plastic tape and marking all copies with a neon library sticker or writing the school name on the cover to encourage students to read and return rather than collect the graphic novels. A number of online resources about graphic novels are available, including publisher's Web sites, discussion groups such as www.topica.com/lists/GNLIB-L, and reputable sites with information on recommended graphic novels. Expanding Your Knowledge with the Internet 10-2 provides more information on these Internet sites about graphic novels.

Francisca Goldsmith notes that graphic novels provide information as well as tell stories and that they "require active, critical participation by the reader who must not only be able to decode text, but also follow its flow and grasp essentials of narrative mood, character or plot through images" (Mooney, 2002, p. 18). Working with library media specialists, teachers should review all graphic novels for content, language, sexist and cultural stereotypes, and overall appropriateness for the particular class. Connecting Adolescents and Their Literature 10-2 provides ideas on ways to have young adults serve on youth advisory committees to assist in the selection.

Graphic novels can contribute to interdisciplinary thematic units or can serve as an introduction to a specific content area. For example, in the social studies, they can help students develop an understanding of history and/or appreciation for differing cultures and, in the sciences, they can help adolescents explore complex and sometimes confusing topics. Earlier in this chapter, we mentioned several graphic novels that could support science and social studies units. In addition, graphic novels offer subject matter and viewpoints that students might not otherwise consider. For example, by providing an account of his parents' lives in England, Brigg's *Ethel and Ernest* (1998) shows how ordinary individuals reacted to major events like World War II (Schwartz, 2002).

EXPANDING YOUR KNOWLEDGE WITH THE INTERNET 10–2

A variety of Internet sites exist where you can find information about graphic novels. A few are listed below. Links to these and many additional sites are found on this book's Companion Website at www.prenhall.com/bucher.

DC Comics
www.dccomics.com

Tokyopop
www.tokyopop.com

No Flying, No Tights—A Website Reviewing Graphic Novels For Teens
This site was created by Robin Brenner of the Cary Memorial Library in Lexington, MA, to provide brief, informative reviews of graphic novels and information on the books and their creation.

www.noflyingnotights.com/index2.html

CONNECTING ADOLESCENTS AND THEIR LITERATURE 10–2

As Gorman (2002a) suggested, create a graphic novel youth advisory committee to help select graphic novels for a school library or classroom collection.

- Let members review new purchases and suggest ways to promote the graphic novel collection.

- Involve as many students as possible by having several small groups instead of one large group.

- Identify young adults who are familiar with graphic novels or who are interested in learning more about them.

- Provide guidelines and explain that the books should, at a minimum, be examined for content, reading level, language, sexist and cultural stereotypes, and overall appropriateness.

- Encourage the students to add other criteria.

- Remind students that their role is advisory and that, while they can recommend novels for purchase, the school might not be able to purchase everything that they recommend.

- Use the committee to review graphic novels that you are considering purchasing or that have been recommended by others.

Educators can use graphic novels to give new voices to minorities and people with diverse viewpoints. In H. F. Kiyama's (1999) *The Four Immigrants Manga,* young adults can examine the lives of four Japanese immigrants in San Francisco, CA, from 1904 to 1924 while, in *Still I Rise* (Laird, Laird, & Bey, 1997), they can examine the history of African Americans (Schwartz, 2002).

Crawford (2003a) suggests some graphic novels can be used with mature adolescents to address National Council of Social Studies (NCSS) Standards that deal with individual development and identity and with power, authority, and governance. *A Jew in Communist Prague* (Giardino, 1997) chronicles a young Jew's coming of age in an era of communism and anti-Semitism. *Stuck Rubber Baby* (Cruse, 1995) examines racism and homophobia in the American South in the 1960s. To provide insight into the conflicts and power struggles of the 20th century, educators can use graphic novels such as *The Complete Maus* (Spiegelman, 1997), *Palestine* (Sacco, 2002), and *Fax from Sarajevo* (Kubert, 1998) (Crawford, 2003a). Suggestions for Collaborative Efforts 10-2 suggests ways teachers and librarians can work together to add graphic novels to the school.

From Page to Screen identifies some film adaptations of comics and graphic novels and has suggestions for comparing the film and print versions.

SUGGESTIONS FOR COLLABORATIVE EFFORTS

Teachers and library media specialists should work together to add graphic novels to the library's collection.

- Get the support of the school administration and the district library supervisor.
- Determine how the graphic novels will be:
  - put in the library,
  - circulated,
  - displayed, and
  - publicized.
- Determine who (students? teachers?) will be involved in the selection process and who will be responsible for reviewing each novel before it is placed in circulation to teenagers (Mooney, 2002).

Magazines

At the end of the 1990s, the readership of teen magazines was strong, and several new magazines for young adults, especially girls, entered the market (Fine & Kinney, 2000; Norton, 2002). However, by 2003, the market was "overcrowded" (Tyre, 2004, p. 59). The result was that *Teen* magazine folded in 2002 and previous favorites such as *Seventeen, Teen People,* and *YM* lost readers and advertising revenue. In contrast, several new magazines such as *CosmoGirl* and *Teen Vogue* grew in sales (Tyre, 2004). In this section, we take a look at the changing field of magazine or periodical publishing for young adults, provide information on a representative sample of current publications, and suggest guidelines for selecting and using popular magazines. Our focus will be on the magazines that are targeted directly to adolescents and not on the adult magazines that young adults read.

One problem that many school librarians face is deciding which, if any, popular magazines to purchase. With rising subscription costs, shrinking budgets, an emphasis on curriculum content, and the use of periodical databases for research, some school library media specialists have decreased the number of periodicals that they purchase for entertainment and have, instead, looked for magazines that are both educational and entertaining. This has become more difficult as publishers of traditional quality periodicals are resorting to more glitz, glitter, and gloss (Fine & Kinney, 2000) in an effort to reach young adults who, increasingly, are turning to the Internet for information and entertainment. One result has been the growth of Webzines, or Web sites that focus on topics of interests to teenagers. Another has been that sex and glamour are now found more frequently in the pages of teen magazines (Mosford & Henry, 2000). Finally, some traditional teen magazines are now being read by younger children as adolescents turn to magazines that appeal to older readers including "celebrity weeklies *In Touch, US Weekly,* and the *Star*" (Tyre, 2004, p. 59).

FROM PAGE TO SCREEN

Comic Books and Graphic Novels

Comic books and graphic novels present unique critical opportunities when adapted to the screen. Because of their often hip and edgy realism, many of the best graphic novel adaptations, such as 2000's Ghost World *and 2003's* American Splendor, *receive an R-rating, making them unsuitable for sharing with adolescents.*

Comic books are often adapted for the screen in a much more general way than novels. Filmmakers pick up threads from several different issues and attempt to match the overall tone of the comic book series. When viewing these big screen comic book heroes, you'll want to compare the film's faithfulness to the overall vision the comic book series has of its hero, and discuss whether or not the film's take on the story and characters is as valuable as the original text.

Hellboy
2004, PG-13
★★★

Adapted from a series of popular graphic novels, Hellboy *is a surprisingly high-quality film. Director Guillermo del Toro brings humor and dark style to Mike Mignola's story of a demon child raised by a kindly scientist. The film grasps at familiar adolescent issues of isolation and belonging. The moving force behind this entertaining film, however, is Ron Perlman, whose performance as the cat-loving romantic trapped in a demonic form is a revelation.*

Batman
1989, PG
★★★ 1/2

Tim Burton's original phenomenon relies heavily on his trademark dark yet campy style for interest, but a scene-stealing performance by Jack Nicholson as the Joker is what keeps the film relevant. Compare the genesis of the characters with that laid out in the comics, and compare the tone of the film with the TV series and other installments in the film series to see which version comes closest to the DC Comics tenor.

Spider-Man 2
2003, PG-13
★★★ 1/2

Director Sam Raimi's video game-like visual style and Tobey Maguire's everyman good nature give this blockbuster a color, action, and human quality missing from some of the darker, more brooding superhero flicks. With less exposition, a finer-tuned villain, and more investment in Peter Parker's humanity and personal storyline than in special effects, the sequel is superior even to the impressive original film.

FROM PAGE TO SCREEN

Hulk
2003, PG-13
★ ★ ★

Controversial and disappointing when released because it strayed so far from audience expectations, this film is an excellent choice for comparison and contrast to its comic book roots. Director Ang Lee, quite uncharacteristically, chose to focus audience emotions on the entirely computer-generated Hulk, creating one-dimensional characters of the human counterparts. This artistic decision explores the tragically human quality the comic book series gave Hulk, but relegates his human side to the realm of unimportant side note. Is Lee too unfaithful to the tone of the comic book foundation for his monster?

X2: X-Men United
2003, PG-13
★ ★ ★

With less exposition and more thrills, this sequel to 2000's X-Men is in many ways superior to its predecessor. Director Bryan Singer, whose Usual Suspects *(1995) launched him as a filmmaker with an eye for action sequences and gift for character intrigue, capitalizes on stronger actors (Ian McKellen, Hugh Jackman, Brian Cox) to ground the plot, freeing the rest of the cast to engage in high energy character indulgence.*

Reasons For Using and Teaching with Magazines. Traditionally, magazine writers and publishers have produced magazines with appropriate reading levels, topics, and formats to interest young adults, especially reluctant readers and teens who feel challenged when asked to read a complete novel or even a long short story. Focusing on young adult concerns such as beauty, fitness, the opposite sex, cars, friendships and relationships, sports, and hobbies, these magazines have a variety of short and medium-length articles that are written in an exciting and enthusiastic style and can be read at one sitting. In recent years, the traditional print format has been challenged by Webzines, or magazines on the Internet. Connecting Adolescents and Their Literature 10-3 looks at one way to build on the popularity of Webzines.

Characteristics of Magazines For Young Adults. Just as with all young adult literature (i.e., series or informational books), magazines vary in quality and educators need to evaluate and select them carefully. Considerations for Selecting Young Adult Literature: *Magazines* provides some questions you should ask when examining magazines.

Magazines For Young Adults. As with all literature, young adults prefer visually appealing magazines that appeal to their interests. While many young adults read *People,*

CONNECTING **ADOLESCENTS AND THEIR LITERATURE 10–3**

Webzines (magaZINES on the Internet) use the power of the Internet to provide young adults with a wide range of choices in teen magazine literature. Many of these Internet magazines focus on topics that interest young adult girls (Norton, 2002). Review a few Webzines. Then follow the suggestions of Christie "CJ" Bott (2002) in *Zines—The Ultimate Creative Writing Project* and have students make their own Webzines as part of a creative writing project. Links to a few Webzines are found on this book's Companion Website at www.prenhall.com/bucher.

Time, Newsweek, or *Sports Illustrated,* there are special current events magazines for young adults including *New York Times Upfront, Teen People, Teen Newsweek,* and even *Kids' Wall Street Journal.* To support the curriculum, there are magazines like *Muse,* which focuses on science, history, and the arts; *Cicada,* a literary magazine; and Archaeology's *Dig.* Two magazines that feature the writing of adolescents are *Merlyn's Pen: Fiction, Essays and Poems by America's Teens* and *Teen Ink.* In 2004, author Michael Cart began a semi-annual journal entitled *Rush Hour* for older adolescents. Looking more like a collection of short stories than a magazine, the literary journal includes short fiction, poems, nonfiction, and essays by recognized young adult authors.

Teachers and library media specialists should be careful to avoid stereotyping either gender. However, it appears that, while some magazines appeal to both genders, others appeal primarily to either boys or girls. Magazines that appear to cater to female's interests

CONSIDERATIONS | **For Selecting Young Adult Literature** | **MAGAZINES**

When examining magazines for adolescents, ask the following questions:

- ◉ Is the magazine visually appealing to adolescents?

- ◉ Does the content of the magazine appeal to the interests of adolescents?

- ◉ Is the content (both text and illustrations) of the magazine developmentally appropriate for adolescents?

- ◉ What is the reading level of the magazine?

- ◉ Does the magazine directly support the curriculum of the school?

- ◉ Is the magazine a good choice for recreational reading? Will it appeal to reluctant readers?

- ◉ Does the magazine avoid stereotyping or exploiting genders?

- ◉ Does the magazine duplicate information that can be found more easily in another resource (such as a database or on the Internet)?

EXPANDING	*YOUR KNOWLEDGE WITH THE INTERNET 10–3*

 Listed below are a few Web sites for young adult magazines. Links to these and many additional sites are found on this book's Companion Website at www.prenhall.com/bucher.

Cricket Publishing—Muse and Cicada

www.cricketmag.com

Dig

www.dig.archaeology.org

Teen People

www.teenpeople.com

---

include *American Girl, Seventeen,* and *YM (Young and Modern).* Catering to males are periodicals such as *Beckett Baseball Card Monthly, Thrasher, TransWorld SKATEboarding, Snowboarder,* and *BMX Plus.* Expanding Your Knowledge with the Internet 10-3 provides URLs for a few of these popular magazines.

Suggestions For Selecting and Using Magazines. Suggestions for Selecting Young Adult Literature: *Magazines,* earlier in this chapter, listed questions to ask when evaluating magazines. It is important to remember that young adults want to read about an appealing subject and do not want to struggle through difficult or unfamiliar vocabulary. Although adults often want to provide magazines that challenge young adults' reading levels and enhance their interests, few adolescents (although exceptions exist) will read magazines that seem uninteresting or that are frustrating to read. Similarly, while educators might question the appropriateness of topics (especially in schools) such as beauty/fitness; the opposite sex; extreme sports; rap, grunge, or hip-hop music; and friendships and relationships; these topics interest young adults and should be represented in the magazines that we provide for adolescents.

Realistically speaking, the content of some magazines is a concern for teachers and library media specialists. Even though magazines do not always have to "fit the curriculum" and may be purchased to meet the needs of adolescents for recreational reading, the mere fact that the periodicals are in a school library or classroom collection may give legitimacy to the publication. Educators must consider how parents and community members might respond to some of the content explored in young adult magazines. For example, *Seventeen* and *YM* sometimes have articles that, while not sexually explicit, deal with the sexual aspects of relationships. In fact, school librarians complained about a "salacious ad" (Margolis, 2001, p. 24) in an issue of *Seventeen* magazine. In response, the publisher announced that it would not repeat the ad (Margolis, 2001).

Some individuals also question whether young adults should be reading about skateboards or extreme sports in school. Thus, educators need to be prepared to justify the inclusion of these materials on the basis of interest and appropriate reading levels since to do otherwise would be to censor well-written materials that appeal to many adolescents. In a survey sponsored by the American Library Association, 64% of the boys indicated that they read sports magazines (Cox, 2003).

With magazines, there is always a need to balance literary merit and popularity. Some educators want young adults to have magazines that will challenge readers to new heights and acquaint them with some of the classics of literature or with articles that expand their intellectual horizons. However there are those educators who view magazines as one way to tempt the reluctant reader or to provide reading materials that academically challenged youth can enjoy. They believe that the immediate goal should be to encourage young adults to read and that once the love of reading is nurtured in young adults, these students will develop a desire to read more scholarly or educational materials. The perennial debate focuses on how to find a balance between these extremes. With budget cuts and the rising cost of periodical subscriptions, the temptation is to cancel the subscriptions to any magazines that do not support the curriculum. For some educators, the decision not to purchase popular periodicals is made easier because of the shift toward edgier articles that address sexual issues, and the belief that many of the popular magazines have an extreme emphasis on beauty or dangerous or violent sports. While professional educators have a responsibility to challenge readers, they also need to understand the popularity of the topics addressed in these magazines and the need for young adults to read. We encourage you to examine a number of different magazines for young adults, talk to adolescents about their reading preferences, and, then, make up your own mind.

Magazines can be used in a number of ways throughout the curriculum. Obviously, some periodicals have subject tie-ins such as *Muse* for the arts, *Dig* in science, and the many teen news magazines in social studies. Suggestions for Collaborative Efforts 10-3 looks at ways teachers and library media specialists can help young adults to get their writing published by focusing on literary magazines.

SUGGESTIONS FOR COLLABORATIVE EFFORTS

10-3

Some young adults would probably love to have their writing published. However, breaking into the publishing world can be difficult to do. Teachers and library media specialists can work together to help adolescents learn about magazines such as *Merlyn's Pen: Fiction, Essays and Poems by America's Teens* and *Teen Ink* that regularly publish student work. Librarians need to have these publications available for students to read and teachers need to help learn how to write for publication.

Some tips on writing for publication (Kellaher, 1999) include:

- Help adolescents get to *know* the publication where they will submit their work by examining current issues to determine:
    - the target audience (age group) of the magazine
    - the types of articles published

- the length of the articles
- the required submission format (paper or electronic)
- the submission process
- Encourage young adults to write about people, places, events, and issues they know about.
- Discuss plagiarism—what it is, the consequences, and how to avoid it.
- Remind young adults to consider Webzines that might be interested in receiving student work.
- Encourage young adults to be realistic in their expectations, not to take rejections personally, and to revise and resubmit.

CONCLUDING THOUGHTS

Comics, graphic novels, and magazines can motivate young adults to read. Unfortunately, some educators once thought, and perhaps some still do, these three types were not "real" genres or "real" literature and did not deserve recognition and use in schools. However, many young adults *do* read and enjoy them. Some teachers have been very successful in using comics, graphic novels, and magazines for instructional purposes. Others use them to motivate students or supplement instructional resources. Comics have been read by many students since their earliest years; graphic novels appeal to students who grew up on video games and television; and magazines offer interesting possibilities for directing attention to young adults' concerns and interests. With their potential for getting young adults to read, comics, graphic novels, and magazines deserve serious consideration rather than being relegated to second-class status or ignored altogether. Visit this book's Companion Website at www.prenhall.com/bucher for additional information about comics, graphic novels, and magazines including review questions, self-assessments, Internet sites, and young adult literature and readings.

Young Adult Books

This section includes young adult titles recommended or mentioned in this chapter. Check the Companion Website at www.prenhall.com/bucher to find additional suggestions of current young adult literature.

Comics

Refer to Table 10–1 for a list of some recommended comic book series.

Graphic Novels

Table 10–2 contains additional recommendations of graphic novels.

9-11 artists respond. (2002). Milwaukie, OR: Dark Horse Comics. Artists look back at the attacks on September 11, 2001.

9-11 the world's finest comic book writers and artists tell stories to remember. (2002). New York: DC Comics. Here are more stories of the September 11, 2001, attack.

Aragones, S. (2002). *The Groo maiden.* Milwaukie, OR: Dark Horse Comics. Groo is in love as he tries to get the most dangerous female warrior around. Another book about Groo is *Groo and Rufferto.*

Arnoldi, K. (1998). *Amazing "true" story of a teenage single mom.* New York: Hyperion. After being raped, a young girl finds she is pregnant.

Bendis, B., & Bagley, M. (2002). *Ultimate Spider-Man: power and responsibility.* New York: Marvel Comics. This is the first volume in a series that takes a fresh look at a well-known character.

Briggs, R. (1998). *Ethel and Ernest.* New York: Pantheon Books. This book takes a look at England through the eyes of an average family.

Busiek, K. (2000). *Astro City: Life in the big city.* Minneapolis, MN: Sagebrush. Astro City has a large number of superpowered human beings—the catch is the superheroes have human problems that supernatural powers cannot fix.

Claremont, C., & Byrne, J. (2003). *The Dark Phoenix saga.* New York: Marvel Enterprises. This is the second volume in the X-Men Legends series.

Cooke, J. B., & Morrow, J. (Eds.). (2000). *Streetwise: Autobiographical stories by comic book professionals.* Raleigh, NC: TwoMorrows Publishing. This book contains biographies of individuals in the comic book industry.

Cruse, H. (1995). *Stuck rubber baby.* New York: Paradox. This frank coming-of-age story looks at the Civil Rights movement as well as a young man's emerging sexual identity.

Eisner, W. (1978). *A contract with God.* New York: DC Comics. This work began the graphic novel genre.

Eisner, W. (2002). *Sundiata: A legend of Africa.* New York: NMB. In this African legend, a crippled boy grows up and leads the fight against the evil Samanguru.

Eisner, W. (2003). *Fagin the Jew.* New York: Doubleday. This is *Oliver Twist* from a different perspective.

Fujishima, K. (2003). *Oh my goddess! Mystery child.* Milwaukie, OR: Dark Horse Comics. Imagine being a boy in a house filled with goddesses. This is just one entry in a long series.

Gaiman, N. (1993). *The Sandman: A game of you.* New York: DC Comics. A young witch leads a group of women on a quest to destroy the evil Cuckoo. There are additional books in this multivolume award-winning fantasy series with mature content.

Gaiman, N. (1994). *Death: The high cost of living.* New York: DC Comics. Every 100 years, Death comes back to earth in this work for mature readers.

Gaiman, N. (1996). *Black Orchid.* New York: DC Comics. Black Orchid tries to put together the pieces of her past and the biological tests that created her.

Gaiman, N. (2004). *The books of magic.* New York: Morrow. In this book with advanced themes, a young boy gets involved in a world of magic.

Giardino, V. (1997). *A Jew in communist Prague: Volume: Loss of innocence.* New York: NBM. In this book for older adolescents, readers follow Jonas as he grows up in Prague in the 1950s.

Golden, C. (1999). *Buffy the vampire slayer: Origin.* Milwaukie, OR: Dark Horse Comics. Buffy becomes a vampire slayer.

Gonick, L. (1997). *Cartoon history of the universe.* New York: Broadway Books. Fun and fact are combined in this look at history. A similar book is *The Cartoon Guide to Statistics* (1993) by Gonick and Smith.

Heuet, S. (2001). *Remembrance of things past.* New York: NBM. Proust's work emerges as a graphic novel.

Hosler, J. (2000). *Clan apis.* Columbus, OH: Active Synapse. Follow the life cycle of a honeybee and explore the environment in which it lives.

Hosler, J. (2003). *The sandwalk adventures: An adventure in evolution told in five chapters.* Columbus, OH: Active Synapse. This easy-to-read graphic novel presents Darwin's theory of natural selection.

Kiyama, H. F. (1999). *The four immigrants manga.* Berkeley, CA: Stone Bridge Press. Young adults can examine the lives of four Japanese immigrants in San Francisco, CA, from 1904 to 1924.

Kubert, J. (1998). *Fax from Sarajevo: A story of survival.* Milwaukie, OR: Dark Horse Comics. In this intense and sometimes explicit book, Kubert takes an up-front look at the horrors of war.

Kuper, P. (2003). *The metamorphosis.* New York: Crown. Kuper adapts Kafka's classic story.

Laird, R. O., Laird, T. N., & Bey, E. (1997). *Still I rise: A cartoon history of African Americans.* New York: Norton. This is a history of African Americans.

Marz, R. (2002). *Mystic vol. 1 rite of passage.* Oldsmar, FL: CrossGeneration. In a world run on magic, Genevieve Villard was in line to become the great leader, but during the Rite of Ascension, something went wrong.

Marz, R., et al. (2002). *Sojourn, vol. 1: From the ashes.* Oldsmar, FL: CrossGeneration. In this action/adventure book, the troll armies and the legendary weapon meet to create an epic quest.

Marz, R., Durrsema, J., et al. (2001). *Star Wars: Darth Maul.* Milwaukie, OR: Dark Horse Comics. This is about one of *Star Wars'* darkest villains.

McCraw, T. (1999). *Legion of super-heroes: The beginning of tomorrow.* New York: DC Comics. Here are adventure and romance in the 31st century.

Miller, F. (2000–2001). *Daredevil: Visionaries.* New York: Marvel Comics. There are three volumes in this series about the man who has no fear. Other superhero series by Miller are *Batman* and *X-Men.*

Miller, F., & Varley, L. (1999). *300.* Milwaukie, OR: Dark Horse Comics. The Spartans and Persians meet in the Battle of Thermopylae.

Ottaviani, J. (2001a). *Fallout.* Ann Arbor, MI: G. T. Labs. Examine the events that led to the creation of the atomic bomb.

Ottaviani, J. (2001b). *Two-fisted science: Stories about scientists.* Ann Arbor, MI: G. T. Labs. These short stories feature real scientists such as Isaac Newton and Galileo.

Ottaviani, J. (2003). *Dignifying science.* Ann Arbor, MI: G. T. Labs. This anthology presents biographies of famous women scientists.

Rall, T. (2002). *To Afghanistan and back: A graphic travelogue.* New York: NBM Publishing. Rall recounts his trip to Afghanistan during the American bombing against the Taliban.

Robinson, J. (2000). *Leave it to Chance: Shaman's rain.* New York: DC Comics. Following in her father's footsteps, 14-year-old Chance Falconer wants to become a famous paranormal investigator

Russell, P. C. (2002). *The Ring of Nibelung.* Milwaukie, OR: Dark Horse Comics. This series retells Richard Wagner's Ring cycle opera.

Sacco, J. (2002). *Palestine.* Seattle, WA: Fantagraphics Books. Sacco describes his life among the Palestinians under Israeli occupation. Another of his books is *Safe Area Gorazade: The War in Eastern Bosnia 1992–1995*.

Sakai, S. (2000). *Usagi Yojimbo: Grasscutter*. Milwaukie, OR: Dark Horse Comics. Delve into Japanese mythology in this tale of the recovery of the lost sword of the gods.

Sanderson, P. (2003). *X-Men: The ultimate guide*. New York: DK. The mutants with super abilities move from comic to graphic novel and Sanderson traces their history.

Shanower, E. (2001). *A thousand ships*. Orange, CA: Image Comics. In this first book in the Age of Bronze series, Shanower begins his story of the Trojan War.

Spiegelman, A. (1997). *The complete Maus*. New York: Pantheon. In this Pulitzer prize-winning graphic novel, Spiegelman looks at his family's struggle to survive as the racism of Nazi Germany spreads across Poland.

Takahashi, R. (1996). *Rumiko Takahashi's Rumic Theater*. San Francisco: Viz Comics. This is a collection of stories from a great female manga author.

Takahashi, R. (1998). *Rumic Theater: One or double*. San Francisco: Viz Comics. This second collection from Takahashi contains more stories.

Talbot, B. (1995). *The tale of one bad rat*. Milwaukie, OR: Dark Horse Comics. A young girl tries to recover after sexual abuse.

Tanaka, M. (2000). *Gon*. New York: DC Comics. This is a wordless manga graphic novel.

Toriyama, A. (2002). *Dragonball Z*. San Francisco: Viz Comics. Son Goku and friends must overcome enemies who want to destroy the earth.

Wenzel, D. (2001). *The Hobbit: An illustrated edition of the fantasy classic*. New York: Ballantine Books. Wenzel brings Middle-Earth to life in this adaptation.

Winnick, J. (2000). *Pedro and me: Friendship, loss, and what I learned*. New York: Henry Holt. Winnick looks at AIDS in his examination of his friendship with the late Pedro Zamora, an HIV-positive AIDS activist.

Magazines

(Check the chapter for URLs for most of these.)

American Girl. This positive and upbeat magazine will appeal to younger adolescents.

Black Beat. This magazine addresses African American interests with a focus on musicians and music.

BMX Plus. Packed with pictures of BMX bikes and articles about maintenance, tricks, and safety, this magazine will probably appeal to more boys than girls.

Cicada. With poetry and prose, this literary magazine features works by outstanding young adult authors as well as teens.

GamePro. This magazine features information on the latest games and tips for playing them. A similar title is *Game Players Sega Nintendo*.

Merlyn's Pen. This magazine contains fiction, plays, short stories, essays, and poetry written by young adults.

Muse. Published by Cricket, this magazine explores science, history, and the arts.

New York Times Upfront. Published by Scholastic during the school year, this periodical looks at science and technology, current events, and teen issues.

Right On! A look at popular entertainment personalities written especially for African American young adults.

Teen Ink. A periodical written by teens about teen issues.

Teen Newsweek. *Weekly Reader* and *Newsweek* have combined on this current events magazine.

Teen People. Similar to *People* Magazine, this magazine is targeted to 11 to 18-year-olds and is available in a Spanish edition.

YM (Young and Modern). This magazine contains information on entertainment, fitness, careers, beauty, and fashion for young women.

Suggested Readings

Bussert, L. (2005). Comic books and graphic novels: Digital resources for an evolving form of art and literature. *College & Research Libraries News 66*(2) 103–106.

Frey, N., & Fisher, D. (2004). Using graphic novels, anime, and the Internet in an urban high school. *English Journal, 93*(3), 19–25.

Ogle, J. P., & Thornburg, E. (2003). An alternative voice amid teen 'zines: An analysis of body-related content in "Girl Zone." *Journal of Family and Consumer Sciences, 96*(1), 47–56.

Scordato, J. (2005). Talking with Wendy and Richard Pini: The team behind ElfQuest. (2005). *Library Media Connection 23*(6), 46–49.

Scordato, J. (2005). Top 10 Graphic novels for youth. *Booklist 101*(14), 1304.

References

(Note: All young adult literature referenced in this chapter are included in the Young Adult Books list and are not repeated in this list.)

Alvermann, D. E., Moon, J. S., & Hagood, M. C. (1999). *Popular culture in the classroom: Teaching and researching critical media literacy.* Newark NJ: International Reading Association.

Archie Comics' Note to Parents. Retrieved March 2, 2004, from www.archiecomics.com/arcade/sunday/stumper/forparents.html.

Bott, C. (2002). Zines—The ultimate creative writing project. *English Journal, 92*(2), 27–38.

Comic books for young adults. (2001, December 5). Retrieved December 11, 2003, from http://ublib.buffalo.edu/libraries/units/lml/comics/pages/reading.html.

Comics worth reading March 2004 previews. Retrieved March 2, 2004, from http://www.comicsworthreading.com/previews/0403.html.

Cox, R. (2003). From "Boys' Life" to "Thrasher:" Boys and magazines. *Teacher Librarian, 30*(3), 25–26.

Crawford, P. (2002). Graphic novels: Selecting materials that will appeal to girls. *Knowledge Quest, 31*(2), 43–45.

Crawford, P. (2003a). Beyond Maus: Using graphic novels to support social studies standards. *Knowledge Quest, 31*(4), 41–42.

Crawford, P. (2003b). Graphic novels of 2002: Superheroes and more. *Knowledge Quest, 31*(5), 46–47.

Fine, J., & Kinney, M. (2000). Magazine mania. *School Library Journal, 46*(8), 40–43.

Gorman, M. (2002a). What teens want: Thirty graphic novels you can't live without. *School Library Journal, 48*(8), 42–44.

Gorman, M. (2002b). More of what teens want. Retrieved December 30, 2002, from http://slj.reviewsnews.com/index.asp?layout=articlePrint&articleID=CA261476.

Kellaher, K. (1999). Get kids' work published! Top tips on how to do it from children's magazine editors. *Instructor, 108*(6), 14+.

Kennedy, M. H. (2003). Wisdom from the Old Master: Will Eisner discusses the graphic novel. *Library of Congress Information Bulletin, 62*(5), 110–111.

Lubbock (Texas) City-County Library. (library.ci.lubbock.tx.us/opac/)

Margolis, R. (2001). Ad nauseam: School librarians complain about a salacious ad in *Seventeen* magazine. *School Library Journal, 47*(3), 24.

McDonald, H. (2002). The year of the graphic novel. *Publishers Weekly, 249*(51), 21–22.

Mooney, M. (2002). Graphic novels: How they can work in libraries. *Book Report, 21*(3), 18–19.

Mosford, D., & Henry, J. (2000, January 28). Sex ousts pet pooch in ten mags. *The Times Educational Supplement,* p. 9.

Norton, B. (2002). When is a teen magazine not a teen magazine? *Journal of Adolescent & Adult Literacy, 45*(5), 296–299.

O'Kelly, J. (2001). *Son of invisible art; Graphic novels for libraries.* Aylesbury: Library and Information Service for Schools.

Overstreet, R. M. (2004). *Official Overstreet comic book price guide: Comics from 1828–present included.* New York: Gemstone.

Raiteri, S. (2003a). Graphic novels. *Library Journal, 128*(8), 94.

Raiteri, S. (2003b). Graphic novels. *Library Journal, 128*(14), 138.

Reid, C. (2002). Asian comics delight U.S. readers. *Publishers Weekly, 249*(51), 26.

Reid, C. (2003). Manga is here to stay: Tokyopop's format leads manga into the bookstore market. *Publishers Weekly, 250*(42), S6.

Sabin, R. (2001). *Comics, comix & graphic novels: A history of comic art.* London: Phaidon.

Schwartz, G. E. (2002). Graphic novels for multiple literacies. *Journal of Adolescent & Adult Literacy, 46*(3), 262–265.

Simmons, T. (2003). Comic books in my library? *PNLA Quarterly, 67*(2), 12, 20.

S. Rep. No. 83–62. (1956). *Comic books and juvenile delinquency.* Retrieved March 1, 2004, from www.geocities.com/Athens/8580/kefauver.html.

Tyre, P. (2004, April 19). No longer most likely to succeed. *Newsweek* p. 59. Retrieved April 8, 2005 from: Lexis-Nexis database: http://web.lexis-nexis.com/universe/document?_m=7d9e29807226cec1445c470701e16544&_docnum=2&wchp=dGLbVtz-zSkVb&_md5=1b670dbf5c0202dad10bc5355255d6bb.

Weiner, R. (2001). Graphic novels in libraries. *Texas Library Journal, 77*(4), 130–135.

Weiner, S. (2001). *101 best graphic novels.* New York: NBM.

Weiner, S. (2003). Building a strong collection. *School Library Journal, 49*(5), 33.

TEACHING, USING, AND APPRECIATING YOUNG ADULT LITERATURE

In a school library two high school students look at the shelves and mutter while they consult a list, look at a book on the shelf, and then return to the list. If we listen very closely we may hear one of them say: "Aren't there any short books on this list? If I have to read a book, why can't I read what I like instead of the lame books on this list?"

Educators encourage and even require adolescents to read books. However, rather than appealing to student interests, many English teachers have tried to identify books, often classics, that they believe are worthy of students' time and attention. History or science teachers often assign "informational book reports" or other activities requiring students to read and digest content material. Although these approaches undoubtedly prove effective for some students, many students read as little as they can to "get by." These lists and assignments have not motivated the students or encouraged a love of reading. Fortunately, newer trends such as using literature across the curriculum and literature-based instruction have grown in popularity, suggesting more productive ways to use young adult literature. Rather than working in isolation, many educators now make collaborative decisions on curricular themes and use young adult literature that crosses subject areas and helps students see new and different perspectives about issues and subject content. This chapter explains how young adult literature can be used in single subject areas, shows how appropriate books can cross curricular boundaries, and offers a strong recommendation for incorporating young adult literature across the curriculum.

FOCUSING POINTS   **In this chapter, you will read about:**

1. Essential considerations for using literature.
2. Considerations for planning effective literature-based teaching-learning experiences and the roles of teachers, school librarians, and public librarians.
3. Aspects related to literature-based instruction—its definition, rationale, and advantages.
4. Suggestions for including young adult literature in regular subject areas and a strong endorsement for incorporating literature throughout all curricular approaches.
5. Considerations for reaching and encouraging reluctant readers.
6. Recommendations for developing a community of readers and teaching for lifelong reading.

ESSENTIAL CONSIDERATIONS

Whether you are using a single poem with a lesson, reading a book with a unit, or including multiple texts in a thematic approach, there are several things you should remember when teaching young adult literature. While other considerations (perhaps some of equal importance) undoubtedly exist, we selected these three because, if you remember to include them in your teaching, you will be a more competent and enthusiastic teacher or school library media specialist.

View Literature as Entertaining as Well as Challenging

Think back to your own days as a young adult. Can you recall reading books and poems that you considered "dry as dust"—books on reading lists that someone labeled as "must" reading for all students sometime in their education? How did reading those materials make you feel? Now, ask yourself how a teacher can help adolescents develop a love for reading and a desire to become a lifelong reader if the assignments actually seem designed to convince teenagers that books are difficult, boring, or totally uninteresting?

This is not to say that teachers should not challenge students or use good literature. However, there must be a balance between quality and interest; the terms are not mutually exclusive. Adolescents do have the desire to read well-written materials that encourage them to think about what they are reading. They will even read "long" books (just look at the length of some of the fantasy novels that they avidly read). When teachers select quality young adult literature that is interesting, appropriate, and challenging, students will enjoy both the reading process and the literature itself.

Become Familiar with a Wide Range of Literature

There are several advantages to knowing a wide range of young adult literature. In addition to planning better teaching units, especially literature-based units (discussed later in the chapter), you will be able to suggest young adult books for students' special interests or bibliotherapeutic needs, and books that compare and contrast issues and perspectives in a variety of subjects. You will also be able to discuss the books that your students are reading, comparing your reactions to theirs, suggesting similar books, and learning new titles from your students. When you know a wide range of titles and authors of young adult literature, you should feel comfortable and competent in your teaching role and should be able to make more connections to the young adults in your classes.

Share Literature with Adolescents

We believe that all teachers need to be teachers of literature. No, that does not mean that science teachers need to worry about teaching the elements of fiction. What it does mean is that all teachers need to have the skills to share literature with their students. They need to be eager and able to read to their students and to share literature that will interest, intrigue, amuse, and excite adolescents. The effective teacher must be able to give oral performances (i.e., poetry and drama need to be read aloud). While an English teacher may read a poem and then help students explicate it, a social studies teacher may read a poem written by a Holocaust survivor as an introduction to the study of World War II. Although these teachers have different motives for reading poetry and one teacher may focus on the form of the poem more than the other, both teachers need to be proficient with reading literature and must be comfortable reading aloud to students. In addition, English teachers need to be able to teach students how to use the techniques of dramatic and oral interpretation in their own reading and presentations.

Generally, teachers who have the skills and confidence for dramatic and oral interpretation are more interesting and enthusiastic. By modeling enthusiasm and appreciation of literature, these teachers can be powerful role models for students. What about teachers who do not feel comfortable reading aloud? In addition to taking a course (perhaps a speech, drama, or storytelling course or workshop) in which they can learn oral reading techniques, teachers can seek help from a more proficient teacher or the library media specialist. Once they know skills and techniques, teachers can practice alone, perhaps in front of a mirror. To hone skills even more, teachers can participate in a community storytelling league and take storytelling and creative dramatics classes offered by a local public library. Connecting Adolescents and Their Literature 11–1 provides some ideas for using recordings and audiobooks to present literature orally to adolescents.

| CONNECTING | ADOLESCENTS AND THEIR LITERATURE 11–1 |

As Marjorie M. Kaiser (1999) says, when we listen to a story we no longer have the tendency to rush through it, can appreciate the words more, and can "relish the choice image or phrase" (p. 18). By providing a way for educators to bring a skilled reader into every classroom, audiobooks allow all adolescents to listen to quality literature. Rather than being viewed as a substitute for books, audiobooks are a "natural complement to print books" (Austin & Harris, 1999, p. 242) and an "authentic literary experience" (p. 242). Kaiser (1999) explains that, for some readers/listeners, the narrator can help shape the understanding of characters, define the setting more clearly, and bring the story to life. According to Whitten (1998), high school teachers have reported that, after listening to audiobooks, their students had an appreciation for and love of literature. Teachers can:

- Encourage school and public librarians to develop collections of quality audiobooks.

- Use all or part of a book on tape or CD with an entire class.

- Use earphones to allow individuals or small groups to listen to selections.

- Set aside a short portion of a class on a regular basis so that students can have an expert reader share an audiobook with them.

 Deborah Locke (2001) lists a number of Internet resources to help teachers integrate audiobooks into the classroom and provides a list of "starter titles" (p. 28) for an audiobook collection. Links to this site and other resources on audiobooks are on this book's Companion Website at www.prenhall.com/bucher.

DEVELOPING A YOUNG ADULT LITERATURE PROGRAM

Teachers and library media specialists are most effective in encouraging adolescents to read for enjoyment, interpret events in books, and develop an awareness of authors and titles when they work collaboratively to implement a literature plan or program. This plan can be very informal, with a goal to increase reading in the school or to encourage every teacher to use at least one piece of young adult literature during each grading period; or very formal, with specific assignments or programs such as Sustained Silent Reading (SSR) or Accelerated Reader (AR). To develop this plan, teachers and library media specialists (LMS) need to know the young adults in their school, and know a wealth of appropriate books. Only then can they begin to make the right match between reader and book, to suggest the right book for a literature-based thematic unit, and/or to recommend an appropriate book for a reader who is struggling with a problem or special challenge.

Purposes

Remember that young adults read books and teachers assign books for a number of reasons. While one student might read *The Land* (Taylor, 2001) because she or he enjoys reading about American history, another student might read the book only because a social studies teacher assigned it. However, regardless of whether students read by personal choice or by teacher assignment, reading is usually done for three broad purposes: enjoyment, learning and interpreting, and/or developing literary awareness.

A major purpose of any literature program is to provide young adults with an opportunity to enjoy books and other forms of literature. While some adolescents will read only assigned materials, all students should be encouraged to read and have an opportunity to enjoy reading. One of the best ways to teach young adults to appreciate novels and other literature is to provide an interesting, diverse, and well-written selection of literature that includes all the genres discussed in this book. Rather than dictating tastes or telling readers what they will like, teachers and LMS should encourage students to browse through books and make their own selections. Teaching young adults to enjoy literature and the reading process should be a major priority in any literature program.

The literature program should also teach adolescents to interpret literature. Literature can have many meanings, some clear and others abstract. To understand these levels of meaning, adolescents need to learn that a passage with deeper meanings may have to be read several times, digested, and, then, thoughtfully considered. It takes time, thought, and skills to examine and interpret events, settings, themes, characters, the author's style, and, if applicable, the illustrations to determine the author's meanings. Adolescents need help to gain confidence in expressing their beliefs, their interpretative decisions, and their conclusions. Later in this chapter, we will provide some examples of strategies teachers can use.

Finally, the young adult literature program must help adolescents develop literary awareness. This means that teachers and LMS need to convey a sense of appreciation for novels and other genres of literature. To do this, educators must teach about authors and their books, and how or why they write as they do. An author's name should bring to mind other books by the same author or by other authors who write in the same style or on the same topics. For example, educators should use and teach adolescents how to make concept maps or book webs showing relationships among books. As with appreciation for literature, awareness skills will likely increase over time and will differ among individuals.

Teachers' and Library Media Specialists' Roles and Environments

Teachers and library media specialists must set the tone for any literature program. If they are committed and enthusiastic, they will serve as models for other adults who are involved in the program and for the adolescents in the school. Educators might sometimes underestimate their powerful role and influence. If a teacher assigns a book with an attitude of drudgery or says "I had to suffer through it—you should have to suffer too," he or she will not motivate young adults to read the book or to become lifelong readers. However, by modeling respect, enthusiasm, and appreciation for novels and other genres of literature, an educator can have more far-reaching effects than by merely assigning books and being sure books have been read.

The teachers and LMS must be committed to the literature program and to an educational environment that reflects literature and a respect for reading. This commitment can take many forms such as providing a sufficient quantity and quality of books written for young adults, providing students with time to read in class, helping students locate appropriate books for reading enjoyment and special school projects, creating a welcoming atmosphere in the school library media center, or inviting the LMS and/or public librarian to give booktalks to students in classrooms and to teachers in faculty or departmental meetings. Connecting Adolescents and Their Literature 11–2 provides more information about the use of booktalks.

From our experiences as a school library media specialist, public librarian, and classroom teacher, we have seen the importance of making a variety of good books available for young adults. In one school with a library media center (LMC) full of quality

---

CONNECTING | **ADOLESCENTS AND THEIR LITERATURE 11–2**

Doing a booktalk is like dangling bait in front of a fish. The idea is to talk about a book in a way that tantalizes your listeners and entices them to read the book. According to Terrence E. Young (2003), you need to be enthusiastic and passionate about the books that you are recommending. The "talk" on each book is usually short and tells just enough to "hook" the reader without giving away too much of the story.

Teachers and librarians have many occasions to do booktalks.

- A formal presentation of several books on a related theme or topic to a whole class.

- A brief talk to fellow teachers at a faculty meeting to recommend new titles.

- A talk to individual students who are looking for something good to read.

 Young has some excellent suggestions as well as a list of Web resources to help you booktalk. You can find the link to this article in the Chapter 11 weblinks on this book's Companion Website at www.prenhall.com/bucher.

There are also several excellent books about booktalks: *Tantalizing Tidbits for Teens: Quick Booktalks for the Busy High School Media Specialist* (2002) by Ruth E. Cox; *Booktalks Plus: Motivating Teens to Read* (2001) and *Booktalks and More: Motivating Teens to Read* (2003) by Lucy Schall; *Teenplots: A Booktalk Guide to Use with Readers Ages 12–18* (2003) by John Thomas Gillespie and Corinne J. Naden; *The Booktalker's Bible: How to Talk about the Books You Love to Any Audience* (2003) by Chapple Langemack; and *Still Talking That Book! Booktalks to Promote Reading Grades 3–12* (2003) by Cathlyn Thomas and Carol Littlejohn.

interesting books and classrooms with additional shelves of age- and interest-appropriate books; specific times in all classes to read; teachers and LMS who read and talk about books; activities such as student book clubs; and opportunities before, during, and after the school day to visit the LMC and to check-out books from both the LMC and the classroom collections, adolescents saw the value of reading and responded positively. From the circulation statistics in the LMC, the "wear and tear" on the books, and the discussion of young adult literature in classes throughout the curriculum, it was evident that the students in this school were reading. To us, messy shelves and a few tattered books are well worth it if our students are reading and enjoying books. Connecting Adolescents and Their Literature 11–3 has some suggestions that you can use to develop classroom collections to encourage reading.

Library Media Centers

A confusing array of names exist for what used to be called the "library." In this book, we follow the lead of the American Association of School Librarians and use the term *library media center* (LMC) to reflect the expanded services and materials that support the curriculum of the school and the reading interests of the school's students and teachers. The LMC's collection contains a wealth of resources including books, videotapes, DVDs, CD-ROMs, databases, and computers with Internet access.

CONNECTING   **ADOLESCENTS AND THEIR LITERATURE 11–3**

A number of ways exist to find quality books to put in classroom collections in schools. However, no matter which method you use to develop your collections, remember that you must select the materials carefully, applying the selection criteria that you have read in this book. The idea is not just to "fill the shelves" but to provide young adults with a chance to read quality literature.

- Ask for donations from parents and former students. Check with the LMS to see if your school has a policy for donated materials and be sure that everyone understands that materials which you cannot use in your classroom will be donated to another agency such as the public library for their annual book sale. Do not forget to check out those library book sales to add to your classroom collection.

- Haunt the thrift shops and secondhand stores. Often they have quality paperbacks at rock bottom prices.

- Visit the used book stores in your area. If you let the owners know what you are trying to do, they may be on the lookout for inexpensive books for you.

- Go to yard/garage sales. We have found wonderful books for 10 cents each just because the teens in the home left for college.

The LMC should be an inviting place where teachers, students, and parents can find a wealth of carefully selected materials. A licensed professional school library media specialist must know these materials and their potential use, foster literature appreciation, and teach information literacy skills to both students and teachers. This LMC should be open all day to serve both students and teachers, and the LMS should encourage free access to materials at all times while supporting intellectual freedom. In addition, the LMS works as an instructional partner with teachers throughout the curriculum, developing literature programs that will meet both the instructional and recreational reading needs of young adults. In the LMC, students can access information from both print and non-print resources, locate information on the Internet, evaluate that information before using it, work on projects, engage in other media- and book-oriented activities, and locate books for recreational reading. To ensure that this happens, the LMS must

- engage in cooperative planning with teachers throughout the curriculum and help develop instruction (rather than only selecting books for specific assignments);

- utilize technology to provide improved access to the collection;

- evaluate the impacts, outcomes, improved grades and test scores, and positive youth development that come from their efforts (Jones, 2002).

Public Libraries and Young Adult Services

Public libraries have also changed from repositories of books and now include many of the same types of resources that are found in school libraries, although the public library's charge is to meet the needs of all citizens rather than to support the curriculum of a particular school. At the same time that the increased population of teenagers places more demands on library services, public librarians are facing the tremendous task of integrating technology and information literacy into their programs while they maintain and expand other types of resources and programs (Jones, 2002). Adolescent patrons challenge public libraries in several ways: they want teen-friendly library spaces, more-relevant materials and services, increased computer access and instruction, improved customer service, and a review of policies and hours (Meyers, 2001).

An influx of young people can be an exciting challenge for public librarians who are constantly trying to attract this most discerning and easily distracted age group. Although public libraries want adolescents to feel welcome in the library, to be part of the community, to obtain leadership skills, to be culturally aware, and to be advocates for the library, the trickiest challenge for most public librarians is to get adolescents to use public libraries and to see what they have to offer (Ishizuka, 2003). Part of the problem lies in the differences between the library culture and adolescent culture. While adolescence is a time of energy and conversation, many public libraries have a culture of solitude.

To help adolescents learn that libraries have unique resources to balance solitude and social experience, a modern library staff must provide an array of young adult programs and services. Machado, Lentz, Wallace, and Honig-Bear (2000) identified some best practices in public libraries that accommodate the needs of adolescents. These include (a) formal tutoring-style homework centers, (b) drop-in style homework centers,

(c) career development/mentoring programs, and (d) cultural/recreation programs. Public libraries must also plan ways to cross the digital bridge that separates adolescents who have access to information and those who do not, use a wide variety of print and electronic information formats, and work with the school LMS and teachers (Jones, 2002). Suggestions for Collaborative Efforts 11–1 provides some suggestions for educators and public librarians.

Some public libraries are making the effort to form partnerships with youth agencies such as Boys and Girls Clubs, Boy and Girl Scouts, park districts, art centers, and faith-based groups. Together they can provide adolescents with safe places, constructive opportunities, the guidance of respectful adults, and the companionship of peers during nonschool time. Public libraries are especially important because they encourage a disposition toward lifelong, self-directed learning, which is essential to employment, health, and participation in civic life, home management, and recreation (Costello, Whalen, Spielberger, & Winje, 2001). Expanding Your Knowledge with the Internet 11–1 highlights some programs that public libraries have developed to reach young adults.

SUGGESTIONS FOR COLLABORATIVE EFFORTS

Educators can find a ready partner in most public libraries to help provide materials and services to young adults. The first step is for a teacher or school LMS to contact the public library (before a project or assignment is due), learn what the public library has to offer, and plan appropriate programs to utilize the resources of both the public library and the school. Diane P. Tuccillo (2003) lists a number of services of public libraries including:

- Booktalking in the school library and classroom
- Coordination of resources with the school library for programs such as Accelerated Reader
- Teen library Web pages with links to resources for young adults
- Teen advisory boards for the public library with educators recommending members
- Newsletters about resources and programs
- Teen literary magazines
- Tours of the public library
- Recommendations on professional materials for educators
- Internet pages with links for educators
- Meetings with educators to explain programs and services
- Homework alert services where the school notified the public library in advance of assignments that will require the use of library resources.

EXPANDING **YOUR KNOWLEDGE WITH THE INTERNET 11-1**

 A number of public libraries have Web sites just for young adults. Here are a few of them.

Berkley Public Library Teen Services

www.infopeople.org/bpl/teen/index.html

Providence Public Library Teen Power

www.provlib.org/teenpower/teenpower.htm

Mansfield/Richland County Public Library Teen Zone

www.mrcpl.lib.oh.us/TeenZone/index.html

Visit this book's Companion Website at www.prenhall.com/bucher to link directly to these and many other public libraries.

LITERATURE-BASED INSTRUCTION THROUGHOUT THE CURRICULUM

Traditionally, teachers have used young adult novels and other forms of literature only in English classes. However, the increase in quantity and quality of young adult literature (often called trade books as distinguished from textbooks) makes it possible for teachers to develop a literature plan to use these books across the curriculum. The result is that adolescents can now see that reading books is something that does not happen only in "literature class" and that books can play a major role in all content areas.

In many schools, especially middle schools, educators have begun to use literature-based integrated curricular plans in which students read trade books to develop reading skills, content knowledge, and an appreciation of literature. Connecting Adolescents and Their Literature 11–4 looks at one teacher's success story. Naturally, change is often slow and some educators feel uncomfortable with literature-based approaches. While some teachers may work in teams or groups to adopt a total literature approach, others may elect more limited approaches. Figure 11–1 shows the progression of usage of young adult literature. We believe that all teachers, not just English/language arts educators, should muster the initial effort, commitment, open-mindedness, and time to incorporate young adult literature into their curriculum. Literature does not have to be used in every class or with every unit of study; and a combination of both literature-based and traditional approaches may be most effective. Thus, educators will move back and forth on the pyramid depending on the instructional content of the units they are teaching.

Definition

Literature-based instruction is the use of young adult literature (e.g., trade books containing nonfiction, novels, poems, drama, and other literary forms) in place of or in addition

CONNECTING | *ADOLESCENTS AND THEIR LITERATURE 11–4*

Rebecca J. Joseph (1998) writes of her success in starting each year with a "provocative young adult novel" (p. 21) to help her students develop literature skills, make connections between literature and life, and "initiate a great conversation" (p. 21). In an urban middle school, she used Mary E. Lyons' *Letters from a Slave Girl: The Story of Harriet Jacobs* (1992) in a variety of ways:

Reading: Comprehension questions that center on the skills tested on Maryland's functional reading test.

Writing: (a) City-wide prompts that are used to prepare students for a high-stakes state test were adapted to use materials from the book. (b) Open-ended writing activities to connect the book to real life with some small-group discussion of responses.

Journals: Topics related to the book or student reactions to the text.

Grammar: Teacher reads the journals and writing, identifies the skills they need to improve, and adapts the grammar text assignments to fit the novel.

Vocabulary/Spelling: Words are taken from the novel.

Poetry: Connections are made between the novel and poetry. For example, she matched Lyons' book with African American poetry on the same theme.

Interdisciplinary Connections: A social studies teacher focused on the geography of the novel as well as the political climate of the 1800s. A science teacher tied a lesson on muscles to the story.

Supplementary Literature: Joseph booktalked similar novels and used excerpts from nonfiction to supplement the story.

to the traditional textbooks used in schools. For example, teachers in middle or high school social studies can use novels such as Karen Hesse's *Out of the Dust* (1997), Kathryn Lasky's *True North: A Novel of the Underground Railroad* (1996), or Carol Matas' *Greater Than Angels* (1998) to bring the Depression, slavery, and the Holocaust to life for readers. They can complement these fiction books with nonfiction such as Jerry Stanley's *Children of the Dust Bowl: The True Story of the School at Weedpatch Camp* (1992) (An Orbis Pictus Award winner), Tom Feeling's narrative paintings in *The Middle Passage: White Ships, Black Cargo* (1995), and Anita Lobel's biography of her experiences in the Holocaust in *No Pretty Picture: A Child of War* (1998). By carefully matching curricular objectives and young adult trade books, teachers can ensure that students learn appropriate social studies and history concepts. These same books can then be used in the English/language arts classroom for a study of literature. The ultimate goal should be to incorporate as much young adult literature as possible into the curriculum and to use young adult books to make curriculum connections across disciplines.

FIGURE 11–1 *Integrating Literature into the Curriculum*

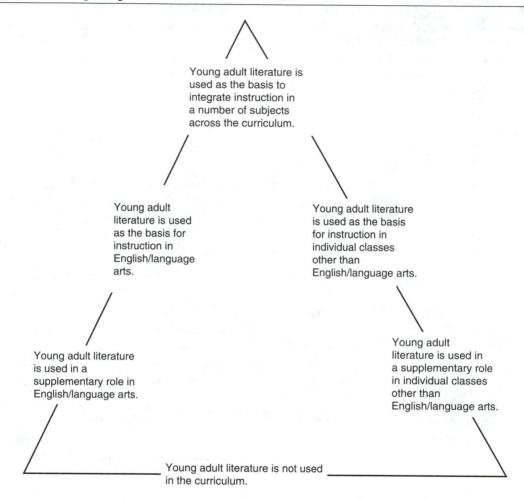

Young adult literature is used as the basis to integrate instruction in a number of subjects across the curriculum.

Young adult literature is used as the basis for instruction in English/language arts.

Young adult literature is used as the basis for instruction in individual classes other than English/language arts.

Young adult literature is used in a supplementary role in English/language arts.

Young adult literature is used in a supplementary role in individual classes other than English/language arts.

Young adult literature is not used in the curriculum.

Rationale and Advantages

Students do not learn "subject content" only from textbooks. In fact, textbooks often break knowledge down into formal clusters of information that do not encourage reader interest, content acquisition, and meaningful retention (Smith & Johnson, 1993). In contrast, young adult trade books have the potential for making the curriculum content more understandable, comprehensible, and meaningful. For example, rather than reading in a science or health textbook about good nutrition, healthy eating, and food disorders, adolescents can read appropriate literature including both fiction and nonfiction as shown in Figure 11–2. While the fiction books can form the basis for class discussion, the nonfiction books can be used to provide additional health information for adolescents.

FIGURE II–2 *Books for Healthy Eating*

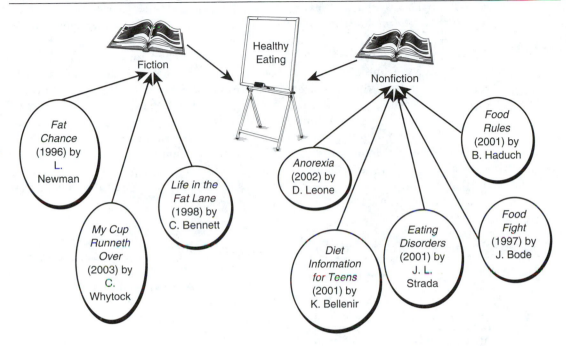

There are many benefits from using literature-based instruction. By reading and responding to young adult literature, students:

■ learn content material in all curricular areas and learn to identify meanings in what they read;

■ discover knowledge and make meaning by examining age-appropriate problems, values, issues, and concerns;

■ reinforce other language skills including talking, writing, and listening;

■ respond, analyze, synthesize, and organize ideas in meaningful content; and

■ read and write often about their thoughts and ideas rather than simply concentrating on the mastery of facts and concepts in a given subject (Gerlach, 1992).

As you think about using young adult literature throughout the curriculum, you might wonder if there are enough quality books that support the curriculum. Fortunately, with the steadily increasing quantity and quality of young adult books, with the skills to select quality literature, the advice of a qualified library media specialist, and the resources of school library media centers and public libraries, all teachers who are committed to using appropriate young adult literature will be able to locate sufficient resources. It is important for teachers and LMS to work collaboratively and identify appropriate books for young adults to read in the various content areas. Although we cannot provide an exhaustive listing of books for each content area, we can show some representative examples. Then, you can use these examples to guide you as you develop more specific lists for your own subject content.

In most cases, educators can use a selection of both fiction and nonfiction books (as we did in the previous example) in all of the subject disciplines. While nonfiction will inform the reader of the facts of a particular event or issue, fiction will show how the topic, event, or issue affects humans—the decisions, the happiness, the sadness, the triumphs, the failures, and the injustices. While educators must be sure that they help students understand the differences between fiction and nonfiction and keep from confusing the two, adolescents can gain considerable insights as they read fictional accounts. Figure 11–3 shows fiction and nonfiction that could be used with a curriculum unit on the conflict in the Middle East and central Asia, and Figure 11–4 shows literature that could be used with a science unit on ecology.

FIGURE 11–3 *Literature on the Conflict in the Middle East and Central Asia*

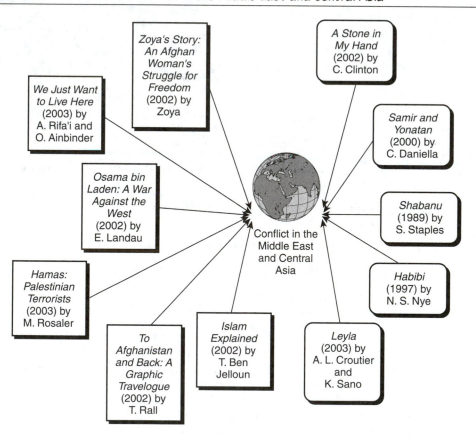

FIGURE 11-4 *Literature on Ecology and Conservation*

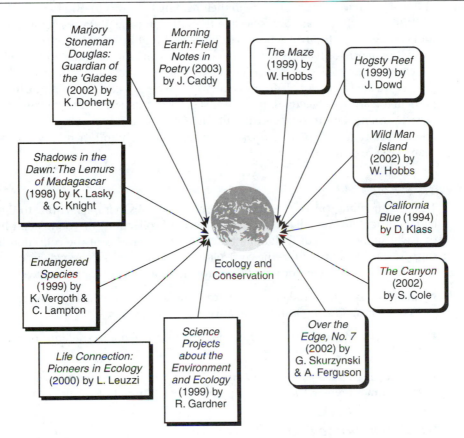

Feasibility

Can literature-based approaches be implemented in all curricular areas? From a realistic perspective, teachers in some curricular areas such as mathematics (particularly more advanced subjects such as algebra and trigonometry) will likely experience difficulty locating appropriate trade books. However, even with mathematics there are some young adult books that teachers can use. Pinchback (2000) reports using *A Gebra Named A1* (Isdell, 1993) with gifted middle school students. The novel combines fiction with real math and science to tell the story of a frustrated algebra student. Other good choices for a mathematics class are David Blatner's *The Joy of [Pi]* (1997) and Hans Magnus Enzensberger's *The Number Devil* (1998). Whitin's and Wilde's *Read Any Good Math Lately?* (1992) and Kathryn Kaczmarksi's *Exploring Math with Books Kids Love* (1998) are excellent resources for teachers. We believe that all teachers can find at least one book per grading period or semester that relates to the topics being taught. Literature-based instruction can help readers perceive relationships between curricular areas, develop an appreciation for both young adult literature and the reading process, gain an awareness of literary characteristics, and extend their reading horizons to other areas.

While we wholeheartedly believe in the value of using literature across the curriculum and as a basis for instruction, we also believe that it is important to determine the feasibility of using literature with a particular topic before planning literature-based instruction. Some topics simply do not lend themselves to a literature-based approach. Also, there are times when educators might not feel they can use literature to teach the particular learning objectives. In these instances, rather than adopting a contrived approach, teachers need to teach without a literature-based approach or to use literature (poetry, short stories, picture books) as an introduction and/or reinforcement rather than the core of the lesson.

Educators' Roles

Teachers and library media specialists have essential roles in implementing the literature-based curriculum. Together they need to develop collections of young adult literature that will support the curriculum and then identify portions of the collection that will support specific units within the curriculum. They also need to provide learning activities and educational environments that provide students with opportunities to:

- make choices about the books they read, the projects in which to engage, whether to work individually or in Cooperative Learning Groups.

- learn tasks relating to or building upon existing schema or students' previous learning and life experiences.

- learn cooperatively and collaboratively in an accepting and nonthreatening environment where they feel both physically and psychologically safe.

Identifying Appropriate Books

Before making a decision concerning whether to use literature with a particular unit, educators need to identify and consider the availability of appropriate books. Teachers and LMS should work collaboratively to determine:

- Are novels, nonfiction, and/or other forms of literature available for use? In the LMC? Public library? As classroom sets?

- Are these books on appropriate reading and interest levels?

- Do the books meet the criteria for good literature in their genre?

- Do these books provide accurate and unbiased perspectives?

- If the topic relates to multicultural issues, are the books free of stereotypes?

- Do these books show more than one dimension or perspective (i.e., an appropriate book on war shows the various perspectives and participants of war)?

- Do these books logically lend themselves to the subject areas and the particular topics under discussion?

- Do these books show well-rounded characters in more than one-dimensional terms?

- Will these books motivate young adults to think critically about what they read and to relate the events to what they have learned previously and what they are presently learning?

- Do these books promote higher-order thinking?

When necessary, educators can use picture books and easy reading chapter books as well as young adult literature, nonprint resources, and expository texts from various sources including newspapers, the Web, and magazines to build background knowledge on either the topic or the theme. It is important that educators select the best literature, rather than just choosing a book because it is available. In Chapter 2 and throughout the genre chapters in this book, we have noted resources that educators can use to identify appropriate young adult literature. These range from best books lists and award winners to Internet sites and print bibliographies.

Full-Length Young Adult Literature. Educators have always faced the dilemma of whether to use full-length books or selections from an anthology. Increasingly, educators are using full-length books for both large- and small-group instruction. Whether all students in the class read the same book or small groups of students with similar reading and overall ability levels read a particular book, this practice builds students' appreciation for literature; teaches story structures, genres, and themes; and increases both reading abilities and broadens reading interests. This does not mean that educators should not use shorter pieces of literature such as short stories or poetry. Both are excellent choices for SSR as well as for introductions and reinforcement.

Young Adult Literature and the Classics. A number of teachers are reluctant to use young adult literature as a basis for instruction in middle and high schools and, for a number of reasons, prefer to focus on "the classics." While some of these teachers are successful, others succeed only in alienating adolescent readers and convincing them that reading is pure misery. Our favorite response to the question "Why shouldn't adolescents read the classics?" is to use the example of a fish and vegetables. You do not go fishing by putting a piece of broccoli on a hook and dangling it in a lake. Instead, you put a nice tasty worm or a professionally endorsed lure on your fishing rod. Quality, well-written young adult literature can be the tasty worm in your classroom that will encourage adolescents to read and maybe, eventually, to feel comfortable tackling the classics.

If you do want to include some classics in your literature instruction, we encourage you to team the classics with young adult literature. One way to do that is to look for books with similar themes or plots. For example, *Romiette and Julio* (Draper, 1999) has a similar plot to Shakespeare's *Romeo and Juliet,* while *Witness* (Hesse, 2001) addresses some of the issues found in *To Kill a Mockingbird. Soldier's Heart* (Paulsen, 1998) can likewise be paired with *The Red Badge of Courage.* Young adult novels can also be used to provide additional information about a period in history or about a particular setting or event in preparation for the reading of a classic. A number of resources are available to help teachers identify literature pairings such as the series *Adolescent Literature as a Complement to the Classics,* which is edited by Joan F. Kaywell (1993–2000); *From Hinton to*

Hamlet: Building Bridges Between Young Adult Literature and the Classics (1996) by Sarah K. Herz with Donald R. Gallo; and *Heirs to Shakespeare: Reinventing the Bard in Young Adult Literature* (2000) by Megan Lynn Isaac.

Reader Response and Young Adult Literature

Teachers who use literature as the focal point of instruction need to be familiar with reader response theory, sometimes called a *transactional view of literature,* in which a reader draws meanings from and makes response to literature based on her or his background experiences. Rosenblatt (1978, 1989) describes reading literature as a transaction between the reader and the text, whether a novel, poem, short story, or play. Whenever students read, they take a reading stance (i.e., readers read literature for enjoyment or appreciation (which Rosenblatt terms *aesthetic*) or for learning (which she calls *efferent*)). While a reader's stance may remain constant in some works, it may vacillate within others. For example, a student may take an efferent stance while reading nonfiction but may switch to an aesthetic stance when viewing the illustrations (which appeal to a reader's past experiences or values) in the same book.

Drawing upon past experiences, personality, and memories, readers relate to the new experiences found in literature and make decisions about the theme, the characters, setting, plot, conflict, contrasts, and the author's style. On another transactional level, readers decide what the book means and make inferences about the meanings of the literature. Readers, as individuals, enter into their own transaction with the text, and each reader's transaction will be unique. In a group, each reader will respond differently, based upon her or his individual and personal sense of consciousness. Similarly, if a teacher or LMS reads literature aloud, the reader's tone, emphasis, and ability to read aloud may influence young people's meaning-making. While readers will make personal meanings and responses from their readings, the teacher or LMS should help readers interpret the various literary aspects and help readers identify clues that contribute to meaningful responses, provide time for experiencing personal meanings, and encourage readers to develop respect for both their and others' initial meanings.

Reading/Responding Activities to Encourage Learning. When young adults read and respond to literature, they should do more than memorize facts or summarize the plot. Instead, they should employ the full range of mental traits that comprise critical thinking (Gerlach, 1992).

According to Gerlach (1992):

> If the literature is to have meaning for readers, the readers must construct it and order it for themselves. They must respond, analyze, synthesize, organize, apply, and evaluate—all of which are tools of learning—in order to make meaning and demonstrate an understanding of literature as it applies to their own lives.
> Through reading and responding to young adult literature, readers come to search for and make knowledge of their worlds. (p. 120)

Thus, educators not only need to motivate students to read novels and other literature, but they also need to teach students to respond to books, question characters' actions and motives, and ask why authors chose a particular style or point of view. Reading requires thought. When young adults simply read words without paying attention to detail, issues, and events, they are not gaining the skills necessary for learning and the dispositions to become lifelong readers. To help students develop these skills and attitudes, teachers and LMS need to talk individually with readers or establish Cooperative Learning Groups in which adolescents can engage in reading and responding activities with their peers. In turn, these practices will help eager and enthusiastic adolescents read, enjoy, and share the books they read. Connecting Adolescents and Their Literature 11–5 explores one way to encourage reading. Later in this chapter, you will discover other strategies to allow adolescents to respond to literature.

Literature-Based Reading Guide. There are many ways to incorporate literature into a unit and to encourage adolescents to respond to that literature. However, in a true literature-based unit, the literature will become the core. In that instance, a single book may be used for all students or there may be a core book that everyone reads and then four or five supplementary books that are read by small groups of students. When a single book takes the central role, teachers need to develop or identify activities that

CONNECTING   *ADOLESCENTS AND THEIR LITERATURE 11–5*

According to Dreher (2003), adolescents like oral reading—they like teachers to read aloud and they like to read aloud to each other. One of the benefits of reading aloud is that it increases the engagement, confidence, and ability of all students.

To take advantage of these preferences, teachers can do the following:

- Form three groups. In one group students can be read to, in another they can read aloud to each other, and in the third group they can read silently.

- 3–4 days a week, devote 25–40 minutes (of a 55-minute class) to reading. Use the remaining time to
  - clarify questions,
  - discuss the day's readings,
  - prepare for more formal discussions, and
  - share journal reflections.
- Allow the students to change groups as they move through the unit.

Dreher (2003) found that, on some days, students wanted to listen, while on other days they wanted to read silently, and on other days, they wanted to read aloud. Still, almost every student moved through all three groups.

There are several ways to expand this reading aloud activity. In addition to reading aloud in their own classroom, adolescents can read aloud to younger students in an elementary school or in a public library. They can also use their oral reading skills to read aloud in other classrooms in their school or in the school library.

pertain to each of three reading stages: Pre-reading, during-reading, and after-reading. Table 11–1 identifies some sample strategies for each stage that teachers can modify to meet the needs, interests, and abilities of young adults in their classrooms. Then, Suggestions for Collaborative Efforts 11–2 shows how two teachers used a single young adult book in English and music.

TABLE 11–1	*Literature-Based Reading Strategies*

While there are a variety of instructional strategies that educators can use to help adolescents explore literature, the following are a few basic suggestions.

Pre-Reading Strategies

Set the stage and provide a foundation for reading.
Identify and organize students' prior knowledge of the book or topics in it.
Establish any necessary background.
Determine where students stand on issues they will encounter.
Arouse curiosity in the book.
Motivate students to read.

Sample Strategies

1. *Anticipation questions:* Use questions that ask students to think critically about the issues that they will find in the book. Responses may be oral or written in a journal.
2. *New vocabulary:* Present a list of new words found in the book.
3. *Booktalk:* Booktalk the novel to spark interest. This is especially effective when several books are used in a thematic unit.
4. *Predictions/Forecasting:* Use the cover and/or the title as the basis for making predictions about possible characters, actions, and problems that may arise in the story.
5. *Agree/Disagree statement:* Provide three to five controversial or thought-provoking statements related to the topics in the books. Students either agree or disagree and explain their reasons.
6. *Shared pairs:* Use a short sentence, poem, or list of words from the book and have each student quickly list as many associations as she or he can. Then pair students to share their lists. Next, have each pair share with another pair. Finally, have the groups of four share with the entire class.

During-Reading Strategies

Facilitate comprehension.
Focus attention on characters, issues, themes, or details.
Engage students in their reading.
Relate information from the book to the students' knowledge base.
Foster literary exploration of the elements of fiction.
Encourage reflection and personal responses to the reading.

TABLE 11–1	continued

Sample Strategies

1. *Maps, webs, and sketches:* Provide a visual representation of the characters, the plot, the conflict, or the issues. In character maps, include the main and/or supporting characters and their characteristics. Plot maps can identify major events, conflicts, and resolutions; while conflict maps can focus on the conflict, cause, participants, sources of support, and resolution, and issue maps show how a particular theme or issue is explored in the book and who supports it.
2. *Response journals and logs:* Write responses to teacher- or student-posed questions, make predictions, or provide reactions (written or visual) to the reading.
3. *Compare and contrast charts/activities:* Use charts to examine the similarities and differences between characters or between this book and another one.
4. *Discussion:* Use both small- and large-group discussions or literature circles to provide an opportunity for students to discuss their reading. Assign roles to each member of a small group such as discussion leader (develops and asks questions), illustrator (depicts a scene from the reading), travel tracer (maps the flow of the action from place to place), literary luminary (identifies passages that illustrate the author's style of writing), vocabulary enhancer (identifies and defines new vocabulary), and connector (makes connections with real life or other books).
5. *Dramatics:* Role-play or act out interactions between characters.
6. *Poetry:* Expand the format of the "Book Lice" poem from Paul Fleischman's *Joyful Noise: Poems for Two Voices* to compare and contrast the characters from the book (Van Horn, 2000).
7. *Writing:* Create biopoems, the diary of a character, dialogue between or among characters, or an essay evaluating the use of the elements of fiction.
8. *Dialogue journals:* Use dialogue journals in which students express their thoughts about the book or respond to questions. Journals are passed between a student and the teacher or between pairs of students for responses. Dionisio (1994) finds this is an excellent way to engage adolescents in a discussion of the elements of literature.
9. *Forecasting:* Predict outcomes based on current reading.
10. *Problem solving:* Determine what a character's problem is. Then list alternatives and criteria for solving the problem.
11. *Artistic representation:* Illustrate a scene or draw a character.

(continued)

TABLE 11–1	continued

After-Reading Strategies

Continue and pull together the during-reading activities.
Provide closure to the unit.
Move beyond the book itself.
Critically analyze and evaluate the book.
Relate the book to personal experiences.

Sample Strategies

1. *Drama:* Provide an oral interpretation (Readers' Theater) of important scenes from the book or develop a script for a follow-up scene. Gauweiler (2003) suggests extending the Readers' Theater idea by having students make a video production of a book.
2. *Analysis of literary style:* Re-read sections of a book to identify the elements of the author's style (similes, metaphor, repetition, etc.).
3. *Relationship web:* Use a graphic organizer to compare this book to others by the same author or on the same themes or issues. You can also use webs to compare the characters in the book to those in another book or to compare the elements of fiction in this book to another.
4. *Art:* Use art to create a collage or mobile with artifacts and quotes from the book, new dust jacket/cover for the book, diorama of a scene, T-shirt with a message from the book, or a quilt with each square representing the book. Deringer (2003) has additional visual response ideas.
5. *Music:* Write a song based on the book.
6. *Newspaper:* Create a newspaper using the information from the book with ads, news, features, and cartoons.
7. *Research:* Research and report on a topic that comes from the story.
8. *Storyboards:* Reconstruct the story or write a sequel by creating major incident cards that represent the flow of the plot.
9. *Menu:* Develop a menu for a restaurant that one of the characters in the book might open. For help in developing the menu, read the article by Susan H. Smith (2003).
10. *Poetry:* Create "found poems" (Hobgood, 1998) by selecting a passage in the novel and turning it into a poem.

Thematic Literature Studies

While individual pieces of literature are often the focus of a unit, a thematic literature unit can add depth to the topic(s) being studied. Kettel and Douglas (2003) argue that the one-text-at-a-time tradition "reinforces a student's beliefs that each text is an island, that each text stands alone" (Kettel & Douglas, 2003, p. 43). Instead, they call for multiple

11–2

SUGGESTIONS FOR COLLABORATIVE EFFORTS

While teachers often complete a literature unit within a single classroom, many opportunities exist for collaboration. Rief and Ervin (1994) describe a unit in which the reading of Katherine Paterson's *Lyddie* (1991) served as the basis for a research project and the development of an original musical. After reading *Lyddie,* students

- researched the Industrial Revolution,
- wrote their own story,
- turned it into a script, and
- developed the poetry for the lyrics of the songs in their Language Arts class.
  Then, in their music class, they
- refined the script and lyrics and
- set the lyrics to music.
  The final presentation occurred before parents, teachers, and other students.

text-single theme teaching. By selecting books with a similar theme but various levels of difficulty, teachers can involve all students in discussions. In addition to helping young adults see connections among books, this approach helps students of diverse reading abilities. By examining issues from a variety of perspectives, integrating information from diverse sources, and building upon young adults' own interests with materials that are consistent with the students' developmental levels, teachers can use literature to create units that are beneficial, meaningful, and relevant (Smith & Johnson, 1995).

Thematic units include some of the same activities as those presented previously in Table 11–1; however, they require slightly different planning by the teacher and LMS. Table 11–2 outlines this process. To be successful, teachers may need to forsake some traditional, teacher-directed instruction to provide time for group activities that may develop as part of the overall unit. The classroom environment will undergo changes and will reflect the student-centered, participatory nature of thematic units (Smith & Johnson, 1995). Expanding Your Knowledge with the Internet 11–2 provides links to a few literature units that you can examine for more ideas.

Book Discussions

In both single-book and multiple-text thematic units, educators use book discussions as an instructional strategy to encourage young adults to consider what they read. Sometimes these occur as whole-class discussions, while at other times teachers may use small literature circles or even one-on-one literature conversations (Beers & Probst, 1998). Although discussion plans should reflect the abilities and interests of a specific group of young adults and will vary with the specific books or books under discussion,

TABLE 11–2	Developing a Thematic Unit

In developing a thematic literature unit:

- Identify the theme
  - Review the state or district curricular framework for possible topics.
  - Informally survey students to determine their interests and prior knowledge.
- Set goals and select literature
  - Identify learning outcomes—Student knowledge and skills.
  - Consult with the LMS to identify possible literature.
  - Read possible selections and select the most appropriate.
  - Ensure a variety of literature with different perspectives including biographies, fiction, informational books, short stories, and poetry.
- Develop the instructional plan
  - Plan the learning activities for the unit.
  - Collaborate with the LMS and other teachers to identify specific content and interrelated concepts to be studied.
  - Plan specific lessons that develop the skills as well as knowledge needed to meet the learning outcomes.
  - Identify individual, small-group, and whole-group activities.
- Plan the unit assessments
  - Develop both formative and summative evaluations for students matching the assessments to the identified student outcomes.
  - Prepare rubrics for those assessments.
  - Develop an instructional assessment to evaluate the unit itself.
- Gather/prepare resources
  - Collect and organize materials and resources.
  - Schedule guest speakers, field trips, etc.
  - Schedule any special spaces such as labs, LMC, or the auditorium.
  - Inform administrators and parents of the scope and sequence of the unit.
- Implement the plan
- Evaluate the unit plan and your implementation of it (Based, in part, on Smith & Johnson, 1995)

some basic activities can be done with most literature. Table 11–3 provides some suggestions for discussions. Then, Suggestions for Collaborative Efforts 11–3 profiles a student/parent/teacher book discussion group.

LITERATURE FOR THE RELUCTANT READER

Unfortunately, it is a rare educator who does not have to deal with reluctant readers. Even young adults who enjoy reading are sometimes reluctant to read a particular book

EXPANDING | **YOUR KNOWLEDGE WITH THE INTERNET 11–2: SAMPLE BOOK UNITS**

A number of Web sites have sample book units (or links to sites) and thematic units featuring young adult literature. For example, there are K–12 literature: Lesson plans and classroom activities by book title at members.aol.com/DonnAnCiv/Literature.html and Florida State— English Education—WebQuests on literature (Classics and Young Adult) www.fsu.edu/~CandI/ENGLISH/web.htm. In this book's Companion Website at www.prenhall.com/bucher you will find links to these and other resources on literature units.

and may go through a transitory stage where they do not want to read. To help reluctant readers, teachers and LMS need to identify the cause and utilize a number of strategies to address the problem. Too often, the stereotype of a reluctant reader is a boy who has below grade level reading ability and little literature and/or encouragement to read at home. This stereotype might prove dead-wrong because often good readers are reluctant to read.

Young Adult Literature and the Reluctant Reader

One way to encourage reluctant readers is for educators to use quality young adult literature that addresses the needs of reluctant readers.

- Authors write young adult literature with adolescents' age level and interests in mind.

- While usually shorter and with an age-appropriate reading level, young adult literature can be well-written and more attractive than a reading book.

- The language and the plots of young adult literature are similar to what students are accustomed to finding in real life, on television, and in movies.

Methods of Encouraging Reluctant Readers

Educators are often concerned about why students begin to read less around the middle grades and how to motivate reluctant readers. With increased socialization, more difficult reading materials, and peer pressure that overshadows personal preferences, some adolescents read only for information and do not enjoy reading for pleasure. However, while it is helpful to understand why students read less, it is more productive to determine ways to motivate them to read.

Perhaps the best way to encourage reluctant readers is to get to know individual adolescents—their reading and interest levels and their reading preferences. Then, try some of the following strategies to encourage them:

- Provide a variety of books, both fiction and nonfiction, with appropriate reading levels.

TABLE 11-3	Suggestions For Book Discussions

The following suggestions can be modified for discussions of a variety of young adult literature. In addition, you will want to develop content-specific questions to include in the discussion.

Discussion after the first chapter(s)

1. What is your first reaction to this book?
2. What characters have you met and what do you know about them? How do you feel about these characters?
3. What types of conflict do you anticipate might occur in this book? What predictions can you make about the character's reactions to the conflict?
4. How would you describe the author's style of writing?
5. What are the setting and the point of view for the story?

Discussions during the first part of the book

1. Who are now the main characters in the book? Are they the same as in the initial chapters? How have they changed? What has caused the changes? Are there any characters that you particularly like or dislike? Why?
2. What now appears to be the main conflict in the book? Has it changed since the first chapter(s)? How are the characters dealing with the conflict? Are some handling the conflict better than others? Do any have a conflict style that might lead to trouble?
3. At this point in the book, knowing the conflict and the conflict styles of the characters, what predictions can you make?
4. Are there any characters who need to learn something about conflict management style? What should they know or be taught? Are they capable of change?
5. Whose point of view is the book told from? Does this person give us an honest story? Would other characters tell us different information?
6. Are there any parallels between this book and another book that you have read or with this book and real life?
7. How successful is the author in plotting the story and describing the characters?

Discussions at or near the end of the book

1. Review all of the choices that led up to the climax. Discuss the character's decision. At this point does the character have a real choice?
2. Have the characters learned anything or changed because of their experiences in the book?
3. What is the theme of the book? (Bushman & Haas, 2001; Stanford, 1996).

SUGGESTIONS FOR COLLABORATIVE EFFORTS

Book discussions are not limited to the classroom. In fact, a number of schools and some public libraries have successfully used book discussions as a way to bring young adults and literature together. Breen and Rubin (2003) describe a program in which more than 100 middle school students, their parents, and their teachers meet four times in the evening during the school year to discuss books. The program begins with a kick-off full of booktalks, skits, videos, and contests with refreshments to "melt the hearts of any doubting eighth-grade boys" (p. 9). After each parent/child team selects one of the four book choices for the month, they "locate the book, read it, discuss it at home, and come prepared for a book discussion at the following meeting" (p. 9). At the meeting (which also has door prizes and refreshments), the student/parent teams meet with others who have read the same book. While the initial discussions are led by teachers, later discussions are led by student facilitators.

- Stay in touch with adolescents' current interests and provide books that reflect these interests.

- Use booktalks to entice adolescents and to showcase a variety of books.

- Read books aloud and model enthusiasm for reading by carrying a book with you.

- Use audiobooks in classrooms and encourage adolescents to listen to them.

- Allow students to "self-select" their own books.

- Encourage an interest in short stories, graphic novels, and magazines and work up to full-length books.

- Use alternatives to traditional book reports.

- Give extra academic credit for books read while trying to get learners to read for more intrinsic rewards.

- Encourage students to realize they can read and still be accepted by peers.

- Use Internet resources to find out more about favorite authors.

- Respect the reading interests of young adults and do not expect them to enjoy only the books you suggest.

- Encourage parents and families to set aside "reading times" at home.

- Relate reading to video reinforcement—read the book, see the video.

- Provide an atmosphere conducive to reading—respect for books and comfortable places for reading—and perhaps appropriate background music.

- Encourage businesses and community organizations to donate age- and interest-appropriate books.

- Encourage student "booktalks," so adolescents can share the pleasures of motivating others to read.

- Encourage educators in all curricular areas to provide adolescents with reading opportunities.

- Form "reading clubs" and book discussion groups that provide adolescents an opportunity to discuss.

- Investigate the use of reading incentive programs such as Accelerated Reader where students receive points for reading and redeem the points for prizes.

- Encourage learners to bring their own books to school, ones they find interesting.

- Provide time for recreational reading, so learners realize reading is not always schoolwork.

- Incorporate more young adult literature into the curriculum to develop interest in and a love for books.

- Provide young adults with attractive book lists, divided by subject, interest, and reading levels. Be sure there are some "thin books" on the list.

- Have a classroom collection of books that students can check out.

Educators can use some resources to locate books for reluctant readers and to provide more ideas for reaching this audience. These include *More Rip-Roaring Reads for Reluctant Teen Readers* (1999) by Bette D. Ammon and Gale W. Sherman, *Reaching Reluctant Young Adult Readers: A Handbook for Librarians and Teachers* (2002) by Edward T. Sullivan, and *Radical Reads: 101 YA Novels on the Edge* (2002) by Joni Richards Bodart. Suggestions for Collaborative Efforts 11–4 looks at forming partnerships to reach reluctant readers.

SUGGESTIONS FOR COLLABORATIVE EFFORTS

Working collaboratively with other teachers, the library media specialist, one or two parent volunteers, and the public librarian, decide how to most effectively address the needs of "reluctant readers." Do you recommend special books? Special rewards? How can you determine why readers are reluctant to read? Perhaps your agenda could be: (a) determining problems and needs of reluctant learners; (b) planning a literature program (e.g., books, methods, motivational techniques) that addresses those needs; and (c) planning a means of evaluation to determine program success and needed changes.

DEVELOPING A COMMUNITY OF READERS

When educators incorporate literature across the curriculum, they can create a "community of readers" in which students develop the desire to become "lifelong readers" who read to gain information and to learn as well as read for pleasure. To create such a community, teachers and library media specialists need to promote reading by convincing students of the benefits of reading, modeling respect for and enjoyment of books and other forms of literature, providing well-written reading materials, and using literature across the curriculum to show how reading relates to all aspects of one's life. By creating an atmosphere conducive to learning and appreciating literature, having well-written books and other reading materials readily available, allowing students to select books and reading materials based upon their interest, and making time available for reading during class, educators have an opportunity to foster a love of literature and promote a community of readers that will continue to read as adults. Expanding Your Knowledge with the Internet 11–3 has more ideas for reaching young adults and turning them into readers.

CONCLUDING THOUGHTS

To foster lifelong reading, teachers and library media specialists need to know appropriate books and other types of literature and make a powerful commitment to incorporating literature in as many curricular areas as possible. While literature should be a focal point in individual curricular areas, the greater emphasis should be on a literature-based curriculum using full-length young adult books. Such an approach will show readers how literature has a place in all curricular areas and also contribute to the concept of a community of learners and the promotion of lifelong readers. The success of these efforts will depend upon educators' commitment to plan and teach young adult literature throughout the curriculum. Visit this book's

EXPANDING **YOUR KNOWLEDGE WITH THE INTERNET 11-3**

Find more ideas for reaching reluctant readers and for turning adolescents onto the Internet at sites such as those listed below. Links directly to these resources and others like them are on this book's Companion Website at www.prenhall.com/bucher.

ALA Quick Picks For Reluctant Young Adult Readers

www.ala.org/yalsa/booklists/quickpicks

Cool Books For Tough Guys

scholar.lib.vt.edu/ejournals/ALAN/fall94/Baines.html

Companion Website at www.prenhall.com/bucher for additional information about teaching young adult literature including review questions, self-assessments, Internet sites, and young adult literature and readings.

Young Adult Books

 This section includes young adult titles recommended or mentioned in this chapter. Check the Companion Website at www.prenhall.com/bucher to find additional suggestions of current young adult literature.

Bellenir, K. (Ed.). (2001). *Diet information for teens: Health tips about diet and nutrition.* Detroit, MI: Omnigraphics. This book contains general sections on meal planning and specialized diets as well as information on eating disorders.

Ben Jelloun, T. (2002). *Islam explained.* New York: New Press. In addition to relating the history of Islam, the author explains Muslim beliefs.

Bennett, C. (1998). *Life in the fat lane.* New York: Delacorte. Lara cannot understand why, despite all of her attempts to diet and exercise, she keeps gaining weight.

Blatner, D. (1997). *The joy of [Pi].* New York: Walker. History, poetry, humor, and math collide in this book.

Bode, J. (1997). *Food fight: A guide to eating disorders for preteens and their parents.* New York: Simon & Schuster. Bode provides helpful information about anorexia, bulimia, and compulsive overeating.

Caddy, J. (2003). *Morning earth: Field notes in poetry.* Minneapolis, MN: Milkweed Editions. Poetry about nature and the seasons.

Carmi, D. (2000). *Samir and Yonatan.* New York: Scholastic. A Palestinian boy finds himself in an Israeli hospital with a broken leg.

Clinton, C. (2002). *A stone in my hand.* Cambridge, MA: Candlewick. In the violence in Gaza between the Jews and Palestinians, Malaak's father and brother join the Islamic Jihad.

Cole, S. (2002). *The canyon.* New York: HarperCollins. When a land company wants to develop a canyon, Zach leads the opposition.

Croutier, A. L., & Sano, K. (2003). *Leyla: The black tulip.* Middleton, WI: Pleasant Company. In the 1720s, a young girl in Turkey tries to help her family and ends up on the Topkapi Palace in Istanbul.

Daniella, C. (2000). *Samir and Yonatan.* New York: Arthur A. Levine. The story of a young Palestinian boy who becomes the friend of an Israeli boy.

Doherty, K. (2002). *Marjory Stoneman Douglas: Guardian of the 'Glades.* Brookfield, CT: Twenty-First Century. Douglas was a strong environmentalist who devoted her life to protecting the Everglades.

Dowd, J. (1999). *Hogsty Reef.* Atlanta, GA: Peachtree Publishers. While helping their father study reef ecology, Jim and Julia become involved in a mystery. The sequel is *Rare & Endangered* (2000).

Draper, S. (1999). *Romiette and Julio.* New York: Atheneum. An African American girl and a Hispanic boy meet on the Internet and fall in love.

Enzensberger, H. M. (1998). *The number devil.* New York: Holt. When his math teacher refuses to let him use a calculator, Robert gets help from a strange person.

Feelings, T. (1995). *The middle passage: White ships, black cargo.* New York: Dial. Feelings uses 64 paintings in his depiction of the middle passage.

Gardner, R. (1999). *Science projects about the environment and ecology.* Hillside, NJ: Enslow. Projects for middle and high school students.

Haduch, B. (2001). *Food rules: The stuff you munch, its crunch, its punch, and why you sometimes lose your lunch.* New York: Dutton. This book is filled with fun food facts along with good nutrition information.

Hesse, K. (1997). *Out of the dust.* New York: Scholastic. In a series of poems, Billie Jo tells about growing up in Oklahoma during the dust bowl.

Hesse, K. (2001). *Witness.* New York: Scholastic. Everyone has his or her own story to tell when the Ku Klux Klan comes to Vermont in the 1920s.

Hobbs, W. (1999). *The maze.* New York: Morrow. Can Rick and a bird biologist protect the condors in a remote canyon?

Hobbs, W. (2002). *Wild man island.* New York: HarperCollins. A storm strands Andy on remote Admiralty Island, Alaska.

Isdell, W. (1993). *A gebra named Al.* Minneapolis, MN: Free Spirit. Julie, a frustrated algebra student, takes a journey to the Land of Mathematics.

Klass, D. (1994). *California blue.* New York: Scholastic. The butterfly that John found may mean that the mill where his father works will have to close.

Landau, E. (2002). *Osama bin Laden: A war against the west.* Brookfield, CT: Twenty-First Century Books. Landau presents information about militant Islamic leader Osama bin Laden and the beliefs that fuel his terrorist actions.

Lasky, K. (1996). *True north: A novel of the underground railroad.* New York: Scholastic. Fourteen-year-old Lucy helps a fugitive slave girl.

Lasky, K., & Knight, C. (1998). *Shadows in the dawn: The lemurs of Madagascar.* San Diego: Harcourt. The authors showcase the work of a primatologist to show the relationships of people and animals in a fragile habitat.

Leone, D. (Ed.). (2002). *Anorexia.* San Diego: Greenhaven. This is a collection of personal essays.

Leuzzi, L. (2000). *Life connections: Pioneers in ecology.* New York: Scholastic. Leuzzi profiles eight scientists.

Lobel, A. (1998). *No pretty picture: A child of war.* New York: Greenwillow. Anita Lobel takes readers back to her experiences as a Jewish child in Poland in World War II, her capture by the Nazis, and her later life in Sweden after the war. This was a 1999 Orbis Pictus honor book.

Lyons, M. E. (1992). *Letters from a slave girl: The story of Harriet Jacobs.* New York: Aladdin. Through letters, Lyons tells this fictionalized version of the life of Harriet Jacobs in North Carolina in 1842.

Matas, C. (1998). *Greater than angels.* New York: Simon & Schuster. The people of Le Chambon-sur-Lignon in France are prepared to risk their lives to protect Jewish families.

Newman, L. (1996). *Fat chance.* New York: Putnam. Judi is obsessed with being thin. But can she become too thin?

Nye, N. S. (1997). *Habibi.* New York: Simon & Schuster. Liyana's father moves the family from St. Louis, MO, to Jerusalem.

Paterson, K. (1991). *Lyddie*. New York: Dutton. A young girl becomes a mill girl in Lowell, Massachusetts.

Paulsen, G. (1998). *Soldier's heart: Being the story of the enlistment and due service of the boy Charley Goddard in the first Minnesota volunteers*. New York: Delacorte. Charley leaves Minnesota full of the glory he will find in the Civil War. He returns full of the horrible images of the war.

Rall, T. (2002). *To Afghanistan and back: A graphic travelogue*. New York: NBM. Rall uses the format of a graphic "novel" to recount his experience in a war zone in this frank, often disturbing book.

Rifa'i, A., & Ainbinder, O., with Tempel, S. (2003). *We just want to live here: A Palestinian teenager, an Israeli teenager—An unlikely friendship*. New York: St. Martin's. First meeting in an exchange program in Switzerland, two teenagers exchange the letters that make up this book.

Rosaler, M. (2003). *Hamas: Palestinian terrorists*. New York: Rosen. This book presents the history and activities of this terrorist group.

Skurzynski, G., & Ferguson, A. (2002). *Over the Edge, No. 7*. Washington, DC: National Geographic Society. The life of a scientist studying condors in the Grand Canyon is threatened.

Stanley, J. (1992). *Children of the Dust Bowl: The true story of the school at Weedpatch Camp*. New York: Crown. Stanley tells of the school that was built for the children of migrant workers during the Depression.

Staples, S. F. (1989). *Shabanu: Daughter of the wind*. New York: Knopf. In Pakistan, 11-year-old Shabanu is pledged to marry an older man.

Strada, J. L. (2001). *Eating disorders*. San Diego: Lucent. Strada looks at bulimia, anorexia, and binge eating and what they tell teens about self-perception.

Taylor, M. (2001). *The land*. New York: Phyllis Fogelman. The son of a plantation owner and a slave, Paul-Edward Logan tells his story of life during reconstruction in the American south.

Vergoth, K., & Lampton, C. (1999). *Endangered species*. New York: Scholastic. This book provides an excellent overview of the subject.

Whytock, C. (2003). *My cup runneth over: The life of Angelica Cookson Potts*. New York: Simon and Schuster. Angel loves to cook and to eat, but she is concerned about getting too fat.

Zoya with Folian, J., & Cristofari, R. (2002). *Zoya's story: An Afghan woman's struggle for freedom*. New York: Morrow. A young woman from Afghanistan tells of her life under the rule of the Taliban and the Mujahideen.

Suggested Readings

Blau, S. (2003). Perfomative literacy: The habits of mind of highly literate readers. *Voices from the Middle, 10*(3), 18–22.

Bowman, C., & Edenfield, R. (2003). Adrian Fogelin's fiction in the middle school classroom. *The ALAN Review, 30*(2), 10–12. (Author Unit)

Carger, C. L. (2003). Stitches in time: Two novels about embroidery. *Book Links, 12*(6), 7–11. (Thematic literature unit)

Carroll, P. S., & Gregg, G. P. (2003). Literature-based instruction for middle school readers: Harry Potter and more. *The ALAN Review, 30*(3), 60–64.

Johnnessen, L. R. (2003). Strategies for initiating authentic discussion. *English Journal, 93*(1), 73–77.

Quinn, K. B., Barone, B., Kearns, J., Stackhouse, S. A., & Zimmerman, M. E. (2003). Using a novel unit to help understand and prevent bullying in schools. *Journal of Adolescent & Adult Literacy, 46*(7), 582–591.

Schneider, D. (2003). Zimbabwe 2194: A future odyssey. *Book Links, 12*(5), 28–31. (Single book unit)

References

(Note: All young adult literature referenced in this chapter are included in the Young Adult Books list and are not repeated in this list.)

Ammon, B. D., & Sherman, G. W. (1999). *More rip-roaring reads for reluctant teen readers.* Englewood, CO: Libraries Unlimited.

Austin, P., & Harris, K. (1999). The audio argument, of sound advice about literature. *The New Advocate, 12*(3), 241–247.

Beers, K., & Probst, R. (1998). Classroom talk about literature or the social dimensions of a solitary act. *Voices from the Middle, 5*(2), 16–20.

Bodart, J. R. (2002). *Radical reads: 101 YA novels on the edge.* Lanham, MD: Scarecrow Press.

Breen, M., & Rubin, T. (2003). Readers are survivors: A middle school student/parent/teacher book discussion group. *Voices from the Middle, 10*(4), 8–10.

Bushman, J. H., & Haas, K. P. (2001). *Using young adult literature in the English classroom.* Upper Saddle River, NJ: Merrill/Prentice Hall.

Costello, J., Whalen, S., Spielberger, J., & Winje, C. J. (2001). Promoting public library partnerships with youth agencies. *Journal of Youth Services in Libraries, 15*(1), 8–15.

Cox, R. E. (2002). *Tantalizing tidbits for teens: Quick booktalks for the busy high school media specialist.* Worthington, OH: Linworth.

Deringer, M. L. (2003). Visual responses to YAL that encourage higher level thinking. *Voices from the Middle, 10*(4), 11–12.

Dionisio, M. (1994). Responding to literary elements through dialogue journals and minilessons. *Voices from the Middle, 1*(1), 12–17.

Donahue, D. (2003). Reading across the great divide: English and math teachers apprentice one another as readers and disciplinary insiders. *Journal of Adolescent & Adult Literacy, 47*(1), 24–37.

Dreher, S. (2003). A novel idea: Reading aloud in a high school English classroom. *English Journal, 93*(1), 50–53.

Fullner, S. K. (2003). Quickie kamishibai booktalks. *Library Media Connection, 21*(4), 31–33.

Gauweiler, C. N. (2003). From page to stage. *Voices from the Middle, 10*(4), 29–30.

Gerlach, J. M. (1992). The young adult novel across the curriculum. In V. R. Moneau & G. M. Salver (Eds.), *Reading their world: The young adult novel in the classroom* (pp. 113–131). Portsmouth, NJ: Boynton/Cook.

Gillespie, J. T., & Naden, C. J. (2003). *Teenplots: A booktalk guide to use with readers ages 12–18.* Westport, CT: Libraries Unlimited.

Herz, S. K., with Gallo, D. R. (1996). *From Hinton to Hamlet: Building bridges between young adult literature and the classics.* Westport, CT: Greenwood.

Hobgood, J. M. (1998). Finders keepers: Owning the reading they do. *Voices from the Middle, 5*(2), 26–33.

Isaac, M. L. (2000). *Heirs to Shakespeare: Reinventing the bard in young adult literature.* Portsmouth, NH: Boynton/Cook.

Ishizuka, K. (2003). Preparing teens for the future: A new mix of life skills and career programs has teens rushing to their local libraries. *School Library Journal, 49*(7), 46.

Jones, P. (2002). New directions for serving young adults means building more than our collections. *Journal of Youth Services in Libraries, 15*(3), 21–23.

Joseph, R. J. (1998). "Is this really English?" Using young adult literature in an urban middle school. *Voices from the Middle, 5*(2), 21–25.

Kaczmarski, K. (1998). *Exploring math with books kids love.* Golden, CO: Fulcrum.

Kaiser, M. M. (1999). Listen my children and you shall hear: Audio books for young adults. *The ALAN Review, 26*(3), 18–20.

Kaywell, J. (Ed.). (1993–2000). *Adolescent literature as a complement to the classics* (Vols. 1-IV). Norwood, MA: Christopher-Gordon.

Kettel, R. P., & Douglas, N. L. (2003). Comprehending multiple texts: A theme approach incorporating the best of children's literature. *Voices from the Middle, 11*(1), 43–49.

Langemack, C. (2003). *The booktalker's bible: How to talk about the books you love to any audience.* Westport, CT: Libraries Unlimited.

Locke, D. (2001). Heard any good books lately? *Book Links, 11*(2), 26–29.

Machado, J., Lentz, B., Wallace, R., & Honig-Bear, S. (2000). A survey of best practices in youth services around the country: A view from one library. *Journal of Youth Services in Libraries, 15*(2), 30–35.

Meyers, E. (2001). The road to coolness: Youth rock to the public library. *American Libraries, 32*(2), 46.

Pinchback, C. L. (2000). Using literature in mathematics: Gifted students' comments. *Gifted Child Today, 24*(1), 36–43.

Rief, L., with Ervin, D. (1994). Threads of life: Reading, writing, and music. *Voices from the Middle, 1*(1), 18–28.

Rosenblatt, L. M. (1978). *The reader, the text, the poem: The transactional theory of the literary work.* Carbondale, IL: Southern Illinois Press.

Rosenblatt, L. M. (1989). Writing and reading: The transactional theory. In J. M. Mason (Ed.), *Reading and writing connections* (pp. 153–176). Boston: Allyn and Bacon.

Schall, L. (2001). *Booktalks plus: Motivating teens to read.* Englewood, CO: Libraries Unlimited.

Schall, L. (2003). *Booktalks and more: Motivating teens to read.* Englewood, CO: Libraries Unlimited.

Smith, J. L., & Johnson, H. A. (1993). Bringing it together: Literature in an integrative curriculum. *Middle School Journal, 25*(1), 3–7.

Smith, J. L., & Johnson, H. A. (1995). Dreaming of America: Weaving literature into middle school social studies. *The Social Studies, 86,* 60–68.

Smith, S., with Hickey, B. (2003). Menu magic! *Voices from the Middle, 19*(4), 13–15.

Stanford, B. (1996). Coping with conflict in adolescent life and adolescent literature. Presentation at the National Council of Teachers of English, Chicago, IL, November 23, 1996.

Sullivan, E. T. (2002). *Reading reluctant young adult readers: A handbook for librarians and teachers*. Lanham, MD: Scarecrow Press.

Thomas, C., & Littlejohn, C. (2003). *Still talking that book! Booktalks to promote reading grades 3–12*. Worthington, OH: Linworth Publishing.

Thorp, C. (2002). Reading and writing in the content areas. *Educational Leadership, 60*(3), 96.

Tuccillo, D. P. (2003). Getting teens hooked on reading: What public librarians can do for teachers today. *The ALAN Review, 30*(2), 63–65.

Van Horn, L. (2000). Young adult literature: An entrée into the joys of reading. *Voices from the Middle, 8*(2), 40–48.

Whitin, D., & Wilde, S. (1992). *Read any good math lately?* Portsmouth, NH: Heinemann.

Whitten, R. F. (1998). A+ for audiobooks. *Audiobook Reviews & Information, 6*(9), 17–19.

Young, T. E. (2003). Working booktalks and bookchats; Tidbits that tantalize. *Knowledge Quest, 32*(1), 62–63.

12

PROTECTING INTELLECTUAL FREEDOM

CHAPTER OVERVIEW

What do Phyllis Reynolds Naylor's Alice series of books, John Steinbeck's *Of Mice and Men,* J. K. Rowling's Harry Potter series, Mark Twain's *The Adventures of Huckleberry Finn* (1885), and Katherine Paterson's *Bridge to Terabithia* (1977) have in common? All of these books reside among the top 10 of the American Library Association's Most Frequently Challenged Books of 1990–2000 (American Library Association, "The 100 Most Frequently Challenged Books of 1990–2000").

As you can see from the diversity among these books, censorship can happen to any type of literature. Thus, teachers and library media specialists need to be aware of the problems caused by censorship and must support and protect intellectual freedom. Unfortunately, authors, educators, young people, and all individuals who value the freedom to read or to write whatever they wish often face the threat of censorship from people who try to impose their value systems or set restrictions on what others can read or write.

As you read this chapter, you should understand that we firmly believe in the rights of all individuals to freedom of expression and the right to read. We also believe that parents have the right and responsibility to make decisions for their own children. However, our concerns arise when a single individual or group tries to dictate what all individuals in a school may read and when materials are removed from a school without following the materials reconsideration policies of that school division.

| FOCUSING POINTS | In this chapter, you will read about: |

1. Definitions of censorship, intellectual freedom, and the relationship between the two.
2. Differences between censorship and selection.
3. Relying on review sources and awards.
4. Parental rights versus censorship.
5. Forms of censorship.
6. Censorship through the ages.
7. Landmark court decisions that affect intellectual freedom.
8. Censorship today and contemporary motives and targets of censorship.
9. Professional organizations that support intellectual freedom, their goals, and efforts.
10. Documents that support intellectual freedom.
11. Ways to cope with censorship and assaults on intellectual freedom.

DEFINING CENSORSHIP, INTELLECTUAL FREEDOM, AND SELECTION

Censorship is nothing new and its effects are constantly felt throughout society. As a result, authors may be afraid to write about certain topics and may intentionally delete or change language or characters that some readers might find offensive. Publishers may reject manuscripts that contain controversial topics, and libraries and schools may decide not to purchase materials if they believe those materials might be the target of censorship. In order to understand what is happening in each of these instances, it is important to understand the differences between censorship and intellectual freedom as well as the difference between censorship and the selection of materials.

Censorship, Intellectual Freedom, and the Relationship Between Them

The American Library Association defines *censorship* as the suppression of ideas and information that certain individuals, groups, or government officials find objectionable or dangerous (American Library Association, "Intellectual freedom and censorship: Q & A"). In general, people act as censors when they examine books, periodicals, dramas, films, television and radio programs, and other forms of communication in order to identify and even suppress the parts that they consider offensive. The rationale for their actions lies in their belief that they have the correct view of what is truthful and appropriate and that they must impose these views on others in order to protect three basic social institutions: the family, the church, or the nation (Konvitz, 2003). These people assume that if a book goes against their personal beliefs, then it must be wrong,

TABLE 12–1	Reasons For Censoring Items

The following reasons for censoring items are listed in order from most frequent to least frequent.

American Library Association[1]	Analysis by Curry[2]
Sexually explicit material	Profanity
Offensive language	Heterosexual activity
Unsuited to age group	Homosexuality
Occult theme/promoting occult or Satanism	Sexual activity deemed immoral or illegal
Violence	Religion/witchcraft
Homosexual theme	Violence/horror
Promoting religious viewpoint	Rebellion
Nudity	Racism/sexism
Racism	Substance use/abuse
Sex education	Suicide/death
Anti-family	Crime
	Crude behavior
	Depressing/negative

Developed from information in the following sources:
[1]American Library Association. Challenged and banned books. Retrieved March 1, 2004, from www.ala.org/ala/oif/bannedbooksweek/challengedbanned/challengedbanned.htm.
[2]Curry, A. (2001). Where is Judy Blume? Controversial fiction for older children and young adults. *Journal of Youth Services in Libraries, 14*(3), 28–37.

offensive to others, and might negatively influence young minds. Table 12–1 identifies some of the most common reasons for censoring materials.

In their quest to mold the thinking of young adults, censors often believe that adolescents must read or see only the things that they, the adults, deem appropriate; that reflect the adults' views on living; and that espouse the positions that the adults support. These individuals may fear any reading that possibly deviates from their perception of the ideal (Greenbaum, 1997). Sometimes they distrust the inclusion in books of those topics and subjects that differ from when they were young. Thus, they may consider abortion, homosexuality, and incest to be inappropriate topics for young people to read about. While groups often lead the movement to censor certain items, censorship can be as simple as a single individual stating: "Don't let anyone read the book, or buy that magazine, or view that film, because I object to it!"

In contrast to censorship, *intellectual freedom* is the right of every individual both to seek and to receive information from all points of view without restriction (American Library Association, "Intellectual freedom and censorship: Q & A"). A basic tenet of a democratic system, intellectual freedom protects the rights of individuals to have free access to all expressions of ideas, and to examine all sides of a question, cause, or movement before making up their own minds. Traditionally, libraries and schools have provided the ideas and information, in a variety of formats, to allow people to become well-informed citizens. Intellectual freedom encompasses this freedom to hold, receive, and disseminate ideas (American Library Association, "Intellectual freedom and censorship: Q & A").

Censorship is tied very closely to intellectual freedom. A relationship also exists between censorship and freedom of speech, with censors exercising the freedom that they want to deny to others. Would-be censors are exercising their right to free speech, the same right that is also held by the creators and disseminators of the materials to which the censors are objecting. However, the rights of censors to voice their opinions and try to persuade others to adopt these opinions is protected only if the rights of the creators and disseminators to express those ideas are also protected. Unless the rights of both sides are protected, neither's rights will survive (American Library Association, "Intellectual freedom and censorship: Q & A"). In Expanding Your Knowledge with the Internet 12-1, you will find examples of Web sites that have basic information about intellectual freedom and censorship.

The Difference Between Censorship and Selection of Materials

Freedom and Johnson (2001) maintain that most censorship efforts have focused on the issue of who should have the authority to select the materials that are purchased for and used in schools. Undoubtedly, parents and guardians have the right to determine what their own children should read. However, the responsibility for selecting the materials that will form the basis for the curriculum and the school library collection usually falls on the shoulders of teachers and school library media specialists who identify books and other materials that have the potential to engage young adults and that are cognitively, socially, emotionally, and psychologically appropriate for them.

There is, however, a fine line between this selection of appropriate materials and censorship. In general terms, censorship is often associated with the removal of materials

---

EXPANDING | *YOUR KNOWLEDGE WITH THE INTERNET 12–1*

A number of Internet sites have information about intellectual freedom and censorship. A few are listed below. Visit this book's Companion Website at www.prenhall.com/bucher to link directly to these and many other sites.

American Library Association, Office of Intellectual Freedom
www.ala.org/ala/oif/Default622.htm

Banned Books Week
www.ala.org/ala/oif/bannedbooksweek/bannedbooksweek.htm

ProQuest/SIRS Intellectual Freedom Awards
www.sirs.com/corporate/freedom.htm

from a library or school; materials that have already been selected by educators to support the curriculum or to meet the needs of young adults for recreational reading. In contrast, selection calls for evaluation and a deliberate judgment (Sipe, 1999) to identify appropriate materials for adolescents that can be included in a school or library. As author Cynthia Grant noted: "the best collection is one that always makes you feel slightly uneasy" (Grant, 1995, p. 50).

Sometimes, however, the boundaries between censorship and selection begin to blur, and what one individual calls selection may actually be censorship. According to Suhor (2003), when teachers and librarians "select" materials they look at a wide range of items and decide what is best for the students and programs. However, when educators "censor" they intentionally look for undesirable language, characters, and themes. In a title analysis of the young adult book collections in a sample of Texas high school libraries, Coley (2002) found signs of self-censorship in over 80% of the schools.

Exclusion Versus Inclusion. There are instances when, as a school library media specialist or teacher deliberately and conscientiously selects books and other materials to include in a library collection or to incorporate into instruction, censorship consciously or unconsciously results. For example, a teacher might decide to exclude a book from a reading list because, even though the book is an award winner, there may be individuals in the community who would object to the book. Or, a library media specialist (LMS) might not order a particular book in spite of the fact that the book had excellent reviews. The LMS might rationalize this choice by citing budget limitations when, in actuality, the LMS thought there were passages in the book to which someone might object. There may also be instances where a subject or a particular author might remind the educator of a previous experience where censorship occurred or where someone made an actual complaint. In these cases, the educator does not really engage in a selection process because the book is never seriously considered. Suhor (2003) maintains that selection means that teachers develop lists of good books that are circulated as suggestions rather than prescriptions, while censorship means that teachers develop lists of "approved" books and specify ones that cannot be used.

Control Versus Advice. As these terms imply, teachers and library media specialists may feel pressure to select or not to select a book. For example, parents, community members, or groups may try to *control* the materials that are available in a school library or taught within the curriculum. If powerful, these censors can influence the school administration or the school board, and may be successful in preventing books from being used in the curriculum, appearing on reading lists, or being placed on library shelves by applying pressure or threatening legal action. By claiming that certain topics should not be discussed or presented in schools, these censors want to control what is appropriate for all young people. For example, if an educator knows that there is a very vocal group in the community that objects to the theory of evolution, the educator may refrain from purchasing books on evolution for the school library or using books in the classroom that talk about evolution. Rather than subjecting the books to the selection criteria of the school district, the educator has allowed the threat of censorship to control his or her actions.

While not as strong as control, *advice* can have an effect on selection or become a form of censorship. An individual or group may give advice about what schools should teach in the curriculum and/or add to the library's collection. Generally, those who give advice are more open to dialogue than those who seek to control. Unlike "censorship by control," advice can be beneficial if it opens a constructive dialogue in which individuals and educators are able to consider the positions of others.

Indoctrinate Versus Educate. Educators want to select and use books and works that offer a balanced perspective of issues and that *educate* or enlighten young adults to something new or unique. These materials should allow young adults to make their own informed decisions that are free from prejudice. In contrast, books and other reading materials that *indoctrinate* provide only one view of an issue. While it is possible to use these materials in a school, educators have to be careful to balance them with materials that present opposing points of view, and to be sure that all of these materials are equally accessible by young adults.

Isolation Versus the Work as a Whole. Sometimes when selecting materials, individuals can become censors when they fail to consider the entire work and focus only on a single "dirty" word or a so-called "controversial passage" (e.g., a sex scene, one or two uses of profanity, or a reference to one's sexual orientation). Educators must be careful that this form of censorship does not sneak into the selection process. For example, Jane Leslie Conly's *Crazy Lady* (1993) was chosen as a Newbery Honor Book, an ALA Notable, and an ALA Best Books for Young Adults. In the book, there are two mild profanities that upset some people (Reeder, 2002). When considering this book for a classroom or school library, an educator may be tempted to look only at these two words rather than to consider the entire book before making a decision on its appropriateness and whether to use it with young adults.

Relying on Review Sources and Awards: Benefits and Pitfalls

Although all teachers should read the books they plan to use in their classroom and preview all other materials, teachers may not have the time to read all the books on a booklist. Certainly, school library media specialists cannot read all of the materials that they select to include in the school library's collection. Instead of relying on the name recognition of an author (for example, Shel Silverstein wrote for *Playboy* as well as for children) or publishers' recommendations (publishers promote, not review, their own products), educators must turn to review sources and awards to assist in the selection process. In general, as you read in Chapter 2, most reviews are done by experts or at least readers who are genuinely interested in young adult literature. Reviews are readily found, usually in respected journals and magazines known for their focus on young adult materials. Even on Internet sources such as Amazon.com and Barnesandnoble.com, educators can locate reviews from reputable review sources.

There are, however, pitfalls in using reviews. In most instances, reviews are just one person's opinion and might reflect only that person's taste. Although most selection journals have written selection criteria, some reviewers may have a personal bias. In addition, published reviews do not always reflect local standards or values. A book or video that a reviewer finds acceptable for one community might be deemed offensive in another community. One of the authors of this book attended a panel discussion by book review editors that was held at a national conference. During the discussion, all of the panel participants noted that they did not feel it was necessary for their reviewers to note parts of the books that might be open to censorship challenges or that might be objectionable to some group.

Thus, an individual review source and/or award should be only one factor contributing to the selection of a book or other material for use in a school. The ideal is to locate several reviews or a combination of reviews and awards, to read each review completely, and to know exactly why the award is given and by whom. When there are conflicting reviews or when the reviews raise questions, teachers and library media specialists have a responsibility to read the book or view the item themselves, discuss the appropriateness with others in the school or community, and consider community norms and expectations before making a final selection. Throughout the selection process, educators need to keep in mind the selection policies of the school division in which they work as well as the documents that promote and defend intellectual freedom. Suggestions for Collaborative Efforts 12-1 points out the need for teachers and library media specialists to work together when selecting materials.

Parental Rights Versus Censorship

A fine line exists between the supervisory rights of parents and guardians and censorship. As we have stated before, parents are ultimately responsible for raising their children. Thus, educators should try to cooperate whenever a parent or guardian makes a request about specific materials that his or her child reads, hears, or sees in school. Following the

12-1

SUGGESTIONS FOR COLLABORATIVE EFFORTS

Teachers and library media specialists need to collaborate when selecting materials for the curriculum and for the library collection. For example, if an individual teacher wishes to select a book to supplement a unit in the curriculum, Edward Sadler (1995) suggests that the teacher take a positive approach.

- Develop a rationale for the book:
    - include his or her intentions for selecting that particular book
    - identify what students will get out of the book
    - link the book to the specific unit objectives
- Work with the library media specialist to collect reviews of the work and identify any awards or honors that it might have won.
- Develop informal groups within the school to provide support for members should there be a censorship challenge in the school.

rulings of the courts, most school divisions have a procedure under which a parent, guardian, or individual student may request the opportunity to read a different book than the one that is being read by the entire class. In addition, many teachers use a "parental permission to read" form whenever they are assigning any materials that they believe may be controversial.

Another issue concerns parental requests that a school librarian restrict what an adolescent can check out. While some library media specialists would honor the request, Anderson (2002) cites three reasons she would not. First, depending on the size of the school, keeping track of individual student restrictions may be practically impossible. Also, because most school libraries have student assistants working at the circulation desk, it would not be appropriate or ethical for these students to know about the restrictions placed on their schoolmates. Second, restricting students' access to information violates the ALA "Code of Ethics" and the AASL (American Association of School Librarians) "Access to Resources and Services in the School Library Media Program: An Interpretation of the Library Bill of Rights." Finally, Anderson (2002) points out that, through reading, adolescents have the opportunity to explore diverse ideas and values and to experience vicariously what might prove dangerous in the real world.

The line between parental rights and censorship begins to blur when individuals or groups make a request that would limit access by all the students in a school rather than just their own children. For example, in Fairfax County (VA), PABBIS (Parents Against Bad Books in Schools) has lobbied to have teachers provide "written notice of any sexual depictions or graphic violence in books students might read in class" (Glick, 2002, p. 26). Also, the organization asked for a "rating system" (p. 26) that would alert parents to sex or violence in a book. In response to requests by PABBIS and supportive school board members, the district superintendent proposed having review panels in each school examine classroom materials for "cultural and ethnic differences, language or word choice, religion, disabilities, violence, and implied or explicit sexual situations" (p. 26). Connecting Adolescents and Their Literature 12-1 suggests one strategy that teachers and library media specialists can use when groups of students or parents consider the use of potentially controversial materials.

PABBIS (Glick, 2002) has gone on to challenge several books in Fairfax County (VA) school libraries, including Morgan Llywelyn's *Druids* (1991), Lois Duncan's *Daughters of Eve* (1979), and Ken Follett's *The Pillars of the Earth* (1989). When a school district committee voted to keep the books in the schools, PABBIS appealed to the school board, which removed *Druids* and *Daughters of Eve* from middle school libraries and made *The Pillars of the Earth* available only to high school students in 10th grade and above.

Forms of Censorship

As you can see from the actions of PABBIS, once an item has been selected for inclusion in a curriculum or school library media center, a parent can ask that his or her child not be allowed to read a certain book, a community member can object to the inclusion of a specific book in the school library, or an organized group can present a list of items that they find objectionable. The result can be a restriction of what one student is allowed to read, the complete removal of an item from a school, the removal of an item

CONNECTING | *ADOLESCENTS AND THEIR LITERATURE 12–1*

Joanne M. Marshall (2003) suggests that teachers should use open discussions to help students (and their parents) consider the use of potentially controversial books in the classroom. Her framework consists of seven steps:

1. Ask participants if they have read the book or, when appropriate, if they have seen the movie.
2. Briefly summarize the story.
3. Make a "For" and "Against" list and quickly brainstorm ideas to support or not to support using the material.
4. Introduce the concept of finding common ground and initiate a discussion by asking participants to try to see the opposing point of view.
5. Use a handout to get participants to work in small groups, to think about the events in the book, and to examine the impact of those events. Include questions about the protagonist, antagonist, violence, sex, religion, culture, moral lessons, and response to authority. For example, Marshall (2003) uses a three-column handout. In the first column, she puts questions such as: Who is the villain and who does the villain fight? What is the message behind the villain's role? In the next column, participants record answers based on their knowledge from the book. In a third column, they indicate whether they believe the book is a positive, negative, or neutral influence.
6. Compile the responses from each small group and then lead the entire group in a discussion of the responses.
7. Ask the group to make an overall statement about the book's value or appropriateness. An alternative is to have each group member write a short persuasive essay supporting his or her position.

from a booklist, or the deliberate exclusion of an item from a library collection. Thus, censorship in schools can take a number of different forms.

Non-Selection. As you read earlier in this chapter, one form of censorship is the non-selection of materials. Suhor (2003) called non-selection an "insidious form of book banning" (p. 7). In several recent instances, school boards and school administrators have effectively censored items in advance of any challenge, not by adopting formal selection criteria or approving selection procedures, but by identifying one administrator to be a "gate-keeper." In the selection process, groups of teachers may have the responsibility to choose novels and supplementary materials. However, their selections must be approved by the "gate-keeper" who may base the selection decision on personal choice or by applying his or her own definition of community standards. Either way, the effect is the same—the selection process actually becomes a censoring device.

An educator can actually engage in censorship without being aware of it. Take the following example. A teacher has five books from which to choose one to use with a particular unit of study. In a nearby school division, there have been problems with some of the works written by the author of the first book under consideration, so it is excluded. Now, the educator has four books to consider. He or she picks the fifth book because it is the safest. That means that the remaining three books were not selected and, in fact, never even seriously considered. Nothing may be wrong with these three books, but the educator never even subjected them to a deliberate and conscious selection process. Rather than selecting any potentially risky books, the educator took the safest route and made the final selection.

Orders From a Higher Authority. Sometimes intellectual freedom is curtailed when a higher authority dictates that books and other curricular materials must be removed. Administrators, either principals or individuals at the school district level, can make arbitrary decisions to remove potentially damaging books to avoid censorship threats. One example is the demand of a Virginia school principal to remove Alice Walker's Pulitzer Prize-winning book *The Color Purple* (1982) from a high school library before any complaint was received. Considering the book potentially controversial, and acting without consulting teachers or librarians, the principal simply ordered the removal of the book. Of course, this made the book an instant best-seller at the local bookstores and actually led to more adolescents reading the novel once it was banned than had read it while it was on the shelves of the school library. This unilateral act of censorship is the same as removing a book from a school based on one complaint without listening to opposing points of view.

Personal Opinion of Educators. While censorship by special interest groups, minority groups, and fundamentalist religious groups is blatant and usually attracts attention, another form of censorship—consisting of teachers and library media specialists censoring materials—sometimes occurs and often goes undetected. These educators might subscribe to the beliefs of the special interest groups or they might be acting on their own personal beliefs and opinions. Unfortunately, this form of censorship often goes unnoticed and undetected. For example, a single teacher went to the school library's bookfair and demanded that a book of short stories be removed from the sale because it contained a story about ghosts. Her request was based solely on her personal beliefs about one story in the entire collection.

Fortunately, most educators support the freedom of expression and the freedom to read. While they may not personally support a particular position or belief, they respect an individual's right to express that belief in writing, music, or art; and they respect the rights of other individuals to read, view, or listen to that expression. At times, however, a problem arises when the individuals doing the reading, listening, or viewing are young adults. As Small (2000) writes, especially in the Internet age, some teachers feel obligated to monitor and sometimes make difficult decisions about what students read and observe. Again, there is the fine line between selection of what is appropriate for adolescents and censorship.

Some teachers and library media specialists attempt to censor materials prior to any controversy erupting (O'Neal, 1990), possibly because they fear these materials will lead to confrontations with parents, community members, or school administrators (Freedman & Johnson, 2001). They may also be afraid that they will not be supported by the administration of their own school or by the district level administration. Thus, by providing access only to literature that does not discuss sex, politics, or violence, or that does not question the role of adults, some teachers and library media specialists may believe that they are protecting themselves. However, they are also influencing young people's minds. To help educators make wise selections and to eliminate the problems of self-censorship, school divisions need to develop sound policies for selecting and removing materials from the curriculum and the school library (O'Neal, 1990). When teachers abandon their right and responsibility to select literature and other curriculum materials, they sacrifice their students to protect themselves. Self-censorship silences both teachers and students (Freedman & Johnson, 2001).

Community Pressure. Community organizations and other groups of people can pressure educators to remove materials from schools. Although most school boards and individual school libraries have planned procedures for dealing with censorship, defending a censorship challenge can still be time-consuming and emotionally draining and may sometimes lead to costly legal battles. At times, community pressure can be so powerful that educators may decide that it is easier to remove the material altogether; remove the material for a time until the controversy has quieted; restrict access to the material; or remove the item from a reading list. Unfortunately, a school or an individual educator may not have the resources (e.g., people, money, legal expertise) to engage in a possibly long, drawn-out defense. In addition, members of elected school boards may find it is politically more advantageous to remove an unpopular item than to support intellectual freedom. Finally, a school may not be willing to face the loss of community support by retaining challenged materials in the library or in the curriculum. Thus, schools often give in to community pressure.

Filters. Although it is beyond the scope of this young adult literature book to discuss Internet filters in detail, we mention them because censorship challenges to print materials in schools have dropped dramatically in the past several years as some attention has shifted to materials that are available on the Internet ("Censoring school literature in the cyber age", 2001). With the *Communications Decency Act,* the Amendment to the Telecommunications Act of 1996, the federal government attempted to prohibit posting "indecent" or "patently offensive" (Kravitz, 2002, p. 134) materials in a public forum on the Internet, including Web pages, newsgroups, chat rooms, and online discussion lists. At a basic level, this would mean that the texts of classic fiction such as *The Catcher in the Rye* and *Ulysses,* although offensive to some, would be censored on the Internet while they would enjoy the full protection of the first amendment if published in a newspaper, magazine, or book (Kravitz, 2002).

Internet material is unselected, and most secondary schools do provide computers so that adolescents can access Internet resources both in the classroom and in the school library. Thus, in response to federal laws that require filtering software on all computers purchased for schools with federal funds, and to accommodate parental and community concerns, many schools have established policies regarding student Internet use and/or have installed filtering software. However, policies can be broken and filters can sometimes restrict access to inoffensive materials by mistake while allowing access to some offensive materials. Just ask the teacher who typed the name "Seymour Simon" (author of many nonfiction books) in a search engine and was rewarded with a listing for nude celebrity photos. As she said, that was more of Simon than she wanted the class to see. While the Internet may represent the next big censorship battleground, easy access to information will be difficult to combat ("Censoring school literature in the cyber age," 2001).

Alteration. Rather than blatantly removing books from a classroom or library, sometimes censors just make alterations by deleting words or passages that they find offensive. This alteration might be a few changed words in a new edition of Roald Dahl's classic *Charlie and the Chocolate Factory* (1964), the use of a marking pen to "raise" the bodice of a young woman on the cover of a modern romance story, the removal of a complete page that discusses wet dreams in Judy Blume's *Then Again, Maybe I Won't* (1971), or the revision of a quote so that it no longer praises California "wine" (Kleinfield, 2002). The New York Board of Regents adopted Sensitivity Review Guidelines and used them to censor literary excerpts from authors such as Chekhov, I. B. Singer, or Annie Dillard in the English Regents' Examination. The Regents insisted they were only shortening the excerpts, not censoring them (National Coalition Against Censorship, 2003).

One of our college students reported that, during her practicum, the teacher she was working with received a book that had been purchased by the school division to supplement the science and literature curriculum. When the teacher reviewed the book, she found that two pages were stapled together. Curious, the teacher removed the staples and found sketches of the development of a human baby, something the school division obviously did not want the students (or the teacher) to see. In these examples of censorship by isolation rather than consideration of the work as a whole, only the objectionable parts are considered and altered in some way.

Elimination From Booklists. Using exclusion instead of inclusion, individuals or groups can censor books by keeping them off school lists or out of library collections. The idea is that if someone has problems with a book, it is easier to exclude the book based on his or her own beliefs or fears of what the censors might say, rather than to worry about responding to a censorship challenge. For example, we know of one instance in which a high school teacher refused to add Lois Duncan's *Killing Mr. Griffin* (1978) to a booklist in spite of student requests because there had been an objection in a neighboring middle school. This elimination of a work from booklists or a library collection is a matter of concern for many educators who think that young adults should have the opportunity to read a wide range of materials and that selection should be made on the basis of established selection criteria and the content of the curriculum.

Relocating Controversial or Challenged Books. Another form of censorship is the relocation of controversial or challenged materials. While public librarians might move controversial young adult books to the adult section, school librarians might remove controversial material on topics such as date rape, drugs, and witchcraft from the regular collection, place them in the librarian's office, and provide them only to adolescents who specifically ask for them. Because any mention of these materials may be removed from the library's catalog, adolescents have to know that the materials are available and that they can request them. In some cases, this means that adolescents may have to face the embarrassment of asking for information on what they see as very personal subjects. In other libraries, the materials may be placed in a restricted "Teachers' Collection" (Curry, 2001, p. 28) or on bookshelves that can be accessed only by adolescents who have permission from a guidance counselor, therapist, or parent. Although educators often justify this relocation because it may defuse a situation while still retaining some access to the material, Curry (2001) called this relocation of materials a "disturbing trend" (p. 28).

Removal From the Library or School. Perhaps the most extreme form of censorship is the complete elimination of materials. In this case, teachers, library media specialists, or administrators actually remove the book or other material from the library and/or the entire school, either in reaction to a censorship challenge or as a precautionary move to prevent censorship efforts.

While a few educators may be able to overlook some of the other forms of censorship, to most, the actual removal of an item from a school is an assault on intellectual freedom. When an item is removed from a school, young adults do not have access to that item unless they can find it in a public library or purchase it from a local or Internet bookstore. If the decision to remove the item was based only on the beliefs of a single individual or did not follow the school division's policies, this removal has diminished intellectual freedom in the school and has constrained the rights of young adults to read, view, or listen to the item.

CENSORSHIP THROUGH THE AGES

Censorship is nothing new. In fact, it has persisted throughout the ages with early censorship often tied directly to government and religion.

Early Examples

Even in ancient Greece where the freedom to speak openly was a respected right, Socrates committed suicide rather than have his teaching censored. A general belief existed in ancient Rome that only those in power, particularly members of the senate, could speak freely. Thus, Ovid and Juvenal, two Roman poets, were banished (Konvitz, 2003). The church also played a role as a censor. Once Christianity was established as the religion of the Roman Empire, both the government and the church persecuted anyone who deviated from orthodox doctrine or practice. Later, in the 15th century, Gutenberg's invention of movable type along with the printing press made it possible to censor works before they were published. In 1487, Pope Innocent VIII required all printers to submit manuscripts to church authorities and to publish them only after church approval was given. The *Index of Forbidden Books* was first issued in 1559 by Pope Paul IV. Later, in England, King Henry VIII banned and then burned copies of the English translation of the New Testament. He also established a licensing system that existed for approximately 150 years and resembled the prepublication censorship of Pope Innocent VIII. The English poet John Milton protested against such censorship in his classic *Areopagitica* (1644) (Konvitz, 2003).

Many famous authors, scientists, philosophers, and historians saw their works censored, including Galileo, Jean-Jacques Rousseau, Frances Bacon, and Victor Hugo. Voltaire was thrown in prison because he "libeled King Louis XIV" (Kravitz, 2002, p. 75).

Censorship in the Modern Age

Modern democratic countries display an emphasis on toleration and liberty; and freedom of expression and freedom of religion are generally accepted constitutional principles. However, although the modern period began in the 18th century with the Age of Enlightenment and the American and French Revolutions, these freedoms did not come easily or to all peoples. Except for a brief period in France after the Revolution of 1789, political censorship flourished in most of continental Europe until the rise of republican governments in the mid-19th century. Even in the 1900s, in totalitarian countries, state censorship remained severe. One event that galvanized support for the anti-censorship movement was the May 10, 1933, book burning by the Nazis in Germany (Cronon, 2003). In spite of this, censorship has remained an accepted fact of life in many countries where governments control or carefully scrutinize all media from books to movies. In the 1970s, a book by Nobel prize winner Nadine Gordimer was banned in the Republic of South Africa because it "endangered the safety of the state" (Kravitz, 2002, p. 75). The works of Alexander Solzhenitsyn and Boris Pasternak were censored in the former Soviet Union because of their criticism of communism. It may, however, be considered a sign of political and social progress that, in most countries today, people pay lip-service to the ideal of liberty and that no country admits that it is committed to a policy of religious, intellectual, artistic, or political censorship (Konvitz, 2003).

Censorship in the United States

The First Amendment to the United States Constitution forbids Congress from enacting laws that would regulate speech or the press, either before or after publication. This has not, however, stopped attempts to censor what Americans can see and read. For example, in the years directly before the American Civil War, southern states outlawed abolitionist literature. More recently, in 1971, there were attempts to censor portions of a 47-volume classified report on U.S. policy in Vietnam that was published in the *New York Times* and in book form as the *Pentagon Papers*. In this instance, the U.S. Supreme Court refused to bar the newspaper from reprinting the report.

Until the 20th century, government policies strictly suppressed so-called "obscene" publications and prohibited these materials from being sent through the U.S. mail or from passing through customs. These prohibitions were successfully challenged in the courts in the 1930s when *Ulysses* by Irish author James Joyce was found not to be obscene and was allowed into the country. Later, however, in the case of *Roth v. United States,* the U.S. Supreme Court noted that obscene materials were not protected by the Constitution and were "without redeeming social importance." This case also applied a new test of community standards when determining obscene materials, which was later defined to mean the national "community" of the country rather than any local standards.

In spite of the freedom guaranteed by the U.S. Constitution, censorship challenges continue to arise. Although some of the challenges are to newly written materials, others are to books that have come to be considered part of the literary canon. Here are a few comments about some of these works:

- Plato's *Republic* ("This book is un-Christian")

- George Eliot's *Silas Marner* ("You can't prove what that dirty old man is doing with that child between chapters")

- Jules Verne's *Around the World in Eighty Days* ("Very unfavorable to Mormons")

- Nathaniel Hawthorne's *The Scarlet Letter* ("A filthy book")

- Shakespeare's *Macbeth* ("Too violent for children today")

- Fyodor Dostoevsky's *Crime and Punishment* ("Serves as a poor model for young people")

- Herman Melville's *Moby Dick* ("Contains homosexuality")

- D. Salinger's *The Catcher in the Rye* ("A dreadful, dreary, recital of sickness, sordidness, and sadism") (*NCTE guideline: The student's right to read,* 2003)

Censorship in the Schools

Censorship reaches into American education when groups and individuals attempt to control what is taught in the curriculum, what textbooks are used, and/or what other books and materials are available in classrooms and school libraries. These objections have ranged from a challenge to the *Wizard of Oz* because the characters did not pray to God and to *Goldilocks* because the main character trespasses on the bears' private property (Kravitz, 2002), to the call for removal of *Annie on My Mind* (Garden, 1982) from a school because it contains a lesbian relationship (Curry, 2001), and to the censorship of *Fallen Angels* (Myers, 1988) for offensive language, violence, and racism ("10 Most . . . Challenged Books of 2000," 2001). In Panama City, Florida, Robert Cormier's *I Am the Cheese* (1977) was challenged for being anti-government.

Textbooks were challenged in Tennessee (Basic Reading series published by Holt, Rinehart and Winston) for promoting "idolatry, demon worship, gun control, evolution and feminism" (Kravitz, 2002, p. 70) and in Kanawha County (WV) because of a conflict between the religious views of groups of citizens and the multicultural content of the *Interactions* reading series. In the latter instance, the conflict "turned into a violent, all-out war" (p. 34) with "right-wing extremist organizations" (p. 35) from throughout the country lending their support to the protestors at "boycotts, pickets, and strikes at the coal mines" (p. 37). What began as a protest against a textbook spread to a call to censor *Moby Dick, The Good Earth,* and *Paradise Lost* and threats to firebomb the schools. When new selection guidelines were established and a settlement was finally reached, the parents were given a form on which they could identify the books that they did not want their children to read. The National Education Association commented that "if given the interpretation obviously meant by their proponents, the guidelines would not only bar the disputed books from Kanawah county classrooms, but would proscribe the use of any language arts textbooks, including the *McGuffey's Readers*" (p. 39).

Although a separation of church and state exists in the United States, some groups have charged that "secular humanism," a philosophy that advocates human rather than religious values (*American Heritage Dictionary of the English Language,* 2000), is taught in public schools. Thus, several conservative religious organizations such as Focus on the Family headed by James Dobson and the Educational Research Analysts run by Mel and Norma Gabler have spearheaded the drive to combat secular humanism in the schools by calling for the elimination of courses in drug education, sex education, values clarification, and multicultural education and for a shift from an emphasis on problem solving to one of mastering the content of the disciplines (Kravitz, 2002). The Eagle Forum protested a curriculum in Michigan that included decision-making skills and "holistic health principles" (Kravitz, 2002, p. 71).

Landmark Court Decisions That Affect Intellectual Freedom

Often, the struggles between individuals and groups who are attempting to censor items and those who are arguing on behalf of intellectual freedom are played out in the court system, with a few cases going all the way to the U.S. Supreme Court. A number of cases, listed in Table 12–2, have dealt with topics such as a school board removing books from a classroom or school library, parents and other groups challenging a textbook or textbook series, and a teacher being fired for using inappropriate materials in the classroom.

Most of the court cases have centered around the following issues:

1. According to the school division's policies, who has the final authority to select materials for a school and under what circumstances?

2. Is there a procedure to follow if materials are challenged and was the procedure followed?

3. Who ultimately has the right to remove materials from a school and under what specific circumstances?

4. What are the rights of individuals who challenge materials that are in the schools and were the individuals provided these rights?

5. What is the difference between the compulsory use of materials and optional use of them?

6. If students are excused from using certain materials, what effect will that have on the students and on the students' learning?

TABLE 12-2	Court and Other Legal Cases

Year	Case	Issue
1969	Tinker v. Des Moines Independent Community School District	Students wore black arm bands to protest war.
1972	Presidents Council, District 25 v. Community School Board No. 25 (NYC)	School board removed books from the school library.
1976	Minarcini v. Strongsville (OH) City School District	School board removed books from school library.
1978	Right to Read Defense Committee v. School Committee of the City of Chelsea (MA)	Poetry anthology banned from the school library.
1980	Bicknell v. Vergennes (VT) Union High School Board	School board removed books from the school library.
1980	Loewen v. Turnipseed (MS)	School board refused to approve textbook.
1982	Pratt v. Independent School District No. 831 (MN)	Film removed by the school board from the curriculum.
1982	Island Trees (NY) v. Pico	School board removed eight books from the library.
1985	Grove v. Meade School District No. 354 (FL)	Parents objected to book on basis of secular humanism.
1986	Mozert v. Hawkins County (TN) Board of Education	Parents challenged reading textbooks.
1987	Fowler v. Board of Education of Lincoln County (KY)	Tenured high school teacher discharged for showing movie she had not seen.
1988	Hazelwood (MO) School District v. Kuhlmeier	Principal removed articles from student newspaper.
1989	Virgil v. School Board of Columbia County (FL)	Parents complained about literature textbook.
1994	Brown v. Woodland Jt. School District (CA)	Parents challenged reading series.
1994	Fleischfresser v. S.D. 200 (IL)	Parents challenged reading series.
1994	Guyer v. S. B. of Alachua County (FL)	Halloween celebration challenged as promoting religion of Wicca.
1998	Gibson v. Lee County (FL) School Board	Use of the New Testament to teach history.
2002	Chamberlain v. Surrey (B.C.) School District (Canada)	School board removed picture books that depict same-sex marriage.
2002	Counts v. Cedarville (AK) School Board	Harry Potter book placed on restricted list.

Although there are too many cases to discuss in detail in a single chapter, there are several that contain important rulings.

One of the landmark cases confirming intellectual freedom in schools was *Island Trees (NY) School District v. Pico* (1982), in which four high school students and one junior high school student challenged the legality of the school board's removal of nine books from the district's school libraries. A conservative group had told board members about several books in the libraries that were on a list of objectionable items. Ostensibly, the board removed the books in order to read them. However, when a review committee recommended that seven of the books be returned to the library, with five to be placed on the open shelves and two to be in a restricted area, the board voted to remove eight of the books entirely. The case reached the U.S. Supreme Court, which found that, while a school board may have "significant discretion in determining curriculum content" (Ishizuka, 2001, p. 17), school officials "may not remove books from school library shelves simply because they dislike the ideas contained in those books" (Ishizuka, 2001, p. 17). The court also found that "school boards do not have unrestricted authority to select books and that the First Amendment is implicated when books are removed arbitrarily" (Reichman, 1993, p. 153). The Court did suggest, however, that books could be removed from schools when the decision to do so was based on educational suitability, when there was a recognized materials review system with reconsideration guidelines in place, and when those guidelines were followed in the removal process.

The use of identified criteria in the selection of materials for a school can be very important. In *Loewen v. Turnipseed* (1980), the Court found that a rating committee must follow its own stated criteria and cannot substitute personal opinion when selecting textbooks. Court decisions such as *Minarcini v. Strongville* (1976) and *Right to Read Defense Committee v. School Committee of Chelsea* (1978) supported the rights of young people to have access to appropriately selected materials that represent diverse points of view.

The *Hazelwood School District v. Kuhlmeier* (1988) case dealt with school journalism and the school newspaper rather than young adult literature, but it has had an impact in other federal cases. In Hazelwood, Missouri, when a principal objected to two stories that dealt with teenage pregnancy and divorce and banned them from the school newspaper, the student newspaper staff filed a suit. The U.S. Supreme Court finally ruled that school administrators can exercise considerable control over student expression that is not consistent with the basic educational mission of the school. Although the Hazelwood case involved only the conflict over the contents of a student newspaper, the Court's decision had implications for censorship of school plays, library holdings, and classroom instruction. In 1989, when the school board of Columbia County (FL) locked up a state-approved literature textbook that contained selections by Aristophanes and Chaucer, some parents filed a lawsuit. The federal judge in the case of *Virgil v. School Board of Columbia County* based her decision on the Hazelwood case and ruled in favor of the school board (Whitson, 1993).

CENSORSHIP TODAY

Judging from the lists of challenged and banned books, it appears that many people believe they have the right, or even the obligation, to define the literary canon. Young adult literature is well represented on the lists of challenged materials with problem novels making a strong showing (LeMieux, 1998). While this censorship may be done by individuals, many times an organized group is behind the challenge. Table 12–3 provides a list of some of these groups. In Expanding Your Knowledge with the Internet 12-2, you will find the URLs for some of these organizations.

Motives for Censorship

According to Konvitz (2003), censors identify materials that they believe are immoral or obscene, heretical or blasphemous, seditious or treasonable, or injurious to the national security. While there are many factors that motivate individuals to become censors, the following are a few reasons that seem to occur most frequently.

TABLE 12–3	Organizations or Pressure Groups That Have Been Associated with Censorship or Intellectual Freedom Challenges.

American Christians in Education (CURE)
American Family Association
Arizona Parents for Traditional Education
Christian Coalition
Citizens for Community Values
Citizens for Decency
Citizens for Excellence in Education
Citizens United for Responsible Education (CURE)
Concerned Women for America
Eagle Forum
Educational Research Analysts (Mel and Norma Gabler)
Family Friendly Libraries
Family Research Council
Focus on the Family
Heritage Foundation
John Birch Society
Let Our Values Emerge (LOVE)
Let's Improve Today's Education (LITE)
Morality in Media
National Coalition for the Protection of Children and Families
Parents Against Bad Books in Schools
People of America Responding to Educational Needs of Today's Society (PARENTS)
Save our Schools (SOS)

| EXPANDING | *YOUR KNOWLEDGE WITH THE INTERNET 12–2* |

Many organizations, such as the examples listed below, have taken positions on censorship and intellectual freedom. Visit this book's Companion Web site at www.prenhall.com/bucher to link directly to these and many other similar organizations.

Educational Research Analysts (Mel and Norma Gabler)
http://members.aol.com/TxtbkRevws/

Family Friendly Libraries
www.fflibraries.org/

Parents Against Bad Books in Schools
www.pabbis.com

Family Values. Most frequently, challenges to materials in schools are brought by parents, perhaps because they feel helpless sending their children into a world that seems increasingly plagued with hazards over which they have no control (Kravitz, 2002). They may also fear books and other materials that might encourage adolescents to think on their own or that contain things that conflict with their own values or moral views. Often, a problem arises when parents want to influence not only what their children read, but what everyone in the school may read.

Political Views. Except for sexual issues and religion, few topics inflame people more than politics. While most people agree that young adults should learn about diverse political philosophies, there are problems actually implementing this idea. Conservatives have charged that history and social studies textbooks often criticize America. Liberals may raise the issue of political correctness and contend that events have been oversimplified (Reichman, 1993).

Religion. Although challenges by religious groups have always existed, the majority of America's broad-based religious groups do not favor censoring (Kravitz, 2002). However, some individuals and organizations have questioned the role of women and the portrayal of moral issues, religious themes, sexual issues, and witchcraft in school materials. In addition, some teachers face the dilemma of teaching evolution, creationism, or some combination of both. Almost with certainty, whichever they decide to do will draw the ire of some irate parent or community member, with advocates of creationism usually seeking to add rather than delete materials from the school curriculum (Reichman, 1993).

Minority Rights. During the 1980s and 1990s, a wide range of groups and individuals, including peoples of color, women, the elderly, homosexuals, and the disabled, challenged school materials based on a concept that became known as political correctness

(Kravitz, 2002). Their complaints ranged from the words used to describe racial, ethnic, and minority groups to the manner in which members of minority groups were represented (i.e., physical characteristics, work ethic, social habits, abilities) in books and other materials. While educators must be concerned when an author stereotypes characters based solely on cultural background, gender, sexual orientation, or other distinguishing characteristics, it is also realistic to assume that the whole range of individuals in society, with their flaws as well as their strengths, will be represented in literature.

The Primary Targets of Censorship

In Table 12–1, you saw some of the primary reasons why individuals and groups attempt to censor materials. In the following section, we combine the two lists and look at a few of these reasons for censorship in more detail. As with most other lists, some of the categories overlap and some of the books that are mentioned in one category have been challenged in other categories as well.

Profanity/Curses/Offensive Language. Writers usually do not advocate the use of "bad language" (Kravitz, 2002, p. 82) when they use it in their novels. However, they do use language to portray life as it really is and to allow characters to speak as they would in their everyday lives (Kravitz, 2002). We remember the instance of a high school library media specialist who was approached by a parent demanding that she remove a book from the library that depicted the U.S. Marines landing on the beaches of a Pacific Island during World War II. Under heavy enemy fire, the Marines' language included a few instances of mild profanity, which the parent did not believe belonged in a school library media center. The LMS simply explained the benefits and "worth" of the book in regard to the curriculum, and asked the parent to consider the realism of the book and how mild the few expletives were in contrast to what the Marines might actually have been saying. As the LMS recounted to us: "I just asked him if he thought it would be realistic for the Marines to be saying 'Gee whiz, they're shooting at us'." After considering the issue, the parent agreed that the book should remain in the school library.

A number of books have recently been challenged because of language that ranges from traditional curses (i.e., damn, hell, bitch) to taking the Lord's name in vain (Curry, 2001). You have already read about challenges to the language in Walter Dean Myers' *Fallen Angels* (1988) and Jane Leslie Conly's *Crazy Lady* (1993). In addition, Katherine Paterson's *The Great Gilly Hopkins* (1978), Harry Mazer's *Last Mission* (1979), Robert Cormier's *The Chocolate War* (1974), Christopher Collier and James Lincoln Collier's *My Brother Sam Is Dead* (1974), Judy Blume's *Blubber* (1974) and *Here's to You, Rachel Robinson* (1993), Robert Lipsyte's *One Fat Summer* (1977), Chris Lynch's *Iceman* (1994) and *Shadow Boxer* (1993), and Johanna Reiss's *The Upstairs Room* (1972) have all been challenged because of profanity or foul language.

There are other challenges in which individuals object to the use of offensive language in books. Sometimes authors use street language or dialects that differ from standard English. For example, in *A Hero Ain't Nothing but a Sandwich* (1973), Alice Childress uses street language to show the life of a young boy who is drawn into drug use.

In other instances, the challenges center on words, which, while once used in our culture, are no longer acceptable. Sometimes these words are used in a contemporary but derogative sense while in other times they appear in historical fiction or books that were written years ago when the use of these words was accepted. The paradox is that, in the historical books, the words are historically accurate although painful to some people; to change them would be to attempt to change history. A classic example is the use of racial slurs in *The Adventures of Huckleberry Finn,* which was written by Mark Twain in 1885. Some people object to the use of the word *squaw* in Sally Keehn's historical fiction book *I Am Regina* (1991), and the word *nigger* in several historical fiction titles including James Lincoln Collier and Christopher Collier's *Jump to Freedom* (1981) and *War Comes to Willy Freeman* (1983), Paula Fox's *Slave Dancer* (1973), William H. Armstrong's *Sounder* (1969), and Barbara Smucker's *Underground to Canada* (1978).

Heterosexually Explicit Materials. The inclusion of sexual situations and topics in books for adolescent readers has always been a target for censors in spite of the so-called sexual revolution of the 1960s and the inclusion of more graphic sexual scenes in movies and on television. Some censors either think reading about sex in fiction or nonfiction will make young people more likely to engage in sexual experimentation or they think all sexual matters and issues are inappropriate for young people.

One of the pioneers of young adult literature was Judy Blume. While her books are very popular with adolescents, her books are often challenged because they explore the sexual feelings of young people and answer many adolescents' questions about the changes happening to their bodies and in their lives. As recently as 2004, her coming-of-age novel *Deenie* (1973) was challenged by the parent of a 7th-grade student in Hernando County (FL) Schools. The book was retained but can be read only by students with "written parental permission" ("Deenie defeats detractors—sort of," 2004, p. 15).

A series of books that is consistently among the top challenged books is the Alice series by Phyllis Reynolds Naylor. In 2003, it even replaced the Harry Potter series as the most-challenged books ("Alice series tops most-challenged list," 2004). Complaints have ranged from "too explicit—graphic—sarcastic—mentions underwear—... inappropriate for any age group" (Bucher & Manning, 2002, p. 10) to "preachy—didactic—contrived" (p. 10). At the same time, other critics called the series "full of vitality—readable—laughable—... sensitive—true to life—... age appropriate—cheerful, upbeat writing with a positive emphasis" (p. 10). As Naylor said, "In my Alice series . . . I promised myself that I would write about everything that a girl would wonder about, and I am sticking to that promise. . . . I refuse to back away just because it's controversial" (West, 1997, p. 181).

In nonfiction, Robie Harris in *It's Perfectly Normal* (1994) assures adolescents that it is normal to have a wide variety of thoughts and feelings about sex and physical changes. In addition to topics such as male and female anatomy, physical changes at puberty, and fertilization, the book includes discussions of gay and lesbian relationships, masturbation, and abortion (Bayne, 2002). Harris tries to make the point that sexual matter is appropriate for developing readers, and it is perfectly normal for them to be interested. Still, the book has been the subject of considerable criticism and censorship efforts.

A number of other well-known young adult books have been challenged because of sexually explicit materials or sexual activity that censors deem immoral or illegal. These range from Chris Crutcher's *Chinese Handcuffs* (1989) and Alane Ferguson's *Show Me the Evidence* (1989) to Hadley Irwin's *Abby, My Love* (1985), Louise Rennison's *Knocked Out by My Nunga-Nungas* (2002), Norma Fox Mazer's *Up in Seth's Room* (1979), and several of the works of Norma Klein such as *Mom, the Wolfman, and Me* (1972), *Family Secrets* (1985), and *That's My Baby* (1988).

Homosexual Themes. Censors sometimes condemn books about sexual orientation as immoral and perhaps even damaging to young adult readers. However, sexual orientation is a significant issue in contemporary American life (Broz, 2002). Whether because of external pressures or their own initiative, many educators have promoted tolerance of gays and lesbians and opposed discrimination. Trying to recognize and accommodate the needs of all students, they have attempted to provide materials that include characters from diverse sexual orientations. According to Patti Capel Swartz (2003), young adult literature provides an awareness of the issues surrounding sexual orientation and can be used to counter homophobia in the schools.

However, some people have a difficult time dealing with gay and lesbian issues discussed in young adult books or middle and high school classrooms. As a result, while there has been a growth of gay-oriented literature for adolescents, there has been a corresponding rise in the challenges to this material in some school districts (Reichman, 1993).

When *Annie on My Mind* (Garden, 1982), an American Library Association "Best of the Best Books for Young Adults," and one of the "most influential books of the 20th century" (Jenkins, 2003, p. 50), was provided to 42 schools in and around Kansas City by an organization called Project 21 to promote accurate, positive materials about gays and lesbians in libraries and curricula, groups and individuals raised their voices in protest. As a result, the school districts removed copies of the book. In response to that move, other individuals protested to retain the book. When the controversy ended up in court, the judge ruled that *Annie on My Mind* had been unconstitutionally removed from the shelves (Garden, 1996). Speaking about her book, author Nancy Garden noted:

> . . . it's . . . important to prepare teens for the world they'll meet as adults, and to help them understand it and form their own reactions to it. One can't do that by keeping the world from them. Far better for them to encounter difficult subjects when they still have adults—like their parents and teachers and librarians—to talk to than to keep them so sheltered that they know nothing of the world until they're thrust into it as independent kids in their 20s." (Jenkins, 2003, p. 50)

While other books may not have achieved the notoriety of *Annie on My Mind* (Garden, 1982), several have been challenged because of homosexual themes. *Am I Blue: Coming Out From the Silence* (1994), edited by Marion Dane Bauer, is notable as the first collection of stories to address gay and lesbian themes. Censors complained that the book was inappropriate for middle school students, emphasized suicide, confused adolescents about sexuality, and promoted the gay and lesbian agenda (Broz, 2002). When

CONNECTING | *ADOLESCENTS AND THEIR LITERATURE 12–2*

> Discussions of sexual orientation are disconcerting to some readers. However, educators need to challenge heterosexual readers to read literature that realistically portrays lives that differ from their own and to understand the challenges faced by gay and lesbian young adults. In addition, gay and lesbian readers need books that validate the struggles that they may face.
>
> Educators can ask all adolescents to read a book that focuses on homosexuality such as Frank Mosca's *All American Boys* (1983), Bette Greene's, *The Drowning of Stephan Jones* (1991), or Nancy Garden's *Annie on My Mind* (1982). Then, ask students to write an essay or prepare a PowerPoint presentation that focuses on the:
>
> - summary of the book
> - challenges that the characters faced because of their sexual orientation
> - similarities and dissimilarities of a gay or lesbian lifestyle and heterosexual lives
> - ways American society can change for heterosexuals to be more tolerant of gays and lesbians (and vice-versa) or how any group can become more tolerant of a group that is different from them

Francesca Lia Block told the story of a gay man in *Baby Be-Bop* (1995), her work was censored as well. In 2002, *Achingly Alice* (Naylor, 1998) was banned from a Missouri school library for promoting homosexuality (Doyle, 2003). Other books that have undergone censorship challenges for homosexual themes include Frank Mosca's *All American Boys* (1983), Susan and Daniel Cohen's *When Someone You Know Is Gay* (1989), and Ann Heron's *Two Teenagers in Twenty* (1994). Connecting Adolescents and Their Literature 12-2 looks at a plan for creating reading and learning experiences around these books.

Witchcraft/Occult/Religion. Sometimes the depiction of witchcraft, extrasensory perception, the occult, paranormal phenomena, or even diverse religions in young adult literature prompts complaints and threats of censorship. While Roald Dahl's popular novel *The Witches* (1983) has been a perennial target (Bergson-Shilcock, 2002), more recently J. K. Rowling's Harry Potter series has gained equal or greater notoriety for its wizardry theme. Other books that censors target for their inclusion of witchcraft include Bruce Colville's *The Dragonslayers* (1994), Mary Downing Hahn's *Wait Till Helen Comes* (1986), and Alvin Schwartz's *Scary Stories 3* (1991), which includes scary stories, songs, poems, and rhymes that appeal to a wide range of ages, interests, and tastes (Majak, 2002). Elizabeth George Speare's Newbery medal-winning classic *The Witch of Blackbird Pond* (1958) was challenged in a Connecticut middle school in 2002 (Doyle, 2003). Also, complaints have been lodged against Shakespeare's *Macbeth* because of its portrayal of witches (Morris & Ellis, 1996).

Concerned with the treatment of Christianity in young adult literature and the representation of Biblical teachings and religious beliefs, some individuals and groups have questioned the inclusion of books such as Doerkson's *Jazzy* (1981) and Godard and Ribera's *The Ultimate Alchemist* (1983) in schools. Other challenges have centered on Judy Blume's *Are You There God, It's Me, Margaret* (1970) and the positive portrayal of a non-Christian religion such as Taoism in Laurence Yep's *Dragonwings* (1975).

Violence/Horror. Unfortunately, violence is a part of the American society; therefore, it has become an integral part of young adult literature. Some contend that, even when violence is absent from the lives of adolescents, books and the media make it part of the adolescent experience (Isaacs, 2003). As a result, numerous censorship complaints have been filed, either to protect young adults or to prevent them from engaging in similar violent acts.

Johnston (2002) told of Lois Duncan's *Killing Mr. Griffin* (1978) in which students plot to frighten and ridicule their English teacher. What censors fail to realize is that Duncan was attempting to show how a teacher challenges students to do their best rather than live a wasted life. Instead of focusing on violence, the book deals with peer pressure, failures of communication, and inabilities to recognize potential problems among students.

Many other books have been condemned for violence. Set on a 1920s Vermont farm, Robert Newton Peck's *A Day No Pigs Would Die* (1978) has been attacked because of its violence, hatred, and animal cruelty (Curry, 2001). Caroline Cooney's *The Terrorist* (1997) has a theme of violence that censors thought was unsuitable for the age group. *Fallen Angels* (Myers, 1988) has been criticized for the violence in its portrayal of the Vietnam War; while *My Brother Sam Is Dead* (Collier & Collier, 1974), applauded for its high literary quality and strong character development, has been challenged for its depiction of the American Revolution (Short, 2002). Even *The Devil's Arithmetic* (1988), Jane Yolen's story of the Holocaust, has been challenged for being too violent (Curry, 2001).

Racism/Sexism. Many adults have concerns about the depiction of racial and ethnic minorities and about the treatment of women in young adult literature. While *The Little Engine That Could* was challenged in California because the engine was portrayed as a male (National Coalition Against Censorship, 2003), most censorship challenges have dealt with charges of racism rather than sexism (Curry, 2001). While many people realize how long-held stereotypes and prejudice have affected various cultural and racial groups, others find fault with some literature on the basis of bad language, suggestive situations, questionable literary merit, and ungrammatical English (*NCTE Guideline: The Student's Right to Read,* 2003).

As you have read, a debate exists over the use of specific words that, while no longer accepted, were historically accurate during the time in which they were written or the time represented in the book. However, other censorship challenges have focused not on individual words but on the depiction of minority groups in general. For example, people have objected to Mildred Taylor's *Roll of Thunder, Hear My Cry* (1976) both for having an anti-white racial bias and for having an anti-black racial bias

(Curry, 2001). *The History of the American Nation* was called biased and misleading in its presentation of minority groups, women, the Civil Rights movement, and the Vietnam War (Reichman, 1993). Other books that have been challenged because of the representations include Theodore Taylor's *The Cay* (1969), Laurence Yep's *Dragonwings* (1975), and Bette Greene's *Summer of My German Soldier* (1973).

Substance Use and Abuse. Censors often complain about descriptions of substance abuse in young adult literature. Perhaps they believe adolescents will be tempted or influenced to experiment with drugs. Many books, however, present a message that young people have the power to organize and be heard and they can make changes in their schools, communities, and their lives (Morgan, 2002). Challenged books in this category include Luis Rodriguez's *Always Running* (1993), Beatrice Sparks' (formerly listed as Anonymous) *Go Ask Alice* (1971), Norman Klein's *Learning How to Fall* (1989), Robert Cormier's *We All Fall Down* (1991), and Todd Strasser's *Angel Dust Blues* (1979). In books like *Road to Nowhere* (1993) and *Die Softly* (1991), Christopher Pike has upset censors for three reasons: sex, horror, and drug use. Some censors have even attacked M. E. Kerr's *Dinky Hocker Shoots Smack* (1972) based solely on the title and not the content of the book itself.

Scientific and "Historical" Theories. Scientific and historical theories have long been the focus of controversy in schools with the teaching of evolution being a frequent target. According to a survey conducted by the National Science Foundation, a substantial majority of U.S. citizens think that evolution should be taught and that it is not incompatible with a belief in God (Crabcraft, 2004).

This has not, however, prevented challenges in a number of states. Georgia's proposed biology program is drawing fire from science educators because it leaves out the word *evolution* in what critics say is a nod to proponents of creationism ("Ga teachers cry foul . . . ", 2004). Other topics excluded are human origins, the Big Bang theory, human reproduction, and much of plate tectonics ("Ga teachers cry foul . . . ", 2004). In Texas, the State Board of Education rejected arguments by Religious Right groups and voted 11–4 to approve a series of biology textbooks that had favorable treatment of evolution ("Texas ed. board rejects religious right . . . ", 2003). The Worland, Wyoming, school board hoped to adopt a new policy that critics say will water down the teaching of evolution. While the New Mexico Board of Education voted unanimously to retain science standards that emphasize evolution and do not mention creationism, North Carolina's Board of Education is reviewing state standards, and education officials in one community are lobbying to include creationism ("New Mexico rejects effort to add creationism . . . ," 2003).

Other Objections. The previous categories outline the most frequently given reasons for challenging books in schools. There are, however, other reasons. For example, people in Oregon raised objections to *Eli's Songs* (Killingsworth, 1991) because it includes instances of "logger bashing" (Reichman, 1993, p. 35) and because male characters drink (Curry, 2001). Other challenges have occurred over Phyllis Reynolds Naylor's *Outrageously Alice*

(1997) (fosters rebellion), Astrid Lindgren's *The Brother's Lionheart* (1975) (too depressing), and Fran Arrick's *Tunnel Vision* (1980) (too depressing).

Lois Lowry's *The Giver* (1993) presents a futuristic society in a work of social criticism of the pressures put upon young people for conformity, anti-intellectualism, and the drive of mass communication to make everyone look and act alike (Avi, 2002). In the multiple award-winning book, twins are illegal and a baby twin boy is "released" from life with a fatal injection. For this and other reasons such as black magic and euthanasia (Curry, 2001), Lowry's book was no. 11 on ALA's list of most challenged books of the 1990s with challenges in at least five states since 1999 ("Lowry novel frequent censorship target," 2001).

SUPPORTING INTELLECTUAL FREEDOM WHEN MATERIALS ARE CHALLENGED

While it is important to support intellectual freedom on a daily basis, educators must also know what to do if there is a challenge to materials in a school or library. Teachers and school library media specialists must prepare themselves in advance by knowing who to turn to if a challenge arises, what documents support intellectual freedom, and what procedures to follow to deal with a censorship challenge.

Professional Organizations That Support Intellectual Freedom

Hopkins (2003) noted that, when faced with a censorship challenge, it is important for educators to seek support from outside the school because such support is a "primary factor in the retention of challenged materials" (p. 32). In spite of this, in a national survey, only 50% of the library media specialists (LMSs) involved in a censorship challenge sought help from others in the school and only 22% of the LMSs looked outside the school for assistance. Those LMSs who received support during a challenge reported that they appreciated "information about the challenged materials, including reviews, awards, and distinctions" (p. 34).

There are a number of organizations that work to address censorship issues and that provide assistance of varying degrees. Table 12–4 provides selected examples of some of these organizations. In Expanding Your Knowledge with the Internet 12-3, you will find the URLs for some of these organizations.

Supplementing these national organizations, state and local groups, such as state affiliates of the American Library Association and the American Association of School Librarians, can provide help when there is a censorship challenge.

Documents That Support Intellectual Freedom

In addition to providing support, some organizations have produced well-thought-out documents that promote intellectual freedom and provide support during a censorship challenge. These resources vary from position papers and sample selection documents to resolutions and forms (e.g., book rationale forms) for protection against censors. Table 12–5 provides a list of some representative documents, while Expanding Your Knowledge with the Internet 12-4 contains links to the actual documents.

| TABLE 12-4 | Organizations That Support Intellectual Freedom |

Visit Expanding Your Knowledge with the Internet 12-3 on this book's Companion Website at www.prenhall.com/bucher for additional information.

Alliance for Intellectual Freedom in Education
American Booksellers Foundation for Free Expression
American Civil Liberties Union
American Film and Video Association (Formerly the Educational Film Library Association)
American Library Association—Office for Intellectual Freedom—Freedom to Read Foundation, and the Intellectual Freedom Action Network
Association of American Publishers—Freedom to Read Committee
Comic Book Legal Defense Fund
Computer Professionals for Social Responsibility Cyber-Rights
Directors Guild of America
Electronic Frontier Foundation
Freedom Forum
Freedom to Read—Canada
Freedom to Read Foundation
KidSPEAK: Where Kids Speak Up for Free Speech
National Coalition Against Censorship
National Council of Teachers of English
National Education Association
People for the American Way
Thomas Jefferson Center for the Protection of Free Expression

| EXPANDING | YOUR KNOWLEDGE WITH THE INTERNET 12-3 |

Many organizations, including the examples listed below, support intellectual freedom. Visit this book's Companion Website at www.prenhall.com/bucher to link directly to these and many other sites.

Comic Book Legal Defense Fund
www.cbldf.org/

Freedom to Read Foundation
www.sirs.com/corporate/newsletters/read/readtoc.htm

National Council of Teachers of English
www.ncte.org/about/issues/censorship

TABLE 12-5	*Documents Supporting Intellectual Freedom*

American Library Association
Access for Children and Young People to Videotapes and Other NonPrint Formats
Access to Electronic Information, Services, and Networks
Access to Resources and Services in the School Library Media Program
Free Access to Libraries for Minors
Library Bill of Rights
Restricted Access to Library Materials
Statement on Library Use of Filtering Software

Association for Educational Communications and Technology
Statement on Intellectual Freedom

International Reading Association
School Censorship in the 21st Century: A Guide for Teachers and School Library Media Specialists—book offering interesting insights and solid information about the past, present, and possible future of school censorship challenges.
On Opposing Abridgment or Adaptation as a Form of Censorship—this IRA resolution reflects a concern among reading teachers about the publishing practice by which important works are abridged and sometimes altered for textbooks without adequate explanation from the publisher

National Coalition Against Censorship
The Sex Panic—report of the conference on NCAC's Working Group on Women
Censored—article on six banned children's books
Free Speech Guidelines—guidelines for people considering protests against speakers
25 Years: Defending Freedom of Thought, Inquiry, and Expression—highlights significant censorship battles
Freedom Is Not a Dirty Word—one-page flyer showing how censorship affects all people
Public Education, Democracy, Free Speech: The Ideas That Define and Unite Us—booklet stressing the link between public education and the constitutional right to free speech and inquiry

National Council of Teachers of English
Students' Right to Read
SLATE (Support for the Learning and Teaching of English)
Anti-Censorship Center
Rationales for Teaching Challenged Books
Reconsideration of Materials (sample form)

Dealing with a Censorship Challenge

The benefits of intellectual freedom are great for both educators and students. However, the realities of promoting intellectual freedom sometimes lead to difficulties. For example, although the literature program at Mowat Middle School in Lynn Haven, Florida, was recognized as a Center of Excellence in English language arts, the superintendent

| EXPANDING | *YOUR KNOWLEDGE WITH THE INTERNET 12-4* |

The Internet provides links to many of the documents that support intellectual freedom such as the examples listed below. Visit this book's Companion Website at www.prenhall.com/bucher to link directly to these and many other resources.

AECT Statement on Intellectual Freedom
www.bloomington.k12.mn.us/distinfo/P&R/R6160AECT.html

Freedom to Read Statement
www.ala.org/ala/oif/statementspols/ftrstatement/freedomreadstatement.htm

IRA: On Opposing Abridgment or Adaptation as a Form of Censorship
www.reading.org/positions/abridgment.html

NCTE Students' Right to Read
www.ncte.org/about/over/positions/category/cens/107616.htm

wanted to ban 64 books including Shakespeare's *Twelfth Night*. Because of their support of intellectual freedom, two teachers at the school received national awards including the PEN/Newman's Own First Amendment Award; however, one of these teachers transferred to another school while the other resigned (Tomasino, Zarnowski, & Backner, 2003).

Developing a Proactive Position. To cope with censorship challenges, educators must develop a plan before a censorship challenge occurs. This positive and objective written plan should defend young adults' right to read literature of their choice, provide guidelines for the selection of materials for classrooms and the school library media center, identify local selection criteria, include rationales for students reading young adult literature, contain procedures to educate school faculty and administration about intellectual freedom and dealing with complaints, and include guidelines for teaching controversial material. The plan should also establish a clearly defined strategy for dealing with challenges to library or classroom materials (i.e., to whom should the complainant be referred), provide a request for reconsideration form that the complainant can complete (all complaints should be filed in writing and signed by the individual or group making the complaint (Virginia Library Association, 1997)), and outline the exact procedures to be followed if a complaint is made including the makeup of any and all review committees that will hear the complaint. Finally, the plan should also detail any appeal process and the responsibilities of all teachers, library media specialists, staff, and administrators, and should encourage teachers to prepare written rationales for materials that might be challenged.

After the plan is approved by the central administration of the school district and the school board, all personnel should strictly adhere to the policies and follow the procedures outlined in the plan. Suggestions for Collaborative Efforts 12-2 provides suggestions for involving the community in these proactive efforts.

SUGGESTIONS FOR COLLABORATIVE EFFORTS

Simmons and Dresang (2001) suggest creating an "open, exploratory environment" (p. 6) in the school by involving school library media specialists, teachers, parents, students, and community members in an open dialogue before there are any censorship challenges. They suggest:

- Creating a citizen's panel to discuss broad censorship issues.
- Building faculty consensus in the school.
- Meeting with parent and community groups for discussions of books that might be used in the curriculum.
- Preparing outreach statements that explain the selection criteria, the curricular goals, and the rationales for using certain materials.

In addition, Sadler (1995) suggests:

- Reading and discussing the "Library Bill of Rights" with students and asking them if they can think of situations in which these rights may have been violated.
- Having students prepare presentations on the subject of censorship or censored books.

Finally, educators can work with the local public library to

- Celebrate Banned Books Week.
- Encourage community discussions of these and other challenged materials.
- Keep track of legislation pertaining to intellectual freedom and First Amendment rights (Virginia Library Association, 1997).

Another proactive strategy is for all educators to know about the school and the community in which it is located. Sipe (1999) suggests that educators learn the answers to questions such as the following:

- How well does your school communicate with parents and community members?

- Do parents and community members feel a connection to the school and to the decision-making process?

- Do the school and district have clear, current, appropriate policies and procedures for selecting materials? What are they?

- Does the school have a policy on academic freedom and actively support it (Sipe, 1999)?

Preparing Rationales For Frequently Challenged Materials. When teachers and library media specialists are considering purchasing or using books that have been censored in other places, it may be beneficial to prepare a rationale for the book. This procedure will help the educator focus on such things as who will be the target audience for the book, how the book will be used, why the book is appropriate for the intended audience, how the book supports the objectives of the lesson or the curriculum of the school, and what the reviewers have said about the book. The rationale should also include an examination of the book in light of the selection criteria of the school district. While individual school districts can develop their own forms for the rationale, the National Council of Teachers of English has an excellent discussion of how to write a rationale on their Web site. In addition, Table 12–6 provides an example. McClain, Goss, and Moe (1996) suggest that a variation of the rationale can provide the basis for a permission form that teachers can use to obtain approval from a parent or guardian before students read or view controversial materials.

A number of resources to assist teachers contain rationales. Barlow (2002) recommends *Rationales for Teaching Young Adult Literature* (Reid & Neufield, 1999), a book containing rationales for 22 books. Karolides' (2002) *Censored Books II: Critical Viewpoints* is a collection of essays that were written to support a number of *controversial* titles including *Killing Mr. Griffin* (Duncan, 1978), *Fallen Angels* (Myers, 1988), and *The Drowning of Stephan Jones* (Greene, 1991). In *Teaching Banned Books: 12 Guides for Young Readers,* Scales (2001) includes a number of books read by adolescents including *My Brother Sam Is Dead* (Collier & Collier, 1974) and *Roll of Thunder, Hear My Cry* (Taylor, 1976).

Responding to a Challenge. No matter how prepared you think you are, responding to an actual censorship challenge can be difficult. It is important to be calm and objective (Virginia Library Association, 1997) and to deal professionally with the complainant.

- Listen carefully and courteously to the complaint.

- Attempt to resolve the complaint informally and/or to defuse the situation without making judgments or making promises about any actions other than the written school policy (i.e., providing a copy of the request for reconsideration form and/or the selection guidelines).

- Be prepared to refer the complaint to the next level of authority as outlined in the plan.

- Notify the appropriate administrators of the complaint and provide a summary of the discussion with the complainant. Do this even if it appears that the complaint has been resolved.

- If a formal written complaint is filed, follow the procedures outlined in the plan. For support, contact the organizations identified earlier in this chapter.

- Keep notes on the process and maintain a file of all correspondence.

- Continue the use or circulation of the material until the entire review process is completed.

- Conduct the review openly, and inform the community through local media or other communications.

- Once the complaint has been reviewed according to procedure, communicate the results of the reconsideration process to the complainant in writing, explaining both the reevaluation procedure and justification for the final decision (National Coalition Against Censorship, "NCAC on the Issues"; Virginia Library Association, 1995, 1997).

In Expanding Your Knowledge with the Internet 12-5, you will find the URLs for some sample materials reconsideration forms and policies.

TABLE 12–6	Rationale For the Purchase/Use of Materials

Title of the Material: _____

Copyright Year: _____ Type of Material: _____

Grade(s): _____ Curriculum Area: _____

Intended Audience: _____ LMS/Teacher: _____

Provide a summary of the item:

How will this item be used in the library or classroom?

_____ Placed in general circulation in the LMC

_____ Placed in restricted circulation in the LMC

_____ Placed in an individual classroom collection

_____ Included in a booklist of recommended readings

_____ Included in a booklist of required readings

_____ Read/viewed/heard by an entire grade level

_____ Read/viewed/heard by one/several classes

_____ Read/viewed/heard by small groups of students

_____ Read/viewed/heard by individual students upon educator's recommendation

What are the reasons for selecting this material?

Have you read/seen/heard this item in its entirety? If not, why not?

What reviews (if any) has this material received? Where did the reviews appear? (*Note:* Publisher's catalogs are not review sources.)

What specific curricular objectives is this material designed to meet?

Does this material support the state standards of learning? If so, how?

What are the expected changes in students' skills, attitudes, and/or behaviors as the result of the use of this material?

What other materials could be used to meet these same objectives in case of parental concerns?

What objections might be raised to the purchase or use of this material? How would you counter them?

| **EXPANDING** | **YOUR KNOWLEDGE WITH THE INTERNET 12–5** |

A number of Internet sites provide sample intellectual freedom handbooks and resources. Here are a few of them. Visit this book's Companion Website at www.prenhall.com/bucher to link directly to these and many other resources.

Intellectual Freedom Toolkit
www.ala.org/ala/oif/iftoolkits/intellectual.htm

MAME—Michigan Association For Media in Education Intellectual Freedom
www.mame.gen.mi.us/ifl.html

Virginia Library Association Intellectual Freedom Manual
www.vla.org/ifc/toc.htm

CONCLUDING THOUGHTS

Censors want to control the minds of the young. They are fearful of the educational system because students who read learn to think. Thinkers learn to see. Those who see often question. (Scales, 2001, p. 2)

Intellectual freedom should be at the forefront of all teachers' and library media specialists' concerns. Undoubtedly, individuals and groups will continue to file complaints about what young adults can read, view, and hear. Educators must also remain vigilant unless they, too, fall into the role of censor rather than selector of quality materials that meet the social, cognitive, and emotional needs of young adults. To avoid being caught off-guard when censorship complaints arise, it is important for educators to have a deliberate and methodical plan to deal with censorship. The plan should be based more on careful thought than emotional reactions. Only then will educators be able to explain a rationale for the use of specific materials and be able to convince censors of young adults' right to read, view, and listen. Censorship battles will continue as long as censors believe their opinions should provide the basis for what others read. All educators need to be prepared for those challenges and to support intellectual freedom in schools and libraries.

Visit this book's Companion Website at www.prenhall.com/bucher for additional information about intellectual freedom and censorship including review questions, self-assessments, Internet sites, and readings.

Young Adult Books

This section includes young adult titles recommended or mentioned in this chapter. Check the Companion Website at

www.prenhall.com/bucher to find additional suggestions of current young adult literature.

Armstrong, W. H. (1969). *Sounder*. New York: Harper & Row.

Arrick, F. (1980). *Tunnel vision*. Scarsdale, NY: Bradbury.

Bauer, M. D. (Ed.). (1994). *Am I blue: Coming out from the silence*. New York: HarperCollins.

Block, F. L. (1995). *Baby be-bop*. New York: HarperCollins.

Blume, J. (1970). *Are you there God, it's me, Margaret*. Scarsdale, NY: Bradbury.

Blume, J. (1971). *Then again, maybe I won't*. Scarsdale, NY: Bradbury.

Blume, J. (1993). *Here's to you, Rachel Robinson*. New York: Orchard Books.

Blume, J. (1973). *Deenie*. Scarsdale, NY: Bradbury.

Blume, J. (1974). *Blubber*. Scarsdale, NY: Bradbury.

Childress. A. (1973). *A hero ain't nothing but a sandwich*. New York: Avon.

Cohen, S, & Cohen, D. (1989). *When someone you know is gay*. New York: Evans.

Collier, J. L., & Collier, C. (1974). *My brother Sam is dead*. New York: Scholastic.

Collier, J. L., & Collier, C. (1981). *Jump to freedom*. New York: Delacorte.

Collier, J. L., & Collier, C. (1983). *War comes to Willy Freeman*. New York: Delacorte.

Colville, B. (1994). *The dragonslayers*. New York: Simon and Schuster.

Conly, J. L. (1993). *Crazy lady*. New York: HarperCollins.

Cooney, C. (1997). *The terrorist*. New York: Scholastic.

Cormier, R. (1974). *The chocolate war*. New York: Pantheon.

Cormier, R. (1977). *I am the cheese*. New York: Dell.

Cormier, R. (1991). *We all fall down*. New York: Delacorte.

Crutcher, C. (1989). *Chinese handcuffs*. New York: Greenwillow.

Crutcher, C. (1993). *Staying fat for Sarah Byrnes*. New York: Greenwillow.

Dahl, R. (1964). *Charlie and the chocolate factory*. New York: Knopf.

Dahl, R. (1983). *The witches*. New York: Farrar, Straus and Giroux.

Doerkson, M. (1981). *Jazzy*. New York: Beaufort Books.

Duncan, L. (1978). *Killing Mr. Griffin*. New York: Little Brown.

Duncan, L. (1979). *Daughters of Eve*. New York: Little Brown.

Ferguson, A. (1989). *Show me the evidence*. New York: Bradbury.

Fienberg, A. (2000). *Borrowed light*. New York: Delacorte.

Follett, K. (1989). *The pillars of the earth*. New York: Morrow.

Fox, P. (1973). *Slave dancer*. Scarsdale, NY: Bradbury.

Garden, N. (1982). *Annie on my mind*. New York: Farrar, Straus and Giroux.

Godard, C., & Ribera, R. (1983). *The ultimate alchemist*. New York: Dargaud International.

Greene, B. (1973). *Summer of my German soldier*. New York: Dial.

Greene, B. (1991). *The Drowning of Stephan Jones*. New York: Bantam.

Hahn, M. D. (1986). *Wait till Helen comes*. New York: Harper Trophy.

Harris, R. (1994). *It's perfectly normal*. New York: Free Spirit.

Heron, A. (1994). *Two teenagers in twenty: Writings by gay and lesbian youth*. Boston: Alyson.

Irwin, H. (1985). *Abby, my love*. New York: Atheneum.

Keehn, S. (1991). *I am Regina*. New York: Philomel.

Kerr, M. E. (1972). *Dinky Hocker shoots smack*. New York: Harper & Row.

Killingsworth, M. (1991). *Eli's songs*. New York: Margaret K. McElderry Books.

Klein, N. (1972). *Mom, the wolfman, and me.* New York: Pantheon.

Klein, N. (1985). *Family secrets.* New York: Dial.

Klein, N. (1988). *That's my baby.* New York: Viking.

Klein, N. (1989). *Learning how to fall.* New York: Delacorte.

Lindgren. A. (1975). *The brother's lionheart.* New York: Viking.

Lipsyte, R. (1977). *One fat summer.* New York: Harper & Row.

Llywelyn, M. (1991). *Druids.* New York: Morrow.

Lowry, L. (1993). *The giver.* New York: Dell.

Lynch, C. (1993). *Shadow boxer.* New York: HarperCollins.

Lynch, C. (1994). *Iceman.* New York: HarperCollins.

Mazer, H. (1979). *Last mission.* New York: Delacorte.

Mazer, N. F. (1979). *Up in Seth's room.* New York: Delacorte.

Mosca, F. (1983). *All American boys.* Boston: Alyson.

Myers, W. D. (1988). *Fallen angels.* New York: Scholastic.

Naylor, P. R. The Alice Series consisting of:

(1985). *The agony of Alice.* New York: Atheneum.

(1989). *Alice in rapture, sort of.* New York: Atheneum.

(1991). *Reluctantly Alice.* New York: Atheneum.

(1992). *All but Alice.* New York: Atheneum.

(1993). *Alice in April.* New York: Atheneum

(1994). *Alice in-between.* New York: Atheneum.

(1995). *Alice the brave.* New York: Atheneum.

(1996). *Alice in lace.* New York: Atheneum.

(1997). *Outrageously Alice.* New York: Atheneum.

(1998). *Achingly Alice.* New York: Atheneum.

(1999). *Alice on the outside.* New York: Atheneum.

(2000). *Grooming of Alice.* New York: Atheneum.

(2001). *Alice alone.* New York: Atheneum.

(2002). *Simply Alice.* New York: Atheneum.

(2003). *Patiently Alice.* New York: Atheneum.

Paterson, K. (1977). *Bridge to Terabithia.* New York: Crowell.

Paterson, K. (1978). *The great Gilly Hopkins.* New York: Crowell.

Peck, R. N. (1978). *The day no pigs would die.* New York: Knopf.

Pike, C. (1991). *Die softly.* New York: Pocket Books.

Pike, C. (1993). *Road to nowhere.* New York: Simon Pulse.

Reiss, J. (1972). *The upstairs room.* New York: Crowell.

Rennison, L. (2002). *Knocked out by my nunga-nungas.* New York: HarperCollins.

Rodriguez, L. (1993). *Always running.* East Haven, CT: Curbstone Press.

Rowling, J. K. Harry Potter series. (1998). *Harry Potter and the sorcerer's stone.* New York: A. A. Levine Books.

(1999). *Harry Potter and the chamber of secrets.* New York: A. A. Levine Books.

(1999). *Harry Potter and the prisoner of Azkaban.* New York: A. A. Levine Books.

(2000). *Harry Potter and the goblet of fire.* New York: A. A. Levine Books.

(2003). *Harry Potter and the order of the phoenix.* New York: A. A. Levine Books.

Schwartz, A. (1991). *Scary stories 3.* New York: HarperCollins.

Smucker, B. (1978). *Underground to Canada.* New York: Harper & Row.

Sparks, B. (Originally published as Anonymous). (1971). *Go ask Alice.* Upper Saddle River, NJ: Merrill/Prentice Hall.

Speare, E. G. (1958). *The witch of Blackbird Pond.* Boston: Houghton.

Strasser, T. (1979). *Angel dust blues.* New York: Coward, McCann & Geoghegan.

Taylor, M. (1976). *Roll of thunder, hear my cry.* New York: Dial.

Taylor, T. (1969). *The cay.* Garden City, NY: Doubleday.

Twain, M. (1885). *The adventures of Huckleberry Finn.* New York: Webster.

Twain, M. (1876). *The adventures of Tom Sawyer.* Hartford, CT: American Publishing Co.

Walker, A. (1982). *The color purple.* New York: Pocket.

Willhoite, M. (1990). *Daddy's roommate.* Boston: Alyson.

Yep, L. (1975). *Dragonwings.* New York: HarperCollins.

Yolen, J. (1988). *The devil's arithmetic.* New York: Viking Kestrel.

Suggested Readings

Dresang, E. T. (2003). Controversial books and contemporary children. *Journal of Children's Literature, 29*(1), 20–31.

Howard, J. P. R. (2003). Tolerance in the school system: Should teachers be held to one standard and their teaching tools to another? *Education Canada, 43*(2), 40, 42–43.

Kelley, P. (2003). "When I Was Puerto Rican" by Esmeralda Santiago: Responding to a censorship challenge. *Ohio Media Spectrum, 55*(1), 19–26.

McCarthy, M. M. (2004). Filtering the Internet: The children's Internet protection Act. *Educational Horizons, 82*(2), 108–113.

References

(Note: All young adult literature referenced in this chapter are included in the Young Adult Books list and are not repeated in this list.)

10 most. . . challenged books of 2000. (2001). *Teacher Librarian, 29*(2), 56.

Alice series tops most-challenged list. (2004). *American Libraries, 35*(4), 6.

American Heritage Dictionary of the English Language. (2000). Boston: Houghton Mifflin.

American Library Association. (2004a). The 100 most frequently challenged books of 1990–2000. Retrieved April 2, 2004, from www.ala.org/ala/oif/bannedbooksweek/ bbwlinks/100mostfrequently.htm.

American Library Association. (2004b). Challenged and banned books. Retrieved March 1, 2004, from www.ala.org/ala/oif/bannedbooksweek/ challengedbanned/challengedbanned.htm.

American Library Association. (2004c) Intellectual freedom and censorship: Q & A.

Retrieved February 17, 2004, from www.ala.org/ala/oif/basics/intellectual.html.

Anderson, J. (2002). When parents' rights are wrong. *School Library Journal, 48*(11), 43.

Avi. (2002). Lois Lowry's *The Giver.* In N. J. Karolides (Ed.), *Censored books II: Critical viewpoints, 1985–2000* (pp. 173–175). Lanham, MD: Scarecrow.

Barlow, D. (2002). Rationales for teaching young adult literature. *The Education Digest, 68*(2), 77–78.

Bayne, N. (2002). Sexual development: Letting kids know *It's Perfectly Normal.* In N. J. Karolides (Ed.), *Censored books II: Critical viewpoints, 1985–2000* (pp. 259–263). Lanham, MD: Scarecrow.

Bergson-Shilcock, A. (2002). The subversive quality of respect: In defense of *The Witches.* In N. J. Karolides (Ed.), *Censored books II: Critical viewpoints, 1985–2000* (pp. 446–451). Lanham, MD: Scarecrow.

Broz, W. J. (2002). Defending *I Am Blue. Journal of Adolescent & Adult Literacy, 45*(5), 340–350.

Bucher, K. T., & Manning, M. L. (2002). Growing up with the *Alice* series. In N. J. Karolides (Ed.), *Censored books II: Critical viewpoints, 1985–2000* (pp. 10–19). Lanham, MD: Scarecrow.

Censoring school literature in the cyber age. (2001). *The Education Digest, 66*(9), 32–36.

Coley, K. P. (2002). *School library media research, 5.* Retrieved May 4, 2004, from http://vnweb.hwwilsonweb.com.

Crabcraft, J. (2004). The new creationism and its threat to science literary and education. *BioScience, 54*(1), 3.

Cronon, B. (2003). Burned any good books lately? *Library Journal, 128*(3), 48.

Curry, A. (2001). Where is Judy Blume? Controversial fiction for older children and young adults. *Journal of Youth Services in Libraries, 14*(3), 28–37.

Deenie defeats detractors—sort of. (2004). *American Libraries, 35*(4), 15.

Doyle, R. P. (2003). Books challenged or banned in 2002–2003. *Illinois Library Association Reporter, 21*(2), insert 1–7.

Freedman, L., & Johnson, H. (2001). Who's protecting whom? I hadn't meant to tell you this, a case in point in confronting self-censorship in the choice of young adult literature. *Journal of Adolescent & Adult Literacy, 44*(4), 356–369.

Ga teachers cry foul over omission of "evolution". (2004, February 2). *Education Daily,* 1–2.

Garden, N. (1996). Annie on trial: How it feels to be the author of a challenged book. *Voices of Youth Advocates, 19*(2), 79–84.

Glick, A. (2002). Parents wage anti-porn campaign against schools. *School Library Journal, 48*(1), 26.

Grant, C. (1995). Tales from a YA author: Slightly uneasy. *School Library Journal, 41* (October), 48–50.

Greenbaum, V. (1997). Censorship and the myth of appropriateness: Reflections on teaching reading in high school. *English Journal, 86*(2), 16–20.

Hopkins, D. M. (2003). The value of support during a library media challenge. *Knowledge Quest, 31*(4), 32–36.

Isaacs, K. T. (2003). Reality check. *School Library Journal, 49*(10), 50–51.

Ishizuka, K. (2001). Librarian in censorship case honored. *School Library Journal, 47*(10), 17.

Jenkins, C. A. (2003). Annie on her mind. *School Library Journal, 49*(6) 45–50.

Johnston, S. L. (2002). In defense of *Killing Mr. Griffin.* In N. J. Karolides (Ed.), *Censored books II: Critical viewpoints, 1985–2000* (pp. 285–289). Lanham, MD: Scarecrow.

Karolides, N. J. (Ed.). (2002). *Censored books II: Critical viewpoints, 1985–2000.* Lanham, MD: Scarecrow.

Kleinfield, N. R. (2002, June 2). The elderly man and the sea? Test sanitized literary texts. *New York Times,* 0–1.

Konvitz, M. R. (2003). Censorship. Retrieved December 15, 2003, from http://encarta.msn.com/text.

Kravitz, N. (2002). *Censorship and the school library media center.* Westport, CT: Libraries Unlimited.

LeMieux, A. C. (1998). The problem novel in the adult age. *The Alan Review, 25*(3). Retrieved June 17, 2003, from http://scholar.lib.vt.edu. journals/ALAN/spring98.

Lowry novel frequent censorship target. (2001). *Newsletter on Intellectual Freedom, 50*(5), no page numbers.

Majak, C. G. (2002). Conquering our fears: Alvin Schwartz's *Scary Stories* series. In

N. J. Karolides (Ed.), *Censored books II: Critical viewpoints, 1985–2000* (pp. 366–371). Lanham, MD: Scarecrow.

Marshall, J. M. (2003). Critically thinking about Harry Potter: A framework for discussing controversial works in the English classroom. *The ALAN Review, 30*(2), 16–19.

McClain, R., Goss, C., & Moe, M. S. (1996). What if I get in trouble: Self-censorship and the classroom teacher. Presentation of the National Council of Teachers of English, Chicago, IL, November 23, 1996.

Morgan, P. E. (2002). *Always Running* from the real issues: Why kids *should* read about gangs and drugs. In N. J. Karolides (Ed.), *Censored books II: Critical viewpoints, 1985–2000* (pp. 28–38). Lanham, MD: Scarecrow.

Morris, D. M., & Ellis, L. (1996). Deep trouble in the heart of Texas. *Teaching and Learning Literature, 5*(5), 2–7.

National Coalition Against Censorship. (2003). Accountability in public schools. *Censorship News Online, 90.* Retrieved April 30, 2004, from www.ncac.org/cen_news/cn90publicschools.htm.

National Coalition Against Censorship (NCAC). (2004). NCAC on the issues. Retrieved February 23, 2004, from www.ncac.org/issues/ciparuling.html.

NCTE guideline: The student's right to read. (2003). Retrieved December 15, 2003, from www.ncte.org/print.

New Mexico rejects effort to add creationism to science standards. (2003). *Church and State, 56*(9), 16.

O'Neal, S. (1990). Leadership in the language arts: Controversial books in the classroom. *Language Arts, 67*, 771–775.

Reeder, C. (2002). In defense of *Crazy Lady*. In N. J. Karolides (Ed.), *Censored books II: Critical viewpoints, 1985–2000* (pp. 120–125). Lanham, MD: Scarecrow.

Reichman, H. (1993). *Censorship and selection: Issues and answers for schools.* Chicago and Arlington: American Library Association and American Association of School Administrators.

Reid, L., & Neufield, J. H. (1999). *Rationales for teaching young adult literature.* Portland, ME: Calendar Islands.

Sadler, G. E. (1995). The killing of a great book: Censorship and the classics. *Teaching and Learning Literature, 5*(5), 31–37.

Scales, P. (2001). *Teaching banned books: 12 guides for young readers.* Chicago, IL: American Library Association.

Short, K. G. (2002). *My Brother Sam Is Dead:* Embracing the contradictions and uncertainties of war. In N. J. Karolides (Ed.), *Censored books II: Critical viewpoints, 1985–2000* (pp. 305–310). Lanham, MD: Scarecrow.

Simmons, J. S., & Dresang, E. T. (2001). *School censorship in the 21st century: A guide for teachers and school library media specialists.* Newark, DE: International Reading Association.

Sipe, R. B. (1999). Don't confront the censor, prepare for them. *The Education Digest, 64*(6), 42–46.

Small, R. C. (2000). Censorship as we enter 2000, or the millennium, or just new year: A personal look at where we are. *Journal of Youth Services in Libraries, 13*(2), 19–23.

Suhor, C. (2003). Prior censorship—Flying under false colors. *The Council Chronicle, 13*(1), 7.

Swartz, P. C. (2003). Bridging multicultural education: Bringing sexual orientation into the children's and young adult literature classrooms. *Radical Teacher, 66*, 11–16.

Texas ed. board rejects religious right attempt to alter science texts. (2003). *Church and State, 56*(11), 16.

Tomasino, K., Zarnowski, M., & Backner, A. (2003). Of professional interest:

Controversial books support critical literacy. *Journal of Children's Literature, 29*(1), 93–97.

Virginia Library Association. (1995). *Resource guide to intellectual freedom.* Norfolk, VA: Author.

Virginia Library Association. (1997). *Intellectual freedom manual.* Norfolk, VA: Author.

West, M. I. (1997). Speaking of censorship: An interview with Phyllis Reynolds Naylor. *Journal of Youth Services in Libraries, 10*(2), 177–182.

Whitson, J. A. (1993). After Hazlewood: The role of school officials in conflicts over the curriculum. *The ALAN Review, 20*(2), 2–7.

INDEX